LINCOLN CHRISTIAN COLLEGE AND SEMINARY

P9-CEG-644

THE MINISTERS MANUAL FOR 1954

THE VOLUME FOR THIS YEAR, BEING A STUDY
AND PULPIT GUIDE, AND HANDBOOK OF SUG-
GESTION AND INSPIRATION FOR PASTORS,
EVANGELISTS, MISSIONARIES, BIBLE
READERS AND ALL OTHERS REGU-
LARLY CALLED UPON FOR
CHRISTIAN ADDRESS FROM
PULPIT OR PLATFORM

TWENTY-NINTH ANNUAL VOLUME

Books by Rev. M. K. W. Heicher, PH.D.

LIVING ON TIPTOE
MEDITATIONS FOR DAYS AND SEASONS

Also Co-editor of

THE MINISTERS MANUAL, 1943-1952

Books by Rev. G. B. F. HALLOCK, M.A., D.D.

---

210 MORE CHOICE SERMONS FOR CHILDREN
THE PRACTICAL USE CYCLOPEDIA OF SERMON SUGGESTION
NINETY-NINE NEW SERMONS FOR CHILDREN
2500 BEST MODERN ILLUSTRATIONS
THE MINISTER'S WEEKLY MANUAL
FRATERNAL SERMONS AND ADDRESSES
PRAYERS FOR SPECIAL DAYS AND OCCASIONS
BEHIND THE BIG HILL. A YEAR OF SIX-MINUTE SERMONS FOR CHILDREN
THREE HUNDRED FIVE-MINUTE SERMONS FOR CHILDREN
HOLY COMMUNION CYCLOPEDIA
CYCLOPEDIA OF PASTORAL METHODS
CYCLOPEDIA OF FUNERAL SERMONS AND SKETCHES
CYCLOPEDIA OF SERMON OUTLINES FOR SPECIAL DAYS AND OCCASIONS
CYCLOPEDIA OF COMMENCEMENT SERMONS AND BACCALAUREATE ADDRESSES
ONE HUNDRED CHOICE SERMONS FOR CHILDREN
ONE HUNDRED BEST SERMONS FOR SPECIAL DAYS AND OCCASIONS
THE EVANGELISTIC CYCLOPEDIA
NEW SERMONS FOR SPECIAL DAYS AND OCCASIONS
SERMON SEEDS
THE HOMILETIC YEAR
BEAUTY IN GOD'S WORD
THE TEACHING OF JESUS CONCERNING THE CHRISTIAN LIFE
THE MODEL PRAYER
JOURNEYING IN THE LAND WHERE JESUS LIVED
CHRIST IN THE HOME
GROWING TOWARD GOD
UPWARD STEPS
GOD'S WHISPERED SECRETS
THE WEDDING MANUAL

Also Editor of

THE MINISTERS MANUAL, 1926-1954

The
MINISTERS
MANUAL

(Doran's)

A Study and Pulpit Guide
for the Calendar Year 1954

TWENTY-NINTH ANNUAL ISSUE
OF THIS "MINISTERS WORKING TOOL"

Compiled and Edited by
Rev. G. B. F. HALLOCK, M.A., D.D.
and
Rev. M. K. W. HEICHER, PH.D.

HARPER & BROTHERS PUBLISHERS
NEW YORK

THE MINISTERS MANUAL FOR 1954

Copyright, 1953 by G. B. F. Hallock and M. K. W. Heicher

Printed in the United States of America

FIRST EDITION

I-C

The Christian Endeavor Topics and the Sunday School Lessons in THE MINISTERS MANUAL FOR 1954 have been taken from the following copyrighted sources:

CHRISTIAN ENDEAVOR TOPICS FOR 1954

Copyright, 1953 as Christian Endeavor Topics
by the International Society of Christian Endeavor

SUNDAY SCHOOL LESSONS FOR 1954

Copyright, 1953, by the International Council of Religious Education

Library of Congress catalog card number: 25-21658

Foreword

"This book has raised the level of American preaching." The remark was made by a well-known minister as he took up a copy of *The Ministers Manual* from the table of a friend. The editors like to feel that that is true. They intend to produce each year a volume that suggests and inspires better preaching and a finer ministry.

Of course the remark did not refer to any particular volume of the Manual. He was thinking of the twenty-eight volumes that have been published. This is the twenty-ninth. We believe that this volume, too, will add value to the whole series of manuals, and will do the work it is intended to do.

The form of the book is much the same as in previous years, continuing the features which have been more recently added, such as the sections on the Conduct of the Holy Communion, Outlines and Themes for Lenten Services, and For Missions and Missionaries.

Section VII which contains Outlined Sermons for Sunday Mornings and Sunday Evenings for the Entire Church Year is the body of the book. Especially in the Morning Service for each Sunday do the editors seek to present a full service which has a "felt unity." Dean Sperry of Harvard Divinity School has written, "I doubt our ability, as preachers, to gear an unconventional and unpatterned sermon into a total act which is otherwise patterned. To this extent the whole service should be in its style a felt 'unity.' The preacher should not be like a restless colt, irked by the fences which bound his pasture, and intent to jump those fences and run loose on his own account. We ought to accept the fact that the whole service of worship is, of necessity, a patterned act, of which the sermon is a part." From the suggestions given for each Sunday morning we believe ministers can build up services and sermons upon useful and reliable patterns.

In the Manual for 1952 there were 282 scriptural texts which received comment. This year's volume includes as many. We believe that a text is of initial and continuing importance in the composition and reception of sermons. "The text is often the preacher's strongest argument; it is psychological as well as homiletical wisdom to let it stand before all else." Where is the preacher who on occasions does not have to go text hunting? This book is a mine of useful texts.

During the year we have had unusual commendation for the suggestive sermons for children in the Junior Pulpit which is Section VIII. These messages meet a great need. They are upon a great variety of subjects suggesting many other subjects which ministers can develop in their preaching to boys and girls.

G. B. F. H.
M. K. W. H.
Brick Church, Rochester, N. Y.
Community Church, Altadena, Calif.

116366

CONDENSED TABLE OF CONTENTS

(A Complete Alphabetical Subject Index Immediately Follows)

CONTENTS ACCORDING TO SUBJECT

General Alphabetical Index

SCRIPTURAL INDEX

Complete with the exception of references to which there is practically no comment or material.

SECTION I. Calendars and Other Convenient Clergy Helps

1. Civil Year Calendars for 1954 and 1955

1954

JANUARY								APRIL								JULY								OCTOBER						
S	M	T	W	T	F	S		S	M	T	W	T	F	S		S	M	T	W	T	F	S		S	M	T	W	T	F	S
—	—	—	—	—	1	2		—	—	—	—	1	2	3		—	—	—	—	1	2	3		—	—	—	—	—	1	2
3	4	5	6	7	8	9		4	5	6	7	8	9	10		4	5	6	7	8	9	10		3	4	5	6	7	8	9
10	11	12	13	14	15	16		11	12	13	14	15	16	17		11	12	13	14	15	16	17		10	11	12	13	14	15	16
17	18	19	20	21	22	23		18	19	20	21	22	23	24		18	19	20	21	22	23	24		17	18	19	20	21	22	23
24	25	26	27	28	29	30		25	26	27	28	29	30	—		25	26	27	28	29	30	31		24	25	26	27	28	29	30
31	—	—	—	—	—	—										—	—	—	—	—	—	—		31	—	—	—	—	—	—

FEBRUARY								MAY								AUGUST								NOVEMBER						
S	M	T	W	T	F	S		S	M	T	W	T	F	S		S	M	T	W	T	F	S		S	M	T	W	T	F	S
—	1	2	3	4	5	6		—	—	—	—	—	—	1		1	2	3	4	5	6	7		—	1	2	3	4	5	6
7	8	9	10	11	12	13		2	3	4	5	6	7	8		8	9	10	11	12	13	14		7	8	9	10	11	12	13
14	15	16	17	18	19	20		9	10	11	12	13	14	15		15	16	17	18	19	20	21		14	15	16	17	18	19	20
21	22	23	24	25	26	27		16	17	18	19	20	21	22		22	23	24	25	26	27	28		21	22	23	24	25	26	27
28	—	—	—	—	—	—		23	24	25	26	27	28	29		29	30	31	—	—	—	—		28	29	30	—	—	—	—
—	—	—	—	—	—	—		30	31	—	—	—	—	—																

MARCH								JUNE								SEPTEMBER								DECEMBER						
S	M	T	W	T	F	S		S	M	T	W	T	F	S		S	M	T	W	T	F	S		S	M	T	W	T	F	S
—	1	2	3	4	5	6		—	—	1	2	3	4	5		—	—	—	1	2	3	4		—	—	—	1	2	3	4
7	8	9	10	11	12	13		6	7	8	9	10	11	12		5	6	7	8	9	10	11		5	6	7	8	9	10	11
14	15	16	17	18	19	20		13	14	15	16	17	18	19		12	13	14	15	16	17	18		12	13	14	15	16	17	18
21	22	23	24	25	26	27		20	21	22	23	24	25	26		19	20	21	22	23	24	25		19	20	21	22	23	24	25
28	29	30	31	—	—	—		27	28	29	30	—	—	—		26	27	28	29	30	—	—		26	27	28	29	30	31	—

1

1955

JANUARY						
S	M	T	W	T	F	S
—	—	—	—	—	—	1
2	3	4	5	6	7	8
9	10	11	12	13	14	15
16	17	18	19	20	21	22
23	24	25	26	27	28	29
30	31	—	—	—	—	—

APRIL						
S	M	T	W	T	F	S
—	—	—	—	—	1	2
3	4	5	6	7	8	9
10	11	12	13	14	15	16
17	18	19	20	21	22	23
24	25	26	27	28	29	30
—	—	—	—	—	—	—

JULY						
S	M	T	W	T	F	S
—	—	—	—	—	1	2
3	4	5	6	7	8	9
10	11	12	13	14	15	16
17	18	19	20	21	22	23
24	25	26	27	28	29	30
31	—	—	—	—	—	—

OCTOBER						
S	M	T	W	T	F	S
—	—	—	—	—	—	1
2	3	4	5	6	7	8
9	10	11	12	13	14	15
16	17	18	19	20	21	22
23	24	25	26	27	28	29
30	31	—	—	—	—	—

FEBRUARY						
S	M	T	W	T	F	S
—	—	1	2	3	4	5
6	7	8	9	10	11	12
13	14	15	16	17	18	19
20	21	22	23	24	25	26
27	28	—	—	—	—	—

MAY						
S	M	T	W	T	F	S
1	2	3	4	5	6	7
8	9	10	11	12	13	14
15	16	17	18	19	20	21
22	23	24	25	26	27	28
29	30	31	—	—	—	—

AUGUST						
S	M	T	W	T	F	S
—	1	2	3	4	5	6
7	8	9	10	11	12	13
14	15	16	17	18	19	20
21	22	23	24	25	26	27
28	29	30	31	—	—	—

NOVEMBER						
S	M	T	W	T	F	S
—	—	1	2	3	4	5
6	7	8	9	10	11	12
13	14	15	16	17	18	19
20	21	22	23	24	25	26
27	28	29	30	—	—	—

MARCH						
S	M	T	W	T	F	S
—	—	1	2	3	4	5
6	7	8	9	10	11	12
13	14	15	16	17	18	19
20	21	22	23	24	25	26
27	28	29	30	31	—	—

JUNE						
S	M	T	W	T	F	S
—	—	1	2	3	4	
5	6	7	8	9	10	11
12	13	14	15	16	17	18
19	20	21	22	23	24	25
26	27	28	29	30	—	—

SEPTEMBER						
S	M	T	W	T	F	S
—	—	—	—	1	2	3
4	5	6	7	8	9	10
11	12	13	14	15	16	17
18	19	20	21	22	23	24
25	26	27	28	29	30	—

DECEMBER						
S	M	T	W	T	F	S
—	—	—	—	1	2	3
4	5	6	7	8	9	10
11	12	13	14	15	16	17
18	19	20	21	22	23	24
25	26	27	28	29	30	31

2. *Ecclesiastical Year Calendar for 1954 (Including the Movable and Immovable Feasts)*

JANUARY
1—Fr. Circumcision.
3—Su. 2nd Sunday after Christmas.
6—We. The Epiphany.
10—Su. 1st Sunday after The Epiphany.
17—Su. 2nd Sunday after The Epiphany.
24—Su. 3rd Sunday after The Epiphany.
25—Mo. Conversion of St. Paul.
31—Su. 4th Sunday after The Epiphany.

FEBRUARY
1—Mo.
2—Tu. The Purification.
7—Su. 5th Sunday after The Epiphany.
14—Su. Septuagesima Sunday.
21—Su. Sexagesima Sunday.
24—We. St. Matthias.
28—Su. Quinquagesima Sunday.

MARCH
1—Mo.
3—We. Ash Wednesday.
7—Su. 1st Sunday in Lent.
10—We. Ember Day.
12—Fr. Ember Day.
13—Sa. Ember Day.
14—Su. 2nd Sunday in Lent.

21—Su. 3rd Sunday in Lent.
25—Th. The Annunciation.
28—Su. 4th Sunday in Lent.
31—We.

APRIL
1—Th.
4—Su. 5th (Passion) Sunday in Lent.
11—Su. Palm Sunday.
12—Mo. Monday before Easter.
13—Tu. Tuesday before Easter.
14—We. Wednesday before Easter.
15—Th. Maundy Thursday.
16—Fr. Good Friday.
17—Sa. Easter Even.
18—Su. Easter Day.
19—Mo. Easter Monday.
20—Tu. Easter Tuesday.
25—Su. 1st Sunday after Easter.
26—Mo. St. Mark*.
30—Fr.

MAY
1—Sa. St. Philip and St. James.
2—Su. 2nd Sunday after Easter.
9—Su. 3rd Sunday after Easter.

* Transferred from April 25.

16—Su.   4th Sunday after Easter.
23—Su.   5th (Rogation) Sunday after Easter.
24—Mo.   Rogation Monday.
25—Tu.   Rogation Tuesday.
26—We.   Rogation Wednesday.
27—Th.   Ascension Day.
30—Su.   Sunday after Ascension.
31—Mo.

JUNE

1—Tu.
6—Su.   Whitsunday (Pentecost).
7—Mo.   Whitsun Monday.
8—Tu.   Whitsun Tuesday.
9—We.   Ember Day.
11—Fr.   Ember Day.
12—Sa.   Ember Day.
13—Su.   Trinity Sunday.
14—Mo.   St. Barnabas.*
20—Su.   1st Sunday after Trinity.
24—Th.   Nativity of St. John Baptist.
27—Su.   2nd Sunday after Trinity.
29—Tu.   St. Peter.
30—We.

JULY

1—Th.
4—Su.   Independence Day (3rd Sunday after Trinity).
11—Su.   4th Sunday after Trinity.
18—Su.   5th Sunday after Trinity.
25—Su.   St. James (6th Sunday after Trinity).
31—Sa.

AUGUST

1—Su.   7th Sunday after Trinity.
6—Fr.   Transfiguration.
8—Su.   8th Sunday after Trinity.
15—Su.   9th Sunday after Trinity.
22—Su.   10th Sunday after Trinity.
24—Tu.   St. Bartholomew.
29—Su.   11th Sunday after Trinity.
31—Tu.

* Transferred from June 11.

SEPTEMBER

1—Mo.
5—Su.   12th Sunday after Trinity.
12—Su.   13th Sunday after Trinity.
15—We.   Ember Day.
17—Fr.   Ember Day.
18—Sa.   Ember Day.
19—Su.   14th Sunday after Trinity.
21—Tu.   St. Matthew.
26—Su.   15th Sunday after Trinity.
29—We.   St. Michael and All angels.
30—Th.

OCTOBER

1—Fr.
3—Su.   16th Sunday after Trinity.
10—Su.   17th Sunday after Trinity.
17—Su.   18th Sunday after Trinity.
18—Mo.   St. Luke.
24—Su.   19th Sunday after Trinity.
28—Th.   St. Simon and St. Jude.
31—Su.   20th Sunday after Trinity.

NOVEMBER

1—Mo.   All Saints' Day.
7—Su.   21st Sunday after Trinity.
14—Su.   22nd Sunday after Trinity.
21—Su.   Sunday next before Advent.
28—Su.   1st Sunday in Advent.
30—Tu.   St. Andrew.

DECEMBER

1—We.
5—Su.   2nd Sunday in Advent.
12—Su.   3rd Sunday in Advent.
19—Su.   4th Sunday in Advent.
21—Tu.   St. Thomas.
25—Sa.   Christmas Day.
26—Su.   St. Stephen.
27—Mo.   St. John Evangelist.
28—Tu.   Holy Innocents.
31—Fr.

3. Prominent Church Year Dates for Three Years

Ash Wednesday, 1954, Mar. 3.   1955, Feb. 23. 1956, Feb. 15.

Palm Sunday, 1954, Apr. 11.   1955, Apr. 3. 1956, Mar. 25.

Good Friday, 1954, Apr. 16.   1955, Apr. 8. 1956, Mar. 30.

Easter, 1954, Apr. 18.   1955, Apr. 10.   1956, Apr. 1.

Trinity Sunday, 1954, June 13.   1955, June 5. 1956, May 27.

Ascension Day, 1954, May 27.   1955, May 19. 1956, May 10.

Whitsunday, 1954, June 6.   1955, May 29. 1956, May 20.

First Sunday in Advent, 1954, Nov. 29.   1955, Nov. 27.   1956, Dec. 2.

4. A Table of Easter Sundays for the Years 1940-2000

1940, March 24.
1941, April 13.
1942, April 6.
1943, April 25.
1944, April 9.
1945, April 1.
1946, April 21.
1947, April 6.
1948, March 28.
1949, April 17.
1950, April 9.
1951, March 25.
1952, April 13.
1953, April 5.
1954, April 18.
1955, April 10.
1956, April 1.

1957, April 21.
1958, April 6.
1959, March 29.
1960, April 17.
1961, April 2.
1962, April 22.
1963, April 14.
1964, March 29.
1965, April 18.
1966, April 10.
1967, March 26.
1968, April 14.
1969, April 6.
1970, March 29.
1971, April 11.
1972, April 2.
1973, April 22.

1974, April 14.
1975, March 30.
1976, April 18.
1977, April 10.
1978, March 26.
1979, April 15.
1980, April 6.
1981, April 19.
1982, April 11.
1983, April 3.
1984, April 22.
1985, April 7.
1986, March 30.
1987, April 19.

1988, April 3.
1989, March 26.
1990, April 15.
1991, March 31.
1992, April 19.
1993, April 11.
1994, April 3.
1995, April, 16.
1996, April 7.
1997, March 30.
1998, April 12.
1999, April 4.
2000, April 23.

5. List of Wedding Anniversaries with Distinctive Gifts

Pastors when asked find it convenient to have the full list, which follows. The most important are the "Silver" after 25 years, the "Golden," after 50 years, and the "Diamond," after 60, 70 or 75 years.

1st, Paper.
2nd, Cotton.
3rd, Leather.
4th, Fruit.
5th, Wooden.
6th, Candy.
7th, Wool.
8th, Pottery.
9th. Willow.
10th, Tin.
11th, Steel.
12th, Silk.

13th, Lace.
14th, Ivory.
15th, Crystal
20th, China.
25th, Silver
30th, Pearl.
35th, Coral.
40th, Ruby.
45th, Sapphire.
50th, Golden.
75th, Diamond.

6. CHOICE FILMS FOR CHURCH USE

The films listed below are recommended by Mr. Kenneth L. Holst, 1399 N. Lake Ave., Pasadena, Calif. Write him concerning any film problems you may have.

How to use audio-visuals effectively:
1. Fit them carefully into your program; they are teaching tools, not entertainment.
2. Preview before showing.
3. Set up equipment well in advance of showing.
4. Prepare audience before showing— what to watch for, why you are showing material, what to do after showing.
5. Follow up with discussion, offering, prayer of commitment or program of action.

To estimate cost of rental. The average rate is about $8 for 30 minutes.

"Challenge of Africa." Missionary. Highlighting the problems of Africa in a new world. 30 min.

"Strength of the Hills." Color. Church work among Indians of S. Dakota. 30 min.

"The Living Bible." Series: Birth of the Savior, Childhood of Jesus, First Disciples, Woman at the Well, Jesus at Nazareth and Capernaum, Jesus and the Lepers, Thirty Pieces of Silver, The Upper Room, Betrayal in Gethsemane, Jesus before the High Priest, Trial before Pilate, The Lord Is Risen, The Lord's Ascension. 15 min. units.

"On Mission Frontiers." Color. Tour of American Baptist Foreign Mission Fields. 28 min.

"Forward with Christ." A new lesson in Christian Stewardship. 30 min.

"Bantu Girl." Color. Missionary. A day in the life of an African girl. Fine for youth. 13 min.

"Brightest Night." Color. Christmas film for children. 14 min.

"Naw Iris, Burma Nurse." Color. An inspiring film which will prompt viewers to re-examine their own lives in the light of Christ's command, "Heal the sick." 25 min.

"Windows on the Sky." Color. Life of a Navajo family and the work of the Good Shepherd Mission. 25 min.

"An End to Darkness." Africa. Good for youth groups, mission study. 27 min.

"Walt Disney Films." Color. Not religious. Entertaining. Good for fillers. Delightful for children. 15 to 26 min. Some titles: Kitty Hawk, aviation; Disney Cartoon Parade.

"The Search for Christ." Color. 12 Episodes. Jesus Has Two New Followers, Miracle at Cana, Treasures in Heaven, Nicodemus, The Samaritan Woman, Rejected at Nazareth, Healing —Jesus Prays, Faith of Four Friends, Prodigal Son—Raising of Widow's Son, Parable of Sower and Mustard Seed, Stilling of Storm—Jairus' Daughter, Feeding of Crowd—Walking on Water, Peter's Confession—Jesus' Prediction of Death. Usable with children as well as with youth and adults. Each episode 12 min.

"Talents." An excellent stewardship film. About 30 min.

"I Beheld His Glory." Easter film. New. Not yet shown at this writing. Probably about 30 min. Promises to be an excellent film.

"The Street." It carries a message vital to the church in all times and at all places. 22 min.

"On Common Ground." To stimulate discussion on the problems of the rural church. 28 min.

"The New Pioneers." Film on the new Israel. 20 min.

"One God." Portrayal of religious practices among Protestants, Catholics and Jews in America. 37 min.

Older Films that repeat well: "All That I Have"; "Second Chance"; "King of Kings"; "Pilgrimage Play"; "For Good or Evil"; "Like a Mighty Army"; "Torn between These Two."

"Light of the North." Color. Story of the Church's work in Alaska. 28 min.

"Northern Outpost." Color. The Church in Alaska. 30 min.

"No Other Gods." Power, money and fame are not true life goals. 20 min.

"The Guiding Star." A popular Christmas film, for a Sunday night Christmas program, pleasing to children. 30 min.

7. ANNIVERSARIES OF INTEREST FOR CHURCH OBSERVANCE IN 1954

List to choose from:

1,700 years. Origen died in A.D. 254. The most distinguished and most influential of all the theologians of the ancient church, with the possible exception of Augustine.

1,600 years. St. Augustine was born in A.D. 354, Aug. 28. Author of *Confessions* and *City of God.* "No man since the apostolic age has been more influential as a Christian example or a Christian thinker than he."—Walker.

1,350 years. Gregory, surnamed The Great, died in 604. Under his pontificate were carried on the two great missionary enterprises to Britain, that of St. Augustine in 596, and that of Melletus and Paulinus and others in 601.

1,200 years. The year 754 is said to be the death year of St. Boniface, the first English missionary to Germany. Born about June 5, 680. See *The First Christmas Tree* by Henry van Dyke.

400 years. Sir Philip Sidney was born on Nov. 30, 1554. English poet, statesman, soldier. Hero of the often-told story that he refused a cup of water in favor of a dying soldier with the words, "Thy need is greater than mine." Story is in keeping with his character.

350 years. Roger Williams was born in 1604. Founder of the colony of Rhode Island in America and pioneer of religious liberty. Established what is considered the first Baptist church in America. Friend of Cromwell and Milton.

350 years. John Eliot was born on Aug. 5, 1604. Founder of missions to American Indians. He early learned their language, preaching to them and teaching them. His translation of the Bible into an Indian language, completed 1663, was the first Bible printed in North America. Joint author of the *Bay Psalm Book.*

250 years. John Locke died Oct. 28, 1704. Widely influential in the political, educational and philosophical thought of his time; a source of inspiration for the Founding Fathers of America. "The intellectual ruler of the 18th century."

200 years. King's College opened in New York City with eight students and a single instructor, Dr. Samuel Johnson. In 1784 it became Columbia College, later Columbia University.

200 years. Andrew Fuller was born. See *A Bunch of Everlastings,* Frank W. Boreham.

150 years. Joseph Priestly died Feb. 6, 1804. English nonconformist minister and philosopher who became the first great chemist in America. Discoverer of oxygen.

150 years. Immanuel Kant, philosopher, died on Feb. 12, 1804.

150 years. March 10. Upper Louisiana formally transferred by France to the U.S.

150 years. Nathaniel Hawthorne, New England novelist and short-story writer, was born on July 4, 1804.

100 years. Sir James George Frazer was born on Jan. 1, 1854. Scottish anthropologist, one of the world's greatest authorities on folklore, author of *The Golden Bough.*

100 years. On March 31, 1854, the first Treaty of the United States with Japan—a "Treaty of Peace, Amity and Commerce." The ports of Hakodate and Simoda were opened to ships of the U.S. The Expedition of Matthew Galbraith Perry.

100 years. James Montgomery, died April 30, 1854. Writer of more than four hundred hymns, one hundred of which are still widely sung. Ranks with Wesley, Watts and Doddridge. Biography interesting. Hymns: "Angels, from the Realms of Glory," "In the Hour of Trial," and others.

100 years. George Eastman was born on July 12, 1854. American pioneer in

the photographic industry. Philanthropist, patron of music.

100 years. William C. Gorgas, Surgeon-General of the United States, and fighter against disease, was born on Oct. 3, 1854. Eradicated yellow fever from the Panama Canal Zone.

100 years. June 7. First American Young Men's Christian Assn. met in Buffalo, N. Y.

8. FUNERAL MEDITATIONS

In general it is wise to conduct a funeral service that is short. The great scripture passages which are read come to the bereaved with more than usual power. They comfort. They strengthen. They bring peace. No other spoken word can take their place. But a few words spoken from the heart of the minister are often most helpful. Here are a few funeral meditations. They can be repeated at will.

Topic: The Death of His Saints.

TEXT: Precious in the sight of the Lord is the death of his saints. Ps. 116:15.

The word "saints" does not mean those extraordinary characters, which to many of us are not attractive because their lives seem distorted and unreal; but just ordinary people who trusting in God have lived well and whom on such a day as this we delight to honor.

Death does not seem precious to us, and yet perhaps it should. We may be looking from a different point of view than does the Lord. We are apt to think of death as a kind of blind alley, a dead-end street; but from the Lord's point of view it is not. Death is a thoroughfare. It is going through. It is stepping upward. It is going into another room. It is journeying into a better country.

The door of death seems very dark and dull and drab to us, because from our angle only the light of earth falls upon it and that light is mostly darkness. Remember that from the other side the light of heaven shines upon the door. It is bright and splendid. It might be a very precious and lovely thing to see one coming through that door from the other side.

Think of the things the saint leaves behind when passing through the door of death—pain and illness, sin and evil, sorrow and tears, limitations and frustrations. Think of the blessings acquired—wholeness, righteousness, joy and achievement.

We know that there are good things left behind, chiefly friendships, kinships, human loves—but let us not be too sure that these are not still enjoyed. At least they shall be renewed. It seems that there is nothing worth keeping that shall not be kept.

Let us have faith that in the eternal city there is the presence of Christ. God himself is there in some fashion far beyond his presence with us here. There, too, truth is still to be discovered, and beauty is to be appreciated and perhaps created, and there is always higher goodness to be attained. Truth and beauty and goodness are ever beyond us and calling us to greater activity and a larger quest. I believe this is so. Think not of heaven as a do-nothing place. I foresee it as a place of great activity. From the Lord's point of view it must be a great blessing, a very precious thing, to enter the heavenly kingdom.

And from his point of view it may be well for us that our loved ones have gone through the door. This may kindle our own hope of glory. This may strengthen our own faith. We take our bereavement and we transmute it into activity and consecration unto good and ourselves live better lives.

We could go on with such meditation for a long time for the happiness of the new country must be beyond our imagining and the blessings of eternity must be inexhaustible.

Precious in the sight of the Lord is the entrance of ——— ——— into the eternal kingdom.—M. K. W. H.

Topic: A Very Present Help

TEXT: "God is . . . a very present help in trouble." Ps. 46:1.

Yes, that is what we need and generally want in time of trouble—we want God. Yesterday we were busy. Yesterday we didn't seem to need him. Occasionally we stopped a moment to remember that God is; this fleeting thought passed through our mind. Or in some little emergency we breathed a prayer. But today—trouble, death. We want to be sure of God.

To be sure of God we must first find him in our own hearts. After that we may find him revealed in his handiwork, in the lives of good men, in the Bible. He comes to us in the Christ, but first of all we meet him in our hearts. In the restlessness of our hearts we discover a desire for him. In our consciences we learn that he desires us to be righteous. In our appreciations of truth and beauty and goodness we learn to know him. In the awe that breaks over our souls, in the quiet peace that sometimes descends upon us we touch the hem of his garment. But it is in the life of him who once walked in bodily form upon the earth, and who today is a spiritual presence with us, who has found a way into our lives—by the Christ we know that God is and that he is a very present help in time of trouble.

How does he help us? He gives us strength, or as Jesus said, he gives us comfort. Comfort means being strong together. His presence is our strength. We can lean upon him.

God thus becomes our refuge—like a place unto which to fly, like a strong rock under which to hide against the wind and the storm; like a mountain valley where one may find peace.

Strength and refuge bring peace. Jesus said, "Peace I leave with you, my peace I give unto you: not as the world giveth, give I unto you. Let not your heart be troubled, neither let it be afraid." Peace comes as the gift of Christ. It is the peace of adequate spiritual resources, the peace of clean hands and a pure heart—the peace of a presence by our sides and in our hearts. "Lo, I am with you always, even unto the end of the world."

This same Psalm of our text speaks of a river the streams whereof make glad the city of God. The river of God's grace brings refreshment, cleansing, power, beauty, buoyancy. There is much to be received from the river of grace which flows from the throne of God. God is a very present help in time of trouble.—M. K. W. H.

Topic: Time and Eternity

I. Because Christ came into time we can enter into eternity.

II. The way to live serenely and deeply, steadfastly and joyfully, is to live in time while holding eternity in our hearts.

III. One may be very poor in the things which belong to time, but very rich in the things which belong to eternity.

IV. There are three things which we can possess in time which belong to eternity—faith and hope and love. These we must seek with all our hearts.

9. GRACE BEFORE MEAT

a. God we love thee, thou art good,
And we thank thee for this food.
           Amen

Father, bless this food we take
And bless us all for Jesus' sake.
           Amen

God is great and God is good
And we thank him for this food.
           Amen

b. Heavenly Father, make us thankful to thee and mindful of others as we receive this food. In Jesus' name. Amen.

c. O Thou who art the giver of every good and perfect gift, bless this food to our use and us in thy service. Amen.

d. Come, Lord Jesus, be our Guest and let our daily bread be blest. Amen.

e. For these and all they mercies we thank thee, our Father, and pray that thou wilt bless them to our use and us in thy service. Amen.

f. Lord, help us to receive all good things as from thy hand and use them to thy praise. Amen.

g. We thank thee, our heavenly Father, for all thy mercies, new every morning and fresh every evening. Help us in return to give thee the love of our hearts and the service of our hands. In Christ's name we ask. Amen.

h. Morning. For thy watchcare through the night and the blessings of the new day we thank thee. Wilt thou bless the food provided for our bodies and strengthen us for the duties and privileges of the new day. In Christ's name. Amen.

i. Evening. For the blessings of the day and evening we thank thee, our Heavenly Father. We bless thee for these tokens of thy love. Let thy presence go with us through the evening and may we be grateful for all thy loving-kindness. In Christ's name we ask. Amen.

j. Heavenly Father, make us thankful to thee and mindful of others as we receive these blessings. In Jesus' name. Amen.

k. To be sung. (Tune: "Old Hundred")
We thank Thee Lord for daily bread,
As by thy grace our souls are fed.
Grant us to grow more like to thee
This day and through eternity.

l. To be sung. (Tune: "Doxology")
Be present at our table Lord;
Be here and everywhere adored.
Thy children bless and grant that we
Through fellowship grow more like thee.

m. Noon. To be sung. (Tune: "Jesus Calls Us")
Father, for this noonday meal
We would speak the praise we feel;
Health and strength we have from thee,
Help us Lord to faithful be.

n. To be sung. (Tune: "Old Hundred")

Father, we thank Thee for the night
And for the pleasant morning light,
For rest and food and loving care,
And all that makes the world so fair.

10. PRAYERS WITH THE CHOIR

It is a good custom with very many ministers to offer prayer with the choir in the chapel or choir room before entering the service in the church sanctuary. The offering of such a prayer is in every way commendable and its influence good.

a. Grant us, O Lord, the help of thy spirit in our hearts, that we may enter into thy holy presence with reverence and gladness and render a service acceptable unto thee; through Jesus Christ our Lord. Amen.

b. Our Father, we bless thee that thou hast given us voices to speak forth thy praise. Help us to worship thee with our lips and with our lives. Help us to show forth thy goodness in praiseful song. Amen.

c. As we enter thy sanctuary, our Father, wilt thou bestow the spirit of worship upon us. While we sing the songs of Zion may our words and worship be acceptable unto thee, O God. In Christ's name we ask. Amen.

d. Grant us, O Lord, the help of thy Spirit in our hearts, that we may enter into thy holy presence with reverence and gladness and render the service of leading thy people in praise in a way acceptable unto thee and to the edification of all. In the name of Christ our Lord. Amen.

e. May our hearts be in tune with our voices this day, and may our lips bring peace to the people. We would bless thee at all times; may thy praise be ever upon our lips. In the name of Christ. Amen.

f. Grant, O Lord, that what we sing with our lips we may believe in our hearts and practice in our lives; that being doers of Thy Word and not hearers only, we may obtain everlasting life. Through Jesus Christ our Lord. Amen.

11. OPEN CHURCH INVITATIONS

More and more the churches are open for meditation and prayer, not only on Sundays but on weekdays as well. Below are samples of statements for use in the Church Calendar.

a. Friend, there is a welcome in this
   Church for thee;
Come in, and rest, and think, and
   kneel, and pray;
What men have builded for God's
   glory, see—
Give thanks, and so go on thy way.

b. The front door of our sanctuary is unlocked every day from 8:00 A.M. to 6:00 P.M. in order to give anyone who wishes it an opportunity to come in, apart from the hurried world, to meditate, to pray, to think. You are invited to avail yourself of this opportunity of spiritual enrichment and you are urged to tell others about it also.

c. Our beautiful church is always open for private prayer and meditation. The pastor may be seen at any time by appointment for personal counsel.

d. When the side door of the chapel is open the pastor is in the Pilgrim House next door and is available. The chapel is, indeed, a place of prayer where we may bring our troubles as well as our joys and sorrows. But often in times of crisis or emotional strains (we all have them) the assistance of a kind and understanding pastor will bring ease and strength. The front doors of the chapel are always unlocked and when the side door stands open it is a sign that your pastor is available.

e. To all who are tired and need rest, to all who are lonely and need companionship, to all who sin and need a Savior, and to all who seek to serve their fellow men, this church opens wide its doors and, in the name of Jesus, bids you WELCOME.

f. AN INVITATION—To all who would know God and do his will—To all who would live and serve to make a Christian world—To all who seek comfort and would find rest—To old and young, wise and unlearned, rich and poor, saint and sinner, this church opens wide its doors and in the name of Jesus, the Christ, bids welcome to our Father's house.

ENTER TO WORSHIP!   DEPART TO SERVE!

g. THIS CHURCH IS OPEN. ENTER, REST AND PRAY.

OPEN. From dawn to dark the door is open. You need no key. You need not ask permission. Most doors are locked. Usually you have to state your business. BUT NOT HERE.

ENTER. Your welcome is Christ's welcome. "Whosoever will may come."

REST. The church knows how men need rest. A place of quiet. A rest from noise. Rest from the mind's uneasiness, the soul's weariness. Come in and find rest.

PRAY. Here in the dim quiet the peace of God begins to fall upon your soul, and the driven heart beats more slowly. You are somehow reminded of home. You are moved to think of your Father. I will go to my Father.

h. Whosoever thou art that entereth this church, remember it is the House of God. Be reverent, thoughtful and prayerful; and leave it not without a prayer to God for thyself, for those who minister, for those who worship here, and for all men everywhere.

i. The master is within and calleth for thee.

j. A church of the open door, the open mind, the friendly spirit, and the community heart.

k. I am the door: by me if any man enter in, he shall be saved, and shall go in and out, and find pasture.

l. The chapel within is open for your devotions during all daylight hours. You are not only invited, but urged to use it.

SECTION II. Pleas from the Pews. The Question-box, Panel, or Forum Method for Responding to the People's Interrogations and Desires

The writer must be conscious of his reader lest he write only to himself. The speaker must be conscious of his hearer lest he speak only to himself. We can become more conscious of our hearers if we listen to the questions that they are asking. Question 32 was asked by a small boy after arranging for a conference with his pastor. The question seems too simple and naïve. But it was a matter of deep concern to the boy and the simple answer which he received gave him much satisfaction. The questions people ask should be taken seriously. Here are 106 questions which were quite important to those who asked them.

QUESTIONS

1. How can the church aid in building a strong democracy?
2. "Delinquent Dads" and "Dominating Delilahs" are found in many homes—what can be done about it?
3. Is it possible to overcome fear and hate and discover new powers in oneself as the early disciples did?
4. What are the standard by which we can measure our spiritual growth?

5. What do you think constitutes a happy marriage?
6. When do prejudices start?
7. How are prejudices learned?
8. Are parents and teachers aware of prejudices in children?
9. How do children of different environments compare in the nature and extent of their prejudices?
10. How can democratic attitudes be taught effectively?
11. Is communism a religion?
12. Will you clearly define communism, socialism and capitalism?
13. Do you think giving has any connection with the spiritual side of religion?
14. How can I make sure that my giving will help me spiritually?
15. What does church membership involve?
16. What can we young people do to make our church have larger influence?
17. What is the outreach of our church in our community and in the world?
18. How can we apply the golden rule to the race problem?
19. Can a person be a Christian and not be a good citizen?

11

20. In what respects are church members today like the first-century Christians? unlike them?

21. What were the sources of courage among the early disciples?

22. I hear some people talk about the "St. James Bible"; others about the "King James Bible." Which is correct? Why?

23. What is the best version of the Bible for a young person to use?

24. What did Jesus mean when he said that we should call no man "Father"?

25. Can we believe intelligently in the goodness and power of God in view of the fact that so many people suffer so unjustly through war?

26. I am about to establish a home; how can I make it a center of community service?

27. What is spirituality?

28. What do the letters IHS mean—they are often placed on the cross?

29. How can I be sure that I will know my loved ones in heaven?

30. What is the unpardonable sin?

31. Do you think that small children should be put in prenursery schools?

32. A small boy's question—My Sunday School teacher says that God speaks to us; does God know all the languages of the earth?

33. Aren't the good people rather mediocre, while people not so good are apt to be talented?

34. Are the Declaration of Independence and the Constitution of the United States inspired writings?

35. How does one get on top of irritability and depression?

36. Was all the effort and money put into Chinese missions wasted?

37. Jesus said, "Let a man deny himself . . . ." What did he mean?

38. Isn't it too late to seek a better world?

39. How does God reveal himself?

40. Is it true that we assume immortality just because we want it?

41. I know something about the Reformation, but I do not understand what is meant by the Counter Reformation. What was it?

42. How can we settle what is right and what is wrong?

43. Is there any connection between beliefs and character?

44. How can I begin the Christian life?

45. What is the meaning of the Trinity?

46. How can a person increase his influence?

47. Why is the Bible called "the world's greatest book"?

48. What can we Christians do for peace?

49. How can we make our homes more truly Christian?

50. Can we help God answer our prayers?

51. How shall we think of our Christian dead?

52. What is the Apocrypha?

53. What was Christ's attitude toward those who did wrong?

54. Why is the tongue the "most unruly member"?

55. How other than by speech can we bear false witness?

56. What is the Christian meaning of love?

57. How can the Christian family be a more adequate home for love?

58. How may Christian experience bless sex and marriage?

59. What forces are at work when we love?

60. How does Christian love enrich marriage success?

61. In this world of chaos how can a modern youth follow the straight and narrow path?

62. Should a girl marry a boy of a different race?

63. How young may a person be to make a happy marriage? Is it all right for a girl not yet graduated from high school to marry?

64. How does one get over an inferiority complex?

65. Is "My country right or wrong" a slogan which a patriotic Christian man can adopt?

66. Is war curable?

67. Is society ill?

68. Can modern society be Christian?

69. How does one know when one has achieved maturity?

70. How can I cultivate the mind of Christ?

71. What is the difference between an occupation and a vocation?

72. I heard a man say that the vocation of garbage collecting is just as noble as that of a minister. Is that true? If so, why is it true?

73. Do you believe that Malachi 3:10 works out in practical living?

74. How can the young people best serve our church?

75. Does one become a helpful Christian by withdrawing from the world?

76. In what ways can we best express our loyalties to Christ?

77. What are the needed qualities for living a full life?

78. How can intolerance and race prejudice be overcome?

79. Are God's gifts for all?

80. Why is Sunday different from other days?

81. Do young people "sow wild oats" today?

82. Why do we call slander "green-eyed"?

83. What do we mean by saying "money is spiritual power"?

84. What do you most desire to see in life?

85. Does true gratitude to God make giving easy?

86. How does God choose workers for Kingdom tasks today?

87. What was the significance of Jesus' last supper with his disciples?

88. Have church members today the joy of the first-century Christians?

89. Can one study effectively with the radio on?

90. What are some of the sources of interracial hatreds?

91. What would be the result if everybody did exactly as he pleased?

92. Why is character more important than beauty as a basis for marriage selection?

93. How can one choose the good from the bad in dates or courtship?

94. What is the difference between being happy and having fun?

95. What reward is there for humility?

96. What are the incentives for doing our best?

97. What is gambling?

98. What is conscience? How can I train my conscience?

99. Why do we have a conscience at all? How does it grow?

100. Why does disobedience to conscience "chloroform" it?

101. In what way do the books we read affect our devotional life?

102. How did democracy come to be?

103. Does it make any difference whether or not we believe in a future life?

104. What is the ultimate goal of Christian effort?

105. How can we make money work for us?

106. How can we escape the worship of "other gods"?

SECTION III. Vital Themes for Vital Preaching, Being Church-Year and Other Sermons in Germ

STUDIES IN NEGLECTED TEXTS

A flash of illumination on a text that may seem unusual or obscure often makes it brilliant with suggestion. Its various phases of truth become glowing and glorious. In utter frankness, the aim of this section is at being both provocative and picturesque in the way of sermon starts. Here are nearly half a hundred starting-point studies of striking texts and themes. Each year we are giving increased and more careful attention to the quality and suggestiveness of this section of the Manual. The warm commendation it has received shows that it is accounted especially useful.

Our purpose is to present a body of practical-use suggestions, also to bring to attention scores of texts almost wholly passed over by the pulpit, yet vital, full of beauty and spiritual value. There is decided gain in the direction of freshness and force in the selection of texts and themes from the comparatively unknown and neglected portions of Scripture. The preacher does well who often treads the unfamiliar byways of the Bible, visiting regions somewhat new and strange. The use of unusual and striking texts promotes attention, good hearing, interest, and resultful retention in the memory of hearers. The truths uttered are more likely to strike and stick. They need be none the less vital and essential, for ministers are well aware that there is a direct road to Christ from every portion of the Word.

1. Topic: The Chambers of Imagery.

TEXT: "Then said he unto me, Son of man, hast thou seen what the ancients of the house of Israel do in the dark, every man in the chambers of his imagery?" Ezek. 8:12.

Read verses 6-12. Though this was a vision it was intended to present the corrupted state of Judah. The people were falling into heathen idolatry in its most depraved forms, worshiping pictured images of creeping things, abominable beasts, and idols. Ezekiel's mission was to bring them back to God.

I. These "chambers of imagery" may be taken as the type of a blind materialism. Worshiping the created instead of the Creator. Only one thing can save, a living faith in God.

II. These "chambers of imagery" may be taken as the symbol of a secret ungodliness. But some "hole in the wall" betrays the secret. Sham religion. False religion. Idolatry.

III. These "chambers of imagery" may be taken as the emblem of our im-

14

pure imaginations. Watch your reveries. Guard your imagination. Beware of anything that tends to defile the imagination, impure actions, impure companionships, impure pictures, impure literature. "Blessed are the pure in heart, for they shall see God."—T. C. F.

2. Topic: This Feeling of Frustration.

TEXT: "Ye looked for much, and, lo, it came to little; and when ye brought it home, I did blow upon it. Why? saith the Lord of hosts." Hag. 1:9.

I. A prevalent feeling. Blame the government. Blame the times. Blame civilization.

II. Real reasons. Getting off center. Emphasis of thinking is on the wrong thing. Right aims but wrong methods.

III. The need for patience. George Muller put his finger on the right spot when he said, "I must wait for four things. First, to know whether a work is God's work. Second, to know whether it is my work. Third, to know whether it is God's time. Fourth, to know whether it is God's way.—C. W. P.

3. Topic: They Asked for a Miracle.

TEXT: "And Jesus stopped and called them, saying 'What do you want me to do for you?' They said to him, 'Lord let our eyes be opened.' And Jesus in pity touched their eyes, and immediately they received their sight and followed him." Matt. 20:32-34 (R.S.V.).

I. The man who made the offer.

How marvelous that he should condescend to serve two roadside beggars! And yet this is just what we would expect him to do. The offer was a test of their faith. What will they ask him to do?

II. A basic request. We can imagine a beggar simply asking for larger alms than usual—a dollar instead of a dime in the tin cup. Not these men—they wanted their sight. Suppose Jesus should ask us, "What shall I do for you?" What would we ask? The beggars asked for a miracle and got it.

III. The miracle was followed by discipleship "They received their sight and followed him!" Is Christ's favor

toward us always followed by discipleship?—M. K. W. H.

4. Topic: The Church Invisible.

TEXT: "The kingdom of God cometh not with observation: Neither shall they say, Lo here! or, lo there! for, behold, the kingdom of God is within you." Luke 17:20, 21.

If the church is to be patterned after the kingdom of God it must seek its being and salvation:

I. In inward dignity, not in outward splendor.

II. In spiritual power, not in show of numbers.

III. In inward growth, not in mere outward extension.

IV. In inward peace, not in freedom from external conflict.

5. Topic: The Trial of Faith.

TEXT: "That the trial of your faith, being much more precious than of gold." I Pet. 1:7.

I. We may smother our faith through fear. We sometimes count the cost of following Christ too great. Did we ever think of the cost of not following him!

II. Faith may be smothered by preoccupation, as a success in business, and social prestige. When life is overcrowded we give religion no chance to breathe.

III. Faith is smothered for lack of thought. We are sometimes carried away with a flood of undigested knowledge. True faith needs room. It needs air to breathe, a chance to express itself. Granted these it will thrive in many of the unsuspected places of life.

6. Topic: A Soul's Open Window.

TEXT: "His windows were open in his chamber toward Jerusalem." Dan. 6:10.

Millet's *Angelus* is a valuable painting because it portrays a great idea, a fundamental soul principle; viz., a life open to God. Even greater is this prophet's portrayal of Daniel's open window.

I. Truly a spiritual connection—not the lattice of the room merely, but the "inner man" open to God. "It is the soul that sees"—is a familiar motto in blind asylums. Religion is the eye of the soul.

II. Practical usefulness, enabling (1) the farther sight. Daniel saw a nobler morality; imminent divine helpfulness; and a solution to a perplexing situation. (2) Incoming strength—as the window admits light and warmth to the plant; so Daniel found new courage and enthusiasm.

III. It must be opened from within and must have the "right outlook." There are windows in every home rarely opened because of the dark outlook. So in life. Then, there is the alertness of interest. John Ruskin often awakened his guests at Brantwood with the call, "Are you looking out?" It was inspiring preparation for the day.

7. Topic: Religion's Essentials.

TEXT: "For in Jesus Christ neither circumcision availeth any thing, nor uncircumcision; but faith which worketh by love." Gal. 5:6.

Religion, like every other business, must have certain primary essentials by which it is known and distinguished from other forms of thought and activity.

I. Faith is the first. This is where religion started for Jesus. Belief is the mind's acceptance of the reality of God, and in the New Testament this is always associated with faith in Christ.

II. Life is the second essential. Life is of two kinds—spiritual and material. Beauty, for example, is only a generalization until we see it in a flower. So is faith until it is demonstrated in action. Faith is a life, and so is unbelief. The worshiper wears the character of his God. We become like the things we contemplate. Therefore, the Christian has two sides to his life. First, spiritual fellowship with his Lord for which the church exists, and second, the daily surrender of all that constitutes life as we know it to the cultivation of his mind and will.

III. Service is the third essential. Christ was always doing something for others, and he was always sending others to do things for himself and his universal commission to his church is that they "go." It is true to the constitution of our nature. Study and service, leisure and toil, work and play go hand in hand. Every Christian is a worker on behalf of the cause for which Christ died. By such service faith is justified, life is enriched and hope is guaranteed.—R. M.

8. Topic: Shifting Scenery (New Year).

TEXT: "The fashion of this world passeth away." I Cor. 7:31.

The image is drawn from a shifting scene in a play represented on a stage. Human life, indeed, is a drama, and its conditions and mutations are merely the stage settings that are ever shifting.

I. The New Year season is a good time to consider the serious import of living. To be actors in earnest in a play that is real.

II. The New Year season is a good time to discriminate between what is essential and what is stage setting and scenery.

III. The New Year season is a good time to play a part fitting to the scenery of the occasion. To repent, to resolve, to renew as the personal need demands.

9. Topic: The Universality of Jesus

TEXT: "And Pilate wrote a title also, and put it on the cross. And there was written, JESUS OF NAZARETH, THE KING OF THE JEWS. . . . and it was written in Hebrew, and in Latin, and in Greek." John 19:19, 20 (A.S.V.).

INTRODUCTORY: The common custom in those days, when a criminal was executed, of publicly placarding his crime.

But why three languages? Pilate's desire that all might be able to read and understand. Did Providence have a hand in it? Greek and Latin and Hebrew were the three great languages of the world. Each was the vehicle and expression of a great world movement.

DISCUSSION: I. It was written in Greek. Language of culture. The Greeks were the genius people who created the culture of the world. 1. Jesus was claiming the realm of culture for his own. 2. There is a type of culture in the world today which definitely leaves Jesus out. 3. Everywhere, in art, literature, ethics, society, our standard is to be the character of Christ.

II. It was written in Latin. Language of government. Down the centuries the history of the Romans had stood for law and government. 1. Jesus was claiming the realm of government for his own. 2. There is a type of rule which ignores Jesus. 3. Christ must reign! "Unto us a child is born, unto us a son is given: and the government shall be upon his shoulder."

III. It was written in Hebrew. Hebrew was the language of religion. Down the centuries the history of the Hebrew has stood for revealed religion. 1. Jesus was claiming the realm of religion for his own. 2. In the realm of religion Jesus cannot be ignored. "Christ is the greatest character in history."—Clutton-Brock. "Jesus is the saint, the type and model of all men."—Goethe. These are not mere words. Jesus is greater. 3. He is "King of Kings and Lord of Lords."

CONCLUSION: I beg you, in this realm of religion, which means in the deepest intimacies of your life and the most secret fastness of your soul—make Jesus King.—James S. Stewart.

10. Topic: Forgetting the Past (New Year).

TEXT: "But this one thing I do, forgetting those things," etc. Phil. 3:13, 14.

I. The text suggests doing one thing, but we all know that it is most difficult to do that one thing—"forgetting the past."

II. Both friends and enemies remind us of the past. What we are is the product of the past. Being what we are makes it probable that we will choose and act in the future as we have done in the past.

III. Forgetting the past when it can be done is the great step toward a new and better kind of future.

IV. Starting with a clear mind and a fresh unburdened spirit would be wonderful. Our natural question is, can it be done?

V. The text gives us the secret and answer Yes. By fixing the attention upon the goal of "God's heavenward call in Christ Jesus." Only by such concentration and devotion will we ever be able to forget a past that blights and hinders.—A. A. S.

11. Topic: This Is a Wonderful Christmas (Christmas).

TEXT: "For unto us a child is born." Isa. 9:6.

Alternative Topic: The Seven Wonders of Christmas.

I. The Wonder of the Fact. A festival may lose the fact upon which it is based. The birthday of the babe has escaped oblivion.

II. The Wonder of the Story. The beginning of the story. The unfolding. The continuance. This Christmas is a part of the story.

III. The Wonder of the Contrasts. Darkness vs. light. Hatred vs. Love.

IV. The Wonder of the Halos. Halos above shepherds, wise men, motherhood, childhood, fatherhood.

V. The Wonder of the Hope. We must keep on singing of peace on earth, good will to men.

VI. The Wonder of Grace. Grace came through Jesus Christ.

VII. The Wonder of Revelation. In the babe we see God.—M. K. W. H.

12.. Topic: Lincoln.

TEXT: "Commit thy way unto Jehovah; trust also in him, and he will bring it to pass." Ps. 37:5 (A.S.V.).

I. The greatness of Lincoln's work. Seen in: 1. Victory in great Civil War. 2. Emancipation of the slaves. 3. Preservation of the Union.

II. In and for all this—his reliance upon God for accomplishing his work (see extract from his letter to Quakers of Iowa, and inaugural addresses).

III. The elements which such reliance furnishes for all lives. 1. Strength—Sir Galahad,

My strength is as the strength of ten,
Because my heart is pure.

2. Determination. The spirit in which the power is used. 3. Courage, especially moral courage. 4. Hope; see Lincoln's Second Inaugural.

13. Topic: Insolvent Debtors (Financial Canvass).

TEXT: "How much owest thou unto my Lord?" Luke 16:5.
I. The creditor. 1. Our Creator. 2. Our Benefactor. 3. Our Redeemer.
II. Our indebtedness. 1. What have I received? 2. What have I paid?
III. Our means of payment. 1. All our works are insufficient. 2. God releases us by a ransom.

14. Topic: The Inner Light.

TEXT: "For this commandment . . . is not hidden from thee, neither is it far off. . . . But the word is very nigh unto thee, in thy mouth, and in thy heart." Deut. 30:11, 14.
There is then an inner light to guide us along the paths of duty and obedience.
I. We look so much to laws and statutes to settle everything for us when all the while our better, wiser selves are waiting to guide us. We look up and out for God's laws; we are slow to look for them within. The good counsels of life are in our own clearest visions.
II. We must, of course, try to make these inward voices wise; let love instruct us and a wisdom beyond our own advise us. We are truest then to God's laws and nearest his order when we are truest to our highest selves.
III. Then no duty is beyond our power, then every high command finds happy, inner response.—Gaius Glenn Atkins, D.D.

15. Topic Setting Him at Nought (Good Friday).

TEXT: "And Herod with his men of war set him at nought, and mocked him." Luke 23:11.
The pity, the tragedy of this passage is in that single sentence. For Jesus it meant the cross; for Herod it meant his own doom.
I. We need to take care what we make light of. And equally that to which we give weight. Naturally, "Herod and his soldiers" gave no weight to Jesus. (The sword has always made light of the cross.) His weights and balances belonged to another order than theirs. There was some little excuse for them.
II. But for our Herods and their soldiers there is no excuse at all, only the indictment of a terrible stupidity. For what they give no weight to strikes and will strike the balances in the scales of destiny.
III. All the losses of life are in making light of the way, the truth and the life of Jesus Christ. All our victories are in risking everything for love and goodness and the Master's Way, giving them sovereign strength.
O God who has appointed for all thy children a war to wage and a kingdom to win, forgive us that we make so little of love and make mockery of gentleness and scourge the Prince of Peace. Teach our rulers that gentleness alone can make them great and that only the meek shall inherit the earth. In His conquering Name. Amen.—G. G. A.

16. Topic: Behold the Man! (Good Friday.)

TEXT: "Behold the man!" John 19:5.
I. The feelings with which these words were or may be uttered. 1. Pity. 2. Mockery. 3. Faith. 4. Admiration.
II. Let us by faith behold the Christ. 1. Behold the Man of dignity. 2. Behold the man of humility. 3. Behold the Man of purity. 4. Behold the Man of suffering. 5. Behold the Man of glory.

17. Topic: The Crowning Miracle (Easter).

TEXT: "Now is Christ risen from the dead." I Cor. 15:20.
It was many years after the resurrection had been accomplished as a fact that Paul wrote these words, and yet he speaks of it in the present tense.
I. This is the right way for Christian minds to think of the crowning miracle of their faith.

II. We do not worship a dead Christ nor one whose victory over death has become merely a fact of history. His resurrection is fresher and has for us a more vitalizing interest than the happenings of yesterday of which we read in today's newspaper.

III. We worship a risen Christ whose resurrection is for us a glorious fact of the present tense. He is now risen from the dead, and in the firm security of that dynamic fact we shall rise also.—E. W. Caswell, D.D.

18. Topic: The Unreturning Soldier (Memorial Day).

TEXT: "Weep sore for him that goeth away: for he shall return no more, nor see his native country." Jer. 22:10.

Shallum, who went away never to return, is the type in this one respect of the brave soldier boy whose going away had no return.

I. His life was the toll of war. Widowed love and orphaned dependence wept in vain.

II. His eyes never saw again the land which his patriotism rescued or enriched. Ours is a blood-bought privilege.

III. But his memory is garlanded with the floral tokens of sincere mourning and warm affection. Marble and Memorial Day keep alive our patriot dead.—H. R.

19. Topic: Sins against Children (To Parents on Children's Day).

TEXT: "Do not sin against the child." Gen. 42:22.

The importance and value of children. Sin not against them. How they may be sinned against:

I. By depriving them of good parents.

II. By depriving them of the privilege of play.

III. By depriving them of good home life.

IV. By depriving them of secular education.

V. By failure to bring them up in the nurture and admonition of the Lord.

20. Topic: The Training of Children (Children's Day).

TEXT: "Train up a child in the way he should go; and when he is old, he will not depart from it." Prov. 22:6.

I. Training involves an ideal. The ideal—Christ's estimate of greatness.

II. Training involves personal discipline. What we are the boy will be.

III. Training involves a recognition of certain facts. 1. Capacity of evil in the child. 2. Capacity of good in the child. 3. The grace of God to overcome evil.

IV. Training a matter of education. Special considerations should be given each child.

V. The manifold nature of training. 1. Teach that the child belongs to Christ. 2. Teach that sin is the child's enemy. 3. Train by precept. 4. Train by example. 5. Train by efficient teaching of God's Word. 6. Train by carefully planned programs of worship and service.

21. Topic: An Ascended Yet Ever-present Lord (Ascension).

TEXT: "Lo, I am with you always, even unto the end of the world." Matt. 28:20.

These are the final words of a gospel, but the inaugural words of a ministry. They seem to mark the close of a dispensation, yet they open a perspective to the "end of the world." They mark the end of a temporal relationship, but the beginning of an eternal one.

I. This seems not impossible when the unique speaker is taken into account—Emmanuel, glorified and risen.

II. The only condition of fulfillment devolves upon the human chosen ones who receive and obey.

III. The resultant comfort is especially adapted to human longings. 1. In temptations. "Temptations lost their power when thou art nigh." 2. In sorrow or adversity: "Though I walk through the valley of the shadow of death, I will fear no evil, for thou art with me."—Rev. Claude R. Shaver.

22. Topic: Christ's Going Away (Ascension).

TEXT: "It is expedient for you that I go away." John 16:7.

I. His reasons for going.

II. His manner of going.

III. The effects of his going.

23: Topic: Real Values.

TEXT: "Can a man be profitable unto God?" Job 22:2.

These words come into the great drama of Job's life where they seem to imply the familiar query: "What's the use of religion; why strive for the highest?" The answer depends upon the spiritual nature of the inquirer. He is of no value if his life is self-centered.

I. On the other hand, the divine economy creates nothing without a value; insects, poisons, etc. Even though imperfect.

II. Imperfect human life may approach nearer perfection than any other creature's. Hence its value.

III. To deny is a reflection on Almighty wisdom. "Never thought that way," says the nonreligionist. No; but he acts it by ignoring the real agency of life development—the religion of faith and aspiration.

IV. Value has been shown: 1. In the perfect life of Christ. 2. In the price paid for man's redemption. 3. In the power of the endless life "breaking forth from the Easter tomb."

24. Topic: The Effects of Sin.

TEXT: "All have sinned, and come short of the glory of God." Rom. 3:23.

I. A well-attested fact.

II. A great equalizing fact. All have sinned.

III. A tragic fact. Sin deteriorates, curses, kills.

IV. A condemning fact.

25. Topic: A Multitude in Amazement (Whitsunday—Pentecost).

TEXT: "And they were all amazed, and were in doubt, saying one to another, What meaneth this?" Acts 2:12.

I. Note a multitude gathered from all parts of the world, vv. 9-18. The nations here enumerated spoke seven or eight different languages. The places mentioned covered the then known world. Suggests the widespread influence of the Gospel.

II. The multitude had gathered for religious purposes. They had come to the feast of Pentecost.

III. The multitude astonished by a miracle. 1. They heard Galileans speak in other tongues. v. 7. (Galileans proverbially ignorant and uncouth.) 2. They heard in their own tongues every man the wonderful works of God. The subject was one, the languages many.

IV. A multitude variously affected. All were amazed. Some inquired. Some mocked. Some said, "What meaneth this?" v. 12. Others said, "They are full of new wine," v. 13. Regarding the religion of Jesus Christ as fanaticism.

How does the gospel affect us?—F. W.

26. Topic: Fruits of the Spirit. (Pentecost).

TEXT: "But the fruit of the Spirit is," etc. Gal. 5:22, 23.

I. Their origin.

II. Their quality.

III. Their abundance and variety.

IV. Their testing.

27. Topic: The Power of the Spirit (Pentecost).

I. Wind. John 20:22.

II. Water. John 7:38, 39.

III. Fire. Acts 2.

28. Topic: The Holy Spirit's Work (Pentecost).

TEXT: "He shall testify of me." John 15:26.

I. Of the value of Christ's sacrifice.

II. Of the prevalence of his intercession.

III. Of the dimensions of his love.

IV. Of the suitableness and sufficiency of his salvation.

V. Of the beauty and glory of his person and character.

29. Topic: Fighting against God (Pentecost).

TEXT: "Ye do always resist the Holy Ghost." Acts 7:51.

To resist the Holy Ghost is a sin of deepest guilt. It is of the nature of basest ingratitude against God, for it is opposing the very means which God in his infinite love and mercy freely offers for our salvation.

I. The office of the Holy Spirit. 1. Convincing. 2. Entreating. 3. Admonishing. 4. Threatening.

II. The means he uses. 1. The Word. 2. Examples. 3. Conscience. 4. Providential dealings.

III. The modes of resisting him. 1. Inattention. 2. Procrastination. 3. Grieving, or quenching. 4. Contradiction.

IV. The tremendous consequences of resisting the Holy Spirit. Compunction of conscience gradually abates until resisters are "past feeling." "My Spirit shall not always strive," etc. "Ephraim is joined to his idols, let him alone." "Woe unto him that striveth with his Maker."

30. Topic: Life's Completion.

TEXT: "I came not to destroy, but to fulfill." Matt. 5:17 (A.S.V.).

I. Christ takes from life nothing that is worth keeping.

II. Christ demands the relinquishment of nothing that is not harmful to us.

III. Christ offers to life everything that is worth possessing.

31. Topic: Moving Forward (Rally Day).

TEXT: "Speak unto the children of Israel, that they go forward." Ex. 14:15.

Briefly relate the story of the exodus up to this point.

I. It was a time of inactivity. 1. They expected God to work a miracle. 2. God said they had a part to perform.

II. It was a time of testing. 1. How unusual was God's command! 2. God's way is always forward.

III. It was a time of crisis. 1. Defeat or victory lay in their hands. 2. God's purpose for the Jew. Would his people fail him?

IV. It was a time of victory. 1. What Moses' obedience did. 2. Israel did march forward, and to victory.

This message is greatly needed in our day. In this very trying time God says to us, "Go forward." Go forward in faith. Go forward against evil. Go forward in personal religious living. Go forward in religious work. Go forward to the promised land. There are rich promises for us.—R. H. B.

32. Topic: The Feast of Ingathering (Thanksgiving).

TEXT: "And thou shalt observe . . . the feast of ingathering at the year's end." Ex. 34:22.

Our Thanksgiving Day is our feast of ingathering, memento of God's goodness.

I. Its educational value. 1. It aids reflection. 2. It stimulates piety. 3. It tends to national virtue.

II. Its epochal character. "At the year's end." Sacred seasons are punctuation marks. Stop and think. Stop and thank.

III. Its joyous phenomena. 1. The joy of gathering. 2. The joy of using. 3. The joy of celebrating.—S. B. Dunn, D.D.

33. Topic: Paul's Social Teachings (Labor Day).

TEXT: "Let him that stole steal no more: but rather let him labour, working with his hands the thing which is good, that he may have to give to him that needeth." Eph. 4:28.

I. Reformation. "Let him that stole steal no more."

II. Industry. "Let him labour with his hands."

III. Honesty. "The thing which is good."

IV. Property. "That he may have."

V. Charity. "To give to him that needeth."—H. V. D.

34. Topic: Perilous Enticements.

TEXT: "My son, if sinners entice thee, consent thou not." Prov. 1:10.

The greater number of those who have been landed at length in degradation and ruin have been enticed by sinners into the way of it.

I. The danger of being enticed by sinners is not confined to any one period of life. Youth may be the most dangerous, but not the only dangerous period; as accidents on railways or highways often occur in most unlikely places.

II. The enticing is often unexpected. 1. As to time. 2. As to place. 3. As to persons. The tempter sometimes even goes to church!

III. It is of the enticing of sinners the text speaks, not of open calls. Fishes are enticed. Birds are enticed. Wild animals are enticed. And you are enticed. That is to say that you will have something offered you that looks good but only covers that which is really bad, harmful, dangerous.

IV. How to meet these enticings. "Consent thou not." 1. Say "No" at once. 2. Do not parley with them. 3. Think of the results, as well as of present gratification.

V. Remember, too, that Christ entices you. 1. The way to get strength to say "No" to Satan is to say "Yes" to Christ. 2. Though Christ entices you he does not offer you his best first. He reserves the best to the last. John 2:10.—J. C.

35. Topic: The Man of Manhood.

TEXT: "Mark the perfect man, and behold the upright: for the end of that man is peace." Ps. 37:37.

"Mark the perfect man." It cannot imply positive perfection, for that is impossible. Each child of God is perfect in Christ. "By one offering he has perfected forever them that are sanctified."

I. Let us make a brief analysis of perfect manhood. 1. He has bodily health. 2. Mental balance. 3. Moral vigor. He is "upright." He does not deceive his own heart. He is no hypocrite. He is sincere. His life and conduct are good, in private, in his family, in his community. He sets a good example of devotion to God and righteousness of demeanor.

II. This symmetry of character is produced by the Gospel. 1. It preserves the physical health. 2. It expands and quickens the intellect. 3. It sanctifies the affections and will.

III. The natural results of this character—the end. His present condition is blessed, and the end, however chequered the way, is peace. 1. He has peace in life. 2. He has tranquillity in death. "Mark him." He is a monument of God's grace and mercy.

36. Topic: Paul the Seer.

TEXT: "I will show him how many things he must suffer for my name's sake." Acts 9:16 (A.S.V.)

There is a vast difference between a "mere visionary" and a seer of heavenly visions. Paul was a seer of heavenly visions.

The five recorded visions of Paul are as follows:

1. The Damascus vision—a vision of Christ.
2. The Macedonian call vision—a vision of man.
3. The Corinthian vision—a vision of assurance.
4. The Jerusalem vision—a vision of exalted privilege.
5. The shipwreck vision—a vision of exalted privilege.

These are practical visions for everyone desiring best things. Do we wish them? If so, let us remember that they are each and all visions of service and visions of suffering. They will lead us to supply the magnificent demand of the twentieth-century world for heroes and heroines for God.—C. E. P.

37. Topic: The Voice of the Lord.

TEXT: "The voice of the Lord is powerful; the voice of the Lord is full of majesty." Ps. 29:4.

This sacred poem is most elevated and sublime. All God's works praise him, but there are some which praise him more than others. The voice of God is ever full of majesty. It is true. It is commanding. It is powerful.

I. God sometimes speaks through the destructive powers of nature. Breaketh the cedars, v. 5. Divideth the flames, v. 7. Shaketh the wilderness, v. 8. Thunderings and lightnings, Ex. 20: 18-20.

II. The Lord speaks to us in times of bodily affliction and death. "Wilt thou be made whole." "I am the resurrection and the life."

III. God often speaks to us by his Holy Spirit. Think whose voice it is.

IV. God constantly speaks through conscience. "The still small voice." "Speak, Lord, for thy servant heareth." "Be still and know . . . God."—W. C. W.

38. Topic: The Greatest of Graces.

TEXT: "The greatest of these is love." I Cor. 13:13 (A.S.V.)

All Christian graces are but the reflection of Christly love.

I. Christian joy is the exultation of Christly love.

II. Christian peace is the rest of Christly love. It is unruffled by sacrifice and undisturbed by outward storms.

III. Christian long-suffering is the patience of Christly love. The secret of the great apostle's patient endurance was love of Christ that constrained him.

IV. Christian beneficence is the activity of Christly love. As we partake of God's loving nature our active beneficence increases.

V. Christian faith is the heroism of Christly love. The lives of the heroes of faith spoken of in the eleventh chapter of Hebrews were inspired by love for the One whose they were and whom they served.

VI. Christian hope is the expectation of Christly love. The true Christian is the real optimist.—H. A. T.

39. Topic: Paying Our Vows.

TEXT: "What shall I render unto the Lord for all his benefits toward me? . . . I will pay my vows unto the Lord." Ps. 116:12, 14.

A searching question: "What shall I render unto the Lord?" An honest answer: "I will pay my vows." What do we owe unto the Lord?

I. The obligation of money (also of time and talent, producers of money). All men have this obligation, whether they accept it or not. The Jews accepted it. They paid a tithe of money—plus gifts and offerings. They gave one day in seven—plus holy days and seasons. God rightfully expects us to accept it. "Will a man rob God?" "Let each one lay by." I Cor. 16:2.

II. Obligations of love and gratitude. We cannot pay all our debts by means of a check. Love begets love. "We love God because he first loved us." Lack of gratitude is unnatural. Even a dog or a horse will show gratitude for kindness. God needs our love more than he needs our money. Christ said the first commandment is, "Thou shalt love the Lord."

III. Obligation to live uprightly. We cannot pay our debts by check plus flattery. It is possible to pay financial obligations to God and country and still be an undesirable citizen. Possible to express appreciation for benefits received, and yet break the heart of the benefactor. Life is the most valuable gift one can make: to family, to country, to God.—A. P. H.

40. Topic: Wrestlers.

TEXT: "And Jacob was left alone; and there wrestled a man with him until the breaking of the day." Gen. 32:24.

I. We are wrestlers still, wrestling with our ignorances and our divided selves, our difficulties, our perplexities— so much in the dark and so sadly alone. Wrestlers all. Life does not offer us its best on easy terms.

II. There is one secret of victory— "I will not let thee go except thou bless me." We must not, cannot, dismiss any experience till we have found its meanings for our lives and won from it some added wealth of spirit.

III. Easy? Never. But that is what life is for. As though God said: "This, wrestlers in the dark, is the price of better, braver selves and I am on your side though I seem to oppose you."

IV. We do often enough come limping from such experiences, but we face the dawn as we leave them behind and in such wrestlings win our souls.— G. G. A.

41. Topic: The New Will.

TEXT: "He is the mediator of the New Testament." Heb. 9:15.

I. The new will was grounded on a promise.

II. There was an estate to be divided —an eternal inheritance, an actual spiritual value to be bequeathed.

III. By the Spirit a new principle of heirship was formed in the regenerate heart.

IV. The values in the will were available only on the death of the testator.

V. This will had to be probated or passed upon in the judgment work of Christ's death, recognized when he ascended to glory.

VI. Christ as risen from the dead, "ever liveth" and becomes the executor of his own will.

VII. As heirs, we must: 1. Appear and claim under the will, or 2. Resort to the law for our heritage. Let us choose to accept under the will.—H. C. M.

42. Topic: The Way of Evil Men.

TEXT: "Go not in the way of evil men." Prov. 4:14.

God only recognizes two classes of characters. The way of the wicked is:

I. A dark way.

II. A slippery way.

III. A hard and thorny way.

IV. A crooked way.

V. A lonely way.

VI. A degrading way.

VII. A mean way.

VIII. A dangerous way.—Rev. Robert Brewin.

43. Topic: Inferences of Redemption.

TEXT: "For by grace are ye saved through faith; and that not of yourselves; it is the gift of God: not of works, lest any man should boast." Eph. 2:8, 9.

I. The first inference to be found here is that each one of us needs to be saved.

II. The second inference is that personal merit will not avail to save us.

III. The third inference is that only God's grace meets our need.

IV. The fourth inference is that Christ is the provision God makes for our salvation.

V. The fifth inference is that faith is the medium of availability.—Rev. William H. Prichard.

44. Topic: A Great Change.

TEXT: "Who hath delivered us from the power of darkness, and hath translated us into the kingdom of his dear Son." Col. 1:13.

We are here told of a great moral translation, a wonderful transformation. It is effected by redemption.

I. It is a translation from the darkness of ignorance to the light of truth. Darkness denotes ignorance. Ignorance denotes danger. It brings discomfort and fear. It leads to error. In darkness we have neither light nor sight.

II. It is a translation from guilt to reconciliation.

III. It is a translation from misery to peace.

IV. It is a translation from suspicion to confidence.

V. It is a translation from dislike to affection.

VI. It is a translation from disobedience to cheerful compliance.

It is a Divinely wrought change. It is a happy change. It is a momentous change. Out of captivity into the "kingdom of his dear Son."—H.

45. Topic: Dangerous Gods.

TEXT: "And their gods shall be a snare unto you." Judg. 2:3.

The Old Testament prophets and moralists waged a long fight against the gods of Canaan. They were dangerous gods because they made a cult of desire and asked for sacrifice only the indulgences of sense.

I. If life is empty when its shrines are empty what care we need to take about our loyalties and devotions!

II. There are still dangerous gods. A religion of race and blood enshrines dangerous gods. So do strife for power and possession and the allurements of sense. Whatever bows the sacred capacities of the spirit before low altars is dangerous. It takes our best and leaves us only the bitter taste of the ashes of our faiths and enthusiasms; or such tragedy as has wasted half the world.

III. What is the matter with the world? Dangerous gods.

Lord of the Searching and the Lasting, whose altars are high and holy, teach us the sacredness of our faith and loyalties and forbid that we should spend them upon the base or the fugitive. Be thou the guardian of our altars. Forgive us all the gods we set up in place of thee and thy causes. In his name who has lifted our vision to thy Fatherhood and made this world thy temple. Amen. —G. G. A.

46. Topic: Feeding on the Wind.

TEXT: "Ephraim feedeth on wind, and followeth after the east wind." Hos. 12:1.

The east wind, in Palestine, coming from Arabia and the Far East over large tracts of sandy waste, is parching, scorching, destructive to vegetation, and oppressive to man. It is violent and destructive both on the sea and on the land. In leaving God and following idols Ephraim fed on what is unsatisfying and chased after that which is destructive. If a hungry man were to feed on wind it would be light food! If he overtook the east wind it would harm him. The thought is of worthless soul-food. The words have been translated, "Ephraim grazeth wind." The idea is of a soul seeking satisfaction and support in those things which are utterly unsubstantial and worthless—"wind."

I. Sensual indulgences are worthless soul-food. The soul cannot eat straw like an ox.

II. Worldly distinctions are worthless soul-food.

III. Religious formalities are worthless soul-food.

47. Topic: The Cultivation of Self-respect.

TEXT: "And he said unto me, Son of man, stand upon thy feet, and I will speak with thee." Ezek. 2:1 (A.S.V.)

I. As a man cultivate self-respect. Recognize the dignity of life. Cultivate manhood, foster its best qualities, safeguard it.

II. As a member of society cultivate self-respect. Preserve your independence. Resist low motives. Cherish lofty ideals.

III. As a patriot also, live above personal pique, interested flattery, intimidation, selfish party considerations.

IV. As a Christian especially, possessing not only manhood, but redeemed manhood, being an heir of all the ages.

V. As a God-employed laborer, in business, school, or home, guard jealously thy gifts, privileges, opportunities.

VI. As a student in the university of knowledge, be eclectic. Abstain from mud baths. Avoid knowledge which entails a curse. Covet knowledge which ripens on the tree of life. Cultivate self-respect. Stand upon thy feet and God will speak to you, and will commission you.

48. Topic: Conditions of Success in Business.

TEXT: "Cast thy bread upon the waters: for thou shalt find it after many days," etc. Eccles. 11:1-6.

The writer of the book of Ecclesiastes took a very practical view of life. In these verses we may think of him as recounting conditions of success in business.

I. Consider some of the means suggested for adoption. 1. "Cast thy bread upon the waters," meaning that for the man who would succeed there is the necessity of venturing somewhat. 2. Be prudent in dividing risks. "Divide the portion into seven," etc., which seems to enforce the old rule "not to put all your eggs into one basket." 3. Confidence in going forward. "He that observeth the wind shall not sow." That man will make a poor farmer who is too much frightened to proceed for fear of the weather. 4. Diligence. Work is the secret of success. It is "the hand of the diligent that maketh rich."

II. Consider also some of the motives

to be cherished. 1. Expectation. Bread: "Thou shalt find it after many days." The seed-sowing, the venture of business, will generally prove successful. 2. Prudence. As no one can foresee the future, the prudent man lays his plans to "divide the risks." 3. Redoubled energy. "In the morning sow thy seed, and in the evening withhold not thine hand," believing that in the end labor will be crowned with success.

Business is not incompatible with religion. True religion is no hindrance to business. Christian character and business may be helpful to each other. Both should be, and are, a source of blessing to the world.—T. W.

49. Topic: Our Saviour.

INTRODUCTORY: The word "Saviour" is "the most valued and most endearing and most tender of the names of Jesus." The association of the word "Josua"; "Thou shalt call his name Jesus; for it is he that shall save. . . ."

TEXT: "They said to the woman, 'It is no longer because of your words that we believe, for we have heard for ourselves, and we know that this is indeed the Savior of the world.' " John 4:42 (R.S.V.). This is the only time in the Four Gospels where anyone applied the word "Saviour" to Jesus. In Luke an angel uses the word, and it falls from the lips of Mary, but not as applied to Jesus.

He did not come to judge the world
He did not come to blame;
He did not only come to seek—
It was to save He came:
And when we call Him Saviour,
Then we call Him by His name.

DISCUSSION:
I. The Saviour of One—The Samaritan woman.
  1. An experience of being found.
  2. An experience of being forgiven.
II. The Saviour of Many. "And many more believed because of his word." V. 41.
III. The Saviour of the World. The Samaritans called him that. He is then my Saviour, yours!—M. K. W. H.

50. Topic: The Ladder of Degradation.

TEXT: "Look not thou upon the wine when it is red, when it giveth his color in the cup, when it moveth itself aright. As the last it biteth like a serpent, and stingeth like an adder." Prov. 23:31, 32.

We call upon Christian people to pay renewed attention to the dangerous practice of drinking. We ought to see that there is a kind of ladder of degradation involved in what we sometimes brightly call "social drinking."

I. First step—occasional drinking.
II. Second step—habitual drinking.
III. Third step—active alcoholism, inability to control oneself.—Harold A. Bosley.

SECTION IV. Outlines and Themes for Lenten Services. Ash Wednesday to Easter

FOR DEEPENING THE SPIRITUAL LIFE

The Lenten period gets its name from the fact that the days now perceptibly lengthen, but of course has its real significance in the forty days which prepare for Easter. In the reckoning Sundays are omitted, since these are always feast days, commemorating the resurrection of our Lord. In the fifth century the forty days' fast was thought to have had Apostolic origin. Some believe it came from the fact that Jesus spent forty hours in the tomb. Others relate it to our Saviour's temptation and fasting for forty days in the wilderness.

Lent is a period now very widely observed. The traditional aim and purpose of the season has always been to focus the attention of the serious-minded Christian upon the figure of Christ himself. Spiritual exercise of prayer and meditation, worship and personal devotion, fasting and good works, have been directed by the Church mainly in order that the Christian believer might more sympathetically follow Jesus through the major events and aspects of his ministry. So doing, one gains a new apprehension of him as the Word of God to us, the children of God, expressed in events which constitute the decisive turning point in history.

Lent calls for release from excessive social occupation, freedom from indul-

gences and a little more time for reflection and consideration of the deeper meaning of life. This means broadening and enriching life, making it real and shaping its course toward more definitely spiritual ends.

The period begins with Ash Wednesday with its call to repentance. As we approach the great Divine Act which brings forgiveness to sinful men, penitence becomes the normal attitude of earnest men and women. The very first person for the minister to consider is himself. Then, so far as he can accomplish it, he leads his people, and as many others as possible, into communion with Christ and the deeper experiences of the Christian life.

Lenten Pause

The group of skyscrapers in New York City known as Rockefeller Center occupies some twelve acres of land owned by Columbia University and leased until the year A.D. 2015 for a rental of three million dollars a year. The plot of ground is bisected by a short street sixty feet wide running between 48th and 51st Streets. This street is a private thoroughfare, though used freely by the public. Every July, on a chosen day, the trustees of Columbia University rope off this street for twelve hours, between sunrise and sunset, in order to retain the University's property rights. Otherwise by reason of use the street might become

27

a public thoroughfare and be seized as the property of the city.

The Christian life must be lived in the midst of the world with much passing traffic. How important then the need for stated moments when all of life is rededicated to God. Without such periodic commitments of one's soul to God, the world will soon assert its common law rights and come to claim its possession.—F. C. K.

1. Theme: Repentance (Ash Wednesday).

TEXT: "God . . . now commandeth all men everywhere to repent." Acts 17:30.

INTRODUCTORY: Has the human race outgrown repentance? Apparently, for one hears little about it these days. But repentance is still a good word. It has not been taken out of the dictionaries. I also find that repentance is a good Bible word. Many words and phrases have had to be changed to meet the changed conditions. For example, simplest and best known among many examples, the "charity" of I Corinthians is not charity as we know it, but love. Repentance, however, is just as good a Bible word as ever.

I. A good word, potent in Scripture, repentance is also vital in life. There is no substitute for repentance. One may ride in an automobile instead of an oxcart; it is an excellent method of vehicular travel. One may cross the ocean in a steamship instead of a sailboat; he is wise to do that. But one cannot ride into heaven, he cannot acquire the graces of the Christian faith, nor achieve the triumph of Christian character by way of New Year's resolutions, or by nonchalantly saying, "Let bygones be bygones." Repentance is the proved way to God, life, and light. It is the good old way our fathers trod. And it is no less the good way of our new scientific age. There is no substitute in human experience for repentance.

II. Repentance presupposes sin. One can scarcely expect a little babe to repent, for a little babe has not sinned. But we have sinned. "All have sinned and come short of the glory of God."

That is true not because the Bible says it; the Bible says it because it is true. "Let him that is without sin cast the first stone," said Jesus. How many stones were thrown? Not one. Let any preacher stand before his well-dressed, well-fed Sunday morning congregation and ask the question, "All without sin lift the right hand." He would conclude that the congregation was afflicted with an epidemic of arm paralysis, for not one hand would be raised. There are degrees of sin, and different kinds of sin, of course. Not all men are libertines, but there are sins other than the sin of evil thinking. Not all men are drunkards, but there are sins other than the sin of drunkenness; there is the sin of gluttony. Not all women are drug addicts, but there are sins other than the narcotic way of slow suicide; there are the deadly narcotics of envy, hate, jealousy, covetousness. There are the sins of false standards, of doing less than we ought to do; sins of neglect, fear, indifference, silence when we should speak. There are ugly sins for which we have nothing but disdain, and there are pink parlor sins that get us without our knowing it. We would not steal a dollar from anyone, but we would steal almost anyone's good name if we take the notion. We would violently resent the idea of throwing ourselves away in drunkenness, or walking the exhilarating but precipice-end-path of the narcotic, but we will throw ourselves away in unchristian social rivalries, in an idleness we have not earned and a leisure we do not know how to use. There are social sins as well as individual sins. We would not deliberately take the life of anyone, but our ruthless machine age crushes the individual, soul and body, by putting the machine above the man. What more need be said to establish the fact that sin is still in the world and that repentance is not an outgrown fancy but a present, pressing necessity?

III. The immediate first step of repentance is acknowledgment. Some would call it confession. The name does not matter. Confession to whom? To

God, of course. The simple act of repentance is right-about-face. The superb result of repentance is a changed life. The barren field now produces a harvest. Wilfred Grenfell, nominal Christian, became Wilfred Grenfell, crusader for Christ. The divine element in repentance crowns all else. After all it is God who forgives.

Out of my shameful failure and loss,
  Jesus, I come, Jesus I come;
Into the glorious gain of Thy Cross,
  Jesus, I come to Thee.
—B. S. W.

2. Theme: In Quiet Places Apart.

TEXT: "Led by the Spirit into the wilderness, being forty days." Luke 4:1, 2. "Departed into a solitary place, and there prayed." Mark 1:35.

How hard it is in these days to claim time for quietness alone! We live in an age of speed accelerators and space eliminators. Nearly everyone has a crowded date book and is constantly faced with the necessity of rushing from one place to the next. We become so concerned about increasing our efficiency—which too often means multiplying the number of things we dabble in—that often we overlook the elements supremely essential both to efficiency and to satisfactory living.

I. No one was ever busier than Jesus in the great days of his ministry in Galilee. But the busier he was, and the more gigantic his task appeared as it confronted him, the more he realized and claimed the absolute necessity for quiet times apart. The records tell us that after his baptism he departed into the desert and there for forty days—nearly six weeks—he meditated upon his great problem, seeking guidance and strength through fellowship with God in prayer. There the great God-given purpose of his life was thought through anew. There the principles upon which he must proceed were reaffirmed.

II. When the pressure of multitudes was at its height he often stole away for quiet communion with the Father, that his perspective might be regained. One little sentence in Mark tells expressively that when the ordinary hours were so full to overflowing he rose up early—a great while before the dawn—and stole away by Himself to a quiet place and there prayed.

Does it not seem that most of us need more of these times for spiritual renewal? Can our lives in these significant days attain their possible richness without them? If Jesus so definitely felt the need of reliance upon Divine invisible resources and could come out from such moments apart, refreshed and empowered for greater accomplishments, can we afford to neglect these opportunities in our day?

III. But some practical one replies, "What is the use of prayer?" The answer is, obviously, "It depends upon your conception of and your experience in prayer." If prayer means merely the repetition of fixed formulas and the stringing together of pious phrases it may be anemic indeed. If prayer means just going by force of habit to your room or to your church and adopting a certain posture for a few minutes of the day or of the week it may easily lack vitality. But for the follower of Jesus, these are exactly the conceptions which the Master in his teaching and practice sought constantly to supplant and rule forever out of life.—R. B. B.

3. Theme: A Great Evil and an Urgent Question.

TEXT: "Why then is this people of Jerusalem slidden back by a perpetual backsliding?" Jer. 8:5.

I. The great evil mentioned is departure from God, here called backsliding. It is a great evil from its very nature. 1. Because it involves the basest ingratitude. 2. Because it involves also the violation of the most solemn vows.

II. It is a sin also very evil in its influence. 1. Upon oneself. It arrests the progress of the soul. It darkens its prospects. It curtails its liberty. And it destroys its usefulness. 2. Upon others. it encourages unbelievers. It deters inquirers. It embarrasses the friends of truth.

III. The urgent question. "Why?" I. It comes not by force of circumstance over which we have no control. No power in the world can drive us back and away from God against our will. 2. It comes not by God's withdrawal of willingness to help. 3. The causes are in ourselves. Such as the neglect of the means of spiritual improvement. Neglect of the study of God's Word. Neglect of attendance on the means of grace. Or the cherishing of some secret sin.

Remember from whence you have fallen. Repent. Return.

4. Theme: God's Nearness.

TEXT: "Thou art near, O Lord." Ps. 119:151.

There is one thing above all others that we need in the midst of these difficult, trying days—and that is a sense of the immanence of God; to feel that he is not remote or far distant, that he is not indifferent to our needs or separate from our lives but very near, within easy reach of all who need him.

I. If we have that deep conviction, we shall be prepared to meet the discipline of life's most tragic days with steady eyes and valiant hearts. No suffering will be too severe to be endured patiently, no disappointment too bitter to be faced courageously, no loss too great to be withstood bravely, and no sorrow too intense to be borne with fortitude.

II. Among the many gifts which our Christian faith bestows on us, none is more precious than that of the constant, close fellowship of our Saviour. He found his greatest source of strength in his unshaken conviction of his Father's nearness to him. He never felt alone and, in the loneliest moments of his life, when all human companionship failed him, he was surest of the Divine Presence.

III. As we face all the perplexities of these most difficult days, may we never lose the sense of his nearness—always nearest and dearest when needed most.

We shall then be girded with strength to go on from day to day, undismayed and unafraid, in the knowledge of his presence near at hand.—R. B. B.

5. Theme: The Accepted Call.

TEXT: "When thou saidst, Seek ye my face; my heart said unto thee, Thy face, Lord, will I seek." Ps. 27:8.

Here is a call and a response, an accepted call.

I. God's call. "Thou saidst." 1. True religion originates with God. 2. And here is indicated what true religion is. "Seek ye my face." 3. This implies honest endeavor. "Seek."

II. Man's reply. "Thy face, Lord, will I seek." The reply is almost an echo of the call. The Psalmist practically said, "I mean just what God means." "Thy face, Lord, will I seek." 1. It is personal. "I." 2. It is prompt. "When thou saidst." 3. It is emphatic. "Thy face, Lord, will I seek." 4. It came from the right place. "My heart said." Lips may lie, the heart never.—T. K.

6. Theme: Belonging to Christ.

TEXT: "I of Christ." I. Cor. 1:12.

We are not now conisdering why there were any sects among early Christians, some saying, "I am of Paul; and I of Apollos; and I of Cephas; and I of Christ." We are only thinking of what such words as "I of Christ" should signify.

I. They should mean to own his essential dignity as God's Son.

II. They should mean to acknowledge his Divine Mission in the world.

III. They should mean to believe in his truths, his teachings.

IV. They should mean to rely on his sacrifice.

V. They should mean to love his Person.

VI. They should mean to obey his will.

There are many other things which belonging to Christ should and does mean, but these are a few that are central and essential.—H.

7. Theme: Spiritual Refreshment.

TEXT: "But whosoever drinketh of the water that I shall give him shall never thirst; but the water that I shall give him shall be in him a well of water springing up into everlasting life." John 4:14.

There are two kinds of wells: one a reservoir, the other a spring. The latter is the one referred to in this verse. It has the activity of a fountain: motion, not rest, motion derived from itself. That is what Christ promises to us—his indwelling spirit. The resulting life will be a consequence of that indwelling, continual spiritual refreshment. How much we need it!

I. A fountain within. Most people nourish themselves from without but the things they take never satisfy; they only create further desires for the same things. I think the same holds true of wisdom, knowledge, culture, and intellectual development. Nothing that ministers to but one part of our nature wholly satisfies. If, however, we have the spirit of Christ in our hearts, then under all circumstances peace is possible. Joy, contentment, hope, and quiet; everything the soul desires comes from this indwelling fountain and the supply is inexhaustible.

II. This gift is a springing fountain. Water may yield to gravity or it may be pumped up or it may roll as it does in the sea, drawn by the moon, driven by the winds, controlled by the currents. But this spring rises by an energy implanted within itself, self-generated, self-regulated. So with this spirit of Christ: it is not stagnant but is constantly active, a wonderful thing, a relief from the monotony of accustomed tasks, from ennui; emancipation from the possible drudgery of duty, freedom from the tyranny of external circumstances, liberty from the bondage of imposed necessity, glorious deliverance from bondage to externals.

III. It is a leaping fountain of refreshment, a fountain springing up into eternal life. The water of a fountain rises by its own impulse but it falls back into its own basin. This fountain of spiritual refreshment rises higher and higher reaching its source; it is eternal in its duration; not subject to change, not differing in content, quality, or quantity; ever and always the same, rising to the level of its source!

If you desire a life that reaches its goal, in which your spiritual desires are satisfied, a life full of joyous energy, a life free from the tyranny of circumstance and externals, open your hearts wide to the gift of this great source of spiritual refreshment. It is unceasing, unfailing, everlasting. The joy of it is that you may have just as much of it as you really desire. That is not true of any other thing. There are so many material things you may want and cannot have; but you can have as great a supply of spiritual power as you really and truly want.—R. B. B.

8. Theme: The Broken Yoke.

TEXT: "And [they] shall know that I am the Lord, when I have broken the bands of their yoke, and delivered them." Ezek. 34:27.

It appears from the text that there is a process by which God's people are brought to know him. The process is that in which he breaks the bands of their yoke. Then they know that he is God, the Lord.

I. Many yokes which God's people bear they cannot break themselves. Yet there is no yoke God cannot remove. One yoke is a tendency to unbelief. Some Christians are loaded with a yoke of trouble. Some have the yoke of poverty, others of ill health.

II. Christians experience a great deliverance when the yoke is broken. The yoke removed and the Lord revealed! That is the order. 1. We believe that God is powerful. There is nothing too hard for him to do. 2. We believe that he is wise. He knows the way we take. He knows the end from the beginning. We can well afford to trust him. 3. We believe that he is loving. He will do what is best for us. 4. The special hand of God is often seen in the breaking of the yokes of his people.

III. The effect upon God's people of

realizing so great and precious a promise as this. 1. "They shall know that I am the Lord." They do know it. They come to realize it. 2. It leads them to admire, and love, and worship and obey the Lord.

Do we realize and admire such a promise as this? Do we trust, rest upon it? Are we trusting God to supply our needs? It ensured to the Israelites great happiness and continued security in their inheritance. Canaan was typical of heaven. It is typical of our "home over there."—C. H .S.

SPECIAL GOOD FRIDAY SERVICE

1. Theme: Beneath the Cross of Jesus.

TEXT: "And they crucified him." Matt. 27:35.

Yes, there they crucified him.

I. The deed transforms the place. Calvary, the place of crucifixion, has become the center of the world's history and the world's salvation. The great central event of all history is the death of our Lord and Saviour Jesus Christ. The centuries circle round the cross.

II. The cost of salvation smites all indifference to religion. If Christ was willing to die that we might be saved, what ought not we to do?

III. Those who watch Christ may find in him a King, a Redeemer, an Example, or if they themselves are bad, only a subject for mockery and insult. Which company shall we join?

IV. The cross expresses God's feelings toward sin, his readiness to forgive sin, the terrible evil and danger of sin that cost such a sacrifice for deliverance from it. No one would suffer so much to save others from a slight evil or little danger.

V. The cross declares in "letters that can be read from the stars" God's love for man. The atonement on the cross was a voluntary sacrifice. When the Greeks were besieging Troy and met with ill success, the priest Calchas told them that the only way to appease the offended goddess and gain the victory was to sacrifice to Diana Iphigenia, the beautiful daughter of Agamemnon. And these brave men of old are said to have taken her by strategy and force and brought this innocent girl to the altar to slay her. This sacrifice (though she was rescued) was mean and unjust beyond words to express. But when any persons have offered themselves, as Horatius and his comrades at the bridge of Rome, or the nobles of Calais to Edward VI, the sacrifice has been the height of heroism. The sacrifice of Christ expressed the highest love possible.

VI. The cross furnishes every possible motive for turning from sin, touching the heart with love, showing our danger, giving us the hope of forgiveness and life, teaching the law of duty which prefers death to failure or neglect. It shows the value of our souls, the value of salvation, and the worth of eternal life in heaven.—P.

2. Alternate Good Friday Theme: The Superscription on the Cross.

TEXT: "And a superscription also was written over him in letters of Greek, and Latin, and Hebrew, *This is the King of the Jews.*" Luke 23:38.

It was the custom of the Romans in order that the justice of their proceedings might be vindicated, when they crucified anyone, to make public the cause of his death. This was done by placing over the head of the crucified a tablet written in capital letters publishing the cause of his death.

I. Let us consider first the words of this inscription. *"This is the King of the Jews."* They formed a most extraordinary title. Instead of proclaiming Christ's crime they vindicated his innocence. They were written in three languages, in Greek, in Latin, in Hebrew. In Greek because of the Hellenic Jews who were then in Jerusalem for the Passover. In Latin, which was the language of the Roman government under which the crucifixion took place. And in Hebrew, the language of the people to whom Christ belonged. The words and languages of this eulogy and epitaph seem almost prophetic. Hebrew was the language of religion; Greek the language of wisdom and learning; Latin the language of power. It has been claimed that Providentially the superscription was designed to signify that the Gospel of Christ is to be preached to all nations, beginning at Jerusalem, and to be read in all languages.

II. Let us think further for a few moments of the writer of the superscription. It was Pilate. Pilate was the judge. He now becomes, quite unconsciously, Christ's vindicator as also his herald to proclaim his coming glory. That superscription was both a vindicating title and a predicting and presaging message. It was also an immutable title. Pilate was urged to change it, but he determinedly said, "What I have written I have written."

Yes, it was an extraordinary title. Instead of proclaiming Christ's crime it vindicated his innocence. It was public, written in three languages. It was honorable, for thus the cross became a throne of majesty. It was a vindicating title. It was a predicting and presaging title. It was an immutable title. Pilate left it there, *"This is the King of the Jews."*

III. The cross was the best place for that superscription. Yes, the cross explains the title. The cross sets forth the character and mission of "The King of the Jews." Let men do what they will, they cannot cause Christ to abandon his purpose, his work, his mission, and come down from the cross.

IV. Pilate was the best writer of that superscription. Who else could have written it? Not Peter or John or any disciple. It was Pilate, the very judge who had pronounced the sentence on Christ. In God's providence he was the one to supply the true statement, the vindicating title, the superscription of Christ's majesty. Christ was "the King of the Jews," and his reign is extending to the very ends of the earth.

V. In closing let us note that this crucifixion day was the best time for the publication of that superscription. Just at the moment when Jesus on the cross was vindicating his claim to rule the hearts of men he is hailed as King. Men from many countries and all parts of Palestine were present. The time was just when there was a great confluence of all sorts of people to take notice. This must have had much to do with the carrying of the supremely important facts to many parts of the world.

Let it be noted that the providence of God can and often does overrule the counsels and actions of the worst of men to his own glory. He is never at a loss for means to promote his own ends. Pilate would not recede from what he had written on Christ's behalf. Then how shameful a thing for Christians to retract or go back upon what they have said or done on Christ's behalf. Did Pilate fix such an honorable and vindicating title on the cross? Then the cross of Christ is a dignified cross.

Wilt thou do less than Pilate? Come crown him as your King. Say as well as sing:

In the cross of Christ I glory,
  Towering o'er the wrecks of time;
All the light of sacred story
  Gathers round its head sublime.
                                —H.

QUOTABLE LENTEN POETRY

LENT

Oh happy time of blessed tears,
Of surer hopes, of chast'ning fears,
Undoing all our evil years.
  Oh hearken when we cry,
    Chastise us with Thy fear;
  Yet, Father! in the multitude
    Of Thy compassions, hear!

We, who have loved the world, must learn
Upon the world our backs to turn,
And with the love of God to burn.
  Oh hearken when we cry,
    Chastise us with Thy fear;
  Yet, Father! in the multitude
    Of Thy compassions, hear!
                        —F. W. Faber

THE MARCH TO CALVARY

The Saviour King goes forth to die!
  Goes forth in all his glory bright!
And angels from the realms on high,
  Look down to see the wondrous sight.
On, on to Calvary's fateful hill,
  Reviled by those he came to bless;
But in his suffering bearing still,
  The Majesty of Righteousness!
The Saviour King goes forth to die!
                    —Shapcott Wensley

HIS CROSS—MY CROSS

His cross was heavy, awkward, large,
  So very plain;
Designed to cause the utmost sense
  Of human pain.
My cross is made of yellow gold,
  A pretty thing;
I wear it, yet it has no weight,
  Or painful sting

His cross bloomed from the blood-sweat
  of Gethsemane,
And bore salvation through the heat
  Of Calvary.
My cross has never felt the drip
  Of blood and sweat,
And not through choice or force has it
  And Calvary met.

His cross still sheds upon the world
  A deathless glow;
My cross just dangles from a chain,
  Exposed for show.
                    —George W. Wiseman.

GOOD FRIDAY

You drove the nails in his white, white
  feet;
  I pierced each tender hand:
And we laughed as we lifted the cross
  on high—
  Too wise to understand.

You gave him the gall and vinegar;
  I thrust the lance in his side;
Yet they say it was years and years ago
  That the Saviour was crucified.
                    —Edgar Daniel Kramer.

HIS HANDS AND HIS FEET

Lord, when I am weary with toiling,
And burdensome seem Thy commands,
If my load should lead to complaining,
Lord, show me Thy hands—
Thy nail-pierced Hands, Thy Cross-torn
  Hands.
My Saviour, show me Thy Hands.

Christ, if ever my footsteps should falter,
And I be prepared for retreat,
If desert or thorn cause lamenting,
Lord, show me Thy Feet—
Thy bleeding Feet—Thy nail-scarred
  Feet.
My Jesus, show me Thy Feet.

O God, dare I show Thee
My hands and my feet?
                    —Unidentified.

THERE WAS A GARDEN

A cross—One staggering beneath the
  weight.
(Golgotha shivered, but knew not why)
A mob—goading with spears of scarlet
  hate
This One condemned to die.

"Now in the place where he was crucified
There was a garden." Her olive trees
Leaned over the wall and shuddering
  sighed
To the sobbing breeze.

The lilies stirred from sleep and wept at
  the sound
Of the tumult cleaving the day;
And the grasses said; "We stand on holy
  ground—
It was God who passed this way."

Men mocked him. Their frenzy billowed
  and grew
To ghastly impact on Calvary's sod.
Only the garden bowed her heart and
  knew
He was the Son of God.
                    —Marie Barton.

THE NEW TOMB

Fast-sealed the crypt
  They laid Him in,
But death is stripped
  Of power to win;
The sov'reign word through rock and sod
Proclaims, "Awake, thou Son of God."

Again He rests,
  Unwept, unknown,
In hearts once blest,
  Cold hearts of stone,
In brutish lives for which He died,
In Mammon's tomb the Crucified.

Great God of Light,
  The rayless gloom,
The dayless night
  Of sin's new tomb
Thy grace implores: revive us men;
O Christ, rise up in us again.

—N. S. Reeves

OUTLINES AND THEMES FOR LENTEN EVANGELISM

Fellow pastors, evangelism is our supreme duty and most resultful endeavor. The lenten season is most adapted to intensified preaching of the evangel and to the ingathering of souls. The reception of new members, both young, from the Communion or Confirmation Classes, and those who are older, about Easter time, mark this as the climax of the year. There is great call and great need for this work. "O Lord, revive thy work in the midst of the years, in the midst of the years make known."

1. Topic: A Disciple of Christ.

TEXT: "Will ye also be his disciples?" John 9:27.

This word "disciple" was the first name attached to Christ's followers. He was known as Teacher, therefore those who received his instruction were known as disciples. "The disciples were first called Christians at Antioch."

I. Let us think first of what is implied in being a disciple of Christ. 1. It implies surely that we accept him as being truly the Christ, the Messiah, the Saviour of men. 2. It implies also that we accept and rest upon him as our personal Saviour. 3. It implies too that we try to know and follow his teachings. 4. And also that we imitate his example of meekness, humility, long-suffering, acts of love, and show zeal in promoting his kingdom and interests.

II. What are some of the happy privileges of discipleship? Many are implied in the above statements. 1. They are also beloved of God as his children. 2. They are heirs of his promised blessings. 3. God is their refuge and support. 4. They will be the Lord's when he comes to make up his jewels.

III. There remains the all-important question: "Will ye also be his disciples?" 1. There is no compulsion. "*Will* you?" You have the power of choice. 2. It is a personal inquiry. "Will *you?*"

2. Topic: The Gracious Invitation.

TEXT: "Whosoever will, let him take the water of life freely." Rev. 22:17.

What beautiful language as regards the Gospel of Christ! What a gracious invitation!

I. As to the Inviter. It is Christ himself. He invited once on earth, "Come unto me." He now invites from heaven with the same urgency and love.

II. The persons invited. The athirst. Do you want to be happy? Joy is here for you whoever and whatever you are.

III. The blessings invited to. "The water of life." Water, living and life-giving. A quickening well. A well of water springing up unto everlasting life. Its vivifying and resuscitating influence!

IV. The price. "Freely." Free to each one as he is, even the thirstiest of men, even the chief of sinners. Consider the freedom with which it should be received.

V. The time. At the time when the invitation is given. No! It comes here at the close of this closing book of Revelation. It comes as Christ's last words in the book and meant for a weary thirsty world.

VI. The unlimited extent to which it is addresesd. "Whosoever will." No one who comes will be denied. This is a God-thirsty world. "Come." You are a God-thirsty soul. Come. The Spirit says, "Come." The Christian Church (the Bride) says, "Come." The mere hearer is commanded to say, "Come." This all reveals God's mercy toward a soul-thirsting world.

3. Topic: God's Loving-kindness.

TEXT: "How excellent is thy loving-kindness, O God! therefore the children of men put their trust under the shadow of thy wings," etc. Ps. 36:7, 8.

I. Let us think first of God's loving-kindness. 1. It is unmerited. 2. It is disinterested. 3. It is costly. 4. It is munificent. 5. It is endless.

II. What is the duty such loving kindness places upon us? 1. That of trust for our temporal wants. 2. That of trust for our preservation and comfort in the trials of life. 3. That of trust for grace to continue and progress in the Christian life.

III. Think of the happiness such loving-kindness causes Christians to expect, both, 1. Here on earth. 2. In God's house in heaven.

4. Topic: Plenty of Room.

TEXT: "Yet there is room."   Luke 14:22.

The parable compares the kingdom of heaven to a feast of joy. Yet there were guests who excused themselves.

I. "Yet there is room"—where? At the feast, at the table, in the house, in the kingdom of God. 1. Room with Christ himself. He calls "Come." 2. Room at his table. Fullness of joy. Yet he still cries, "Compel them to come in." 3. Room with his company, which is yet too small.

II. "Yet there is room"—for whom? 1. Not for those who feel secure and careless as sinners. 2. Not for those self-righteous ones who depend on their own goodness, virtue, etc. "Because thou sayest I am rich, and increased with goods, and have need of nothing, and knowest not that thou art wretched." But there is room for sincere and penitent souls, every one! If you wish to be saved through Christ's grace, then there is plenty of room.

III. "Yet there is room"—how long yet? "Yet"; that means now, at this moment. Be admonished by that word "yet." Today "yet!" But tomorrow may mean no, too late. Consider where there is room, for whom there is room, and how long there is room. "Now is the accepted time. Today is the day of salvation." "Him that cometh unto me I will in no wise cast out."

5. Topic: Seeking the Lord.

TEXT: "Seek the Lord, and ye shall live." Amos 5:6.

In the days of Amos the prophet the rebellious people of Israel were bringing ruin upon themselves by their sinful conduct. But their case was not hopeless for the prophet assured them if they would seek the Lord they could live. And his words are applicable to us and to all men.

I. Think first of the duty urged. "Seek the Lord." 1. How the Lord may be found. By earnest seeking. "Oh that I knew where I might find him." This is the attitude and language of the penitent. 2. We are to come to the Lord in his own appointed way. Confessing our sin. Forsaking our sin. Faith in the Lord Jesus Christ.

II. Notice, second, the encouragement given. "And ye shall live." Sin brings death, but grace brings salvation. 1. "Ye shall live" in happy communion with God. 2. In full exercise of your God-given powers. 3. And for all time. "Whosoever believeth in him shall not perish, but have everlasting life."

III. "It is time to seek the Lord."

6. Topic: An Important Question.

TEXT: "What shall I do then with Jesus?" Matt. 27:22.

I. Let us think seriously of this question propounded by Pilate. 1. It was an imperative question. Pilate was compelled to do something with Jesus. 2. It was a troublesome question. Pilate believed Jesus innocent, but he feared the people. There are many who acknowledge the just claims of Christ upon them. They are troubled, but lack courage to ally themselves with him. 3. It was a personal question. "What shall I do with Jesus?" God holds us individually responsible.

II. Think, second, of the New Testament answer to this question. It tells us plainly what to do with Jesus. Our present and eternal salvation depends upon our making the divinely appointed use of Jesus. 1. Believe in him. 2. Trust in him as your personal Redeemer. 3. Receive him in his fullness to save. 4. Abide in him. Draw your sustenance from him in prosperity, in adversity, in life, in death.

7. Topic: Christ's Gracious Favor to Us.

TEXT: "Who gave himself for us, that he might redeem us from all iniquity," etc. Tit. 2:14.

I. The recipients of this favor. "For us." Though unworthy, sometimes ungrateful, even sometimes rebellious.

II. The voluntary character of this favor. "Who gave."

III. The richness of this favor. "Who gave Himself." How much that means! Love unspeakable!

IV. The object of this gracious favor. 1. That he might redeem us. 2. That he might cleanse us "from all iniquity." 3. That he might make us his people, pure in heart and life. 4. And so a "peculiar people," governed by peculiar motives, surrounded by a peculiar spiritual atmosphere, engaged in a peculiar work—a zealous people.

8. Topic: A New Creature.

TEXT: "If any man be in Christ, he is a new creature." II Cor. 5:17.

I. His judgments are new. He makes right estimates of himself, of God, of the purpose of life, and in what true happiness consists.

II. His purposes are new. It becomes his great purpose to serve God and do his will. Every other purpose becomes subservient to this.

III. His desires are new. "Whom have I in heaven but thee," etc. He is moved by a great love. The love of Christ constraineth us."

IV. His conversation and conduct are new. He walks in Christ, tries to honor Christ in his daily life. He has the sense of Christ's grace and companionship. The change is such that he may be counted "a new creature." In fact he is a new creation, a new creature.

9. Topic: The Prodigal's Resolve.

TEXT: "I will arise and go to my father." Luke 15:18.

The young man, son of a rich man, was thoroughly destitute. Hungry and in rags, it flashes upon him, "I will go home."

I. This resolution was made in disgust at his present position. This is no condition for a rich man's son, feeding swine! "I will arise and go to my father." Conviction!

II. This resolution was formed in sorrow at his past behavior. It occurred to him in deep penitence how badly he had treated his father. Repentance!

III. The resolution was formed in a feeling of homesickness. How long had he been gone? We don't know, but it is very certain from the reading of the passage that he was homesick. There is much homesickness for God. Heart hunger!

IV. The resolution was immediately put into execution. "He arose and came to his father." If you resolve to become a Christian next year, next month, or tomorrow, it is worth nothing. As the prodigal says "I will arise and go to my father" he starts. In an instant he is on his way. If you feel your need of your heavenly Father, why not seek him *now*? Return!

You know the reception that boy was given!

10. Topic: Advice to the Newly Enlisted.

TEXT: "Look to yourselves, that we lose not those things which we have wrought, but that we receive a full reward." II John 8.

The newly enlisted are objects of great interest to their churches and pastors. Each one must look to himself or herself so as not to lose the blessed ground which each occupies. Each one may well heed such advice as the following drawn from the Word of God and from the lessons of experience.

I. Obey principle rather than emotion.

II. Be intelligent and sound in the faith.

III. Strive to grow in grace. Growth is the law of healthy life.

IV. Study the Bible regularly, prayerfully, and diligently. Its treasures are inexhaustible.

V. Use all God's appointed means of grace, in closet, family, sanctuary. You can never rise above their need.

VI. Cultivate an enlightened and tender conscience.

VII. Do not follow the common course of the world. The broad and thronged way is likely to be the wrong way.

VIII. Be a faithful and truthful witness for Christ. He is depending on you.

IX. Be a working Christian. Christ wants to save others through you. Serve the Lord with gladness as a free soul. Bear in mind also that apathy is one of the greatest inconsistencies and perils of the Christian.

11. Topic: A Manly Christianity (To the Newly Enlisted).

TEXT: "Watch ye, stand fast in the faith, quit you like men, be strong. Let all your things be done with charity." I Cor. 16:13, 14.

This is an important exhortation. There are here certain demands which Christianity makes upon all men.

I. First there is a demand for vigilance. "Watch ye." The duty of watchfulness implies its need. It implies a care for our souls. There are many outward temptations. There are many inward temptations. We must watch over our thoughts, our affections, our words, our actions, as also against outward enticements.

II. Second, there is the demand for stability, steadfastness. "Stand fast in the faith." The man who watches is likely to stand. He will not be wavering, vacillating, "tossed about with every wind of doctrine." This steadfastness is needed to withstand the influence working against us. To this end we need more than a feeble conviction of the truth.

III. And, third, there is the demand for manliness. "Quit you like men."

These words have a martial air about them. They sound like the words of a great general on the eve of a critical battle. The call is for spiritual heroism. Be courageous, invincible, well equipped, manly. Be an ideal man. There is nothing greater than this. If the religion of Christ be true it is manly to confess it and to act out our belief.

IV. There is also the demand for strength. "Be strong." The spiritual life is capable of great strength. That is clear from the characters of the faithful in all ages. Be strong in conviction. Be strong in will. Be strong in experience and purpose, immovable, always abounding in the work of the Lord. The stronger your graces are the weaker will your temptations be.

V. But there is also demand for charity. "Let all things be done with charity." That word "charity" is love. Guard against temptation. Hold fast your principles. Act with courage. Persevere with constancy. Then do all things in the spirit of love. Love is a supreme duty. Love is the supreme motive. "The love of Christ constraineth us." Love makes service easy. Love makes duty a delight.

12. Topic: In the School of Christ (To the Newly Enlisted).

TEXT: "Learn of me," etc. Matt. 11:29.

In the school of Christ there must be docility, obedience, and a willingness to learn of him. All Christians, young and old, are pupils in his school.

I. Notice first Christ's fitness to be our Teacher. 1. He understands our nature. 2. He understands all those things we need to know. 3. He understands perfectly the art of imparting knowledge. 4. And he is an affectionate, winsome teacher.

II. Then consider, second, the methods by which he teaches. 1. By his words, works, character as made known in the Bible. 2. By the truths he now imparts to the human heart by the Holy Spirit.

III. What is the affect of his teaching? Rest. "Ye shall find rest to your souls." 1. His instruction leads to the pardon of sin. 2. It leads to the assurance that we are reconciled to God. 3. It leads to the removal of all fear. Rest is the opposite of fear.

IV. What evidence have we that we are learning in this school of Christ?

1. One very desirable evidence is that if we are becoming like him. "They took knowledge of them that they had been with Jesus." 2. We should all desire and submit to be taught in the school of Christ. Let us "learn of him."

SECTION V. The Conduct of the Holy Communion

At the close of the last Passover Christ instituted the Communion of the Supper which has come down through many generations. It has gone forth into all the world as the remembrance of his death and a pledge of the blessings it has purchased for us. Empires have risen and fallen, society has been tossed in wild confusion, and still it holds on its way. And it will do so, for Christ himself is in it, with that heart of love which shall yet bless a whole sinful world. It is a blessed commemorative ordinance designed to call into vivid remembrance, by the significant symbols of his own appointment, his dying love.

From the very beginning of her history the Christian Church has regarded the Lord's Supper as a rite of primary importance. It has many most important uses. It has a historical use. It is a memorial or monument sacred to the memory of Christ bearing sure attestation to his reality and religion. It has a doctrinal use. Seeing that Christianity is a historical religion, its doctrines rest upon the great facts of the gospel history. The Supper expresses indeed the creed of Christendom. It has a devotional use. The ordinance is an act of worship The condition of mind required for acceptable and profitable observance is that of a worshiper. It has a use of edifying. It is a principal "means of grace," in which believers are strengthened in faith and greatly enriched and blessed. It has a witness-bearing use. It is a powerful testimony to the world regarding the faith and hope of the Church. And it has a prophetic use. It is a pledge as well as a symbol. It has a hand of hope which points to the future. Both the symbols and the actions employed in the Holy Communion are very simple, but how touchingly suggestive and how eloquent they are. It is the number and importance of the uses to which it lends itself that makes the Lord's Supper the supreme rite of the Christian Church.

Feeling at Home at the Table

"Let a man examine himself," said St. Paul, reminding us that there can be no true participation in this sacred mystery without awe and godly fear and deep searchings of heart. Yet today I would fain help you to realize how simple and how friendly is this feast. In that lovely book, the *Life of Temple Gairdner,* it is told that one morning in the Church at Cairo, before Communion, Gairdner was kneeling at the altar, praying for God's blessing on his people in the Sacrament, when a child stumped up quite close to his praying form, and passed into the vestry where he had left a toy. Someone afterward made an apology, but Gairdner with a smile replied, "I liked it! I thought the little fellow seemed so much at home in his

40

Father's House." What Gairdner there felt about the House of God I would we all could feel about the Table to which by a royal summons we are now invited.—James S. Stewart.

SUGGESTIVE SERMON-MEDITATIONS AND OUTLINES

1. Theme: The Prepared Table.

TEXT: "Thou preparest a table before me in the presence of mine enemies: thou anointest my head with oil; my cup runneth over." Ps. 23:5.

In this brief and beautiful Psalm we have two pictures: that of God as Shepherd and that of God as Host. The second is the subject for our communion meditation. Think of the exalted privilege of having God for our host. Once Rudyard Kipling was the guest of the king and queen of England and much was said about it because thirty years before he had gotten the disfavor of the English royalty by writing of Queen Victoria as "The Widow of Windsor." The human race once got the disfavor of God because of sin, but Christ reinstated man, so that he is now the guest of God. As God's guest, man finds:

I. First, preparation. "Thou preparest a table." The communion table has been prepared and we are invited by him to come, "for all things are now ready." Every consideration has been made for the guest. This preparation was made by the gift of his Son who said, "I go to prepare a place for you."

II. Second, plenty. The table suggests an abundance, for it is no scanty meal that is prepared. It is a banquet table laden with the mercies of God—"My cup runneth over." There is both room and plenty for all.

III. Third, protection. "Thou preparest a table before me in the presence of mine enemies." The divine Host not only provides abundantly for the guest, but also furnishes calm and repose for him while he partakes. The guest may feel safe as long as he is at God's table. The child may feast at his Father's meal in spite of his enemies. "Behold, what manner of love the father hath bestowed upon us, that we should be called the sons of God."—Rev. Neill G. Stevens.

2. Theme: Never Lose Heart (Beginning of Year).

TEXT: "I never lose heart," that is the text. It is found in the writings of Paul, II Cor. 4:16. In the usual versions it reads, "We faint not." But Moffatt, Goodspeed, Weymouth translate it, "I never lose heart."

Who is this that never loses heart? The Apostle Paul—and that means that it is not some little two-by-four personality that never loses heart—but a real man that has been up against life; he seems always to have been up against hard things.

If you want a fine exercise in Bible study take a concordance and find the passages which speak of a man fainting or not fainting—fainting is the key word. Then change the word in your mind to the modern phrase, "lose heart."

You will come to an experience in the life of Jacob and his heart fainted, Gen. 45:26—Jacob lost heart.

Here is David in the 27th Psalm, "I had fainted." *I had lost heart* "unless I had believed to see the goodness of the Lord. . . . Be strong, and let thy heart take courage" (A.S.V.). David also was no two-by-four personality.

Here is Jonah who writes (2:7), "When my soul fainted within me"—when *I lost heart.*

Proverbs 24:10 "If thou *lose heart* in the day of adversity, thy strength is small."

I. By such study one comes to the conclusion that the tendency to lose heart is rather universal—everybody gets into the dumps.

But here is Paul who writes, "I never lose heart." Let us look into his experience. Read on! He says: "Even though our outward man does waste away, yet our inward man is renewed day by day" (Weymouth).

Our outward man wastes away—what is it Paul?—arthritis, diabetes, heart trouble, asthma, tuberculosis, or just growing old—there is a Pennsylvania

Dutch word which covers a wide scope —*opnemma*. What is the matter with John Schmidt? He has the *opnemma*—that is tragic. He has the *wasting away*. Babies get the *opnemma*. Youth get it. Of course it is probably a corruption of the German *anf-nehmen, op-nemma* —wasting away. It covers a lot of ignorance, but it is something to worry about —life diminishing, getting weaker and weaker. Paul says—when I get the *op-nemma*, I never lose heart.

When Time says, "Move on!" When time gathers unto itself undue circumstance and grabs Paul by the throat and says, "I'll get you down"—Paul says, "I never lose heart." Three cheers for Paul.

II. Read on—for our light and transitory affliction is achieving for us. What is this you are talking about Paul— *light* and *transitory* affliction?

I'd like to make this man read his own words in this very letter—I'd like to put the 11th chapter before his face and make him read, "Five times I have received floggings, lashings from the Jews, forty lashes all but one. Three times I have been beaten with rods, once I have been stoned, three times I have been shipwrecked, once hanging on to a bit of timber for twenty-four hours in the water before being picked up. I have travelled much, amid dangers from rivers, robbers, enemies. I have faced dangers in the cities, deserts, on the sea, from false brethren. I've had to labour and toil with many a sleepless night, hunger, thirst, cold, lack of clothing. Worried because of the churches. A thorn in the flesh—some weakness of body."

And here he writes that this is light and transitory affliction! I never lose heart! Why not? He has learned the secret of experience. Experience says, "Go through!" He has learned a secret from his Master who said, "A man ought always to pray and not to faint, not to lose heart."

"In the world you have tribulation; but be of good cheer, I have overcome the world" (R.S.V.).

Tribulation—it is light affliction: I go through—I never lose heart.

I read Moffatt's translation—"The slight trouble of the passing hour results in a solid glory past all comparison." There is something heroic, tremendously heroic about this—making tribulation work out to solid glory past all comparison.

Going through the dark valley to stand with solid footing on a mountain peak. Going through sorrow and coming out with a sweetened instead of an embittered life. "A man loses his fortune, and it makes him a kinder, a more understanding, a more deeply spiritual person, instead of a hard, cynical and resentful person."

"Here is a woman whose little child dies, and the experience turns her to God. Who are the men and women whom you name in any roll-call of spiritual giants—they are those who have gone through tribulation to take a solid stance on a higher level."

Resume your journey with gladness of heart—go through! Never lose heart. Just keep on going through! What do you do when life tumbles in? You just keep on keeping on.

III. Never lose heart. We must resume our journey catching the thrill of aspiration. Hearing the call: Come up! It is what Paul calls the *solid glory* calling to a man. What is this *solid glory?*—something that won't wobble when you stand on it, something that won't shake in earthquake, something that won't cave in in depression, something that holds you up when you stumble, something that won't disappear like a mirage, something that won't dissipate like the morning mist. Now anything as solid as that can't have material solidity—material solidity wobbles, shakes, caves in, fluctuates, passes away—it is only spiritual solidity that holds. It is spiritual solidity that a man gets when he goes through—and of course Paul knew what spiritual solidity is—he writes it out fully and carefully, "And now abideth faith, hope, love." A man goes through to higher faith, a keener hope, a fuller love. These things stand. These things call a man! Come up! These things never fail—in spite of everything, they hold.

I never lose heart—look what's ahead of me—faith, hope, love—solid glory.

IV. I never lose heart, because my eyes are on the unseen, not on the seen, for the seen is transient, the unseen is eternal.

What does he mean? I take it that he means, I never lose heart because my eyes are on God whom I cannot see. I never lose heart because God is a fact— a present fact.

I never lose heart because God is an eternal fact—time can't change him. He is the same yesterday, today, tomorrow. Everything else is transient, except that God gives it eternity.

In the first verse of this same chapter Paul writes, "By God's mercy to me, I never lose heart." Now you are getting into the crux of the whole matter. I never lose heart because of God's mercy —I never lose heart because God has a heart. I never lose heart because God's heart is one of loving-kindness.

I never lose heart because everything that happens to make one lose heart— failure, sin, sorrow, loss, weakness—all that he takes into his own heart. He bears us and redeems us through it.

That is the meaning of the cross—that is the reason that sometimes you hold a crucifix before the eyes of a dying man; he knows that by the heart of God he need not lose heart even though he goes through the valley.

That is the reason we sing a hymn, "Earth has no sorrow that heaven cannot heal"—we let God channel our sorrow through his own heart, and we can be of good cheer.

I never lose heart—not even as a sinner—I look up to the unseen—the God of love and mercy—and once more as I have done many times before, I penitently let him bear my sin and bring my redemption. Again I resume my journey with gladness of heart.

The Sacrament is a token of the mercy of God: the bread the symbol of his broken body, broken for me; the wine the symbol of his shed blood, shed for me—that by the partaking of this bread and wine I might lift my eyes above them—and see that which is unseen— that which is a fact—even God, an eternal fact, an eternal Person, a merciful person revealed to us through the Christ and the cross—and so I resume my journey with gladness of heart— and no matter how time says "Move on!" no matter if Experience says "Go through!" and Aspiration calls "Come up!"—I never lose heart. My eyes are set, my heart is strong, my life is free, I live above!—M. K. W. H.

3. Theme: Remembrance Unites.

TEXT: "And he took bread, and gave thanks, and brake it, and gave unto them, saying, This is my body which is given for you: do this in remembrance of me." Luke 22:19.

Once I read an account of the experiences of a Church of England minister in North Africa at the time of World War II. On an Easter Sunday he administered the Sacrament of Holy Communion to English troops who were in a prisoners-of-war camp. About forty to fifty Germans stood near by and watched the proceedings very eagerly. After the service was over, the minister asked the officer in charge to let him know whether there were any Protestant Germans among these who would care to have the Sacrament administered to them. It was discovered that there were eighty. Arrangements were made, and the Sacrament was administered to these men. The minister shook hands with them as they left the service. This was his way of sharing with these German friends their woes and joys.

I. Some describe this occasion as the Eucharist, others call it the Sacrament, while we generally refer to it as the Communion service. There is one term, however, which all Christians can use to describe this occasion. It is a "Remembrance." The Lord's Supper, to me, is a memorial. I would not say simply a memorial, since it has other implications as well. But we all know this service as essentially a memorial of our Lord, Christ.

Everything that makes us "remember" has pictorial value. When we see the bread we remember how our Lord gave his body; how his body was abusively used by those to whom he entrusted it. The wine, too, reminds us of his "blood and sweat"; how he allowed his blood to be shed in order to open up a way of life for the salvation of the human race from sin. The Lord's Supper, to me, is a picture of Jesus' giving of himself entirely, without counting the cost.

If we as Christian people wish to show by an outward sign our allegiance to our Lord, then, we are present to see this picture and to dwell upon it as frequently as possible.

II. If I were asked for one of several principles upon which all branches of the Christian church could be united, I would say without hesitation, here is one—"I believe that the Last Supper is a service of remembrance." Allow me to recall an experience which I had in 1933, of being one of about two thousand students gathered for divine worship at St. Giles' Cathedral, Edinburgh. Forty nations were represented in that vast congregation, including representatives of every branch of the Christian church. Why were we there? Because we all remembered Christ our Lord.

III. Here in this remembrance of Christ we have a power which stands out beyond every other to unite people together. The present world problems will be solved only in so far as the peoples of the nations learn the dependancy of this Power. As we call to mind our Lord at the service of remembrance he himself comes to us and gives us the moral dynamic that reinforces our weak wills into right action for the work of the kingdom of God on earth. Through this picture, I see Jesus shedding his blood and giving his body to save me and all mankind from sin. It matters not if, as Christians, we interpret the meaning of the cross in different ways. What matters is that through the pictorial effect of the meal of remembrance, we discover the significance of the cross. It is through this that we know Christ as Lord and Saviour of the world.—W. M. J.

4. Theme: The Upper Room.

TEXT: "And he will shew you a large upper room furnished and prepared: there make ready for us." Mark 14:15.

The upper room is an institution in the social life of the East: the "upper room" has become equally significant in the redemption life of the world. It is the trysting place of privacy and intimacy, a "secret place of the Most High." To enter there is to withdraw from the lower room of worldliness and to be secluded in the "upper room" of intimacy with God. The "upper room" was no mere accident or incident in the institution of the Sacrament of the Supper: it was also a selected place, selected by the Lord's providence, which went ahead and sent the man with the pitcher to show the disciples the way.

I. It was the upper room of fellowship. Discipleship admitted. Jesus was there. There were the disciples. There was nothing to mar their communion with one another. The upper room of unholy selfishness when the supper was instituted had given place to common forebearance and love.

II. It was the upper room of harmony. Those who sat at the first communion were acknowledged by this act to be Christ's friends and were made partakers of great privileges. They feed upon Christ by faith, have their union with him confirmed, are strengthened against sin, encouraged and quickened in duty, inspired with new life and zeal, and have peace of conscience and happy hopes of eternal life.

III. It was the upper room of prayer. It was a room separated from the noise and interruptions of the street. Christ prayed there, his great intercessory prayer for his disciples. They reverently participated in that prayer.

IV. It was the upper room of preparation. Their life and service in the world and for the world was in front of these men. What wonderful preparation was the Supper here in the presence and fellowship of Christ!

V. It was the upper room of prophecy. The Lord's Supper is a prophecy of his second coming, of the perfect triumph of his kingdom, for we are to celebrate it till he comes. It contains a hope and promise of victory and heaven. Our last view of Christ in the Gospels is not of death, but of an ever-living Saviour. Christ did not say to his disciples, "This do in remembrance of my death," but, "This do in remembrance of me." And thus he desired them to remember his birth and example and leading, as well as his cross, and to think of him as he is now, at the right hand of the Father.

THEME PRAYER: Father, we thank thee today for the simplicity of the relationship between our souls and thine; ourselves foolish, inconsequent, feeble; thyself wise, stable, omnipotent, how can the one have converse with the other? Yet thou hast taught us that as a little child depends for its life upon its mother, so we depend upon thee. O Almighty Father, here once again, a worthless gift, we give ourselves to thee, thy happy, grateful children, eager to do thy work today and all the days.—J. S. Hoyland (Adapted).

5. Theme: The Sacrament of the Lord's Supper.

TEXT: "This do in remembrance of me." Luke 22:19.

There is no institution more delightful to the Christian than the sacrament of the Lord's Supper. It is a touching remembrance of the Redeemer's love, a refreshing means of grace to the soul, a happy communion for the Lord's believing family, and a gladdening foretaste of the marriage supper of the lamb.

I. The partaking of the Sacrament is an act of remembrance. When our Lord gave the bread and wine to his disciples he said, "Do this in remembrance of me"; and when these elements are given to us we receive them in remembrance of Christ. We know in common life what a value we put upon any token of affection, a book, a ring, a picture, which has been given as a memorial by some dear departed friend. It

becomes sacred in proportion to our love to the one who gave it, and when that love is strong we care far more for it than for other things of comparatively greater value. When we receive the bread and wine we set to our seal that Christ is our soul's beloved, that we live on his grace, and can never forget his mercy.

II. But we do not merely show our remembrance of his person and character. The Communion is especially a remembrance of his death. It was appointed on the very night before his crucifixion, and the broken bread represents his body crucified, while the wine is a figure of his blood so freely shed for our sins. "As often as ye eat this bread, and drink this cup, ye do show the Lord's death until he come." Now, there never was an act so full of love as that. Never, therefore, must that love of Christ be forgotten or disregarded by the Christian. It is our hope, our life, and our only source of peace.

III. But the Lord's Supper is also a means of spiritual food and sustenance. The soul requires to be fed as well as the body. And as the body lives by outward food, so the believing soul feeds on Christ. He is the living bread which came down from heaven, the heavenly manna provided for his people. So this sacrament is a divinely appointed means whereby believers feed on Christ. We do not mean that there is anything remarkable or mysterious in the elements received. But when with the lips we receive those elements in faith, the Holy Ghost within the heart is graciously pleased to pour life into the soul.

IV. The bread is a figure of the body, as the wine is a figure of the blood. If a person were showing a gallery of pictures he might say, "This is St. Paul," "This is St. Peter," and "This is St. John," and he would mean thereby that those pictures on the canvas were representations of the persons whose names they bore. So, again, when our Lord said, "I am the vine" and "I am the door," he did not mean that he was a real vine or a real door, but that the vine and door were figures and emblems of his offices. Just so in the Lord's Supper, when he said, "This is my body" and "This is my blood," he did not mean that the bread or wine were changed into real flesh or real blood, but that they were signs and emblems of his sufferings and sacrifice, of his body broken and his blood so freely shed for man. It is not, therefore, from any mystical property in the bread and wine themselves that we expect a blessing, but from the gift of the Holy Spirit to those who receive them in obedience and faith.

Thus to hungering and thirsting souls the Communion becomes inestimably precious. When we feel our weakness we rejoice to come before him that we may be strengthened with might by his Spirit in the inner man.

V. There is another point of view in which the Lord's Supper is presented in this passage. It is as a foretaste of the marriage supper of the Lamb. "For as often as ye eat this bread, and drink this cup, ye do show the Lord's death till he come." Each celebration has a reference to the present, to the past, and to the future. To the present for we cast our sins and burdens of the day upon him; to the past, for the heart is full with the recollection of his death and passion by which alone we have remission of our sins; and to the future, for our present delightful Communion is a faint but true image of the blessedness of that glorious hour when the whole company of God's people shall be gathered to the marriage supper of the Lamb.—E. H.

6. A Thanksgiving Communion Service.

SUGGESTED SCRIPTURE READING: Col. 3:12-17.

SELECTED HYMNS: "Come, ye thankful people, come."—Henry Alford. "O love of God most full."—Oscar Clute. "Blest be the tie that binds."—John Fawcett. "Saviour, again to thy dear name we raise."—J. Ellerton. "Praise to God, immortal praise."—Anna L. Barbauld. CALL TO WORSHIP: "Enter into his gates with thanksgiving, and into his courts with praise; be thankful unto him, and bless his name."

PRAYER: In this Thanksgiving week shed abroad in our hearts, O Lord, that most rare and precious gift, the spirit of gratitude.

Grant unto us such heightened appreciation that no blessing of life may seem common, no relationship of life ordinary, no experience of life insignificant, and may we be quick to discern thy particular dealings with us along our several ways.

We thank thee that the field hath not withheld its bounty and the orchard its abundance, that the earth hath yielded treasure into our hands. We thank thee for materials and for inventive gifts to shape them into things for use.

We rejoice in such blessed gifts as color and music, fragrance and taste by which our lives are enriched.

We thank thee for work and play, for love and worship. We thank thee for kinships, parenthood and friendships, the privilege of having friends and being friendly.

We are glad for virtues and graces, for faith and hope and love, for humility and goodness, for loyalty and justice. We praise thee for the many times we see these drawn out in the living lines of human life and character.

We thank thee for this lovely place in which we live so full of beauty, with institutions for our advancement and welfare, for homes and gardens, for libraries and schools.

By thy providence and grace we live in a land full of abundance, blessed with peace, ennobled by the name of Christian. For this we are thankful.

We are grateful above all for thine own nature of righteousness and love, for the moral law and for thy mercy. We thank thee for the revelation of thyself in Christ, for his teaching, his life, his death, his saviorhood, his resurrection, our hope of glorious immortality.

By our lives more than by our lips, by our deeds more than by our words, by our charity more than by our thought about it may we express our thanks-givings.

Continue to bless us, O Lord. Help us to become more worthy of blessing. Use us to build thy kingdom and to redeem this world from sin and sorrow until the whole earth is filled with the knowledge of the Lord as the waters cover the sea. Amen.

MEDITATION: May I turn our attention to several phrases in our morning prayer: "Grant unto us such heightened appreciation that no blessing of life may seem common, no relationship of life ordinary, no experience of life insignificant, and may we be quick to discern thy particular dealings with us along our several ways."

I. No blessing of life is common. Take, for example, bread. Never take bread for granted.

It is not common in its *origin*. For back of the loaf, back of the mill and the flour, back of the sunshine and shower is God. God said, "Let the earth bring forth plants yielding seed. . . . and it was so." Call not that common which God has made.

Bread is not common in its *function*. Bread sustains life. Anything that sustains life is marvelous. The marvel and mystery and miracle of life reflects upon the thing which sustains it.

Bread is not common because there is always *need* for it. Whether the world has ever had sufficient bread I don't know. But this I do know that many to-day do not have enough bread. There is famine, and where there is famine there is fault. Surely not God's fault —man's!

Bread is not common because of its *symbolism*. Jesus said, "I am the Bread of Life." Bread is a token upon our table. The broken bread is the broken body of him who meditated unto us salvation and eternal life by his brokenness.

So, I say no blessing of life is common. Test a cup of water by its origin, the sustenance it gives, the need for it, its token value.

After I saw men die upon a battlefield it seemed to me that all our common blessings are red-tinged, bought with human sacrifice. They are not common, and for them we should give uncommon thanks.

II. No relationship of life is ordinary. Is it ordinary to be the child of a mother? The strangest thing in the world I think is the manner of our coming into the world. How marvelous the imagination of God when he ordained the manner of our birth and gave the world motherhood.

Fatherhood is not ordinary. "Fatherly love is so meaningful and so capable of expanding discovery that it became the great theme of Christian experience— God is our loving Father."

Is it ordinary for a man to be wedded to a woman, a woman to a man—the relationship without which all life would end, the family cease, the state fall, the world become unpeopled? This relationship is exalted as the token of the relationship that exists between Christ and his church.

Relationships are not ordinary—not brotherhood or any kinship. Nor is friendship without great luster. I am always depressed when I see a man break friendship easily, and no time is there that I feel more sorrowful than when I lose a friend.

To be a neighbor is not ordinary as Jesus taught us in the parable of the good Samaritan.

And what of being a child of God? To have a Saviour?

Call no relationship of life ordinary. For each relationship give extraordinary thanks.

III. No experience of life is insignificant. Of experience of love in relationship we have spoken. Play is significant—the happy play of children wherein girls feel their dawning motherhood and boys achieve the manual and mental skills useful in their manhood vocations. The play of re-creation for men and women.

Work is blessing sometimes unrecognized. Unhappy is the man who finds his work his doom.

Whatever experience comes, wise men and women know that the experience which is grievous to be borne wraps up a blessing, and they are wise who undo the wrapping.

No experience of life but what gives an opportunity to display a virtue. No experience whether great or small, high or low, joyous or sorrowful, is insignificant.

Thank God that life is marvelously meaningful.

IV. "May we be quick to discern thy particular dealings with us along our several ways."

Here we face the fact that we are particulars, peculiar persons, unique personalities. We are not lost in the crowd, only a part of the mass. No, I am a particular person in the sight of God. He knows me by name. My experience is my own. It does not belong to another. Down the pathway of my own nature God comes to me in blessing. Let us each thank God for his own uniqueness and that God's love is so great that, though loving us together, he loves us separately. Christ died for the world; and yet he died for me.

Let these thoughts shape our Thanksgiving: There is no blessing that is common. There is no relationship that is ordinary. There is no experience that is insignificant. There is no person without God's love.

Let us give thanks through our Sacrament, and make this ceremony a Eucharist—a Thanksgiving.—M. K. W. H.

An Invitation to the Lord's Supper.

We are accustomed to come to the Lord's Table in a repentant spirit, feeling the need of forgiveness for sins of omission and commission. We renew our vows to lead a new life, following the commandments of God, and walking from henceforth in his holy ways. In this spirit let us come to the Sacrament.

We are accustomed also to come to the Lord's Table as a token of our mutual love and charity with fellow Christians—in a spirit of forgiveness, forgiving others as we ourselves are forgiven. In this spirit let us come to the Communion.

We come hungering and thirsting after righteousness, aware that the grace of God is poured into our lives for strength, for courage, for healing. We receive food and drink. Let us bring our hunger and thirst to the Lord's Supper.

But today come to make this a true Eucharist—this is an ancient word for the Sacrament—Thanksgiving. Today come in the spirit of the 103rd Psalm.

> Bless the Lord, O my soul;
> And all that is within me, bless
>   his holy name. . . .

7. Theme: Consider Christ.

TEXT: "Wherefore, holy brethren, partakers of the heavenly calling, consider the Apostle and High Priest of our profession, Christ Jesus." Heb. 3:1.

All the means of grace are designed to turn our thought to Christ. This one. To know him we must think of him, contemplate him.

I. Contemplation of Christ fixes the thought upon that which is essential to Christianity and sufficient to the Christian. Essentials, not doctrines, not good works, not ritual, but a Person. That Person sufficient for all.

II. Contemplation of Christ corrects our tendency to contemplate one another. We gauge our piety too often by human standards, compare with one another, judge one another.

III. Contemplation of Christ fixes our gaze intently upon the cross. He is our "Apostle and High Priest." Accept his work for us. Do this gladly. Too often at the table we think of our sins. Let there be gratitude, love, hope, assurance when we consider him.

IV. Contemplation of Christ prepares us for, and inspires us to, service. It gives sympathy with his work, deepens convictions, arouses zeal.

V. Contemplation of Christ makes us like him. Transformed by beholding. Changed into the same image. Let Christ's glory into thy soul.

8. Communion: Talk to Young People.

As you young people sit here this morning you see before you this Communion Table set in pure white and upon it only bread and the fruit of the vine. I think you sometimes wonder what all this is for, or what it means. I feel sure were I to ask, you would be glad to have me try to tell you as much as I can in these few moments just what it does mean.

I am confident that there is here in our church this morning someone or more than one who has at home a little private drawer. In the drawer are letters. Possibly they have been in the drawer for quite a while. They are keepsakes, from someone who now lives far away, maybe out West, or in another country, or possibly no longer alive here on this earth. The friend here happens to open the drawer, maybe reads one or two of the letters, and then says to himself or herself: "What a lovely person my friend was! What good times we used to have together!" While looking at the letters love was freshened up, almost as if they had had a visit together. It was because of remembrance.

There is a woman in this city who has a tiny pair of white shoes and little baby ornaments laid away somewhere. Every once in a while she goes to the place where they are, looks on the little keepsakes, and says to herself: "How sweet and beautiful our little baby was! How dear to us all! To me!" And her love is wonderfully freshened up as she calls to mind the little one who is gone. That is remembrance.

Still more personal to you young folks: I know a young girl who when she was about ten years of age moved with her family to California. She had a playmate friend here of whom she was very, very fond. When the girl was bidding goodby to her friend she gave her something as she said "to remember her by." I have forgotten what it was, but it was a ring off her finger or a bracelet, and she said: "Every time you look at this you will think of me." When the girl looks at that ring, or keepsake, she says to herself: "What a dear girl she was! She was my pal! What good times we had together!" As she looks at the keepsake her love is freshened up. And it is so every time she sees it. That is because of remembrance.

Now, my dear young friends, when cleared of all mystery, this is just what the Lord's Supper is and what it means. It is a memorial—a memorial feast. A remembrancer. Jesus said, "This do in remembrance of me." He said, "Keep on doing it." And every time we do it we freshen up our thought of him, our memory of him, our love for him. We think of him. We recall his love. We commune with him, talk with him. So our love is greatly freshened up, and because of this we give ourselves to him again, and determine anew that we will be his and serve him as long as ever we live.—H.

PRAYERS BEFORE, AT, AND AFTER THE SUPPER

1. Invocation Prayer.

We bend in worship and adoration before thee, our God. Lord, teach us to pray. Make us wise with heavenly wisdom as we draw near to thee, and even in our ignorance and unwisdom may our hearts ever be true and right with thee. We thank thee for the Lord Jesus, the Captain of our salvation. We thank thee for the love no words can tell in which he gave his life a ransom for us. Make us deeply conscious that we are not our own, but redeemed unto thee with the precious blood of Christ. May the power of his sacrifice rest upon our hearts, enabling us to drink of his cup, and to serve one another in love for his sake. We thank thee that thou seekest the love even of our hearts and the service even of our hands. Bless all who are walking together in Jesus' steps. Restore those who have wandered or fallen. Have mercy on those who are self-confident and proud. Forgive our sins, that our souls may be at liberty to serve thee. Loose our bonds that we may do thy will. Compass us with thy favor as with a shield, and suffer us not to be overcome of evil. We ask in Jesus' name. Amen.

2. Invocation Prayer.

Most merciful Father, we thank thee that we are the children of promise, and that we are invited to a table laden with provision of grace. Thou dost not mock thy children. Thou dost not make our souls to hunger and then hold the bread beyond our reach. Thou dost not invite us to thy fellowship and then absent thyself. Before we hunger the bread is ready, and before we thirst the water is at hand. Thou are waiting for thy guests, and all things are ready to meet and satisfy our needs. Mercifully give to us a strong and apprehending sense of thy presence. May our souls realize that this house is filled with thy glory. Possess every ministry in this service. Let nothing be formal and empty. May our communion be deep, spiritual, and fruitful. Help us to break the bonds of custom and rise into the liberty of the children of God. O living Christ, lift us up to sit with thee in heavenly places. Give us the wings of faith to lift us above the things of sense, and may we move with joy and freedom among things unseen and eternal. These mercies we ask for thy name's sake. Amen.—J. H. J.

3. Invocation Prayer.

Our Lord and Saviour, who loving thy disciples didst love them unto the end, and under the shadow of the cross didst institute this Holy Supper and ordain it to be to the end a memorial of thy love and sacrifice, grant that with sincere preparation of heart, in a true repentance of all sin, and a simple trust in thee, with unfeigned love of the brethren and desire to grow in thine image we may this day come to the table of thy love, may find thee present to cheer and rejoice our hearts, and be made strong for days to come. May thy love be shed abroad in our hearts and all of us together be richly blessed in our communion with thee. We ask in thine own name. Amen.

4. Prayer on Approaching the Table.

Almighty God, our heavenly Father, we praise and bless thee for all thy gifts and benefits toward us, but above all else we thank thee for Jesus Christ, thine unspeakable Gift. Not as we ought, but as we are able, we praise thee for his birth in our nature, for his life on earth for his sufferings and obedience unto death, even the death of the cross, for his resurrection from the dead, and his ascension to thy right hand. We give thanks for the coming of the Holy Ghost, and for his abiding presence and work in the church and in the world. We praise thee for the Word, sacraments, and prayer, and for the fellowship of thy house on earth, and for the hope of heaven.

And now do thou bless and sanctify with thy Word and Spirit these elements of bread and wine set before us, and grant that we may become partakers of the body and blood of Jesus with all his benefits to our spiritual nourishment and growth in grace. O Lamb of God, that takest away the sin of the world, grant us thy peace. We ask in thine own name. Amen.

5. Prayer on Approaching the Table.

And now, most merciful Father, look upon us we most humbly beseech thee, as we make that memorial of thy Son's most blessed sacrifice which he hath commanded us to make. Send down thy Holy Spirit to bless and consecrate these thine own gifts of bread and wine which we set before thee. May the bread which we break be unto us the communion of the Body of Christ, and the cup which we bless the communion of the Blood of Christ. May we receiving them by faith be made partakers of all his benefits to our spiritual nourishment and growth in grace, and all to the glory of thy name.

O Lamb of God, that taketh away the sins of the world, have mercy upon us. O Lamb of God, that taketh away the sins of the world, grant us thy peace. We ask through Christ our Lord and Saviour. Amen.

6. Prayer at the Table.

O God, who by the life and death and rising again of thy dear Son hast con secrated for us a new and living way into the holiest of all; cleanse our minds, we beseech thee, by the inspiration of thy Holy Spirit, that drawing near unto thee with a pure heart and conscience undefiled, we may receive these thy gifts without sin, and worthily magnify thy Holy Name; through Jesus Christ our Lord. Amen.

7. Prayer at the Table.

Gracious Father, who didst send forth thy Son Jesus our Lord to utter all thy will for man in a life of charity and self-sacrifice, we remember his great humility in that he took upon him the low estate of a servant and was subject to the pains and distresses of our humanity; we remember his agony in the garden; his acceptance of thy holy will; his prayer for those who ignorantly slew him; his confidence that at last all evil will be destroyed and all ignorance dispelled; and his return to thee to be our everlasting Friend and Saviour. We remember also and give thanks for the immortal longings which he quickened in the souls of men; for his promise of new heavens and a new earth wherein shall dwell righteousness; for the works which his servants, sustained by him, have wrought, and for the sorrows they have healed and prevented; for the comfort he has brought to our souls, and for the confidence with which in his company we face the unknown journey that yet remains. Amen.—H. C.

8. Prayer after the Supper.

Almighty and most gracious Father, who this day hast given thy servants to remember the Lord Jesus in the Sacrament of the Supper; grant that that mind which was in him may also be formed in us that we may take upon us the burdens and duties which have been appointed us and follow in his steps, bearing contradiction patiently, subduing in ourselves every lawless and guilty desire, setting ourselves steadfastly against every evil work, and by our willing services and sacrifices bringing comfort and hope to those who are distressed; through the name of our Saviour Jesus Christ. Amen.—H. C.

9. Close of Service with Offering.

THEME PRAYER: We thank thee, O God, for the rewards of love. We thank thee for the deeper fellowship with thee, for the favor of our fellow man, for the commendation of thy Spirit in our inner lives. Help us to be uncalculating in our love, and yet to rejoice in the richness of love's recompense. Amen.

OFFERTORY SENTENCE: "Do good unto all men as ye have opportunity, especially to those who are of the household of faith."

OFFERTORY PRAYER: O God, our heavenly Father, we thank thee for the gift of thy dear son. Grant that we who have received him in our hearts may joyfully go forth with him on many errands. Bless those who toil for thee in far-off places. Comfort and sustain them in their loneliness and unite our work to theirs as we bring our offerings this morning. Graciously accept and bless and use these gifts of thy people to the extension of thy kingdom in the world and bless us as we bring them. We ask in Christ's name. Amen.

10. Close of Service with Offering.

THEME PRAYER: Today and from this day forward help us, O Lord, to live a life of intimate communion with thee. Lift our prayers above the mere asking for help in our day of need. May we know thee as the sharer of every experience of life as Savior and Friend. Amen.—M. K. W. H.

OFFERTORY SENTENCE: "Charge them that are rich in this world, that they do good, that they be rich in good works, ready to distribute, willing to communicate."

OFFERTORY PRAYER: We hear thee saying: "Upon the first day of the week let every one of you lay by him in store as God has prospered him." Of that which thou hast given us we bring to thee. Accept and use these gifts for the extension of thy kingdom in the earth. In Christ's name we ask. Amen.

11. Close of Service with Offering.

THEME PRAYER: O thou wounded Christ, lay balm upon our wounded hearts. Lift thy hands above us in blessing, hold them out in proof, with them break the Bread of Life unto our souls. And help us so to live that we may be numbered among those who comfort others because we ourselves have been comforted of thee. It is in thy name we ask. Amen.—M. K. W. H.

OFFERTORY SENTENCE: "For ye know the grace of our Lord Jesus Christ, that, though he was rich, yet for your sakes he became poor, that ye through his poverty might be rich."

OFFERTORY PRAYER: We consecrate this offering O Lord, unto the advancement of thy church. It is a gift of our hands. Teach us how to make more precious offerings than these—gifts of prayer, of service, of witnessing. Bless our gifts and our selves unto they great purposes of righteousness and love. In Jesus' name. Amen—M. K. W. H.

SUGGESTIVE LORD'S SUPPER TEXTS AND TOPICS

A Dying Wish Respected: "This do in remembrance of me." Luke 22:19.

A Personal Question: "What mean ye by this service?" Ex. 12:26.

Duty and Obligations of Christians to Keep the Communion Feast: "Therefore let us keep the feast." I Cor. 5:8.

Good to Draw Near to God: "It is good for me to draw near to God," Ps. 73:28.

At the Last Supper: "Now when the even was come," etc. Matt. 26:20.

After Thoughts: "So when they had dined." John 21:15.

Encouragement for the Timid: "As for me, I will come into thy house in the multitude of thy mercy," etc. Ps. 5:7.

Invited Closer: A Day of Communion: "Master, where dwellest thou? . . . Come and see." John 1:38, 39.

Love's Question: "Lovest thou me?" John 21:16.

A Joyful Approach: "I went with them to the house of God, with the voice of joy and praise, with a multitude that kept holyday." Ps. 42:4.

The Guestchamber of the Soul: "The Master saith, Where is the guestchamber, where I shall eat the passover with my disciples?" Mark 14:14.

The Eucharist a Renewal of the Covenant: "This cup is the new testament in my blood, which is shed for you." Luke 22:20.

The Action: "This do ye." I Cor. 11:25.

The Paschal Lamb: "Christ our passover." I Cor. 5:7.

The Bequest of Jesus: "Peace I leave with you, my peace I give unto you." John 14:27.

The Gospel Festival: "A feast of fat things, a feast of wines on the lees, of fat things full of marrow, of wines on the lees well refined." Isa. 25:6.

The Bread of Life: "For the bread of God is he which cometh down from heaven," etc. John 6:33.

Communion a Spiritual Feast: "In this mountain shall the Lord of hosts make unto all people a feast of fat things," etc. Isa. 25:6.

God and Man Meet in the Communion: John 6:56.

The Heart's Sacred Places: "Surely the Lord is in this place." Gen. 28:16.

The Large Upper Room: "And he will shew you a large upper room furnished and prepared." Mark 14:15.

Christ at the Feast: "I will come in to him, and will sup with him, and he with me." Rev. 3:20.

Preparation for the Feast: "How amiable are thy tabernacles, O Lord of hosts," etc. Ps. 84:1, 2.

Close to Christ: "Cleave to that which is good." Rom. 12:9.

The Friendship of Jesus: "Ye are my friends, if ye do whatsoever I command you. Henceforth I call you not servants," etc. John 15:14, 15.

Danger of a Too Busy Life: "Come ye yourselves apart into a desert place, and rest a while." Mark 6:31.

The Hymn at the First Communion: "And when they had sung an hymn, they went out into the mount of Olives." Matt. 26:30.

Remember Jesus Christ. "Remember that Jesus Christ of the seed of David was raised from the dead according to my gospel." II Tim. 2:8.

CHOICE LORD'S SUPPER ILLUSTRATIONS

1. Receive Him Joyfully.

Cleopatra entertained Mark Antony with a feast beyond price. Pearls were melted in the wine, and every lavish expenditure was made to impress him with her welcome. Such is not what Christ asks of us, but at the Holy Supper we should receive him joyfully, and perform the duties that will invite his approval. Furthermore, do not fail to trust him. Keep no secrets from him. Confess your faults to him. Assert your love for him and let him know that you accept his.

What are some of the special blessings of having him with us? One is companionship. We cannot feel alone when he is with us. "I will fear no evil, for thou art with me." Another is quickening of love. Our hearts will burn within us as he talks with us by the way. Let us constrain him to tarry.

2. The Upper Room.

Separated from the noise and interruptions of the street, a friend of mine, who is widely known, and who has difficulty securing uninterrupted privacy even in his own home, had an important paper to prepare. He went to a hotel and secured a room, and spent a whole week in seclusion doing that work. He considered it just that important. He gave it "an upper room." I have another friend whose hands are full of hard work every day in the year. Traveling across the continent, he stopped over at one city and spent a whole day in a hotel room alone for prayer over a certain matter which he regarded as supremely vital. The "upper room" showed his estimate of that thing. These are extreme cases, but they help one to understand what is due to our Christ—the very top, the uppermost, the best—our exclusive attention.—W. C. Smith.

3. A Furnished Room.

Some equipment was necessary for the supper table—vessels, seats, or reclining places, food and drink, lights, and so on. See to it. Have a good clearprint Bible. Get a good one that will wear well and that you will enjoy handling. Take advantage of every opportunity to train your minds and your hands in Christian service; seek the fellowship of others doing the same thing—in Sunday School, church, or conferences. surround yourselves with every Christ-loving, Christ-serving influence. That is a part of it; you will think of other ways to furnish the large, upper room. —W. C. Smith.

4. The Lord's Supper.

In the course of the passover meal in the upper chamber in Jerusalem a few hours before his betrayal Jesus instituted the observance of the Lord's Supper by taking part of what was provided for the meal and giving it a new meaning as a symbol of himself. Shedding of blood in connection with the making of a covenant was common. At the making of the covenant at Sinai between God and Israel blood had been sprinkled on the people. So in the covenant foreshadowed by that the forgiveness of sins was secured through the pouring out of Christ's blood, which was represented by the fruit of the vine. He was sharing the cup with his disciples for the last time under earthly conditions; in the future they were to have spiritual communion.

5. First, Then.

First, the Lord's Supper, and then the Lamb's Supper. All who partake of the former as members of Christ's body will partake of the latter as members of his bride. Self-deception here is fatal.

6. United with Christ.

An aged Christian spoke with so much confidence of her salvation that a friend thought to chide her a little for over-confidence. He said: "What would you think if you were to slip through the fingers of Christ, after all?" "Oh, I cannot," she said, "I am one of his fingers." That was Scriptural: "Now ye are the body of Christ, and severally members thereof." He has constituted himself our very selves, even including this body of ours; for, "Know ye not that your bodies are members of Christ?" How even our physical bodies, together with our whole being, can be joined in literal union with the eternal Christ we cannot understand; but he plainly would have us accept this by faith. I am not a material instrument he can lay aside or let slip. I am a member of the body of Christ.—H.

7. A Simple Devout Service.

The Lord's Supper is no more a didactic ordinance addressed to the head, than it is a pompous ceremonial addressed to the eye. It is a simple, devout service of worship springing from the heart. Its single purpose is to awaken memory of Jesus, to arouse gratitude, and to kindle love. Everything that diverts our hearts from this is an intrusion. Everyone that comes between us and our atoning Saviour is an intruder.

When our Lord was eating the last passover with his twelve apostles, and but a few hours before he was betrayed, he saw fit to institute a service which should remind his people of his sufferings and death, in such a manner as no precept alone could possibly have done. Separating two simple elements, which were before them on the table —the bread to represent his body broken, and the wine to represent his blood poured forth—he distributed them to his disciples, saying of the bread, "This is my body"; and of the cup, "This is my blood of the new testament, which is shed for many"; and then giving it in solemn charge, "This do in remembrance of me." It was a permanent ordinance, so given and so understood; for more than twenty years

afterwards Paul enjoined its observance on the Corinthian church as a well-known institution, saying "For I have received of the Lord that which also I delivered unto you; that the Lord Jesus, the same night in which he was betrayed, took bread," etc.

Conscientious Christians have to this day, by almost universal consent, observed the Lord's Supper. It is an ordinance peculiar to the church of Christ, and to be statedly observed there until "he shall appear the second time, without sin unto salvation." Notwithstanding this general admission of the obligation to observe this sacrament, there are those who neglect it.

8. Help to Be Religious.

We cannot always sit at the Communion table. We partake of the feast not so much as a luxury, though it is that, but to give us strength to work. We think our Sabbath services, our prayers, our Bible readings, are our religion. It is not so. We do these things to help us to be religious in other things. These are the mere meals, and a workman gets no wages for his meals. It is for the work he does. The value of this Communion is not estimated yet. It will take the coming week to put the value upon it. In itself it counts little; we shall see what it is by what we shall be.—Henry Drummond.

9. Confession of Faith Obligatory.

The duty of confessing Christ before men is incumbent on everyone who hears the Gospel. It is spoken of in Scripture in immediate connection with saving faith. "If thou shalt confess with thy mouth the Lord Jesus, and shalt believe in thine heart that God hath raised him from the dead, thou shalt be saved." In like manner, the duty of commemorating the death of Christ at his table is binding on all who have been made acquainted with his gracious work. Impenitence and unbelief, while they disqualify for right performance, afford no excuse for neglect. It is the sin and not the apology of the sinner that he has no faith to profess and no love to testify.—J. W. A.

10. Preparation of Heart.

To benefit from this feast the only preparation we can make is preparation of heart. Greed and selfishness and self-confidence and cowardice are all out of harmony with the occasion and must grieve the Lord who, though unseen, spreads the feast and presides at it. Let us seek that heart-fellowship with him which his followers enjoyed after Pentecost.

11. The Perpetual Reminder.

The sacrament of the Lord's Supper began with the present dispensation and is to continue till Christ's return whose right it is to close the records of the present dispensation and make sacraments no longer necessary. Till then, let us observe it with unceasing regularity. Wisdom leads us to follow the Divine pattern; and loyalty demands it.

Among the stories of our childhood days is that story of "Sinbad the Sailor" on the Indian Ocean. His vessel was gradually drawn toward a magnetic rock in midocean that lay concealed just beneath the surface. Silently and gradually the bolts and rods of his vessel were drawn from it till of a sudden it collapsed and precipitated the crew into the ocean and they helplessly sank to their watery grave with wreckage all about them. So the magnetic rocks of unbelief and self-pride have menaced our old ship of Zion. Penitence and prayer and church attendance and Bible reading and godly living and Baptism and the Lord's Supper are the bolts that have braced our glorious ship against all storms and tides. These were in the original pattern of the divine builder and arrogance and unbelief must not be left free to draw them out.

The Communion Service! What a time for thought! To the devout in heart it can have no rival. "While I was musing the fire burned," said the Psalmist. What a holy fire burns on the altar of the heart while we "muse" about the Table of our Lord.—Rev. M. E. Harlan.

12. Means of Grace.

Jesus has provided "means of grace" —appointed ways by which spiritual strength may pass from him to us. The Lord's Supper is one of these means. It has no magical virtue, but when approached in the right spirit it becomes a great refreshment and enrichment to our spiritual lives. Remembering Jesus' love, and the price he paid to show it, will make us tenderhearted, grateful, and courageous to resist evil.

13. I Accept.

Coming to Communion is an acceptance of Christ. A pastor was telling his congregation of a custom following World War I. He was telling his people how French women visiting the new-made soldier cemeteries near their villages would chalk over their signatures on the rude wooden crosses the words, "I accept." It meant that these good women would be responsible for keeping green these graves of boys whose loved ones, who would otherwise perform this ministry, were far away in distant lands. The incident beautifully suggests to us, this pastor said, that the finished work of redemption is represented by a cross that stood near an open tomb, and upon which we must by faith inscribe those words of eternal import, "I accept."—*Sunday School Times.*

14. Freshening Up Our Love.

There is a legend about Zacchaeus, that when he was old he still dwelt in Jericho, humble and pious before God and man. Every morning at sunrise he went out into the fields for a walk, and he always came back with a calm and happy mind to begin his day's work. His wife wondered where he went in his walks, but he never told her.

One morning she secretly followed him. He went straight to the tree from which he first saw the Lord. Hiding herself to see what he would do, she noticed that he took a pitcher, and carrying water, poured it about the tree's roots, which were getting dry in the sultry clime. He pulled up some weeds here and there. He passed his hand fondly over the old trunk; then he looked up at the place among the branches where he had sat that day when he first saw the Lord Jesus. After that he turned away, and went back home.

His wife afterward referred to the matter and asked him why he took such care of the old tree. His quiet answer was, "It was that tree which brought me to Him whom my soul loveth." Every Communion season is such a reminder, opportunity for such a freshening up of love.

15. Why Remember Jesus?

Why did Jesus want to be remembered? First, for his own sake. He had a craving for human friendship and could not bear the thought that his own disciples might forget him and his very name thus pass into oblivion. God himself must have his human children; having created them and brought them into his life he cannot be the same without them. "The Father seeketh such to worship him." And Jesus also wanted the disciples to remember him for their sake. Their devotion to his teaching and laws and life, service and sacrifice, depended upon their faithfulness to his person and memory. If they were to forget his spirit would soon fade out of their hearts and his kingdom vanish from the world. Memory is the storehouse of all the accumulated treasures of life, the tie that binds us to all that is precious in the past, and Jesus used this powerful means of perpetuating his own spirit and service in the hearts of his disciples and in the world.

16. Till He Comes.

In the celebration of the Lord's Supper we are commanded to observe it in remembrance of Christ. It is, however, no commemoration of defeat, for our Lord gained his greatest victory and his most signal triumph in his death upon the cross for the sins of men. It was through his vicarious atoning death that he bore our sins and carried our sorrows. It was through the cross that he achieved for his people the great deliverance. In commanding his people throughout all ages to remember his death in this helpful sacrament, he is virtually saying: Commemorate my victory, my triumph over sin and death and hell. Do this that you may with faith and patience await my return. "For, as oft as you eat this bread and drink this cup, ye do show the Lord's death till he come."

17. The Unworthy Invited.

Many excuse themselves from coming to the Lord's Supper on account of their unworthiness. They do not consider that the greater the sickness the more need of a physician. Christ came not to call the righteous, but sinners to repentance.

18. All Equal Here.

The Duke of Wellington once took part in the Lord's Supper in a country church. A poor countryman entered the church and walked down the aisle, taking his place at the table next to the duke. One of the pew openers touched the old man on the shoulder and whispered to him to wait until the duke had received the bread and wine. The duke heard the whisper. He took the old man by the hand and prevented him from rising; then he said, "Do not move; we are all equal here." At the Lord's table we are all God's children, and he does not think whether we are rich or poor. We are just children.

QUOTABLE LORD'S SUPPER POETRY

THE LORD'S TABLE

The table of the Lord
  Is set with care,
That hungry souls may feed
  On heav'nly fare.

We dare not to eat or drink
  From plate or cup
Except we love the Lord
  With whom we sup.

We sit in mockery
  About this spread
If sin is in our hearts
  And love is dead.

If hate and envy rule
  Our heart or mind,
He has no seat for us
  Or peace to find.

Now let this Host Divine
  All souls make clean,
That we may eat and drink
  With Him, serene.
                    —Irwin E. Bradfield.

THE CLOSING HYMN

They sat within the "upper room"
  At evening dim,
He spoke of His impending doom;
  And then, as fell the gathering gloom,
They sang a hymn.

I wish I could have heard that song;
  'Twas sweet, I know;
For loving John would sing out strong,
And Peter's bass would roll along
  So rich and low.

Voice after voice took up the strain
  As it arose;
The sweetness of the grand refrain
Excluded thoughts of loss or pain,
  And cruel foes.
                    —Unidentified.

COMMUNION

As I bow down before Thee, Lord,
  And take this bread and wine;
Accept me, sinful as I am,
  Through Thy rich grace divine.

Forgive me, Lord, where I have erred
  And gone my willful way,
Allowing hatred, prejudice,
  And greed to have full sway.

O, save me from self-righteousness,
  Conceit, and stubborn pride;
Cleanse Thou my soul from every stain
  And then therein abide.
                    —B. Schoonmaker.

THIS IS MY BODY

He was the Word that spake it,
He took the bread and brake it;
And what that Word did make it,
I do believe and take it.
                    —Anon. (16th Century).

ALONE WITH GOD

  Alone with God—
That He may counsel give,
With strength divine to live
Above each ill and care,
To overcome each snare,
  As Guide and Friend.

  Alone with God—
To ask that He will come
And make my heart His home,
My life to enter in,
Its aims for good to win,
  A Saviour, Friend.

  Alone with God—
That I my joys may tell,
And gratitude as well,
For all His gifts to me
And loving-kindness free,
  My Maker, Friend.
                    —R. H. Lyon.

ACCEPTING MORE LOVE

Oh, help me, Lord, to take, by grace
    Divine,
Yet more and more of that great love
    of Thine:
That day by day my heart may give to
    Thee
A deeper love and growing constantly.

Naught but Thy love can satisfy my
    heart,
Constrain my will from self and sin to
    part;
In love so great Thou givest Thyself to
    me;
For Thou art Love—to all eternity.
                    —Unidentified.

O BREAD OF LIFE

O, bread of life! By love and grace
bestowed
To feed our souls—straight from the
Heavenly Board—
Which towards poor, hungry, dying
men, hath showed
Such holy kinship from our Father,
Lord;
In penitence, we at Thy footstool fall;
Feed us, in mercy! Saviour, heed our call.

By faith, dear Lord, we on Thy Body
feed,
Drink of the Life-wine from Thy
sacred veins:
From earthly care and trammel to be
freed
We would be cleansed from sin's
besmirching stains.
Bending at this, Thy Feast, we plead
Thy Word;
Feed us, Thou Living Bread; Almighty
Lord.

—W. T. Pearman.

SOME SUGGESTED
COMMUNION HYMNS

My God, and is thy table spread.—
P. Doddridge.
My Shepherd of souls, refresh and
bless.—J. Montgomery.
How condescending and how kind.—
I. Watts.
Here, O my God, I see thee face to
face.—H. Bonar.
Not worthy, Lord, to gather up the
crumbs.—E. H. Beckerseth.

By Christ redeemed, in Christ re-
stored.—G. Rawson.
According to Thy gracious word.—J
Montgomery.
Jesus, to Thy table led.—R. H.
Baynes.
Bread of the world in mercy broken.
—R. Heber.
O Bread to pilgrims given.—J. Conder.
Jesus, Thou joy of loving hearts.—
Bernard of Clairvaux.
Bread of heaven, on Thee I feed.—
J. Conder.
At the Lamb's high feast we sing.—
Anon.
A parting hymn we sing.—A. R.
Wolfe.
Beneath the Cross of Jesus.—E. C.
Celphane.
Sweet feast of love divine.—E. Denny.
At Thy feet, our God, and Father.—
J. D. Burns.
When I survey the wondrous cross.
—I. Watts.
Sweet the moments, rich in blessing.—
W. Sherley.
O blest memorial of our dying Lord.
—J. R. Woodford, Jr.
O Love, that wilt not let me go.—G.
Matheson.
O for a closer walk with God.—W.
Cowper.
Draw nigh and take the body of your
Lord.—J. M. Meale.
Break thou the bread of life.—M. A.
Lathbury.
At Thy command, our dearest Lord.
—I. Watts.
Fairest Lord Jesus.—Anon.
Majestic sweetness sits enthroned.—
S. Stennett.

SECTION VI.   For Missions and
Missionaries

Everything about the gospel seems to be world-wide in its design. Christ announced a world-wide enlightenment: "I am the light of the world." As such, he has thrown light upon all the complex problems of human life—on life, death, character, duty, and destiny. He claimed a world-wide field of activity: "The field is the world." In his parable of the leaven he gives us to understand that the truth of the kingdom will ultimately permeate the entire race. When Christ broke the bands of death and came forth from the tomb with the keys of death and the grave swung to his girdle, he issued his marching orders to the church, announcing a world-wide evangelization: "Go ye therefore, and make disciples of all the nations, baptizing them into the name of the Father and of the Son and of the Holy Spirit." When the disciples came to inquire as to the time for restoring the kingdom, Christ replied: "It is not for you to know times or seasons, when the Father hath set within his own authority. But ye shall receive power, when the Holy Spirit is come upon you; and ye shall be my witnesses both in Jerusalem and in all Judea and Samaria, and unto the uttermost parts of the earth." It was not the work of the disciples to be sitting up in Jerusalem reigning, but to go out and bear this revolutionizing and elevating truth of Christ to all the world.

In his wonderful Apocalyptic vision on Patmos, John "saw a new heaven and a new earth; for the first heaven and the first earth are passed away; and the sea is no more." He also "saw the holy city, new Jerusalem, coming down out of Heaven from God." The purpose, therefore, of the kingdom was not to take a few individuals away from the earth and transfer them to heaven, but to transfer heavenly influences and powers and principles to earth and by means of these to make it new.

The church has been slow in carrying out its commission for missions, but there are evidences that it is feeling a new impulse in this direction. For both missionaries and home pastors this department is intended to give aid. It has been warmly welcomed by both. We have ample testimony that missionaries find this department and the whole book suited to their needs. Also home pastors value the department as a help toward their frequent messages on missionary themes.

SOME STARTING-POINT STUDIES FOR MISSIONARY SERMONS AND ADDRESSES

1. Topic: The Assured Success of Missions.

TEXT: "The earth shall be full of the knowledge of the Lord, as the waters cover the sea." Isa. 11:9.

59

I. He who sides with God. Someone once said to Abraham Lincoln during the Civil War: "I hope the Lord is on your side." "I am not very much concerned about that matter," was the great man's answer. "Why?" asked the shocked listener. "I am vastly more concerned as to our being on the Lord's side," Lincoln replied. To be on God's side is to succeed eventually, and that is just the reason that the cause of missions will succeed. It is God's purpose that the world shall be evangelized. People forget that the theme of missions is the central thought running through the whole Bible. Take missions out of Book and you would have almost nothing left. God sent his Son that the "world might be saved," and we are told that "the kingdoms of this world shall become the kingdom of our Lord and his Christ," also that "the earth shall be full of the knowledge of the Lord as the waters cover the sea."

II. The power of the Gospel. Missions will succeed because the Gospel is the "power of God unto salvation to every one that believeth." There is not a country on the face of the earth where the Gospel has not shown its power to save men from sin. Other religions do not do this. Mohammedanism, Buddhism, Confucianism and the other religions of the world, while having good moral precepts, have not the power to save men from their sins. The Gospel is the only power that redeems humanity.

III. The hunger of man's soul. Someone has said that the whole human race is homesick for God. There is great truth in the statement. This is the hope of missions. Heathen people are hungry without God and never will be content till they find God. In the Gospel they find him and have peace. Throughout the whole heathen world you will find people seeking for God. They do it in strange, sad ways, through idols, pilgrimages, self-punishments, long prayers. But this shows they are hungry; that deep down in their hearts is an unsatisfied longing. The missionary goes to these people. He teaches them the truth. They sometimes cannot see it for a long while, but when they do they are made glad.

IV. The Gospel was made to spread. It was never intended that Christianity should be bottled up, that it should satisfy the wants of some local territory and never go out into the ends of the earth. The Christian religion is universal. It is its very genius to spread and it must. It will be powerful only as it does spread. Some people seem to think that the Gospel gets thinner as you spread it. No, it is rather like the fire in the forest, becoming more powerful as it does spread. In early days they thought they could overcome Christianity by persecutions; that they could stamp it out. They bound the followers of Christ, but they could not bind his religion. It spread more, the more they persecuted.

V. The quality of foreign Christians. Much encouragement comes to missionary success by the quality of the converts on the field. Of course they are not all true there, as here, but the majority of converts in foreign lands are noble follows of Jesus. Men and women are brought from the lowest idolatry and degradation into the light of the Gospel and become changed people. Stories come of heroic faithfulness on the mission fields that would put many of us to shame at home.

VI. The success attained. The marked success of modern missions gives great hope of final success. In Christ's time the whole world lay in darkness. Get now the latest statistical report of converts, churches, hospitals, schools, orphanages, etc. What has done this much can carry the work on to completion, till the whole world is influenced. The people will come from the east and from the west, from the north and from the south and sit down in the kingdom of God.—S. J. Corey.

2. Topic: The Great Commission.

TEXT: "Go ye therefore," etc. Matt 28:19, 20.

The natural religions of the world cannot be compared with Christianity.

Those religions are the product of human thought, from man to God; Christianity is a divine revelation, from God to man. They, at best, are seeking after God; Christianity, from first to last, is a finding of God. Christianity is a Person. Christ is the center, the circumference, the all in all of Christianity; hence, he is the One whom we are to present and proclaim. The New Testament throbs with this thought, because its very heart is Christ.

I. The One who commands. The position which Christ occupies as related to his church is that of Saviour and Lord. As Saviour, he is the possessor of those whom he has redeemed; as Lord, he is the director of those whom he possesses. It is, therefore, his inherent and unlimited right to ask of his people what he pleases, to require what he asks and to command what he requires. His words, therefore, are fiats, which, being uttered, call for immediate, full and continued obedience, until they are fulfilled.

II. Those who are commanded. The Christian lives in consequence of a sacrificial act which saved him from death. There is, therefore, not a moment of time when he can consider himself independent of that act or under little or no obligation to it. He must look upon himself as one who is required to learn his Redeemer's wish and to do his will. Not to act thus indicates that he has little appreciation of what has been done for him and what he owes in return. In other words, the whole church is under sacred obligation to fulfill Christ's command to evangelize the world, and each Christian in his own appointed way is to be at it and always at it.

III. The thing which is commanded. Christ has given to his church many commands. But one command is primal and pre-eminent. It is to preach the Gospel to every creature. This mandate is clear in its intention and expression, so that its meaning cannot be misunderstood. Also, it is plain, both as to its content and extent. As to content, we are told to preach one thing, not less or more, namely, the Gospel; as to extent, the preaching is to be continued until every person has heard.

IV. The way the command is to be fulfilled. The good, as we all know, is often the enemy of the best. Social reform is good, but it is not the Gospel. Education is good, but it is not the Gospel. Medical work is good, but it is not the Gospel. If a missionary keeps the balance between the primary and the secondary, he has a true conception of the Great Commission. Truth is the essential which God requires and which the condition of the world demands. Our commission, therefore, is this: to preach the truth, that is, the Gospel.

It was largely this conception of things which sent of old so many noble men and women into the regions beyond. For the love they bore their Master, they obeyed his Word, went to lonely places, lived often in sordid surroundings and laid down their lives, slowly or suddenly, in willing sacrifice for the One whom they served and for those who needed the Gospel that they preached. Hence, in their places of service, they turned the world upside down and innumerable lives were turned right side up. It will be so with any man who will follow in their steps.

Let us to our tents, O Israel, and our knees. There in the secret place of prayer and dedication let us hear what Christ would say to us. Then let us rise and go forth, to do God's work, in God's place and in God's way.—H. W. F.

3. Topic: The Cry of the Nations.

TEXT: "Come over . . . and help us." Acts 16:9.

I. The first fact is that all who are ignorant of the Gospel need help. They are in a state of ignorance, of darkness, of bondage. They know not God.

II. Those in the same state as were the people of Macedonia are crying, Come over . . . and help us."

III. It is incumbent on the Christian church to send help to the nations that are in darkness. 1. It is Christ's command. 2. We can do it. 3. It is a reasonable requirement.

IV. In consequence of this obligation we ought to send the Gospel by those means God has appointed. 1. The Gospel excites attention. 2. It is adapted to impress.

V. It is incumbent on Christians to use methods to send them the Gospel. 1. Pray. 2. Contribute. 3. Exert influence.

VI. The motives to the performance of this duty are most powerful. 1. The command of Christ. 2. Millions are perishing for lack of knowledge. 3. The promise of Divine Presence and aid.—B.

4. Topic: The Gospel for the World.

TEXT: "Go ye into all the world, and preach the gospel to every creature." Mark 16:15.

These words are a part of the last Great Commission, spoken by the Lord to his apostles after his resurrection from the dead, and before his ascension to heaven. Consider,

I. The Speaker. The words are those of him who once was dead, but is now alive forevermore, and has in his hands the keys of death and the grave; of him to whom is committed all power and authority both in heaven and on earth. Therefore, all he proposes he is able to carry out; and all he promises he is abundantly able to perform.

II. The persons addressed. The commission was given to, 1. The Apostles. 2. Their number. 3. Their qualifications were complete. They had been with and learned of Jesus, and afterward were miraculously endowed by the Holy Spirit. 4. All Christians. A part of the charge to the apostles was to teach all things he had commanded them. So the charge is binding upon all Christians, and will be to the end of time.

III. The duty enjoined. The first duty enjoined in the text is "Go." One cannot sit down in idleness and accomplish anything. The second duty is to "preach the Gospel." The Gospel is the good news of salvation, on the terms proposed by Christ. 1. It consists of facts to be believed. 2. Commands to be obeyed. 3. Promises to be enjoyed.

IV. The Gospel field. The field is described or bounded by two expressions in the text. The work was to begin in Jerusalem, the place of Christ's death; then it was to extend to Judea, then to Samaria, then to the uttermost parts of the earth. The apostles themselves observed this order. The duty resting upon all Chritsians is to continue the work along the same lines. This includes the whole human race; the high and the low, the rich and the poor, the black and the white, the Chinese and the Japanese. Our duties as Christians in this respect will not be done until salvation is offered to "every creature."

5. Topic: The Inevitable Claims of Foreign Missions.

TEXT: "Go ye into all the world," etc. Mark 16:15.

Foreign missions are not optional. Neither are they secondary. The claims of foreign missions are primary and unavoidable. The work of preaching the Gospel to every creature and making disciples of all nations is not the responsibility of a department or the enthusiasm of a few. It is the work of the whole church. The duty of the church to the heathen does not rest upon considerations of expediency and compassion. The claims are inevitable, because they are rooted in the very nature of Christianity, and in the essential character of the church. Foreign missions are often advocated in the interests of commerce and civilization. The missionary is the pioneer of trade and the forerunner of social progress. Such by-products of missionary enterprise have their value, but it is not for these the church of Christ sends forth its messengers. Nor it is upon social humanitarian benefits its plea can prevail. It is not a question of expediency, but of loyalty to Jesus Christ and his redeeming purpose in the world.

I. The claims of foreign missions are inevitable because they are inherent in the character and calling of the church.

The doctrine of the church is summed up in one word: it is the body of Christ. That is not a figure of speech; it is the supreme and final statement of a fact.

The practical bearing of this doctrine is, first, that Christ identifies himself with the church; and, second, that he is dependent upon his church for carrying out his work in the world. The inevitable claim of foreign missions lies in this fundamental fact: the life of the church is the life of Christ, and the life of Christ is the life of the church.

II. The inevitable claim is set forth in the commission with which Christ sent forth his church into the world. The church is under orders. No provision is made for the modification of the charter granted between Easter and Pentecost; the manifesto is entirely missionary. Christ's kingdom is imperial, and his Gospel universal.

The God of the Bible is a missionary God; his purposes of grace have never been less than world-wide. The only alternative of obedience is treason. The church has no choice.

If the commission is to "all nations," so also is the Gospel for "every creature." The Gospel is neither good advice nor good programmes. It is good news. It is good news which all men need, and which fits all men's deepest needs. The inevitable claim is an obligation of faithfulness to Christ, and a debt due to "every creature" to whom the Gospel is sent.

III. The inevitable claims go beyond both Kingdom and Gospel to the Person of Christ himself. After all, it is neither a kingdom nor a gospel that is the church's responsibility, but a Person. Christianity is not simply a new religion with a more exalted code or a clearer light. Christianity is Christ. The mission of the Church is to preach Christ and to carry Christ to all people. Our debt is to him first, and through him to all, without whom he cannot be complete or satisfied.

The solemnity of the charge deepens when the issues are considered. Jesus Christ has placed the keys of the kingdom in the hands of his church. His work of redemption is in our hands. The destiny of nations has become our responsibility. If any people know not the Christ, it will be laid to our account.

Great trusts involve great issues. God has conditioned the life of the church itself upon its attitude to missions. The church that ceases to be missionary dies. Missionary enthusiasm can only be sustained by spiritual fellowship with Christ. The Head of the Church cannot live in a Church that does not respond to his mind and will.—Rev. Samuel Chadwick.

6. Topic: The Gospel Is to Prevail.

TEXT: "All the ends of the world shall remember and turn unto the Lord: and all the kindreds of the nations shall worship before thee." Ps. 22:27.

I. A description of true religion. 1. It includes remembering. 2. It includes turning unto the Lord. 3. It includes worshiping before him. It implies the Gospel and its results.

II. A prediction of the universal prevalence of this religion. 1. This prediction is contained in the Book of God. 2. It is accompanied with the promise of an agency that secures its fulfillment. 3. It is already partially fulfilled. 4. There is no natural improbability in its literal fulfillment.

SOME PRAYERS FOR MISSIONS AND FOR MISSIONARY OCCASIONS

1. Comprehensive Prayer for Missions.

Almighty God, our Father in heaven, we have beheld thy glory and thy goodness, shining in the face of Jesus Christ, the Saviour of mankind. Send forth thy light and thy truth, we beseech thee, and draw all people that on earth do dwell into the fellowship of Jesus and the joy of thy salvation. O thou who hast so greatly loved the world, that thou hast given thine only-begotten Son, the Redeemer, communicate thy love to the heart of all believers, and inspire thy

Church to preach the Gospel to every creature. O thou who rulest by thy providence over land and sea, defend and guide and bless the messengers of Christ. In danger, be their shield; in darkness, be their hope; enrich their word and work with wisdom, joy and power, and let them gather souls for thee in the far fields white unto the harvest. O thou who by thy Holy Spirit workest wonders in secret, open the eyes that dimly look for light to see the day-star in Christ; open the minds that seek the unknown God to know their heavenly Father in Christ; open the hearts that hunger for righteousness to find eternal peace in Christ. Deliver the poor prisoners of ignorance and captives of idolatry. Break down the bars of error, and dispel the shadows of the ancient night. Lift up the gates, and let the King of Glory and the Prince of Peace come in. Thy kingdom, O Christ, is an everlasting kingdom! Strengthen thy servants to pray and labor and wait for its appearing. Forgive our little faith and the weakness of our endeavor. Hasten the day when all nations shall be at peace in thee, and every land and every heart throughout the world shall bless the name of the Lord Jesus, to the glory of God the Father. Amen.

2. A Comprehensive Prayer for Missions.

Our Father who art in heaven; who because thou didst so love the world gaveth thine only begotten Son for its salvation, grant to us to have that new world-wide consciousness which was of old in thy heart and in the heart of thy Son our Saviour. He said that many should come from the East and the West to sit in thy kingdom. He answered the petition of the heathen widow. He blessed the wicked woman of Samaria whose people, he said, knew not whom they worshiped. In his words the note of world-wide love and world-wide triumph constantly appears. He, the country carpenter who never touched in his short life the great ones of earth, loved by few, hated and slain by the leaders of Church and State, bade us make all na-

tions his disciples. Many have dreamed such dreams, but he alone dreamed true. We bless thee that always that world-wide consciousness has flamed in some true hearts, like William Carey cobbling shoes and gazing at the map of the world which his Master was to conquer. We bless thee that in our days that world-wide consciousness leaps from heart to heart and from land to land as never before, and that today, led by countless consecrated missionaries, millions of converted heathen worship thee.

May this world-consciousness possess our hearts, making great our small souls, glorifying, as we daily walk with thee in the path of the world's salvation, our little lives, our petty opportunities, our weak endeavors, for Christ and the world's sake! Amen.

3. Short Prayer for Missions.

O God our Father, who didst send thy Son to save the whole world; we pray thee to bless all who work for thee at home and in distant lands. Make us glad to help in thy work; so that all thy children everywhere may learn to know thy love, and to share with us the joy that comes through our Saviour Jesus Christ. Amen.

4. Short Prayer for the Coming of the Kingdom.

We pray thee, O God, for the spread of thy kingdom and the triumph of righteousness. Rule and overrule in the lives of men and nations until pride and prejudice, selfishness and exploitation shall be vanquished and men shall live together in freedom and good will without fear. Our hearts thrill at the vision of the New Jerusalem established among men. May it be granted to us to lay its foundations by lives that are wholly devoted to the common good because they are wholly consecrated to Jesus Christ our Lord and Saviour. In his name we ask. Amen.

5. An Invocation Prayer.

We thank thee, O God, for the good news of the Gospel of Jesus Christ, our

Lord. We thank thee for the revelation of his face and for the wonderful words of life. We cannot number the blessings that have come to us through our knowledge of Jesus. We would sacrifice all else for him. We would give up all rather than part with him. He is our Life, our Joy, our undying Hope. The riches of his grace in us, O Lord, is but the measure of our obligation to thee and to those who do not know thee. We would have all men rejoice in our Gospel. We would have India, and China and Africa know Jesus even as we do. How can the nations be glad and sing for joy until they know the Gospel? O, sent out thy light and thy truth unto all the earth. Bless all missionaries, and native teachers, and native workers. Bless the church in our land, and out of her increasing wealth may she freely give and freely go that the world may be saved, and that Jesus may see the travail of his soul, and be satisfied. For his name's sake. Amen.

6. For a Missionary Meeting.

We wait upon thee on behalf of our brethren who labor in distant parts of the earth for the Gospel of Christ. We give thee thanks for service rendered in thy name, and for endurance amid danger and distress. Let not their spirit be broken by opposition and persecution, but like the Psalmist of old may they still hope in God who is the health of their countenance. Break down the barriers of darkness before them, and let thy light and thy truth lead them whither they know not into new and grander conquests for Christ. Bless their homes with Christian love that out of them may continue to pour upon needy hearts the sweet graces of the Spirit, and upon all the special movements for the advancement of thy kingdom may there descend the promised showers. To thee we look and for thy presence we wait. Through Christ our Lord. Amen.

7. A Brief Prayer for Missions.

O God, our heavenly Father, who didst manifest thy love by sending thine only begotten Son into the world that all might live through him; pour thy Spirit upon thy church, that it may fulfill his command to preach the Gospel to every creature; send forth, we beseech thee, laborers into thy harvest; defend them in all dangers and temptations; and hasten the time when the fulness of the Gentiles shall be gathered in, and all Israel shall be saved; through the same thy Son Jesus Christ our Lord. Amen.

8. Prayers following Missionary Offerings.

(1) For the privilege of engaging in the great enterprise of the kingdom we give thee thanks, O Father. It lifts us out of petty and trifling things; we are no longer circumscribed in our activities; we are no longer limited in the area of our influence; we can serve men far and near. For the broadening and emancipating call of the Gospel to service we give thee thanks. Bless our offering. For Jesus' sake we ask. Amen.

(2) Our dear heavenly Father, we bring our gifts to thine altar this day. All we have is thine; the cattle on a thousand hills belong to thee. Help us to feel our dependence on thee. Accept these offerings and use them for the extension of thy kingdom in the world. We ask in the name of Christ. Amen.

(3) Almighty Father, whose grace doth ever keep and whose love can never fail us, we would commit ourselves and our ways unto thee. May we be glad in the Lord, and in the beauty of holiness worship thee. May we invite thy mercies through our charities and thy great love through our pure and unselfish affections. Make us wise to know thee and faithful to obey thee. Receive and bless and use to thy glory and the good of men the offerings we bring this morning. In the name of Christ, we ask. Amen.

(4) As we bring these our thank offerings to thine altar our prayers are for all who are seeking to do thy will and to set forward thy kingdom, that they may be inspired with grace and truth, with zeal for promotion of the brother-

hood, and renewed devotion to thy service. Through Christ we ask. Amen.

(5) We pray, our Father, that this offering may be blessed of thee unto the great ends for which Christ came to earth and lived and died and rose again. May it carry the message of the Gospel far and near and bring release to the captives who are bound by low ideals and the enslavement of sin. In the name of Christ we ask.—M. K. W. H.

(6) O thou God of patience, teach us how to labor and to wait; how to walk and not faint. Thy kingdom come, in us, in others, in all the world. To this end accept and bless the offering we bring this day. In the name of Christ we ask. Amen.

(7) We bless thy name, our Father, for the privilege of this act of worship. May our giving be with gladness and a true desire to aid in the extension of thy kingdom on earth. We ask in the name of Jesus. Amen.

SUGGESTED MISSION TEXTS AND THEMES

The Transforming Gospel: "These that have turned the world upside down are come hither also." Acts 17:6.

The Kingdom of Christ: "Thou sawest till that a stone was cut without hands," etc. Dan. 2:34, 35.

The Shepherdless Multitudes: Matt. 9:36-38. 1. Christ's compassion. 2. The harvest. 3. The laborers. 4. The praying. 5. The sending.

Christ the World's only Saviour and Christianity the World's only Hope, Acts 4:12.

The Regions Beyond: II Cor. 10:15, 16. 1. The hearer enlarging the preacher. 2. The church enlarging the Gospel.

A Glorious Vision: The redeemed from all lands. Rev. 7:9.

"Doing Good unto All Men": Gal. 6:10. A glorious opportunity entailing a sublime responsibility.

Missionary Heroes and Heroines: II Cor. 4:1-18. The spring of missions is belief. Belief (1) in God's love, (2) in human need, (3) in Christ's sacrifice, and

(4) in the all-sufficient salvation which he offers.

Incentive to Missionary Work: I John 4:19.

Encouragements in Missionary Work: Ps. 22:27, 28.

The "Good Samaritan" Deeds of Medical Missions: Luke 10:33-35.

The Missionary and the Home Church.

The Missionary and His Methods.

The Inner Life of the Missionary.

First Missionaries: Acts 8:4-8.

The Missionary Spirit: Isa. 50:4-9.

"Where is Abel thy brother?" Gen. 4:9.

Scattering that Increases: Prov. 11:24, 25.

The Regions Beyond: II Cor. 5:15, 16.

How Missionaries Have Helped Business.

CHOICE ILLUSTRATIONS ON MISSIONARY THEMES

1. A First Missionary Qualification.

A missionary made his first visit to a village in South America and read to a group of natives the New Testament narrative of Jesus' life and death and resurrection. The next day the same people came together and asked to hear the story again. Once more the missionary read the old, old story of Jesus and his love. "Do you know the Man in the Book?" asked one of the listeners. In telling about the incident the missionary said: "Thank God that I did know the Man in the Book. I knew him as my Lord and Saviour and was able to introduce my Friend to those who had never met him before."—Rev. W. D. Cavert.

2. Where There Are Men.

When a volunteer missionary to Polynesia was told of dangers to be met, he asked whether there were men there. "Yes," he was answered, "horrible cannibals." "That settles it," said he; "wherever there are men, there missionaries are bound to go."

3. Dust, Well and Wisely Mixed.

While Campbell Morgan stood one day in the vestry of the Fifth Avenue Church in New York, a man stepped up to him, took his hand and looked into his face affectionately, and said: "Don't you know me?" "I seem to know your face," said Dr. Morgan. "I am Griffith John," said the man. Dr. Morgan said he felt that he stood in the presence of one of the great apostles. Under the spell of that moment, Dr. Morgan asked him for his blessing, and this is the benediction he quickly gave him: "I have had fifty years in China, and I'm going back." "Well," said Dr. Morgan, "aren't you coming to see us in the old country?" "Oh, no," he said, "I've very little interest in the old country." "Don't you want to see Wales?" pressed Dr. Morgan. "No," he said, "I love China more. Wales is a beautiful memory to me, but I must live and die in China, and mix my dust with hers." That is the way for a man to manage his affairs and "mix his dust," even in the interest of a world-wide gospel deliverance.—*Religious Telescope*.

4. Getting Offerings for Missions.

Church officers who are beginning to consider budget plans for the ecclesiastical year will appreciate the story recently heard of a farmer and his cow: "Does your cow voluntarily give much milk?" asked a summer boarder. "Well," replied the farmer, "I can't just say how voluntary it is. If we can get her headed into a corner, and tie her there while an active, able-bodied man gets hold of her, she'll yield up considerable."

5. The Best for Missionaries.

Out of five men gathered at Antioch waiting upon the Lord in prayer, God takes the chiefest two and sends them away to those who have not heard of him. Our method of preaching would be to keep Paul and Barnabas and make them ministers at Antioch, but the Spirit's method was "ever onward, ever farther out—the best to the regions beyond!"

6. Missions a Spreading Tree.

In the Botanical Gardens in Calcutta, India, is a banyan tree that shades a larger area than any other tree in the world. The main trunk is sixty feet in circumference; and, in keeping with the nature of this strange tree, hundreds of air roots descend from its branches to the ground, so that it is really many trees in one. And it spreads out so far that a whole army could rest in its shade. Jesus planted a wonderful tree, an organism, a brotherhood; and he called it his church. And from the main trunk of that tree branches have spread and have taken root in every part of the earth. Also, as each new offspring of the banyan tree remains vitally united with the parent tree, though rooted in its own soil, so every true church, however dependent on the human soil where it is, remains, through the Spirit, vitally united with Christ. Moreover, the spiritual church which Jesus planted is destined to grow and spread till the great army of those who are weary and heavy laden—even under the "heavy burdens and grievous to be borne" laid on many by ecclesiastical authorities not united with Christ—will find rest and peace beneath its shade.—Gordon Hurlbutt.

7. The Living Line.

Akbar the Great, who reigned in India at the time Elizabeth was queen of England, summoned his ministers on one occasion, when his mother lay ill at Ajmer, two hundred miles from Agra, his capital, and stated that he required an hourly bulletin regarding her condition. When told by his ministers that the thing was impossible, there being nothing but fleet horses to carry any such messages in those days, he asserted that the thing must be done—and got the messages. He stationed a man at the palace gate at Ajmer, another a few furlongs down the city, then another and another, and carried his line of men right across the desert to Agra. Every hour the man at the palace gates got the message and called it aloud to the next, and so across the desert that living telegraph bore the message to the waiting Akbar every hour at Agra. It is by means of a living telegraph that we can communicate the great message of salvation to the world today, but if those who are in that line of communication have no message to pass on, nothing gets through.—Bishop T. B. Bradley.

8. Missions Pushing the Desert Back.

Thomas Tyson was a great man in Australia. They say he left twenty-five millions when he died. He made it his entire lifework to set the desert back. He declared himself an enemy of the desert; and what he enjoyed was to push farther and farther out on the sands of Australia the fertile fields and forests, and the great herds of cattle. At the time he died he had twelve hundred farms laid out on the actual sands of the desert, to which he was going to bring water in a few days and make them as rich as any garden in the world. How true that is of Christ and Christians in the world! Paul was setting the desert back. Missions are setting the desert back.

9. Results of Missions (In Old Korea).

There has been wonderful progress in the work of the Christian church in Korea. A few years ago there were two Christian churches in the city of Pyeng Yang—a Presbyterian and a Methodist. Now there are ten churches of the Presbyterian and Methodist missions there, and two churches carried on by the Japanese Congregationalists, one among the Koreans and one among the Japanese. We spent the whole of one Sunday going about from church to church and from Sunday School to Sunday School, ending the day with two meetings, one for men and one for women, that packed two of the largest churches. I wish that all the friends of the work in Korea might have been at the men's meeting, when two thousand men and boys crowded every square foot of space, and might have heard them as they sang, at our request, the hymn that we had heard across the plains and through the valleys of Korea eighteen years ago, "Nothing

but the Blood of Jesus."—*With Speer in Korea.*

10. The Civilizing Religion.

Africa is coming to be belted with brickyards out of whose product houses, churches, schools, and all the structures of civilization are built. The artisans who built the splendid edifice of the Free Church of Scotland at Blantyre were natives whose fathers had never seen a white man. It is the genius of the religion to civilize where it touches. —Cyrus C. Adams.

11. Flourish or Decay Together.

By an eternal law, home work and foreign work flourish or decay together. Contributions to home work have never been diminished because the work of the church abroad has taken its proper place in our parochial organizations. On the contrary, they will grow and increase, for foreign work acts and reacts on the home work. Schools, Bibles, classes, services in church, are all stronger, brighter, healthier in proportion as the duty to preach the Gospel to the unevangelized is recognized.

12. Missionaries Voluntary Exiles.

The missionaries go as voluntary exiles from home and church, from all the social connections, from all the literary surroundings, which are as dear and delightful to them as to you and me. They go out for an isolated work, seemingly dreary and desolate, as those tarrying behind look upon it. And yet they are full of gladness and of triumph, from the beginning onward. They are the most self-sacrificing, as we say, of the disciples of the Master, and also the most full of jubilant rejoicing and of triumphant courage.—R. S. Storrs, D.D.

13. The Hindrance of Drink.

A missionary recently said, "In the interior of Laos I saw shops with long rows of bottles labeled 'Scotch Whiskey,' 'French Brandy,' and 'Australian Beer.' In Bangkok I read the English sign, 'Place for drinking of the delightful juice.' Near the Silliman Institute, where we are teaching Filipino boys, there is a building bearing the infamous inscription, 'American Saloon.' That was a great day on which Congress passed the law 'forbidding any American to sell intoxicants, opium or firearms in any islands of the Pacific not governed by a civilized power.' If in Islands why is it not wrong and preventable to debauch the Pacific Continentals? Why should the streams of influence pouring into Asia and Africa from Christian nations be polluted by slime from the pit?"

14. More Gospel, Less Rum.

The first letter written in English by a native of the Congo was written to the Archbishop of Canterbury. It was this, and surely there is a lesson in it for Christendom: "Great and Good Chief of the Tribe of Christ: Greeting, The humblest of your servants kisses the hem of your garment, and begs you to send to his fellow-servants more gospel and less rum. In the bond of Christ. Ugalla."

15. Christ's Onward March.

There are no backward steps in Christ's march down the centuries and across the nations to universal victory. —Rev. Dr. Judson Smith.

16. Honor for Missionaries.

When the first American missionaries reached India, the English government refused them a landing. "Go back," was the imperious order; "go back in the ship in which you came." In the General Assembly of the Church of Scotland, when it was first proposed to send the Gospel to the heathen, reverend gentlemen declared against the scheme. But much over a century has passed since that time; yet now all Christendom rings with gratulation over the achievements of Christian missions; and no other class of men are so reverently canonized in the affections of the church as her missionaries to the unevangelized world.—Prof. Austin Phelps.

17. Transformation.

At the beginning of the nineteenth century there was a large stone in Tahiti, red with the blood of slain children. Years ago it was hollowed out and is now used as a baptismal font in a Christian church.

18. Missionaries Witness-bearing for Christ.

On the English coast there are two objects that never fail to attract and interest. One is a lighthouse, standing on a headland some five miles along the coast; the other, a lightship, anchored about seven miles out at sea, at the point of a dangerous reef of sandbanks. The former is strong, stately, a costly as well as a beautiful building. The other is just a stout, clumsy tub of a ship, with one mast set in her center for the purpose of carrying the lantern. When the shadows of night begin to fall, a light shines from each of these out across the waters, to guide and warn the shipmasters, who trust implicitly to their friendly beams. But for them, how many thousands of lives would be lost on this ocean highway!

God has placed some men like the lighthouse—men of high rank, of great wealth, or of exceptional mental gifts —to uphold his cause in the world. Others, of lesser power, in humbler stations, are equally used by him. "The spirit of man is the candle of the Lord," and wherever the soul is indeed set on fire by the love of Christ, there the light of a pure and holy life will shine out. Just as lighthouses are needed all along a dangerous coast, and lightships far out at sea, by lonely rocks and treacherous sandbanks, which ships and sailors must pass at the peril of commerce and life; so in every land, and among all ranks and classes, men and women of God are needed, by their influence, their example, their sympathy, to warn their fellows of the dangers of sin, and to guide them across life's stormy ocean to the haven of eternal peace.—Rev. J. W. W. Moeran.

19. The Permeating Power of Missions.

Said a learned Indian judge, the Hon. Sir Narayan G. Chandavarker, to a meeting in Bombay some years ago: "Let me tell this great country with its more than 350 millions of people, there should come from a little island, unknown even by name to our forefathers, many thousands of miles distant from our shores, a message so full of spiritual life and strength as the gospel of Christ. This is a marvel, if ever there was one. The ideas that lie at the heart of the gospel of Christ are slowly, but surely, permeating every part of Hindu society and modifying every phase of Hindu thought."

20. An Investor in Missions.

One day a boy said to his mother: "I am going down to the church tonight to hear the missionary from Africa, for when he was here before I gave him five cents, and I want to know what he has done with it." We should give intelligently, and follow up our gifts with our interest.

21. Brotherhood, "Where Is Thy Brother?"

If I had to put the meaning of Christianity into a single word, the best I could do would be "brotherhood." The Elder Brother come down from heaven, and we are our earthly brother's keeper. And that one word, "brotherhood," defines missions also. How wide is your conscious brotherhood?

22. Make Not Yourself Too Cheap.

Do not make yourself too cheap. A noted artist lately offended his government and a reward was placed on his head. He was greatly offended for the price was so small! The old offer "a penny for your thoughts" was no compliment to the mental grist of the grinder. If you want to keep humble over your missionary benevolences, sit down and make an exact memorandum of what you have given, and then compare that with some of your other expenses or indulgences. Do not make yourself too cheap.

SOME QUOTABLE MISSIONARY POETRY

OUR PART

The restless millions wait
The light whose dawning
Maketh all things new.
Christ also waits;
But men are slow and late.
Have we done what we could?
Have I? Have you?
—Unidentified.

MISSIONARY PRAYER

Whither thou sendest,
Whither thou leadest,
Thither my journey.
Eastward or westward,
Northward or southward,
Dayward or nightward,
Joyward or woeward,
Homeward or starward,
So be it Thee-ward,
Thither my journey.
—Author Unknown.

BREAD FOR THE NEEDY

"Go break for the needy the Gospel bread"—
These words unto me the angel said.
"And must I keep giving again and again?"
My petty and pitiless answer ran:
"Ah, no," said the angel piercing me through,
"Just give till the Master stops giving to you."
—Author Unknown.

THE GREAT COMMISSION

The Christian knelt in prayer,
Alone with God:
"Reach, Lord, oh, reach the souls of men
And lift their load."

"Grant them thy love and light.
Dispel their gloom."
His words were hushed: A Holy Presence stood
Within the room.

"On Calvary, for men,
  My Love, my Life I give,
I have. Do thou—do thou
  Go forth and save."
          —Annie S. Wallis.

AFRAID

A little Chinese girl, who escaped from the bandits tells how, gun in hand, they asked the missionary, J. W. Vinson, if he were afraid. "No," he replied; "if you shoot, I go straight to heaven." His decapitated body was found later.

Afraid? Of what?
To feel the spirit's glad release?
To pass from pain to perfect peace,
The strife and strain of life to cease?
  Afraid—of that?

Afraid? Of what?
Afraid to see the Saviour's face,
To hear His welcome, and to trace
The glory gleam from wounds of grace?
  Afraid—of that?

Afraid? Of what?
A flash—a crash—a pierced heart;
Darkness—light—O heaven's heart!
A wound of His a counterpart!
  Afraid—of that?

Afraid? Of what?
To do by death what life could not—
Baptize with blood a stony plot,
Till souls shall blossom from the spot?
  Afraid—of that?
          —E. H. Hamilton.

STAND STILL AND SEE

"I'm standing, Lord.
There is a mist that blinds my sight.
Steep, jagged rocks, front, left, and right,
Lower, dim, gigantic, in the night.
  Where is the way?

"I'm standing, Lord.
The black rocks hem me in behind.
Above my head a moaning wind
Chills and oppresses heart and mind.
  I am afraid!"

He answered me, and on His face
A look ineffable of grace,
Of perfect, understanding love,
  Which all my murmuring did remove.

"I'm standing, Lord.
Since Thou hast spoken, Lord, I see
Thou hast beset; these rocks are Thine;
And, since Thy love encloses me,
  I stand and sing!"
    —Mrs. Elizabeth Alden Scott Stam,
      Martyred Missionary.

SECTION VII. Outlined Sermons for Sunday Mornings and Evenings of the Entire Church Year. With Recognition Also of Special Days and Occasions and Thematic Aids to Public Worship

SUNDAY: JANUARY THIRD

MORNING SERVICE

Theme: The Ships That Never Sailed (New Year).

SUGGESTED SCRIPTURE READING: LUKE 16:1-13. After-petition: May God's Spirit bless this lesson to our needs as we enter the New Year.

SELECTED HYMNS: "Another year is dawning."—F. R. Havergal. "O God, our help in ages past."—I. Watts. "While with ceaseless course the sun."—J. Newton. "Days and moments quickly flying."—Anon. "For thy mercy and thy grace."—H. Downton.

PREPROCESSIONAL CHOIR PRAYER: Fill us, our Heavenly Father, with the true spirit of praise. For the New Year grant a new song in our hearts. As in former days we have worshiped thee, accept our fresh offering of praise. In the name of Christ we ask. Amen.

CALL TO WORSHIP: "Wait on the Lord, be of good courage, and he shall strengthen thine heart. Wait, I say, on the Lord." "They that wait upon the Lord shall renew their strength; they shall mount up with wings as eagles; they shall run and not be weary; they shall walk and not faint."

INVOCATION PRAYER: We come before thee, our Father, this first Sunday of the year in the sacrament of worship. Our souls desire those gifts of thine which are both present and eternal. Truth we desire, which knowing now we know eternally. Beauty we desire, which seeing now we see in deathless splendor. Purity we desire which adoring now we shall adore forever. Joy we desire, deep, quiet, radiant, which shall never die. Love we desire, immortal, infinite, perfect even here and now. Simplicity we desire, after thine own heart most childlike. Courage we desire, thy courage as it dwelt in thy Son our Saviour. Knowledge we desire, knowledge of thy truth, thy love, thyself. Truly it is thyself we desire more than thy gifts. Give us this day thyself. In the name of Christ do we ask. Amen.—Adapted from J. S. H.

Theme: The Ships That Never Sailed (New Year).

TEXT: "Jehoshaphat made ships of Tarshish to go to Ophir for gold: but

72

they went not; for the ships were broken at Ezion-geber." I Kings 22:48.

INTRODUCTORY: Solomon the Magnificent built a navy. He was not content with coasting vessels. His passion for wealth led him to covet the riches of faraway countries. There were the treasures of Tarshish to be gathered and the gold of Ophir brought for his enrichment. No one knows where Tarshish is and it would seem that in Solomon's own day the name had come to stand for any far-distant place.

Long years after Solomon's day there sat upon his throne Jehoshaphat. He, too, longed for the wealth of distant lands. He, too, would build his ships of Tarshish to make the adventurous voyages. He built his ships of Tarshish and moored them at Ezion-geber, the most southerly point of Edom on the Gulf of Akabah. The restless sailors were waiting for the order to cast off and begin the long quest. But the order did not come. Then one night, down the mountain gorge above Ezion-geber swept the mighty resistless hurricane and the proud ships of Jehoshaphat were smashed to pieces by its overwhelming power. They were the ships that never sailed.

"Jehoshaphat made ships of Tarshish to go to Ophir for gold; but they went not for they were broken at Ezion-geber."

We do not know why the sailors did not put to sea from Ezion-geber, but we may suggest three out of many possible reasons.

I. They lacked the will. It may be they were in no hurry to start, even though they had every intention of starting someday. Why start today? Tomorrow the weather may be more propitious. And so another day goes by. It is not difficult to find excuses for delay. This New Year which God has granted to us provides the occasion for new voyaging. What are we to make of the opportunity? It is the time for new resolutions, and it may well be that in the quietness we have made them; but when do we put them into effect?

For ever against our dillydallying there stands the great word of the New Testament, "now." "Now is the axe laid to the root of the tree." "Now is the accepted time, now is the day of salvation." In a world that stands in bitter need of the faithful labors of good men how shall we excuse ourselves if we neglect to do that which God has revealed as our duty?

II. It may be the sailors lacked the courage to set sail. They knew the treachery of the hurricane and the relentless motion of the sea. They could wait for fair weather rather than face the dangerous hazard.

This is surely the mood of many people in our day. We have lived through two great wars and we are just emerging from the horrors of the most terrible war the world has ever known. The call is to build new ships and set sail once more, but have we the courage to venture?

We live in an age which is desperately in need of worthy moral standards. In our own age when all the virtues our fathers esteemed are called in question it is not easy to stand up for moral values at all. Only the man of moral courage will make the voyage. He will need to face criticism, ridicule, cynical amusement, direct opposition, and none of these blows is easy to endure.

III. Why did the sailors not put to sea from Ezion-geber? It may be they lacked faith. The hazards of life are so many, its uncertainties so vast that it must be faced in faith. We must believe in the future, that the voyage is worth the making, that there is treasure to be found. It is often that faith that we lack. The prevailing mood is one of faithlessness. Do we really believe that the time will come when the will of God shall be done on earth as it is in heaven? Do we believe that the kingdoms of this world shall become the kingdom of our God and of his Christ and that he shall reign for ever and ever?

The world is beginning to reject the easy policy of *laissez faire* and to feel the deep conviction that there is need to plan events and to plan them wisely. For the Christian life always offers momentous decisions. Jesus calls us to adventure. He bids us believe in the rich things which the Father has prepared for his children, a blessedness transcending the gold of Ophir and the wealth of Tarshish, and the strong ships of Tarshish are waiting for us to man them. May he give us the will, the courage and the faith to cast off from the Ezion-geber ere it be too late. And if the sea be rough and the wind contrary and our hearts grow faint, may it be ours to see him near us and to hear him call: "Be of good cheer! it is I, be not afraid."—R. H. T.

THEME PRAYER: Ever-living God, by whose mercy we have come to the gateway of another year; grant that we may enter it with humble and grateful hearts; and confirm our resolution, we beseech thee, to walk more closely in thy way and labor more faithfully in they service, according to the teaching and example of thy Son our Lord. Let not the errors and offenses of the past cling to us, but pardon us and set us free, that with a purer purpose and a better hope, we may renew our vows in thy presence and set forth under the guidance of thy Spirit, to travel in that path which shineth more and more unto the perfect day. We ask in the name of Christ. Amen.

OFFERTORY SENTENCE: "Wherefore do ye spend money for that which is not bread? and your labour for that which satisfieth not?"

OFFERTORY PRAYER: Whether we experience wealth or poverty during this year upon which we have entered, our Father, may we gather wealth that is spiritual—treasures of life and character and service as a heavenly portion. Bless the offerings which we bring thee now and us as we bring them. In Christ's name. Amen.

Illustrative Material

SEED THOUGHTS, HOMILETIC AND EXPOSITORY. Ships that Never Sailed: They illustrate resolutions that were never kept.

We have read of a ship departing from one of the New England ports in the early period of the colony. She never reached her destination. She was never heard of afterward. The narrative went on to say that one pleasant summer afternoon, long after, the New England people were standing by the sea when they saw a vessel approach the shore which they knew by its build and rigging to be the very missing ship. It drew nearer and nearer until every line of rigging was visible and even the faces of those on board. Then suddenly the vision faded, the sails dissolved in cloud, the spars were lost in the mist of the sky, the hull disappeared beneath the waters, the specter-barque was no more. So have we made resolutions that dissolve into thin air, like the ships at Ezion-geber that never sailed.

Fading Resolutions: Resolves perish into vacancy, that if executed, might have been noble works.—H. Giles.

Sudden Resolutions: Sudden resolutions, like the sudden rise of the mercury in the barometer, indicate little else than the changeableness of the weather.—Hare.

The Disappointed Shipbuilder: I. The ships of Jehoshaphat brought black no gold from Ophir. This man was foiled in his enterprise. II. And yet the sacred historian thinks it not unworthy to record that Jehoshaphat made ships to go for gold. That was the main incident. "But they went not." That was an untoward accident. And the great thing to be recorded about any of us is just that we made ships to go to Ophir. III. And while Jehoshaphat's sinking ships are settling let them speak to us also of the venture of immortality. That is the last voyage. That is a far-off Ophir indeed, and very precious the gold that awaits us there. —Hubert L. Simpson.

Choice Illustrations on the Theme

RESOLUTIONS THAT NEVER SAILED. Is it not the fact with us that we have our moments of illumination when we see with crystal clarity what we ought to do and we make our resolutions, good strong resolutions like the ships of Tarshish, able to sail in the stern waters of adversity? But how often are they broken ere they can sail from Ezion-geber because we have not the will to send them forth into action. How many of us, on looking back, must see our lives strewn with the wreckage of half-finished things, of works begun but never tried out, of plans conceived but never operated, of opportunities granted but never seized!—Rev. Ralph H. Turner.

RESOLUTIONS MAKE REVOLUTIONS. Joke-smiths make fun of New Year's resolutions; but resolutions create revolutions. Before ever there was a great change in a single life or in a nation there was a purpose in somebody's heart. Revolutions are merely resolutions come to fruit.

All of the noisy celebrations in great cities of the arrival of a new year are of less significance than the unrecorded and unknown resolutions in single spirits.

There is a Christian word for all these lofty self-dedications: it is consecration. The consecration vows of Christians at New Year's Day are heard in heaven, beyond the tumult of all lesser celebrations.—J. W. G. Ward, D.D.

"SHIPS WERE BROKEN AT EZION-GEBER." This statement is more than a mere incident from the naval annals of Judah. It is a universal experience with many of life's ambitions. Who is there who has not set his heart upon something as precious in his eyes as the far-famed gold of Ophir? Who has not built his ships and made his plan for them to go and come again? "But they went not." Is not that just the sum of many a life's tragedy? Where was your Ezion-geber, sir? Is there anything more haunting than the pathos of eyes that grow weary watching for the ships that will never come in? Some there are, the very music of whose life never gets beyond a *nocturne*. Their swift ships of desire have all foundered in perilous seas forlorn. They were on the eve of some momentous discovery when some stubborn element whose presence they

had forgotten or ignored rose up to confound their hopes and shatter their prospects. . . . They made ships to go, ships that should have gone—but they went not."—Hubert L. Simpson.

MEN OF THE SEA. *Man and the Sea* is the apt title of the book by the late Dr. J. Holland Rose, professor of maritime history in the University of Cambridge, in which he seeks to capture for us the romantic spirit of the sailors of many lands. The sea has its enchantment for all who know it. Those of us who were born within sound of its music have a feeling of exile if we are kept long away from it, and even those born in the inland places yearn for its ceaseless song. It is not the sea air which calls us to make holiday on the coast but the sea itself, at once so vast, so full of changes and so relentless. The British people have their great traditions as lovers of the sea. We are never far from wild sea-girt coasts. Our history is often maritime history.—Rev. R. H. Turner.

Quotable New Year Poetry

PRAYER FOR THE NEW YEAR

To grow a little wiser day by day,
To school my mind and body to obey,
To keep my inner life both clean and
    strong,
To free my life from guile, my heart
    from wrong,
To shut the door on hate and scorn
    and pride,
To open up to love the window wide,
To meet with cheerful heart what comes
    to me,
To turn life's discords into harmony,
To share some weary worker's heavy
    load,
To point some straying comrade to the
    road,
To know that what I have is not my
    own,
To feel that I am never quite alone—
This would I pray from day to day,
For then I know my life would flow
In peace until it be God's will I go.

New Year Resolution

Faithfully faithful to every trust;
Honestly honest in every deed;
Righteously righteous, and justly right,
This is the whole of a good man's creed.
—Josephine Pollard.

Beginning the New Year

At the beginning of this year,
Dear Lord, help us to spread the cheer
That comes from living close to Thee;
Help us to keep our spirits free
From everything that might abase,
To give Thee always highest place;
To listen to the still small voice.
Whatever comes, may we rejoice
And trust in Him who knows what's
best;
Give us the strength to meet each test.
At the beginning of this year
Lord, free our hearts from thoughts of
fear.
—Pearl Holloway.

The Road

Heave no sigh for things undone,
For the prize you might have won;
Don't bewail the yester-sun;
All your yesterdays are gone—
Gone!
Are you ready for today?
Roads are stretching far away;
You will stumble, you will stray,
You will have to pay your way—
Pay!
Mate thy staff and guide thy star;
Bush or stone be not thy bar;
How we fight is what we are;
Let your aim be onward far—
Far!
—Philip M. Raskin.

New Year Resolution

I do resolve to seek the worth
Of every hour Time brings to birth,
To keep the faith with every friend
That heaven may see fit to send,
To try to do each duty shown,
And meet each obligation known.
I do resolve to give a thought
To every honest problem brought,
To render as the days go past
Some service that will really last,
To try to live through sun and rain
So the year will not be in vain.
—Clarence E. Flynn.

The Set of the Sails

One ship drives east, and another west
With the selfsame winds that blow;
'Tis the set of the sails
And not the gales,
Which decide the way to go.
Like the winds of the sea are the ways of
fate,
As we voyage along through life;
'Tis the will of the soul
That decides the goal,
And not the calm or the strife.
—Unidentified.

EVENING SERVICE

Theme: Beginning the Year with God (New Year).

Text: "In the beginning God." Gen. 1:1.

Introductory: How to begin? That is the question that faces everyone who would accomplish any task worth his while. How shall we begin? How enter the new year so full of possibilities, so mysterious, so pregnant with destiny for each of us?

I. In the first place, we must begin as the Book itself begins, and as creation began—with God. "In the beginning God." If the coming year is to have any real meaning or purpose, any worth or dignity; if it is to lead us to any goal worth while, to any loftier level of manhood or womanhood, then he who is the source of all life and the inspiration of all noble living—God—must stand with us on the very threshold of the year, and step out with us on its undiscovered highways. You and I are sons of God, created for companionship with the Almighty, and, because of this, to start the new year without him is to get hopelessly off the track. If the new year is to be a year of spiritual growth for you,

you must "in the beginning" and all the way through have God for your Companion, Counselor and Guide.

II. Again, to begin the year with God will mean strength and courage for the tasks and struggles of the twelve months ahead.

On the last day of the year 1868 the historian, W. H. Lecky, wrote in his journal the prayer of the old Breton sailors: "Keep me, my God, for my boat is so small and thy ocean so wide." And it is in the spirit of that prayer that you and I should face this new year. In this new year every one of us will have to confront situations requiring the utmost wisdom and patience and strength. How then can we go forward without the God of all wisdom and strength to help us? In the beginning start out with God, and keep step with him all through the year, and peace and power, gladness and strength will be yours to the end.

III. To begin the year with God also means that there will be abiding spiritual comfort to you in the hour of your deepest need, no matter what trials or tribulations the year may bring to you.

Trials and troubles will surely come. Are you ready to meet them? Remember there is only one way to meet them victoriously. It is to begin this year with God, to take him as your personal friend and companion every step of the way; to listen to his counsel, follow his guidance and to obey his commands all through the days and hours of the next twelve months.

IV. Finally, let us remember that if we begin with God, if we put ourselves under his control, and determine to follow his guidance throughout the year, he will finish what he began. He will see us safely and triumphantly through to the end. He has declared: "I will never leave thee, nor forsake thee."

Take God as your counselor and friend. Make him the companion of your days and hours. Consult him about your plans. Obey his commands. Follow his leading, and sure as the sun rises in the east each morning and the stars shine in the vault of heaven when day is done, he will be with you in every need, stand by you in every difficulty, and give you the victory in every struggle. In the beginning God! And on to the end God!—Rev. Alfred E. Cooke.

Suggestive New Year Texts

"Ye have not passed this way heretofore." Josh. 3:4.

"I will go in the strength of the Lord." Ps. 71:16.

"The Lord shall be thy confidence, and shall keep thy foot from being taken." Prov. 3:26.

"Things not seen as yet." Heb. 11:7.

"They went every one straight forward." Ezek. 10:22.

"He hath sent me . . . to proclaim the acceptable year of the Lord." Isa. 61:1, 2.

"Who knoweth whether thou art come to the kingdom for such a time as this?" Esther 4:14.

"Redeeming the time, because the days are evil." Eph. 5:16.

"The time is fulfilled, and the kingdom of God is at hand." Mark 1:15.

"As for me and my house, we will serve the Lord." Josh. 24:15.

"All the congregation said, Amen, and praised the Lord. And the people did according to this promise." Neh. 5:13.

"I am resolved what to do." Luke 16:4.

MIDWEEK FELLOWSHIP MEETING TOPIC

(Church Night or Suggested Sermon Subject)

Theme: Strength and Power (New Year).

TEXT: "As thy days, so shall thy strength be." Deut. 33:25.

The future in fact and character is wholly involved in the present.

I. The duties, needs, interests and thoughts of the present as they are met and attended to determine the future. "Now is the essential time." "The inward man is renewed day by day." "Give us this day our daily bread." "Take no anxious thought for the morrow." These and many more passages like them indicate our true attitude toward life. Our desire is prone to run ahead of this and live in the future.

II. This is just as unreasonable as living beyond one's means. Strength comes in the day and in the use of the day. A man is not a man born; we are all born as babes. We grow day by day. We walk step by step. We learn experience. Our maturity dawns when we learn how to sing "One step enough for me." This is the law and procession of life. Strength is given, not for the day, but in the day. God makes us strong as the day is employed to that end.

III. Strength is not something given to us to lay in store against the time of need. Strength develops in the struggle. Power to do lies in the doing. It grows as we grow. It is life itself, a present and never a future. Act today, fight today, be true today and you will be strong today. You will be strong tomorrow in proportion as you have been strong today.

IV. At best, we are on the way. Therefore we can have but relative strength, relative knowledge, relative truth. We can never have full knowledge, full power, but day by day. We are not only in transit, but also in progress. Increased strength is the gift of each day as it comes. Back of every strong tomorrow lies a strong today, and back of every strong today a strong yesterday. Strength is not stored but current power—R. B.

BULLETIN BOARD SLOGANS FOR THE MONTH

By Earl Riney

Get your direction before you try for distance.

Difficulties are opportunities.

A train of thought is a good thing if it is going somewhere.

Remember the weekday to keep it holy.

You can't finish the job you never start.

We learn to make decisions by deciding.

A new year—a new purpose, new power, new life.

Christian life has no ending but a lot of beginnings.

The finger of God fashions destiny.

Many who have a fast tongue have a slow mind.

It is more important to be kind than to be clever.

The set or direction of our lives should be Godward.

CHRISTIAN ENDEAVOR SOCIETY TOPIC

Jan. 3. What Is Sin? Rom. 7:13-25; I John 3:4; 5:17a.

SUNDAY SCHOOL LESSON

Jan. 3. God Revealed in Christ. John 1:20; 30-31.

Memory Verse: "These are written that you may believe that Jesus is the Christ, the Son of God, and that believing you may have life in his name." John 20:31 (r.s.v.).

The lessons of this quarter are taken from the Gospel of John. This is the Gospel of Light and Love and Life.

The prologue of the Gospel, chapter 1:1-17, has been called "the profoundest page of the New Testament." Much is implied by calling Jesus the Word. A word is spoken. Jesus is the speech of God. Or a word is written. Jesus is the document of God. In him God reveals "his will, his intention, his decree, his world-plan, his love." He is not only the medium of God's telling; he is also the message that God tells.

SUNDAY: JANUARY TENTH

MORNING SERVICE

Theme: A New Thing (Post New Year).

SUGGESTED SCRIPTURE READING: Isa. 43:8-21. After-petition: May the Lord incline our hearts to keep this law.

SELECTED HYMNS: "Soldiers of Christ arise."—C. Wesley. "Ye servants of the Lord."—P. Doddridge. "Lead on, O King Eternal."—E. W. Shurtleff. "Forward! be our watchword."—H. Alford. "Onward, Christian soldiers."—Sabine Baring-Gould.

CALL TO WORSHIP: "Blessed is the man whom thou choosest, and causeth to approach unto thee, that he may dwell in thy courts."

INVOCATION PRAYER: Eternal God, our heavenly Father, who has fashioned all things after the pattern of thine own will, without whom nothing is strong, nothing is holy; as we worship together this day grant us a vision of that true fellowship into which thou art calling us and all thy people. Help us to kindle the fires of our enthusiasm and hope for the rebuilding of our common life. Help us to develop and to dedicate all our powers of mind, all our deepest insights, and all our acquired skills to the bringing upon the whole earth thy kingdom of love and peace and good will, so that the men and women and children of ours and every nation shall come to know, to love, and to serve thee. This we pray through Christ our Saviour. Amen.

Theme: A New Thing (Post New Year).

TEXT: "Behold, I will do a new thing." Isa. 43:19.

INTRODUCTORY: This "new thing" resembles the opening of a path in the wilderness. God will make a way, a road upon which his people will travel in security and with certainty to their appointed destination. "Behold, I will do a new thing" speaks to our need. It reminds us of God, great and mighty and loving. It challenges us to worship with fidelity and devotion him who is Lord over all. It calls us to bring him our faith, humility and service. And it kindles a new flame of hope in our hearts, telling us to expect great things from God. Thus the prophet pleads with the people to look away from their own plight to God's love and power. "Behold, I will do a new thing."

I. May we not believe, first of all, that God will do a new thing for the nations of the earth? God's plainly declared will for all mankind is lasting peace and true prosperity, the nations learning to live together as one family. Christ taught us to pray, "Thy kingdom come, thy will be done on earth as it is in heaven." He never mocks men. Never would he have taught us that prayer were it not to have an answer.

II. May we not believe also that God will do a new thing for his church in the world? God's spiritual resources are not exhausted. Surely they are not so fully exploited and exhausted that he can no longer guide and help his people to anything new. "Expect great things from God. Attempt great things for God." Have faith in God. He will yet do many new things for his church. He is today swinging open before his church a great door of opportunity. May he make us willing to enter that door in the day of his power!

III. We believe that God will also do a new thing for our own local church and community. Our situation. Our need. Our opportunity. How large is our faith? He says, "According to thy faith be it unto you." Amplify to the local situation.

IV. And further we may most surely believe that God will do a new thing for us individually. This is the new year season. The new year is a new way. It brings a new and fresh opportunity. But we are all conscious of how much we need to have God by his Holy Spirit to work in our lives a miracle of cleansing and transforming grace. We remember our weakness against temptation, our failure to resist sin, our fitfulness in prayer, our ineffectiveness in service. But let us not be unduly disheartened, for God is the same to us that he was to Israel long ago. He says, "Behold, I do a new thing." If we look to him in humility and faith he will do a new thing now in us and for us. "If any man be in Christ, he is a new creature: old things are passed away; behold, all things have become new."—H.

THEME PRAYER: O Thou who inhabitest eternity and from whose hands our days are measured out, may we take them reverently as thy gifts and so spend their irrecoverable hours that, though we be poorer in time, we may be richer in life. Forgive us wasted hours and bless what we have sought to do well. Send us forth in the year before us to do our best to forward thy kingdom in the word. We ask in Christ's name. Amen.

OFFERTORY SENTENCE: "And Jesus sat over against the treasury, and beheld how the people cast money into the treasury."

OFFERTORY PRAYER: We would remember, our Father, that we are not our own, that we are bought with a price; we would therefore glorify thee in our bodies and our spirits, which are thine. We would be true helpers of thy kingdom. It is to this end that we bring thee our offerings this day. Wilt thou graciously receive and bless both the gifts and the givers. We ask in Christ's name. Amen.—H.

Illustrative Material

SEED THOUGHTS, HOMILETIC AND EXPOSITORY. Opening a New Path: I. The promise of a "new thing" is promise of new help and supply even under circumstances most difficult. It is compared with a path in the wilderness and the supply of rivers of waters in the desert. II. It is intended as an encouragement to repentance and renewed consecration to God. III. It is the old message over again that God will give to all who look to him everything that is requisite for spiritual progress and success.—T. S.

New Things: Is there anything whereof it may be said, see, this is new? I suggest that we take up that old challenge. What are some of the ways in which Christ may be said to have broken in upon the monotony of human life with something new? I. He has brought us the possibility of a new likeness to God. II. He has brought us assurance of the possibility of forgiveness of sins. III. He has brought us a new life.—W. R. H.

Choice Illustrations on the Theme

A NEW THING FOR THE WORLD. More than one hundred years ago two men sat by their campfire under the eastern stars by the headwaters of the Euphrates. All their camping kit and baggage was carried by a single pack animal. For months they had been journeying on foot and on horseback through the unknown valleys and plateaus of Asia Minor, for a new world was spread before them. These were the scouts of civilization, the explorers who first pierced into the unknown life of the Near East.

For more than a year their journey took them through Armenia, Kurdestan and Persia, and the record of their journeyings, often written in secret by the light of their campfire, relates the standard authority on the country, inhabitants and their home life for the heart of the Turkish Empire.

Smith and Dwight were the pioneer missionaries in that great land that now has such a prominent part in the affairs of the world.—*World Outlook.*

A NEW THING IN THE SOUL. One of the best definitions of religion we have heard is that given by a statesman to university students some years ago. Speaking at Oxford, the late Ramsay Macdonald said: "The chief function of religion is to keep alive a springtime freshness in the soul."—Archer Wallace.

A NEW THING FOR A MAN. For the true Christian "Behold all things are become new." It is a visible change. "Behold!" There is a change without as the expression and effect of a change within. It is an admirable change. The "Behold!" is to attract attention, admiration. It is a thorough thing. All things are become new." It is therefore a permanent thing, a lasting thing. Because a new creature and in Christ the Christian has a new impulse, a new social standard, a new spiritual history.

A NEW THING IN SOCIETY. The situation in our day is not radically different from the conditions prevailing in Jesus' day. Social, economic, moral and spiritual chaos existed then as it exists today around the world. Into that ancient situation a Saviour came, and we do well if we would solve our problems to inquire as to his methods of dealing with it. All the opportunists of his day said "Gather the discontented groups and break through to freedom." "Dazzle them with miracles." "Make terms with the world," said the Arch Politician; "all these things will I give thee, if thou wilt fall down and worship me."

The answer of Jesus is the answer for us today. "Not by might, nor by power, but my Spirit, saith the Lord." The world could be saved only as men became inwardly renewed.—Adapted from Allyn K. Foster.

A NEW THING FOR THE CHURCH. A revival of religion is a miracle of Divine grace. It cannot be secured by any kind of machinery, and yet its coming to a church is not so mysterious and so apart from human agency and the use of means as some good people think. God is always ready to pour out his Spirit. Indeed, the Spirit is poured out. The Spirit is around us like the light and will enter our hearts as soon as we open them. The Spirit is pressing against the stubborn wills of impenitent men and women, like water against the head gate of a mill. He will come in and start all the wheels of moral action as soon as the gate is open.

Every local church can have a revival if it plans for it, organizes its forces, believes in a saving Christ, presents a vital gospel and goes out after the lost and brings them in. God is ready to do a new thing for each church.

EVENING SERVICE

Theme: Redemption.

TEXT: "In whom we have redemption through his blood, the forgiveness of sins, according to the riches of his grace." Eph. 1:7.

Creation was glorious, but redemption is the most glorious work of God. Redemption is a great word. It is a great fact. It is a supreme reality, a supreme concern, a supreme attainment. The mind of Paul delighted to dwell upon this theme.

I. The necessity of redemption. Sin makes the necessity. Men are represented as sin's captives, needing the interposition of a Redeemer. 1. Captive to sin. "Whosoever committeth sin is the servant of sin," John 8:34. 2. Captive to Satan. 3. Captive to law. "Shut up in prison," Gal. 3:22. It is a state of wretchedness and misery.

II. The Agent of redemption. "In whom," etc. Jesus is the Redeemer. "Ransom for many," Matt. 20:28. 1. He became incarnate, John 1:14. 2. He possessed the highest dignity and glory, John 1:1-5. 3. He was perfectly holy. "Knew no sin." "Offered without spot to God."

III. The means of redemption. "Through his blood." He took the sinner's place, Isa. 53:6. 1. He paid the penalty due to the transgressor. 2. He destroyed the power of men's enslavers.

IV. The blessed fruits of redemption. "Even the forgiveness of sins," etc. The greatest possible blessing we can have in this world. The fruitful source of all true blessedness in time and in eternity.

V. The source of this redemption.

"According to the riches of his grace."
1. Therefore not of works, nor merit.
2. But of Divine grace, the unmerited love of God, II Tim. 1:9; Gal. 2:2.
3. The Gifts of God are munificent, "according to the riches," etc. Kingly gifts by the King! Infinite ability. Infinite love. Infinite gift, redemption.

Suggestive Evangelistic Texts and Themes.

A Friendless Soul: "Sir, I have no man, when the water is troubled, to put me into the pool." John 5:7. (A helpless man near a remedy. How distressingly sad!)

God's Quiet Work: "Whose heart the Lord opened." Acts 16:14.

Acquaintance with God: "Acquaint now thyself with him, and be at peace: thereby good shall come unto thee." Job 22:21.

A Good Resolution: "I will arise and go to my father." Luke 15:18.

The Heart Asked For: "My son, give me thine heart." Prov. 23:26.

The Joy of Religion: "Rejoice evermore." I Thess. 5:16.

MIDWEEK FELLOWSHIP MEETING TOPIC

(Church Night or Suggestive Sermon Subject)

Theme: The Transient and the Eternal.

TEXT: "The heavens are the work of thy hands. They shall perish, but thou shalt endure. . . . Thou art the same, and thy years shall have no end." Ps. 102:25-27.

On the Hudson some miles above New York there is a great house in the dining room of which are carved in stone above the fireplace the figures of a group of sun worshipers..

I. Christians are grateful for the sun and its light and heat, but they do not worship the sun. They worship him who made the sun. This is the sentiment of the Psalmist, who has all of a poet's love for nature, but who knows that nature is not changeless, but that the God of nature is. So we pray, "O thou that changest not."

II. The sun changes. Science makes note of its varying phases. God is the same, yesterday, today and forever. Scripture affirms his immutability and human experience attests the Psalmist's words, "Thou art the same." History is a graveyard of nations. The rise and fall of empires, the growth and decline of nations, the swift panorama of world politics, and the certainty that nothing material abides give us a deep sense of insecurity.

A little child, riding in a carriage, fording a stream, grew dizzy and cried out to his father who was driving, "The carriage is floating away." His father simply said, "Don't look at the water—look at the shore." When the child lifted his eyes from the swift flowing water to something permanent, his dizziness passed.

III. It is good that amidst the ceaseless flux of things we may fix our mind on God. It steadies us, gives us the calmness and the strength to pursue our journey knowing that though all things else may perish, God endures. His word endureth forever. Christ is the King Immortal.—C. C. A.

CHRISTIAN ENDEAVOR SOCIETY TOPIC

Jan. 10. Sins of the mind. Tit. 1:15, 16; Phil. 4:4-8.

SUNDAY SCHOOL LESSON

Jan. 10.　Jesus Uses His Authority. John 2:13-25.

MEMORY VERSE: "God is spirit, and those who worship him must worship in spirit and truth." John 4:24 (R.S.V.).

The dark picture of the profaned temple is placed over against the bright, festal scene described in the former part of the chapter. This incident reveals the power of Jesus' personality. It gives us a picture of the indignant Christ.

We note his authority, his sense of mission, his enthusiasm. Jesus "spake of the temple of his body." It is the privilege of every man to be joyously aware of the same sublime possession. Enthusiasm for the sanctity of the human temple ought to characterize every Christian.

SUNDAY: JANUARY SEVENTEENTH

MORNING SERVICE

Theme: A Whole-time Religion.

SUGGESTED SCRIPTURE READING: Mark 12:28-34; James 1:19-27. After-petition: May God bless to our understanding this message from his Word.

SELECTED HYMNS: "Ye servants of the Lord."—P. Doddridge. "Jesus calls us o'er the tumult."—C. F. Alexander. "Who is on the Lord's side?"—F. R. Havergal. "O happy band of pilgrims." —J. M. Neale. "Dear Lord and Master Mine."—T. H. Gill.

PREPROCESSIONAL CHOIR PRAYER: O God, our heavenly Father, who hast called us to the sacred ministry of praise in the service of thy church, make us ready now to worship thee in spirit and in truth. Teach us to love the place where thine honor dwelleth, and make all that we say and do this morning acceptable unto thee and edifying to the people. Through Jesus Christ our Lord. Amen.

CALL TO WORSHIP: Who shall ascend into the hill of the Lord? or who shall stand in his holy place? He that hath clean hands, and a pure heart; who hath not lifted up his soul unto vanity, nor sworn deceitfully. He shall receive the blessing from the Lord, and righteousness from the God of his salvation.

INVOCATION PRAYER (Note: The Invocation can be one of the most significant elements in a service of worship. The very name of the prayer, Invocation, reveals the nature of the thing attempted. It is the simple, humble, quiet invitation to God to be present. It is, or should be, the outgoings of the hearts and souls of the worshipers, not alone of the preacher, to God in active seeking. Surely a very deep thing. It can be one of the most important elements in the church's service of worship. Let us try to make it so.) : O God, infinite and eternal, Creator of the universe, fearful in might and glorious in holiness, we bow in awe and reverence before thee, acknowledging our utter dependence.

O God in Christ, we come to thee. We come in the boldness inspired by thine own grace and impelled by our dire needs. Have mercy upon us; forgive our sins; regenerate our lives; reconstruct our society in accordance with truth and justice and love.

Through thy Holy Spirit clarify our minds, strengthen our wills and fill our hearts with love so that we may do justly, love mercy, and walk humbly with thee. Grant to men everywhere wisdom, and courage for the facing of the conditions of this hour in Christian faith and hope, that out of our present confusion there may come a new order of life among men and nations which will conform more nearly to the mind of Christ.

Bless us each and all together as we worship in thy house this day, and grant help for the whole of the week upon which we have entered. We ask all in Christ's name. Amen.—Acknowledgment to J. A. S.

Theme: A Whole-time Religion.

TEXT: "With part thereof . . . he roasteth roast, and is satisfied: yea he warmeth himself . . . and the residue thereof he maketh a god." Isa. 44:16, 17.

INTRODUCTORY: We cannot read a passage like this and say there is no humor in the Bible. It might well laugh idolatry out of existence. It pictures a primitive savage at work. He cuts down a tree. Part of it he uses to make a fire to warm himself. Part of it he uses to roast his food. Then, being warmed and fed, he sees the remnant and betakes himself to making out of it the image of a god. To this he bows down saying, "Deliver me; for thou art my god."

I. Translate this into modern terms, and we have a living picture of the place which religion holds in the life of many people. 1. We parcel out our time, so much for business, so much for pleasure, so much for worship and prayer. That is a perfectly right thing to do. Life is not properly balanced if any of its big interests are left out. 2. We apportion our money in the same way. If we are careful in its management, we use so much for food, so much for pleasure, so much for religion and philanthropy. 3. If we are wise, also, we apportion our thinking. The mind should not always be traveling in one groove. We have to think of business most of the time, but we should find time for reading. 4. We should find time, too, to think of God and the meaning of life. But how easily the part we give to religion begins to shrink. It often depends on how much time is left over when pleasure or business have had their share. "The residue thereof he maketh a god." After we have warmed and fed ourselves, the rest we devote to God. After we have spent the whole day in other interests, till mind and strength are gone, there may be five odd minutes for prayer. After a busy week, Sunday worship will have to take its chance of whether or not we feel inclined for it. Many people decide the question of Sunday worship by the strength they have over after the hectic pleasure of the evening before. "The residue thereof he maketh a god." 5. It is the same with giving. How much of our giving is calculated and propor-

tioned? How often is it dependent on what we have left over, when the other things have had their full share? It is the same with thinking.

II. This opens up a very difficult question for some of us. The struggle of life is hard. It is not easy to satisfy the needs of the body. Food and shelter are grim necessities and the most of life is taken up with getting these.

But this way of thinking of religion as a special department of life is all wrong. There was one interesting thing about this savage. Religion was one of his big needs, as essential as food and shelter. Religion is not merely one of the needs of life. It is an attitude to God that we must take all through our life. This man should have practiced his religion in the way he cut his tree and made his fire. Not on one day only or at one special time of the day, but every day and all the time. Religion is a whole-time business or it is nothing. It is a continuous way of life, a constant fellowship with God. It comes to shape the spirit of all the work and struggle and enjoyment of life. It is not an addition to the things we do, but a way of doing everything. It is not setting apart a bit of time for God. It means the whole of life tuned to the spirit of devotion.

There is nothing that is exempt from the religious spirit. Nothing is to be kept out of our fellowship with God. The work of the shop or the office or the house must be lifted into the service of God. His purpose must guide and fashion all our ambitions. "That woman sings to God," said a friend to me once, as we listened to a fine singer.

III. That was part of the service Christ did for religion. He took it out into the open. He set it working in the home. He brought it into all his relationships with people. The whole of life is the field for religion.

But this does not mean that no special time need be set apart for definite communion with God. This truth can be made plain by a simple illustration. If a violin is to produce true music it must be constantly retuned. Worship and prayer are the means of retuning our minds and spirits to the will of God. To be content with worship without seeking to live out our faith is like tuning a violin without attempting to play a tune. But to try to play the violin without retuning it means that the strings become limp and useless. The same kind of thing happens with our souls when worship is left out and no time is set apart for making touch with God. The strings of faith and devotion will produce no music of Christian living. The man who knows what a glorious thing real religion is will want to renew from day to day his touch with God. He will want time to shake off the grip of the world with its fear and its seduction. He will seek a special time to be alone with God that he may find the power to give it all to him.—J. R.

THEME PRAYER: O Lord, our heavenly Father, we offer and present unto thee ourselves, our souls and bodies, to be a reasonable, holy and living sacrifice unto thee. Take us as we are, and make us more fit for thy service. Use us for thyself and for the furtherance of thy church. We are not our own, but thine, bought with a price. Therefore, claim us as thy right, keep us as thy charge, use us as thou wilt and when thou wilt, to the glory of thy holy name and the good of our fellow men. Through Jesus Christ our Lord. Amen.

OFFERTORY SENTENCE: "Every man according as he purposeth in his heart, so let him give; not grudgingly, or of necessity: for God loveth a cheerful giver."

OFFERTORY PRAYER: Touch our hearts, O Lord, with a spirit of compassion. Open our eyes to human need and grant us that grace which shares another's suffering and pain. Bless our offering today unto the good of our fellow men. Use it, Lord, unto the redemption of the world from sin and suffering. In Jesus' name. Amen.—M.

Illustrative Material

SEED THOUGHTS, HOMILETIC AND EXPOSITORY. Residual Religion: Is it untrue to say that there are many men who live after this fashion, that when they have supplied their own wants, when their body has been amply fed, when the conditions of their life have been cared for so that they are well provided with the warming comforts of life, then, out of the residue of their time, out of the residue of their money, out of the residue of their thought, they will perchance consecrate something to God?—W. B. C.

The Idolater's Folly: I. Neither the idol nor its god knows anything. II. Neither the idol nor its god can do aught. III. Neither the idol nor its god is aught. But God knows all, is almighty, and is the Perfect Personality, loving, wise, true, and his worship exalts and saves the soul.—W. S. A.

The Idolater's Folly: With a dash of pungent satire Isaiah shows what a silly man this is. We have seen here the whole process of god-manufacture. —J. T. D.

Choice Illustrations on the Theme

TAKE TIME FOR RELIGION. There is a grove of trees outside Stratford-on-Avon that I have driven past many a night. It was an ordinary grove of trees as I rushed by. One evening my host asked if I would like to hear the nightingales sing. He drove me to the familiar grove of trees, and, stopping the car, said, "Now we will sit quietly and listen." And, oh, what music! I had rushed by it other nights. You see, we refuse to believe we can really talk with God only when we refuse to stop and listen.— J. Burford Parry.

THE NEW IDOLATRY. To educated persons the more primitive kinds of idolatry have ceased to be attractive. They find it easy to resist the temptation to believe that particular natural objects are gods, or that certain symbols and images are the very forms of divine entities and as such must be worshiped and propitiated. Like drinking and prostitution, the primitive forms of idolatry are tolerated, but not approved. Their place in the accredited hierarchy of values is among the lowest.

How different is the case with the developed and more modern forms of idolatry! These have achieved not merely survival, but the highest degree of respectability. They are recommended by men of science as an up-to-date substitute for genuine religion and by many professional religious teachers are equated with the worship of God. —Aldous Huxley.

THE LOST PENDULUM. "Many people," says James Reid, of England, "are like a clock which has lost its pendulum. You wind it up, and off it goes at a furious pace of whirring wheels which is soon finished and played out. But attach the pendulum, and the result is a movement which is peace—stable, restful, calm, purposeful. What has happened? The law of gravitation has come into play—the law which rules the resistless tides of ocean, with its feverish heart, has been taken up into a mighty movement, and there is peace. That is what our lives need. We are born to take our part in a movement which is far larger than ourselves. While our lives are moving in the orbit of selfishness there is sure to be confusion."

It is a suggestive thought and hits off the essential lack of numbers of lives—restless, feverish, yet without impressiveness, purpose or endurance. Their prime need is religion. For religion is to the life what the pendulum is to the clock.—F. C. H.

HOW MUCH DOES YOUR RELIGION MEAN? An American who had wrecked his mind and body by the incessant and uncontrolled scramble for money went to see a great nerve specialist. He was considerably surprised when he was asked this question: "How much does your religion mean to you?"—so surprised, in fact, that he was unable to reply. The famous doctor then explained that there was one class of people he scarcely ever saw in his consulting room—the people who believe and practice the Christian religion.—F. A. Atkins.

EVENING SERVICE

Theme: Who Is Satan?

TEXT: "Now there was a day when the sons of God came to present themselves before the Lord, and Satan came also among them." Job 1:6.

INTRODUCTORY: Whether drama or poetry, or both, the practical character of the Book of Job is manifest. Some look upon it as true history. Whether poetry, drama or history, each one of us knows by experience that the thing talked about in the book is real. Where is the boaster who has never known temptation? Poetry and drama suggest. Prose states. But in either case we have here a meaningful representation of the contrast of evil and good in the realm of the eternal.

I. Whether in poetic description or highly sublime personification, who is Satan? In this passage we have the Scriptural idea of the Evil One. He has, for example, personal existence. Acting as a person he "goes to and fro in the earth." The personality of his existence is declared in Scripture and confirmed by human history. He is called by different names, Devil, Old Serpent, Dragon, Prince of the Power of the Air, Beelzebub, etc.

II. He is an intruder into the sacred. Wherever the sons of the Almighty assemble he is among them to bias their minds and to pollute their feelings.

III. He is a vagrant in the universe. His "going to and fro" implies two things: first, homelessness, and second, zealousness.

IV. He is a slanderer of the good. He slanders man to God, and he slanders God to man. He is Diabolus, breaking the harmony of God's moral universe by slander.

V. He is a compasser, and is so entitled, which means a tempter. The "earth" signifies all the people of the earth. It is as if he had said, "I come from going to and fro in the earth tempting, compassing all the people of the earth." He compasseth all men. By his wicked arts he sometimes compasseth even good men.

VI. There is a limitation upon him. He can act only by permission. While evil and Satan exist they are conditioned by the sovereignty of God. Satan is neither omnipresent nor omnipotent.

He is conditioned by the Almighty, acts only by permission of God or when used by him as an instrument.

There is a great tendency among men to forget the real nature of Satan.

We should be warned against his adroitness. In striving to defeat men he sometimes compasses them with business and cares and quarrels and even promised pleasures. He uses any method that seems to him most promising of success.—H.

Suggestive Texts and Themes

Attending to Our Attitudes: "He looked for a city which hath foundations, whose builder and maker is God." Heb. 11:10.

Building for Permanence: "If any man's work shall abide which he built thereon, he shall receive a reward," etc. I Cor. 3:10-15 (A.S.V.).

The Impossibility that Everybody Tries: "No man can serve two masters." Matt. 6:24.

Wanted—the Foundation Stone (Missions): "For other foundation can no man lay than that which is laid, which is Jesus Christ." I. Cor. 3:11 (A.S.V.).

Living on the Level of the Purposes of God: "Fear not, little flock; for it is your Father's good pleasure to give you the kingdom." Luke 12:32.

MIDWEEK FELLOWSHIP MEETING TOPIC

(Church Night or Suggested Sermon Subject)

Theme: Sympathy and Service.

TEXT: "And I sat where they sat." Ezek. 3:15.

Ezekiel was one of those Jews who lived in the humiliating conditions of captivity. At first he was withdrawn from his fellow captives in a kind of spiritual isolation; but God does not make prophets that way, so Ezekiel was brought into close contact with his people. He writes: "I sat where they sat." We cannot help people if we stand aloof. One of the best manifesta-

tions of the Christian life is seen in brotherly sympathy and service.

I. "I sat where they sat" would cure all pride in Christians.

II. It would settle denominational jealousies.

III. It would cure all prejudice in race relations.

IV. It would remedy all unfair business competition.

V. It would heal and cement the relations between capital and labor and between labor and capital.

There is food for thought in the following anonymous rhyme:

I used to think him heathen,
    Just because—well, don't you see,
He didn't speak God's English,
    And he didn't look like me.
He had a burnt complexion,
    Which is heathen goodness knows;
He ate a heathen's rations,
    And he wore a heathen's clothes.
But there's a s'prising skinful
    In that bloke from far away;
He fights like any Christian,
    And I've heard the beggar pray;
He's kind to little kiddies,
    And there's written in his eyes
The willingness to render
    All a Christian sacrifice.
Yes, you'd know him for a heathen
    If you judged him by his hide;
But, bless you, he's my brother,
    For He's just like me—inside!"

CHRISTIAN ENDEAVOR SOCIETY TOPIC

Jan. 17. What Is the Gospel? I Cor. 15:1-10.

SUNDAY SCHOOL LESSON

Jan. 17. The New Birth. John 3:1-16.

MEMORY VERSE: "God so loved the world, that he gave his only begotten Son, that whosoever believeth in him should not perish, but have everlasting life." John 3:16.

What is the new birth like? For some it is the simple experience of changing one's mind. Sometimes it is an experience of re-evaluation. W. L. Watkinson says that it is often "the expulsion of the monstrous." In Galatians there is a "dismal catalogue" of the monsters that live in human lives —fornication, uncleanness. The new birth is also like magnetization; "if any man be in Christ he is a new creature"; new fire, power, attractiveness—magnetism is there. Again the new birth is like illumination. The new birth may be like growth, like the germination of a seed. Like liberation, a man feels that the shackles are off; there is liberation unto happiness, goodness, love. This miracle in a man's life is like cleansing. Or it is like integration.

Such is the new birth. It is not culture; it is not reformation; it is not amelioration: it is re-creation by the Spirit of God.

SUNDAY: JANUARY TWENTY-FOURTH

MORNING SERVICE

Theme: Preconceptions and Misconceptions.

SUGGESTED SCRIPTURE READING: II Kings 5:1-27. After-petition: May God reveal to our minds and hearts the great truths contained in this portion of his Word.

SELECTED HYMNS: "My Jesus, as thou wilt."—B. Schmolek. "Father, whate'er of earthly bliss."—A. Steele. "Thy way, not mine, O Lord."—H. Bonar. "Father, I know that all my life."—A. L. Waring. "I do not ask, O Lord."—A. A. Procter.

PREPROCESSIONAL CHOIR PRAYER: O Lord, whose favor is life, and in whose presence is fullness of joy, we give thee thanks for these thy servants who have dedicated their special talent of song to thee and to the leading of thy people in worship. May all thy people through the ministry of music see visions of a nobler life, find the doors of their spirits unlocked, and be moved in their hearts to devout worship this morning. We ask in the name of Christ. Amen.

CALL TO WORSHIP: "Thus saith the high and lofty One that inhabiteth eternity, whose name is Holy; I dwell in the high and holy place, with him also that is of a contrite and humble spirit, to revive the spirit of the humble, and to revive the heart of the contrite one."

"Draw nigh to God, and he will draw nigh to you."

INVOCATION PRAYER: O Lord, our God, we desire to feel thee near us in spirit and in body at this time. We know that in thee we live and move and have our being, but we are cast down and easily disquieted and we wander in many a sad wilderness where we lose the conscious experience of thy presence. Yet the deepest yearning for our hearts is unto thee; enter thou into them and fit them for thyself, making them pure with Christ's purity, loving and lovable with his love. We thank thee for this day, for all churches and all worshiping companies. Reveal to us anew how much we receive when we enter through a church door, how much we miss in our sore need if we do not enter, and help us to love and serve our own churches that they may be high in spirit though their spires are low, and blessed in fellowships though their numbers be few. In the Name of Christ we ask. Amen.

Theme: Preconceptions and Misconceptions.

TEXT: "Behold, I thought." II Kings 5:11.

INTRODUCTORY: Recite the story. Naaman was angry—terribly angry. It was humiliating in the extreme. "Behold," he said. "I thought." Yes, indeed, and that was where he made the mistake. He wanted the cure, but he wanted it on his own lines. He had his own preconceptions of a cleansing, but, fortunately or unfortunately, they were misconceptions. And not until he became a subject of abject obedience to the prescribed conditions of a cure did his flesh become as the "flesh of a little child."

There is something very human in that story. Many of us are willful like that. We sadly stand in need of some great blessing, but for all that we want it so badly we want it only along our own lines. The trouble is so often with our preconceptions that they are misconceptions.

I. The truth can have relevance to our prayers and our proposals before God. How often have we come to God with our minds made up as to how God should answer our prayers. And how often he has taken his own way and sent us home again, saddened and disappointed. We have said: "Behold, I thought." He would answer my prayer as I asked; that he would certainly grant my request along the lines of my own suggestion, only to find out what misconceptions our preconceptions have been.

What we do well to remember is that we are only humble suppliants before God after all. We always need to bend our wills to his, and be prepared to sink our own preconceptions, if need be, in favor of his wiser orderings.

II. The same truth can have relevance also with regard to life's pathway and to life's plans.

How often, in setting out upon life, we have planned things for ourselves, determined our own way, and having done so, submitted our plans to God, only to find that he has cross-purposed them that he may lead us in another way altogether. Then in a somewhat resentful spirit we have said, "Behold, I thought he would surely grant my requests and favor my desires," only to find that our preconceptions were misconceptions after all.

And why? It is not always possible to tell. We can only surmise; better still, we can only trust. Maybe our way was not the most suitable for us; maybe he had better plans for us.

III. Finally, our preconceptions can be misconceptions with regard to God's appointed way of cleansing and salvation. We can harbor a spirit of prejudice just there. We can have our own ideas as to how we would like to be cleansed, which may not necessarily fit in with God's ideas. "Dip in Jordan," says God; but we may say, "Jordan, that miserable stream—why not Abana and Pharpar those lovely aristocratic waters of Damascus?" But no! it is not Abana or Pharpar, it is Jordan, much as we may dislike it. So we have to put our prejudice on one side.

Cannot he but wave the hand and by some miraculous means rid us of our guilt without our plunging into Jordan? So we argue only to find how silent God can be and how wrong our preconceptions.

But how does this story finish? It finishes by Naaman putting his feelings on one side, and, stepping into Jordan, losing his leprosy, so that his flesh becomes as the flesh of a little child.

So it is that when we, like Naaman, put our mistaken preconceptions on one side and accept God's way, we find that we are treading the way of truest blessing.—J. R. T.

THEME PRAYER: Preserve us, our Father, from the folly of pride and preconceptions. Grant unto us such a sure sense of how much we need compared with what we have of wisdom, grace and goodness that our willingness to be taught may be the opportunity for thy truth; our longing to be good the door through which thy transforming spirit may reach and change us. Amen.

OFFERTORY SENTENCE: "Now ye have consecrated yourselves unto the Lord, come near and bring sacrifices and thank offerings into the house of the Lord."

OFFERTORY PRAYER: We love, O God, because thou didst first love us. Having received, we give. Having benefited, we desire to become benefactors. Having been shown mercy, we would be merciful. This offering is prompted by our thanksgiving for thy exceeding goodness shown unto us through Jesus Christ. Grant thy blessing upon it, we pray. Amen.—M. K. W. H.

Illustrative Material

SEED THOUGHTS, HOMILETIC AND EXPOSITORY. Behold I thought: The danger of misconceptions. Naaman has heard of a man who could cure his leprosy. So he thought out how it would be accomplished. He made a plan in his own mind. I. How could we expect to find out the way of salvation by our own thoughts? II. Should the plan of salvation be arranged according to our will and judgment? III. By what rule are we able to preconceive that plan?—C. H. S.

Dangers of Preconceptions: I. It is common to have them. We picture the face of a person we expect to meet, or the scenery of a country. II. Regarding conversion, we preconceive the strength of conviction of sin. Wait for a certain kind and intensity. III. It is the same regarding religious experience. We count on a certain intensity of enjoyment. IV. Why should we not be influenced by preconceptions? 1. We are likely to be unhappy if we run short of our expectations. 2. God works along the line of individuality and temperament. 3. Our conceptions have nothing to do with our salvation.—J. L. E.

Choice Illustrations on the Theme

GOD'S WILL BEST. Ann Brontë's experience, as denoted in her lovely hymn, is a case in point as to the need of bending our wills to God's will. What fond hopes she cherished of life. What preconveived ideas she had of what she would like life to be, only to find that they issued in the saddest denial. "I hoped," she sang,

That with the brave and strong
My portioned task might lie;
To toil amid the busy throng

With purpose pure and high;
But God has fixed another part,
And He has fixed it well,
I said so with my breaking heart,
When first this trouble fell.

It is always best to bring one's thoughts along the lines of God's thoughts; to lay aside our preconceived ideas if they are misconceived, in favor of the higher wisdom of God.—A. Russell Tomlin.

FIND GOD'S PLAN. Many years ago you may have set your heart on obtaining a definite position in life, winning a certain success, and now, as the years have rolled by, you find yourself a long distance from the point you expected to reach and you are "bewildered, disheartened, oppressed by a deepening sense of failure." May I suggest to you that the remedy will lie in revising your standards of success, in trying to discover what is God's plan for your life rather than your plan? It may be that you are filling now exactly the place that God ever intended you to occupy and that boundless opportunities of service are awaiting you if you can but realize that "the place whereon you stand is holy ground."—John Sutherland Bonnell, D.D.

FOOLISH PRECONCEPTIONS. Elder Yi, one Sabbath morning, said to his class, "When we built the first bell tower in Chung Ju churchyard, we had to place the rope inside a long box so the boys would not ring the bell. Thus you could not see how the bell was rung. So a neighbor watched it ringing and thought, "How strange to see a bell ring of itself!" Do you think he was foolish? Let me tell you that he was not a bit more foolish than the people who think that this wonderful world we live in, along with the more marvelous one above us, were made and move of themselves.—Missionary in Korea.

PRECONCEIVED ANSWER TO PRAYER. Being true to me, God in his greater wisdom will not grant all my petitions. I remember vividly a childhood visit to a zoo when I pleaded with my parents to let me have a bear cub to take home. Never having seen anything so appealing as those little fuzzy cinnamon bears, I thought my father quite lacking in sympathy when he refused my request. He knew, as I did not, that bears grow up—even innocent little bears—to be dangerous pets. So it is with our prayers to our heavenly Father. There are some things he must deny us for our own happiness. He will not, I may be sure, grant me something that glitters now but will pauperize me later, as did Midas' gold in the fairy tale.— Clergyman's Testimony.

EVENING SERVICE

Theme: Under Repairs.

TEXT: "Thou shalt be called, The repairer of the breach." Isa. 58:12.

INTRODUCTORY: In the naval department of every government there is kept a correct list of ships. Some are for home service, others are on foreign stations, a portion of the fleet is "laid up in ordinary," and some are under repairs. And we have sometimes thought that there may be tabulated for the information of the younger sons of light a correct list of worlds, with their names, position, history and mission. And in the absence of positive evidence to the contrary we may reverently assume that our world occupies a lonely line, that it stands out in awful solitude, the only one which demands and receives the solicitude, study and rapturous devotion of all the ministering spirits who are sent forth "to minister to the heirs of salvation." And as they bend over us, and behold the reflection of so Divine a love, perhaps there is no sentiment more definite, more unique, more welcome to their hearts than that we are "under repairs."

I. First we are deeply aware that damage has been done. 1. Damage to the Divine image in man. How battered, disfigured, how changed men are! 2. Damage to the relationships of man. His relationship to God how altered; to his brother how alienated! The first-

born was a murderer; the second-born his bruised and bloody victim.

II. But it is also true that damaged man is under repairs. These repairs go on by the authority and under the superintendence of God. 1. The method is his. "There is none other name under heaven given among men, whereby we must be saved." 2. The materials are his. The life cries, the heart throbs, the death pangs of the Redeemer, are they not his? 3. The ministries are his. The angelic, "Are they not all ministering spirits?" The human, called, qualified, placed in their lot, their steps ordered who by the mighty impulses of their mission "beseech in Christ's stead to be reconciled to God." 4. The memorial is his. A living, perfect, beatific monument of unmeasured, unrivaled, unending love. "Unto him that loved us," etc.

III. It is a further and solemn fact that these repairs must be accomplished in time. No repairs are done either in heaven or in hell. "He that is unjust let him be unjust still," etc. Time is defined by the Son of God as "space to repent" (Rev. 2:21).

How much time has been absolutely wasted! How little really improved! The remaining portion is little enough for the work!—Rev. H. T. Miller.

Suggestive Texts and Themes

All Things are Ready: "Behold, I have made ready my dinner; my oxen and my fatlings are killed, and all things are ready: come to the marriage feast." Matt. 22:4 (A.S.V.).

Today: "Son, go work today in the vineyard." Matt. 21:28 (A.S.V.).

The Principle of Sacrifice: "I lay down my life, that I might take it again." John 10:17.

The Riches of Reality: "If therefore ye have not been faithful in the unrighteous mammon, who will commit to your trust the true riches?" Luke 16:11.

The Secret of Getting: "But this I say, He that soweth bountifully shall reap also bountifully." II Cor. 9:6.

MIDWEEK FELLOWSHIP
MEETING TOPIC

(Church Night or Suggested Sermon
Subject)

Theme: Following Jesus.

TEXT: "And he left all . . . and followed him." Luke 5:28.

Toward the close of his life Phillips Brooks was talking about his sermons and said to a group of his friends, "I have preached a great many sermons in my life, but as I review them, they may all be included in a single one. I have had but one theme, and one plea." It was sublimely true of that princely preacher. The enrichment of life by the acceptance of Jesus Christ as the absolute revelation of the Infinite was Phillips Brooks' theme in youth and maturity, and he never grew old. Nor did his theme grow old or tiresome.

I. It is capable of infinite variations. The primary colors are few, but think what beauty flashes from them. The musical notes are few, but think how love and life with all their emotions are expressed by those few notes.

II. Jesus had but one theme. All other themes led up to it. God as the Father, life lifted upon high levels, sin conquered in the human heart, peace flowing like a river, joy rising to ecstasy, great hope for the future—it is all one theme, and it was Jesus' theme at Matthew's feast. It is my theme as I remind you of this occurrence long ago. It might have occurred but yesterday.

III. Human life is the same. Burdens are still heavy. Phantom lights still beckon us which, if we follow, lead us into deep morasses or over perilous precipices. Selfishness is as selfish now

as then. And God is near. We have as much to leave as Levi had. And we have as much to gain by leaving it—and as much to lose if we hear the voice that says, "Follow me," and fail to follow Him.—C. C. A.

CHRISTIAN ENDEAVOR
SOCIETY TOPIC

Jan. 24. What does the Surrendered Life Mean? Gal. 2:20; Rom. 12:1; II Tim. 2:19-26.

SUNDAY SCHOOL LESSON

Jan. 24. Crossing Man-made Barriers. John 4:1-42.

MEMORY VERSE: "We have heard for ourselves, and we know that this is indeed the Savior of the world." John 4:42 (R.S.V.).

Look at the principal characters of this story. Catch the contrasts. 1. An Oriental man; and an Oriental woman. In those days and in some places a man would not recognize his own mother, sister, wife or daughter in a public place. The division between the sexes was sharply drawn. 2. A Jewish man; a Samaritan woman. Racial and national prejudice is not a new thing in the world. 3. Unmistakably he is a good man; she is a woman of bad repute. The barriers of sex, race, character are evident. Note how skillfully he breaks them down by means of the conversation in which he first becomes a supplicant and she is made a benefactor. Later he becomes the benefactor and she the suppliant. It is a climax when she is on the way to Sychar, the first missionary of the Gospel of Christ.

SUNDAY: JANUARY THIRTY-FIRST

MORNING SERVICE

Theme: The House of Worship.

SUGGESTED SCRIPTURE READING: Isa. 60:1-22. After-petition: May God's Word be a lamp unto our feet and a light unto our path.

SELECTED HYMNS: "I love thy kingdom, Lord."—T. Dwight. "How charming is the place."—Stennett. "City of God, how broad and fair."—S. Johnson. "Glorious things of thee are spoken." —J. Newton. "The Church's one foundation."—S. J. Stone.

PREPROCESSIONAL CHOIR PRAYER: We thank thee, O God, for the long succession of thy singers who have lifted thy people's hearts and brightened their way with sacred song. Bless these, thy servants, who are to lead us in thy praises this day. In the name of Christ. Amen.—H.

CALL TO WORSHIP: "Great is the Lord, and greatly to be praised in the city of our God, in the mountain of his holiness. Beautiful for situation, the joy of the whole earth is mount Zion."

INVOCATION PRAYER: O Almighty and Everlasting God, our heavenly Father, we bless thee that thou has brought us to the beginning of this day of fellowship in thy house. May it be a day of great renewal in our experiences of thy grace. Renew our faith, and hope, and love. Renew our wills, that we may serve thee more gladly and watchfully than ever. Renew our delight in thy Word and thy worship. Renew our joy in thee, and our longing that all men may come to know thee. Renew in us also our desires and labors to serve thee and others. Give thy kindly light to all within thy courts this day. May our fellowship together be strong and sweet, and may our experiences be so enriching that we shall all be led

into a closer walk with thee. In the name of Christ we ask. Amen.

Theme: The House of Worship.

TEXT: "I was glad when they said unto me, Let us go into the house of the Lord." Ps. 122:1.

I. "The House of the Lord." That is what the Psalmist called the Temple or the Synagogue. Jesus thought of the Temple as his Father's house, and called it a "house of prayer." It is the place where God meets with his children in the unity of a family. It is the place where the most intimate relations are recognized and developed and realized in a common life, in a most sacred communion. It is the place which God designates for the fulfillment of some of his most precious promises, and where he bestows some of his richest blessings. As a house of prayer, it is the place where his children enjoy the highest privileges possible to them in the worship of God. It is there that God waits to bestow upon them the blessings of grace, through his Word and his Sacraments, in the assurance of the forgiveness of sin, in the direction of the true life, in the strengthening of faith, in the gift of grace for every need.

When the "House of the Lord" means so much to God, how can it ever mean little to me?

II. The Home of the Congregation. The Christian congregation is the body in which the heart of the church dwells. That body requires a home, and the house of the Lord is the home of the congregation. It is there that Christians meet on common ground, with common interests of most essential importance. It is there that they affirm the unity in Christian love, and an equality in personal relationships not

94   THE MINISTERS MANUAL FOR 1954

found and not possible anywhere else among men. This is true in spite of the disagreements and dissensions sometimes found in congregations on account of the imperfections of some Christians. It is there that the truest and most beautiful fellowship among men is expected and experienced and enjoyed. And it is there that the little children are given to the Lord and are received by him into his family of the saved. It is there the young people are joined in the sacred bonds of marriage and are committed to the perpetuation of the Christian home, the social unit of both church and state. It is there that co-operative service is planned and directed.

III. The Heart of the Church. Because the House of Prayer is the House of the Lord, it becomes, spiritually speaking, the "Heart of the Church." It is there that the communion of saints on earth is most fully realized. It is there, in the congregation, that the very life of the church exists and functions. There its life is nurtured and strengthened, and its work is inspired and directed. It is there that the unity of the church is cultivated and developed. There the support of the church is secured and its mission in the world is advanced.

IV. The Haven of the Soul. Because the House of the Lord is the heart of the Church and the home of the congregation, it is the spiritual haven of the individual soul. When one enters he can leave the world and its trials behind. There, in the very presence of God, he may approach the throne of grace boldly, in personal communion with God in ways and degrees not possible anywhere else. In the House of the Lord he has everything to help him to the fullest possible realization of the very essence of his religion, whether he enter for public worship with the congregation, or for private prayer and meditation. In very truth the House of the Lord is the haven of the soul.

THEME PRAYER: For thy Church in the world and for all that it means and has meant we thank thee, O God. Deliver us from mere formal or nominal religion. We would keep the fire burning, the fire of the earnest study of thy Word; the fire of redeemed manhood and womanhood; the fire of Christian brotherliness; the fire of childhood and youth preserved in purity and strength through faith, in Jesus' name. Amen.

OFFERTORY SENTENCE: "If there be first a willing mind, it is accepted according to that a man hath, and not according to that he hath not."

OFFERTORY PRAYER: We would render unto thee, our Father, the glory due unto thy name; we would bring an offering and come into thy courts. Remember in thy gracious favor those who have brought these gifts; remember also the causes for which they are given. So follow with thy blessing that thy purposes shall be advanced in the world. We ask in the name of Christ. Amen. —H.

Illustrative Material

SEED THOUGHTS, HOMILETIC AND EXPOSITORY. Happiness and Worship: Probably this Psalm was composed for the use of the Israelites when journeying up to worship at Jerusalem on the great annual festivals and solemnities. It suggests gladness in the prospect of worship. I. It suggests thought of the Lord himself, and of going to the house of the Lord. II. And thoughts of the exercise of worship. How pleasant to praise! What relief in the confession of sin! How soothing is prayer! How helpful is Christian and united fellowship!—S. M.

Gladness and Worship: I. The words show that the Psalmist was thinking about worship. "The house of the Lord." II. And that he was thinking about social worship. "Let us go." Solitary worship is good. But social worship, with "the fellowship of kindred minds" is also very important and helpful. III. There is suggestion also about invitation to social worship. Commendable. Not to be neglected. The human invitation seems to echo the Divine welcome.—U. R. T.

To know real and undying happiness the soul must be bent away from earth and bound back to God. This is religion.—R. S.

Gladness of God's House. I. Why glad? That we have a house of the Lord to which we may go. II. Glad that any feel enough interest in us to say, "Let us go," etc. III. Glad that we are able to go. Bodily, mental and spiritual health. IV. Glad that we are disposed to go.—J. G. B.

Choice Illustrations on the Theme

WHY NOT GO TO CHURCH? If religion gave you the entire Lord's Day, what is one hour, that you should begrudge it to religion?

What better indication can be afforded of a man's good intentions that his willingness to meet God for an hour once a week and to listen to instruction on how to live a better life?

A man who is immersed in business all the week would better come up for a breath of air on Sunday.

When you hear the sermon it may bore you, but when you apply it in your life, it will arouse the enthusiasm of your friends.

The most beautiful sight from the pulpit is a whole family seated together in a pew. The church service is not a convention, that a family should send a delegate.

Churchgoing is a means of grace, and divinely appointed. It is helpful and restful. A fine investment of your time. It develops the best powers of men. But how easily neglected. Absence from next Sunday's services will make it easy to stay away the next week. The slightest irregularity in attendance will work havoc with a good habit. Then we reach for excuses which we shall find aplenty except good ones. If you will attend church regularly one quarter, you will want to go. Try this remedy. Begin next Sunday. We shall look for you.—Authors Unidentified.

MORE THAN A STORM CELLAR. Sometimes we wonder if the blessings of the church are not too easily accessible, if people would not appreciate the church more if it exacted greater demands and required more devoted service. In all communities there are people who have a church to stay away from, to criticize, to neglect. Inevitably the time comes when life caves in, when physical, financial or moral disaster strikes. When the shock comes, they then realize how utterly indispensable the church is. But Christianity is something more than a storm cellar. It is something more than present help in time of trouble. It is a way of life—a way so glorious and so crowned with victory that commonplaceness should never blind us to the glory of it.—Selected.

IS MY PLACE EMPTY? I once read a description of an obscure church somewhere in the British countryside where candleholders had been built along the pews; when a parishioner took his place, his candle was lighted by the sexton. Particularly during the evening service, the dark place occasioned by one's absence was conspicious. Perhaps it will require some painful realization of just what absenting ourselves from church means to the Christian cause to bring us back to our places within the sanctuary.—H. L. Toner.

WHY I DON'T GO TO PICTURE SHOWS.

1. I was made to go too often when I was young.

2. No one ever speaks to me when I go there.

3. When I go, they always ask for money.

4. The manager never called to ask why I had not been lately.

5. The people there don't live up to what they are shown on the films.

6. The music is very poor.

7. I was ill for weeks, and nobody from there came to see me.—*Church Magazine.*

THE BOARD OF ABSENTEES

We are the Board of Absentees;
We attend our church about as we please;

We judge it will run of itself, you know
And, Sundays, we're just too tired to go!
We are the Board of Absentees;
At business meetings our chance we
seize
To tell exactly how things should be
run,
But we lift not a finger to get them
done.
We are the Board of Absentees;
Men and women of all degrees;
"Shall we give up the church? O never,
never!"
"Shall we go today?" Well, scarcely
ever!
We look for a world far better than
this,
A world of peace and of moderate bliss,
A day of right through the Seven Seas—
Just now we're the Board of Absentees!
—Anon.

MORNING SERVICE

Theme: A Good Name (Young People's Day).

TEXT: "A good name is rather to be chosen than great riches, and loving favour rather than silver and gold." Prov. 22:1.

INTRODUCTORY: There are some strange things about names. One is that we have no choice in the matter of our names. The thing that does matter is what one wishes of his name. A number of years ago a historical society issued a booklet commemorating the anniversary of the death of William McKinley. The pamphlet was chiefly concerned with an accurate account of the visit of the martyred President to the Pan-American Exposition, but it had a brief introductory biography. It began with the boy in Niles, Ohio. There he was a lad like any other lad, probably barefoot in summer, playing in the lanes and the fields of Niles. The name of William McKinley meant little then. But through the years that followed he clothed his name with meaning and beauty.

I. Young people, it doesn't matter a snap what your name is; but it mat-

ters tremendously what you make of your name.

"If my name is so valuable," said Robert E. Lee to a group of men who simply wanted to use his name, the price thereof to be a liberal salary for no work done, "then I must be very careful how I use it. No, I cannot do it." So he kept the name Lee untarnished, synonymous with all that is noble and true.

II. Names develop synonyms. In time a name comes to stand for honesty or dishonesty, kindness or meanness, sympathy or indifference, rightness or baseness, good citizenship or graft. In the cathedral in Liverpool, England, there is a chapel having a series of magnificent art-glass windows commemorating the deeds of good women. The name of the woman is given, then the quality which causes her to be remembered. That quality is the synonym of her name: Victoria—Noble Queen. Susannah Wesley—Devoted Mother. Catherine Gladstone—Loyal Wife. Agnes Jones—Devoted Nurse. Grace Darling—Courageous Maiden. Christina Rossetti—Sweet Singer.

III. Then, too, names carry weight, some more weight than others. I do not know your habit, but I often find myself opening a letter and before reading it looking at the signature. If the name carries weight, I read the letter eagerly. I receive many letters from a man in another state. Whenever I see his name signed, I do not like to read the letter; often I put off reading it for a while, because he is always asking something, never giving. When it was known that a man named Herbert Hoover was to journey from Washington to Detroit to address a convention of the American Legion, the great hall could not begin to contain the number who desired to hear him. More than that, what he said carried weight because the name Herbert Hoover was behind the voice and words. A good name that carries weight is rather to be chosen than great riches.

IV. There are many other names that deserve attention besides the names of individuals. Names of books, business firms, organizations, periodicals—they too appreciate the value of a good name. If I were a young man going into business, profession or trade, I would make my aim to do the very best possible in my work. I would build a good name. A good name will stand one in good stead when hard times come.

There is a good name. Isaiah caught its certain foregleam, St. Paul its fadeless glory. All humanity inherits its divine power.

Through all the depths of sin and shame,
Drops the plummet of His name,
Never yet abyss was found
Deeper than His name could sound.
—Adapted from Rev. Bruce S. Wright.

Suggestive Texts and Themes

The Righteous Judge: "We know that the judgment of God is according to truth." Rom. 2:2 (A.S.V.).

Fear as a Motive: "I will warn you whom ye shall fear." Luke 12:5 (A.S.V.).

The Power of Precedent: "There is none of thy kindred that is called by this name." Luke 1:61.

The Teaching of the Trees: "Behold the fig tree, and all the trees." Luke 21:29.

The Supreme Authority: "But I say unto you." Matt. 5:22.

The Constant Companions: "Ye are they that have continued with me in my temptation." Luke 22:28 (A.S.V.).

MIDWEEK FELLOWSHIP MEETING TOPIC

(Church Night or Suggested Sermon Subject)

Theme: The Perfect Will of God.

TEXT: "That ye may prove what is that good, and acceptable, and perfect, will of God." Rom. 12:2.

Most people think of the prayer "Thy will be done" as adapted to use only in times of trial and suffering.

I. But life is not all suffering.

What of all the unclouded days? What of our sheltered childhood? What of love and friendship, of labor and its rewards? As we stand secure in the affections of our friends and in the respect of our community, do we ever stop to think that this is a part of the perfect will of God concerning us?

II. The point is: God's will covers the whole compass of life. The magic and mystery of God's will is that we may adopt it without impairing the freedom of our own wills in any degree. We simply consent to be guided. Do we lose the freedom of our wills when we follow a guide over a mountain pass, or obey the orders of a pilot as we sail through the narrows? Do we surrender our liberty when we deliberately choose God to be our guide? "The law was our schoolmaster to bring us to Christ," Christ is our schoolmaster to bring us to God, and God is our schoolmaster to bring us to—what?

III. To ourselves; to the fulfillment of life; to the richest and deepest experiences of righteousness and peace and joy.

The apostle says, "All things are for your sakes." Then this is for our sakes—God's will and God's way. Our only method of discovering God's will is in the use of reason and revelation. He gave us moral judgment to guide us in the light and the Great Book to guide us in the dark. So where reason ends, faith begins, and "the heart has reasons which Reason alone never knew."—C. C. A.

CHRISTIAN ENDEAVOR SOCIETY TOPIC

Jan. 31. Forward with Christ through My Church. Acts 2:41-47; Matt. 16:13-20.

SUNDAY SCHOOL LESSON

Jan. 31. **Faith That Makes Whole.**
John 5:2-18.

MEMORY VERSE: "I am come that they might have life, and that they might have it more abundantly." John 10:10.

The day of miracles is not over. I have seen miracles. I have seen burdened people strangely strengthened. I have seen them stand erect and walk away; not always freed of their burdens, but bearing them magnificently. I have seen defeated people turn upon the thing that had whipped them for years and give it a sound thrashing. I have never seen a pool stirred and a lame man cured, but I have seen a man's heart stirred by the Master of Souls and his life made whole. I can't explain it. I only know that when hope is great and God is given a chance amazing things happen.—Boynton Merrill.

SUNDAY: FEBRUARY SEVENTH

MORNING SERVICE

Theme: The Lord's Supper (Holy Communion).

SUGGESTED SCRIPTURE READING: I Cor. 11:23-34. After-petition: May God bless to our spiritual profit the reading of this portion of his truth.

SELECTED HYMNS: "Here, O Lord I see thee face to face."—H. Bonar. "Not worthy, Lord, to gather up the crumbs."—E. H. Bickersteth. "Jesus, thou joy of loving hearts."—Bernard of Clairvaux. "According to thy gracious word."—J. Montgomery.

CALL TO WORSHIP: "One thing have I desired of the Lord, that will I seek after; that I may dwell in the house of the Lord all the days of my life, to behold the beauty of the Lord, and to inquire in his temple."

INVOCATION PRAYER: Almighty God, Father of our Lord Jesus Christ, who hast revealed through him thy nearness to humanity, and art graciously inviting us to the fellowship of thy table, make us partakers of thy blessing and let us enter into thy courts with joy. Prepare our hearts that we may receive the symbols of thy love. Work in us unfeigned sorrow for wrongdoing. Confirm our faith in the great mysteries of redeeming grace which we are this day to show forth. In the name of Christ we ask. Amen.—M. K. W. H.

Theme: The Lord's Supper (Holy Communion).

TEXT: "For I have received of the Lord," etc. I Cor. 11:23-26.

INTRODUCTORY: This holy ordinance has been in high estimation by the followers of Christ in every age of the church. The first Christians frequently attended its celebration; indeed it seems to have been the principal object of their meeting together, Acts 20:7. Let us notice the estimate the Apostle Paul puts upon it.

I. He represents it first as a Divine ordinance. "For I received of the Lord," etc.

II. He represents it as a symbolical ordinance. "Took bread," etc. The symbols are bread and wine. They refer to his body and precious blood. Breaking of bread refers to the bruising of his sacred person; the pouring out of wine to the blood shed for our redemption.

III. He represents it as a commemorative ordinance. "Do this in remembrance of me." To keep up a lively remembrance of the Saviour, of his person, his love, his sufferings, and especially of their end and design.

IV. He represents it as a professional ordinance. "Do show forth the Lord's death." Proclaim it, preach it, keep up the remembrance of it in the world, and show our own faith in it, hope through it, and our love and obedience to Christ.

V. It is the Christian's social ordinance. It is not observed in retirement to solitude. It is the family ordinance of the household of faith. It is for all those who are the spiritual kindred of the Saviour.

VI. And it is a perpetual ordinance. "Ye do show forth the Lord's death till he come." From his first to his second coming this ordinance is to be observed, the gospel is to be preached, salvation's streams are to flow, prayer is to be offered, the fact of the Saviour's death is to be celebrated and perpetuated.

What benefits do we receive from the Supper's observance? Increased strength; comfort, peace and joy in the Holy Ghost; and a greater fitness for the fellowship of heaven.—J. B.

AFTER-COMMUNION PRAYER: We give thee thanks, O Lord, for thy rich mercy and invaluable goodness, vouchsafed to us in this sacred communion, wherein we have assurance that we are very members of the mystical body of thy Son, and heirs through hope of thine everlasting kingdom. So enrich us by thy continual grace that the life of Jesus may be made manifest in our mortal body, and thy kingdom furthered through all such good works as thou hast prepared for us to walk in. Amen.

OFFERTORY SENTENCE: "He that soweth sparingly shall reap also sparingly; and he that soweth bountifully shall reap also bountifully."

OFFERTORY PRAYER: Never may this part of our service slip into the matter-of-fact or the commonplace. Help us to use it to express our thanksgivings unto thee, our fellowship with others, our desire for the coming of thy kingdom, and our allegiance unto thy will. Be pleased to follow this offering with thy blessing that it may do much good. Amen.—M. K. W. H.

Illustrative Material

SEED THOUGHTS, HOMILETIC AND EXPOSITORY. Preparing for Communion: "There make ready." Mark 14:15. For us, where make ready? In our hearts I. What the Communion is. 1. The

feast. 2. The provision. 3. The design. II. The necessity of preparation. Often unprofitable for lack of it. III. What is good preparation? It is preparation that brings us into sympathy with Christ. We are to try to get his feelings. 1. About sin. 2. About salvation. 3. About spiritual growth, strength, consecration, etc.—W. R. T.

Christ Expected at the Feast: "What think ye, that he will not come to the feast?" John 11:56. I. What is there to cause us to fear he will not be at the feast? 1. Our sins against him. 2. Our neglect of doing commanded duty. 3. Our lack of love for him. II. On the other hand, what is there to encourage the hope that he will be at the feast? 1. His character. 2. His disposition to forgive. 3. His love.—H.

Choice Lord's Supper Illustrations

CELEBRATION OF THE SUPPER QUICKENS LOVE. Each recurring observance of the Lord's Supper rekindles love. You have an absent friend. You have not thought of that friend for a long time. But something starts a train of thought; and you allow yourself time to meditate. As you sit and think, how all his kindly ways and loving words and deeds come back to you, and you find your love for him burning warm and full. Your meditation of him is sweet. Going through your papers, you open an old letter. It is from a former and almost forgotten schoolmate. But as you read and reflect, that friend seems almost to be at your side again. Just so does the remembrance of Christ in the Lord's Supper bless and quicken love for Him. —H.

THE LORD'S SUPPER YOUR PLACE. After his resurrection Jesus told his disciples to go back to Galilee. Galilee was home for all but one, we believe. They were to go back home, for the heart is more tender back home. They were to go back to the place where they had first met him. Everything at Galilee —the boats, the nets, the lakeside lilies —had associations with him. They were to go back to meet the larger Christ—

the Christ who had passed through the garden, who had endured the cross, who had broken the bonds of death in the Resurrection. They would meet the risen Christ in Galilee.

Each Christian has his Galilee—a place that is the home of the soul, a place where he first met the Master, a place where he may return to have communion with an ever greater Saviour and Lord.—M. K. W. H.

THE LORD'S SUPPER A MONUMENT OF RE- MEMBRANCE. The Lord's Supper is a momument nineteen centuries old whose inscription, "In Memory of Jesus the Saviour," is as legible as when first graven. By partaking of the Lord's Supper, his followers in a dramatic way proclaim the Lord's death. They eat the bread and drink the wine in re- membrance of him. But what is it to remember Jesus? "To remember Jesus is to accept him as our Mediator, to trust him as our Redeemer, to love him as our Friend, to follow him as our Teacher, to obey him as our King, to take him for our all in all." Of all this the symbolic act is a pledge.

ONE WHO KNEW THE FELLOWSHIP OF CHRIST'S SUFFERINGS. The broken body of the Lord Jesus given for us receives a striking illustration in the work and death of Livingstone. In the eighteen years of solitary travel in Africa he was worn out. Reduced by fever, starved, bereaved (the disablement by the lion's jaws was one of the lesser of his physical sufferings), a man of sorrows and ac- quainted with grief, he not only opened up Central Africa by his discoveries, but touched the imagination and heart of the world by his sufferings. It was his death that completed and crowned this break- ing of his body for Africa. Borne in a litter to Chitambo's country, and laid in the hut at Ilala, he finished his course. On his knees he was found dead, arresting forever the attention of the church, and challenging Christians to evangelize Africa. To make the break- ing of his body perfect and manifest for all time, the heart was buried there in the center of the continent, and the body was brought by Susi and Chamah to the coast, and thence to the central shrine of the Anglo-Saxon world. Out of the broken body has sprung the evangeliza- tion of the Congo and of the Uganda; Livingstonia and the mission stations on Nyassa testify to it. It will work its miracles until all Africa is won to Christ.—Robert F. Horton, D.D.

A MEANING OF THE LORD'S SUPPER. A chaplain was speaking to a soldier on a cot in a hospital. "You have lost an arm in the great cause," said the chaplain. "No," said the soldier with a smile, "I didn't lose it—I gave it." And in the same way Jesus did not lose his life— he gave it. That is what the Lord's Supper meant.

Suggestive Communion Texts and Themes

The Worthy Communicant: "But let a man examine himself, and so let him eat of that bread, and drink of that cup." I Cor. 11:28.

The Action: "This do ye." I Cor. 11:25.

The Paschal Lamb: "Christ our pass- over." I Cor. 5:7.

The Bread of Life: John 6:33.

The Bequest of Jesus: "Peace I leave with you, my peace I give unto you." John 14:27.

A Last Wish: "This do in remem- brance of me." Luke 22:19.

The Gospel Festival: "A feast of fat things, a feast of wines on the lees, of fat things full of marrow, of wine on the lees well refined." Isa. 25:6.

Neglect of the Lord's Supper: "And they would not come." Matt. 22:3. "I will sup with him." Rev. 3:20.

The New Passover Feast: "And they made ready the passover." Luke 22:13.

The Surroundings of the Supper: "After the same manner also." I Cor. 11:25.

On the Threshold: "He brought me to the banqueting house." Song of Sol. 2:4.

Eternal Life in Christ: "The gift of God is eternal life through Jesus Christ our Lord." Rom. 6:23.

EVENING SERVICE

Theme: A Symmetrical Character.

TEXT: "And every one had four faces: the first face was the face of a cherub, and the second face was the face of a man, and the third the face of a lion, and the fourth the face of an eagle." Ezek. 10:14.

INTRODUCTORY: There arises a very serious question. Shall we be satisfied with merely one aspect of character and dwell in that aspect, or shall we live in two, or three, or four?

I. That is to say, shall we live in a segment of our destined powers, or in the full circle? To live in one and to ignore the others is to live in perilous exaggeration. It is to maim the character and render it ineffective. For instance, to have the eagle without the lion is to have visions and dreams and reveries, but no massive strength, no firmness of march, no courageous resolution. It is to be an air patrol with no adequate forces on the road.

II. On the other hand, to have the lion without the eagle is to have strength without vision. It is to be in possession of blind force, which can so easily become cruel, and brutal, and destructive.

III. And once again, to have the face of the cherub without the face of the man is to have piety divorced from humanity, and that is weak sentimentalism; it is to have piety sundered from geniality and that is a gloomy asceticism. The cherub without the human face! That is what Wordsworth had in his early days. He worshiped at nature's altar, but no fellow pilgrims joined him in the worship. He saw the glory of the Lord, but he did not see it alongside the pathetic needs of man. And then, later in life, to the face of the cherub came the face of the man, and never again could Wordsworth move in the fair fields of God's creation without hearing what he calls "the still, sad music of humanity." The cherub without the man is remote from our clouded shores, and lives a deformed and ineffective life.

IV. But the man without the cherub is equally partial and maimed. He toils without mystic communion. His labor is divorced from prayer. The human is cut away from the divine, and he never sees the mystic ray, "the light that never was on sea or land." The man without the cherub! His ocean has no heavenly star. His road has no ethereal gleam.—J.

MIDWEEK FELLOWSHIP MEETING TOPIC

(Church Night or Suggested Sermon Subject)

Theme: The Average Man.

TEXT: "He that had received two." Matt. 25:17.

I. His dangers. 1. He will be surely tempted to imitate greatness. 2. He will be tempted to underrate himself. 3. He may lose himself in the crowd.

II. The encouragements of the average man. In some ways he may even have advantages. 1. For one thing, he has the necessary talents. The two-talent man had capital and doubled it. 2. God designed to do the most of his work in the world through the average man. Abraham Lincoln said, "God must love the common people or he would not have made so many of them." In the very nature of things the man who goes beyond the average and the man who falls short of the average, both of them, by their very definition are exceptions. The great continent of human life is made up of average existences, the mass of two-talented capacity and action. It is in the quality more than in the quantity of the talents that their true value lies. 3. A supreme encouragement for the average man is the magnificence of the reward that awaits him. In this parable the two-talent man doubled his capital and had a surprising reward.— F.E.C.

THEME PRAYER: O thou Lover of the common people, we rejoice that thou canst carry on thine eternal plan through the aid of ordinary men. Deliver us, we pray thee, from the curse of self-depreciation and from the paralysis of unbelief. We ask in the name of Christ. Amen.

CHRISTIAN ENDEAVOR SOCIETY TOPIC

Feb. 7. "So Send I You" (Christian Endeavor Day). Luke 10:1-9; Isa. 6:1-8.

BULLETIN BOARD SLOGANS FOR THE MONTH

By EARL RINEY

Character is what you are in the dark. (Moody.)

The only difference between stumbling blocks and steppingstones is the way you use them.

If you want to put the world right, start with yourself.

What you will be tomorrow you are now becoming.

Not failure, but low aim, is shameful.

The gospel is the answer to the question, What is the use?

The parents' life is the child's copybook.

No man is too big to be courteous, but many men are too little.

Success should make us grow, not swell.

To have a friend, be one.

The greatest of faults is to be conscious of none.

SUNDAY SCHOOL LESSON

Feb. 7. Christ, the Living Bread: How Christ Sustains Us. John 6:48-59, 66-69.

MEMORY VERSE: "I am the bread of life; he who comes to me shall not hunger, and he who believes in me shall never thirst." John 6:35.

What is the nature of the food which Christ offers? Lives that are stretching forth to grow must have nutritious bread. Nothing can take the place of nourishing bread. With his plate heaped with all the things that go to make a Thanksgiving dinner a boy ate nothing but bread. He had bread hunger. It was what his growing frame needed most at that time.

Christ offers fresh bread. We recall that the children of Israel could not store up the manna for future use. In this conversation with Jesus, John 6, certain men made reference to the manna which their fathers ate. He used it as the occasion to tell them of the new fresh bread which God was giving them. When they said, "Lord, give us this bread," he answered, "I am the bread of life."

Other questions will open up this lesson and its teachings: How can this bread be obtained? What practical help does the concept of Christ as the living bread have for Christians today? How can this bread be shared?

SUNDAY: FEBRUARY FOURTEENTH

MORNING SERVICE

Theme: The Perilous Vacuum.

SUGGESTED SCRIPTURE READING: Rom. 12:1-21. After-petition: May God bless to our understanding his word as read.

SELECTED HYMNS: "Take my life, and let it be."—F. R. Havergal. "Jesus calls us, o'er the tumult."—C. F. Alexander. "Thy way, not mine, O Lord."—H.

Bonar. "Lead us, O Father, in the paths of peace."—W. H. Burleigh. "I look to thee in every need."—S. Longfellow.

PREPROCESSIONAL CHOIR PRAYER: Grant a special blessing, our Father, upon these thy servants as we enter thy house this morning. Open thou our lips and our mouth shall show forth thy praise. Through the reality of our devotion may we lead others to a deep experience of joy. In Christ's name. Amen.

CALL TO WORSHIP: "We have thought of thy lovingkindness, O God, in the midst of thy temple. According to thy name, O God, so is thy praise unto the ends of the earth: thy right hand is full of righteousness."

INVOCATION PRAYER: O God who dwellest not in temples made with hands, help us to worship this day in the beauty of holiness. Make this place a mount of vision and an altar of consecration. Help us now to commune with thee in the spirit of reverential love. May we find light at the entrance of thy Word, comfort in prayer, and joy in thanksgiving. To us each and all may this be a day of peace and joy and spiritual growth. In Christ's name we ask. Amen.

Theme: The Perilous Vacuum.

TEXT: "When the unclean spirit is gone out of a man," etc. Matt. 12:43-45.

INTRODUCTORY: No one could ever tell a story like Jesus. He was able to express himself in such a way that whatever he said remained indelibly fixed in the minds of the hearers.

Once upon a time, said our Lord, there was a man who owned a house which was occupied by a bad tenant. The place was in poor repair and dirty and the character of the tenant himself was most disagreeable; so the owner had him ejected. When the tenant was gone the house was redecorated and cleaned from top to bottom and then it was left standing empty. The evil tenant, having nowhere else to go, wandered about the streets until one day he came past the place where once he had lived and, looking through the window, he saw its spotless condition. He immediately went and found seven of his friends who were equally undesirable characters, and together with them broke into the house and very soon reduced it to a much worse state than it had ever been in before. That, said Jesus, is a parable of the human heart.

I. One of the great dangers in the spiritual life is to cast out some evil thing and then to leave our hearts unoccupied by any positive good. Nature abhors a vacuum, and if our hearts are left without great ideals and great ideas the vacuum will soon be filled by the sins which so easily beset us. No evil propensity can be got rid of unless it is expelled by a greater good. It is no good merely taking things away if you have nothing positive to put in their place. There is always the need for what Dr. Chalmers of Scotland once called "the expulsive power of a new affection."

II. Here we have clearly the problem of the immediate future. Just as nature abhors a vacuum, so does the soul of man, and if he hasn't any good ideals to live by, then he will develop evil ones. "Man must and will have some religion," said William Blake; "if he has not the religion of Jesus, he will have the religion of Satan and will erect a synagogue to Satan."

III. There is finally only one answer to this question, the question of empty lives. Our great problem is the emptiness and meaninglessness of the average life.

The ancient Greeks knew of an island inhabited by the beautiful-voiced sirens who by their singing would entice the mariners to their destruction. Ulysses managed to bring his ship past the danger when he plugged the ears of his crew with wax, but he only just got by. Orpheus was far wiser, for he sat upon the deck and sang his most beautiful songs, so that to the listening sailors the voices of the sirens seemed harsh and discordant. By giving them something more beautiful to listen to he was able to keep the men on his ship from being lured to destruction. So, if we are to save our civilization we must present to our generation a great and noble ideal which will drive from their thoughts all that is base and unlovely.

We have been speaking about the empty life and the empty heart. It may be that you have often wondered why your life is empty and with little meaning. Perhaps you know that it is untenanted and can "feel the void within." This, then, is the word for you. There stands One without who says, "Behold, I stand at the door and knock: if any man hear my voice, and open the door,

I will come in to him, and will sup with him, and he with me."—R. W. S.

ASPIRATION PRAYER: Be pleased, O Lord, to bless this hour of worship and meditation in thy Word. May it minister to our comfort and spiritual growth. Abide with us during the remainder of this Sabbath, and help us to rejoice in thee; through Jesus Christ our Lord and our Redeemer. Amen.

OFFERTORY SENTENCE: "Ye know the grace of our Lord Jesus Christ, that, though he was rich, yet for your sakes he became poor, that ye through his poverty might be rich."

OFFERTORY PRAYER: We thank thee, our Father, for the law of sacrifice, that by the grain of wheat being lost in the planting it bringeth in thirty, sixty or a hundredfold. May we have the wisdom of one who takes the long view of things. May we know that which is laid down for the spread of the Gospel will come back unto us after many days. Bless our offering in the name of Christ. Amen.—M. K. W. H.

Illustrative Material

SEED THOUGHTS, HOMILECTIC AND EXPOSITORY. Transient Religious Impressions: I. The withdrawal of the evil spirit. The transient religious impression. II. The evil spirit's restless anxiety to return. True to experience this. III. The re-entrance he at length secures. Finds it empty, garnished, but not furnished. Not spiritually indwelt. IV. The possession he again takes. V. The consequences of his repossession. The man will run greater lengths in evil than before. Fearful relapse.—H. B.

The Heart a House: I. The malicious heart for the spirit of envy. II. The drunken heart for the spirit of inebriety. III. The haughty heart for the spirit of pride. IV. The impure heart of uncleanness.—T. A.

The Empty Life: As wealth increases, as life becomes less primitive and more artificial there come to be found a large number of persons, both men and women, who have little or nothing to do, unless they seek to make an occupation for themselves. It is out of such a condition of things that there is sure to arise sooner or later every imaginable evil that can afflict society or ruin the individual soul.—H. C. P.

Choice Illustrations on the Theme

THE HOUSE IS TENANTED. As a loving parent you seek to expel from your child the demons of disobedience, untruthfulness, self-will. You do well in thus sweeping the house. But this is not enough. One deed done by your boy out of love of God in Christ is worth all the sweeping and garnishing in the world, for it indicates that the house is tenanted.—T. C. Finlayson.

OVERCOMING EVIL WITH GOOD. Between a poor woman's house and the next corner were several vacant lots with a path the near way across. But every time she went out she got burrs in the skirt of her dress. Her young son undertook to pull up the bushes that lined the walk. A gardener came along and said to the boy, "That is not the way to get rid of the weeds; sow grass seed." He explained that the weeds would soon come up again; but that if he would get the grass to grow it would take the place of the weeds. The boy followed the gardener's directions, cut down the bushes and weeds, plentifully sowed the grass seed, and by fall the whole place was covered with grass instead of weeds.— *Evangelical Messenger.*

HITLER'S SUCCESS. Hitler's early success in Germany can largely be attributed to the fact that with the decay of a virile religious faith among the German people he filled their empty hearts with a new religion. Their souls were hungry and he satisfied them with Nazism.—Rev. Robert W. Shields.

THE PERILOUS VACUUM. There is an account given of a happening in a district in England just following World War II. A large number of fires were started inside of three weeks in a certain area. A gunner who had returned to his home after long service in the army on pleading guilty of arson could only say in defense that life at home was too boring and slow for him and that he had to find some way of brightening it up! His mind may have been unbalanced, but the occurrence raises the question, What are we going to put in the place of war?—Rev. Robert W. Shields.

SPIRITUAL STRATEGY. Our souls are a picture gallery. Cover the walls of them with things serene, noble, beautiful, and the foul and flashy will seem revolting. "Hang this upon the wall of your room," said a wise picture dealer to a college undergraduate, as he handed him the engraving of a Madonna of Raphael, "and then all the pictures of jockeys and ballet girls will disappear." Try the same experiment within your soul.— *5,000 Best Modern Illustrations.*

REFORMATION IS NOT SALVATION. Here let us suppose is a drunkard whom you are anxious to reform. He is ruining his body, breaking his wife's heart, injuring his family. You succeed in reforming him, a matter for great rejoicing. You have done well in sweeping the house from one vice. But that vice had its root in ungodliness, and if after his reformation the man continues ungodly and irreligious there is great danger of that ungodliness and irreligion breaking out in worse sins than ever.—T. C. Finlayson.

EVENING SERVICE

Theme: Acquaintance with God.

TEXT: "Acquaint now thyself with him, and be at peace: thereby good shall come unto thee." Job. 22: 21.

INTRODUCTORY: People are not acquainted with God. Naturally we are ignorant of him. Ignorance of God is the secret of all opposition to him. It is impossible for anyone to know God and not to love him. The advice of Eliphaz points the way to the highest knowledge and the greatest good. "Acquaint now thyself," etc.

I. First let us think of what acquaintance with God is or implies. True religion rests upon correct views of God, of his character and attributes. Many people assume that they naturally know God. That is not true, thought they have a longing or instinct toward him.

Acquaintance with him includes knowledge of him. It includes friendship toward him. It includes confidence in and communion with him. "Acquaint" is a very forceful word. One rendering of the word is "acquiesce in God." Another is "join thyself to God." Another is "attach thyself to God."

II. What are some of the ways of becoming acquainted with God? To acquaint ourselves with God we must make ourselves acquainted with the revelation he has made us respecting himself and his will. There are two possible ways of coming to knowledge of God. One is speculative. The other is experimental, resting upon personal acquaintance. Both have value, but the experimental is the only solid and satisfactory way to knowledge of him. We should make a heartfelt experimental knowledge of him the object of our unceasing pursuit. By study of his Word, prayer, association with Christians, and in many other ways we can seek acquaintance with God.

III. Further, and especially, let us consider some of the blessed results of acquaintance with God. "And be at peace." There is no deep and abiding peace outside the experimental knowledge of God. Eliphaz speaks of other results. "Thereby good shall come unto thee." How much there is in that word "good"! No doubt Eliphaz thought of temporal blessings, and there are many and desirable. But look at the special blessings of the Christian. Sins blotted out. Heart renewed. Bondage changed into liberty. The power of sin broken. Besetting infirmities overcome. Life made a blessing to others. Death robbed of its sting. Soul peace. Present good. Eternal good. These and such as these are the greatest and happiest that human nature is capable of enjoying—the highest knowledge and the greatest good—H.

Suggestive Texts and Themes

An Exhausted Christ: "Asleep on a pillow." Mark 4:38.

Inner Radiance: "And was transfigured before them." Matt. 17:2.

Freedom to Choose: "If it seem evil unto you to serve the Lord, choose you this day whom ye will serve." Josh. 24:15.

Code and Conscience: "Thou art the man." II Sam. 12:7.

The Will and the Deed: "She hath done what she could." Mark. 14:8.

MIDWEEK FELLOWSHIP MEETING TOPIC

(Church Night or Suggested Sermon Subject)

Theme: The Church's Peace and Prosperity.

TEXT: "Peace be within thy walls, and prosperity within thy palaces." Ps. 122:7.

Note the Psalmist's attachment to God's house. Worthy our imitation.

I. Consider the blessings desired. "Peace and prosperity." A peaceful church. A growing, advancing church. Harmony. Growth. The second depends much on the first.

II. What are some of the evidences of their possession? 1. When unity and love prevail. 2. When its ordinances are cheerfully and regularly attended. "Whither the tribes go up." 3. When many are asking the way to Zion with their faces thitherward.

III. The means of promoting these blessings. How are peace and prosperity secured in the church? 1. When friends pray, "Peace be within thy walls." 2. When this is a true desire and aim. 3. When it is the language of life. First we must say, "Peace be within thy walls." Then comes "prosperity within thy palaces." The latter proceeds from the former.

How important on God's account! How desirable on our own account! "They shall prosper that love thee."—B.

CHRISTIAN ENDEAVOR SOCIETY TOPIC

Feb. 14. Facing Up to Your Prejudices (Race Relations Sunday). John 7:45-53; Gal. 3:28.

SUNDAY SCHOOL LESSON

Feb. 14. Jesus Declares His Deity. John 7:37-44; 8:12-19.

MEMORY VERSE: "I am the light of the world; he who follows me will not walk in darkness, but will have the light of life." John 8:12.

1. Jesus' claim to deity is sustained by his character. "His greatness is full-orbed. He was complete, and in his completeness we find an explanation of his beauty. . . . He pushed every good trait of human character to its utmost limit. His forgiveness was unbounded, his generosity was untiring, his patience was inexhaustible, his mercy was immeasurable, his courage was illimitable, his wisdom was unfathomable, his faith removed mountains, his hope had no shadow in it, his love was infinite."—Charles Jefferson.

2. Jesus' claim to deity is sustained by his power. "The power of Jesus still grows, both in the way of drawing men, subduing them, and uniting them. . . . The religious power of the world is not ideas or truths, powerful as these are, but personalities and their deeds."—P. T. Forsyth.

3. Jesus' claim to deity is sustained by his influence. "His effect on the human soul is greater than any human cause can explain." Consider his effect in history, in the church and its experience.

4. "It is the work of the cross that crowns and carries home the greatness of Christ. There the Master becomes our Lord and our God."—P. T. F.

SUNDAY: FEBRUARY TWENTY-FIRST

MORNING SERVICE

Theme: Discovering the Lordship of Jesus.

SUGGESTED SCRIPTURE READING: Eph. 1:1-23; I Tim. 6:13-16.

SELECTED HYMNS: "Crown him with many crowns."—M. Bridges. "All hail the power of Jesus' name."—E. Perronet. "Mighty God, while angels bless thee."—R. Robinson. "The head that once was crowned with thorns."—T. Kelly. "O for a thousand tongues to sing."—C. Wesley.

CALL TO WORSHIP: "Hear, O Lord, when I cry with my voice: have mercy also upon me, and answer me. When thou saidst, Seek ye my face; my heart said unto thee, Thy face, Lord, will I seek."

INVOCATION PRAYER: We will lift up our eyes unto the hills whence cometh our help. Let us not forget thy goodness, O Lord, in the constant gifts of thy providence and grace. For life and all that makes life worth living, for home and kinship and friendship and the fellowship of saints we thank thee. Blessed be thy name for the assurance that thou art an High Priest who can be touched with a feeling of our infirmities. Enable us to realize that the sufferings of this present time are not worthy to be compared with the glory that shall be revealed in us. Be pleased to pardon our sins, for thy great mercy's sake. We are great sinners; but thou, O God, art a great Saviour! Bless with us all who worship today in the churches of the whole world. Keep them loyal to thy law and true to thy Gospel. And hasten the time when sinners everywhere shall be converted and every knee shall bow in worship before thee. We ask in Christ's name. Amen.—J. D. B.

Theme: Discovering the Lordship of Jesus.

TEXT: "Ye are my friends, if ye do whatsoever I command you." John 15:14.

INTRODUCTORY: Many a soldier has gone forward under orders when otherwise fear would have laid him prostrate. All of us need and the world needs an authority. The freer we are the greater the need for discipline. The discovery of an authority, not tyrannical, not fascist, an authority that can and must make righteous demands and issue benevolent promises with ability and will to fulfill them is one of the greatest needs of the hour. I believe that authority may be discovered in Jesus Christ. The Lordship of Jesus is an introduction to his friendship. "Ye are my friends, if ye do whatsoever I command you."

I. We discover the Lordship of Jesus in simple choices. Simple alternatives are placed in our minds by our parents, society, the church, with Jesus standing on one side. Is not this itself an indication of the dominance of Christ that he has so influenced the common life that we can feel his demand? Simple choices are made all through life which lead to an experience of his Lordship. We borrow lines from Joseph Addington Richards:

One day there passed along the silent shore,
  While I my net was casting in the sea
A Man, who spoke as never man before;
  I followed Him—new life began in me.

Mine was the boat
  But His the voice
And His the call,
  Yet mine the choice.

II. We discover the Lordship of Jesus in critical choices. We think of such a choice as that of vocation. The word "vocation" itself comes from the Latin root *voco*, "I call." It suggests that a man make his daily work an answer to a word previously spoken by God himself. How eloquent is the Old Testament as its leading characters are reviewed and we note those who made their career an answer to God and by that discovered his Lordship in a deep and fundamental way; such characters as Abraham, Gideon, Samuel, Jeremiah, Isaiah and Amos!

In critical choices acknowledging the Lordship of Christ how many noble careers have had to be put aside. Some few like Albert Schweitzer could give up the careers of scholar and physician to become a doctor in equatorial Africa and then find opportunity to take them up again, but others have had to choose to be under Christ in one vocation by laying down another. Burne-Jones could not be both minister and artist; the ministry was laid aside. Robertson of Brighton could not be both soldier and minister; he had to bury Robertson the soldier.

Two young men stood on the corner of Van Ness Avenue and Sacramento Street in San Francisco. It was their first night in that strange city. The choice on that Sunday evening was whether or not to enter the church on that corner. One entered; the other did not. The former became a follower of Christ and one of San Francisco's most useful citizens. The other went his own way and never found Christ's way. It was a moment of crisis in their lives far beyond their knowledge, though later in the perspective of years it was seen as such.

III. We discover the Lordship of Jesus by persistent choices. Of course, we cannot go through life weighing every occasion and event. We often make what becomes a persistent choice by the acceptance of a principle of life. A principle is no substitute for the Person, but often leads to a knowledge of him and acceptance of his authority. "As for me and my house, we will serve the Lord," said Joshua, and many have said it since. Something was done once and for all as Joshua asserted his decision. By the principle of honesty, "swearing to one's own hurt and changing not," men have discovered the mastery of Christ. By the acceptance of the principle of stewardship they have made him dominant. The principles of benevolence, purity, temperance have opened doors into inner rooms where men have learned to know the Master.—M. K. W. H.

THEME PRAYER: O Thou whose Son was willingly uplifted by the cross, that from its redemptive station he might draw all men unto him, so enable us to exhalt him in all our minds and wills and ways that his supremacy may become our salvation. In his Name. Amen.

OFFERTORY SENTENCE: "Offer unto God the sacrifice of thanksgiving; and pay thy vows unto the Most High."

OFFERTORY PRAYER: By our giving, O Lord, we have learned that we receive. As the spring flows it is also replenished. By the exhaustion of our strength we are revitalized. So we give in thy name and in thy name we receive. Bless unto the good of others that which we give and may thy grace given unto us restore and refresh our souls. Amen.—M. K. W. H.

Choice Illustrations on the Theme

CHRIST THE LORD. Before the second World War we had the privilege of studying, in the Rospigliosi Palace in Rome, Guido Reni's great picture "The Aurora." It is a ceiling fresco and can be studied only with greatest difficulty from the floor. But a mirror is so placed on a table that it reflects the picture, and one can study it there with ease and pleasure. God is a spirit, and he is in heaven, "dwelling in light unapproachable." It was not easy to know him there. But the Incarnation, the Word becoming flesh and dwelling among us, was the bringing of the reflection of the glorious person of God down to earth in human form and life. Men looked at Jesus and saw the likeness of God, "the express image of his Person." He was Christ, the Lord.— *5,000 Best Modern Illustrations.*

ONCE-IN-A-LIFETIME CHOICES. Once-in-a-lifetime choices come in many forms. A loved one dies and Christ stands by the bereaved person waiting for a choice between bitterness and the resolve to transmute the bereavement into something noble and useful. One of America's leading citizens of some years past made the quick choice of plunging into North River or entering a mission hall to pray. By the choice of the latter his life was saved and he learned to know the Lordship of Christ. It was a choice made in desperation but the right one.

PERSISTENT CHOICES. I heard a woman say of her husband, "You know Al's been superintendent of the Sunday School for thirty-seven years and he's been clerk of the City School Board for thirty-eight." There he stood, but I had never realized his bigness until then. He had achieved little by little, by persistently choosing the only kind of greatness it was possible for him to achieve. He could hold no high station in state or in church, but by persistently choosing the place of quiet service he had found the Lordship of Christ and Christ had highly exalted him.—A Pastor's Testimony.

DISCOVERING CHRIST'S LORDSHIP. I remember at one of our testimony meetings a man got up and said he had got a great blessing at Keswick. They asked him, "What can you say about it?" "Well," he replied, "I can say this: I was a Christian before I came to Keswick. Christ was my King, but I am afraid he was a constitutional sovereign and I was prime minister. Now he is absolute Lord, and that has made the difference in my life and brought a blessing." Aye, that makes all the difference in the world. Make Jesus King. Crown him Lord of all and you will know the liberty of the glory of the sons of the kingdom.—Rev. W. E. Moore.

STUMBLING ON CHRIST. When Goethe was in his teens, he stumbled on one of the great hours of life. He discovered Shakespeare, came upon that glory of music and art. "I was one born blind," he declared, "who had suddenly been made to see! I rushed out into the open air, and felt as though for the first time I had hands and feet." Would it not be a great thing someday to stumble on Christ?

EVENING SERVICE

Theme: The Life I Should Live.

TEXT: "And Simon he surnamed Peter." Mark 3:16.

INTRODUCTORY: His first name meant an uncertain sort of hearer; his second name meant a rock. And the Lord deliberately displaced the weaker name and supplanted it by a stronger one.

I. "Simon" was a man of fickle impulse, undependable, slipping out of one's grasp like a handful of sand. "Peter" was rock, granite, invincible as the everlasting hills. I wonder how the sand felt the first time it was called rock! Or how should I feel if the Lord were now to appear and address me by that tremendous name? The new name did not describe the man as he was. It described the man he might be, and the man he was to be. It was not the name of a man who had arrived, but the name of a man who was on the journey.

II. Here, then, is a glimpse into one of our Lord's methods in training those whom he had ordained. He fixed his thought on the vast possibilities which stretched before them. He thought of people in terms of what they would be. While they were still learning the alphabet he saw them familiar with the highest literature. When they were just learning to walk he saw them as finished athletes. He was Alpha and Omega, and he saw the end from the beginning. He saw the mighty oak in the fragile sapling, and in its earliest stages. He rejoiced in the King of the forest, the Lord and sovereign of storm and windy circumstance.

III. And so we find our Master continually addressing people in the brilliant titles of their new names, the names which indicate their brilliant possibilities and their coming achievements. "Ye are the salt of the earth!" "He also is a son of Abraham!" When the Lord gave a man a new name it was a call from the heights. And how inspiring it would be! It would rouse like the sound of a bugle. Surely Simon would pull himself together when Christ called him Peter! Surely he stretched himself toward his suggested stature! And so with Zacchaeus when the Lord called him "a son of Abraham." The little man went home that night walking as if he were six feet three!

IV. And this is how our great Saviour thinks of thee and me. He thinks of us now as though we were perfected. And his grace will bring us into the very perfection which we seem to wear in his holy love. We are called "children of God," "children of light," "heirs of God," "joint heirs with Christ," "saints of the household of faith." How greatly he thinks of us!—J.

Suggestive Texts and Themes

Physical Righteousness: "The temple of God is holy, which temple ye are." I Cor. 3:17.

Unhappy Heredity: "Visiting the iniquity of the fathers upon the children." Ex. 20:5.

Dignity of Healthfulness: "Your body is a temple of the Holy Spirit." I Cor. 6:19. (R.S.V.)

Slaves to Appetite: Their Doom: "If ye live after the flesh, ye must die." Rom. 8:13. (A.S.V.)

Heroism of Self-control: "I buffet my body and bring it into bondage: lest . . . I myself should be rejected." I Cor. 9:27.

MIDWEEK FELLOWSHIP MEETING TOPIC

(Church Night or Suggested Sermon Subject)

Theme: How to Gain the Victory.

TEXT: "Be of good cheer; I have overcome the world." John 16:33.

Jesus said, "Be of good cheer." There are three things to do:

I. First, hope in God. If hope has been our ally in the past it still is for the future. Keep up hope!

II. Second, keep a cheerful mind. One of the best tonics for any day is hearty laughter. Laughter comes from a joyous heart and joy is at the heart of the universe. Jesus constantly spoke of his joy and expressed a desire that it should remain in man's life.

III. Third, keep the faith. If "Christians hold the world together" the most important thing in the world today is for them to keep faithful—faithful in duty, in devotion, in worship and prayer life. The reason the successful stewards in the parable of talents were successful was because they were faithful and they were commended for their faithfulness, not their success. Near the close of his life Paul said, "I have fought a good fight, I have finished my course, I have kept the faith." May all Christians be challenged by him to live so they might say the same!

Whatever the unknown future holds you can still hope in God, keep up your spirits by good humor and laughter, and be faithful to the end. Doing this you will gain the victory over the world.— Earl W. Haney.

CHRISTIAN ENDEAVOR SOCIETY TOPIC

Feb. 21. Join Hands with Your Neighbors (Brotherhood Sunday). Rom. 13:10-14.

SUNDAY SCHOOL LESSON

Feb. 21. Sight for Man's Blindness. John 9. Esp. 24-38.

MEMORY VERSE: "One thing I know, that though I was blind, now I see." John 9:25. (R.S.V.)

The miracles of Jesus were performed to meet all sorts of human emergencies. The changing of water into wine met an emergency of embarrassment. The feeding of the five thousand met an emergency of hunger. Other emergencies were sickness, danger, death. This man who was born blind was in an emergency of despair. A man who was blind described his emergency with this word—

despair. This miracle is a revelation of the power of Christ to meet life's most extreme needs.

The experience of the man made him a courageous and effective witness. It may be pointed out that effective witnessing is based upon the reality of Christian experience—the certainty or assurance which is expressed in the memory selection.

SUNDAY: FEBRUARY TWENTY-EIGHTH

MORNING SERVICE

Theme: The Sacrifice of Obedience.

SUGGESTED SCRIPTURE READING: I Sam. 15:1-23. After-petition: May God bless to our instruction this ancient story.

SELECTED HYMNS: "Dear Lord and Master mine."—T. H. Gill. "Lord, it belongs not to my care."—R. B. "Saviour, teach me day by day."—J. E. Leeson.

CALL TO WORSHIP: "Praise waiteth for thee, O God, in Zion: and unto thee shall the vow be performed. O thou that hearest prayer, unto thee shall all flesh come."

INVOCATION PRAYER: O God, by whose hand all living things were made, and by whose blessing they are nourished and sustained; we give thee hearty thanks for all the bounties of thy providence wherewith thou hast enriched our life; and we humbly pray that enjoying thy gifts we may be enabled by thy grace to use them to thy glory. Especially we thank thee for thy great love in sending thy Son to be the Saviour of the world and in calling us into fellowship with him; and we beseech thee to grant us always thy Holy Spirit, through whom we may grow continually in thankfulness toward thee, as also into the likeness of thy Son, Jesus Christ our Lord. Bless us one by one and all together as we worship in thy house this morning. We ask in the name of Christ. Amen.

Theme: The Sacrifice of Obedience.

TEXT: "Behold, to obey is better than sacrifice." I Sam. 15:22.

INTRODUCTORY: The king was guilty of thinking that a self-chosen sacrifice was more important than obedience to Good. He lost his kingdom, and ultimately his life, for his disobedience. The supremely important thing that is so hard for all of us to learn is the importance of unquestioning, implicit, persistent obedience to the divine will.

The great historical illustration is Martin Luther on his way to the Diet at Worms. When his intimate friends tried to dissuade him from going because they knew enemies were waiting there to kill him, his answer was: "Were there as many devils in the way as tiles on the housetops, yet would I go!" And when he was threatened with death if he did not recant his beliefs that he had nailed to the church door, he answered: "Here I stand; I cannot do otherwise; God help me."

It is men of supreme obedience like that who stand forth as makers of history. On the one hand, they do their own thinking, not "tossed to and fro by every wind of doctrine," nor farming out their thinking to other men. On the other hand, having formulated their beliefs and principles, they proceed to express them in terms of common life.

"Ye call me Lord and Master," said Jesus to his disciples, "and ye say well, for so I am." And in exposition of his lordship and mastery he said, "Ye are my friends if ye do whatsoever I command you."

I. Unquestioning obedience. It appears then that God requires the same unquestioning obedience that a captain expects from a soldier in the ranks. We remember a funeral in our earlier ministry of a little boy. The father was rebellious, irreconciled, and told the minister there could not be a God of love and justice or he would not have let his little boy die. The minister said: "You make no pretense to religion, you never attend church, you never give God a thought. Why should God consider you? Were I you, I would repent and sin no more lest a worse thing befall me." And he left the man. In two weeks he sent for the minister, and told him he could not get his words out of his mind. The result was he made a profession of faith and united with the church, and became a faithful Christian.

It is not easy to resist our instinctive curiosity as to the reason of things. We are too much like the boy who takes his father's watch to pieces to see "what makes the wheels go 'round." There are "state secrets" which the "King of kings" keeps to himself, and there are occasions when all we can do is render him unquestioning obedience.

II. Exact obedience. God also expects from men an exact obedience. We have no more right to take liberties with God's commands than did Saul when he spared the king of the Amalekites and some of their flocks and herds for a special sacrifice. The prophet Samuel rebuked him with the words: "Behold, to obey is better than sacrifice, and to hearken than the fat of rams." The thoughtful man knows that God demands exact obedience.

III. Persistent obedience. And God requires persistent obedience. "Be ye faithful unto death, and I will give thee a crown of life." It is the staying quality of our piety that tells.

We are thinking of a ranchman received into the church and baptized after he was a grandfather. Sitting with him the next day, he said to the minister, "I feel like I have lost thirty years of my life." When asked why, he replied: "Thirty years ago I went to Chicago with a train of cattle. I heard that Dwight L. Moody was preaching each night. For four nights I went to hear

him, and felt each night I should accept Christ and unite with the church. But I would not. And now I have done what I ought to have done thirty years ago." But he became a most persistent worker and believer, and was ultimately an officer in that church.

When Christ's earthly ministry was drawing to a close, it was written that "he steadfastly set his face to go to Jerusalem." What an example for those who love and serve and follow him.— T. O. P.

THEME PRAYER: O Lord, give us grace, we beseech thee, to hear and obey thy voice which sayeth to every one of us "follow me." May we disobey no heavenly vision nor fail thy cause in any extremity. Uplift us also to all needed acts of duty or courage that thy Kingdom may come and thy will be done on earth as it is in heaven. Amen.

OFFERTORY SENTENCE: "Thou shalt remember the Lord thy God, for it is he that giveth thee power to get wealth."

OFFERTORY PRAYER: In the name of Christ and unto the spread of his Gospel in the earth we dedicate this offering. May it receive, O Lord, thy blessing to carry unto men a finer appreciation of service, unto women a higher evaluation of their lives, unto children their rightful heritage of Christian nurture, and unto all a saving knowledge of thee. In Christ's name we ask. Amen—M. K. W. H.

Illustrative Material

SEED THOUGHTS, HOMILETIC AND EXPOSITORY. Obedience and sacrifice: I. Sacrifice is only circumstantially necessary, but obedience is essentially so. II. Sacrifice is a relative good, obedience is personal and therefore better. III. Sacrifice is temporary, obedience eternal. IV. Sacrifice is good as a means, therefore to obey, being the end, is better.—W. K.

Hypocritical obedience may please men, but not God, the searcher of hearts. —T. B.

Obedience Better than Sacrifice: I. Obedience must be prompt. II. It must be exact. III. It should be unquestioning. IV. It should be cheerful.—H. R.

The Supremacy of Obedience: I. It is of the moral element in religion, far above ceremonial. II. It is of the essence and spirit of religion while sacrifice is but one of its forms. III. Obedience is itself an end in religion while sacrifice is a means to that end. IV. Obedience is continuous and eternal whereas sacrifice is intermittent and may cease.—H. M.

Choice Illustrations on the Theme

ANGELIC OBEDIENCE. A teacher was explaining to her class the words concerning God's angels, "ministers of his who did his pleasure," and asked: "How do angels carry out God's will?" Many answers followed. One said, "They do it directly." Another, "They do it with al their hearts." A third, "They do it well." And after a pause a quiet little girl added, "They do it without asking any questions."

OBEDIENCE BETTER THAN SACRIFICE. A child was forbidden by her father to go to the shore of a lake. But some fascination drew her to the forbidden place. She gathered a number of beautiful shells, of which he was a great admirer, and carried them to him. But when she put them in his hand he put them away from him, simply saying in explanation, "My child, to obey is better than sacrifice." The lesson was never forgotten.—*Christian Endeavor World.*

OBEDIENCE, NOT PROFESSION. Pharmace sent a crown to Caesar at the same time that he rebelled against him. But Caesar returned the crown with this message: "Let Pharmace return to his obedience first and then I will accept the crown."

PERFECT OBEDIENCE. One noon General Havelock left his son on London Bridge, telling him to stay there until his return. The father intended to be absent but a short time, but he was kept busy with one affair after another, and forgot all about his boy. Not until he went home at night, and his wife inquired, "Where is Henry?" did he recall.

Hastily calling a cab, he drove down to the bridge in great anxiety, and found there his boy standing where he had left him.

EVENING SERVICE

Theme: **The Delusion Prosperity Produces.**

TEXT: "I shall be a lady for ever." Isa. 47:7.

INTRODUCTORY: This was the boast of proud Babylon. It is identical with that of the vain and self-confident in all ages. It is the delusion prosperity produces in so many men and nations, and leads to all sorts of ill results.

I. For one thing, such pride and delusion lead to false security. "I shall be a lady for ever." The Bible speaks of those who "trust in their wealth, and boast themselevs in the multitude of their riches" (Ps. 49:6). Even so good a man as Job, in a time of health and gladness, said, "I shall die in my nest" (Job 29:18). It is sadly true that the tendency of prosperity and honors is to blind the heart to the future, and often to steel it toward God.

II. The natural tendency also of such pride and boasting is that they shall lead to presumption. "I shall be a lady for ever." The one who is rich and prosperous is exceedingly liable to feel so in his own right, and that no contingency can arise to deprive him of his title and wealth. The prosperous man is tempted to forget that he is as dependent upon God now as he was in his days of adversity. The boast of Babylon of being "a lady for ever" shows also a sense of being superior to others. Prosperity is very liable to make people feel superior, that they are in themselves a higher order of being, which is miserable self-conceit and presumption.

III. Another fault prosperity is very liable to produce is that of self-satisfaction. "I shall be a lady for ever." I am that now! I am that sure! No one can dispute it! Even a church of Christ, the Church of Laodicea, when things looked bright about them, talked in that way:

"I am rich, and increased with goods, and have need of nothing," (Rev. 3:17). How dreadful the delusion when anyone speaks in that way! "I am a lady!" "I shall be a lady for ever!" Yes, a self-styled lady—proud, boasting, self-satisfied—dependent, deluded, despised!

IV. There is another serious sin to which this boastful prosperity is very liable to lead. It is that of abandonment to luxury. "I shall be a lady for ever. That is, I mean to be one. I intend to enjoy myself. I intend to live that kind of luxurious life." She is going to "keep up with the Joneses," and will live that way that will do it—even outdo them! If in the New Testament the man who hid his Lord's money was condemned, what shall be the doom of those who use their means only for self-indulgence?

We may well recall the history of proud, self-satisfied and boastful Babylon. She exalted herself to heaven, but was brought down to desolation. For centuries even the location of the city was hardly known.

Suggestive Texts and Themes

The God Who Speaks: "This is my beloved Son . . . hear ye him." Matt. 17:5.

This Is the Life: "He that hath the Son hath life." I John 5:12.

The Great Experience: "Wherefore if any man is in Christ, he is a new creature: the old things are passed away; behold they are become new." II Cor. 5:17 (A.S.V.)

Someone Must Begin: "While he was yet young, he began to seek after the God of David his father." II Chron. 34:3.

The Courier: "Joseph was in Egypt already." Ex. 1:5.

Your Everyday Life: "Only let your manner of life be worthy of the gospel of Christ." Phil. 1:27 (R.S.V.)

CHRISTIAN ENDEAVOR SOCIETY TOPIC

Feb. 28. Quiet Down (Quiet Hour). Isa. 30:15; Ps. 46:10; Isa. 40:28-31; Eccles. 5:1-7.

SUNDAY SCHOOL LESSON

Feb. 28. Christ's Love for All People. John 10:1-11.

MEMORY VERSE: "I have other sheep, that are not of this fold; I must bring them also, and they will heed my voice. So there shall be one flock, one shepherd. John 10:16 (R.S.V.)

"I am the door of the sheep." The door's suggestion is that of intimacy. At the door we call one another by name. "I am the door, by me if any man enter in"; it is a person-to-person relationship. When one moves from the figure of speech to the fact we recall the intimacy of Jesus with a few. There were only twelve in the band that traveled with him in Galilee, or perhaps just a few more. On occasions he took but three with him. And the final "multitude" of his close followers was about one hundred and twenty.

And yet his call is unto all men. The intimacy of the door is the intimacy of invitation. "Come," we say, "my latch-string is out." "Come, and ye shall see," said Jesus to two men who once followed him with embarrassment and hesitation. "Come!" is his blessed word to the weary and heavy laden. "Suffer little children to come to me." The word, echoed by the Spirit and the bride, brings invitation even unto this day unto every man, any man, "Come, I am the door."

SUNDAY: MARCH SEVENTH

MORNING SERVICE

Theme: On the Right Road.

SUGGESTED SCRIPTURE READING: John 14:1-17.

SELECTED HYMNS: "Guide me, O though great Jehovah."—W. Williams. "Through the night of doubt and sorrow."—B. S. Ingemann. "He leadeth me."—J. H. Gilmore. "Lead us, O Father, in the paths of peace."—W. H. Burleigh. "Father of love, our Guide and Friend."—W. J. Irons.

CALL TO WORSHIP: "They that trust in the Lord shall be as mount Zion, which cannot be removed, but abideth for ever. As the mountains are round about Jerusalem, so the Lord is round about his people from henceforth even for ever."

INVOCATION PRAYER: Come, O thou living and loving God: Come in all thy gentleness and make us great. Come to little children as a friend. Come to youth as an ideal. Come to the mature as comrade and helper. Come to the aged as Shepherd of their souls. Unto all of us grant thy Fatherhood, and thy Saviourhood, and the gracious presence of thy Spirit in our worship. We know that the blessings which we ask from thee for our loved ones are very small by comparison with the abundance of all good things which thou art willing to give. Shower thy blessings upon them, we pray, not according to our imperfect asking, but according to thy beneficent will. Enlighten them, that they may accept thy many gifts to satisfy their every need and use all things to thy glory. Bless us now, each one and all together, as we worship in thy house today. We ask in the name of Christ. Amen.

Theme: On the Right Road.

TEXT: "He knoweth the way that I take." Job 23:10.

INTRODUCTORY: The Book of Job has been called "the finest thing ever written with pen." This because of both its literary composition and the clear light it throws upon human trial and its issues. It teaches men to retain faith, to trust in the order of things, and in the God of order. Job cherished absolute dependence upon the divine goodness.

Job was like a traveler on a lonely road. Satan had been permitted to interrupt his course and bruise and lame and strip him of all that he had. Now these so-called friends of his are weaving elaborate arguments to prove that because he is in such a sorry plight therefore he must be on the wrong road. In substance Job answers, "No matter what you think, God knows all about me. If he thought I was upon the wrong road he would tell me. 'He knoweth the way that I take.' "

Let us interpret Job's thoughts under this figure of a road.

I. Job says, " 'He knoweth the way that I take' for he has directed me." The greatest comfort one can have in time of affliction is to know that God wills or permits it. If one can say, "I know that God would not fail or be false to me, neither would he strengthen me in a wrong course": This is walking by faith. The way may be almost trackless. The believer may walk alone, and with difficulty find his way, but he can be sure of going right because he is in the way of God's appointment.

II. Faith can also say, "He knoweth the way that I take," although I have sometimes doubted it. God's guidance is not dependent on our faith. It is not always that the afflicted can feel that all is right. God is true to us however uncertain we may be. Dark hours may come, but what a comfort to know that however doubtful we are God is still faithful and knows our state.

III. So faith can add, "He knoweth the way that I take," and I am sure he will never abandon me. To the believer God's past mercy is a pledge of his future grace and guidance. He never yet has left the soul he engaged to guide. It is only reasonable to conclude that he will continue to bless.

IV. "He knoweth the way that I take"; therefore, I do not need to mind too much some roughness on the road. If God be for me I have every reason for perseverance and for brave endurance. I am satisfied with his dealings with me.

V. "He knoweth the way that I take"; therefore, I must reach the journey's end and home. It does not matter then what the road is like or how I feel therein. I am on the right road and the journey's end makes amends for any roughness of the way. No detour. Keep to the road. It will lead me home.

THEME PRAYER: O thou who art the Way, the Truth and the Life, suffer us not to stray from thee. Speak to us anew in every time of need; perfect us in holy obedience to thy words and revelation, and so keep us secure and on the right road. Deliver us from willful waywardness, and vouchsafe to us an instant readiness to yield ourselves in accord to thy gentlest invitation or thy sternest summons; through Jesus Christ our Lord. Amen.

OFFERTORY SENTENCE: "And this commandment have we from him, That he who loveth God love his brother also."

OFFERTORY PRAYER: We bless thee, our Father, that we can read and see the upward movement of the race in its blind, painful struggle toward light and freedom and truth. Help us to be helpers of men and of thy righteous kingdom. Accept our offering and bless us. In Christ's name we ask. Amen.

Illustrative Material

SEED THOUGHTS, HOMILETIC AND EXPOSITORY. Your way: I. Do you know your own way? Purpose? Where going? How are you going? II. Is it a comfort to you that God knows your way? III.

Do you meet with trials on the way? Sorrows? Storms? IV. Have you confidence in God as to these storms? Can you say, "He knoweth the way that I take"?—C. H. S.

The Good Man's Way: I. The good man's comfort lies in his relation to God. II. The good man's way. 1. It is the way God chooses for him. 2. It is the way of obedience to God's will. 3. It is the way God's Son has trod. 4. It is the way of self-sacrifice for others. III. God's knowledge of the good man's way. 1. He knows it because he knows all. 2. He knows it with a sympathetic interest. 3. He knows it when the path is darkest and roughest. 4. He knows whither it leads. IV. The outcome of the good man's trials. 1. God sees when discipline is needed. 2. He fixes its limits. 3. He guarantees the beneficial results. 4. This will be blessed and well in the end.— I. E. P.

Choice Illustrations on the Theme

THE ROAD OF LIFE. There was once an illiterate fellow who admitted his inability to read. He was not, however, without some accomplishment. "I kin read figgers," he said, "but not words. And when I see a road sign, I kin tell how fer, but not where to."

Obviously, his partial knowledge could do him little good. It would be of no value for him to know how far the road led, if he knew not the direction and destination. The Christian's knowledge of the road of life is of a different nature. He may not know, and he cannot know, how far. But he does know "where to," for the One he follows is himself "the Way." As you and I follow Christ, we have an invaluable knowledge—the direction and the destination. And we know this too: no matter how far, the Companion of the Way will be with us. —Rev. A. A. Amstutz.

WHITHER THE ROAD? David, the Lord's anointed, "made a road" into the land of the Philistines, the enemies of Israel, and dwelt there. He, who had just spared the life of his enemy, King Saul, soon became so like the people among whom he lived that he could go out against innocent nations without provocation, make war against them, and utterly destroy them.

It was a sorrowful day for David and for all his people when he "made that road" into the land of the Philistines, for it was the road that took him away from God. Thus it is today with every Christian who makes a road into the land of sin and disobeys the ways of God. "Whither have ye made a road today?" God is asking us. May it not be a road into the land of the Philistines, that land of sin and death, but rather may it lead to the presence of the Lord Jesus, opening a highway for peace and love and life.—Rev. Charles L. Ruhlen.

JESUS THE ROAD. There are roads that are obstacles to progress rather than means of progress. Dirt roads. And please put the emphasis on "dirt." Roads full of holes and bumps that throw you out of your seat if you are driving. Even when they lead to somewhere, you cannot be sure of getting there. You may break down on the way.

The purpose of a road is not only to guide you to some destination, but to make it easy for you to arrive. It is not a moving pavement. It will not carry you forward. But if you supply the energy, it will perform the function of a good road, reducing friction and helping you to go on with comfort.

Jesus, the way or the road, fulfills this ideal. He leads us to our destination, the goal of the soul. He takes the jar and the friction out of life if we keep in the way. One of his aims is to make life easy. "My yoke is easy," he said. And a yoke is to help us to haul the load.

Jesus' way of living is not only the best way; it is the happiest way, because it is the true way.

Of lost wanderers it is said, "They have gone out of the way." We invite friction, sorrow, disaster, when we leave him. The more we keep in the way,

the more harmonious, peaceful and happy will be the road of life for us, and the more progress shall we make toward our home.

Jesus is the way.—Robert P. Anderson.

THE END OF THE ROAD. A distinguished clergyman in a recent radio talk referred to a California road which begins among olive groves and eucalyptus trees, and ends in Death Valley. Many young people take a road without stopping to ask where it ends. At the start there are gaiety, laughter, song, excitement and thrills. It is hard to believe that it ends with the anguish of broken faith and blasted hopes, with shame, tears and despair.

The road you are taking seems very satisfactory today, but today is not all of life. Look ahead. Where does your road lead? Where will it end?—Young People's Weekly.

ROADS

Answer, soul of mine—which way
Hast thou made a road today?
Hast thou followed Love's sure chain
Over hill and over plain.
Whichsover choice thou'st made,
There another road is laid—
Not a transient, fading trail,
But a path that shall not fail.
Evermore some foot shall stray
O'er the road thou mad'st today.
Ah, let each of us beware
How his thoughts and motives bear!
Every road that we shall choose,
Other pilgrim feet, shall use.
Some will follow where we lead
Long as life shapes life, indeed.
Have a brother's care, and pray
God to mark thy road each day.
—Unidentified.

EVENING SERVICE

Theme: Heart's Desire.

TEXT: "As for me, it was in my heart to build a house unto the name of Jehovah my God." I Chron. 22:7 (A.S.V.).

I. A dream cherished by David. He

did not have it only in mind to build a temple; he had it in his heart. In mind a project remains cold and intellectual. The fervent longing of the heart "is pumped through every channel and passage of your being, permeating you through and through."

When David was prevented from building, because he was a man of war, his heart's desire kept him eagerly and patiently continuing the preparations for building. "He lived faithfully and prayerfully for the plan he was never to see fulfilled."

He kept the dream in the hearts of his contemporaries. He passed it on to his son. He would not permit hope to die. He kept this forever "in the imaginations of the hearts of thy people."

II. A dream commended by the Lord. The Lord said to David, "Thou didst well that it was in thy heart." Decorated with the order "Well done!" This is God cheering. Remember Browning's lines in "Rabbi Ben Ezra":

For thence,—a paradox
Which comforts while it mocks,—
Shall life succeed in that it seems to
    fail:
What I aspired to be,
And was not, comforts me:
A brute I might have been, but would
    not sink i' the scale.
        . . . . .
All I could never be,
All, men ignored in me,
This, I was worth to God, . . .

"We may never build that castle in Spain or that temple in Jerusalem but will you find its plans among your papers when we pass from these scenes of time? Will the great Discerner of the thoughts and interests of the heart say in the end of the day, 'It was well that it was in thine heart?' "

III. A dream fulfilled by David's Son. What compensation to the heart of David to know that a beloved son would put his hands to the task and build the temple after the pattern given him by his father. His own high dreams were in his son's eyes. The heart's desire of the father became the heart's desire of his son. It is a great thing to pass on the next generation the dream cherished in one's heart. It is then not cherished in vain.—H. L. S.

Illustration on the Theme

THE ASPIRING SOUL. Those who are in quest of the good life should read books on mountain climbing, for in mountaineering, as George Meredith wrote, "Every step is a debate between what you are and what you might become." Those who seek to scale some height of character know the nature of such debate.

Though men must ever seek to climb Mt. Everest that we may have the inspiration of their climbing, yet it may be well that the summits should never be reached. Then it can remain the symbol of that Mt. Everest of the soul, the character of Jesus Christ. Though we do not attain to the summit yet we are ever challenged to climb.

When George Leigh Mallory, who lost his life on the slope of Everest, spoke at Harvard Union, he said, "Someone is bound to ask me why I wish to climb to the top of Everest; my answer is, 'Because it is there!' "

We see the Christ stand: that life and character ever calls the aspiring soul to step one step upward from where he is to where he ought to be. "The higher climbers climb, the higher they want to climb."—M. K. W. H.

Suggestive Texts and Themes

Up, Up, for This Is the Day: "And Deborah said to Barak, Up; for this is the day." Judg. 4:14. I. Day of need. II. Day of opportunity. III. Day for strengthening the church. IV. Day for personal commitment, etc.

Jesus' Hands: "Lay thy hand upon her, and she shall live." Matt. 9:18.

The Iron Curtain: "Ye entered not in yourselves, and them that were entering ye hindered." Luke 11:52.

Quenched Lamps: "Our lamps are gone out." Matt. 25:8.

Partners of the Divine Joy: "Enter

thou into the joy of thy lord." Matt. 25:21.

Human Limitations of the Grace of God: "And they prayed, and said, Thou, Lord, who knowest the hearts of all men, show of these two the one whom thou hast chosen." Acts 1:24 (A.S.V.).

MIDWEEK FELLOWSHIP EVENING SERVICE

(Church Night or Suggested Sermon Subject)

Theme: Christian Zeal.

TEXT: "And your zeal hath provoked very many." II Cor. 9:2.

The Macedonian Christians had abounded in liberality to the extent of their power. They were poor, but their zeal had exerted much influence upon others. I. The nature of Christian zeal. 1. It is spiritual in its origin. 2. It is intellectual in its character. 3. It is modest and humble in its pretensions. 4. It is consistent and enduring in its influence. 5. It is diligent and active in its efforts. 6. It is kind and affectionate in its spirit. II. The spheres in which zeal may be exercised. They are numberless, but may be compressed under two statements: 1. In securing all the good within one's power. 2. In communicating all possible good to others. III. The principles on which zeal should be cultivated. 1. As an essential characteristic of true religion. 2. As the distinguishing trait of best men and angels. 3. As essential to the success and triumphs of the cause of Christ.

Cultivate zeal as a principle. Think of the greatness of the objects for zeal. Think of the limited period for our opportunities and endeavors.—B.

CHRISTIAN ENDEAVOR SOCIETY TOPIC

Mar. 7. Manners Attend Church, Too. Eccles. 5:1-7.

SUNDAY SCHOOL LESSON

Mar. 7. **Lord of Life and Death.** John 11:32-46.

MEMORY VERSE: "I am the resurrection, and the life; he who believes in me, though he die, yet shall he live, and whoever lives and believes in me shall never die." John 11:25 (R.S.V.).

Jesus restored Lazarus to light and love and life. All his restorations have these objects. Out of darkness we are brought into the light of day. The ties of love are drawn closer. Life is received more abundantly. This is so when the spiritually dead experience a resurrection.

Consider the marvellous confession of Martha's faith in verse 22 of this chapter, "I know, that even now, whatsoever thou wilt ask of God, God will give it thee." Mark the "even now"! Beautiful it is when a soul's most awful crises are the seasons of its most radiant faith! Beautiful it is when a lamp shines steadily in the tempest, and when our spiritual confidence remains unshaken. Beautiful it is when in our midnight men can hear the strains of the "even now"!—J. H. J.

SUNDAY: MARCH FOURTEENTH

MORNING SERVICE

Theme: Divine Discontent.

SUGGESTED SCRIPTURE READING: Phil. 3:1-16; Eph. 4:1, 14-16.

SELECTED HYMNS: "As pants the hart for cooling streams."—Anon. "Rise, my soul, and stretch thy wings."—R. Seagrave. "Forward! be our watchword."—H. Alford. "More love to thee, O Christ."—E. P. Prentiss. "So let our lips and lives express."—I. Watts.

CALL TO WORSHIP: "Praise ye the Lord. Sing unto the Lord a new song, and his praise in the congregation of saints. Let Israel rejoice in him that made him: let the children of Zion be joyful in their King."

INVOCATION PRAYER: Our Father, we remember on this Sabbath morning thy constant care in all the days of our life. Accept our thanks for these blessings. Help us to worship thee today in the beauty of holiness. May we enter thy sanctuary with glad and expectant hearts. We beseech thee to bless all the families of the earth with a Father's blessing. Look mercifully upon the solitary and the lonely, the weary and the heavy-laden, and grant them rest and peace and grace according to their day. Pity and relieve the sorrows of all mankind. Shed abroad the holy influence of this the Lord's day throughout our land and keep our whole people, with those who are chosen to govern it, in the way of wisdom and righteousness. We also commend to thy Fatherly goodness all who are near and dear to us, wherever they may be today, praying thee to watch over them, to provide for them, to bless them in body and soul, and at last bring them and us into the perfect and eternal joy of heaven; through Jesus Christ our Lord. Amen.

Theme: Divine Discontent.

TEXT: "As for me . . . I shall be satisfied, when I awake, with thy likeness." Ps. 17:15.

INTRODUCTORY: There are things with which it is our bounden duty as Christians to be dissatisfied. Such discontent is divine. Its function is to bring us into true relationship with God and with our fellows. All spiritual religion has its starting point in discontent.

I. First, every one of us ought to be dissatisfied with his or her present self. Our souls turn to God only as we have a profound sense of our moral failure. Because we are made in the Divine Image we cannot remain satisfied with the things of time and sense. Our lives may not be stained with heinous sins, but if we know ourselves at all, we are conscious that again and again we fail to exhibit the godliness revealed in Jesus Christ. We are not selfless. We are not forgiving. We are not completely dedicated to the purposes of God. We are not pure in thought. We are not disinterested even in our best deeds. We do not speak the absolute truth.

We may know this and be unconcerned about it, telling ourselves that we are no worse than others and a great deal better than some, but such complacency spells spiritual stagnation.

Are you so discontented with yourself that you are prepared to embark on a new spiritual adventure? Every un-Christlike thought, word and deed sends us back to him in disgust with ourselves. We can never be content until we awaken in his likeness.

II. Second, we ought to be dissatisfied with the religion of our fathers. Maybe that sounds extreme. But it was because Jesus was discontented with Judaism, in spite of much that was valuable therein, that we have Christianity today.

There is no ground for alarm when men and women are dissatisfied with the traditional expositions of some of the Christian doctrines. That is as it should be. The thought forms of the ages change. The only eternal fact is Jesus Christ himself.

It may be that your dissatisfaction with the religion of your fathers has other ramifications. You are discontented with the personnel and the witness of the church. Here again you are in harmony with Jesus. He, too, was dissatisfied with the church of his day. He strongly deplored the church's lack of interest in the outcast and the irreligious. Is that your discontent with the church? Go on being dissatisfied. Get others into a like state of mind and translate your discontent into a constructive adventure for the kingdom of God.

III. Third, we ought to be dissatisfied with any set of conditions which hinders the full development of human personalities. This has been a characteristic of a long role of men and women whom history acclaims as benefactors of our race. William Wilberforce, Zachary Macaulay, Granville Sharp, John Howard, Elizabeth Fry, Lord Shaftesbury, Octavia Hill—so we might go on. Are there not innumerable phases of national and international life which ought to make us discontented and rouse us to action? Ought we to be satisfied with a world where not more than one third have the slightest contact with Christianity and probably not more than 2 per cent are vitally Christian?

It has been a divine discontent with things as they are which in the past has impelled me to go forth in God's name and in his power to make the affairs of life more after the heavenly pattern. And he that sitteth on the throne said, "Behold, I make all things new." And the earnest Christian can never rest satisfied until he awakens to find its reality on earth.—N. C.

THEME PRAYER: Move us, our heavenly Father, through thy Holy Spirit, to extreme dissatisfaction with every past attainment in spiritual things. Grant to us increasingly to know that which is worth knowing, love that which is worth loving, do always that which is worth doing a little better and through every experience to grow in grace and knowledge of our Lord and Saviour. In whose name we ask it all. Amen.

OFFERTORY SENTENCE: "Bless the Lord, O my soul, and forget not all his benefits."

OFFERTORY PRAYER: O God, of whose bounty we have all received; accept this offering of thy people; and so follow it with thy blessing that it may promote peace and good will among men, and advance the kingdom of our Lord and Saviour Jesus Christ. Amen.

Illustrative Material

SEED THOUGHTS, HOMILETIC AND EXPOSITORY. Divine Dissatisfaction: I. There is no satisfaction in the things of this world. 1. From the nature of the world itself. 2. From the nature of the human mind. II. Satisfaction is realized in the service of God and in the possession of true religion. 1. Religion satisfies the intellect. 2. Religion satisfies the conscience. 3. Religion satisfies the heart.—T. S.

Blessed Satisfaction: I. There is a beatitude of the senses. II. There is a beatitude of the mind. We think. We study. We seek after truth and find it. III. There is a beatitude of the memory. IV. There is a beatitude of conscience. V. There is a beautitude of the heart.—A. S.

Present Satisfaction: I. The high present attainment of the real child of God. II. The interesting expectation. "I shall be satisfied." How much of that held now? III. The solemn assurance. "I shall." "I will." This is the vitality of religion.—J. I.

The opening phrase of this verse is expressive of a noble singularity. "As for me." Others may do otherwise, but "as for me" I will seek higher things. —J. H.

Choice Illustrations on the Theme

SPIRITUAL DISCERNMENT. It is said that a lady looking at one of Turner's pictures delineating some scene of nature, said to the artist, "Mr. Turner, I cannot see in nature what you put into your pictures." The artist's quiet answer was, "Don't you wish you could, madam?" Men of the world observe the raptures of Christian faith, and say with a sneer, "We cannot see such joys as these in religion." It takes the artist's eyes to see the glory of nature; it takes the opened eye of Christian faith to see the glories of God's spiritual kingdom. —*5,000 Best Modern Illustrations.*

AMBITION FOR SERVICE. When William Cary heard that his son Felix had become an ambassador, he simply said, "Felix has dribbled into an ambassador." Though the world would rank young Carey higher than his father, it would be well to remember that ambition for the honors of the world should be as nothing compared to ambition for wholehearted service for Christ.—*5,000 Best Modern Illustrations.*

FALSE AMBITION DEFEATED. When Napoleon marched after the retreating Russians as they led him as far as Moscow, he brought with him a marble statue of himself crowned with laurel, which he intended to erect in the most conspicuous position within the city to proclaim himself the world's conquerer. Providence, however, decreed that that piece of marble folly should become the property of Russia by military conquest, for Napoleon retreated through the deep snows, leaving 175,000 brave French soldiers scattered along the route. Today in the Kremlin museum the traveler is shown the marble statue to illustrate the vanity of selfish pursuits and mad ambitions. History brought upon Napoleon swift vengeance.

THE BUMBLEBEE CANNOT FLY. According to theory of aerodynamics and as may be readily demonstrated through laboratory tests and wind tunnel experiments, the bumblebee is unable to fly. This is because the size, weight and shape of his body, in relation to the total wing spread, makes flying impossible. But, the bumblebee, being ignorant of these profound scientific truths, goes ahead and flies anyway— and manages to make a little honey every day!

BE AMBITIOUS FOR CHARACTER. Be ambitious for knowledge. "If a man empties his purse into his head," writes Franklin, "no man can take it from him." But let us seek first knowledge of God, without whom we can never understand anything aright.

Livingstone is an example of a missionary ambitious to plant the cross in the hearts of the heathen world. All missionaries have been ambitious to win the world to Christ.

EVENING SERVICE

Theme: The Sigh of Jesus.

TEXT: "And looking up to heaven, he sighed." Mark 7:34.

INTRODUCTORY: We must not suppose that our Saviour had no bright and joyous hours on earth. The children of evil have no monopoly on happiness. Guilty happiness! There is no such thing. Why did Jesus sigh? "He sighed," but "looking up to heaven." He did not sigh because of helplessness, because he saw distress he could not cure.

I. We think first that his sigh was a sigh of sympathy. His love went out to the sufferer. It goes out to every sufferer.

II. In our conjecture we think that his sigh was one of prayer. Probably Jesus when here never did any great work without prayer. How much of the real force of prayer may have been concentrated in that sigh! We feel sure there was something like an ejaculatory prayer in this sigh of his soul.

III. We may think of his sigh also as a sigh of sorrow, showing the keenness with which our Saviour felt the evil of sin. It may be he sighed because there is so much trouble in the world everywhere, especially the trouble caused by sin, as also because of the poor work men make of overcoming it.

IV. There may have been in it the sigh of apprehension. What use will the man make of his restored faculties? His tongue has spoken no evil. His ears had heard no evil. What evil might he not now do with his tongue, or hear with his ears!

V. Why did he take the man aside? It is a great thing to be alone with nature, or to be alone with a man of noble heart. How much greater a matter to be alone with Jesus, "aside from the multitude." It would quicken the man's sense of individuality. God made us persons. We lose ourselves in the crowd. Having us alone Jesus awakens us. Alone with Jesus might awaken the man to his spiritual needs. "He touched him." Where? Ears and tongue. There the evil, there the cure. This same may have caused the man to concentrate all his hopes on Christ. Christ may have taken the man aside purely to get away from the multitude and to honor the man's privacy. That act would bind the man all the more strongly to Christ himself.

The touch of Christ! How important to us all!—H.

MIDWEEK FELLOWSHIP MEETING TOPIC

(Church Night or Suggested Sermon Subject)

Theme: Misunderstanding Jesus.

TEXT: "Are ye also yet without understanding?" Matt. 15:16.

The Master marveled more than once at the dullness of mind on the part of his hearers. It is true, he made use of picturesque imagery, which required thought for its complete elucidation. But his pictures do not obscure, they only explain the truth.

I. The language of Jesus does not demand expert literary interpretation. It is a wonder that people do not understand him better. Why are they troubled to understand his meaning, even to this day? Perhaps because "no man ever so spoke" before. The strikingly new is always more or less inexplicable. It is only the commonplace that is wholly intelligible.

II. The ideas of Jesus are so utterly unlike those with which the world is most familiar that he seems to speak a strange tongue. Even yet it is so! Religious truth is conventionally supposed to be mysterious and incomprehensible; the plain and simple statement of truth by Jesus must carry some dark mystery, which the man of the street cannot be expected to understand.

III. We stumble over his simplicity and, by obscurantist methods, keep the world in darkness. His own words are still and always will be the best revelation of his original mind.—W. L. G.

Suggestive Texts and Themes

The Fountain of Justice: "In that day shall the Lord of hosts be . . . for a spirit of judgment to him that sitteth in judgment." Isa. 28:5, 6.

The Possibilities of Manhood: "And a man shall be as an hidingplace from the wind, and a covert from the tempest; as rivers of water in a dry place, as the shadow of a great rock in a weary land." Isa. 32:2.

A Vain Conflict: "And I myself will fight against you with an outstretched hand and with a strong arm, even in anger, and in fury, and in great wrath." Jer. 21:5.

Lost: "For what doth it profit a man, to gain the whole world, and forfeit his life?" Mark 8:36 (A.S.V.).

Found: "For this my son was dead, and is alive again; he was lost, and is found." Luke 15:24.

CHRISTIAN ENDEAVOR SOCIETY TOPIC

Mar. 14. I Believe in God Our Father. Deut. 32:1-6; Isa. 46:8.

SUNDAY SCHOOL LESSON

Mar. 14. Jesus Faces the Cross. John 12:20-32.

MEMORY VERSE: "He who loves his life loses it, and he who hates his life in this world will keep it for eternal life." John 12:25 (R.S.V.).

"If you wish blessedness, head for service: if you wish the crown of joy, take up the cross of sacrifice; if life is to be yours, lose your life in other lives and in causes that have now your love. So far from seeing abundant living and sacrificial service as mutually exclusive, see one as the road to the other."—H. E. F.

This lesson anticipates the experience of Jesus in Gethsemane and reveals his understanding of the final issue of his message and ministry.

SUNDAY: MARCH TWENTY-FIRST

MORNING SERVICE

Theme: The Realm of Silence (Lent).

SUGGESTED SCRIPTURE READING: Ps. 46:1-11; Ps. 85:6-13.

SELECTED HYMNS: "Calm me, my God, and keep me calm."—H. Bonar. "My faith looks up to thee."—R. Palmer. "Sometimes a light surprises."—W. Cowper. "O Light whose beams illumine all."—E. H. Plumptre. "O God of truth, whose living Word."—T. Hughes.

CALL TO WORSHIP: "God is a Spirit: and they that worship him must worship him in spirit and in truth." "Let the words of my mouth, and the meditations of my heart, be acceptable in thy sight, O Lord, my strength, and my Redeemer."

INVOCATION PRAYER: By our awareness of thy presence in this house lift us, O Lord, above the ordinary levels of our lives. By our consciousness of the presence of our friends and loved ones may we feel ourselves bound up in the bundle of humanity. By the knowledge of ourselves, our own need, our aspirations, our strength and our weakness, our faults and failures and sins may we lean hard upon the Saviourhood and friendship of Christ. Send us forth, O God, to live on a higher level of daily living than ever before. We ask all in the name of Christ.—Amen.—M. K. W. H.

Theme: The Realm of Silence (Lent).

TEXT: "Be still, and know that I am God." Ps. 46:10.

INTRODUCTORY: The realm of silence—do we know anything about it? I have seen in Bombay, India, in a quiet grove, the Parsee Temple of Silence. In these days of push and rush and roar is it possible to get any appreciation of the calm and unruffled and retired spaces of existence? The lenten season gives opportunity for this. Let us remember that all depths are silent, depths of space as well as depths of thought.

I. Nature is to a great degree silent. The depths of the sea are a great calm. The air above us and the stratosphere are silent. The earth itself is not noisy. When we "lift up our eyes unto the hills" and incline our ears, the hills are mute. Yet how they do speak of God! Not earth, but only city streets and highways drown out silence. The mountains and the deserts, the heights and the depths, are silent.

II. Growth is silent. Without noise a garden clothes itself with beauty or an orchard with fruitfulness. The human body grows without the creaking of joints or the rattle of bones. Growth is in silence.

III. Love in its deeper expression is silent. The unspoken word is often more eloquent than the spoken. Extreme emotions of all kind are silent. The divinest Gift that was ever made was in a quiet night at Bethlehem underneath the silent stars.

IV. Great power is silent. God's power is not noisy. It is held in by righteousness and love. It is harnessed to great and constructive purposes of good will and peace. A bomb did not explode at Bethlehem, a Baby was born! "Be still, and know that I am God."

V. We must keep silent spaces in our hearts wherein the stillness God may become known. "Be still, and know." It does not come from effort. It comes from reposefulness. There are some forms of knowledge which necessitate stillness. Self-knowledge, God-knowledge—these can never be had until we have learned to be still. This does not mean the stillness of indolence, or indifference, or of stoicism and despair, but of humility, observation, expectation. 1. It means keep near to God. 2. It means keep ready. 3. It means keep still. 4. It means keep expectant.

The late Rev. Dr. John Henry Jowett well said of knowledge through silence, "'Be still, and know.' How can God give us visions when life is hurrying at a precipitate rate? I have stood in the National Gallery [London] and have seen people gallop round the chamber and glance at twelve of Turner's pictures in the space of five minutes. Surely we might say to such trippers, 'Be still, and know Turner!' Gaze quietly at one little bit of cloud or at one branch, or at one wave of the sea, or at one ray of the drifting moon. 'Be still, and know Turner.' But God has difficulty in getting us still. This is perhaps why he has sometimes employed the ministry of dreams. Men have had 'visions in the night.' In the daytime I have a diviner visitor in the shape of some worthy thought, or nobler impulse, or hallowed suggestion, but I am in such feverish haste that I do not heed it, and pass along. I do not 'turn aside to see this great thing,' and so I lose the heavenly vision. If I would know more of God I must relax the strain and moderate the pace. I must 'be still.'"—H. With acknowledgement to M. K. W. H.

THEME PRAYER: Our Father in heaven, we would hear thy voice and know thy meaning. Amid the din of traffic, the din of rival cries, may we be still and know that thou art God. May we hearken to thy words of assurance and hope, of warning and correction, of help on the way. We ask in Christ's name. Amen.

OFFERTORY SENTENCE: "Now ye have consecrated yourselves unto the Lord, come near and bring sacrifices and thank offerings into the house of the Lord."

OFFERTORY PRAYER: We would remember the grace of the Lord Jesus that though he was rich yet for our sakes he became poor, that we through his poverty might be made rich. Help us therefore to count it a great privilege, our Father, in his name and for his sake to bring our offerings this day for the support and extension of his kingdom in the world. Bless the gifts and the givers. We ask in Jesus' name. Amen.—H.

Illustrative Material

SEED THOUGHTS, HOMILETIC AND EXPOSITORY. Be Still, and Know: I. There is implication of resistance. When it is said, "Be still," resistance, turbulence, commotion are implied. We sometimes rebel against the dispensations of Providence. II. There is also an assertion of supremacy. "Know that I am God." III. There is the claim of submission. "Be still." Be silent and submissive.—J. P.

"Be Still": I. The command is assuring. Fear not for the ark, for the kingdom, for yourself. God will not fail. II. Why we need this injunction. 1. On account of our ignorance and presumption. We see but a fragment of God's design and work. If we saw the whole campaign and consummation! 2. On account of the haste and rashness of our judgment. 3. On account of our conclusions without taking God into account. III. The stillness enjoined.

Not that of indolence, inaction, indifference. IV. See God in all, bringing forth judgment unto victory.—H. R.

Choice Illustrations on the Theme

BE STILL AND KNOW. We live in an age of hurry. Life that was formerly likened to a journey, a voyage or a pilgrimage has become a race, a chase, in which not bit and bridle but spurs and whip are deemed the rider's best equipment. A railway train or an airplane should be the emblem on our shield, with the motto "Hurry!" Haste has entered into possession of us. We are hurried so fast that we have no time to "be still, and know God," no place quiet enough to read our Bibles or say our prayers. Character is not a blow struck once, but a growth. And we see this same forcing method in education. Everything must be done rapidly. We have short twelve-lesson modes of learning. "Be still, and know."—A. A. Livermore.

BE STILL, AND BELIEVE. There is a repose of faith. It is not easy to be still in this rough and restless world. Be still, and believe. In all the more delicate cases of surgery the success of the operation is hardly more dependent upon the skill of the practitioner than it is upon the quietness and self-control of the patient. To suppress all irritability and nervous alarms; to submit in entire reliance to the course of discipline recommended; to endure pain without flinching, and to encourage as far as possible every hopeful impression—all these conduce directly to a happy issue.—T. Ainger.

IMPORTANCE OF STILLNESS. A speech by one of our country's most eloquent men was being broadcast. But the young people in the MacGillvary home were busy playing a new game. Father came in an hour later and said, "I suppose you all heard the speech tonight?" "No," they said. "Well, you missed something, let me tell you." There had been a great voice in the room that night, but not one there heard it. There is a price for everything, and the price they would have had to pay was to be still and listen. There are voices calling to us all the time, and above all the Great Voice that speaks to us in the silence of our own hearts. Are we missing the Voice because we do not pay the price of keeping still and listening? "Be still, and know that I am God."—*Forward*.

GOD'S VOICE

Man's voice I know
Through chatt'ring market and roar of mill,
But silent as the flakes of snow,
God's voice is still.
　　　　　　　　—Samuel Adams.

THE IMPORTANCE OF SILENCES. A professor in one of our theological seminaries poses this question to his students: "Have you control over your silences?" To this we might add: "Is there any silence in your lives?" Bishop Francis J. McConnell tells of an acquaintance in New England who excelled as a lifesaver at a coastal emergency station. He was the trainer of a group of young men who came to have marvellous powers of selective listening. As they patrolled the shores they could detect above the pounding of the waves and roar of the winds any sound of human significance. And in the event of distress they dispatched to the scene all the resources of the United States Government within their reach, rescuing many from danger of death. So we need to be alert to hear the still small voice of God as he speaks amid the world tumult, and to hearken to those words that direct us into the paths that he would have us follow.—Rev. John M. Rast.

EVENING SERVICE

Theme: Ill-timed Sleep (Lent).

TEXT: "Let us not sleep, as do others." I Thess. 5:6.

INTRODUCTORY: This caution was addressed to Christians. It is a suitable Lenten caution. It reminds us of some reasons why Christians should not sleep. God has done more for us than for others. And Christians have made promises to God which others have not made. God has made to them great and precious promises which he has not made to others. While Christians sleep the enemy is busy and sinners perish. Life is the time for work. "Let us not sleep, as do others."

I. For such sleep is an indication of ingratitude. Our Saviour has left us work to do and there is but little time in which to do it.

II. Sleep is too often an indication of indifference and thoughtlessness. Of the businessman who lets his opportunities slip by we say, "He must be asleep." The Christian is no less foolish who is asleep spiritually and lets his religious opportunities slip by. He who sleeps in harvest is a fool. A drowsy Christian is an anomaly.

III. The sleep of indolence and inaction is even more blameworthy. Think how many of the Scripture emblems of the Christian life give support to the necessity for activity, earnestness and diligence. Examples: the sower, the worker, the builder. The unadvancing Christian is a practical contradiction.

IV. The sleep of the Christian is a state of insecurity. While the husbandman slept the enemy sowed tares. While the Christian sleeps his treasures fall a prey to the robber. When did you lose your influence and position in the church? When you slept, were backslidden, were fallen from grace. Sleep not as did those disciples who went with Christ to the garden. Sleep not as did Jonah in the ship. Sleep not as did Sisera when Jael slew him. Sleep not as did Samson when his locks were shorn and his strength ebbed away. Sleep not as did those when the enemy came and sowed tares. Sleep not as did the ten virgins while the bridegroom came and the door was shut. Sleep not as did Solomon's sluggard hour after hour. Sleep not as did the fabled Argus of the hundred eyes whose life was the penalty.

V. All that has been said and these examples serve to give emphasis to the Christian's duty of watchfulness, the folly of ill-timed-sleep. All unwatchfulness implies a sad awakening. Watch against thine own sin. Watch for the doing of good. Watch in duties and watch after duties. When the garden is dressed and the seed sown it still needs to be watched against loss through enemies or neglect. Watch! "Let us not sleep, as do others." "It is high time to awake out of sleep!"—H.

Suggestive Texts and Themes

Listening to God: "I will hear what God the Lord will speak: for he will speak peace unto his people." Ps. 85:8.

Quiet Times: "In returning and rest shall ye be saved; in quietness and in confidence shall be your strength." Isa. 30:15.

A Balanced Life: "And Jesus increased in wisdom and stature, and in favour with God and man." Luke 2:52.

The Abiding Record of Sin in our Physical Natures: "His bones are full of the sin of his youth, which shall lie down with him in the dust." Job 29:11.

The Worldling's Faulty Estimate of the Spiritual Man: "Wherefore came this mad fellow to thee?" II Kings 9:11.

The Forces of the Universe against Wrong: "The stars in their courses fought against Sisera." Judg. 5:20.

MIDWEEK FELLOWSHIP MEETING TOPIC

(Church Night or Suggested Sermon Subject)

Theme: The Prayer-hearing God.

TEXT: "In my distress I cried unto the Lord, and he heard me." Ps. 120:1.

What a frank, comforting statement. I believe a great part of the distress we have to endure is due to the fact that we do not look upon our Father as being near at hand.

I. If God has simply set the machinery of the universe in motion, and then stands idly by, what can it all matter to you and me? But if, on the other hand, he is still working in his world, if he knows our frame and remembers that we are dust, and if, in all his wonderful plans, he is planning for us, then the whole perspective changes.

II. Now, I feel convinced that the Psalmist had somehow gotten a firm conviction that God was very near him. The "sharp arrows of the mighty" were pressing him sorely. He desired peace, but war was thrust upon him; even friends had turned from him. And then he did the wise thing: in his distress he took the matter to the Lord, who heard and helped him.

III. Do you believe that God hears your prayer for help? Your need is pressing, sore. You feel a sense of isolation, and like one of old you cry, "Oh that I knew where I might find him!" But have you ever thought that God is as eager to "find" you as you are to find him? And when again you pray, speak to your Father as one who is near at hand, and he will hear, and hearing, will help.—I. D. L.

CHRISTIAN ENDEAVOR SOCIETY TOPIC

Mar. 21. I Believe in Jesus Christ Our Saviour. I Pet. 1:18-21; Acts 4:12.

SUNDAY SCHOOL LESSON

Mar. 21. Jesus' New Commandment. John 13:12-17, 34-35; 14:21-24.

MEMORY VERSE: "A new commandment I give to you, that you love one another; even as I have loved you, that you also love one another." John 13:34 (R.S.V.)

These words derive impressiveness from having been spoken at the last Supper, and on the eve of the Great Sacrifice. The Commandment of Love issued appropriately at the time of the Feast of Love, and not long before the great Act of Love. For the love of Christ was no fine *saying*: it cost him his life to say these words with meaning, "As I have loved you."—F. W. R.

"Within the Christian fellowship each is to be linked to each by a love like that of Christ for each. That is the new commandment and obedience to it is to be the evidence to the world of true discipleship." What if the church were really like that?

SUNDAY: MARCH TWENTY-EIGHTH

MORNING SERVICE

Theme: The Story of Demas (Lent).

SUGGESTED SCRIPTURE READING: John 6:58-71.

SELECTED HYMN:. "Oh for a closer walk with God."—W. Cowper. "Depth of mercy! can there be."—C. Wesley. "Come, Holy Spirit, heavenly Dove."—I. Watts. "O thou, the contrite sinner's Friend."—C. Elliott. "O Jesus, Saviour of the lost."—E. H. Bickerseth.

CALL TO WORSHIP: "Thus saith the Lord: O Israel, thou shalt not be forgotten of me. I have blotted out, as a thick cloud, thy transgressions, and, as a cloud, thy sins: return unto me; for I

have redeemed thee. And ye shall seek me, and find me, when ye shall search for me with all your heart."

INVOCATION PRAYER: O God, give us a vision of thyself today. For this is life eternal, to know thee, the only true God, and Jesus Christ whom thou hast sent. Help us to hide in the cleft of the rock and hear, if nothing more, the rustle of thy garment as thou passeth by. Unveil thy beauty in the face of thine only begotten Son. Show us thy love, the love that passeth knowledge; thy justice and righteousness which are as the high mountains; thy holiness before which angels and archangels veil their faces. Help us to abhor our sins and find the healing comfort of thy grace. Make us grateful for all thy mercies and patient under thy chastening hand. If ever life seems hard and lonely, show us the things which thou hast prepared for them that love thee. Make us brave to live and willing in thy time to enter on the life eternal. Enlarge our hearts to think of others. Bless all whose lot is harder than ours. Remember those who have no Gospel. Reclaim the wandering. Glorify thyself in thy church and in the triumphs of thy grace. In Jesus' name we ask. Amen.—D. J. B.

Theme: The Story of Demas (Lent).

TEXTS: Philomen 24; Col. 4:14; II Tim. 4:10.

INTRODUCTORY: In three of his epistles the Apostle Paul mentioned Demas, and in these three allusions Paul has given us the outline of a story that is all too familiar.

I. In his letter to Philemon the apostle spoke of Demas with warm appreciation, referring to him as "Demas, my fellow-laborer." Demas was evidently an ardent disciple, active in spreading the Gospel of Christ.

Few men have enjoyed such spiritual advantages as were granted to Demas. He was the intimate friend of the greatest Christian of his time. He was Paul's cherished companion. Often he heard the great apostle preach. He prayed with him and came under the spell of his radiant personality. To be so closely associated with a great Christian is a priceless privilege. Many of us recognize a boundless debt to Christian parents, teachers or friends whose lives have revealed to us more eloquently than words ever could the transforming power of the Gospel of Christ.

II. But in Paul's letter to the Colossians we find a second reference to Demas that is strangely devoid of commendation. The apostle merely mentions the name of Demas. That is all. This would not seem significant except that Paul was a very gracious person. He was richly endowed with the grace of appreciation. When he mentioned a fellow worker he usually said something pleasant about him. It was so in this connection. Of one and another the apostle expressed grateful appreciation, which is the mark of a generous spirit, and a good habit to acquire. But of Demas Paul said nothing.

The fellow laborer had become merely Demas. In the light of what was to come, perhaps we may say that the active church worker had become just a nominal member of the church. It is surprising how often that happens. Many churches have rolls of inactive members, some of whom in other days were zealous workers. Their names are still on the church roll, but they no longer count in the life of the church.

III. But there is another chapter in the story of Demas. In the last of Paul's letters, the second epistle to Timothy, the apostle says, "Demas hath forsaken me, having loved this present world." Demas the backslider had become Demas the deserter. The nominal Christian had dropped out altogether. It is a perfectly logical sequence. When Demas the fellow laborer became just Demas, he was already on the way out.

How did it happen? What got into this one-time fellow laborer of the great apostle that he so ingloriously fell away? Paul says it was the love of this present world.

When the apostle warns against the danger of loving this present world, he is not inviting us to close our eyes to the beauties of nature, or to shut ourselves in a hermit's cell. He is warning us against the temptation to live for the things that are sensual rather than the things that are spiritual. He is warning us against loving pleasures and possessions more than we love Christ and the things of the kingdom of heaven. Our only sure protection against the tragic fate of Demas is to keep very close to our Lord.—Henry Wade DuBose, D.D.

THEME PRAYER: Come, Holy Spirit, come. Open our ears to hear thy voice. And make us obedient, walking in the light thou givest until the day break and the shadows flee away; in Jesus' name we ask. Amen.

OFFERTORY SENTENCE: "Render therefore unto Caesar the things which are Caesar's, and unto God the things that are God's."

OFFERTORY PRAYER: We praise thee, O God, from whom all blessings flow, for great has been thy mercy toward us. Great therefore may be our gratitude, and great our response to every call of need. Wilt thou accept and bless our offerings of this morning and use them for the upbuilding of thy kingdom. In Christ's name we ask. Amen.

Illustrative Material

SEED THOUGHTS, HOMILETIC AND EXPOSITORY. Demas: I. His previous history. Philem. 24; Col. 4:14. II. His subsequent faithlessness—falling away. III. The cause. His temporal interests.— T. J. C.

Demas the Deserter: I. What do we know concerning Demas? 1. He was no hypocrite. 2. Nor was he a timid follower of Jesus. 3. Nor was he moved by a passing flow of enthusiasm. 4. Nor was it that he had no religious opportunities and fellowship. II. What was it that ruined him? 1. Was it avarice? 2. Was it love of pleasure? 3. Was it a gradual process of spiritual neglect? 4. Here is the black record: "Demas hath forsaken me, having loved this present world." Demas, thou hast made a bad bargain!—M. G. P.

Worldliness is fatal to religion.—S. C.

The relapsed Christian reminds us of the piteous spectacle of a man emerging from the watery element in which he has been plunged, and for a moment gaining a footing upon the shore, but caught by the returning wave or losing his hold he is once more carried into the deep water with the danger of being finally engulfed, unless by another strenuous effort he should regain the shore and reach a standing above the power of the surge.—J. L.

Choice Illustrations on the Theme

THE APOSTASY OF DEMAS. In the long line of the Doges in the grand old palace in Venice one space is empty, and the black curtain that covers it attracts more attention than any of the fine portraits of the merchant kings. From that panel, now so unsightly, once smiled the sallow face of Marino Falieri, afterward found guilty of treason against the state, and blotted out, so far as might be, from remembrance. The story of Demas reveals the fate of one who filled a much more honored place, and who, yielding to temptation, sank to a still lower depth. Poor, foolish Demas has gained for himself a most unenviable notoriety.—J. N. Norton, D.D.

WHAT KIND OF CHRISTIAN SOLDIER? In the second letter to Timothy, his friend and son in the faith, Paul says, "Thou therefore endure hardness, as a good soldier of Jesus Christ" (II Tim. 2:3). If I were a soldier, and if a battle were impending, and if I were to leave my place in the ranks and go to the rear because the captain of my company did not speak to me when he passed yesterday, or because a lieutenant did speak to me and spoke ungraciously, or because a sergeant hurt my feelings by something he said or did or left unsaid or undone, or because a comrade trod on my sensitive toes—if I were to throw down my arms and go to the rear, what sort of a soldier should I be? Yet have we not known "Christian soldiers" to do just such things?

If a soldier were to absent himself from drill, absent himself habitually and without good reason; if he were to neglect to study the book of tactics, the manual of arms; if he were to criticize his officers in the presence of other soldiers, and thus implant the seeds of dislike or distrust in their minds; if he were in a perpetual state of discontent because the captain did not consult him as to the plans of the campaign; if the army needed recruits, and if this soldier never said to any man, "Come, enlist and bear arms for the cause"; if, by his half-heartedness, he repelled possible recruits, and if he were to attempt to excuse himself by saying, "I am only a nominal soldier anyhow, and I do not pretend to be more," we should have a perfect right to say to him, "You are no soldier at all; you are simply playing soldier; mount a broomstick and gallop away!" A "nominal Christian" indeed! Is there such a thing? Who cares to consult a "nominal tailor," or to eat a dinner prepared by a "nominal cook"? Just how far could one travel on a "nominal train" and how much money would one care to keep in a "nominal bank"? A "nominal Christian" is no Christian at all.—Charles C. Albertson, D.D.

LOSING GOD. The late Rev. F. S. Miller, missionary in Korea, illustrating how a man may lose his consciousness of God, tells of an old native man and his son who were on a train going to Seoul. When they looked for their railway ticket it could not be found. The conductor said he would come through again and for them to keep up their search. They hunted through their clothing and baggage and scolded each other. Finally, the son opened up his underclothing and there in a secret pocket, wrapped up in paper, he found the ticket, all safe and sound. "When you feel you have lost God, do not search the heavens above or the earth beneath, just look in your heart," said Mr. Miller.

REDISCOVERY OF CHRIST. A collector of art treasures visited an old art store in London and, browsing about, he found a stack of old paintings and prints in a neglected corner of the dingy shop. He rummaged carelessly through the pile of worthless pictures until suddenly his trained eyes settled upon a stained and dirty old canvas. All the rest he abandoned quickly and asked the price of this particular one. It was only a pittance; he bought it and rushed to have it cleaned. As the grime and dirt of many a year was washed away the value that the trained eye had seen at first was clearly visible to all. Here was a priceless masterpiece of the living Christ that had been lost and lay forgotten in a dark, neglected corner!

Oh, that we could make such a discovery for ourselves today! Oh, that we could clear from his image the dimming haze of accumulated familiarity and prejudice! My soul, go again, take a fresh look at the Jesus of the gospels.—W. Howard Lee.

Suggestive Lenten Texts and Themes

The Lenten Resolution: "I will be sorry for my sin." Ps. 38:18.

How to Meet Temptation: "Watch and pray, that ye enter not into temptation." Matt. 26:41.

The Realm of Silence: "Be still, and know that I am God." Ps. 46:10.

Having a Form of Godliness: "Having a form of godliness, but denying the power thereof." II Tim. 3:5.

Sin and Separation: "They went to Baalpeor, and separated themselves unto that shame." Hos. 9:10.

EVENING SERMON

Theme: Hiding from God (Lent).

TEXT: "I heard thy voice in the garden, and I was afraid, because I was naked; and I hid myself." Gen. 3:10.

INTRODUCTORY: "Where art thou?" This is the first question in the Bible. It was addressed by God to the first man, and as the result of the first sin. It was a very important question for Adam. It is an important question for us. "Where art thou?" It came from Adam's act in hiding from God.

I. His hiding was a proof of his guilt. 1. His haste to make excuse was an evidence of guilt. Consciousness of evil leads to self-condemnation. 2. His confession of fear proved his guilt. "I was afraid." A child who has done wrong dreads his parent. 3. Adam's morbid moral sensitiveness proved his guilt. "I was naked." "Who told you that thou wert naked?" We cannot escape the chiding of conscience. In hiding after sin Adam represents the average sinner.

II. His vain expedient for escape. "I hid myself." This attempt at concealment on the part of our first parents furnishes a striking example of the dreadfulness of sin. Now with the taint of guilt upon them, they were ready to believe in the efficacy of any subterfuge. They assumed that the mere shade of leaves could conceal them from the eyes of God!

III. What are some common expedients of our more modern days? Among the trees of our gardens! 1. One of the most common of our expedients is complete thoughtlessness, refusal to think. "Forget God." But it is never complete or there would be no conscious hiding. 2. Another is pleasure. Its whirl. 3. The occupations of life furnish another retreat for man when fleeing from God. Man works, works hard that he may hide himself deep. 4. Moralities and forms of religion form other hiding places.

Sin cannot escape from God. Sin cannot stand before God. Sin may find compassion from God. There are two kinds of retreats. The sinner's retreat: thoughtlessness, pleasures, occupations, moralities, forms and observances of religion. The second is the saint's retreat: "I flee unto Thee to hide me."

MIDWEEK FELLOWSHIP MEETING TOPIC

(Church Night or Suggested Sermon Subject)

Theme: Steps to Self-culture.

TEXT: "But ye, beloved, building up yourselves on your most holy faith, praying in the Holy Spirit, keep yourselves in the love of God. . . ." Jude 20, 21 (A.S.V.).

I. "Building up yourselves." Become better human beings, with robust health of body, mind and spirit.

II. "On your most holy faith." Dwell upon positive, not negative ideas. Doubt destroys; faith builds up.

III. "Praying in the Holy Spirit."

This means praying with deep sincerity and purposefulness. A flowing stream keeps more healthful than a stagnant pool. So a praying faith keeps fresh and wholesome.

IV. "Keep yourselves in the love of God." Avoid the lowlands of hatred and bitterness and keep your thoughts and purposes in the bracing mountain air of divine love. Keep in love with nature, humanity, life, but above all, with God and his unfailing love.

CHRISTIAN ENDEAVOR SOCIETY TOPIC

Mar. 28. I Believe in the Holy Spirit Our Guide. John 14: 16-26; Acts 2:1-6.

SUNDAY SCHOOL LESSON

Mar. 28. The Guidance of the Spirit. John 16:1-13.

MEMORY VERSE: "When the Spirit of truth comes, he will guide you into all the truth." John 16:13 (A.S.V.).

Verse 14 continues, "He will glorify me, for he will take what is mine and declare it to you." How marvelously these words are fulfilled as we read the things which belong to Christ in the Gospels! The Spirit takes the things which pertain to Christ and makes them effective in the lives of men.

We have reasons to believe that the Spirit fulfills this function not only through direct action in our conscious lives, as for example through our consciences, but also in the depths of personality where the springs of life are found. In the secret places of our deepest selves the Spirit takes the things that pertain to Christ and makes them effective unto eternal life. God is not only the God who created us; not only the God who redeemed us; but, if we let him have his way in us, he is the God who perfects us.

SUNDAY: APRIL FOURTH

MORNING SERVICE

Theme: Why Don't People Find God? (Lent).

SUGGESTED SCRIPTURE READING: Acts 17: 22-34; Ps. 27:7-14.

SELECTED HYMNS: "O thou the contrite sinner's Friend."—C. Elliott. "Approach, my soul, the mercy seat."—J. Newton. "O Jesus, Saviour of the lost."—E. H. Bickerseth. "Take me, O my Father, take me."—R. Palmer. "The King of Love my Shepherd is."—H. W. Baker.

CALL TO WORSHIP: "Seek ye the Lord while he may be found, call ye upon him while he is near: Let the wicked forsake his way, and the unrighteous man his thoughts: and let him return unto the Lord, and he will have mercy upon him; and to our God, for he will abundantly pardon."

INVOCATION PRAYER: At the dawn of this new Sabbath, Lord, our souls would return to their rest. Wilt thou put the world far from us and receive us into the secret place of thy pavilion, where thou hast promised to commune with those who seek thee. Our souls wait for thee, O Lord; yea, more than they that watch for the morning. Be pleased to make thy presence known. We do believe that thou art here, nearer than hands or feet and closer than breathing. May all blessings come with thee. And help us now to yield ourselves wholly unto thee. We ask in Jesus' name. Amen.

Theme: Why Don't People Find God? (Lent).

TEXT: "Oh that I knew where I might find him!" Job 23:3.

INTRODUCTORY: The greatest quest on which man has ever embarked is the search for God. Why don't people find him?

I. One reason we do not find him is because we do not take time. We do not give our search for God a sufficiently high priority.

II. A second reason God does not seem real is because we consider the essence of religion as in not doing certain things. But no one has ever found God because of what he did not do. There are, of course, certain things in which no Christian can engage. But fundamentally Christianity is a positive religion. It gives us power to do something and to be something. The "thou shalt not" phase is necessary as far as it goes, but alone it never led anyone into the presence of God.

III. A third reason we fail in our quest is because we make our search for God an extension of our own selfishness. Instead of really wanting God we want material blessings for ourselves. Instead of being the chief end of our lives, God becomes a means we try to use for our own interests. There is acute danger in such fair-weather religion. If the dominant drive in our religion is to minister to our own selfish, material needs, God will never be real to us.

IV. The next reason is even more basic. We do not find God because we are not in earnest about our search for him. The reason we are not desperate is because we have a suspicion we can get along fairly well without God. God will not be to us a mere luxury. He must be the chief passion of our life. Perhaps we have not found God, because we have not been in dead earnest about him.

V. But there is a more fundamental reason yet why God is not real to many. Too often we are not ready to make the moral commitments he demands. We would like to have the blessing of his presence, to see him in the beauty of the sunset and the dignity and symbolism of the church worship, but we are not ready to live as he wants us to live.

Much of so-called intellectual doubt is fundamentally an unwillingness to live up to God's moral demands. It is much easier in a college dormitory to argue about what we think of God than honestly to face the question, "What does God think of us?"

God will never be real to us till we surrender our lives wholly to his will. Jesus said to those who doubted him, "If any man will do his will, he shall know of the doctrine." It is not the man who stands off and seeks an intellectual solution to his doubts who finds God, but the man who has made the supreme act of commitment to Christ as his leader.

These are some of the reasons why people do not find God. But more important than our search for God is his search for us. The essence of Christianity is not man's pitiful, stumbling climb to God, but God so loved us he sent to us his only begotten Son, that we might not perish. Behold, he stands at the door of our hearts and knocks. —Rev. William B. Ward.

THEME PRAYER: Lord, help us to realize that we belong to two worlds, and that they are not far apart. Let our conversation be in heaven. Keep our hearts open to the approach of all goodness and closed to the allurements of sin. May be be prepared for whatsoever thou hast prepared for us. Enable us to live as heirs of thy salvation and the praise of that salvation shall be thine forever. Amen.

OFFERTORY SENTENCE: "And whatsoever ye do, do it heartily, as to the Lord, and not unto men."

OFFERTORY PRAYER: Teach us, our Father, in all our giving to thee to give not alone with our hands and of our goods, but from our hearts and with our spirits. May we be eager to bless others with gifts of love and good will. It is with desire to be helpers of thy kingdom that we bring our offerings this morning. Wilt thou graciously accept and bless and use them in the hastening of thy kingdom. We ask in Christ's name. Amen.—H.

Illustrative Material

SEED THOUGHTS, HOMILETIC AND EXPOSITORY. Craving for God: "Oh, that I knew," etc. I. Job asking the deepest question of life. II. If it be true, as it is true, that man has ever sought God, it is a deeper fact still that God has ever sought man. The deep of man's desire has been answered by the deep of God's mercy.—H. B.

Search for God: I. What a longing! What a search! The search for God. II. The search rewarded.—T. M. H.

Search for God: I. Job's condition. II. Job's desire. III. His resolution. IV. His confidence and expectation.—W. J.

Man Desiring God: God comes only into the heart that wants him. Do I really, with my whole heart, desire to find God, and to give myself wholly into his hands?—J. P.

The Soul's Inquiry after God: I. The need of the soul for a personal God. II. The soul in search after a personal God. III. The perplexity of the soul in its search for God. IV. The secret confidence of the soul in the personal God it seeks.—T. H.

Choice Illustrations on the Theme

AUGUSTINE'S LONGING FOR GOD. O Truth, Truth, how did the marrow of my soul pant after thee! They sounded out thy name to me, but it was but a voice. As fictitious dishes served up to one in hunger, so instead of thee they served up to me the sun and moon, thy beauteous works, but not thyself, and I fed upon them, but was not nourished, but famished. For I hungered and famished, not so much after thy works, but after thee thyself, the Truth, with whom there is no variableness, neither shadow of turning.—Augustine.

THE CRAVING FOR GOD. That tragic blindness of the soul to beauty, the beauty of nature and the beauty of holiness, may be illustrated by quoting from Wordsworth's well-known poem, "Peter Bell":

He roved among the vales and streams,
In the green wood and hollow dell.
They were his dwellings night and day—
But Nature ne'er could find the way
Into the heart of Peter Bell . . .
A primrose by the river's brim,
A yellow primrose was to him,
And it was nothing more.

Compare now Wordsworth's own response:

My heart leaps up when I behold
A rainbow in the sky:
So was it when my life began:
So is it now I am a man:
So be it when I shall grow old,
Or let me die.

The heart that "leaps"—that is life's great possession. "The object of life," says Augustine, "is to possess the vision of God."—James Burns.

A LISTENING SOUL. As the flowers follow the sun, and silently hold up their petals to be tinted and enlarged by its shining, so must we, if we would know the joy of God, hold our souls, wills, hearts and minds still before him whose voice commands, whose love warms, whose truth makes fair our whole being. God speaks for the most part in such silence only. If the soul be full of tumult and jangling voices, his voice is little likely to be heard.—A. Maclaren.

FINDING GOD IN MEDITATION. I have a friend who taught school in India. One day he went to call on an Indian businessman who was a Christian. His wife told him he was out—that he had gone up into the hills for a few days to think over the doctrine of the Trinity. If that had happened in America, we would have concluded the businessman was crazy. If we had been told he had gone off into the woods to shoot squirrels, or to pull fish out of the creek, it would have been perfectly normal. But if a businessman should go off into the hills for a few days to meditate about God, we would call the psychiatrist. But it is in periods of quiet meditation that the consciousness

of God's presence means most.—Rev. William E. Ward.

EVENING SERVICE

Theme: The Gospel As a Power.

TEXT: "Yet once more I shake not the earth only, but also heaven." Heb. 12:26.

INTRODUCTORY: There are two shakings here referred to. The first is that of Sinai, the giving of the Law. The second is that of Calvary, the giving of the Gospel. The giving of the Law shook the earth. The giving of the Gospel is to shake earth and heaven. This second shaking began when Christ came. It is going on now. It will continue until world's end. The Gospel cannot build up and make strong without shaking down. It shakes down the evil and builds up the good. It is doing that today and will so continue until Christ's kingdom is consummated. The Gospel is not a weak thing. It is a mighty power.

I. It is a revoluntionary power. Falsehood, evil, corruption, wherever they exist, in hearts, governments, commerce, literature, science or art, Christianity has shaken and will shake.

II. It is a reigning power. It is a "kingdom." Whoever does not receive it as a reigning power does not receive it at all. Whoever does not receive it as a reigning power is exposed to the fate of a rebel against heaven.

III. It is a permanent power. It is a "kingdom which cannot be moved." Its elements, love and truth, are immutable. Its fitness is eternal. Men through all the ages will never outgrow it, will never cease to want it, will never be able to get on without it.

IV. It is a practical power. 1. The mode of acceptable service. "Reverence and godly fear." 2. The qualification for acceptable service. "Let us have grace" thankfully to realize the high blessing conferred upon us and with devout gratitude engage in the work. 3. Motives to acceptable service. One is that "our God is a consuming fire." The

God who rolled thunder and flashed lightnings on Sinai has not changed. His antagonism to sin is as great as ever. He is also a God of grace and love, a great rewarder of all who serve him.

Suggestive Texts and Themes

The Friends of Christ: "Ye are my friends, if ye do the things which I command you." John 15:14 (A.S.V.).

The Enemies of Christ: "For many walk, of whom I have told you often, and now tell you even weeping, that they are the enemies of the cross of Christ." Phil. 3:18.

Unexpected Faith: "After he had ended all his sayings in the ears of the people, he entered into Capernaum. And a certain centurion's servant, . . . I have not found so great faith, no, not in Israel . . ." Luke 7:1-10 (A.S.V.).

The Missing Faith: "And he said unto them, Where is your faith?" etc. Luke 8:25.

The Forgiveness of Sins: "Him did God exalt with his right hand to be a Prince and a Saviour, to give repentance to Israel, and remission of sins." Acts 5:31 (A.S.V.).

MIDWEEK FELLOWSHIP MEETING TOPIC

(Church Night or Suggested Sermon Subject)

Theme: Rich in Mercy.

TEXT: "But God, who is rich in mercy." Eph. 2:4.

What a good thing it is that our Father is rich in the very thing we need most!

I. Of course, he is rich in all good things; but what a calamity it would be if instead of having the comfort of knowing that he has an abundance of mercy, we were to feel that he has only a scant supply. I am always touched by the opening words of the 51st Psalm. What a wonderfully fine argument the writer uses in coming to God for pardon. Not his own worthiness; not even his neediness; but "according to thy lovingkindness."

II. Yes, the cattle upon a thousand hills belong to him; the seams of precious metal in the earth are God's; the starry heavens above are full of God, and stamped with his symbol of ownership; but what is better and even more encouraging for us is the great fact that "God is rich in mercy."

III. If God is rich, we cannot be poor. We may lack some of the paltry things of this world—the things that shall perish amid the crack of doom—but because we are Christ's and Christ is God's, all things are ours, and over and around them all the riches of his mercy.—I. D. L.

CHRISTIAN ENDEAVOR SOCIETY TOPIC

Apr. 4. Person-to-Person Call. Matt. 4:18-22.

BULLETIN BOARD SLOGANS FOR THE MONTH

BY EARL RINEY

Have the will to win and the courage to work.

We need one another.

Laugh calamity straight in the face.

A "Holy Week" is meaningless to an unholy life.

"Come thou with us and we will do thee good."

Most of our sorrows spring from forgetfulness of God.

The way home is the way of the cross.

The Easter message is life—freer—fairer—fuller—life.

"If ye be risen with Christ, seek those things which are above."

Church membership is not an elevator into heaven.

A good deal of laziness of mind is called liberty of opinion.

For our hope of heaven we rest in the character of Christ.

Atheism can never be an institution; it is only a destitution.

SUNDAY SCHOOL LESSON

Apr. 4. Intercessory Prayer. John 17.
MEMORY VERSE: "Whatever you ask in

my name, I will do it, that the Father may be glorified in the Son." John 14:13 (r.s.v.).

This prayer of Jesus is like an expanding spiral. As every Christian prayer should be it is God-centered; it begins with the word "Father." It moves forward with a petition, glorify thy Son, and with the expanding desire that such glory shall be for the blessing of his disciples. Soon the prayer expands to include them directly, *I am praying for them.* Note the various turns of the spiral—*keep them in my name, keep them from the evil one, consecrate them in the truth.*

With this turn of the spiral it moves outward again to include all *those who are to believe in me through their word.* And these in turn are to bring belief to the world beyond them, v. 21. The prayer ends stressing perfect unity, the glory of eternity, and the infinite love of God which Christ and all his followers shall share. The principles set forth in this intercessory prayer are such as we may use in prayer today.

SUNDAY: APRIL ELEVENTH

MORNING SERVICE

Theme: The Triumphal Entry (Palm Sunday).

SUGGESTED SCRIPTURE READING: Matt. 21:1-17. After-petition: May God bless to our hearts and minds this Palm Sunday prophecy of the Kingly Christ.

SELECTED HYMNS: "Ride on, ride on, in majesty."—H. H. Milman. "All glory, laud and honor."—John M. Neal, Jr. "When his salvation bringing."— John King. "O could I speak the matchless worth."—S. Medley. "All hail the power of Jesus' name."—Edward Perronet.

CALL TO WORSHIP: "And the multitudes that went before, and that followed, cried, saying, Hosanna to the son of David: Blessed is he that cometh in the name of the Lord; Hosanna in the Highest."

INVOCATION PRAYER (Holy Week): We praise thee, O God, we acknowledge thee to be the Lord. All the earth doth worship thee, the Father everlasting. With whole hearts we would rejoice and be glad in thee this day. For thou art good, and ready to forgive, and plenteous in mercy to all that call upon thee. Grant to us one and all the spirit of true devotion, that our prayers and thanksgivings may be acceptable in thy sight. We make our plea this day under the cross of Christ. The chastisement of our peace was upon him and with his stripes we are healed. And give us, we pray thee, in full measure the joy of thy salvation, the joy that expresses itself not alone in praise, but in right living and faithful service. Lord, what wilt thou have us to do? Direct us to the place of duty. Equip us for service and make us glad to do thy holy will. Bless thy church today. Give to all preachers the baptism of thy Spirit, and to all hearers the attentive ear and understanding heart. Let the healing shadow of the cross of Christ fall over the world today. We ask in his name. Amen.— After D. J. B.

Theme: The Triumphal Entry (Palm Sunday).

TEXT: "And when they came nigh to Jerusalem," etc. Mark 11:1-11.

INTRODUCTORY: What do we mean by Palm Sunday? We are familiar with the church's manner of celebrating it and every year look forward to it as preparatory to Good Friday and Easter. And yet, familiar as we are with the story of the so-called Triumphal Entry, we have, most of us, I think, a mistaken idea of it. The entry of Jesus into Jerusalem was not, as many conceive it, a spontaneous uprising of the people in honor of Jesus. Our Lord himself planned it. There is a prophecy in the Old Testament known to all the Jewish people: "Shout, O daughter of Jerusalem: behold, thy King cometh unto thee: he is just, and having salvation; lowly, and riding upon an ass, and upon a colt the foal of an ass."

I. Knowing that these words were in the minds of the people, and that they were looking for their fulfillment, he determined thus to make one final dramatic appeal to them. So he found the colt and rode into the city upon it. The men who took part in it were a few Galileans, probably friends of the apostles, with a host of children who always love to follow a procession. The people of Jerusalem were cold or hostile. The only connection they had with it was to stand and gaze in scornful indifference, and to send a delegation to Jesus to protest. Doubtless in the crowd that watched there were some who were friendly, but they had not the courage of their convictions.

II. When we come to Luke we find an incident in the triumphal procession story which he alone records. His account emphasizes the pathos of it all. Jesus had been here over thirty years. No one else had ever lived or spoken as had he. Now he is approaching the end and a poor little procession was the only response of the nation to him. Even the enthusiasm of these few followers was not unopposed. They sent him word, saying, "Rebuke thy disciples." Jesus' reply was: "I tell you that, if these should hold their peace, the stones would immediately cry out."

This is one of the very significant utterances of our Lord. He was facing the darkest hour in his life and in all human history. He had been rejected and was going to his crucifixion. Only a handful of simple men and women and children still followed him.

What if they were silenced? He was not dismayed. He knew that even if all human comfort was withdrawn, God would not fail him. The very stones, nature itself, would speak.

What if the voices of those who witness for God were everywhere silenced? What then? Jesus here gives us the answer. "If these should hold their peace, the stones will immediately cry out." God depends on us, upon our faithfulness to our responsibility as his spokesmen and ambassadors. But what if we fail him? Will the cause fail? No! If we fail, if we hold our peace, the stones will cry out. If we are not true to our trust, he will summon other means to accomplish his work, for the gates of hell shall never prevail against the church of God.

III. Palm Sunday means victory, the final overcoming of evil. We go into the National Museum in Washington, or into the Soldiers Memorial Hall. There we see torn and faded battle flags, reminders of victories long gone and almost forgotten. We are tempted to think of the victory of Palm Sunday as something also which is only a memory.

A week after the apparent defeat of Jesus, he arose to a triumph which has changed the thinking and living of the whole world. Do not be disturbed if men and women you know, who only a little while ago were shouting "Hosanna," are now on the other side crying "Crucify." As long ago, this was only the darkness before the dawn.

IV. Finally, the word which is always associated with Palm Sunday is "Hosanna." This is a prayer. It means "Save now, Lord." Is there anything this troubled world needs more than this prayer? Only Jesus can save.

And so today what we as men and women need, what the church and the world need, what civilization must do if it is not to perish, is to sound again that cry of despair, and yet of eternal hope, which greeted Jesus on his lonely road to Calvary, "Hosanna!" Save now, Lord."—S. N. H.

THEME PRAYER: O Master of the

Palm-strewn Way, help us now to open the hidden and potent ways of our wills and affections to thy grace and glory. May we repeat in our own spirits that procession of triumph so long ago and as we receive thee into our own lives, wilt thou so entirely possess us that we ourselves may establish thy reign in our midst. Amen.

OFFERTORY SENTENCE: "This is the generation of those that seek him, that seek thy face, O Jacob."

OFFERTORY PRAYER: Forgive us, our Father, our vain hosannas to the false and the fugitive. Give us a renewed vision of what endures and blesses. Help us to make our hearts highways for the Lord of love and redemption, and establish us with a grave willingness to follow him. Bless the offerings we bring this morning. Use them for the promotion of his kingdom in the world. We ask in his name. Amen.

Illustrative Material

SEED THOUGHTS, HOMILETIC AND EXPOSITORY. The Triumphal Entry: It was a day of triumphal manifestation, as also of sore disappointment. Great lessons. I. The calm preparation of Jesus for his own death must always be a lesson for his people. II. "The Lord hath need of them" was enough for the owners of the ass and colt. But that message fails to open the purses of many who say they love that very Lord today. III. It is easy to follow the crowd, whether it be into Jerusalem strewing palm leaves, or out to Calvary crying "Crucify him." IV. Everyone was talking about Jesus that day. It is strange how people have kept on talking about him ever since. Everyone talks of an evangelist when in the full tide of preaching he arouses a city. When he goes away they forget him. But always someone remembers the Christ. V. Who would you have said he was had you been there that day? You cannot answer. You were not there. Who do you say he is today? You can answer. You are here. VI. The chief priests and elders tried to make Jesus repress the enthusiasm of the children. He would not. We have no chief priests now; but we have elders. A church without enthusiasm in its children is hopeless. VII. This was the last offer Jesus made of himself to his nation. VIII. Confession of Christ is easy when nothing turns on it. To shout hosanna on the hillside costs nothing.—R. S. H.

Choice Palm Sunday Illustrations

SPREADING OF GARMENTS. We read that when Jesus approached, the people spread their garments in the road for him to tread upon. In India, in the old days before the British took charge, the ponderous car of Juggernaut was dragged through the streets. Hindu devotees, as it passed, threw themselves down before it and were crushed beneath its wheels. It was their poor way of showing that they were the servants of their idol even unto death. These men along the road to Jerusalem were trying to express to Jesus their devotion. Unable to cast themselves before him, they spread their garments instead. This is the gift he asks of all of us.—Stuart Nye Hutchison, D.D.

THE ENTHRONED CHRIST. In the beautiful cathedral of Orvieto, among its brilliantly decorated ornaments of sculptures and paintings, is one of Fra Angelico's greatest works, "Christ Enthroned." By his left hand he steadies the globe. His right hand is raised in divine supremacy. But in that hand is the print of the nail. And it is the wounded hand that is so raised; it is by that hand that he controls the world! Ah, it was by his sufferings that he became the enthroned Christ. His earthly crown was the crown of thorns.

ENDORSEMENT OF ENTHUSIASM. The scene on this first Palm Sunday and Christ's approval of the demonstration assure us that he endorses and is pleased with enthusiasm in his service. There was feeling and thrill and enthusiasm on that day and Christ accepted and endorsed it all. What he endorses on one day he approves on all days. His endorsement of enthusiasm in the first century is his plea for enthusiasm in the twentieth century.—John F. Cowan, D.D.

THE UNIVERSAL KING. There is in Austria, upon one of the bridges over which multitudes pass and repass, a series of statues located similarly to the stations of the cross which represent Christ in the various aspects of his early life. In one he is a carpenter, in another a physician, in another a shepherd, and in another a King. There is a particular Christ, as it were, for each individual. For the working man, he is the carpenter; for the farmer, the sower of seed; for the sick, the physician; and for the weary, the strong burden bearer. Each person finds here an image of the Christ which exactly suits his need. Jesus satisfies the need of every individual. He meets the changing wants of all, and from youth to age there is in him something that satisfies the changing and increasing need of life. "Thou, O Christ, art all I want. More than all in Thee I find."
—Rev. H. T. Kerr.

Quotable Palm Sunday Poetry

THE TRIUMPHAL ENTRY

Hark! how the children shrill and high
"Hosanna" cry;
Their joys provoke the distant sky,
Where thrones and seraphim reply;
And their own angels shine and sing
In a bright ring;
Such young, sweet mirth
Makes heaven and earth
Join in a joyful symphony.
—Henry Vaughan.

THE LORD HAS NEED OF IT

Peter lent a boat,
To save him from the press;
Martha lent her home,
With busy kindliness.

One man lent a colt,
Another lent a room;
Some threw down their garments,
And Joseph lent a tomb.

Simon lent his strength,
The cruel cross to bear;
Mary brought her spices,
His body to prepare.

What have I to lend?
No boat, no house, no lands;
Dwell, Lord, within my heart,
I put it in Thy hands.
—Unidentified.

Suggestive Palm Sunday Texts and Themes

Behold Thy King!: "Behold, thy King cometh unto thee, meek, and sitting upon an ass, and a colt the foal of an ass." Matt. 21:5.

Enthusiasm in Religion: "The whole multitude of the disciples began to rejoice and praise God," etc. Luke 19:37.

The Enthroned Christ: "When the Son of man shall come in his glory." Matt. 25:31.

The Commencement of Christ's Coronation Procession: "And they came to Jericho," etc. Mark 10:46-52.

Entire Consecration: "The Lord hath need," etc. Matt. 21:3.

EVENING SERVICE

Theme: At Home in God's Love.

TEXT: "He that dwelleth in love dwelleth in God, and God in him." I John 4:16.

INTRODUCTORY: This word "dwelling" is a very strong and eloquent term. To "dwell in love"—what is this? What but to make it our element, to reside in it, to make it our permanent resting place, to make it our home? Home is the place where we dwell, where we abide, where our joys nestle and sing, where the springs of our comfort are. How wonderful that God should be our home! That we should be at home in God's love!

I. Loving God is but letting God love us. John, the writer of this book, was the apostle of love. His training, his nearness to Christ, having his spirit ripened by long experience, made him so. Accurately understood faith is just letting God love us. So is love. So is consecration. "He that dwelleth in love dwelleth in God."

II. Loving God is also but letting God live in us. God in us and we in him! We at home in God's love, and God at home in our love! Men as "temples of the Holy Spirit"! To dwell in love as a habitation is not natural, but supernatural, not of the flesh but of the Spirit.

III. How are we to realize this state? How have love as our habitation? How dwell in love? God himself dwells in God-loving hearts. The flesh is selfish and sensual. Obtain a place in the spiritual and divine—in God's house by adoption, in God's nature by regeneration, be born into the kingdom of heaven. The place is to be retained by faith and prayer and communion, communication kept up between God and the soul. Thus love will abound yet more and more. Fellowship with God begets love. Love is the reflection of God.

IV. One other thing should be said. The love must be exhibited. 1. In the tone of our conversation. 2. In unselfish conduct, for "Love seeketh not her own." 3. In generous beneficence toward others. 4. By doing all this constantly to God's glory, inspired by him, seeking to please him. 5. And all this as the habit of the soul. Not the impulse of a season. Not occasionally. Not under unusual pressure, but as our daily life, as the habit of our home-dwelling.—H.

Theme: The Lowly King and His Wide Dominion (Palm Sunday).

TEXT: "Behold, thy King cometh unto thee, meek, and sitting upon an ass, and a colt the foal of an ass." Matt. 21:5.

The story of the Triumphal Entry: When? Where? Who? What? Why? Whatever answer may be given to Why? it was a direct and open fulfillment of the prophecy of Zechariah 9:9, 10. The story as given in the Four Gospels may be studied along with the passage in Zechariah.

I. The sovereignty of Christ. "Thy King cometh!" "He laid his hand on that magnificent prophecy and said, 'It is mine. I am the King.'"

II. The character of Christ. I. Just. 2. Merciful. (See margin of American Revised Version, "having salvation" is "saving victory.") 3. Humble. All the details of the narrative are suggestive of humility.

Conclusion: 1. We can be subjects under his sovereignty. 2. We can be bearers of his character. See Micah 6:8. 3. We can be heralds of his peace.—M. K. W. H.

CHRISTIAN ENDEAVOR SOCIETY TOPIC

Apr. 11. Crosses (Palm Sunday). Matt. 16:24, 25.

SUNDAY SCHOOL LESSON
Apr. 11. Jesus Gives His Life. John 19:17-30.

MEMORY VERSE. "I, when I am lifted up from the earth, will draw all men to myself." John 12:32 (R.S.V.)

The cross is the Love of God seeking that word which will speak to the universal heart of man.—E. P. D.

The cross! The supreme disclosure of the love of God, the supreme disclosure of the holiness of God; the final disclosure of the sinfulness of sin.—J. D. J.

The cross! fountain and origin of all that is divinely fresh and recreative in human life.—F. W. D.

The cross! He bears the sin of the world. "He was wounded for our transgressions." The *our* is not only a corporate, collective pronoun, but it may also be distributive, individual. He was wounded for *my* transgressions, and *yours*. I can make him an offering for sin—the specific sin, my sin.

SUNDAY: APRIL EIGHTEENTH

MORNING SERVICE

Theme: Easter and Gardens (Easter).

SUGGESTED SCRIPTURE READING: Luke 24:1-32.

SELECTED HYMNS: "Welcome, happy morning."—V. H. C. Fortunatus. "The day of resurrection."—John of Damascus. "Christ the Lord is risen today." —C. Wesley. "Angels roll the rock away."—T. Scott.

CALL TO WORSHIP: "Now is Christ risen from the dead, and become the firstfruits of them that slept." "Thanks be to God, who giveth us the victory through our Lord Jesus Christ."

INVOCATION PRAYER: Almighty God, who art the Life and Light Eternal, who hast given us our Lord Jesus Christ to make Easter Day a perpetual prophecy that life shall outlast death, that the rewards of life are divinely given, we pray thee as we enter upon this service that the Easter light may shine in every heart, that always and everywhere we may look up to thee, and especially that at this moment we may see thee as Author of light, Redeemer of life, and the God and Father of our Lord and Saviour Jesus Christ. Comfort all who mourn with the Easter comfort, and bless us individually and all together as we worship in thy house this day. We ask in the name of Christ. Amen.

Theme: Easter and Gardens (Easter).

TEXT: "And in the garden a new sepulchre." John 19:41.

INTRODUCTORY: Easter and Gardens! There were many sacred gardens in the Holy Land. In some of these flowers, plants, nuts and fruits were grown. Some were places of rest, pleasure and prayer. Some were places of burial. We are reminded this Easter day of a number of gardens each of which carries with its name a special meaning.

I. There is, for example, the Garden of the Old Home, the garden of love and care. Well do many of us remember it. It was laid out with carefully formed beds and pathways, all with such precision and exactness as to remind us of the loving care of parents desiring to strew the pathway of the garden of the life of their children with flowers. Many a pleasant evening was spent in the Garden of the Old Home.

II. Earth had another garden, the Garden of Eden. It was a very beautiful garden, but proved to be the Garden of Temptation. When God completed his work of creation he looked upon what he had made and said that it was good. From that which was good he must have selected the very best for the Garden of Eden, where our first parents, created in the image of God, were placed and where they were in harmony with God and nature and in communion with God.

The tempter entered that garden to deceive Adam and Eve. Yielding to Satan's deception they forfeited their heritage. Thus sin and death came into the world, though followed immediately by the first promise of a coming Redeemer and Saviour.

III. Then there is another garden, a garden where prayer and agony met, the Garden of Gethsemane. Jesus went further into that garden than he asks any of his followers to go. And if we surrender our wills to the will of God, then Jesus will walk with us in our gardens of sorrow, assuring us that we are his own.

IV. We recall that there is another garden, the Garden of the Sepulchre. In every garden there is a tomb, a sad side of life. But around every tomb there may be a garden, the joyous side of life. The Garden of Death is transformed into a Garden of Life. Thus Joseph's tomb, in which Christ was laid, became prophetic of immortality. From that tomb came forth a living, victorious Saviour, who shall live forevermore.

The price of victory over death and the grave was paid in a garden, which has become the Garden of Life. Thus the Garden of the Sepulchre, the Garden of Death, has become the Garden of Resurrection, the Garden of Life, the Easter Garden!

V. There is yet another garden, the Garden of Paradise, the Heavenly Garden. We have no language at our command to describe the place, the home, the garden, the heaven which Jesus has gone to prepare for us, and where by and by he will take us to dwell with him forever. The beauties of these our present earthly gardens cannot be compared with the heavenly gardens which Jesus has gone to prepare, for "eye hath not seen, nor ear heard, neither have entered into the heart of man the things which God hath prepared for them that love him." —After O. F. L.

THEME PRAYER: O Thou who through thy Son hast turned the shadow of death into the morning, we praise thee for the everlasting hopes that now rise within our hearts and for the Gospel which has brought life and immortality to light. Receive our thanksgiving, reveal thy presence and kindle our hearts with the spirit of the risen Christ. In his name we ask. Amen.

OFFERTORY SENTENCE: "If ye then be risen with Christ, seek those things which are above, where Christ sitteth on the right hand of God."

OFFERTORY PRAYER: "We bless thee, our Father, for thy great love toward us in the life and death and resurrection of Jesus. Help us being risen with Christ to seek those things which are above, and to seek also the advancement of thy kingdom here upon the earth. To this end receive and bless the offerings which we consecrate

this day to thy cause. In the name of Christ we ask. Amen.

Illustrative Material

SEED THOUGHTS, HOMILETIC AND EXPOSITORY. Love at the Tomb: "Now on the first day of the week cometh Mary Magdalene." John 20:1. I. Love is persistent. At the foot of the cross, at the risk of life—she remained. II. Love is early—she was early, "while it was yet dark." III. "Love laughs at locksmiths." She and the other women came early to the grave not counting on "who should roll away the stone." IV. Love is comforted. Mary and the other women came to the grave in great sorrow. The angelic watcher at the empty tomb said, "Fear not ye" (Matt. 28:5). "Life is ever lord of death; and love can never lose its own." There is approaching a Man. Not a Roman soldier. Not a disciple. Not the wealthy Joseph. Not the caretaker. He speaks the one word, "Mary!" But, oh, it has the old familiar inflection! The tragedy of that first Easter departed! The Son of Righteousness had arisen!—R. V. G.

Choice Easter Illustrations

EASTER IN A SUBMARINE. A young sailor on submarine duty in the Pacific wrote to his pastor a few days after Easter, 1945, saying that he had spent Easter Sunday below the surface of the ocean. Although their submarine was submerged in the shadows of the sea, until they were resting almost on the ocean floor, they nevertheless had an Easter church service. There was no chaplain and no choir, but the captain conducted the service, and a record played a hymn.

"It wasn't like Easter at the old home church," the sailor wrote in his letter, "but it meant a lot to the fellows to know that he was with you, especially on a day like Easter."

THE LIGHT OF EASTER. In some of the great cathedrals the music of the "Miserere" is sung. Sometimes it is sung in a cathedral that is all radiant with light, and as the music moves on in majesty, the lights go out one by one and the music comes to its close in the darkness. There are those who think that life is just like that, but that is not the gospel hope. After the cross is Easter morning, and the music of life which begins in the dark sings itself into the light of a new day. It is always thus in the Christian religion.—Rev. Hugh T. Kerr.

EASTER POWER. When Jesus met his disciples after his resurrection he issued commands to them. The risen Christ is a Christ who requires service—and who has a right to expect service. He has a right to expect service because he has the power to make that service completely successful. As the Easter Christ he has at his command all the power of the universe. Are we ready to serve the risen Christ?

WHERE HE IS. A Christian doctor sat at the bedside of a patient in his last illness. The sick man talked about leaving this life and asked the physician what he thought the future life would be like. The doctor looked in the direction of the door where his dog could be heard scratching and begging to come in. "That dog," he said, "doesn't know what is going on within this room. What he wants is to be near his master. So it is with the future life. I cannot tell what it will be like, but just to be with the Master of Life will satisfy."

Jesus did not give a preview of the life after death. He did something infinitely better. He assured his friends that where he was, there they would be also.

EASTER AS AN ACHIEVEMENT. Heaven is the gift of God's rich grace. Yes, but belief in it is not a gift; it is an achievement. It is the reward of practicing the values of eternal life here in the midst of time. No argument, formula or creed can assure to you the Easter hope; only experience can do that. Dare to live significantly—which in the end means unselfishly—and you will know something of the Christian's joy now. But more, there will be dawn in

your heart, like the light of a glad Easter day, the confidence that such meaningful life will go gloriously on through the portals of death.—Frank G. Fagerburg.

EASTER'S VICTORY. A few years ago a distinguished scientist was conducting a forum in a large eastern city. He had stated his belief that there is a power back of this universe which conserves eternally its spiritual and personal values. In the question period that followed one listener asked: "How can you say that there is a trustworthy divine administration in back of this universe, who guarantees the permanence of spiritual values, when a character as perfect as Jesus suffered defeat?" The reply was eloquent. The speaker paused a minute and then said: "In the light of what Jesus accomplished during his days on the earth and in the centuries since, do you really think Jesus was defeated?" The answer that instinctively comes to the lips of every Christian at Easter is: "No, Jesus was never defeated, and never will be, for his way of life was victorious over death, and is from everlasting to everlasting."

Anyone who has caught the spirit of Christ's way of life possesses here and now life eternal.—William E. Park.

Quotable Easter Poetry

LIFE AGAIN

Out of the dusk a shadow,
  Then a spark;
Out of the cloud a silence,
  Then, a lark;
Out of the heart a rapture,
  Then, a pain;
Out of the dead, cold ashes,
  Life again.

—John B. Tabb.

TWO WORLDS

Impoverished is the man who owns one world,
And one alone; whose soul has never trod
The bold beginnings of the path to God;

Who goes with ne'er a flaming dream
    unfurled
Along the crawling highways of his
    kind,
Clinging to vapors and to husks,
With futile hands, half lost and wholly
    blind,
Fearful of the shadows, yet without the
    mind
To see what stars may fleck his jour-
    ney's dusks,
To him be pity. For his soul shall
    grope
In vain for beauty, and for hope.

—Unidentified.

EASTER DAWN

Nothing to show that Easter is near,
    Gardens still are bare,
Lacking even autumn's cheer
    In the chilly air.

Then the spring comes—musically,
    Things begin to grow,
Pushing with determined strength
    Through brown earth and snow.

Not more wonderful is this
    In the Easter dawn,
Than that we shall one day find
    Life—when life is gone.

—T. Williamson.

LORD OF LIFE

Most glorious Lord of Life, that on
    this day
Didst make Thy triumph over death
    and sin;
And having harrowed hell, didst bring
    away
Captivity thence captive, us to win:
This joyous day, dear Lord, with joy
    begin,
And grant that we, for whom Thou
    diddest die,
Being with Thy dear blood washed
    clean from sin,
May live for ever in felicity.

—Edmund Spencer.

GOING TO EMMAUS

'Twas in the hush of evening,
They walked their quiet way;
Their hearts were sad and burdened
For He had gone away.

The Christ whom they had come to
    love,
On whom their hopes were stayed,
Was dead—and some said lived again,
But they were sore dismayed.

And then a gentle Stranger
Drew nigh with them to walk;
Why look so sad and troubled,
As you wend your way and talk?

Then opened they their hearts to Him;
This Stranger seemed to care
So much they asked Him to abide,
Their evening meal to share.

And then their eyes were opened,
They knew Him—Christ He lives!
No words have they to tell the joy,
This wondrous knowledge gives.

I wonder if with burdened hearts
We do not often go
Not knowing that He walks with us,
The Christ who loves us so.

—Charlotte Noble.

EVENING SERVICE

**Theme: The Power of Christ's Resur-
rection (Easter).**

TEXT: "That I may know him, and
the power of his resurrection." Phil.
3:10.

INTRODUCTORY: The power of Christ's
resurrection has cast a mysterious spell
over about six hundred million people
living in the present day, so that they
love him, and are exemplifying him, in
all the various parts of the world.
This power is universally recognized
everywhere by foes as well as by friends
of Christ.

The fruits of this marvelous power
of Christ's resurrection may be clearly
seen from three angles.

I. It is a personal transforming
power. I. It is seen in the new life in
Christ. Faith in Christ is its basis
(Rom. 4:25). 2. It is seen in the
spiritual knowledge. The best evidences are seen in boots, not in books.
There is no greater force than that
back of the certain "I know," for Chris-

tianity can be attested by personal experience.

II. This marvel is seen in that it is a world-transforming power. 1. See the battle in array. The early problem was a billion pagans against twelve disciples of Jesus. This seems to us of today almost absurd, but the triumph was assured. 2. The internal enemy, too, was conquered by the real thing. Heresy, many times, is worse than paganism, as it is more insidious in its workings, and more difficult to deal with. But Christianity conquered here.

III. The power of Christ's resurrection is seen in that it transforms death. 1. It transforms the angel of gloom into an angel of light. It makes one to sense the Light of the World illumining "the valley of the shadow of death." With a consciousness of Jesus' Real Presence, there can be no death as ordinarily understood. 2. In Christ, in him alone, there is a glorious triumph. Paul in the presence of the martyr's block rejoiced in the "crown of righteousness" (II Tim. 4:7, 8). Jerome of Prague had no fear of physical pain while Christ was near. At the martyr's stake three Quakers in more recent times in England, in their last moments, could clap their hands in holy triumph because they felt the power of Christ's resurrection!

Thus today we may realize the tears; tomorrow we shall know the triumph. Today we may know earth's sorrow; tomorrow we shall know the joy. Today we view the mounded graves; tomorrow we shall view the triumphal glory, and this all because of "the power of Christ's resurrection"!

—C. W. D.

Suggestive Easter Texts and Themes

The Invitation of a Risen Host: "Jesus saith unto them, Come and dine." John 21:12.

The Light of the Tomb: "Now is Christ risen from the dead." I Cor. 15:20.

Easter Banishes Fear: "I declare unto you the gospel . . . wherein ye stand." I Cor. 15:1.

Witnesses That Convince: "This Jesus did God raise up, whereof we all are witnesses." Acts 2:32 (A.S.V.)

The Joy of Easter: "And they departed quickly from the tomb with fear and great joy." Matt. 28:8 (A.S.V.)

Immortal Life: "And they shall see his face." Rev. 22:4.

If Christ Be Not Risen: "If Christ be not risen, then is our preaching vain, and your faith is also vain." I Cor. 15:14.

The Double Message: "He preached unto them Jesus, and the resurrection." Acts 17:18.

Many Infallible Proofs: "He shewed himself alive after his passion by many infallible proofs." Acts 1:3.

Our Sure Resurrection: "He which raised up the Lord Jesus shall raise up us also by Jesus." II Cor. 4:14.

MIDWEEK FELLOWSHIP MEETING TOPIC

(Church Night or Suggested Sermon Subject)

Theme: "The Joyous Message of Easter" (Easter).

TEXT: "For this is the will of my Father, that every one that beholdeth the Son, and believeth on him, should have eternal life; and I will raise him up at the last day." John 6:40 (A.S.V.).

I. Easter is the church's supreme festival. It sounds the highest symphony of Christianity. It echoes the sublimest oratorio of faith. It is the sunrise of hope over this darkened world. All nature seems to dance on Easter Day, and why? Because it tells of life. This is the secret of the universal interest in Easter.

II. The distinctive message of Easter is the affirmation of the fact of immortality. As the shell murmurs the music of the ocean from whence it came, so the soul carries the life of a lovelier land.

III. The Easter message proclaims not only the life of the soul, it asserts the existence of a body in a form that is incorruptible. See I Cor. 15:53. "I will raise him up at the last day."

IV. Heaven is the home of the

beautiful. Easter reassures us of the joy that will be ours in that heavenly meeting.—J. B. R.

CHRISTIAN ENDEAVOR SOCIETY TOPIC

Apr. 18. When I Die, I Live (Easter). Phil. 1:21; Gal. 2:20.

SUNDAY SCHOOL LESSON

Apr. 18. Our Living Lord. John 20:24-29; 21:15-17.

MEMORY VERSE: "Blessed are those who have not seen and yet believe." John 20:29 (R.S.V.).

"My Lord and my God!" Now Thomas has a conviction to stand on!

He has something to go by! He has a task to do, a place to hook in. He has a Friend.

We can well believe that courage never melted out of him again. He was never again toppled over by his doubts. He based life now upon an assertion of the Kingship and the Lordship and the Deity of Christ.

Every man needs something to stand on! Every man needs a finality like that of Thomas' "My Lord and my God!" Every man needs a stance that does not shake. A finality like that of the Lordship and Deity of Christ becomes a master value of life. "Unless there is a master value to assign all lesser values to their station, how can they be stabilized or brought in any kind of order?"

SUNDAY: APRIL TWENTY-FIFTH

MORNING SERVICE

Theme: The Lord's Supper and Personal Faith (Holy Communion).

SUGGESTED SCRIPTURE READING: I Cor. 11:23-34.

SELECTED HYMNS: "Beneath the Cross of Jesus."—E. C. Clephane. "Here, O my Lord, I see Thee face to face."—H. Bonar. "Sweet feast of love divine."— E. Denny. "Bread of the world in mercy broken."—R. Heber.

CALL TO WORSHIP: "And when the hour was come, he sat down, and the twelve apostles with him. And he said unto them, With desire I have desired to eat this passover with you before I suffer: For I say unto you, I will not any more eat thereof, until it be fulfilled in the kingdom of God."

INVOCATION PRAYER: Lord, at thy table we would dedicate ourselves anew to fellowship and service. We seek close companionship with thee and with each other, and we would win this by serving. We want a heart that aches to do

thy will; to do always what will please thee; and we want to be of use to one another. At this holy hour grant us this; the high art of loving usefulness. Our hearts are vacant of high experience because our hands are empty of kindly ministries; Lord, fill them. Give us grace to do good, now; to respond to men's need of sympathy and help, moment by moment. Make our hearts tender. Keep us from thinking too much about ourselves. Melt our hardness. Take away our moral chill. Let other people find us warm. Make us sensitive to human need. And so may we hear thy voice, experience thy saving power, and pass thy life out to those around us. Here at thine altar set us on fire with love of God and man. In Christ's name we ask. Amen.

Theme: The Lord's Supper and Personal Faith (Holy Communion).

TEXT: "The Lord Jesus, the same night in which he was betrayed took bread: And when he had given thanks, he brake it, and said, Take, eat: this is my body, which is broken for you: this do in remembrance of me." I Cor. 11:23, 24.

INTRODUCTORY: The Lord's Supper is a great and meaningful symbol. The bread broken symbolizes that Jesus Christ, dying for our sins, has become the bread of life. The eating of the bread symbolizes the faith of the communicant. Faith thus unites us and Christ inseparably; it gives us an inalienable possession of Christ. Faith then being on our side the great act of the Lord's Supper, let us note more particularly its action therein.

I. First, we in the Lord's Supper confess our faith. "We make a confession," many say, "when we partake of the Lord's Supper." They seem to mean that we profess a certain sanctity, or a certain superiority. Not at all; the taking of the Sacrament is not such a profession; it is rather the confession of our faith. He who partakes confesses he is unable of himself to attain salvation; neither does he point to self and profess to be good or have superiority. "But," say others, "to partake of the Lord's Supper is to profess a great creed." It is of course to profess a certain faith; but is a confession that is experimental, not dogmatic; practical, not theocratic. Instead of pointing to self we point to Christ and confess our faith in him.

II. But the confession involves the exercising of our faith. In the Lord's Supper Jesus Christ is most certainly present. His presence does not wait upon the consecrating word of any minister. Christ is present as truly before as after the consecrating word of the clergyman or minister. The communicant, discerning the Lord's presence and offer, does there and then receive his Saviour, his truth and grace, his love and spirit.

III. This being so, a third fact follows, that in the Lord's Supper we receive nourishment to our faith. The silent, impressive appeal of the symbols, the communion of saints, the presence of the Lord, quicken our faith to appropriate and assimilate Jesus Christ so that our spiritual nature is nourished, as is

our body by partaking of the appropriate food. This nourishment, it must be noted, depends upon the activity of the faith of the communicant.

IV. Also in the Lord's Supper our faith pledges us anew to Christ. If we confess and exercise our faith in Christ, and receive spiritual nourishment in the Sacrament, our hearts involuntarily consecrate us anew to our blessed Lord. An act of consecration, therefore, should accompany the partaking and be a part of the Communion.—A. G.

THEME PRAYER: Gracious Father in heaven, we thank thee that in this holy Sacrament we are made partakers in Christ. So enable us to hold fast to that which has been given us that the life of Jesus may be made manifest in us and thy kingdom furthered through us. In the name of our only Saviour and Mediator. Amen.

OFFERTORY SENTENCE: "Let your light so shine before men, that they may see your good works, and glorify your Father which is in heaven."

OFFERTORY PRAYER: Our Father, we bring to thee the loaves of our offering, and we ask thee to break the bread as did the risen Lord at Emmaus, that we may see the living Christ through our sacrifice. We ask in Jesus' name. Amen.

Illustrative Material

SEED THOUGHTS, HOMILETIC AND EXPOSITORY. The Lord's Supper: I. It is a memorial of the sacrifice of the death of Christ. II. It is a means of present communion with Christ. III. It is the highest act of worship in the church. —C. W. F.

The Lord's Supper: I. The Author of the institution. In every action it is good to know by what authority we do it. II. The duty enjoined. "Do this." Take bread. Give thanks. Eat it. And so of the cup. 1. Its fitness to our present condition. 2. Its profitableness. 3. Its delightfulness. 4. Its necessity. III. When are we to do it? "As oft." Implies often. IV. The end. "In remembrance of me." Memory is a preserver.—G. D. H.

The Lord's Supper: I. "Take." 1. Knowingly take. 2. Humbly. 3. Believingly. 4. Thankfully. II. "Eat." Take and eat, appropriate. III. Uses. 1. Prepare yourselves for this spiritual banquet. 2. Receive it with faith. 3. Feed with thankfulness. 4. Endeavor to get that spiritual nourishment from it so as to serve God better hereafter. —B.

Choice Lord's Supper Illustrations

THE REMEMBRANCE OF CHRIST. I saw behind a hotel in Switzerland a fine garden, and I unexpectedly found there American flowers; and being far away from home and half homesick, they afforded me great pleasure. Every one of them seemed like a message to me full of affection by association. So the remembrance of Christ in the Lord's Supper rekindles our love to him.— H. W. Beecher.

REFRESHING OUR LOVE. There is a legend that after Zacchaeus' conversion he was accustomed to go for a walk each morning and come back happy and refreshed. His wife wondered where he went each day. She secretly followed him on one occasion and discovered that he walked to the tree that he had climbed to see Jesus pass by. It was his way of remembering what Christ had done for him. In a Communion service each of us should spend some quiet moments in going back along memory's lane to recall what Christ has done for us. In such ways will we be kept from forgetting how great a salvation is ours and what a wonderful Saviour we have.

MEETING THE MASTER IN THE LORD'S SUPPER. After his resurrection Jesus told his disciples to go back to Galilee. Galilee was home for all but one, we believe. They were to go back home, for the heart is more tender back home. They were to go back to the place where they had first met him. Everything in Galilee, the boats, the nets, the lakeside lilies, had association with him. They were to go back to meet the larger Christ, the Christ who had passed through the Garden, who had endured the cross, who had broken the bonds of death. They would meet the risen Christ in Galilee.

Each Christian has his Galilee, a place that is the home of the soul, a place where he first met the Master, a place where he may return to have communion with an ever-greater Saviour and Lord.

But warm, sweet, tender, even yet
  A present help is He;
And faith has still its Olivet,
  And love its Galilee.
          —M. K. W. H.

THE LORD'S SUPPER A SACRAMENT OF CONTACT. There is a sense of reality that comes from touch. Thomas said, "Except I shall see and touch his wounds I will not believe." Touch gives a sense of individuality. People will stand in line a long time just to touch the hand of the President of the United States in a handclasp. A moment's touch, but that moment is individual, not mass contact. As Jesus walked along a Capernaum street he said, "Who touched me?" "The crowd," answered his disciples. "No, some one touched me." By individual contact power was drawn from him. And touch gives a sense of spirituality. Touch communicates courage, comfort, sympathy. "His words touched my heart!" There is Old Testament mention of a company of men whose hearts God had touched.

In the sacrament of the Lord's Supper Christ gave us touch tokens of his vicarious death.—M. K. W.

Suggestive Lord's Supper Texts and Themes

Partakers of Christ: "For we are made partakers of Christ, if," etc. Heb. 3:14.

The Culture of the Communion: "This do in remembrance of me." Luke 22:19.

A Joyful Approach: "I went with them to the house of God, with the voice of joy," etc. Ps. 42:4.

Life's Sweet Surprises: "He was known to them in breaking of bread." Luke 24:35.

The Soul's Longing: "How amiable are thy tabernacles, O Lord of hosts," etc. Ps. 84:1, 2.

A Dying Wish Respected: "This do in remembrance of me." Luke 22:19.

A Personal Question: "What mean ye by this service?" Ex. 12:26.

Duty and Obligations of Christians to Keep the Communion Feast: "Therefore let us keep the feast." I Cor. 5:8.

Good to Draw Near to God: "It is good for me to draw near to God." Ps. 73:28.

At the Last Supper: "Now when the even was come," etc. Matt. 26:20-22.

After Thoughts: "So when they had dined." John 21:15.

EVENING SERVICE

Theme: What Memorial Have You?

TEXT: "This also that she hath done shall be spoken of for a memorial of her." Mark 14:9.

INTRODUCTORY: This is a beautiful incident of Christ's last days on earth. It is not likely that the woman knew that Christ was near the end of his life here. But the motive that prompted her act was fine and noble. And there was beautiful courtesy and grace in our Master's readiness to accept the offering and to step in between the woman and her reproof.

I. First, the incident gives encouragement to all who would perform acts of devotion or make gifts to God and his church. The remembrance of this woman is a pledge that God will not forget his people.

II. It is well to bear in mind also that the power of rendering service to God comes from the fact of being Christians. Knowing Whom we serve and sure of being accepted, everything we have becomes a talent we can use for God.

III. In conclusion one may note that doing good is a very pleasant way of getting ourselves remembered. All work done for Christ's sake is both remembered and recompensed. We note an interesting illustration of this thought from the Rev. Dr. Hugh T. Kerr. He says, "We have often been interested at a wedding in seeing the gifts spread out, and someone who knows the secret behind each gift will take us around and say: 'Mrs. So-and-So gave that. And Mr. So-and-So gave that. And the mayor of the city gave that. And this celebrated judge gave that.' We have often thought of the treasures that Christ someday may show to us, and he will say: 'The widow in the temple gave this,' and there will be the two mites which were her whole living. 'And the Samaritan woman gave that. And the woman who came to the tomb on Easter morning gave these spices and fine linen.' Among all the memorials that the Master keeps will be Mary's alabaster box, still broken, and the fragrance of the perfume filling both heaven and earth. And then we will say, 'I wonder if he has anything of mine?'"—H.

MIDWEEK FELLOWSHIP MEETING TOPIC

(Church Night or Suggested Sermon Subject)

Theme: The Earthen Vessel (Post-Easter).

TEXT: "We have this treasure in earthen vessels." II Cor. 4:7.

Paul's sad anticlimax in the text compared with the preceding context. It is like a lark at morning time soaring, songful, toward the sky, arrested in flight and falling back to earth again.

I. The earthen vessel, the mortal body, is the wonderful climax of material evolution—the palace for which everything lower is staging preparation.

II. But it is inadequate and will not endure. 1. It is dust. 2. While it lasts it is inadequate to express the highest life, that is, by speech, facial motion, etc. 3. It is a seat of suffering and pain.

III. Christ's resurrection explains it. 1. Shows that the real evolution of the person is not interrupted when the "earthen vessel" breaks. 2. Points to the spiritual body, to show how, suddenly in Christ, more gradually in us, the "earthen vessel" is transmuted into the enduring body. 3. Shows us in the fact that the resurrected body of Jesus bore the marks of his passion that the ascending scale of pain in the universe does not stop with man. God shares it.

Right theology must include a suffering. Conversely man may enjoy the glory of God in spite of the pangs of the "earthen vessel."

By these marks of the Passion in his "earthen vessel" we shall know Jesus in his glory. They prove that he carried up there sympathy with humanity.

CHRISTIAN ENDEAVOR SOCIETY TOPIC

Apr. 25. Fifteen Words for Christ (Missionary Emphasis). Phil. 2:15, 16a.

SUNDAY SCHOOL LESSON

Apr. 25. **Ahijah Foresees a Divided Kingdom. I Kings 11:29-38.**

MEMORY VERSE: "If thou wilt hearken unto all that I command thee, and wilt walk in my ways, . . . I will be with thee, and will build thee a sure house." I Kings 11:38.

This lesson begins a series of ten in the history of the Northern Kingdom, Israel. It is important to show the historical significance of the rebellion under Jeroboam rooted in the oppression under Solomon. It can be pointed out that in each period of the kingdom's history there was a prophet to proclaim God's will and to urge the people to obey God's commands. Yet one after another of Israel's kings led the people farther and farther from God until the nation was morally degenerate and spiritually impoverished. Jeroboam missed his opportunity to lead Northern Israel in renewed obedience to God. It is possible to find in this story an example of the way in which revolutionary movements become corrupt when they come to power.

SUNDAY: MAY SECOND

MORNING SERVICE

Theme: The Trees of the Lord (Springtime).

SUGGESTED SCRIPTURE READING: Ps. 1:1-6; Rev. 22:1-7.

SELECTED HYMNS: "With songs and honors sounding loud."—I. Watts. "The harp at nature's advent struck."—J. G. Whittier. "The glory of the spring how sweet."—H. H. Gill. "We plow the fields and scatter."—M. Claudius. "Fairest Lord Jesus."—Anon. "Thou art, O God, the light."—T. Moore.

CALL TO WORSHIP: "My voice shalt thou hear in the morning, O Lord; in the morning will I direct my prayer unto thee, and will look up."

INVOCATION PRAYER: Make known thy love to us this day, thou Lover of mankind. Deep in the mind of man and

far across the earth reveal thy beauty. Shine through the mists that close us in, thou glory of Eternal loveliness. Still thou this day the hearts of men into a ceaseless quest for thee, into an ardent yearning that in following thy will they may partake of thy nature. O thou deathless and unchanging One, the only answer to our need, shine through the earth to change it from the awful condition man's lust and greed have made unto the gateway of thy heaven. So shine upon us this day and grant us thy salvation. We ask in Christ's name. Amen.—Adapted from J. S. H.

Theme: The Trees of the Lord (Springtime).

TEXT: "The trees of the Lord are full of sap." Ps. 104:16.

INTRODUCTORY: Trees are among the

most beautiful things in the world. You know the lines of the popular poem:

Poems are made by fools like me,
But only God can make a tree.

Trees are often referred to in the Bible, and often with a strong human interest. The patriarchs planted trees to commemorate events in their lives. They met under trees to make and renew their covenants with God and with one another. They ate and slept in their shadow, and when they died were buried beneath their spreading boughs.

I. The primal joy. The text is a word for springtime. It was written in the spring. Just now the trees are full of sap. Like the rest of us, they have endured months of cold and wind and frost. All the time the moisture has been about their roots, but they could not draw it up. They needed the help of the sun.

II. Men as trees. This fact of nature is full of spiritual suggestion. We may think of ourselves as "trees of the Lord." The Bible encourages us to do that. "The righteous shall flourish like the palm tree, he shall grow like a cedar in Lebanon." "He shall be like a tree planted by the rivers of water." The child of God, in this life, is like a tree. What is the life of a tree? The tree lives because of three things: the soil beneath it, the sun above it, and the sap within it. So man, God's child, lives by three things: the material body, related to all lower creation, conscious mind, by which he makes contact with higher things, and spiritual life, by which divine forces and powers flow within him.

Perhaps the most suggestive thing is this: They all draw upon the same primal forces, but each one grows to a size and shape and strength and structure and beauty of its own.

III. Some trees. 1. The Oak Tree, massive, hard, knotted, strong. Only by tremendous exertion of power can it be broken, but it will be broken before it will be bent. The oak is the symbol of massive strength. The Lord of our life likes to see in us, in our life and conduct and service, the unbending toughness of the oak.

2. The Larch Tree—a contrast to the oak. The larch is an example of slender gracefulness. With tall, straight trunks and feathery tasseled foliage, larches have been called the "ladies of the fir-tree family." The larch will bend, but it will not break easily. The Lord of our life, even if we are not stout and tough as oak trees, can still make use of us if we are faithful to endure.

3. The Horse Chestnut. We have all seen and delighted in this tree; its fine and full proportions, its bursting buds, its great leaves, its rich blossoms. It may stand as the symbol of full-bosomed richness and beauty, beauty of form and flower. The sap that rises in that tree expresses itself in ample proportioned fruitfulness.

4. The Wild Cherry. Of all the trees in the wood, their blossoms were the most perfectly pure white of all the flowers I ever saw. The sap that rose in those trees expressed itself in a constancy that was unfailing, and in a purity that was unsullied. And I know that the Lord of all good life wants to see, in your life and mine, a constancy like that, and a purity like that.

5. The Quivering Aspen. The symbol of that fine sensitiveness to the Spirit of God, the wind of which "thou canst not tell whence it cometh and whither it goeth."

"The trees of the Lord are full of sap." We may be trees of the Lord, planted by him, sustained by him, growing up because his life is within us. May it be our ambition, in the spring and summer of our lives, and on to the autumn and the white winter days, to be strong as the oak, graceful as the larch to show even with slender powers the straight upstanding steadfastness, well-proportioned as the horse chestnut to reveal to the world the balanced beauty of the Lord, constant and pure as the wild cherry, and sensitive as the quivering aspen to every breath of the Spirit of God. May we be trees, so planted in the house of the Lord, that we shall flourish for ever in the courts of our God.—C. N.

THEME PRAYER: O God, we thank thee for the springtime of the world, for the freshness and beauty and gladness which the coming of Christ brought into a dying and weary earth. We thank thee that we are a part of this creative, ongoing movement. Grant us power to contribute our utmost to it that the message of the new life which is intended for all men may be carried to all men. In the name of Christ we ask. Amen.

OFFERTORY SENTENCE: "Many, O Lord my God, are thy wonderful works which thou has done, and thy thoughts which are to us-ward."

OFFERTORY PRAYER: O wondrous Giver of all things, this world is full of thy riches. We thank thee for the splendor and beauty of nature and for thy bountiful provision for the needs of man. Bless the offerings we bring this morning. Use them for the extension of thy kingdom in the world. In the name of Christ we ask. Amen.

Illustrative Material

SEED THOUGHTS, HOMILETIC AND EXPOSITORY. God and Nature: This Psalm is a hymn of praise to God in nature. I. First it sings of the universality of God's workings in nature. 1. In the domain of dead matter—waters, clouds, on crusted earth, "laying foundations." 2. In the domain of living matter—vegetable life, grass, fields, forests. 3. In the domain of sentient life—rational existence, moral minds, etc. II. The personality of God's workings in Nature. 1. He works sublimely. 2. He works incessantly. 3. He works benevolently. 4. He works wisely. 5. He works in nature morally. To make the world morally better and happier.—H.

A Tree by the River: I. The planting. II. Its culture. III. Its fruitfulness. God's tree by God's river must be a fruitful tree.—M. R. V.

The Tree Similitude: Here is a beautiful illustration of the perpetual verdure and fruitfulness of the piety deriving its origin and sustenance from God and his Word. It is compared to a tree whose roots are refreshed by never-failing streams of living water and whose every part is instinct with the life flowing from its roots.—D. C.

Choice Illustrations on the Theme

TREES ENRICH US. Trees enrich us. They give their refreshing coolness, their beautiful and fragrant blooms, their healthful fruits, lumber for our homes, and other useful things. When a man meditates upon the law of the Lord and follows his precepts, he is like a tree that proves a blessing to mankind. St. John had a vision of the New Jerusalem with its river of the water of life. "Blessed are they that do his commandments, that they may have a right to the tree of life."

We have not been promised that life would be easy for the Christian, but we have this wonderful promise: "To him that overcometh will I grant to sit with me in my throne." Those who keep God's law will share divine power with him.—L. T. Guild.

TREE-LIKE PEOPLE. A Brahmin compared the Christian missionary to a mango tree. It puts forth blossoms, and then weights its branches with fruits. For itself? No; for the hungry who come to it for food. By and by the tree is assailed with clubs and stones. Its leaves are torn, and its branches are bruised and torn. It is stripped bare. But does it resent this cruel treatment, and refuse to yield fruit another year? No; next year it is more fruitful than ever.—J. R. Miller.

PLANTING TREES. When we plant a tree we are doing what we can to make our planet a more wholesome and happier dwelling place for those who come after us, if not for ourselves.—O. W. Holmes.

SELF-SURGERY BY A TREE. Why do the branches of the kauri tree of New Zealand escape the encumbrance of the wild vines and clematis? For reasons that seem too wonderful for belief. The kauri tree does not allow its branches to enter too deeply into its life. They are related not to the heart but to the circumference of the tree. The bark slowly but surely underlays the lower branches. These are already burdened with a heavy tangle of vines. With a crash the laden branch is "cut off" and the impediment is carried in wreckage to the floor of the forest. The process is repeated till at last the tree is so lordly tall that none of these clinging growths can so much as touch it. And that is why this tree is free in bark and branch from all those things that hinder.—Principal North.

Quotable Springtime Poetry

HE WHO PLANTS A TREE

He who plants a tree
    Plants a hope;
    Rootlets up through fibres blindly
        grope.
Leaves unfold unto horizon free.
    So man's life must climb
    From the clods of time
    Unto heavens sublime.
Canst thou prophesy, thou little tree
What the glory of thy boughs shall be?

He who plants a tree,
    He plants love:
Tents of coolness spreading out above
Wayfarers he may not live to see.
    Gifts that grow are best
    Hands that bless are blest;
    Plant! Life does the rest.
Heaven and earth helps him who plants
        a tree,
And his work its own reward shall be.
                —Lucy Larcom.

OUT IN THE FIELDS WITH GOD

The little cares that fretted me,
    I lost them yesterday.
Among the fields above the sea,
    Among the winds at play;
Among the lowing herds,
    The rustling of the trees;
Among the singing birds,
    The humming of the bees.

The fears of what may come to pass,
    I cast them all away
Among the clover-scented grass,
    Among the new-mown hay;
Among the hushing of the corn,
    Where drowsy poppies nod,
Where ill thoughts die and good are
        born—
    Out in the fields with God.
                —Unidentified.

Suggestive Springtime Texts and Themes

Springtime Lessons: "He that ploweth ought to plow in hope." I Cor. 9:10 (A.S.V.).

The Good News of Out-of-doors: "And the Lord God took the man and put him into the garden of Eden to dress it and to keep it." Gen. 2:15.

Some Lessons from Springtime: "For, lo, the winter is past," etc. Song of Sol. 2:11-13.

Nature Praising God: "Then shall all the trees of the wood rejoice before the Lord." Ps. 96:12, 13.

The City with Trees: "In the midst of the street of it, and on either side of the river, was there the tree of life." Rev. 22:2.

Firmly Rooted: "And he shall be like a tree planted." Ps. 1:3.

EVENING SERVICE

Theme: Servants on Horses and Princes Walking.

TEXT: "I have seen servants upon horses, and princes walking as servants upon the earth." Eccles. 10:7.

INTRODUCTORY: The books from which God teaches are many. Nature, reason, history, experience, revelation, all teach man great and valuable lessons. Observation will enrich our minds with facts and wisdom.

The language of the text is mainly figurative. Much more is meant than the words definitely state. They are to be thought over, and will yield much spiritual teaching.

I. The text implies or suggests that the moral world presents some strange illustrations of the unfitness of persons and things for the places and circumstances occupied by them. Servants upon horses and princes walking!

1. For example, when a nation sets wicked or ignorant men in its highest places, and treats its best citizens with neglect or contempt. Charles II on the throne and John Bunyan in jail! Herod and John the Baptist, Nero and Paul!

2. Or when debasing passions and appetites are allowed to rule the man, and intellect, reason and noble affections are trampled under foot. Felix, Herod, the prodigal son!

3. Or when recreations and amusements which at best are but servants of the soul are placed upon the throne of the heart and the great and earnest work of life is left neglected and undone.

4. Or when the world is seated on the throne of the affections and Christ, "the King of kings," is allowed to be but a beggar at our feet, pleading in vain for our attention and love.

II. The text plaintly implies that this state of things is surprising, wrong and ruinous.

1. It is surprising. Reason, common sense and divine revelation teach that this ought not so to be.

2. It is wrong, because it insults virtue, humanity and God.

3. It is ruinous. It upsets justice and right both here and hereafter.—R. B.

MIDWEEK FELLOWSHIP MEETING TOPIC

(Church Night or Suggested Sermon Subject)

Theme: "Ready."

TEXT: "So, as much as in me is, I am ready to preach the gospel to you that are at Rome also." Rom. 1:15.

"I am ready" was the motto of Paul the missionary. Ready for anything, anywhere.

I. Ever since he heard the voice, and saw the light on the Damascus road, nothing seemed worth while except to know and do the will of his great commander and friend. The vision of the man from Macedonia with outstretched, appealing hands, crying, "Come, help us," burned in his heart and brain. It burns in many a heart and conscience today, for the same Jesus who spoke to Paul is speaking now—our risen, living Christ—and men and women are saying, "I am ready!" The love of Christ is still constraining the hearts of men.

II. We must not think that the fire that blazed upon the altar of the early Christian church has died away to mere ashes. There have been great upheavals in the nations in recent years, and even yet there comes from earth's sobbing heart a moan of hunger, suffering and death. But, if we have ears to hear above earth's lamentations, we know that the voices of Faith, Hope and Love never cease and are eternally true.

III. Down through the centuries their harmonies ring—"The Lord reigneth, let the earth rejoice!" How good God is to give us who live in this day similar opportunities to those Paul had to waken the triumphant song in all desolate and needy places throughout the world.—W. S. S.

CHRISTIAN ENDEAVOR SOCIETY TOPIC

May 2. What It Takes—to Be a Missionary. Acts 9:20-31.

BULLETIN BOARD SLOGANS FOR THE MONTH

By EARL RINEY

The Christian life lived has no regrets.

Purpose is what gives life a meaning.

God often comes to visit us, but generally we are not in.

A defeat to a great man is only victory deferred.

Faith is the hand wherewith we take everlasting life.

God's crumbs are better than the world's loaves.

The place to spend a happy day—in church.

For the true Christian all the way to heaven is heaven.

Obedience is the organ of spiritual knowledge.

Repentance is more than remorse; it means a change.

You have to think straight before you can be straight.

It is impossible to slip backward uphill; one must climb.

Religion and common sense are divine twins.

SUNDAY SCHOOL LESSON

May 2. Judgment on Jeroboam. I Kings 14:5-10a, 12-16.

MEMORY VERSE: "Beware lest thou forget the Lord thy God, in not keeping his commandments." Deut. 8:11 (A.S.V.).

When Jeroboam turned to idolatry, Ahijah, as a prophet of God, pronounced judgment on Jeroboam and proclaimed his impending doom. It may be shown how the wrong direction given by Jeroboam prevented the Northern Kingdom from fulfilling the purposes of God. It may be shown how rebellious and unwise decisions lead in wrong directions and prevent the fulfilling of God's purpose in our lives.

Judgment pronounced by the phophet is based on the sinfulness of the king, but it implies dire consequences for the nation.

SUNDAY: MAY NINTH

MORNING SERVICE

Theme: The Making of Happy Christian Homes (Mother's Day).

SUGGESTED SCRIPTURE READING: Prov. 31:1-31.

SELECTED HYMNS: "O happy home, where Thou art loved."—C. J. Spitta. "Up to me sweet childhood looketh."—Anon. "The voice that breathed o'er Eren."—J. Keble. "O perfect love."—D. R. Bromfield. "Thou gracious power whose mercy lends."—O. W. Holmes.

CALL TO WORSHIP: "One thing have I desired of the Lord, that will I seek after; that I may dwell in the house of the Lord all the days of my life, to behold the beauty of the Lord, and to inquire in his temple."

INVOCATION PRAYER: Our loving heavenly Father, we thank thee for the love and fellowship of our homes. We thank thee for the strength and joy that we find in the close ties of family life. But, dear Lord, do not let our

happiness blind us to the loneliness of those around us. Make our hearts open to all those who may be lonely, and help us to draw others into the warmth and cheer of our family circle. And be thou, O Christ, our abiding guest. May we witness for thee in our homes by lives of love and helpfulness. May we witness for thee in the community by standing for Christian ideals. And may we witness for thee in the world by sending our prayers, our money, and our sons and daughters to teach all men repentance and remission of sins. We thank thee for one another. Thou hast set the solitary in families, and in thee every family in heaven and earth is named. We rejoice that we are not alone in the world, but have those near us who love us and whom we love. Forgive us for all unkindness to one another, and make our love constant and sincere. Grant thy pity to those who are lonely; and give us a spirit of true brotherliness in Christ for all thy children. So may we be prepared for our life in the home beyond. In the name of Christ we ask. Amen.

Theme: The Making of Happy Christian Homes (Mother's Day).

TEXT: "God setteth the solitary in families." Ps. 68:6.

INTRODUCTORY: The family is fundamental in human society. It is the original source of authority, government, morality and religion. There the church was organized. There human government was instituted. There marriage was solemnized. Without family ties, family government and discipline, family virtue and piety the church could not exist, and society would soon relapse into barbarism and fall to pieces.

I. The Christian home, therefore, is under God the hope of the world. Everything that is good in church or society is first planted and tended, shielded and nurtured in good homes. The church must look for its spring and source, its fountainhead, in the spiritual life of Christian homes. Why should we not expect the Christian home, as in former days, to be the nursery of true piety, where religious principles shall root themselves deeply in the hearts of parents and children alike? Why should we not definitely expect that the genius and temper and spirit of the home shall be such as to foster the fear of the Lord which is the beginning of wisdom? And why not plan and purpose that our homes shall be so hedged about, fenced and safeguarded against the influence and contagion of the world that they shall be places in which Christ himself shall abide, filling them with the aroma of his presence and the atmosphere of his love?

II. And Christian homes are happy homes. They should be, for they are rallying places of the affections. Besides, there are factors which rightly employed wil surely make them blessed and happy.

1. One supreme factor is fellowship with God. Abraham was called "the friend of God." And of him God said,

"I know him, that he will command his children and his household after him." Abraham's home was a central temple. He and his household built home altars and worshiped there.

2. Another factor in home happiness is intimacy with children. And children are great teachers as well as great learners. For centuries the church has been an increasing institution, holding before itself the task of instructing childhood and inspiring maturity with its truths. But great as is the church, we may well face the fact that it is not the main place when religion is learned. The primary institution both for teaching and practicing religion has been, is now, and ever shall remain in the home. Religion is not so much taught as caught. It is largely a home contagion.

III. The home is fundamental, moreover, because it begins its contacts with childhood so early in life. This is universally recognized, and is crucial. It is so also because the contacts with any given child are so continuous. They are not often interrupted by stress of sickness. On the contrary, sickness usually increases the affectionate contacts of home. Then, too, the home opportunity is great because it has more time at its disposal—more than church, and Sunday School, and day school. A further important factor is that parents have a relationship to the child that no one else can get. To the average child father and mother are hero and heroine in his or her regard.

IV. A further great means both to acquaintance with God and to family fellowship is the household altar. Nothing is, or can be, more important than the establishment and maintenance of family worship. Daily if possible. If that is not possible then time surely can be found at least once a week, probably on the Lord's Day, for the family to gather for Scripture reading, affectionate Christian converse, and a brief prayer. Grace at table should, of course, have its place at every meal.

The restoration of family worship in our homes would do much to bring back our lost or obscured ideals, strengthen home ties, increase interest in and knowledge of God's Word, and bring about faithfulness to the church and zeal in Christ's cause.

Think how superior this is to the all-too-modern home now so much in vogue. There is a typical story of a modern girl who said to a real estate agent seeking to sell her a house: "A home? Why do I need a home? I was born in a hospital, educated in a college, courted in an automobile, and married in a church. I live out of the delicatessen and paper bags. I spend my mornings on the golf course, my afternoons at the bridge table, and my evenings at the movies. And when I die I will be buried from the undertaker's. All I need is a garage!"

How far is all that from any true conception of home! How far indeed also from nay realization of the blessings, the happiness, home was intended to bring!

The beginning of worship in the home—how? when? A large proportion of young people have this purpose in mind. Let them not defer it, or neglect it. Too many put off from day to day their commencement of family worship. They thereby miss, or postpone one of the sweetest means of creating a happy and influence-radiating Christian home.

It has been well said, "The sweetest type of heaven is the home."—H.

THEME PRAYER: Our Father, bless thou the homes of thy people. Give them true ideals of helpfulness. Let all that dwell therein have a real sense of the responsibility that rests on each that the earthly home may reflect the blessedness of the eternal home. May our homes be such that the Spirit of Christ may find a true welcome and that he may often be our guest. Amen.

OFFERTORY SENTENCE: "In the morning sow thy seed, and in the evening withhold not thine hand: for thou knowest not which shall prosper, either this or that, or whether they both shall be alike good."

OFFERTORY PRAYER: Give us faith, our Father, in our giving. May we in the morning sow our seed and in the evening withhold not our hand, knowing not which shall prosper, this or that, or whether they shall both be alike good. It is for the forwarding of thy kingdom we bring our gifts this day. Wilt thou graciously accept and bless and use them, and us as we bring them. We ask in Christ's name. Amen. —H.

Illustrative Material

SEED THOUGHTS, HOMILETIC AND EXPOSITORY. Institute of the Affections: The family has been best defined as "the institute of the affections." In its ideal state it is the home of love. It is the place of all others in which the affectionate side of human nature receives its strongest impulse, its freest, fullest development.—S. W. D.

The Family: I. It is a divine institution. II. It is intimately connected with our earthly happiness. III. The family intercourse has the most powerful influence on human character. IV. The earthly family is not a permanent and abiding thing.—W. M. T.

Rallying Place: The paternal hearth, the rallying place of the affections.— Washington Irving.

Home makes the man.—Samuel Smiles.

"What Makes a Home?" I asked my little boy, and this is what he said: "You, mother, and when father comes, our table all set and shiny, and my bed; and, mother, I think it's home because we love each other." You who are old, what would you say?—U.

Choice Christian Home Illustrations

FAMILY RELIGION. There is an automobile story about a man who eagerly desired to purchase a number of accessories for his car. But the only way he could raise the money to do it was to sell the car itself and buy the accessories. So that is what he did. That is what the wild waves are telling us, that we are in danger of allowing the accessories of life to usurp the place of life itself. Just test out the truth of this statement in regard to the realm which all of us know best—the home. Has not the external aid become in many cases the substitute for that inner life, which the word "home" in its highest sense really means? . . . We are all willing to confess that electric irons and hardwood floors and vacuum cleaners are poor substitutes for unfeigned love and family prayers.—H. E. Luccock.

A HOUSE AND A HOME. Those who unduly magnify their house often fail to enjoy a home. There are six things necessary to make a happy home: integrity, tidiness, affection, cheerfulness, industry, and the sense of divine providence. The house has little to do with the making of an ideal home. For home is the resort of love and joy and peace—the sanctuary of our dearest affections. Henry van Dyke says that every house where love abides and where friendship is a guest is a home. Bruce Barton says that many a renter owns his own home, and then adds, "Many a family has successfully saved for a home only to find itself at last with nothing but a house."—D. Carl Yoder.

WHAT HAVE THEY SEEN? A lady had just parted with some friends who had been guests for a few days. She had been happy in having them see her new home and fine furnishings. Sitting down for a moment she noticed her Bible which had not been open during the friends' visit. Opening the Bible, as it were, at random, her eyes fell on the words of God to Hezekiah, "What have they seen in thine house?" Hezekiah had had visitors. He, too, had been proud of his house, but somehow he had not represented God to his visitors and God had penalized him. Do our guests see a family altar in our homes? Do we wait for a "blessing" at our meals? We cannot possibly leave God out of our family program night and morning, whether we have guests or not.—Garden of Prayer.

DOES GOD LIVE IN OUR HOUSE? Five-year-old Margaret and her brother were frequent visitors in the home of a neighbor. One of the never-ending wonders over which little Margaret pondered as she visited in Hortense's home was the prayer time. Hortense's daddy read out of the big black book and afterward talked to God as if he were very near and dear to them all. Sometimes the family would join in singing a song of praise. One morning when Margaret had been present at the prayer time, Hortense's mother suggested, "Margaret, don't you pray at your house?" Margaret shook her head sadly, and said, "No, you see, God doesn't live at our house as He does at yours." Margaret's home was by no means a so-called underprivileged one. It was an average, middle-class American home. But if the little girl wanted to meet God, the Heavenly Father, she had to go next door. He just wasn't included in her family circle.—Sunday School Digest.

Quotable Mother's Day Poetry

THAT'S MOTHER

A little bit of lavender;
A little bit of lace;
A dainty little bonnet, and
A kindly beaming face;
    That's Mother!

Two lips that speak forth godliness;
Two hands, in service, lent;
Two feet, though slow and faltering,
On mercy-missions bent;
    That's Mother!

A mind, alert, in spite of years;
A body worn by cares;
A soul that learned to trust in Him
Who, all her burdens, shares;
    That's Mother!

That's Mother! yes, God bless her ways
And keep her pathway bright,
And through her few remaining days
Make all the burdens light,
    For Mother.
                        —C. E. Hetzler.

MY ALTAR

I have worshipped in churches and
chapels;
I've prayed in the busy street;
I have sought my God and have found
him
Where the waves of his ocean beat;
I have knelt in the silent forest
In the shade of some ancient tree;
But the dearest of all my altars
Was raised at my mother's knee.

I have listened to God in his temple;
I've caught his voice in the crowd;
I have heard him speak when the
breakers
Were booming long and loud;
Where the winds play soft in the tree-
tops
My father has talked to me;
But I never heard him clearer
Than I did at my mother's knee.

—John H. Styles, Jr.

EVENING SERVICE

Theme: Portraits of Nobility.

NOTE: The ingenious minister can
make this service attractive by present-
ing living portraits of the women mentioned below. It is possible to make a
large book and have the portraits as
illustrations in the book. Advice might
be secured from a professional in dramatic production when such a person is
available. Of course, an effective service does not depend upon such pres-
entation.

INTRODUCTORY: The Bible is the greatest portrait gallery in the world. The
famous galleries found in Amsterdam,
Paris, London and Florence cannot compare for a moment with the gallery of
the Old and New Testament; and notable among the portraits found there
are those of the women of the Bible.

Is it because of their beauty that
these women belong to the greatest of
all galleries? Little is said of the physical beauty of any of the women in the
Bible; what is emphasized is the beauty
of soul—a beauty which does not fade
with the passing years, but only becomes

greater as the years go on and the
woman's influence grows, becoming one
of the most powerful forces for good in
the world. Of course, not all the
women of the Bible were good women;
they were not all lofty, noble, godlike,
glorious; in fact, some were base, ignoble, wicked and contemptible, but the
latter would not belong in this great
gallery.

A minister once asked his congregation to vote upon the ten greatest
women of the Bible. They chose Ruth
first and Eve last. With the limited
time I have, I cannot even touch upon
all the great women of the Bible, not
even ten, so I have chosen a few whose
portraits of life may inspire us to radiate
the light of Christian living, and to
know the greatest joy in life, the joy of
serving.

I. Mary. I would not name Ruth
first on my list of great women, but
would give that place to the one to
whom the angel said, "Thou art highly
favored—the Lord is with thee. Blessed
art thou among women," the mother of
Jesus.

There is not a great deal told in the
Bible about Mary, but because she was
the one chosen to guide the early footsteps of the Messiah, she is to each
if us the epitome of consecration and
service. We see her as a young woman
to whom the angel revealed that she
was to bear this wonderful Son, and
we see her thirty-odd years later as a
quiet, devout member of a group of
believers. In those years she has known
a joy deeper than one can imagine, but
she has also known an indescribable
sorrow.

Mary's spiritual intuition was of
great depth and her moral fiber of tremendous strength and power. The love
in her heart was great and beautiful.
We have reason to believe that the most
powerful forces in the development of
the boy Jesus were the piety, faith and
righteousness of Mary and Joseph. As
one author puts it: "Every touch in the
gospels concerning the life at Nazareth,
every implied allusion to it, brings up a
picture of goodness and truth, a parental

care for a growing boy, shared by two who could hear the angels speak, and who both desired only the rightful purposes of God."

And Luke phrases the childhood of Jesus in simple, radiant words that are unequalled, "And he went down with them, and came to Nazareth; and he was subject unto them: and his mother kept all these sayings in her heart. And Jesus advanced in wisdom and stature, and in favor with God and men."

II. Ruth. But not far from this portrait would be the one of Ruth, an ancestress of David, the line of Jesus. It was the attractiveness of virtue, the beauty of sacrifice, and the winsomeness of simple trust in God which were the attributes of this young woman. Her famous words to her mother-in-law, Naomi, "Whither thou goest, I will go; and where thou lodgest, I will lodge: thy people shall be my people, and thy God my God," show her great spirit of loyalty. It was a part of God's plan that she go with Naomi and God guided her, but she exercised her power of choice. She trusted in God and so was guided by him. Because of her loyalty, it was her destiny to become an ancestress of our Lord.

The poet Keats, in his "Ode to a Nightingale," imagines Ruth listening to the entrancing song of that bird in the fields of Jerusalem where she was gleaning:

Perhaps the self-same song that found
  a path
Through the sad heart of Ruth, when,
  sick for home,
She stood in tears amid the alien corn.

I think he was mistaken when he spoke of Ruth as "sick for home." Ruth had willingly and gladly chosen Israel and turned her back on Moab, and nowhere do we find that she regretted her choice.

I am sure we are all familiar with the story of Ruth, how she followed her mother-in-law to her home, how she was sent into the fields of the kinsman Boaz to glean, how she found favor in his sight and married him.

Ruth stands for those whose decision is final and irrevocable. Ruth chose definitely and forever the people of God. And the picture of Ruth comes to mind whenever we think of loyalty.

III. Esther. Our next portrait is of a woman who was really beautiful: her beauty was more than physical, however, for she had that beauty of soul which made her great. Her Persian name "Esther" means star. "Beauty," the wise man said, "is vain." But that is not always true, not when beauty of face and body is joined with beauty of soul. In the Book of Esther we have the story of how God used the beauty of one woman to save a nation from destruction and carry forth his eternal purpose.

At the beginning of the book, before Esther comes upon the scene, very briefly we see another beautiful woman who loved honor and her soul more than life itself. The story of Esther begins with a great banquet given by the king of Persia, a banquet which has probably never been surpassed in wickedness, beauty and length of time. It had lasted seven days and many of the princes had had to be carried out because of their drunkenness. About midnight on the seventh day, when the excitement was beginning to wane, the drunken king, trying to think of something new to entertain his guests, called for his queen Vashti to come in and display her beauty before them. She knew that it meant dismissal from the court, her exile, and maybe even her death if she refused. Yet she did not hesitate to say "No," and had it not been for that "No" of Vashti's, we never would have heard of Esther. Vashti was banished and was never heard of again, but her beauty of character shines forth as a great light amid the debauchery of the king's court.

Then began the original beauty contest. Every province of the empire was searched that another beautiful queen might be found for Ahasuerus. The choice fell upon Esther, the adopted daughter of her cousin Mordecai, who held a post of some importance in the palace.

This is another story with which we are all familiar. Haman, the prime minister of the king, became angry with Mordecai the Jew because he would not bow down to him. So, desiring revenge on Mordecai, he got permission from the king to kill all the Jews in the kingdom, declaring that they were the cause of all the troubles that arose. The Jewish race was saved by the courage of Esther. Her courage more than her beauty gives her a prominent place in the gallery of the Bible.

IV. Martha and Mary. Next we have two sisters, who were famous because they were intimate friends of Jesus. One was the busy, efficient woman, who cooked and sewed, and the other sat at the feet of the Master. At one time in Jesus' life he said that the foxes had holes and the birds of the air had nests, but the Son of Man had nowhere to lay his head. It is a satisfaction to know that in this home of Mary, Martha and Lazarus Jesus always found a welcome and was treated with kindness, sympathy and understanding. One day, as Jesus was traveling with his disciples up from Jericho, he stopped at the home of these friends. Perhaps he sent word ahead, but, at any rate, it was quite a crowd of guests for a small household and we can imagine Martha's hurrying to make ready for so many. Suddenly she thought of Mary and, wondering why she wasn't in the kitchen helping with the preparations, she went to look for her. When she found her sitting in the cool courtyard looking up into the face of the Master, drinking in his words of wisdom, Martha lost her temper and said, "Lord, dost thou not care that my sister hath left me to serve alone? Bid her, therefore, that she help me." And Jesus patiently answered, "Martha, Martha, thou art careful and troubled about many things: But one thing is needful: and Mary hath chosen that good part, which shall not be taken away from her." Jesus did not rebuke Martha for her zeal and industry; someone had to prepare the meal or he and his disciples would have gone hungry. However, it was clear from his words that she put too great emphasis upon the practical side of life to the neglect of the devotional side. The ideal woman must learn to combine the practical and the devotional and not neglect that which is important to the soul. Mary had chosen the good part; she chose to give her heart to Christ, the one thing which was needful, which could not be taken away from her, the Master said. And when she anointed the feet of Jesus with expensive ointment and wiped them with her hair, Jesus said, "Verily I say unto you, Wheresoever this gospel shall be preached throughout the whole world, this also that she hath done shall be spoken of for a memorial of her." Surely these two sisters whom Jesus loved so much that he wept, when they were in sorrow, deserve a place in the gallery of the Bible.

V. Others. And so we could go on adding to this list—Hanna, the mother of Samuel; Rachel, the beloved wife of Jacob; Lois and Eunice, the mother and grandmother of Timothy; Priscilla, who with her husband, Aquilla, befriended Paul, even helping to save his life, when he was in trouble with Demetrius; Lydia, the Christian business woman; and many others who lived nobly.

What a great thing it would be, if we could find a composite portrait, which would unite the tremendous love, strength and power of Mary, the loyalty of Ruth, the courage of Esther, the efficiency of Martha and the pious meditation of Mary. We would indeed have the ideal woman. Fortunately, the picture of an ideal woman is painted for us in the last chapter of Proverbs. "She looketh well to the ways of her household, and eateth not the bread of idleness. She riseth while it is yet night" to labor for her family and to wait upon those of its number who are sick. She is loyal for the Proverb says, "The heart of her husband doth safely trust in her." She is charitable: "She stretcheth out her hand to the poor; yea, she reacheth forth

SUNDAY: MAY NINTH

her hands to the needy." The law of kindness is on her tongue; she has a godly character and she shall be praised because she fears the Lord. She excels them all; her influence abides from generation to generation and "her children arise up, and call her blessed."—Gladys Blackmun Bock.

Suggested Mother's Day Texts and Themes

Our Mothers, An Appreciation: "When Jesus therefore saw his mother," etc. John 19:26, 27.

Promises to Children: "Honour thy father and thy mother." Ex. 20:12.

An Ingenious Mother: "Took for him an ark of bulrushes, and daubed," etc. Ex. 2:3.

An Ambitious Mother: "Grant that these my two sons may sit," etc. Matt. 20:21, 22.

Mothers Builders of the Race: "A faith that was seen first," etc. II Tim. 1:5. (Goodspeed)

MIDWEEK FELLOWSHIP MEETING TOPIC

(Church Night or Suggested Sermon Subject)

Theme: The Ideal Mother (Mother's Day).

TEXT: "Her children arise up and call her blessed; her husband also, and he praiseth her." Prov. 31:28.

The family is the profoundest and most sacred of all our social relationships. It is a type of spiritual relationships and a means of realizing them. In this delineation of the excellent woman the influence of the mother is that she receives the benediction of her own children. They do her honor, speak of her with reverence and love and blessing. What must a mother be in order to inherit such benediction from her children? The ideal mother is characterized in this chapter.

I. She is virtuous, v. 10.

II. She is industrious, vv. 13-19.

III. She is a good manager, v. 16.

IV. She is charitable, v. 20.

V. She gives her husband prestige, v. 23.

VI. She is intelligent, v. 26.

VII. She is reverent and religious, v. 30.

Susannah Wesley was a model mother. She brought up her family so well that all Christendom has cause to bless her name. At her death her children gathered around her bed and sang a hymn of praise in gratitude to God for such a mother. General Garfield used to say, "I owe everything to my mother."

CHRISTIAN ENDEAVOR SOCIETY TOPIC

May 9. What It Takes—to Be a Parent (Christian Family Day). Col. 3:12-24.

SUNDAY SCHOOL LESSON

May 9. Elijah Challenges Baal Worship. I Kings 17:1; 18:17-24; 37-39.

MEMORY VERSE: "How long go ye limping between the two sides? if the Lord be God, follow him; but if Baal, then follow him." I Kings 18:21 (A.S.V.)

The historical setting, when made clear, is most interesting as found in chapters 17 to 19. The kings of Judah in order were Rehoboam, Abijah, Asa. Those of the Northern Kingdom, Israel, were Jeroboam, Nadab, Baasha, Elah, Zimri, Omri and Ahab. This lesson's historical background is the reign of Ahab.

I. *Contrast* Baalism with the worship of the Lord. The Baalim were local gods. Their worship was often idolatrous ad debased by immorality. See Jer. 19:5 which tells of human sacrifice associated with Baal worship.

II. *Proclamation:* This lesson should impress the truth for our day. "The Lord, he is God."

III. *Challenge:* "If the Lord be God, serve him."

SUNDAY: MAY SIXTEENTH

MORNING SERVICE

Theme: Out of Focus.

SUGGESTED SCRIPTURE READING: II Pet. 1:1-21.

SELECTED HYMNS: "Rise up, O men of God."—W. P. Merrill. "What grace, O Lord, and beauty shone."—E. Denny. "How sweet, how heavenly is the sight."—J. Swain. "Blest be the tie that binds."—J. Fawset.

CALL TO WORSHIP: "The Lord is nigh unto all them that call upon him, to all that call upon him in truth. He will fulfil the desire of them that fear him: he also will hear their cry, and will save them."

INVOCATION PRAYER: In that name which is above every name, in the name of Jesus Christ, our Lord, we bow before thee, O God, in prayer. This instinctive need of our hearts to commune with thee and pray lifts us above our fellow creatures of the earth. It is the mark of our humanity. And we pray, our Father, because we are dependent upon thee. We have no power to bid the rising of the sun nor the changing of the seasons. By no power of ours is life given to the seed and the seed caused to grow. We plant and thou dost bring to fruitage. We sow and by thy will the fields become golden unto harvest.

We are dependent upon thy grace, O God, to satisfy the deep personal needs of our hearts. The high ideal and the good example is thy gift unto us in Jesus Christ. In him we find a Saviour from sin unto righteousness, from death unto life. He is strength for our weakness. He finds us when we are lost. He leads us when we aspire. And as we pray, our Father, we remember thy grace, we praise thee for thy goodness, and we pray for that further grace which enables us to appropriate the rich gifts which thou hast provided for us in Jesus Christ. Amen.—M. K. W. H.

Theme: Out of Focus.

TEXT: "He that lacketh these things is blind, and cannot see afar off." II Pet. 1:9.

INTRODUCTORY: "Distance lends enchantment to the view"; so says Gray the poet. But really to appreciate the truth of that, we must be sure that we have the proper focus; for distance can create indistinctness, delusion, deception. Distance can shut out beauty, harmony, meaning. For example, sound. For example, sight.

Is not much of our haziness about life something like that? We are out of focus for we are lacking in the things that go to make for spiritual discernment. "He that lacketh these things [faith, virtue, knowledge, temperance, godliness, brotherly kindness, charity] is blind, and cannot see afar off."

I. Here is a man with whom we differ. We say we cannot understand why he differs. That is true: we simply cannot. We might easily understand it if we understood why we differ from him. So much of our thinking is against others, when really it should be against ourselves. But had we some of the virtues already mentioned we might hear the music in that man's life, and see the beauty of his character.

A man true to his convictions was unpopular among certain of his fellows. One of them said: "Why, he's quite a different person when you get to know him." Have you ever said that of one for whom you had no liking, or of whom you were suspicious? Was not the reason simply this, that you had not risked a little patience or confidence, a little brotherliness or charity; you had not put yourself into the position of know ing the man?

Here is a man who seems very self-centered. We say of him that he might as well be out of the world as in it, for outside himself not one single service does he render. That is our distant view of him. But come nearer. Enter his home; see him in great tenderness minister to his wife who lies on a sick-bed from which she will never rise. Three young children claim this father's love—a love which never tires. This man's day (and it is every day) is crammed with service. And yet as we passed him we thought that selfishness had claimed him. Things are not always what they appear to be. We do not know what men and women have to contend with. Patience, godliness, brotherly kindness, charity—lacking these things we are blind, and cannot see afar off.

II. It has been said that one half of the world does not know how the other half lives. It ought to know, and God means us to know. And the best means of knowing is just to view the other half through the medium of the virtues enumerated. The nearer we draw to humanity, the farther we shall see, and that farther view will help us to be touched with the woes and depriva-tions of fallen and suffering mortals. The nearer we advance the farther we see —it is so where one has perspective; and life is full of perspective.

III. "He that lacketh these things." It was the lack of these things that made the people of Christ's time blind to him. They saw no further than his birthplace, his parentage, his upbring-ing and occupation. Had they drawn near to him in faith and love they would have seen the depth of genuineness in his claim. We cannot blame a man for examining Christianity before accepting it, any more than we can blame a man for considering a business before taking it over; or even knowing something definite of a woman before he makes her his life companion. In these trans-actions he is allowed his choice. The same freedom to choose is given in the

realm of the spirit. Christ can bear inspection. If you come near enough to him you cannot but be drawn to him. When a man gets into focus with Christ he lives a new life, he starts a new career. And a man in getting into focus with Christ gets into focus with himself.—J. L. R.

THEME PRAYER: Lord of all being, we cry unto thee in our blindness, asking thee to grant us the unity of thy Spirit and the bond of peace. Show us the good way out of our differences, the way of brotherhood and co-opera-tion, and quiet the hearts of men with the peace of God that passeth all un-derstanding. Amen.

OFFERTORY SENTENCE: "And God is able to make all grace abound toward you; that ye, always having all-suffi-ciency in all things, may abound to every good work."

OFFERTORY PRAYER: We have heard thy word, our Father, Honor the Lord with thy substance and with the first fruits of all thine increase; so shall thy barns be filled with plenty, and thy presses shall burst out with new wine. It is indeed to honor thee we bring these our offerings this morning and dedicate them to thy cause and king-dom in the world. In Christ's name. Amen.

Illustrative Material

SEED THOUGHTS, HOMILETIC AND EXPOSI-TORY. Spiritual Nearsightedness: Faith oftentimes lies dormant like hibernating insects. A book of Chinese fables tells of a country where the people wake once in fifty days, and take the dreams of their sleep for realities, and the things they are in their waking moments for dreams.—T. G. S.

He is Blind: I. Some people see nothing in salvation but deliverance from wrath. Miserably defective view. The man, who is saved by the forgiving grace of God, neglects to enter into the privilege and fellowship and ennobling spiritual experience to which virtue, knowledge, temperance, patience, godli-ness, brotherly kindness, charity are the successive steps. "He that lacketh these things is blind. II. Or at best his blindness is half blindness. He is nearsighted, shortsighted, "He cannot see afar off." III. Again St. Peter describes the lack of these higher Christian excellences under the figure of an intellectual lapse. "Having forgotten the cleansing from his old sin."—T. G. S.

Choice Illustrations on the Theme

OUT OF FOCUS. The caste system, or the caste spirit, wherever it is found, is but an evidence of prejudicial pride.

A Spaniard in South America, who suffered severely from the gout, refused to accept the services of a noted Indian doctor. "I know," said the afflicted man, "that he is a famous man, and would certainly cure me; but he is an Indian, and would expect to be treated with attentions which I cannot pay to a man of color. Therefore, I prefer remaining as I am."—*Otterbein Teacher.*

OUT OF FOCUS. One may be out of focus by prejudice, or by ignorance, or by a distance too great, or by overnearness. It may have happened that you stood some distance from a picture. There was to be seen in the foreground what seemed to be upright beams and great blotches of dark color. You could not by any stretch of imagination make it out to represent anything known to you. A little nearer you saw that the mass of color was thick foliage. A little nearer yet and you saw the sunset peer through the trees in the distance. A little closer still, and not too close, you saw the artist's motive. The rosy tints fall athwart the figure of a plowman, who, with his team, "homeward plods his weary way." That is the picture. You miss it when you are distant from it. When you draw near to it the lesson of honest toil dawns upon you.—J. L. Rodger, D.D.

GET INTO FOCUS. The former King Edward VIII of England was a fascinating young man. While Prince of Wales he had done many fascinating things. To me, the most fascinating and the most glorious thing he ever did, he did in Bombay. The prince was riding through the streets of the city. The police were trying to hold back something like a million or so untouchables behind rope barriers. The prince saw the struggle going on, rose in' his car and gave a stirring command: "Take down the barriers!" The authorities remonstrated; the untouchables, they said, would mob him, perhaps kill him. "Take down the barriers!" said the prince a second time. The barriers came down. Nothing happened. Those miserable legions of the damned simply stood quietly about the car, looking up into his white face as though he were a god come to rescue them from their fearful condition of life. And the Prince of Wales, heir apparent to the throne of England, stood quietly in his car, and raised his hand in salute to the untouchables of India!

Isn't that the job of the Christians of this generation? To take down the barriers of caste and pride and arrogance and . . . ?

THE BROTHERHOOD FOCUS. An Iowa city had been visited by a severe windstorm which had uprooted a good many trees in the residential section and caused considerable other damage. In a little park at the center of the city a beautiful tree had been a severe sufferer from the wind, but because of the other trees all about which offered support, it had not gone completely down. Tree surgeons came to its rescue, straightened it up, supported it with cables and braces, and in the course of a year or two it sent new roots down into the ground, took a new grip on the earth, and was flourishing again.

Only God can know how many men would have gone down under discouragement if it had not been for the strength furnished them by their associates—other men not quite so badly shaken by the storm.

In no other respect does the church of Christ furnish more ample justification for its existence than at this very point—brotherhood.

No matter how eloquent the preacher or how artistic the choir, that church which does not furnish fellowship is not functioning as a Christian church.—Rev. Roy L. Smith.

TRUTH OUT OF FOCUS. There is a famous passage in Cicero in which he records that a prisoner having spent his life in a dark dungeon, and knowing only what light was from a small fissure in the rock, inferred that if the walls were removed the light would cease to exist because the fissure would be destroyed. Many people live in a similar dungeon and draw the same inference. They think that if the walls they have built to safeguard the light were destroyed truth itself would perish.—*2,500 Best Modern Illustrations.*

GET IN FOCUS. Shortly before the death of the novelist, Joseph Conrad, Epstein the sculptor was engaged in carving a bust of the noted novelist. The sculptor worked twenty-one days at a stretch on this particular bust. At the end he said, "I was glad to spend twenty-one days of my life looking at Joseph Conrad."

When a man gazes on the face of Christ, trying to reproduce it indelibly in his heart, his life will become transformed and transfigured. His confessions will be, "Once I was blind; now I see."

Suggestive Texts and Themes

Neglected Souls: "He maketh both the deaf to hear, and the dumb to speak." Mark 7:37.

The Balance of Power: "They shall not dwell in the Lord's land." Hos. 9:3.

Different Theories: "Whether he be a sinner or no, I know not." John 9:25.

Religion the Laboratory of Life: "O taste and see that the Lord is good." Ps. 34:8.

The Heroism of Noble Despair: "Let us also go, that we may die with him." John 11:16.

EVENING SERVICE

Theme: The Most Christlike Virtue.

TEXT: "Be ye kind one to another, tenderhearted, forgiving one another, even as God for Christ's sake hath forgiven you." Eph. 4:32.

INTRODUCTORY: What is forgiveness? To give up resentment or claim to requital on account of offense or wrong. The Scriptures are rich with illustrations of forgiveness. Examples: Joseph forgives his brethren. David forgives Saul repeatedly.

In the eighteenth chapter of Matthew's Gospel Jesus had been speaking of the sin and peril of our offending others. He then in turn speaks of our proper Christian attitude toward those who offend us, setting forth the parable of the unforgiving servant.

I. First of all, Jesus tells the Christian attitude toward those who sin against us. Make no mistake about it; if Jesus did not escape slander, misrepresentation and wrong, how shall we hope to escape it if we are really following him?

God's Word says: "Be ye kind one to another, tenderhearted, forgiving one another, even as God for Christ's sake hath forgiven you." And beyond that, Jesus says that we are to go to those who have wronged us and seek a loving reconciliation.

II. A second lesson from the parable of the unforgiving servant is that of the urgent necessity of forgiving those who have wronged us. Jesus makes forgiveness the condition for reception into the kingdom of heaven, for regarding the king's treatment of the cruel servant he says, "So also shall my heavenly Father do unto you if ye forgive not every one his brother from your hearts." Note, however, that Christ does not issue a warrant for pardoning every criminal in the land. Forgiveness is a personal relation, not a legal one. In the twelfth chapter of Romans, Paul adds his testimony: "Avenge not yourselves, but rather give place unto wrath: for it is written, Vengeance is mine; I will repay, saith the Lord. Therefore if thine enemy hunger, feed him; if he thirst, give him drink: for in so doing thou shalt heap coals of fire on his head. Be not overcome of evil, but overcome evil with good."

III. Finally, Jesus teaches here the base ingratitude of refusing to forgive others. The servant was forgiven a great debt yet refused to forgive a small one. It is not easy to forgive. It meant a cross for Christ. This is a hard teaching, but it comes from the lips of the Master himself. May God give us grace to remember that once there was a man who into the ugly current of earth's war and hatred poured the healing balm of his own lifeblood to bear away the sins of the race. Never was any man more misunderstood. The ones he loved crucified him on a tree. Each succeeding generation has crucified him afresh. Yet, his voice still echoes down the centuries of time: "Father, forgive them." Therefore, let us "be . . . kind one to another, tenderhearted, forgiving one another, even as God for Christ's sake hath forgiven you."—Rev. Alfred Mathes.

MIDWEEK FELLOWSHIP MEETING TOPIC

(Church Night or Suggested Sermon Subject)

Theme: Delighting in God.

TEXT: "Delight thyself also in the Lord; and he shall give thee the desires of thine heart." Ps. 37:4.

God is worthy of the supreme affection of us all. All other things should be subordinate to him or loved in him.

I. Here is an important duty recommended. "Delight thyself also in the Lord." 1. This presupposes knowledge of God and renewal in him. 2. It presupposes love and sincere pleasure in whatever concerns him. 3. It means to take pleasure in him.

II. The gracious promise made. "He shall give thee the desires of thine heart."

1. The fulfillment depends upon the character of our desires. The desires of a good man are of a righteous nature. 2. His desires are in unison with the will of God. 3. The Christian is not indifferent to temporal wants. God will supply these. 4. The Christian desires to know God better, to have intimate intercourse with him, to be weaned from the world, to have increase of faith. These and all such are desires God delights to meet.—H.

CHRISTIAN ENDEAVOR SOCIETY TOPIC

May 16. What It Takes—to Be a Minister. I Tim. 4:4-16.

SUNDAY SCHOOL LESSON

May 16. Elijah Rebukes Ahab. I King 21.

MEMORY VERSE: "Thou shalt not covet." Ex. 20:17.

Tell the story. It is full of human interest. Catch the contrast, Ahab-Jezebel vs. Naboth-Elijah. Covetousness, deceit, graft, perjury, theft, murder vs. honor, loyalty, religious conviction, righteousness, courage. The world needs men like Naboth who will stand up and say, "I will not give thee my vineyard." "God forgive us that in our folly we have sold so much, and at so cheap a price. But it is still open to every one of us to make a stand at last, and to say with an accent of determination which nothing can shake and no man dare dispute: 'I will not give thee my vineyard.'" The world also needs men like Elijah, fearless, outspoken leaders and people who will act as a conscience for society.

SUNDAY: MAY TWENTY-THIRD

MORNING SERVICE

Theme: The Passing and the Permanent.

SUGGESTED SCRIPTURE READING: Heb. 12:1-29.

SELECTED HYMNS: "How firm a foundation."—Anon. "A mighty fortress is our God."—M. Luther. "Supreme in wisdom, as in power."—I. Watts. "Your harps, ye trembling saints."—A. M. Toplady. "Call Jehovah thy salvation."—J. Montgomery.

CALL TO WORSHIP: "I will bless the Lord at all times: his praise shall continually be in my mouth. . . . O magnify the Lord with me, and let us exalt his name together."

INVOCATION PRAYER: Thou God and Father of all goodness, we thank thee for the call to worship. And for the promise of thy presence we thank thee. Let us know and feel that thou art here. Draw us with the cords of thy love and make us glad together as we commune with thee. We bless thee for all the benefactions of thy providence and grace. May thy goodness lead us to repentance. Save us not only from the penalty of sin, but from the bondage of it; cleanse us from its guilt and power. Lead us into the glorious liberty of thy children, the liberty of truth and righteousness. Defend us from the danger of conformity to this world and help us to seek the things which are unseen and eternal. Relieve our sorrows, according to thy holy will; and make us ever patient in the sphere in which thou hast put us and faithful in serving thee. And whatever we desire for ourselves we ask also for our friends and for all in the household of faith. Bless the community in which we live. Bless our country and its rulers. Bless all lands, especially such as lie in darkness and the shadow of death. Give wings to thy Gospel that it may fly to the uttermost parts of the earth, and give glad hearts and willing feet to those who are commissioned to declare it. All of which we ask in the name of Christ. Amen.

Theme: The Passing and the Permanent.

TEXT: "Wherefore we receiving a kingdom which cannot be moved, let us have grace, whereby we may serve God acceptably with reverence and godly fear." Heb. 12.28.

INTRODUCTORY: Often we hear it said of some invention, some improvement which ingenuity has added to the possession of man, that "it has come to stay." Of other things it may be said, "They have come to pass." No element of permanency is in them. They are merely phases of a passing day.

I. The passing.

1. One of the phases of life that comes to pass is opportunity. When the good Samaritan, hurrying along the Jericho road, came upon the helpless man lying in the path, his chance to serve and save had come to pass. He must do it now.

2. We think of religion, of Christ, as facts which are always here. This is not the truth of the Gospel. Jesus Christ passes by. Christian faith is an opportunity. If we let it pass, it comes not again.

3. Again, time comes to pass. As we grow older we are more and more conscious of the swift flight of the years.

4. Moreover, suffering and pain come to pass. Our afflictions are only for the moment. God has mercifully ordained it so, otherwise the burdens of life would become heavier than we could bear.

II. Let us turn now to the other side. What are the things that remain?

1. First, God did not come to pass. Above all the tumult and change the Lord reigneth.

2. And God's Word remains. "Heaven and earth shall pass away, but my words shall not pass away." Ever since the days of Celsus and Julian, fifteen hundred years ago, the Bible has been assailed. The men who attacked it have passed. They came to pass, and they are gone. But the Bible remains, and it will remain when these storms of criticism have died down into the silence of the ages.

3. Life itself did not come to pass. We have all seen those whose lives were bound up with ours pass beyond our sight and ken. They have gone, but they have not passed away. They did not come to pass. Many things concerning God we do not know, but this we do. He did not create us only to cast us into the void. We did not come to pass.

The late W. J. Dawson wrote a little book at the close of the World War I called *The Father of a Soldier*. In it he speaks of a soldier's belief in immortality. These men who live on such intimate terms with death, who look it in the face every day, he tells us, ought to know something about it. The soldier believes that life does not come to pass. He sees his comrade, yesterday moving, thinking, being, destroyed by a shell in an instant. He speaks of him as "gone west." This is a significant expression. It means home. The men who used it, the British soldiers and the Americans, came from the west. The west meant to them the best things in life, the farm and ranch house, the home, the wife and children, the father and mother, and rest and peace. He has not passed away. He has only gone west. The poor body is not the man. He is somewhere else, with his strength and courage and consecration. He did not come to pass.

Let us rejoice today that in an age of change and decay there are things that cannot pass.—S. N. H.

THEME PRAYER: We pray thee, Lord of the Steadfast, for steadfast wills and purposes perfected in obedience to thee. Forbid that through our want of patient strength any bright promise of good in us or the work we share shall wither away. Make us strong in wisdom and virtue by thy grace, through Jesus Christ, our Lord. Amen.

OFFERTORY SENTENCE: "The righteous giveth and spareth not."

OFFERTORY PRAYER: O thou who art the Giver of every good and perfect gift, it is with humble gratitude we bring our offerings this morning. With our gifts we give ourselves and pray for the coming of thy kingdom of love and peace and good will in all the world. Be pleased to use these our offerings to the extension of thy kingdom in the world. We ask in Christ's name. Amen.

Illustrative Material

SEED THOUGHTS, HOMILETIC AND EXPOSITORY. The Immovable Kingdom: I. There is a kingdom. II. This kingdom cannot be moved. III. There are many temporal kingdoms, but this one is spiritual and divine. The King is God. The Administrator-General is Christ. IV. The subjects are believing saints. This kingdom cannot be moved, is not movable or alterable because Prince, people, laws and administration continue forever.—G. L.

The Immovable Kingdom: I. The immovability of the Gospel dispensation. 1. It is the perfection of all prior dispensations of religion. 2. The Lord Jesus is the Head. "Head over all things to the Church." II. It is obvious that anything which can be termed the "kingdom of God" must be immovable. What changed and passed and disappeared are not of the essence of religion. That remained. The historical Christ, the Christian church, the post-Christian era only illustrate and explain and illumine the truths which are eternal.—L. D. B.

Choice Illustrations on the Theme

THE PASSING AND THE PERMANENT. One of the Red Republicans of 1793 was telling a good peasant of La Vendee, "We are going to pull down your churches and your steeples—all that recalls the superstitions of past ages, and all that brings to your mind the idea of God." "Citizen," replied the good Vendeean, "pull down the stars then."—W. Baxendale.

THE PASSING OF FAME AND POPULARITY. Fame and popularity come only to pass. French historians tell of the triumphant entry of Louis Napoleon into Paris in 1868. He was the idol of the French people. The streets were thronged with happy subjects, cheering and strewing flowers in his path. Two years later a terror-haunted man, with a price on his head, crept out of the city at dead of night, mounted a horse and rode to the coast from whence he escaped to England. It was the same Louis Napoleon whom the French had feasted and feted a little while before.—S. N. Hutchinson, D.D.

A WONDERFUL KING. I heard a man describing the meeting of the Baptist Alliance in Berlin with representatives from sixty nations. One of the last meetings was choral, led by a choir of twenty-five hundred voices. They swept on through Mendelssohn and Brahms and Haydn, but the first number was "All Hail the Power of Jesus' Name," the last was the "Hallelujah Chorus." "Jesus shall reign" was their slogan. I heard one describing a general convention of Episcopalians with the diocesan roll call: Alabama, Alaska, Angkin, Atlanta . . . Haiti, Harrisburg, Honolulu—the world. "Jesus shall reign" was their slogan. I heard one describing a meeting of the Pan-Presbyterian Alliance in Belfast— the world. "Jesus shall reign" was their slogan. I heard one describing a Eucharistic Congress in St. Peters—the world. "Jesus shall reign" was their slogan. Sweep away certain superficial differences of form and the end and aim are one. The ringing slogan is the same— "Jesus shall reign." And inevitably like a great force of nature, his regnancy frees man—frees us where we stand individually, frees all the wide world of men.—Harry M. Edmunds.

A WORLD WITHOUT GOD. There is a story that comes to us from the pen of Jean Paul Richter, the celebrated man of letters, in his *Dream of a World without a God*. He dreamed he was in a churchyard. Thunder, lightning and earthquake filled his heart with terror. Christ appeared. The dead came to life. They asked, "Is there no God?" And the sad reply comes from the Christ: "There is none. I have traversed the worlds, I have risen to the suns, with the milky ways I have passed athwart the great waste spaces of the sky. There is no God. And I descended to where the very shadow cast by being dies out and ends, and I gazed into the great gulf beyond and cried, 'Father, where art thou?' But no answer came, save the eternal storm which rages on. We are orphans all, both you and I. We have no father." Every soul seemed the victim of "mad," unreasoning chance. Every soul in this "great corpse-trench of a universe" seemed utterly alone. Then he awoke. And Richter says his "soul wept for joy that I could still worship God—my gladness and my weeping and my faith, these were my prayers." Life would be intolerable without God.— Elmer George Homrighausen, D.D.

THE PROMISE OF A KINGDOM. Professor John Knox in his book *He Whom a Dream Hath Possessed* tells of an American traveler who once walked over a great English estate with the head gardener. Noting a strange plant he asked what it might be. The gardener replied, "It is a century plant, sir; my father planted it and cared for it for forty years, I have cared for it nearly that long, and my sons will care for it after I am gone. My father never saw it bloom, I shall never see it bloom, and when they do they will think of my father and me." Dr. Knox adds to this story: "Can it be that this living universe has inherent in its very structure the promise of a blossom time? Yes, it must be so. But although men of many generations, laboring with blood and tears, have watched for it wistfully, it has not yet come. But someday it will come, and when it does the glory of humanity's fulfillment will be shared in, in some vicarious way, for all the suffering generations of the sons of men." —Bliss Forbush.

EVENING SERVICE

Theme: Things of Others.

TEXT: "Look not every man on his own things, but every man also on the things of others." Phil. 2:4.

INTRODUCTORY: It has been happily said of Henry Drummond that he was so deeply interested in you that you never learned anything about himself. He had the power of losing himself in the interest of others, and for the simple reason that he found other people more interesting than himself.

I. But really to see other people requires a very fine sight. Indeed, it requires more an intuition than a perception; it is more an instinct than an inference. There is a rare power of apprehension which is known as "understanding." We say to some poor soul who has been pouring out before us some tale of sorrow, "Yes, I understand, I understand!" But the understanding does not mean a mental comprehension of her affairs; it means rather a fellow-feeling with her grief. We are sympathetically drinking of the cup that she drinks of, and she knows that we have tasted her bitterness. Now it is that exquisiteness of feeling, fine as a divining rod in its discernment of the hidden pools which is imperatively needed if we are to look on the things of others.

It is, therefore, no wonder that this word is also spoken of Henry Drummond, that "in his dealings with a fellow man, no one had a more delicate realization of his confidant's personality." He knew what was in man. He could feel a yung man's seriousness behind an assumed frivolity. He could discern the spiritual dryness behind the forced laughter. He knew when there was tragedy in the heart, even when there was comedy on the immediate stage.

II. And how can we get this divining rod of spiritual intuition? First of all, it is a gift of grace. We can nourish it, we cannot create it. It is like every other kind of lofty vision; it comes only with a pure heart. It is a sensitiveness which accompanies spiritual cleansing. And, therefore, we must do as Drummond did; we must turn to the Lord and ask and receive the cleansing of his grace. And having obtained the cleansing, our sight will not be limited to "that which is near"; we shall see God, and we shall have the talent to profound communion with our brother.—J.

MIDWEEK FELLOWSHIP MEETING TOPIC

(Church Night or Suggested Sermon Subject)

Theme: A Cloud Received Him (Ascension Day).

TEXT: "And a cloud received him out of their sight. And while they were looking stedfastly into heaven as he went, behold two men stood by them in white apparel; who also said, Ye men of Galilee, why stand ye looking into heaven?" etc. Acts 1:9-11 (A.S.V.).

The Ascension was from a place familiar to the disciples and filled with haunting remembrances. "The closed book of wonders must be followed by an open book of acts." He was coming back; but sky-gazing would not bring him back. Daydreaming would not bring him back.

I. It is not star-gazing to go onward in the power of the Presence, "Lo, I am with you always."

II. It is not star-gazing to go forward with a new sense of the worth of the individual.

III. It is not mere star-gazing to carry from the place of ascension a shatterproof conviction that the cross is a source of redeeming grace powerful to regenerate men.—Adapted from Josiah Daniel.

Suggestive Texts and Themes

Sifted as Wheat: "And the Lord said, Simon, Simon, behold, Satan hath desired to have you, that he may sift you as wheat: But I have prayed for thee, that thy faith fail not." Luke 22:31, 32.

How to Retain Our Zest and Freshness in Christian Work: "Occupy till I come." Luke 19:13.

The Hymn of Creation in Genesis and

in Science: "In the beginning God created the heaven and the earth," etc. Gen. 1:1.

Will and Gladness: "I will be glad and rejoice in thee: I will sing praise to thy name, O thou most High." Ps. 9:2.

The Challenge of the City: "And when he was come near, he beheld the city, and wept over it." Luke 19:41-42.

CHRISTIAN ENDEAVOR SOCIETY TOPIC

May 23. Working with Spanish-speaking Americans. Acts 8:1-8.

SUNDAY SCHOOL LESSON

May 23. Micaiah Withstands False Prophets. I Kings 22:1-40.

MEMORY VERSE: "As the Lord liveth, what the Lord saith unto me, that will I speak." I Kings 22:14.

This is a most dramatic chapter. The story should be told out of a broad historic background showing the feud between Israel and Syria, and the alliance between Ahab, king of Israel, and Jehoshaphat, king of Judah. Ahab and Jehoshaphat plan to take the city of Ramoth-gilead from the king of Syria. For such an undertaking they desire the divine sanction. Four hundred prophets, ready to please the king, give the sanction falsely. When Micaiah is called to prophesy, though he had been informed what word would be pleasing to the king, he stood alone against the king and the four hundred. His first statement, v. 15, seems to be in agreement with the false prophets, but Ahab caught the tone of scorn which rang through the assenting words. Then Micaiah spoke truly. His vision seemed to hint at the death of the king. His defense accused the four hundred of a lying spirit. The events proved later that Micaiah had spoken the truth, the four hundred had prophesied lies.

"One Against Four Hundred" makes a striking title for this story; or "Alone Against the World." This lesson gives opportunity to emphasize the duty of the individual Christian to stand for truth and righteousness fearlessly even if this is in opposition to all that the people and their leaders wish to hear.

SUNDAY: MAY THIRTIETH

MORNING SERVICE

Theme: The Pearl Trader.

SUGGESTED SCRIPTURE READING: Matt. 13:31-45.

SELECTED HYMNS: "I love thy kingdom, Lord."—T. Dwight. "Glorious things of thee are spoken."—J. Newton. "Lord, of life and our salvation."—P. Pusey. "Lord, with glowing heart I'd praise thee."—F. S. Key. "Come, thou Fount of every blessing."—R. Robinson.

CALL TO WORSHIP: "O God, thou art my God; early will I seek thee: my soul thirsteth for thee, my flesh longeth for thee . . . to see thy power and thy glory, so as I have seen thee in the sanctuary."

INVOCATION PRAYER: O God, our Father, who hast such riches for the children of men, prepare our hearts for thy blessings. Win our minds away from material things. May we not be easily daunted nor turned aside but may we move toward thee and there abide. Thou who dwellest in the secret place, take the darkness from our eyes that we may behold thy glory. Our lives are thine for thy service, but alas, how we have been deceived! Our ways have not been thy ways. Forgive our selfishness and indifference, and grant to us a true spirit of surrender that in obedience to thy will we may learn to find our highest joy. We thank thee for life, its youth and its age, its joy and its sorrow, its growth and its decay. We are in thy hands for time and eternity. Help us to see the purpose of life in the light of thine everlasting love. Bring us closer to thy side by our fellowship with Jesus and in all the labors of the years grant us the hope of eternal rest. For thy name's sake. Amen.

Theme: The Pearl Trader.

TEXT: "Again, the Realm of heaven is like a trader in search of fine pearls; when he finds a single pearl of high price, he is off to sell all he possesses and buy it." Matt. 13:45, 46 (Moffatt).

INTRODUCTORY: Look at this old pearl trader in our parable. He has shrewd eyes and a trained mind; he knows pearls when he sees them. Throughout a long business life he has purchased pearl after pearl at many fishing stations, but none of them really satisfies him. Probably he went home many a time and said to his wife, "I got a fine lot today." But still he went on searching for something better. Life is like that until we find the real thing. It is continually bringing up from its mysterious depths, like a pearl diver from the depths of the sea, some shining thing, and calling to us, "Here is the thing you seek." But none of them really satisfies us.

When they are sparkling in front of us, we "rush upon them," as Augustine said, because we feel they are what we seek. But soon they are lost. And so people often say that life is a cheat, and that the lure of beauty is a will-o'-the-wisp.

I. But Jesus says there is an answer to the deepest hunger within us. He calls it in our parable the Pearl of Great Price. He himself is the diver that plunged into the mysterious ocean at the cost of his life to bring it up for men. He likened the kingdom of God, the goal of human desire, to a single pearl of exquisitely soft luster and beauty. That pearl is the whole universe and its luster is the grace of God shining

through every part of it, for grace means beauty of form, beauty of action, beauty of character. Wherever God reigns there is his kingdom, and wherever his kingdom is there his grace shines. The whole universe shines like a pearl with his glory.

II. Everything shines with the same beauty and grace, everything except man and things that man has made. But the beauty shines in man, too, sometimes and in the things that he makes. A baby in its cradle, a little child laughing in the sunshine, St. Francis kissing the leper's wounds, Da Vinci's "Last Supper," York Minster, the *New World Symphony*. We cannot help feeling that these belong to the same kingdom as the beauty of the stars and the sea, but on a higher level. But there is much that man does that is not inside that kingdom that spoils the perfect form and luster of the pearl. The slums, class hatreds, drunken men and women, the divorce courts, unhappy homes, your selfishness and mine. In these things we fall outside the rule of God, and become divided within ourselves. Jesus says that what we are really seeking is to get into the kingdom of God, to submit to God's rule, so that we may be lovely with his loveliness and joyful with his joy.

III. And the way to do that is to believe in him. To believe in him is not only to believe that he will forgive your sins; it is to identify yourself with him, to think as he thinks, to act under the control of his spirit. He was completely under the rule of God. He was the living expression of the kingdom of God. He yielded to God completely and the beauty and grace of God were in him. When we come to him and live in him all things are ours, and the beauty for which we have hungered all our lives becomes ours. It cost him a cross to remain within the kingdom of God. It may cost us the same. But just as he shone with his greatest glory when he suffered most for love's sake, so it will be with us.—J. M.

THEME PRAYER: Lord of the unfailing promise, we pray for all seeking souls. May they in seeking find thee. We pray also for all teachers, leaders, truth seekers, and dreamers of a better world. Give them faith and patience, and assure them anew that no service to thee and thy children is ever in vain. May they see of the travail of their souls and be satisfied. In the name of Christ we ask. Amen.

OFFERTORY SENTENCE: "Take heed and beware of covetousness; for a man's life consisteth not in the abundance of the things which he possesseth."

OFFERTORY PRAYER: Thou giver of every good and perfect gift, we would call upon our souls and all that is within us to bless and magnify thy holy name. We would forget not all thy benefits, but gratefully remember them. It is to this end we bring these our morning offerings and dedicate them to the work of thy kingdom. Amen.

Illustrative Material

SEED THOUGHTS, HOMILETIC AND EXPOSITORY. The Parable of the Pearl: I. The soul seeking good. II. The soul seeking good will always want a better. III. The soul seeking good wants a better until it finds Christ, the Best.

How Must the Pearl of Great Price Be Sought? I. Diligently. II. With skill and wisdom. III. With full purpose and resolution of heart and soul. IV. As one who knows the great want and need and necessity of Christ. V. As one who is convinced of the great worth and excellence of Christ. VI. Believingly, not doubting. VII. With longings after him. VIII. With a heart touched with the loadstone of his love.—B. K.

A Great Bargain: One Pearl: I. The merchantman seeking. 1. His mind aroused. 2. His heart engaged. 3. He has a fixed and definite object, pearl hunting. 4. His object far from commonplace, not common stones, but pearls. 5. He sought with diligence. II. His finding. 1. It was a remarkable one. 2. Resolved that he would have it. III. His selling out. 1. Of old prejudices. 2. Of self-righteousness. 3. Of sinful pleasures. IV. The buying. 1. An immediate purchase. 2. A joyful one. 3. An enriching one. 4. A final purchase.

5. A purchase he never regretted.—C. H. S.

Choice Illustrations on the Theme

HUNGER FOR GOD. The wisest philosophers have called man "a religious animal" because through all ages men and women have had a hunger for God as real as their hunger for food. A little girl born blind and deaf, whose spirit was imprisoned in utter darkness and silence, was told about God by touch signs on the palm of her hand. Her face lighted up with the joy of a new discovery as she signaled back: "God! Is that what you call him? I have known him a long time, but I never knew his name." Sooner or later we too discern that there is in the world "the true light which lighteth every man."—Berth Condé.

HUNGER OF SOUL. One of the most moving pages in *The Life of General William Booth* is that which tells of an old man who stood before the tablet commemorating that pioneer in social and religious work. The tablet was in the humble rooms where General Booth had met the poor and prayed many of them into the kingdom of God. "Can a man say his prayers here?" the old man asked. He was told that he could, and he knelt and prayed, "O God, do it again! Do it again!"—*Watchman-Examiner.*

SEEKING AND FINDING. A strange sight was seen on the Mystic River in Massachusetts. Some boys who were constructing a shanty on the flats dug up a pot containing about three hundred dollars in old silver coins. The dates on the coins found by the boys ranged between 1717 and 1838. There were coins of England, France, Greece, Spain, all of the South American countries, and also American pieces. Most of the American money was minted between 1828 and 1838. The place where the money was found is within a stone's throw of the historic Craddock House, of Revolutionary fame, and on the site of one of the shipyards which fifty years ago fronted both sides of the Mystic. The discovery brought out an army of men who dug up the whole river bank for lost treasures, and were rewarded by an additional find of thirty-five dollars in coin. If men were only as deeply concerned in looking for the hidden treasures of the kingdom of heaven, they would surely find.—*5,000 Best Modern Illustrations.*

GOD ALSO SEEKS. The Rev. Dr. Robert Bruce, whom Alexander Whyte called the most finished divine of Scotland, was educated for the bar, but against the wish of both parents the Lord had set him apart for the Edinburgh pulpit. Listen to what he says: "I would rather walk through a mile of burning brimstone every night than spend over again those midnight hours when I fought against the call of God."—*5,000 Best Modern Illustrations.*

EVENING SERVICE

Theme: Heritage.

TEXT: "I have a goodly heritage." Ps. 16:6.

INTRODUCTORY: We stand on this Memorial Day in the presence of those who have stepped before us and ahead of us into the life beyond. According to our Christian faith they are not dead but gloriously alive. If we wish it so they can still serve us. They are still powerful in our lives. We idealize them, recalling some virtue or trait of character which each of them possessed, and by such idealization we become better men and women. In days of difficulty we touch the tokens of their former presence with us, or visiting their graves, we draw strength from them and go again about our own tasks, meeting our own responsibilities with higher courage and deeper fortitude.

We draw inspiration from them to follow them. We recall how Douglas carried the heart of Bruce in a casket about his neck. When the battle was hard and hung in the balance he took the casket, threw it ahead of him, crying, "Douglas will follow thee or die!" We shall follow!

But these have done, and do still, more than give us a virtue to idealize, some token to strengthen us, a way to follow. They have placed in our hands an inheritance, a heritage. I am thinking especially of our fathers and mothers, those who have died for their country, the martyrs of the Christian faith, the generations that have preceded us, the line that reaches backward into history.

How best can we honor their memory? By accepting from them that which they gave us. By appreciation of our inheritance. By evaluating it at its true worth. By passing it on, this heritage of ours, enhanced, to our children and our children's children.

What is our heritage? May I state our heritage in three words. The first is *America*.

I. AMERICA

1. The Land Is Our Heritage

Our fathers gave us a land called America. America is our heritage.

At first they were not aware of the wonder of the land. It was a narrow stretch that lay between the Appalachians and the sea, but very lovely, trimmed as it was with pine and spruce and ash and elm and maple; the clear waters of the rivers teeming with fish, and rendezvous of wild fowl. Little did our Founding Fathers know of the great streams of the midland, their sources in the lakes, the alluvial valley of Ole Man River. And less did they know of the high mountains and the broad desert and the long ranges, with the coastal plain where now we dwell.

Finally they possessed the land. They crossed the barriers—mountains, rivers, the terrible desert. All frontiers came down. They explored the land, surveyed it, planted seed upon it, dug shafts into its mountains for coal and gold, carried water to the desert, which bloomed and blossomed like a rose. This land is our inheritance.

We must appreciate it. We must appreciate it the more because all is not well with this fair land. There are rivers, now polluted, where the fish cannot live and the wild fowl refuse to gather. There are forests, once so green, which mile after mile show nothing but blackened stumps. Virgin soil has become dust bowl. Lovely hillsides, where trickling waters nourished the hardwoods, are now baked clay broken by ugly gullies.

Every man and woman of us bears responsibility toward the heritage of the land itself. Every true American should be a conservationist.

2. Liberty Is Our Heritage

What is our heritage? America—but not alone the land. America is synonymous with liberty.

Not that I could tell exactly what liberty is. Not even naming the freedoms defines liberty. Of course it is freedom of thought and speech and worship, freedom from want and fear—but what is freedom of thought, without ability to think? or freedom to speak, without power of expression? or freedom to worship, without desire to pray? Liberty is more than negation of poverty and fear.

There is something gloriously positive in liberty. It is not license. Give a man license with a great pipe organ and he may smash it; but a man who has true liberty will play upon it the great compositions of Bach and Beethoven.

America means liberty. It is liberty for which men died and women bore heavy burdens and little children paid a price. The generations pass and every generation must itself pay some price for this heritage lest it be lost, lest it be denied to their children.

On every side there are evidences that our liberty is slipping away from us. We let our rights lapse. We refuse the duties which they involve. We have become complacent and irresponsible. Each man has his heart set too much upon his own affairs. What concerns *me* is most important. There is too much selfishness at the grass roots of America, breeding corruption in high places.

As we have inherited the land and by that each one of us should be a conservationist, so we have inherited liberty and each one should be a true patriot, ready to sacrifice even life itself for this great blessing.

3. An Ideal Is Our Heritage

Our heritage of America is the inheritance of an ideal. America has always meant that. Here in this land should be established a great nation. Here liberty should bring forth her fruits. With such ideals our fathers crossed the frontiers.

The frontiers, east, west, north and south, are gone. We are dwelling in the whole land. The frontiers are now in the direction of the ideal. No longer can we extend America in the directions of the compass, but we can extend America upward. The old expansionist policy must be revived; it must be redirected.

Expand America upward! What a task! How difficult, yet how urgent! That which does not grow dies. Here is the direction of our growth. This is our great duty and privilege—no finer acceptance of our heritage than this, to dedicate ourselves to follow that shining ideal which every true American carries in his heart.

The land, liberty, the ideal—these belong to the heritage called America.

II. CHRISTIANITY

1. The Church Is Our Heritage

We have a second inheritance from our fathers. It is the heritage of Christianity. Many of us felt this heritage come to us through our fathers and mothers who were men and women of prayer. Many of them had family altars in their homes. They worshiped God on the Sabbath Day. They achieved a high morality.

Back of them were Christian lines, generations of men and women devoted to Christian ideals and purposes. We remember that many who came to America crossed the wide and stormy sea that they might have freedom of worship. They were true to their consciences.

We have spoken of the land itself; when they explored and settled the land they established the church. It is said that when the railroads crossed the plains and the first trains went through there was always a Methodist preacher sitting on the cowcatcher. So it came to pass that the Church of Christ was spread abroad in the land. Every village has its meeting house; every town its chapels and churches; every city its churches and cathedrals. Our Methodist fathers gave us a heritage of evangelistic fervor; the Presbyterians a high regard for education; the Congregationalists carried with them the spirit of democracy. Every denomination of Christians served the common good. This Church in all its ramifications, both Protestant and Catholic, is an American heritage. It should be highly treasured.

2. The Book Is Our Heritage

Our fathers gave us a Church in the land; they also placed in our hands the Christian Book. That Book is a part of our heritage.

Once an African chieftain asked Queen Victoria what was the secret of England's greatness. She handed him a copy of the English Bible with the words, "This is the secret of England's greatness."

If we but knew it, whatever greatness belongs to America may have come to us from the Book. It contains the foundations of morality in the Ten Commandments and the Sermon on the Mount. It carries a gospel of salvation from sin and victory over death that can be found nowhere else. It exalts that service and sacrifice by which the great institutions of the land have been built. The Book belongs to our heritage. Think deeply before you despise it. Think soberly before you neglect it. It is both American and Christian to read it, obey it, teach it. Its place is in homes as well as in our churches. It should be in our hands and its precepts and promises should be written upon the minds and hearts of our children.

3. The Christ Is Our Heritage

Our heritage in Christianity is also the Christ. I have no dogma to utter concerning him at this place. That would be thoroughly improper. Find him whatever you will—whether man or God, whether only one who lived nobly long ago or a presence by your side—you cannot accept from the Christian line Christianity without accepting, appreciating, coming under the influence of that matchless character, Jesus of Nazareth.

This is a marvelous heritage: America; the land, liberty, the ideal; Christianity: the Church, the Book, the Christ.

III. GOD

1. God Is Our Heritage

A third word: our heritage is God! The Psalmist wrote, "I have a goodly heritage. The lines are fallen unto me in pleasant places, yea, I have a goodly heritage." That goodly heritage of which he spoke was *God*.

How do we learn to know God? Before we learn for ourselves we must learn from others. God comes to us through our fathers and mothers, a preceding generation, from the line that extends back into history.

We possess God! We possess God as the source of all our national history. The great river of American history rises in the highlands of God. We become aware of this as we read our great American documents; for example, The Declaration of Independence: "Men . . . are endowed by their Creator with certain unalienable Rights, that among these are Life, Liberty and the pursuit of Happiness." "By their Creator"—that is God! Not less are men endowed by God than was this marvelous land given by God. In days of crisis our nation was sustained and protected by God. God is our heritage by the fact of America.

We possess God as the Source of our Christianity—the Church, the Book, the Christ.

We possess God as the Source of our immortal lives. That is a true instinct of the Psalmist—"I will lift up mine eyes unto the hills, from whence cometh my help. My help cometh from the Lord, which made heaven and earth." The source of personal help is in God. God is our goodly heritage.

These three we have received from our immortal dead—America, Christianity, God.

I was the guest of George in his home. His brother Jim was invited in for the evening. After dinner we stood together in the library. I turned to a framed picture on the wall and said, "George, is this a picture of your father?" "Yes," he replied. Then both men came over to the picture: George, a fine, noble, useful man; Jim, a ne'er-do-well, improvident, irresponsible. They looked at the picture a minute or two, then Jim said, "George, we're not as good men as our father!"

I imagine that George was; but Jim was not. Why wasn't he? Both men had received fortunes from their father. But Jim had refused the paternal heritage—that which I have stated as America, Christianity, God. By the unwillingness to accept his heritage he was an inferior man.

Never a day that so badly needed superior men. Perhaps that superiority begins with the acceptance of our heritage.—M. K. W. H.

MIDWEEK FELLOWSHIP MEETING TOPIC

(Church Night or Suggested Sermon Subject)

Theme: A Pleasant Road to Travel.

TEXT: "Her ways are ways of pleasantness, and all her paths are peace." Prov. 3:17.

This Proverb personifies religion as supreme Wisdom. Her way delightfully pleasant and peaceful. We will think of this way under the figure of a good road to travel.

I. First, Wisdom is a high way. It is always reaching upward and out of the low and the little. It ranges at lofty levels. It has the world at its feet.

II. Wisdom's way always has one fixed mark. For that it aims. It casts other things aside as it progresses and goes straight and earnest to a goal, the glory of God. "The chief end of man is to glorify God and to enjoy him for ever."

III. Wisdom's way is a way of usefulness. It always puts usefulness first, before pleasure, before profit.

IV. To go in Wisdom's way is to go in sweet fellowship. They who walk there walk hand in hand. The way is full of sympathies. "The fellowship of kindred minds is like to that above." All love all in Wisdom's way.

V. The pleasures of Wisdom's way are of all others the most enduring. Joy unending! In the best company. With cheerful prospect. Its joyful termination. Above all, Christ is there. They walk with him, are satisfied with him, and they shall travel on and reign with him.—After J. V.

CHRISTIAN ENDEAVOR SOCIETY TOPIC

May 30. Pioneers of Our Faith (Memorial Sunday). Heb. 11:8-16, 24-26, 32-40.

SUNDAY SCHOOL LESSON

May 30. **Discovering Spiritual Resources.** II Kings 6:8-17.

MEMORY VERSE: "If God is for us, who is against us?" Rom. 8:31 (R.S.V.).

The horses and chariots of God! When will we begin to see them and believe in them? . . . Let me point out to you some of the horses and chariots of God—some of the factors that you can count on here and now to tilt the scales of battle against wrong and in favor of right.

Open your eyes to see the active goodness that is at work in the world at the present hour.

Open your eyes to see the dreams and ideals that persist at the present hour.

Open your eyes to see the power of the gospel of Christ at work in the lives of men at this present hour.

Open your eyes to see God as a real Personal Factor in human affairs at this present hour.—Wallace A. Alstow.

SUNDAY: JUNE SIXTH

MORNING SERVICE

Theme: The Secret of Pentecost (Whitsunday-Pentecost).

SUGGESTED SCRIPTURE READING: Acts 2:1-21. After-petition: May God bless to our spiritual profit the reading and hearing of this portion of his Word.

SELECTED HYMNS: "This is the day, at thy creating word."—W. W. How. "Spirit divine, attend our prayers."—Andrew Reed. "O heavenly Fount of light and love."—W. W. How. "Spirit of God, descend upon my heart."—George Croly. "Our blest Redeemer, ere he breathed."—H. Auber.

CALL TO WORSHIP: "They that wait upon the Lord shall renew their strength; they shall mount up with wings as eagles; they shall run, and not be weary; and they shall walk, and not faint."

INVOCATION PRAYER: God of all grace and consolation, who on the Day of Pentecost didst send down thy Spirit upon a multitude, be pleased now to bestow thy grace upon us as a body of worshipers approaching thy throne. Help us to realize thy presence in this place and to worship thee in spirit and in truth. We thank thee for the Gospel. How graciously thou didst bow the heavens and come down to us in the incarnation of Christ thy Son. Thou, O Christ, didst tabernacle in the flesh so that thou mightst be able to be touched with a feeling of our infirmities. Thou didst speak as never man spake of the great problems of the eternal life. Thou didst go about doing good, healing the sick, comforting the bereaved, and directing penitent souls in the way of pardon and peace. And, best of all, thou didst take upon thyself the burden of our sins, bearing them in thine own body on the tree. Then, triumphing over death, thou didst ascend up on high, taking captivity captive; and thou livest forevermore to make intercession for us. But thy dwelling place is not in heaven alone. Thou has left a great promise, "Lo, I am with you always." Let us claim the fulfillment of that promise now. Come to us. Manifest thy presence unto us as we worship this day. And not to us only, but to all those who everywhere worship in thy courts. Prosper thy cause throughout the world, and hasten the coming of the triumphs of thy grace world wide. We ask in Jesus' name. Amen.—D. J. B.

Theme: The Secret of Pentecost (Whitsunday-Pentecost).

TEXT: "Ye shall receive power, when the Holy Spirit is come upon you: and ye shall be my witnesses." Acts 1:8.

INTRODUCTORY: These words were among the last spoken by Jesus before his Ascension. Then the disciples "returned to Jerusalem and were continually in the temple, praising God." They also returned to the upper room and waited in obedience and in utter dependence on their Lord's promise.

See the eleven gathered with their risen Lord in Galilee, rejoicing in his resurrection, but feeling as weak as men can feel and dreading the coming separation. See them again on the day of Pentecost, the birthday of the church, so wonderfully proclaiming the mighty works of God that there were added unto them that day about three thousand souls. Think of it—only seven weeks separate Easter from Whitsuntide, the Resurrection from the coming of the Holy Spirit, but what a change has taken place in these men! There are four words which summarize the history of those wonderful days.

They are Promise, Prayer, Power and Praise.

I. "Give me a fulcrum," said Archimedes, "and I will move the world." A fulcrum is something on which the lever rests. Our fulcrum is the promise of God and it is strong enough. "Heaven and earth shall pass away," says Jesus, "but my word shall never pass away." The words of our text are the promise he gave to the eleven.

There is a condition attached to this promise. "Ye shall be my witnesses." God gives us his Holy Spirit when we ask, not that we may feel good and be happy, but that we may spend time and strength in making Jesus known throughout the world. Still Christ needs witnesses—our surrendered lives.

II. Prayer is the second word that explains the change in the disciples. "These all with one accord continued steadfastly in prayer." Jesus had given them the promise, then they had seen his ascent and had returned to Jerusalem to pray and wait until their prayers were answered. For ten days the praying went on. They would not cease until the answer came.

If we strive in prayer with God, we shall not fail when we strive to be witnesses before men. If we are to be telling witnesses for Christ, we must empty ourselves. No man can bear witness to Christ and to himself at the same time.

III. To receive the Spirit is to receive power. Dr. E. Stanley Jones says: "I have watched the peasants of India laboriously lifting water into their rice fields by a basket suspended on ropes. It is hard, slow work. But I have also watched the sunbeams come and quietly and gently lift the water and drop it down on the fields." Pentecost offers to those who are struggling the gentle but effectual power of the Holy Spirit. Before we can witness to others we must have experienced the power of the Spirit in our own lives, enabling us to overcome the sins that do so easily beset us.

IV. Last of all comes praise. The bystanders, when they saw the wonderful happiness of that first Whitsunday, said: "We do hear them speak in our tongues the mighty works of God." The disciples had received power, but they spoke not of it, but of him who gave it, and so the power increased. Half the blessings God gives to us are lost for the lack of praise, because we will not acknowledge his goodness. "Let the redeemed of the Lord say so." Whenever you have real religion, the dominant note will be praise. Praise and service are duties that we owe to God, to our fellow men, and to our own souls.

The Holy Spirit is not a spiritual luxury for the greatest of the saints. Christ offers Him to everyone. When they were gathered with one accord, suddenly the Spirit came. And he is here, knocking at your heart and mine. —J. B.

THEME PRAYER: Most gracious God, who in our best moments dost give us foretastes of those good things which thou hast prepared for those that love thee, increase our faith, we beseech thee, in thy power and in thy will to do for us exceedingly abundantly above all that we ask or even think. Thou who in time past hast visited thy people with Pentecostal blessing, pour forth thy Spirit upon us in this latter day. May those of us who are young see visions of the better world thou hast in store; may those of us who are old be refreshed with dreams of the endless life to which thou art inviting us. And to all of us, old or young, vouchsafe such a vision of thyself, thy love, thy power, thy wisdom, thy beauty, that forgetting all lesser things we may give ourselves without reserve to thy service, and trusting thee with the simplicity of children, may receive the end of our faith, even life forevermore. Amen.

OFFERTORY SENTENCE: "Wherefore do ye spend money for that which is not bread and your labor for that which satisfieth not?"

OFFERTORY PRAYER: Our Father, make us worthy to receive the bounties of thy goodness; and make us worthy to contribute to the greatest cause on earth. Add thy benediction to our offering, for without thy blessing all we say and do will never feed a hungry soul. We ask in Jesus' name. Amen.

Illustrative Material

SEED THOUGHTS, HOMILETIC AND EXPOSITORY. The Gift of Power: I. Not physical power. Not like that possessed by Samson. II. Not the power of logic. The disciples were to convert souls but not by argument. III. Nor was it the power of eloquence. Though that is not to be despised. IV. The promise was of spiritual power—the power of the Holy Ghost. Power without limit.—J. L. H.

Power: I. The preparation for power, vv. 1-3. II. The baptism of power, vv. 4, 5. III. The source of power, vv. 6-8. IV. The results of power, v. 8. "Ye shall be my witnesses." V. Ascension to power, vv. 9-11. The reception of power by the disciples depended upon his ascension, Luke 24.49. VI. Praying for power, vv. 12-14. The disciples had the promise of power "not many days hence," but they did not wait in idleness for it to be fulfilled.—S. S. T.

Power: The Gospel is a mighty engine, but only mighty when God has the working of it.—T. A.

Choice Pentecost-Whitsunday Illustrations

HAVE YOU GOT IT? When Leslie Weatherhead of City Temple, London, was to speak in Canada, he was prevailed upon to pass through the United States to address the ministers of New York City in the Fifth Avenue Presbyterian Church. His boat was late, so he was taken off by a tug and then rushed up Fifth Avenue under police escort. The church was filled with metropolitan clergy. Dr. Weatherhead stood looking down into the faces of his fellow ministers for a long time, and then he said, "I want to ask one question. 'Have you got it?'"

That is the all-important question for us when we seek to lead others to Christ.—Sidney W. Powell.

LIGHT, HEAT, POWER. Light, heat, power —that is the threefold service rendered by the religion of Jesus Christ. It illumines man's mind, warms his heart, gives power to his will. That was the work of the Holy Spirit upon the early disciples, as they tarried in that upper room in Jerusalem. It transformed the sayings of Jesus, hitherto obscure, into luminous signposts, marking the way they must follow; it filled their lives with an unchanging and unbounded love like that of their Master; it surged through their beings, sending them forth into a hostile world to proclaim the good news with fearlessness and power. Christ's promise was abundantly fulfilled, and through the power given to them, the Christian fellowship was launched upon its world-enriching, world-transforming mission.—Rev. Roy Pfaff.

PRAYER THE LIFTING LEVER. Many years ago when the *Great Eastern*, the largest boat that had been built up to that time, was ready for launching, there was no power that could lift it. Months of time and thousands of pounds were spent in vain. Then came the inventors of the hydraulic jack and the *Great Eastern* was lifted. Just so, there was not power that could lift sinful, fallen humanity to God till Jesus had died and risen again and sent forth his Spirit. But when the promised Spirit came, there was power—and there is power still—to lift a world.—Rev. John Bishop.

THE HOLY SPIRIT AS COMFORTER. A few months ago, while traveling, I saw a little blind girl come into the train. She was not more than seven or eight years old, and had a very bright face. She had been attending a school for the blind and was on her way home, yet no friend or relative was with her. You ask how she could travel alone? Very well indeed, for she was put in charge of the conductor, a kindhearted man, who lived in the same town as she did. When he was not engaged in collecting tickets, he sat by her side and talked with her. She thus reached the end of her journey safely, and I saw her placed in the arms of her loved ones.

That conductor was a "comforter" in the Bible sense of that word, which means, "one who is called to another's side to aid him." Do we realize that we are like this little blind girl—in a world where we know not the way, yet where the Comforter is our ever-present guide, striving to lead us to our heavenly home?—*Sunday School Chronicle.*

THE HOLY SPIRIT. I used to believe that a few men had a monopoly on the Holy Spirit. Now I know that the Holy Spirit has a monopoly on a few men.—James H. McConkey.

THE SPIRIT POURED OUT. A certain prominent man once threw doubt upon sudden conversions. As a result, a letter appeared in the public press from an official in a church who had himself been brought, as it were in a moment of time, into a saving knowledge of Christ. The writer said that as an irreligious man he had plunged into the depths of sin, and was still in the midst of it all when he listened to a gospel addressed in a Sailors' Rest. As he attended, to use his own expression, "sudden as an earthquake," the mighty change took place. Conviction of sin and faith in Christ were in a sense simultaneous. To use another expression from the letter, "Christ made a sudden clean job of it, same as he has for thousands of others." The text of the address that night was, "We have seen strange things today." Suddenly all desire for the things of the world was taken away.—*Record of Christian Work.*

CLEANSING BY THE SPIRIT. Have you ever seen miners going to work with hands and faces as clean as your own? And have you seen them coming back with those hands and faces begrimed? But there is one part of the face that is just as clean as when they entered the mine. That is the ball of the eye, kept continually clean by the little teargland that keeps working all the time and washes away instantly any speck that touches the eye. In the same way, we may be in the midst of sin and uncleanness and yet be kept entirely clean by the power of the Spirit.—Rev. John Bishop.

EVENING SERVICE

Theme: Concealing Knowledge.

TEXT: "A prudent man concealeth knowledge." Prov. 12:23.

INTRODUCTORY: A prudent man is not wont to utter unadvisedly what he knows, but waits for fitting opportunity, either from humility or wise caution. Of course, in some cases reticence is sinful. Sometimes it is as great a sin to say too little as too much. Silence sometimes means unfaithfulness and indifference. Silence is sometimes a crime. The tongue is a talent. Sometimes life and death are in its power. On the other hand, foolish utterances, indiscreet expressions, revengeful words must be guarded against.

But the text is true. There are certain kinds of knowledge and certain occasions when the prudent man is either sparing of words or altogether silent. Let us think of some times when a prudent man concealeth knowledge.

I. But first let us consider some cautions concerning knowledge itself. Knowledge must first be possessed. We cannot hide what we do not have. Knowledge possessed must be prized. Knowledge should never in vanity be displayed. Vanity is one of the weakest traits of humanity. It is usually a sign of little knowledge. And knowledge may sometimes be abused. We may know damaging facts about a neighbor. Charity will urge us in common decency to hide our knowledge. There is much Christian knowledge which when possessed should be wisely imparted. Concealment must never hide from others the good news of God. The Gospel is for the world. All divine truth is for all honest inquirers.

II. When may or should a prudent man conceal knowledge? Truly when it is inopportune. Jesus said, "I have yet many things to say unto you, but ye cannot bear them now," John 16:12.

III. This may be done also when the knowledge is above the capacity of the hearers. You recall that the Apostle Paul said to new converts in Corinth, "I have fed you with milk, and not with meat" (I Cor. 3:2).

IV. Also when it is likely to be misapplied. It was said of the Saviour in one place, "Jesus yet answered nothing" (Mark 15:5). The knowledge of good things may sometimes be misapprehended, abused, misapplied. The revelation may be premature. God did not send forth his Son until "the fullness of time."

V. Knowledge may be concealed when it is sure of rejection. "Cast not your pearls before swine" (Matt. 7:6).

VI. Or when calculated to injure others. "Thou shall not go up and down as a talebearer among thy people" (Lev. 19-16).

VII. And surely when to utter it would be only for self-display. "Let another man praise thee, and not thine own mouth" (Prov. 27:2). A parade of learning springs more from love of adulation than from love of truth. The loyal truth possessor will have little thought of "making an effect" by the exhibition of mental properties.

Suggestive Texts and Themes

Christ the Light: Isa. 9:2-7. In our anticipation of the new world, is this a picture of what is to be?

Christ the Divine Leader: Jer. 23:5-8. These verses point with hope to Israel's future. Has the Messiah been adequately proclaimed?

The Kingdom of Christ: Luke 1:26-33. Thank God today for this revelation of the miracle of the ages which presents, through its fulfillment, a world Saviour!

Preparation for Blessings: Luke 1:76-79. Christ's coming is as the appearance of the morning star heralding the light of a new dawn.

Christ's Glory and Work: Heb. 1:1-4. How can any doubt the Gospel story as the Word of God! Surely, in Jesus, we see God!

Christ's Dominion: Eph. 1:15-23. Do you not feel strangely drawn into an experience of the mighty power of Christ?

The Exaltation of Christ: Phil. 2:5-11. From deep humility to the towering exaltation of Christ we perceive more fully his perfection.

MIDWEEK FELLOWSHIP MEETING TOPIC

(Church Night or Suggested Sermon Subject)

Theme: Godliness Profitable.

TEXT: "Godliness is profitable unto all things, having promise of the life that now is, and of that which is to come." I Tim. 4:8.

It pays to be a Christian.

I. Even if there should be no future immortal life to look forward to and to make preparation for, and if, actually, existence should cease with the grave, it pays, even for our earthly experience, short and restricted as it might be. True religion is of practical advantage to those who practice it, deterring them for many terrible evil results, and leading on to peaceful and advantageous conditions.

II. The Christian life which counteracts everything like falsehood, stealing, drunkenness, impurity and war, just as good health counteracts all forms of disease, is within our reach if we accept it from God through Jesus Christ.

III. The Christian life is, through Christ, the assurance of happy and holy immortality, thus giving peace as we look out into the future.

IV. The Christian life, or godliness, assures one of peace with his fellowmen, and, if all the members of our human race were Christian, there would be harmony and peace universal. The Christian has God as partner in his business, and, instead of having dishonest relations with men that ruin him and others, is on the way to advance all good conditions and secure results that will be for the glory of God.

V. Then, too, the Christian lives in

such a way as to avoid much physical injury and disease, and to maintain physical strength and comfort.—Anon.

CHRISTIAN ENDEAVOR SOCIETY TOPIC

June 6. Little-known Friends of Jesus. John 11:1-11; Luke 7:36-43; 8:1-3.

BULLETIN BOARD SLOGANS FOR THE MONTH

By EARL RINEY

God's law needs no amendments.

A good man must have ideals as well as ideas.

The hearthstone is the cornerstone of family life.

The power of Christianity is derived from the personality of Christ.

The Christ of power is the living Christ in the hearts of men.

The center of our faith is not a ceremony or ritual but a Person.

Hope is the mainspring of life.

Forget differences and ask all people into the church fold.

The church needs to resume its function as a community center.

You cannot vote right into wrong or wrong into right.

Every duty omitted obscures some truth we should know.

Faith is seeing beyond the horizon.

SUNDAY SCHOOL LESSON

June 6. Amos Condemns Social Injustice. Amos 7:10-17; 8:4-8a.

MEMORY VERSE: "Seek good, and not evil, that ye may live; and so the Lord, the God of hosts, will be with you." Amos 5:14 (A.S.V.).

What evils and injustices are there in our own industrial, economic, social and political life? Do these threaten the destruction of the social order, even the nation itself? Are we aware of our sins and the judgment of a righteous God? What can we do to establish and practice a new and higher justice? Note the ideal given in Amos 5:24 (R.S.V.), "Let justice roll down like waters, and righteousness like an ever-flowing stream."

SUNDAY: JUNE THIRTEENTH

MORNING SERVICE

Theme: The Child in the Midst (Children's Day).

SUGGESTED SCRIPTURE READING: Matt. 18:1-14.

SELECTED HYMNS: "I think when I read."—J. Luke. "Saviour, like a shepherd lead us."—D. A. Thrupp. "There is no name so sweet on earth." —G. W. Bethune. "Hushed was the evening hymn."—J. D. Burns. "Jesus, Holy Child Divine."—Anon.

CALL TO WORSHIP: "Suffer the little children to come unto me, and forbid them not: for of such is the kingdom of God."

INVOCATION PRAYER: O God, our Father, we bring to thee our deepest longings for these young lives thou hast given us. We bring to thee our responsibility for them, and our weakness, asking thy help. We come realizing our need for ever-growing sympathy and patience, for more self-forgetting love, for wisdom to guide them. Thou who knowest them altogether, in every possibility of their lives, teach us to understand their need and their experience. We face with them the changing, troubled world of our time. Before them lie new problems, wide opportunities, great tasks. We ask thee, our Father, for wisdom and courage to use this present time in making them ready for high achievement and service to their fellow men. Bless, we pray thee, the church-school teachers who labor earnestly to help us, and thee. Make our homes thy dwelling place, our Father, that our children may there be made ready for the work, the discoveries, the problems, the joys and the achievements thou hast in store for them. O loving Father, cleanse us from selfishness, from weakness, from fear, that we may not fail these children thou hast given us. Amen.

Theme: The Child in the Midst (Children's Day).

TEXT: "Who is the greatest in the kingdom of heaven? And Jesus called a little child unto him, and set him in the midst of them, and said, Verily I say unto you, Except ye be converted, and become as little children, ye shall not enter into the kingdom of heaven." Matt. 18:1-3.

INTRODUCTORY: Thinking of "The Child in the Midst," we realize that the child can teach the adult and that the adult must teach the child, but, most of all, both child and adult must learn at the feet of Jesus. The occasion for this teaching came because of the wrangling of the disciples as to which should be the greatest in the kingdom. In one account we read that they reasoned about who would be the greatest, but in another account we read that this argument had become a dispute. To teach the disciples, and us, a much-needed lesson, Jesus called to him a little child and placed him in the midst.

I. In this the Master shows that the greatest lessons in the kingdom of God are to be learned from a little child. What a poor world this would be were it not for the fresh start that each generation gives! How happy and delightful is the company of little children! The beautiful lessons of love, humility, confidence, perfect trust and obedience may be learned from little children. Mr. Wordsworth said, "Heaven lies about us in childhood." The poetry of life is found in the world of little children.

One of the delightful things about childhood is its willingness to share.

II. Jesus teaches the disciples, and us, that the lovely traits of childhood are the qualities that he desires in the kingdom. The way into the kingdom; the method of advancement is through the spirit of the little child. The Master identified himself with this spirit when he said, "Whosoever receiveth this little child in my name receiveth me, and whosoever receiveth me receiveth him that sent me." The unbroken line is the child, the Christ, the heavenly Father, the kingdom of God on earth and in heaven.

III. The adult must teach the child. There is no influence in the life of childhood that approaches the influence of parents and the close circle of grown-ups. John Quincy Adams declared, "All that I am I owe to my mother." Emerson said, "Men are what their mothers make them." President Lincoln, remembering the great influence of the pioneer mother, said, "All that I am or hope to be I owe to my angel mother." Mr. Dwight L. Moody, whose evangelistic messages shook the continent, paid this tribute: "All that I have ever accomplished I owe to my mother." Benjamin West said, "A kiss from my mother made me a painter."

The power of adult influence in the life of the child is set forth in the words of the proverb maker: "Train up a child in the way he should go, and when he is old he will not depart from it." The saintly Dr. Archibald Alexander, of Princeton, was fond of this proverb, and when asked about his wayward son, said, "My son is not yet old. The promise is that in old age well-trained sons will be found in the way of the Lord." It is interesting to remember that this son, the subject of so many prayers and earnest training, in later years came back to the right way and achieved a reputation for piety and godliness as great as that of his distinguished father.

Let us gratefully remember that the child can teach us; that we must teach the child; and that at the feet of Jesus both child and adult may learn great kingdom lessons. So will the distressing problem of delinquency both in children and parents be solved in the light of him who said: "I am the way, the truth, and the life."—Rev. Ernest Neal Orr, D.D.

THEME PRAYER: We thank thee today, O Father, that better than youth is it to watch the opening of the youth of others, better than strength is it to share what strength we have with others, better than goodness in ourselves is it to discern and strive to help the growth of goodness in others, better than happiness is it to make others happy, better than life is it to give away life for others. Here in thy house this day we thank thee for this law of truth and for the children of a growing generation. Amen.

OFFERTORY SENTENCE: "Upon the first day of the week let every one of you lay by him in store, as God hath prospered him." "Freely ye have received, freely give."

OFFERTORY PRAYER: Dear Father, from whose bounteous hand cometh every good and perfect gift, no offering that we can bring can ever fully express our thanks for thy gift of our children. Bless us as we bring our offering of money into thy treasury, and enable us to dedicate our children unto him who said: "Suffer the little children to come unto me, and forbid them not: for of such is the kingdom of God." We ask in Christ's name. Amen.

Illustrative Material

SEED THOUGHTS, HOMILETIC AND EXPOSITORY. The Peerage of the Kingdom: I. The question. It showed ignorance, pride, selfishness. II. The answer. 1. From it learn the way of entrance into Christ's kingdom. 2. Not merit or greatness.—H. B.

Members of Christ's Kingdom: I. None but the childlike. II. The most childlike are the greatest. That which is most admirable in a Christian man and the mark of truest greatness is childlike humility. III. The children are God's truest representatives in the world.—C.

Greatness in the Kingdom: I. The occasion of this question. II. The persons that asked the question. "The disciples." III. The question itself. The disciples were mistaken in the terms of their question.

Childlikeness: I. Childlikeness is the test of greatness in the kingdom of heaven. I. Not in ignorance or fickleness. But in 1. A teachable spirit. 2. In a consciousness of weakness. 3. In a dependent spirit. 4. In freedom from false ambition. 5. In a forgiving temper. II. The degree of childlikeness is the measure of greatness. 1. Because it qualifies for usefulness. 2. Because it raises the possessor in the scale of excellence.

Choice Children's Day Illustrations

WE NEED THE CHILDREN. A poor woman came to Dr. Joseph Parker's Thursday noon service, bringing her little child with her. The child could not be kept still during the sermon, but kept up his pretty, winsome prattle. At last the mother, fearing to disturb others near her, got up, and was making her way along the aisle when Dr. Parker detected her and said: "I will not have you leave this service with that little child. We need the child in the midst."

AN ANCIENT LEGEND WITH A MODERN MEANING. Different tribes and races have their own versions of the story of the flood. Certain North American Indians are said to have a legend that God, discouraged by the wickedness of mankind but determined to create a better world, tried to achieve his purpose by destroying the older generation and making provision to save and train the children.

The rain descended and the flood came. Finally it became evident that the entire mountain might be submerged so they gathered about a council and prayed long and earnestly that the Great Spirit would show them his will.

Guided by divine wisdom, the Indians agreed on a plan of action. The efforts of all members of the tribe were directed toward the making of a giant canoe. They cut down the largest available tree, hollowed out its trunk, and carried it to the highest peak.

The water crept up the mountainside until the topmost point was nearly covered. The Indians lifted all their children into the canoe and placed beside them all the remaining food. Then the wisest and most trusted young warrior and the purest and truest young woman, who had previously been selected as custodians of the children and dedicated to their responsibility by a special ceremony, were told to take their places in the bow and stern of the boat. Silently the canoe glided out into the gathering darkness while the older Indians, knee-deep in the ever rising water, stood with their hands upraised in prayer.

When the storm ceased and the water subsided, the canoe was brought to a safe landing place. There the guardians of the children built shelters for those entrusted to their care, and began the task of rearing a generation whose lives would conform to the will of the Great Spirit.

God sought to create a new world, according to the Indian tradition, by placing his faith in what could be accomplished with boys and girls when their training was committed to the best-qualified leaders.—Walter D. Cavert, D.D.

GROWING IN THE SHADE. Most of us like to be prominent, don't we? Well, big people are like that too, many of them. Now let me tell you a story that illustrates the virtue of an opposite way.

In many of the dry sections of our great West the only vegetation you can see is clustered here and there in little bunches about a lonely mesquite tree. The tree lives in the poorest possible soil. Its shade makes it possible for one or two species of shrubs to endure the heat. Under the tree and shrubs, and sometimes climbing up either, there is found more than one variety of cactus, possibly a large-leafed "prickly pear," and sheltered by this, some bright flowering grasses and weeds. Unless these plants were willing to grow thus over-shadowed, there might not be a blossom in the desert, nor a sprig of grass for cattle or horse.

Maybe you can make some application of this fact. Let us see. If others in school, in playing games, in your social world, or even in your church associations overshadow you, why not be willing to grow in the shade? It is often the very best place for development and for service. I don't want you to be lazy or unenterprising; but I do wish you to be happy in your lot and to make the very most of your situation as you find it.—H.

A MOTHER'S SUCCESS. No woman ever faced a more baffling task in child training than did Jochebed, the mother of Moses, but she achieved a success which changed the course of history. Her child was adopted as a member of the royal household. She was given the responsibility of caring for him but the environment was hostile to all that she wished to accomplish.

It might have been expected that Moses would grow up as a privileged Egyptian and scorn everything connected with Jewish culture. Yet he emerged as a young man who had evidently profited by Egyptian educational opportunities but was loyal to the Jewish faith.

The Bible story indicates that there were four ways in which the influence of the mother was formative in the life of her son. She taught him to appreciate the heritage of his race so that he gloried in his descent from Abraham instead of boasting that he was the son of a princess. She built into his life such high moral standards that he became the channel through which God gave the Ten Commandments to the world. She developed within him a sympathy for suffering people and a burning indignation at social injustice.

More than all else, she made God a living reality in his life so that he talked to God "face to face" as a man talks to his friend.

Modern parents, who complain about the difficulty of bringing up their children as Christians amid present-day conditions, need to be reminded of the mother of Moses. Environment is a mighty factor in determining the destiny of a child, but the influence of the mother and father, even when the home is beset by unfavorable circumstances, can be made the controlling factor in environment.

The church, out of a deep concern for developing a finer quality of home life, ought to focus its attention on helping parents to establish Christian homes. Every church might well have a standing committee on the home and family life which will form and carry through a plan to give guidance to parents who are willing to accept it.

The Christian church and the Christian home need each other. They will stand or fall together.—Rev. Walter D. Cavert.

Quotable Children's Day Poetry

EVERY CHILD

Every child should have some scrap
Of uninterrupted sky to shout against;
And have one star, dependable and
bright,
For wishing on.
—Edna C. Joll.

THREE THINGS

These are the things to cherish:
A seed, and a dream, and a child;
Else must the nations perish,
And earth fall away to the wild.
These are the things to nourish:
The budding of trees and youth;
So shall the grown things flourish—
Manhood and beauty and truth.
Out of the leaf-falls that perish,
Retrieved from the waste and the
wild,
These are the things to cherish:
A seed, and a dream, and a child.
—Unidentified.

LITTLE HANDS

Soft little hands that stray and clutch,
Like fern fronds curl and uncurl bold,
While baby faces lie in such
Close sleep as flowers at night that fold,
What is it you would clasp and hold,
Wandering outstretched with wilful
touch?
O fingers small of shell-tipped rose,
How should you know you hold so
much?
Two full hearts beating you inclose,
Hopes, fears, prayers, longings, joys and
woes,—
All yours to hold, O little hands!
More, more than wisdom understands
And love, love only knows.
—Laurence Binyon.

EVENING SERVICE

Theme: Groping for the Door.

TEXT: "They wearied themselves to find the door." Gen. 19:11.

INTRODUCTORY: Sodom was doomed. The inhabitants seemed to sense the coming destruction. Suspicious of two strangers who had come to visit Lot, they surrounded his house, pushed inside and slammed the door, vv. 1-11. But they were smitten with blindness, "so that they wearied themselves to find the door."

We may use this occurrence as a picture of people today blindly groping for a door. Many doors are easily found. Admission is on the easiest terms. There is, however, a grave danger in satisfactions that come so soon. It is well that we should examine the doors through which we pass. It may be that in choosing one door we miss a better. Maybe the best door of all is wide open—a door which leads to abundant life. We speak of "missing the boat" and "missing the bus," but how many there are who miss the Door?

I. The quest for the door of pleasure. Pleasure deliberately sought is joy lamentably missed. It is hopeless to go in for the by-product without first reckoning with the parent substance.

The door called "Pleasure" does not lead to the land which satisfies the longings of the soul. It does not even satisfy the body or the mind. Halt before crossing this threshold! It is the door to disillusionment.

II. There is another door about which folk dream. A door which promises deeper things than the first door we discussed. To many it is the door of doors, surely the end of all human seeking. "Marriage!" Who does not anticipate with gladness the day when he or she reaches this sought-for door? Life together! the beloved always at hand! a home! a garden! a family! Oh, how we dream about the family! Oh, how we dream about the broad and beautiful land to which this door will lead! Now let me say at once that marriage is "an honorable estate, instituted of God." It is good and natural and right that men and women should come together as the Creator ordained, that friendship between the sexes should ripen into love and that love should be the basis upon which homes and families are built. What a pity, though, that so many unions end in disappointment, failure and disaster! Stop and think as you stand before the door called "Marriage"! It may lead to very heaven—on certain conditions. Lacking the conditions it will be a fearful dead end.

III. There is another door which men blindly seek, and above it, emblazoned in letters of gold, is the word "Mammon." The desire for this attractive door may enter the human heart early or late. Some stumble across it by pure chance. Others set out deliberately to find it. Possessions and prestige are sought not only to establish personal security in the material sphere but to add power and influence to the pride of the seeker. Christ tells us to beware of the deceitfulness of riches and the snares of Mammon. Hence his stern warnings. The door of "Mammon" is ajar for most of us, and it is a subtle tempter. Pause before you decide to enter! It is Christ who bids you pause.

Where then may a door be found in which there is no disappointment, no disillusionment, no snare and no shame? Where is the door through which we may pass into abundant joy and peace and love? Jesus has the answer: "I am the door," he cries. "By me if any man enter in he shall be saved, and shall go in and out and shall find pasture."—J. E. B.

Suggestive Texts and Themes

Enduring the Fiery Test: "If any man's work shall be burned, he shall suffer loss: but he himself shall be saved; yet so as by fire." I Cor. 3:15.

Is Jesus Wanted on Earth? "And laid him in a manger; because there was no room for them in the inn." Luke 2:7.

Performance, Not Emotion: "Go, and do thou likewise." Luke 10:37.

How It Pays to Be a Christian: "Godliness is profitable unto all things, having promise of the life that now is, and of that which is to come." I Tim. 4:8.

A Life for a Life: "I came that they may have life. . . . I lay down my life for the sheep." John 10:10, 15. (A.S.V.)

MIDWEEK FELLOWSHIP MEETING TOPIC

(Church Night or Suggested Sermon Subject)

Theme: The Little Word "If."

TEXT: "If ye be willing and obedient, ye shall eat the good of the land." Isa. 1:19.

The word "if" suggests a great fact in Christian experience. In our songs and prayers there is no word we use more frequently than "bless" and its equivalents. It is ever on our lips in prayer. We pray for blessing and we expect blessing. And often we forget that there is not a single blessing included in the covenant of grace which is not conditional. There is an "if" attached to it.

I. What does Jesus say? Hear his words: "If ye forgive men their trespasses, your heavenly Father will also forgive you."

Do we want to be forgiven? Do we want the debt we owe high heaven to be canceled and held no more against us? Do we want to move out into the freedom of reconcilement? Then this "if" stands at the very entrance to the path. "If ye forgive men their trespasses."

II. If forgiveness be the first step into the Christian life, then knowledge is the second; knowledge leading to many another step. In the heavenly ladder which the Apostle Peter builds for us in one of his epistles, he makes knowledge the third step in the pilgrim's pathway to perfection: "Add to your faith virtue, and to virtue knowledge." We meet another "if" at the threshold of knowledge. Read Jesus' words in the seventh chapter of John, seventeenth verse: "If any man will do his will, he shall know."

III. There is hope here for struggling souls. We may fail in obedience at difficult times, but if the spirit be willing, even though the flesh be weak, the blessing of knowledge shall be ours. —C. C. A.

CHRISTIAN ENDEAVOR SOCIETY TOPIC

June 13. Little-known friends of Paul. Acts 13:1-5; 27:40-44; 28:7-10; Col. 4:7-14.

SUNDAY SCHOOL LESSON

June 13. Amos Denounces Intemperance. Amos 2:11-12; 4:1-2; 6:1-7.

MEMORY VERSE: "Let us walk becomingly, as in the day; not in revelling and drunkenness." Rom. 13.13.

Amos denounced the evil of drinking as one of the great curses of Israel. Note that this evil persists with an enormously increased consumption of alcohol in our day.

Amos 2:11-12 illustrates the impairment of judgment and the breaking down of standards which result from the drinking of alcohol.

The passage from Amos 4 may be used to illustrate the corrupting influence of intemperance on home life.

The passage from Amos 6 suggests the evil influence of alcohol on society and the nation as a whole.

SUNDAY: JUNE TWENTIETH

MORNING SERVICE

Theme: The New Fellowship.

SUGGESTED SCRIPTURE READING: Eph. 4:1-16; Col. 3:12-17.

SELECTED HYMNS: "Blest be the tie that binds."—J. Fawcett. "I love thy kingdom, Lord."—T. Dwight. "Send down thy truth, O Lord."—E. R. Sill. "City of God, how broad and far."—S. Johnson. "One holy church of God appears."—S. Longfellow.

CALL TO WORSHIP: "I was glad when they said unto me, Let us go into the house of the Lord. Our feet are standing within thy gates, O Jerusalem."

INVOCATION PRAYER: Our Father, who dost scatter our path with blossoms of love and joy, we came before thee to render the thanks of our very souls this day. O Holy Light, shining from the beginning, guiding our race upward from despair and death, shine thou today into these dark hearts of ours. O holy love of God, incarnate in human form, dying for our life, suffering for our grief and pain, striving ever for our perfection, work thou today in these weak hearts of ours. O holy Joy of God, sharing the gladness of the least of all thy creatures, taking delight in all sweet human beauty, filling the world with the music of brooks and birds, be jubilant today in these dull hearts of ours. And O thou great Heart of God, beating so closely with our own, sharing with us thy light, thy love, thy joy, we thank thee for thyself: live thou this day in these dead hearts of ours. Speak to us thy life, thy light, thy love. We ask in thine own name. Amen.

Theme: The New Fellowship.

TEXT: "And they continued stedfastly in the apostles' doctrine and fellowship." Acts 2:42.

INTRODUCTORY: What kind of fellowship was it, and how did it come into being? It was distinctly a new fellowship, and for its origin we go back to Jesus Christ.

I. The emergence of the fellowship. Two factors contributed to the formation of the new fellowship. One was the fact of the risen Christ. If there had been no resurrection there would have been no Christian church and no New Testament.

The second factor was Pentecost, that direct outpouring of the Holy Spirit. A new thing came into the world on the Day of Pentecost; a new society, a new grouping of people who experienced in a fresh way what Jesus meant to them which led directly to the formation of the new fellowship.

Our text says, "They continued . . . in the fellowship." It is one thing to form a new fellowship, but it is quite a different thing for it to continue, and to continue to have life in it.

II. Our own day has given birth to many new cults; whether they will continue time alone will tell. But of the Christian fellowship we may boast that through the centuries it has continued, and it has continued because it has life in it, Christ's life. That is the secret of its vitality. They found in him a new experience of God, a new standard of living, in a word, a new fellowship. As a result of the baptism of the Spirit those disciples became the first-born of a new creation. They stood in the dawning of a new day. They were in Christ and Christ was in them, continuing his work in the world.

III. Its development and expansion. The author of the Acts of the Apostles tells us "his former treatise was concerned with all that Jesus began to do and to teach until the day in which he was received up." He implies in this second volume that he proposes to go on to tell of the continuation of the Lord's work under altered conditions of enlarged activity and less restricted sway.

At first the fellowship was narrow and consisted entirely of Jews and converts to Judaism. But a change was soon to come. Development and expansion must begin, for with Paul the new fellowship assumes a wider significance. The truth came to him with impelling force that Christ's call is a call to all the world without distinction of race or religion . . . a great, world-wide brotherhood.

IV. World brotherhood. This vision of a united humanity—a world at one —is not a mere figment of the imagination, nor is it merely a kind of spiritual utopianism. It is a living spiritual reality which is gradually taking shape before our very eyes. The whole march of practical affairs and of thought today is pointing in this direction. The world has become a neighborhood. The Christian task of today is to make it a fellowship.—J. W. P.

THEME PRAYER: O God our Father, we pray that thou wouldst bind us to our brothers in deeper and more spiritual kinship. Teach us how to live to promote true neighborliness among men. Let us remember that we belong to a great family and may we so live that the life of all men may be enriched and that the brotherhood of nations and of men shall become real. Amen.

OFFERTORY SENTENCE: "Vow and pay unto the Lord your God." "Let all that be round about him bring presents unto him that ought to be feared."

OFFERTORY PRAYER: Our heavenly Father, when we bring thee our best we serve thee only with what is already thine own. Thou hast entrusted us as stewards of thy possessions. As we bring these offerings of thy people we consecrate them to thee and to thy cause in the world. Wilt thou graciously accept the gifts and bless the givers. In Christ's name we ask. Amen.—H.

Illustrative Material

SEED THOUGHTS, HOMILETIC AND EXPOSITORY. "I am a companion of all them that fear thee, and of them that keep thy precepts." Ps. 119:63.

"Ye are all one in Christ Jesus." Gal. 3:28.

Christian Unity: I. Its hindrances. 1. Exaggerated individualism. 2. Social distinctions. 3. Caste of culture. 4. Spirit of faction. II. Practical remedies. 1. Train young members in unity. 2. Organize for work. 3. Practice love.— A. W.

Christian Unity: Charles Reade, M.P., of England, said that he had in his library an old book describing the various denominations of religion. The book belonged to his grandmother, and she had drawn on the flyleaf a rough diagram of a circle, with lines drawn from the circumference like spokes in a wheel. On these converging lines she had written the names of the various denominational bodies, with Christ at the center; and underneath all, this legend: "The nearer to Christ the nearer to each other."—S. S. T.

Unity: Men, when at their best, when most Christian, rejoice to find themselves one with all men of good will, one in hope and one in spirit.

Choice Illustrations on the Theme

ONE WORLD—ONE ENEMY. Before the battle of Trafalgar, the famous Lord Nelson came upon two of his leading officers. They were quarreling so violently that they did not notice the approach of their admiral. He listened for a moment, then breaking in, he said with cutting severity, "Gentlemen, I don't know what is in dispute, this I do know. There is only one enemy. Our fight is with him." Christ is grieved by our divisions, our proneness to take offense.

Our fight is against evil.—*Christian Herald.*

PULLING TOGETHER. On Board a passenger ship crossing the Pacific there was a tug of war between two groups of passengers. The team which was made up of lighter men won three times in succession and their heavily built opponents were amazed. The reason was this: the lighter group had met to practice pulling together, and had gained such aptness in following their leader's signals that they easily defeated the heavier men who did not know how to pull together. United endeavor means strength. Recently we heard a returned missionary say that nothing hurts the progress of the kingdom of God more than unnecessary divisions among Christians.—Archer Wallace.

OUR SECTARIAN CHRISTIANITY. John Wilkes was a dashing English liberal, very popular with wide areas of the people. Soon, however, his followers, calling themselves Wilkites, got out of hand and went wild, and John Wilkes had to explain, as, for example, to George III, that, as for him, he was not a Wilkite. To think we have reduced Jesus to that! For were he here, looking on our sectarian Christianity, he would say, If that is Christianity, I am not a Christian. We may not be able at once to realize our prayer for a united church but one thing we can do, we can take off from Jesus the scarlet robe of our ecclesiasticisms, we can stop identifying him with our sects. For he stands outside them all, above them all, alien to them all, lamenting over them all, praying that they may be one.— Harry Emerson Fosdick.

ONE IN CHRIST JESUS. "For ye are all one in Christ Jesus" (Gal. 3:28). Paul is here speaking about the Christian community spirit. He means that worldwide community of members of the Christian fellowship who look to Christ as life's great example. Such a spirit involves several things: Interdependence, which is the watchword of our generation. We depend upon each other economically, culturally, spiritually.

Brotherhood, which is the heart of the Christian community spirit demands a life freed from hatred, and prejudice, and filled with love and active good will. Unifying faith, which is the main bond that unites men across the world. Our common faith in Christ brings unity—"all one in Christ Jesus."—Rev. Hoover Rupert.

LACK OF UNITY. "Is it true?" asked a student, "that all the people in the world could live in Texas?" "Yes," replied the professor, "if they all were friends. And if they were not friends even the world itself is too small."—*Sunday School Times.*

THE FELLOWSHIP OF UNITY. The folowing incident happened in a small Western town where the people are poor and where, though there are several churches, they frequently borrow one another's equipment and work together in harmony. One evening a church bell was heard ringing vigorously. The family seated round the tea table looked up in surprise. "What bell is that?" they asked in chorus. No one seemed to know until at last one exclaimed, "Oh, I remember now! That is the Episcopal bell ringing for the Baptist revival that begins in the Presbyterian Church tonight!" The churches there evidently had the fellowship of unity. —*Best Modern Illustrations.*

EVENING SERVICE

Theme: The Bottle in the Smoke.

TEXT: "For I am become like a bottle in the smoke." Ps. 119:83.

INTRODUCTORY: This expression has been well translated, "I am become as a wineskin hung in the smoke." We are to study the picture presented rather than the Psalmist's application of it. The wine bottle or water bottle made of a whole goatskin and now hung up iu the smoke presents a picture of a sad life, or a sad condition of life. The unfortunate bottle hung in the smoke is there for a long while, until it gets black and possibly discarded. The bottle is not represented as in a single puff of smoke, but is where the smoke is always going up, always acting upon it, the bottle lives in the atmosphere of smoke.

I. Now here is, first, the picture of a shriveled life. The empty leathern bottles hung up in the homes of the East get dry and shriveled in the heat. And there is such a thing as dry and shriveled human lives. I. Some people get dried up and shriveled in their minds. They do not exercise them, so they become withered, shrunken, atrophied, small and narrow. There is nothing broad or elastic, nothing expansive and interesting in their conceptions. The very term is used stating that they are shriveled or narrow-minded. 2. And some people become shriveled in heart, in their sympathies. They become like the man who is said to have prayed, "Lord, bless me and my wife, our son John and his wife; us four and no more"—if there ever was such a man. Narrow thinking and selfish habits contract the soul that should be large and expansive.

II. Second, there is here a picture of the unlovely life. A shriveled leathern bottle, black with smoke, has nothing about it to admire, nothing to please the eye or invite the touch. It is shriveled. It is hard. It is black. It is unlovely. And so there are lives far too many that are like that, unacceptable, unlovely, not beautiful, but the opposite.

III. And third, there is here in the shriveled and smoky bottle a striking picture of a useless life. An unlovely life is likely to be a useless one. So long as the goatskin bottle is hung up, shriveled and black in the smoky apartment, it is of no service whatsover. And how many people there are in every generation who are like that, of no use in the world!

The smoky bottle certainly gives a warning picture of the unfavorable possibilities of these human lives of ours becoming shriveled, unlovely, useless. It is a picture and possibility we are here well and wisely warned against.

Suggestive Texts and Themes

Articulate Nobleness: "He knew what was in man." John 2:25.

Blessings Are Serious: "I have sent also unto you all my servants the prophets." Jer. 35:15.

Instinctive Prayer: "He went up into a mountain apart to pray." Matt. 14:23.

A Gentle Easter: "There shall ye see him." Mark 16:7.

Religion for Its Own Sake: "Behold, these are the ungodly, who prosper in the world." Ps. 73:12.

How to Treat Children in the Home: "How shall we order the child, and how shall we do unto him?" Judg. 13:12.

MIDWEEK FELLOWSHIP MEETING TOPIC

(Church Night or Suggested Sermon Subject)

Theme: Fruit of the Spirit.

TEXT: "The fruit of the Spirit." Gal. 5:22.

The fruit of the Christian life is the same as the fruit of the Spirit, because the Spirit is to produce the fruit in the life of the Christian.

I. It will not do for a Christian to profess all kinds of Christian virtues and possess none. One cannot be a real Christian twenty or thirty years, and not have something to show for it in the fruit of the Spirit.

II. One of the great purposes of the church is to provide the best conditions for the development of the fruit of the Spirit in the lives of Christian men and women. To be a Christian is more than being saved. It means also to be Christlike. It is to produce in our lives the character that Jesus produced in his.

III. There is more to a Christian life than simply beginning it—just as there is more to a garden than simply planting it—things are to be cultivated in order that fruit may be produced.

The best Christian generally produces the best fruit and the most of it.

The fruit of the Spirit is really vital religion, which expresses itself in love, joy, peace, etc.—W. W. B.

CHRISTIAN ENDEAVOR SOCIETY TOPIC

June 20. Freedom in Worship. John 4:19-26.

SUNDAY SCHOOL LESSON

June 20.   Hosea Pleads with Israel. Hos. 6.

MEMORY VERSE: "I desire goodness, and not sacrifice; and the knowledge of God more than burnt-offerings." Hos. 6:6 (A.S.V.). "I desire steadfast love . . ." (R.S.V.).

This chapter, like the whole book of Hosea, is full of pathos. The words of 6:1-3 are very beautiful. They are a cry of repentance, but of external repentance only. The people do not understand the serious nature of their offense. "They are utterly ignorant of the true nature of the God whom they have so foolishly provoked. They are thinking of an easily satisfied deity who has no moral or ethical standard of righteousness.

In vv. 4-6 we have "the heart cry of a noble lover who has been crushed by the ingratitude and broken vows of the one he has loved. The penitence expressed in vv. 1-3 is only 'skin-deep.' Their poor shallow hearts are incapable of true love. Sin has rendered them callous and unresponsive. They still labor under the impression that forgiveness can be won by bringing the prescribed sacrifices at stated intervals. Such behavior, even though it may qualify as to correctness of detail in forms and ceremonies, is hollow mockery. God wants righteous conduct, devoted loyalty of heart more than sacrifices and outward conformity to ritual requirements." —Kyle M. Yates.

SUNDAY: JUNE TWENTY-SEVENTH

MORNING SERVICE

Theme: Summer Escapes.

SUGGESTED SCRIPTURE READING: Matt. 17:1-8.

SELECTED HYMNS: "Holy, Holy, Holy, Lord God Almighty."—R. Heber. "Holy Spirit, Truth Divine."—S. Longfellow. "Fairest Lord Jesus."—German, 17th cent. "Summer suns are glowing."—W. W. How. "We thank thee, Lord, for this fair earth."—G. E. L. Cotton.

CALL TO WORSHIP: "They that wait upon the Lord shall renew their strength; they shall mount up with wings as eagles; they shall run, and not be weary; they shall walk, and not faint."

INVOCATION: We wait upon thee, O Lord; fulfill this ancient promise in our lives. Grant unto us daily strength for daily need. When our spirits wane revive them. When the vision fades restore it. When the lights grow dim may we greet a sunrise.

By the meditations of this hour may the journey of life take on new incentives, a fresh loveliness, a sweet serenity and deep peace.

Now at the beginning of our worship grant unto us a repentant spirit that we may receive the forgiveness of our sins and be cleansed of all unrighteousness. Amen.

Theme: Summer Escapes.

TEXT: "Finally, brethren, whatsoever things are true, whatsoever things are honorable, whatsoever things are just, whatsoever things are pure, whatsoever things are lovely, whatsoever things are of good report; if there be any virtue, and if there by any praise, think on these things." Phil. 4:8 (A.S.V.) .

INTRODUCTORY. Summer has come . . . . It is easy to miss a summer. One may even go to the ocean and come back with nothing more than a coat of tan

and the memory of eating popcorn on the Pike. Halford Luccock writes of six hundred thousand people having been at Coney Island on a summer Sunday. Asked the meaning of it all, he said, "Just one thing—peanuts." They walked on the boardwalk and ate peanuts.

So one may go to the mountains, and come back with memories of the slot machines, the coke bar, the radio, the movies.

It is easy to miss the tide, the moon, the scent of the salt air that comes untainted across a thousand miles of sea. It is easy to miss . . .

That we may not miss a summer I want to give you a text (Phil. 4:8) and then point out the "radiant isles," "the green valley," and the "sunbright mountains."

Now summer has arrived. Tensions are somewhat relieved; there are holidays and vacations. There are short trips, or long, to the mountains and the sea.

How would you like to come back from your trip or vacation, how would you like to come through a summer with your "inner youth renewed," your "spiritual batteries recharged," your vision clarified, "the deflections of your personal compass corrected, "your sense of proportion restored"? "Your life replanned in accordance with first things and last things," seeing life steadily and seeing it whole, in balance again, healthy of spirit and more healthy of body, integrated, whole, with the lights of your personality turned on, aware of the inner life as a temple of the Spirit, with spiritual vitality, God very real and Christ effective in your life, spirit-filled? I say, How would you like to come back from summer in such condition? Too much. No, I think not. Perhaps the means are too simple.

I. Go to the "Radiant Isles" (Francis Meehan), the radiant isles of silence. Someone called St. Paul's in London "an isle of silence in a sea of sound." 1. Escape noise. Noise evaporates ideas. Noise deafens the ear. Noise deadens the soul. 2. Cultivate silence. Silence gives birth to ideas. Silence quickens the ear. Silence vitalizes the soul. 3. Suggestion: Every day this summer visit a radiant isle of silence and stay there at least three minutes. For some people that is the limit. And in those three minutes do this: think about some true thing, next about some honorable (reverent, awe-inspiring) thing; then some just thing. Then see what happens. Perhaps you will wish to visit the green valley.

II. Visit the Green Valley of Solitude. Review the story of Moses when in solitude he saw the burning bush. There is a Mohammedan proverb, "No prophet except he has been a shepherd"; that is experienced solitude. 1. The crowd degrades values. The crowd lowers standards. The crowd diminishes the stature of the individual, the spirit shrinks, the soul shrivels. 2. Enter the green valley. Values are enhanced. Standards are raised. The individual becomes infinitely and eternally valuable. 3. Suggestion: Every day this summer find a place of solitude and meditate five minutes on something true, honorable, just or of good report. Escape the crowd for five minutes. What great thing might come to pass if in solitude God should speak to you and you should listen and obey!

III. Climb the "Snow-bright Mountains." This will be hard work that stretches the spiritual muscles and leaves them tired. Where are the mountains? "The mountains of our human history are the master accomplishments of master minds." The Book of Isaiah in the Bible is a mountain. The Gospel of John is a mountain. Great books, art, music are mountains.

In other words I am appealing to you not only to escape the noise and the crowd, but escape the trivial. 1. The trivial steals the light from our eyes, dulls our hearing, leaves our personalities filled with litter, dust, dead leaves and ashes. 2. The majestic and mighty give us alertness of mind, escape from turmoil and doubt, contact with reality, ultimate wisdom. 3. Suggestion. Climb! "It is not the summit that matters, but the fight for the summit; not the victory, but the game itself." Grapple with a mountain this summer. —M. K. W. H.

PASTORAL PRAYER: We would give thanks, O God, thanks for eyes to see summer beauty, thanks for ears to hear the song of the sparrow in the hedge, thanks for touch, that blessed gift unto our hands, thanks for hearts which probe beneath the surface and hold communion with other hearts, thanks for minds to think and ponder, to meditate and know, thanks for wills that send us forth to strive and work and do, thanks for souls and thanks for him who is our souls' deepest joy, the Christ. Thanks for this day's worship and the presence of our Lord.

We pray, our Father, for the quickening of our spirits and the elevation of our minds that we may experience during these summer days that which is for our souls' health and peace and joy. Bless us on our holidays and in our vacations and during the untensioned hours that in them we may grow, find growth of spirit and come to our souls' stature.

To some of us may the days and hours of the summer be ministers of comfort, for these have had great sorrow. To some may they restore health and strength after illness. Some need courage and confidence, a sense of assurance, a knowledge that a past has been forgiven and that life in the future may be clean and wholesome. Some need life to be unified, brought together in its parts, made whole and wholesome. Grant these blessings, Lord, to those who need them, and thou knowest well who they are. In thine own name we pray. Amen.

OFFERTORY SENTENCE: Lay not up for yourselves treasures upon earth, where moth and rust doth corrupt, and where thieves break through and steal: but lay up for yourselves treasures in heaven.

OFFERTORY PRAYER: We bring unto thee, O Lord, all the peoples and nations of the earth that righteousness and peace and justice may prevail among them. Grant thy blessing upon our offering multiplying its usefulness in bringing to pass a better world and the establishment of thy Kingdom. Amen.

Illustrative Material

SEED THOUGHTS, HOMILETIC AND EXPOSITORY. Don't lose the summer. It offers: 1. Time. 2. Beauty. 3. Recreation. Use each for God-connection.

Do something practical this summer. 1. Something that will endure rather than something that will pass away. 2. Something important rather than something trivial. 3. Something of token value rather than something only of intrinsic value.

Whatsoever things are true—like the apple that fell from the tree, seen by Isaac Newton; the three angles of a triangle are equal to two right angles; the position of the North Star; Abraham Lincoln was a great man; God is love.

Whatsoever Things are honorable, that stir awe in the soul, like the Holy Ground of Grand Canyon and Crater Lake, a little baby falling fast asleep, Flander's fields where poppies grow, the house where you were born, a mound in the cemetery, a church hallowed by a hundred years of history, a secret place of prayer.

Whatsoever Things are just, like the Declaration of Independence, General Grant telling the Confederate cavalrymen to keep their horses because they will need them for the spring plowing, the fine work of an honest workman, his pay envelope from an honest employer, a Negro girl on her way to school, God's rain falling on a wicked man's garden.

Whatsoever Things are pure, like a drop of gold in an assayer's crucible, bleached linen lying in the sunlight, chaste snow, mother love, the Babe of Bethlehem, the Man of Galilee, the Christ of Calvary.

Whatsoever Things are lovely—a bride, moonlight, *Finlandia* by Sibelius, a western tanager, stained glass, a ruby, a little girl in Sunday clothes, stars.

Whatsoever Things are of good report, like Lindbergh flying across the Atlantic, four chaplains giving their lifebelts to others when the ship is going down, Abraham Lincoln signing a paper giving a guilty soldier a second chance, Jesus washing his disciples' feet, a woman breaking her box of precious ointment to anoint the Christ, the Gospel of John, God so loved the world that he gave his only begotten Son. . . .

Choice Illustrations of the Theme

MEASURING SUMMER. "I think we should measure summer by the approach of the sun toward the summer solstice as well as the retreat. The retreat began last Monday and according to the calendar summer has come. I feel that according to a better reckoning summer would be twice as long, and now summer would be half over. Of course, I am one of those souls who loves the long evenings, the genial days and the cooling nights, and all they contain of beauty and peace."

THE FIGHT FOR THE SUMMIT. It is the ultimate wisdom of the mountains that a man is never more a man than when he is striving for what is beyond his grasp, and that there is no conquest worth the winning save that over his own weakness and ignorance and fear. "Have we vanquished an enemy?" asked Mallory, who died climbing Mt. Everest. And there was only one answer. "None but ourselves." It is not the summit that matters, but the fight for the summit, not the victory, but the game itself." —James Ramsey Ullman in *High Conquest*.

EVENING SERVICE

Theme: Standing In Your Place.

TEXT: "And they stood every man in his place." Judg. 7:21.

INTRODUCTORY: Gideon's soldiers obeyed their orders. "They stood every man in his place round about the camp." They did not rush into the host of Mideon as greedy either of blood or of spoil, but patiently stood to see the salvation of the Lord. They obediently held their lamps, blew their trumpets, broke their pitchers. Breaking into panic, the Mideonites "ran, and cried, and fled," fell upon one another in their fright. The victory was complete.

I. Notice first their unity. There were no divisions, no quarrels, no mutinies among them. They stood as they were ordered to stand. What might not be done by a united church in our day?

II. Notice, second, their courage. Though so few in number they displayed no fear. They were united. They were obedient. They were courageous. In its conflict with the world today the church calls for men of fiber, men of courage. God is with us. Let us be brave.

III. In the third place, note the faith of these men. The victory was a victory of faith. "Faith is the victory!" Oh, what a theme for contemplation! The victories that faith can furnish!

IV. With obedience, unity, faith and courage, how triumphant the success! The victory was complete. The men stood in order round the camp as commanded. At the given signal they raised their shouts, broke their pitchers, and flashed their torches. They stood and watched the consternation of the enemy. It was a victory which was God-given and full.

Consider an illustration from more recent times. On the field of Waterloo there was a regiment which stood under fire through all that awful day, and were not once permitted to charge against the foe. They held the key to their position, and as again and again they asked permission to advance, the answer came, "Stand firm!" When they had nearly all fallen, the message came back for the last time from their commander, "You have saved the day"; and the answer was returned, "You will find us all here." Sure enough, they lay a heap of slain on that fatal yet glorious hill. They had simply stood, and history has given them the reward of valor and imperishable fame of having turned the tide of the greatest battle of the nineteenth century. So God is

preparing crowns for quiet lives, for suffering women, for martyred children, for the victims of oppression and wrong, for the silent sufferers and the lonely victors who just stood at their posts.—H.

Suggestive Texts and Themes

How the Certainty of God Makes Men Great: "Therefore will we not fear, though the earth do change, and though the mountains be shaken into the heart of the seas; the Lord of hosts is with us; the God of Jacob is our refuge." Ps. 46:2, 7 (A.S.V.).

Bearing Witness: "But ye shall receive power, when the Holy Spirit is come upon you: and ye shall be my witnesses." Acts 1:8 (A.S.V.).

The Supreme Claims of God: "All the best of the oil, and all the best of the wine, and of the wheat, the firstfruits of them, which they shall offer unto the Lord." Num. 18:12.

Apples of Gold: "A word fitly spoken is like apples of gold in pictures of silver." Prov. 25:11.

Human Patterns: "In all things showing thyself an example of good works." Tit. 2:7 (A.S.V.).

MIDWEEK FELLOWSHIP MEETING TOPIC

(Church Night or Suggested Sermon Subject)

Theme: Christian Freedom (Independence Day).

TEXT: "Stand fast therefore in the liberty wherewith Christ hath made us free." Gal. 5:1.

"For freedom did Christ set us free."

I. Christian freedom is freedom from the bondage of sin. 1. This underlies Paul's discussion of the nature of freedom. 2. Brought out by Jesus in John 8:31-36.

II. Freedom from bondage to the law. 1. The condition of bondage to the law. Show Paul's thought in chapter 4. 2. The condition of freedom in Christ. Not license, but liberty.

III. Freedom for service. 1. Paul's description of himself as the bond servant of Jesus Christ. 2. Free service the best service.

IV. Relation of Christian freedom to national freedom. Show how the condition, thought, purposes and ideals of the individual affect the national life.—E. H. K.

CHRISTIAN ENDEAVOR SOCIETY TOPIC

June 27. Freedom in Disciplined Living. II. Tim. 2:8-19.

SUNDAY SCHOOL LESSON

June 27. Judgment Comes to Israel. II Kings 17:5-14, 18.

MEMORY VERSE: "The ways of the Lord are right, and the just shall walk in them: but the transgressors shall fall therein." Hos. 14:9.

This lesson may be treated as a culmination of the quarter's studies. A brief summary of the history of the Northern Kingdom would be in order. The long series of wrong decisions, disobedience and spiritual lapses weakened the Northern Kingdom and led to a defeat in battle with the Assyrians and to a long captivity. It would be indicated that the dissolution of the kingdom was gradual and that the final downfall was the result of disobedience and internal moral decay. This lesson gives opportunity to point out the law of reaping what is sown. God sends spokesmen to give warning of the consequences of violating his laws. When these warnings are not heeded destruction comes.

SUNDAY: JULY FOURTH

MORNING SERVICE

Theme: Like a Tree.

SUGGESTED SCRIPTURE READING: Ps. 1: 1-6; Matt. 7:17-19; Rev. 22:1-5.

SELECTED HYMNS: "For the beauty of the earth."—F. S. Pierpont. "Fairest Lord Jesus."—Anon. "This is my Father's world."—M. D. Babcock. "God of the earnest heart."—S. Johnson. "O Master, let me walk with thee."—W. Gladden.

CALL TO WORSHIP: "Blessed is the man that walketh not in the counsel of the ungodly, nor standeth in the way of sinners, nor sitteth in the seat of the scornful. But his delight is in the law of the Lord; and in his law doth he meditate day and night. And he shall be like a tree planted by the rivers of water, that bringeth forth his fruit in his season; his leaf also shall not wither; and whatsoever he doeth shall prosper."

INVOCATION PRAYER: Our blessed God and Father, let our worship of this hour be acceptable unto thee as the morning sacrifice. Help us to pray and praise in the beauty of holiness. Worthy art thou to receive glory and honor and praise and dominion forever and ever, for thou hast redeemed us by thy Son. We thank thee for our place in the great family of believers who in many lands and languages on earth are worshiping thee as King over all, blessed forever. One family we dwell in thee. Give us the mind of brotherly love, the helping hand, and a great passion for souls. In every relation of life, whether at home, in business or in social fellowship, keep us true to our Christian name. In our trials may we find strength in thee. Give us a deep sympathy for all sufferers. Do good in thy good pleasure to Zion. Prosper every good cause, and magnify thy name throughout the earth. We ask in Jesus' name. Amen.—J. D. B.

Theme: Like a Tree.

TEXT: "And he shall be like a tree," etc. Ps. 1:3.

INTRODUCTORY: This picture of the good man as a tree not alone reminds us of the secret of his goodness, it hints at other characteristics of his as well. Wherever you meet a good man whose goodness is nurtured by his faith in God, you will find that he has at least three qualities.

I. First, firmness. "He shall be like a tree planted." Planted—what a suggestion of strength there is in the very word! We can picture the roots of that tree as they strike deeper and deeper and stretch ever wider and wider. And we have only to think of some of the good men and women we have known to recall with profound gratitude the firmness that characterized them. We always knew where to find them. Having taken their stand on the side of right, nothing could move them to depart from it. They were not blown about by the winds of expediency, as so many of us often are. And when we thought and talked about them we spoke of their "strength of character." "Like a tree planted." Firmness is one of the characteristics of the good man.

II. Second, fruitfulness. "He shall be like a tree planted by the rivers of water, that bringeth forth his fruit in his season."

Sometimes our fruitgrowers have a disappointing year. Trees which in former years had been laden with fruit happen, for once, to bear none. There are men and women who resemble these trees. They have great gifts of mind and body and, in addition, fortune is kind to them. They have their full share and more of the sunshine of prosperity. But judged from a more discerning standpoint, they have to be placed among the world's failures. There are others whose goodness is rooted in their "delight in the law of the Lord," and the world therefore is more wholesome for their presence in it. They brought forth fruit—the only fruit that counts—in its season.

III. Third, freshness. "His leaf also shall not wither." So the Psalmist describes the third characteristic of the good man. The picture is that of a tree whose leaves remain green not only through all the seasons of the year but throughout the whole life of the tree. How different it is with those whose lives are not "harnessed consistently to great and serious purposes"! Here is a man whose leaf does not wither. On the contrary, he keeps in age the freshness and the zest of youth, and finds life more and more meaningful and increasingly blessed as the years go by. And if you were to ask him his secret he could only tell you that, for his part, he has always delighted in the law of God, and somehow life in God's company never palls.

What a poor world this would be if there were left no trees in it! There is a story which tells how, when General Allenby and one of his staff officers were standing on a height in Palestine, the officer asked, "What does this land really need?" Allenby replied in one word: "Trees." And what does this world need now or at any time but good men and women who are as trees planted by the rivers of water? Take them away and what a wilderness is left! Yes, there are men who beautify the world, and hold it together, and enrich its life for the generations to come. God give us always a multitude of such men! God make us such men ourselves, good after the pattern and by the power of the Lord of all good life, our Saviour, Jesus Christ!—G. H. W.

THEME PRAYER: We are resolved, our God and Father, to live a better and more useful life, firmly planted, more beautiful, and more fruitful in good. Be pleased graciously to give us thy help. We would be more like Christ, more thoughtful and prayerful and zealous for thee. Help us to carry out our resolves, and thou shalt have all the praise, in Jesus' name. Amen.

OFFERTORY SENTENCE: "So then each one of us shall give account of himself to God."

OFFERTORY PRAYER: O Thou who hast committed to us the great and solemn trust of life, we thank thee for the goods thou hast put into our keeping. Forgive us our derelictions, give us wisdom and strength for what thou dost expect of us, and, being true to thee, may we be true to all who trust us. Bless these offerings we bring today and use them to thy glory. We ask through Christ. Amen.

Illustrative Material

SEED THOUGHTS, HOMILETIC AND EXPOSITORY. Religion and prosperity: I. Religion, with gratitude, to God contributes in a high degree to enliven prosperity. II. Religion affords to good men peculiar security in the enjoyment of their prosperity. III. Religion forms good men to the most proper temper for the enjoyment of prosperity. IV. Religion heightens the prosperity of good men by the prospect it affords them of greater happiness to come in the future world.—H. B.

Like a Tree: I. Contented. II. Health. III. Roots. IV. Importance. V. Symmetry. VI. Fruit-bearing.—F. S. R.

Like a Tree: I. Variety of nature and uses. No one by becoming a servant of God loses all his distinctiveness. II. Divine culture. The good man is not like the tree that grows wild. He is like a tree planted. Favorably placed, by rivulets of water, in promising parts of God's garden. III. Result, the tree's fruitfulness. 1. "His fruit," not any other tree's fruit. 2. "In his season." The seasons are different for different fruits. The fruit-righteous character is seasonable.—M. R. V.

Choice Illustrations on the Theme

FIRMNESS. Anatole France tells the story of a young French writer who once brought the whole of Paris to his feet. Literary critics acclaimed him as a genius, and all the drawing rooms of fashionable society were thrown open to him. It was an experience which might easily have spoiled him and robbed him of all his vision and power. "You keep your head, young man," said France to him one day. "Sir," replied the young writer, "before I knew the drawing rooms of Paris I dwelt in the Louvre and the great cathedrals." And what did he mean but that he had been living among the big things, the things that were true and lovely and of good report: and that these had made him strong to withstand all the temptations of success and had bred in him a firmness against which all the flatteries of the fashionable world could do nothing at all? "Like a tree planted." Firmness is one characteristic of the good man. —G. H. W.

FRESHNESS. Who are the happiest people on earth? This question was answered once as follows: "A mother, at the end of a busy day, bathing a baby. A craftsman whistling over a job. A child building sand castles. A doctor who has finished a successful operation."

Each of these four happy persons finds happiness in doing something so interesting that he becomes entirely forgetful of self. The energies of life are directed to ends that absorb the imagination.—H. B. Blakely.

FRUITFULNESS. Have you ever seen an old apple tree that was bent, gnarled and scarred, with limbs twisted and broken, but bearing as sweet apples as you ever ate? And did you not forget all the blemishes of the old tree and regard it with mingled pity and admiration for its faithful fruit-bearing despite its scars? And you probably have seen another tree, pretentious in its luxuriant foliage, yet as barren as a post. God judges a man, not by the profession of his lips, but by the occupation of his soul.—Gordon Hurlbutt.

FRESHNESS. Dr. Robert E. Speer, on his return from India, said that he could pick out the Christians there from the light on their faces. It is not only in mission lands that Christians have bright, happy faces. A factory girl in England who had given herself to Christ was walking up and down the platform of a railway station, waiting for her train, when a lady of title, wealth and culture called to her from the window of a train that was standing there, and asked, "What makes you look so happy?" The girl told her story and the result of that brief conversation was that her questioner was led to seek and find the Saviour. The late Dr. G. Campbell Morgan knew them both, and told the incident.

FERTILIZING WATERS. When the Nile begins rising its waters are at first red, and then green, because the great Abyssinian branch, the Blue Nile, flows in first; and then the White. A rich fertilizing mud is discharged, with which the fields are covered to the average depth of about six inches thick in one hundred years. The bed of the river rises about four feet in one thousand years. The extent of the fertilized land is constantly increasing, reaching out over the adjacent desert. It has increased about one third since A.D. 1450. The priest proclaimed how the flood in the Nilometer stood; the husbandmen made preparations for an abundant or a scanty harvest accordingly.—Henry M. Field.

EVENING SERVICE

Theme: Stand Fast.

TEXT: "Stand fast therefore in the liberty wherewith Christ hath made us free, and be not entangled again with the yoke of bondage." Gal. 5:1.

INTRODUCTORY: This phrase, "stand fast," is a military term. It alludes to the duties of soldiers on military service. When marshaled in their ranks soldiers are expected to stand firm, never yielding their ground. When placed as sentinels they must stand upon their guard and permit no enemy to surprise them. So must the soldier of Christ stand on guard against evil and be valiant for the truth.

I. This Scripture speaks first of an accomplished fact. Liberty. "Stand fast therefore in the liberty wherewith Christ hath made us free." Freedom lies at the very foundation of character. Freedom is not looseness. Freedom is not immunity from evil. Christian

liberty is the liberty of faith. Faith receives the truth, and it is truth believed that makes men free. Christian liberty is the liberty of hope, a hope which maketh not ashamed because based on Christ's accomplished work. Christian liberty is the liberty of love. The sense of the Saviour's love draws believers to him and makes service a delight because the heart is in it. "Stand fast in liberty." The people of God are, or should be, free from the bondage of ignorance, knowing the beauty of Christ and his Word. They are, or should be, free from the bondage of the flesh, no longer slaves to their passions. They are, or should be, free from the bondage of this world, its pleasures having lost their charm in the far greater delight of Christian experience and hope. "Stand fast therefore in the liberty wherewith Christ hath made us free."

II. The apostle speaks, second, of an earnest duty. "Stand." "Stand fast." Which means that we are to guard our freedom, highly prize our emancipation. "Standing fast" implies watchfulness. What an important duty! "Watch and pray that ye enter not into temptation." What a needed grace, in order that no one shall either induce or surprise us back into captivity. This standing fast implies also a strong resolution. Evil must be both watched against and firmly resolved against. The Christian soldier must be also a resister, standing fast in the good and fighting manfully against evil.

III. Then there is revealed here, in the third place, a solemn and cautioning warning against a possible danger. What is that danger? The apostle tells us: "And be not entangled again with the yoke of bondage." To the Christian then there is the danger of entanglement. It is our conviction that the true believer cannot be again brought into a state of absolute slavery; yet by negligence and folly he may become so entangled, entrammeled of evil, as to lose many of the joys of freedom. Even Paul expressed himself as fearful of the possibility that, after having preached to others, he himself should become a castaway.

Let us heed the challenge, "Stand fast." Stand fast in Christ to whom we have been brought. Stand fast in the truths of the Gospel in which we have been instructed. Stand fast in the service of Christ into whose cause we have enlisted. Stand fast to the end, for Christ says, "Be thou faithful unto death and I will give thee a crown of life."—H.

Suggestive Independence Day Texts and Themes

The Bible and Patriotism: "Thou shalt read this law before all Israel in their hearing." Deut. 31:11.

A Nation's God: "Happy is the people . . . whose God is Jehovah." Ps. 144:15 (A.S.V.).

The Wellspring of a Nation's Life: "Take fast hold of instruction; let her not go: keep her; for she is thy life." Prov. 4:13.

The Peril of Prosperity: "They were filled, and their heart was exalted; therefore have they forgotten me." Hos. 13:6.

Safeguarding against Destruction: "Lest . . . he destroy thee from off the face of the earth." Deut. 6:15 (A.S.V.).

How a Nation May See Its Way: "For the commandment is a lamp." Prov. 6:23.

A Nation's Textbook: "And they taught in Judah, having the book of the law of Jehovah with them." II Chron. 17:9 (A.S.V.).

MIDWEEK FELLOWSHIP MEETING TOPIC

(Church Night or Suggested Sermon Subject)

Theme: Christian Elevation.

TEXT: "Thou hast lifted me up." Ps. 30:1.

The idea here seems not to be so much that of God lifting us up after we have fallen into some pit of sin; rather, the Psalmist seems to be thinking of some height from which one can get a new and more glorious view of the things that abide forever and where nothing that the world can do can bring harm to one's soul. God will always do that for us if we will give him the opportunity.

Though God's people today may not be lifted up like the Psalmist in a temporal point of view, yet they are all, like him, lifted up in a spiritual point of view.

I. They are lifted above the danger of the wrath of the final judgment.

II. They are lifted to the possession and enjoyment of spiritual life.

III. They are lifted to a place in God's graciously adopted family.

IV. They are lifted above all fatal evil from enemies whether of a temporal or a spiritual description.

V. They are lifted to assurance of a safe and final inheritance in heaven. But to know such experience we must first be surrendered to his love. The heart that is disobedient or indifferent or rebellious is never privileged in holy things.

CHRISTIAN ENDEAVOR SOCIETY TOPIC

July 4. Freedom in Christian Citizenship. II Cor. 3:17; 4:11.

BULLETIN BOARD SLOGANS FOR THE MONTH

By Earl Riney

If we neglect the Bible, we are simply uneducated.

Statesmanship is guardianship of the future.

It is never worth while arguing about the religion you haven't got.

The most direct way of serving the country is by loyalty to religion.

Be not proud of race, face, place or grace,

A prayerless soul is a Christless soul.

Custom in sin kills consciousness of sin.

Beware of the angler with the golden hook.

He who sows thorns should not go barefoot.

Saving is a greater art than getting.

The reward of one duty done is power to do another.

Patience is failing nineteen times and succeeding the twentieth.

Virtue is the reward of virtue.

SUNDAY SCHOOL LESSON

July 4. **Jesus, Our Example.** Luke 2:40-52.

MEMORY VERSE: "Jesus increased in wisdom and stature, and in favour with God and man." Luke 2:52.

Growth in Christian Living is the theme of this quarter's lessons. The course is based upon the principle that Christians are expected to grow continuously in Christian faith, character and life and that there are means which God has provided for this growth. This emphasis on growth in Christian living does not ignore the fact that the Bible teaches the necessity for repentance and deep dependence on the grace of God and the power of the Holy Spirit in the Christian life.

Compare the questions which the secular world asks concerning a man: How much money has he made? Has he been successful? What positions has he held? etc. Compare these with the vital question, Has he grown?

Luke 2:52 points out Jesus as a perfect ideal for growth in living.

SUNDAY: JULY ELEVENTH

MORNING SERVICE

Theme: God's Gift of Quietness.

SUGGESTED SCRIPTURE READING: "Mark 4:35-40; Luke 10:38-42; Heb. 5:9-11.

SELECTED HYMNS: "We bless thee for thy peace, O God."—Anon. "In heavenly love abiding."—A. L. Waring. "While Thee I Seek, protecting power." H. M. Williams. "O blessed life! the heart at rest."—W. T. Watson. "Peace, perfect peace, in this dark world of sin."—E. H. Bickersteth.

CALL TO WORSHIP: "O come, let us worship and bow down: let us kneel before the Lord our maker. For he is our God; and we are the people of his pasture, and the sheep of his hand."

INVOCATION PRAYER: O God, our heavenly Father, renew in us the sense of thy gracious presence, and let it be a constant impulse within us to peace, trustfulness and courage on our pilgrimage. Let us hold thee fast with a loving and adoring heart, and let our affections be fixed on thee, so that the unbroken communion of our hearts with thee may accompany us in whatsoever we do. Teach us to pray heartily; to listen for thy voice within, and never to stifle its warnings. We bring our hearts as a sacrifice unto thee: come and fill thy sanctuary, and suffer nought impure to enter there. In Christ's name we ask. Amen.—Adapted from Gerhard Versteegen.

Theme: God's Gift of Quietness.

TEXT: "When he giveth quietness, who then can make trouble?" Job 34:29.

INTRODUCTORY: In our inmost being there is a yearning for what Elihu here calls quietness. It is the same as Paul in the New Testament describes as "the peace that passeth all understanding," and what Jesus promised to the "weary and heavy laden," rest. The heart of man pants for peace. Tired of the weary struggle within and the strife of the world without, many long indeed for peace and quiet. But this desire is not universally obtained. Why? Because so often people seek peace in almost every way but the right way. Some seek it in the scenes of gaiety, some in the attainment of wealth. Some seek it in the teachings of philosophy, and some in retirement from the world and monastic solitude. There are many other such resorts; however, experience shows that these things only mock rather than satisfy the cravings of the peace-seeker. But, on the other hand, there are people who can attest that they have not alone sought but have found a peace of such a sort that no enemy can rob them of the treasure. In the words of our text they can truly say, "When he [God] giveth quietness, who then can make trouble?"

I. Notice first that such calmness, such quietness of mind and heart, is the gift of God. "God giveth quietness." It is his prerogative. At his bidding the wildest storm gives place to the gentlest calm. It is man that makes war. Sin is war. God is the Prince of Peace, the giver of peace, and shows the ways of peace for the hearts of men as also in the nation and in the world.

II. Consider also the nature of this blessing. It is quietness, calmness, repose of mind and heart, and of conscience. It is internal peace, contrasted with anything external. It is something independent of all the vicissitudes of life and the testings of time. It is peace in God. It is quiet in him. It is the quiet of confiding love. It is the quiet of hallowed devotion. It is the quiet of sweet satisfaction. It is the quiet of a cheerful hope. It is the quiet of full assurance for both time and eternity.

III. But the practical question is this, How is this blessing of quietness, of Christian calm, to be attained? 1. The first step is to make sure we are in a state of right relations with God. 2. The second step is to live closely with him in fellowship, in obedience, and in consecrated service. 3. And also we must learn to cast our cares on him in full assurance that he careth for us. 4.

Also, we should acquire the habit of carrying our anxieties and sorrows directly to him. The result will be a pacified conscience. "Conscious innocence makes the best pillow." Very blessed are all those who know something of the quietness God gives when he pacifies the conscience. Discontent also is one of the greatest enemies of peace of mind and heart. It is the murderer of men's happiness. But this is removed as we permit our heavenly Father to work within our souls a contented disposition. The murderer of happiness is overcome when God giveth quietness by delivering us from all anxiety concerning the future. The future is a seven-sealed book. Happy the one who can look calmly and fearlessly upon that book.

IV. Besides the blessings mentioned there is intimation of a wonderful safeguard and result. "Who then can make trouble?" This is true because all things are subject to God's disposing. When God gives inward peace the Christian can suffer no great inconvenience from outward trouble. He who has peace with God has that within him which swallows all outward ills whatsoever. He is so far provided against, fortified against trouble. Yes, when God gives this quietness, this peace, there is assurance that all outward calamities are actually even working for good. "When a man's ways please the Lord, he maketh even his enemies to be at peace with him." "All things work together for good to them that love God, to them that are called according to his purpose." "When he giveth quietness, who then can make trouble?"—H.

THEME PRAYER: Our heavenly Father, whose ways and works are peace, vouchsafe unto us in the midst of our many tribulations the sovereign power of a quiet mind: through Jesus Christ our Lord. Amen.

OFFERTORY SENTENCE: "Blessed be the Lord, who daily loadeth us with benefits, even the God of our salvation."

OFFERTORY PRAYER: New every morning and fresh every evening have been thy good gifts to us, our Father. It is with thankful hearts we bring thee these our offerings this day. Wilt thou graciously receive them as tokens of our gratitude for all thy mercies, and use them for the advancement of thy kingdom in the world. In Christ's name we ask. Amen.

Illustrative Material

SEED THOUGHTS, HOMILETIC AND EXPOSITORY. Study to be Quiet, I Thess. 4:11. God has always seemed to have trouble in getting men to listen. "Oh that my people would hearken unto me," he says. And again: "Be still, and know that I am God." Paul admonished the Thessalonians to "study to be quiet," and the oft-repeated injunction of the Master was, "Peace, be still." What advice could better be suited to our mad, rushing age than the Lord's admonition to his disciples: "Come ye yourselves apart, and rest awhile"?

Study to be Quiet: I. The quiet to be aimed at. II. Difficulties in the way of a quiet life. III. The unobtrusive life of Christ.—A. C.

Quietness signifies humility, modesty, sobriety of mind. It begets tranquillity and peace. It indicates a good disposition and produces good effects.

Choice Illustrations on the Theme

PEACE ATTAINABLE. Mr. William E. Gladstone had for forty years on the wall of his bedroom this text: "Thou wilt keep him in perfect peace whose mind is stayed on thee." These were the first words on which the great statesman's eyes opened every morning, and they were one of the sources of his calm strength.—*Sunday School Chronicle.*

THE GIFT OF PEACE. More than six hundred years ago the poet Dante stood before the doors of a monastery. Three times the monks asked him what he sought. At last the weary man said, "I seek peace." The quest for spiritual peace is as old as humanity; men seek it as eagerly in the twentieth century as their forefathers did in the remote past. One thing is certain: spiritual peace is not the result of any combination of outward circumstances. Jesus gave a parting gift to his disciples —peace. "Peace I leave with you; my peace I give unto you."—Archer Wallace.

PEACE GIVEN BY CHRIST. An automobile does not make the road smooth, but springs, snubbers and "knee-action" built into an automobile make it run smoothly over rough roads. For passengers the riding is comfortable, even over extremely rough highways. Christ built into our lives does not clear life's highway of all stones, grade down the hills, or tunnel under the mountains, but he does enable us to travel life's hard roads with inner peace and joy and assurance.

To know Christ is to know the Truth, and the Truth makes us free. The Christ Way is the way of the "more abundant life," the one and only worthwhile way, the one safe way. And it leads to life eternal.—Author Unknown.

PEACE REPRESENTED. In the old Pitti Palace at Florence are two pictures hanging side by side. One represents a stormy sea, with its wild waves and black clouds and fierce lightnings flashing across the sky. In the waters a human face is seen, wearing the expression of the utmost agony and despair. The other picture also represents a sea tossed by a fierce storm, with as dark clouds; but out of the midst of the waves a rock rises, against which the water dashes in vain. In a cleft of the rock are some tufts of grass and green herbage, with sweet flowers, and in a sheltered place in the midst of these a dove is seen sitting calmly on her nest, quiet and undisturbed by the wild fury of the storm. The first picture represents "Distress," and fitly sets forth the sorrow of the world where all is helpless and despairing. The other is a beautiful representation of "Peace," fitly showing forth the sorrows of the Christian no less severe, but in which he is kept in perfect peace, because he nestles in the bosom of God's unchanging love.—*2,500 Best Modern Illustrations.*

TRANQUILLITY. The oceans have very deep areas. Parts of the Atlantic are over nine miles in depth; some places in the Pacific deeper still. Yet the severest storms—hurricanes that cast huge ships upon the rocks—do not disturb the oceans for more than a few hundred feet. Deep in the ocean's heart, storm or no storm, there is quiet. One who had been close to many great men said that the quality they possessed in common was their serenity. They were never worried and rarely hurried. They all had a leisurely serenity about them which suggested adequate inner resources. There is a tranquillity of spirit which is the gift of God.—Archer Wallace.

EVENING SERVICE

Theme: God in the Desert.

TEXT: "And the Lord spake unto Moses in the wilderness of Sinai." Num. 1:1.

INTRODUCTORY: There is much in our life that seems like a desert experience. In the desert there is barrenness. In the desert there is homelessness. In the desert there is pathlessness. In the desert there is perilousness. Each of these may typify spiritual lacks or dangers. But there are compensations for desert experiences.

I. God is in the desert, the divine presence. "And the Lord."

II. There is divine communication in the desert. "The Lord spake unto Moses in the wilderness of Sinai." God's voice is never silent. He is ever speaking in the sounds and silences of nature, through the Scriptures, and by his Holy Spirit.

III. There is divine provision in the desert. "The Lord will give grace and glory; no good thing will he withhold from them that walk uprightly."

IV. There is divine direction in the desert. By the leading of his providence, by the teachings of his Word, by the influences of his Spirit.

V. There is divine shelter and rest in the desert. The shadow of a great Rock. "Lord, thou hast been our dwelling place, in all generations."

VI. There is divine protection in the desert. "No weapon that is formed against thee shall prosper." "Who is it that will harm you, if ye be followers of that which is good?"

So it is that life in the desert gives us an illustration of the life of the good in this world.—W. J.

Suggestive Texts and Themes

Christianity's Challenge to Christians: "And if ye salute your brethren only, what do ye more than others? Do not even the Gentiles the same?" Matt. 5:47 (A.S.V.).

Ordering My Prayer: "O Jehovah, in the morning shalt thou hear my voice; in the morning will I order my prayer unto thee, and will keep watch." Ps. 5:3 (A.S.V.).

Fighting it Out to a Finish: "I have fought the good fight, I have finished the course." II Tim. 4:7 (A.S.V.)

Decision Development: "Be strong, and do it." I Chron. 28:10.

Men Possessed by a Force; Men Obsessed with a Formula: "Now when they beheld the boldness of Peter and John, and had perceived that they were unlearned and ignorant men, they marvelled; and they took knowledge of them, that they had been with Jesus." Acts 4:13 (A.S.V.).

MIDWEEK FELLOWSHIP MEETING TOPIC

(Church Night or Suggested Sermon Subject)

Theme: Serving, Obeying, Loving.

TEXT: "Thou shalt love Jehovah thy God." Deut. 11:1 (A.S.V.).

God made all things. He rules all things. He is supreme.

I. If we do not bow before him in recognition of his sovereignty, sometime our knees will bend and our souls will cower in fear. But such fear is not his wish. He pledges his limitless power for those who obey him. He is entitled to willing, grateful service in return.

II. But how shall we love Jehovah? Can love be constrained? If, instead of brooding over the things of life that we wish different and blaming God for them, we consider his kindnesses, his patience, his benefits to us, can we help being grateful? A hard heart is slow in melting. It tries not to soften. But if one puts aside his self-will and in all fairness looks upon the mercies and favors he has received and the love God has shown, answering love will well up in his own heart.

III. It is not enough that we serve and obey God. "Thou shalt love." He merits nothing less than a love that gladly yields everything. And the command, "Thou shalt love," is not merely because it is in our power to give and is due to him, but because it is an offer of blessing to us. "He that loveth, abideth in God." And God is life and light and joy.—J. H. M.

CHRISTIAN ENDEAVOR SOCIETY TOPIC

July 11. I Will Be Sincere. Matt. 19:16-29.

SUNDAY SCHOOL LESSON

July 11. Are We Growing As Christians? I Cor. 3:1-3; Eph. 4:11-16; II Pet. 1:5-8; 3:18.

MEMORY VERSE: "Grow in the grace, and in the knowledge of our Lord and Saviour Jesus Christ." II Pet. 3:18.

I. Christian growth should be continuous. From being babes in Christ we should become mature Christians. We should grow up. I. Cor. 3:1-3.

II. Christian growth may be step by step. The passage in II Peter suggests that each attainment may be supplemented by another.

III. Christian growth is toward a goal. "We are to grow up in every way unto him who is the head, into Christ." Eph. 4:15.

IV. We are dependent upon one another as we seek to attain mature manhood. Eph. 4:13.

SUNDAY: JULY EIGHTEENTH

MORNING SERVICE

Theme: The South Wind.

SUGGESTED SCRIPTURE READING: Acts 27:1-25.

SELECTED HYMNS: "Jesus, Saviour, pilot me."—E. Hopper. "O Maker of the mighty deep."—H. van Dyke. "O Maker of the sea and sky."—H. Burton. "Eternal Father, strong to save."—W. Whiting. "Jesus calls us o'er the tumult."—C. F. Alexander.

CALL TO WORSHIP: "It is a good thing to give thanks unto the Lord, and to sing praises unto thy name, O Most High; to show forth thy loving-kindness in the morning, and thy faithfulness every night."

INVOCATION PRAYER: O God, our heavenly Father, we thy children come now to thy feet with our supplications. We cannot live without thy blessing. Life is too hard for us and duty is too large. We get discouraged and our feeble hands hang down. We come to thee with our weakness, asking thee for strength. Help us always to be of good cheer. Let us not be disheartened by difficulties. Let us never doubt thy love nor any of thy promises. Give us grace to be encouragers of others, never discouragers. Let us not go about with sadness or fear among men, but may we be a benediction to everyone we meet, always making life easier, never harder, for those who come within our influence. Help us to be as Christ to others, that they may see something of his love in our lives and learn to love him in us. We beseech thee to hear us, to receive our prayer, and to forgive our sins, for Jesus Christ's sake. Amen. —J. R. Miller, D.D.

Theme: The South Wind.

TEXT: "And when the south wind blew softly," etc. Acts 27:13.

INTRODUCTORY: When the south wind blew softly, the sailors who were taking Paul to Rome felt quite safe in continuing their journey. But they had not been long on the sea before they ran into a storm.

I. Life has often been called a voyage, and it does seem that we are like the men who go down to the sea in ships. Sometimes the weather is fair and the water is calm and life seems to be a pleasure cruise. And sometimes the winds blow and the waves leap high and the storm is upon us. Life is a voyage and ofttimes in preparing for it we make the same mistake those sailors made. We think that when the south wind blows softly, all is favorable for the voyage of life. We shun the north wind with its bitter cold and its fierce strength. It is so much more pleasant in the south wind of ease and comfort.

II. We don't like the north wind of effort nearly as much as the south wind of rest. We are in favor of labor-saving devices; we think that sweat on the brow is indeed a curse. We are in sympathy with the man who links toil and trouble. If we had our way, we would flee from the north wind of work to the place where we could feel the pleasant breeze of repose. Yet we know that every worth-while thing in life has its price and only those can buy who are willing to pay. A football player must scrimmage and practice until he is weary and sore; a soldier must train and endure hardship; a singer must work long toilsome hours.

They finally achieve their goal, not through enjoying the south wind of rest, but by facing the north wind of effort.

III. The same thing is true concerning the enduring things of the spirit. You cannot buy the best things of life in a bargain basement. Do you want friendship? Friendship is not a ripe fruit to be plucked by any who pass down the road. It is a plant that must be cultivated. Do you want a home? Happy homes do not just happen. They are built with deeds of love and prayers of consecration and patient, earnest effort. Do you want a spiritual experience that will bring comfort in days of distress, that will leave you calm in the midst of the world's turmoil? You must be willing to pay the price—prayer and meditation and worship and service.

IV. The south wind of rest will let a man drift out to where the storms are severest and because he has led an easy existence he has not the strength to fight the storm. Jesus tried to point men to the right way. He never said a man could sleep his way into the worth-while things of life. Instead, he underscored the importance of work: "My Father worketh and hitherto I work. . . . I must work the works of him that sent me while it is day."

V. Most of us shrink from the north wind of sacrifice. We do not want to give up our comforts and our conveniences. We want the hungry people fed but not with the bread from our mouths. We want the world's wrongs made right but we do not want anything to interfere with our plans and purposes. The demands of self loom large before our eyes and we want those demands satisfied. We much prefer the south wind of plenty to the north wind of want. But if the world is to be saved from the storm it will be saved only by many facing the north wind of sacrifice.

VI. We shrink from the north wind of discipline. We want life to flow along like a song. We want to have our way and we want it to be an easy way. We do not want to be hampered by restraints nor dragged around by duty; we do not want to meet the exacting demands of life.

We hear a great deal about the failure of parents to discipline their children. We need to hear more about the failure of people to discipline themselves. It is a whole lot easier to lay down some rules for your child than it is to lay down rules for self. It is easy to police somebody else. It is hard to police ourselves.

Sir Edwin Arnold, addressing the Harvard graduates, once said to them: "Gentlemen, in 1776 you conquered your fathers. In 1815 you conquered your brothers. Will you permit an Englishman to say that your next victory must be over yourselves." Until we have learned that lesson—that the most stubborn foe we have is self—and until we bring self under the mastery of Christ, we will not be able to escape the storm.—Rev. Bernard E. Bain.

THEME PRAYER: Help us, our Heavenly Father, to resist temptation and to refrain our feet from every evil way. Guide our feet in the path that shineth more and more unto the perfect day. So far as our lives serve as a pattern to others, may they find in us examples of fidelity and kindness; sincere though imperfect reflections of the life of Him who is our only pattern, and our Saviour. Amen.

OFFERTORY SENTENCE: "Blessed be the Lord God, who daily loadeth us with benefits, even the God of our salvation."

OFFERTORY PRAYER: In grateful recognition of thee, who art the giver of every good and perfect gift, and who hast richly blessed us with health of body and strength of mind to do our daily tasks and obtain this substance, to thee we dedicate these offerings. Bless them. Use them. And bless us as we bring them. We ask in the name of Christ. Amen.

Illustrative Material

SEED THOUGHTS, HOMILETIC AND EXPOSITORY. A Fair Wind: I. The wind was at first unfavorable. I do not see what right we have as men and women, much less as Christian men and women, to expect everything to favor us. II. The north wind presently became fair. God was brewing the south wind while the passengers and crew were vexing themselves about the north wind. III. As soon as it did become fair the sailors seized the opportunity. "Of course they did," you say. Well, I do not know why "Of course" except that they were men of common sense. I would to God that all had common sense about spiritual things.—T. S.

The Voyage of Life: Analogies: I. Every ship has a captain. II. Every ship has a cargo. III. Sooner or later every ship must encounter storms. We must be ready for bad weather. IV. Every ship in the water is good, but water in the ship is bad. V. Some ships sail more slowly than others. Sometimes delayed by barnacles. Think of barnacles that hold us back in the Christian life.—A. F. S.

Choice Illustrations on the Theme

THE SOUTH WIND SOFTLY. Sir Horace Vere being asked what his brother died of, replied, "He died, sir, of having nothing to do." "Alas," was the rejoinder, "that is enough to kill any general of us all."

The person who has daily, methodical work does not know how much he really has to be thankful for. When he envies the "idle rich" he little realizes what a zest work gives to pleasure, and, indeed, to all life. The holiday may be infrequent, but when it does come he thoroughly enjoys it. He thinks, misguided man, that if life were but a long playtime he would enjoy every minute of it. He has not yet experienced satiety, but that it would come in a very short time all experience proves.—*5,000 Best Modern Illustrations.*

TOO MUCH SOUTH WIND. During his summer vacation, a college student was working as a magazine salesman. Representing one of the farm journals, he tried to sell it to every farmer he met. On one occasion he confronted an old fellow leaning lazily against a rickety fence in front of his dilapidated house. "You ought to take this paper," urged the youth. "It will help you to farm better, and naturally you will make more money." But the farmer shook his head. " 'Tain't no use fer me to take your paper, young feller. I ain't farmin' now as good as I know how." —W. B. Garrison.

NEEDED BOTH SUNSHINE AND SHADOW. A great American once wrote the story of his life and gave it the title, *Sunshine and Shadow*. Most people would agree that the title was a good one as applied to many lives. Yet is it not true that most of the shadows are of our own making? God has made it possible for all, not only to endure pain, but to derive benefit from it. The soul of man is greater than anything that can befall it. Helen Keller, blind and deaf, wrote: "Once I had no hope and darkness lay on the face of all things; then love came and set my soul free. Night fled and love and hope and joy came."—Archer Wallace.

LAZINESS. A bit of Chinese folklore tells of a man so lazy his wife had to feed him to keep him alive. Due to the illness of a family relative it was necessary for her to leave home for a number of days. She made a round ring of the common crusty Oriental bread and hung it about her husband's neck, so that all he needed to do was to bow his head forward and eat. On returning home she found the bread but partly eaten and her husband starved to death! Too lazy to put up his hands and move the bread around!

An American counterpart tells of a tramp who in his utter laziness decided to faint at the roadside in front of a farmer's house. The farmer found him. The man whispered that he was starving. The farmer kindly offered to give him a peck of corn to sustain life. The man looking up languidly asked, "Is it shelled?"—H.

THE BEST MEDICINE. An inquisitive interne asked a white-haired physician which medicine he considered the greatest boon to mankind. The old doctor looked back thoughtfully over a half century of practice. In that time he had used many different remedies, each more or less effective for its purpose. Memories crowded in upon him. But they brought with them a sharp, clear recognition of the one medicine which he believed to be the master medicine of all.

To the interne he said: "This is truly a wonderful medicine. If a man is born stupid, it will make him bright. If a man is born bright, it will make him brilliant. If a man is born brilliant, it will steady him—add to brilliance the stability it so often lacks. With this medicine a man may succeed in getting almost anything he wants; without it, nothing. And the best thing about this master medicine is this: It is not compounded of rare and expensive drugs. That would put it out of reach of too many individuals. It is one of the most commonplace things I know. In truth it is not a drug at all. You can spell the name of this master medicine with four simple letters, W—O—R—K."

EVENING SERVICE

Theme: Suppression of Self.

TEXT: "And they had the hands of a man under their wings." Ezek. 1:8.

INTRODUCTORY: We are to do God's works without noise or notice of ourselves. The angels of Ezekiel's vision had their hands under their wings. Their actions were seen but not their hands. When Manoah catechized an angel, asking, "What is thy name?" the angel would not tell him, but said, "Why asketh thou thus after my name, seeing it is secret?" You cannot find the name of more than two angels in Scripture, Gabriel and Michael. Angels are jealous of God's honor and had rather conceal their hands and names than that God should lose the least degree of his glory.

We are very apt to look at the instrument and neglect the principal.

I. Let us think of the hand under the wing as a symbol of the ideal life of man. Perfect blending of serving and soaring. Man is a child of the skies as well as of the soil.

II. Think of the hand under the wing as a symbol of superhuman energy in connection with human instrumentality. Human skill, tact and eloquence are powerless unless winged by divine might.

III. The right place for the hand of service is under the wing of faith. "Whether ye eat or drink, or whatsoever ye do, do all to the glory of God."

IV. In the noblest service there is need for swiftness and grace. Wings. Movement. Education. Character. Beauty. Power. "I delight to do thy will." If there were more delight in service there would be no need for repeated appeals and resorts to contrivances to get good work done.

V. Let the hand of service be partly hidden by that which gives it speed. Often those whose days are filled with business find time for Christian service of most varied kinds. Angelic way: "They had the hands of a man under their wings." Has your religion a hand in it? Has your religion a wing in it? Has it a hand? Is it practical, human, sympathetic? Has it a wing? Is it lofty, unselfish, inclusive, divine? Religion is the human hand beneath the angel's wing.—H. S.

Suggestive Texts and Themes

Bound in the Bundle of Life: "And though man be risen up to pursue thee, and to seek thy soul, yet the soul of my lord shall be bound up in the bundle of life with Jehovah thy God." I Sam. 25:29. (A.S.V.).

Dwell Deep: "Dwell in the depths." Jer. 49:8. (A.S.V.).

High Roads and High Spirits: "He that giveth, let him do it with liberality; he that ruleth, with diligence; he that showeth mercy, with cheerfulness. Rom. 12:8 (A.S.V.).

The Impregnable Line of our Faith: "For I am persuaded, that neither death, nor life, nor angels," etc. Rom. 8:38, 39.

How to Win Through: "By faith they passed through the Red Sea as by dry land." Heb. 11:29.

Striking the Note of Certainty: "I know him whom I have believed, and I am persuaded that he is able to guard that which I have committed unto him against that day." II Tim. 1:12 (A.S.V.).

MIDWEEK FELLOWSHIP MEETING TOPIC

(Church Night or Suggested Sermon Subject)

Theme: The Eleventh Commandment.

TEXT: "A new commandment I give unto you, That ye love one another; as I have loved you, that ye also love one another." John 13:34.

These words of Jesus have been fitly called the eleventh commandment. Christ himself calls it a new commandment. The words strikingly illustrate the idea of new when he added, "As I have loved you." In this wide and deep sense it is indeed new.

I. The commandment itself. "Love one another." Love includes not alone compassion, sympathy, beneficence, but includes approbation, complacency, oneness, good feeling, good doing, etc.

II. The model on which the commandment is constructed. "As I have loved you." Like Christ's our love must come first, before others love us. Also it may be undeserved. Christ's love comes before we are worthy. Like Christ's it must be self-sacrificing, and it must be practical in its results. It must be to each and every one of Christ's disciples. And it must be abiding. "He loved them to the end."

III. How appropriate the designation of new! "A new commandment." It is a commandment of a new dispensation. It is identified with new grace. It is supplied from new resources; through the work of the Spirit in the soul. It is to be the distinguishing feature of the new kingdom; its sign, its motto, its badge, its glory.

Love. Love is the essence, the substance, the ground of Christianity. Christ's disciples are bound by this commandment. For it there is no substitute. It is the perfection of blessedness and of being a blessing.—J. B.

CHRISTIAN ENDEAVOR SOCIETY TOPIC

July 18. I Will Be Loyal. Matt. 26:31-45.

SUNDAY SCHOOL LESSON

July 18. Growing Through Bible Study. Acts 17:10-11. I Tim. 4:13-16; II Tim. 1:5; 2:15; 3:14-17; Heb. 4:12.

MEMORY VERSES: "All scripture is inspired by God and profitable for teaching, for reproof, for correction, and for training in righteousness, that the man of God may be complete, equipped for every good work." II Tim. 3:16-17 (R.S.V.).

I. By its teaching the Bible gives us a knowledge of God, of man, of life and how to live, of destiny.

II. By its reproof it touches our consciences, brings us to repentance and to the forgiving grace of Christ.

III. By its correction it leads us out of error unto truth; we learn wisdom. We acquire a true and satisfactory philosophy of life. We learn how to live.

IV. By its training faith becomes works. Ideals shine forth in practical deeds of righteousness. The example of Christ influences our lives.

The climax in personal life is that the Christian becomes integrated, whole, complete. He is perfectly equipped for any good work that God calls him to do.

SUNDAY: JULY TWENTY-FIFTH

MORNING SERVICE

Theme: Three Ways of Looking at Life.

SUGGESTED SCRIPTURE READING: Matt. 11:1-19.

SELECTED HYMNS: "When I survey the wondrous cross."—I. Watts. "If thou but suffer God to guide thee."—G. Neumark. "Rise, my soul, and stretch thy wings."—R. Seagrave. "O for a heart to praise my God."—C. Wesley. "More love to thee, O Christ."—E. P. Prentiss.

CALL TO WORSHIP: "Give unto the Lord glory and strength. Give unto the Lord the glory due unto his name; worship the Lord in the beauty of holiness.

INVOCATION PRAYER: On this thy holy day, O Lord, be pleased to lift upon us the light of thy countenance and give us peace. Let this hour be full of thy presence and this place as the gateway of heaven. We thank thee for the blessings of thy providence and grace. We acknowledge our ill desert and ingratitude, and humbly crave the pardon of our sins. Wilt thou graciously make clear the path of duty before us and save us from the eternal shame of having lived a useless life. Put us each in the place of service appointed for us and make us willing to fill it. Bless our kinsfolk, friends and neighbors. Bless all those throughout the world who love the Lord Jesus Christ in sincerity and in truth. Bless the impenitent. Show them thy loving-kindness in such a way that they shall be conquered by it. Bless the preaching of thy Gospel today and hasten the time when thy will shall be done and thy kingdom come from the river unto the ends of the earth. We ask in Christ's name. Amen.

Theme: Three Ways of Looking at Life.

TEXT: "Jesus said, What went ye out into the wilderness to see? A reed shaken with the wind? . . . A man clothed in soft raiment? . . . A prophet?" Matt. 11:7-9.

INTRODUCTORY: It is a common truth that we see in life what we are looking for. The real difference between people is not so much a difference of age or wealth or rank, as a difference of outlook, disposition and character.

In the summertime, for example, the landscape is beautiful—every breeze is laden with fragrance, every field is teeming with fertility, every tree hangs heavy with fruit. Nature, arrayed in all her loveliness, pours of her beauty and bounty into the lap of man. But if a man is cross-eyed or nearsighted, then his testimony about the summer landscape can hardly be trustworthy. The defects of his vision are damaging to his view of the landscape.

Just in the same way the defects of disposition and character are damaging to one's outlook upon life.

Now, it was this common truth, namely, that we see in life what we are looking for, that Jesus had in mind when he asked the multitude, "What went ye out . . . to see?" and the implication seems to be that they might have seen what they wished.

This question of Jesus, "What went ye out . . . to see?" is equally pertinent in our own day; and in the words of the text, Jesus suggests three ways of looking at life.

I. The fatalist way of looking at life. Jesus said, "What went ye out . . . to see? A reed shaken with the wind?" The fatalistic way of looking at life asserts that life is standing in the muck where Chance has placed it, powerless to oppose the powers that sway it to and fro, caught in the vagrant winds of heredity and circumstance. The fatalist believes that the human soul is an arrow shot from the bow of the cradle to the target of the grave. There it

goes sweeping through space, perhaps deflected a little to the right or to the left by some passing breeze of influence, but the general process of its flight is fixed. It is helpless to change its direction. What comfort is there in such a philosophy of life? What burdens has it lifted from overwrought hearts? What tears has it dried from sorrowstained faces? What door has it unlocked to the Temple of truth, the Palace of Beauty, the Halls of Learning, the Shrine of Devotion? If only men and women today would learn to live according to the way of Christ—the way of love, justice, righteousness and peace—then would they come to see that the gratification of power and passion strikes at the security of everything that is beautiful, and sacred, and worth while in life.

II. The materialistic way of looking at life. Jesus said: "What went ye out . . . to see? A man clothed in soft raiment?" This, of course, is the common and popular way of looking at life. We worship at the shrine of wealth and success. We bow down at the altar of mammon. The man clothed in soft raiment is envied and his possessions coveted. Human worth is estimated in cash instead of in character.

There is a better way. Blessed is the man who uses money to make men and not men to make money.

III. The spiritual way of looking at life. Jesus said, "What went ye out . . . to see? A prophet?" This is the best way of looking at life—the spiritual way. The prophet is the man of God, and when we look at life through his eyes, we shall be looking for the evidences of God's presence and the revelations of his will. We shall see that life is a trust from God to be employed to his glory and for the good of man.

The meaning of life is in Jesus Christ. God's purpose for you and me, and for all humanity, is there in Jesus Christ. Christ is the Way, the Truth and the Life! Christ is the one foundation for life which cannot be moved! Christ is the secret of real life! Christ's way of looking at life lifts it up and glorifies it! It keeps the soul mellow with prayer, tender with love, happy in service, and gracious in sympathy!—J. C. A.

THEME PRAYER: Make us loyal to our convictions, O Lord. Impress us with the fact that truth and righteousness and deeds nobly done for Jesus' sake are the eternally enduring things. Make us rich in these however we may lack the things that perish with the using. Give us somewhat of the clear vision and moral courage of Christ, for his name's sake. Amen.

OFFERTORY SENTENCE: "Choose ye this day whom ye will serve."

OFFERTORY PRAYER: Out of thy fullness have we all received, and grace for grace—one measure of blessing upon another. Receive the offerings we bring thee with gratitude for all thy benefits. Use them for the extension of thy kingdom in the world, and bless us as we bring them. We ask in the name of Christ. Amen.

Choice Illustrations on the Theme

MATERIALISM OBSCURING VALUES. Principal Jacks of Manchester College, Oxford, speaks of having once seen a delicate mathematical instrument for indicating the position of the stars, which was made a thousand years ago by a Moslem in India. Around the edge of the fine brasswork was this inscription in delicate Arabic characters: "This is the work of Hussein Ali, mechanic, mathematician, and servant of the most high God." What an effective phrase! "Mechanic and mathematician" indicate the competent skill there displayed. "Servant of the most high God" suggests the high excellence to which Hussein Ali aspired in the accomplishment of his task.

Would that some such inscription could be placed upon this marvelous industrial order which we have created! Mechanic and mathematician have brought the technique of it to a high level of efficiency. But the obscuring of the human values at stake in the workaday world has made it far from

being "the servant of the most high God."—Charles R. Brown, D.D.

VALUE. A lady who had a fine breed of chickens had been shelling corn for them with her own hands when she was overcome to find that a valuable pearl was missing from a ring on her finger. She felt sure it was in the corn, but to find it would be like finding a needle in a haystack; she could only grieve for it as lost. But each morning, before allowing more corn to run into the trough which the fowls had emptied, she looked for it, and at last there it was alone except for some pebbles. The jewel, to her worth more than all her chickens, was to them as valueless as any common stone. The value of a thing depends on the desire there is for it.—Youth's Companion.

SWITCHING THE PRICE TAGS. Some years ago Dr. William Temple, musing on the weaknesses of our world, likened it to a hardware store into which a night prowler had slipped and gleefully switched all the price tags on the merchandise. Entering the store in the morning, we find lawn mowers are two for five cents, nails are twenty-five dollars apiece, and a gallon of paint, a penny. All the values are wrong. Dr. Temple said that that is what has happened to our world. As nations and as persons we will achieve tranquillity only when our price tags tally with God's.

On what things do you place greatest value?

Listing our assets in terms of things that can be counted and measured, some of us count ourselves rich when we are really poor. Perhaps the most common mistake is that made by folks who count themselves poor when they are really rich—rich, that is, in the love of their friends, rich in the respect of the community, rich in treasured memories, rich in peace of mind and self-respect. To be without such things is to know genuine poverty.—Author Unknown.

CORRECTING VISION. A woman sat knitting in the gathering twilight with her little girl beside her. The child noticed that her mother repeatedly looked away to where the distant stars were appearing. She said: "Mother, why do you look at the stars?" The mother replied, "To rest my eyes, dear." It is true that too close application to something near at hand may impair the eyesight and injure vision. In another sense, too, we find rest when we get a larger vision.—Archer Wallace.

EVENING SERVICE

Theme: On Becoming One's Own Friend.

TEXT: "Keep thy heart with all diligence; for out of it are the issues of life." Prov. 4:23.

INTRODUCTORY: The keeping of the heart has important issues. It has outward issues and it has inward issues. It has an issue in the way of becoming one's own friend.

I. Becoming one's own friend is not settling down into complacency and self-satisfaction. It is putting one's own self under the tension of ideals. He is not my friend who expects little of me; he expects my best, my finest, my noblest.

II. Becoming one's own friend is not being easygoing with oneself. It is not finding an escape from discipline. It is rather the opposite, seeking the higher discipline.

III. Becoming ones own friend is not letting oneself down. It is not following the crowd at the cost of surrendering one's honor or integrity.

IV. Becoming one's own friend is living at peace with oneself, integrating self about the highest and the best, tapping the inner sources of strength and courage and power. And it is giving time to oneself, time to appreciate the beautiful, time to achieve the good, time to discover the true. It is inspiring oneself to creative achievement. Also a friend of oneself would introduce the self to the best people in the world, the truly great ones of the past and the noble ones of the present. Edgar Guest wrote: "I have to live

with myself, and so I want to be fit for myself to know," etc. One would exercise the self in the loving of one's fellow men. One would make friends with the Great Friend of oneself and all others.—After M. K. W. H.

Suggestive Texts and Themes

The Victorious Potency of Faith: "And the Lord looked upon him, and said, Go in this thy might, and thou shalt save Israel from the hand of the Midianites: have not I sent thee?" Judg. 6:14.

The Standard of Righteousness: "And he said to David, Thou are more righteous than I: for thou hast rewarded me good, whereas I have rewarded thee evil." I Sam. 24:17.

God's Relation to Sickness: "And the Lord struck the child that Uriah's wife bare unto David, and it was very sick." II Sam. 12:15.

The Secret of Prosperity: "And keep the charge of the Lord thy God, to walk in his ways, to keep his statutes, and his commandments, and his judgments, and his testimonies, as it is written in the law of Moses, that thou mayest prosper in all that thou doest, and whithersoever thou turnest thyself." I Kings 2:3.

MIDWEEK FELLOWSHIP MEETING TOPIC

(Church Night or Suggested Sermon Subject)

Theme: Life in True Proportion.

TEXT: "A month they were in Lebanon, and two months at home." I Kings 5:14.

The great work Solomon was raised up to do was the building of the temple. Silver and gold his father had collected. But for timber and stones he bargained with Hiram, king of Tyre. Solomon's men worked with Hiram's men in a levy, one third always in the mountains of Lebanon. For each levy "one month they were in Lebanon and two months at home."

This suggests thought of life lived in true proportion.

I. We find first a lesson concerning the importance of home and family. "Two months at home." Palestine was where home was. The claims of family demanded one month for Lebanon and two months for home. Pity those who have no home, or abuse home.

II. This thought could well be applied to the question of the proper proportion in our lives of rest and labor. Here we find the ethics of vacations. "Come ye apart . . . and rest a while."

III. A further thought is concerning the importance of the claims of religion and the kingdom of God. These cedars and stones they were cutting were for temple building, God's house.

IV. The same reasoning could well be applied to the question of a suitable combination of the practical and the contemplative in religion. The art of life is in the suitable combination of the two.

CHRISTIAN ENDEAVOR SOCIETY TOPIC

July 25. Why Pray Anyway? Ps. 34:1-8; Matt. 7:7-11; James 1:5-7.

SUNDAY SCHOOL LESSON

July 25. Growing through Prayer and Meditation. Luke 11:1-13. Phil 4:6-7.

MEMORY VERSE: "Rejoice always, pray constantly, give thanks in all circumstance; for this is the will of God in Christ Jesus for you." I Thess. 5:16-18. (R.S.V.) .

Pray constantly. Pray daily. 1. Prayer is reasonable. It is reasonable to build life on unshakable foundations. 2. Prayer is vital. Through prayer a man receives life, love, light, wisdom and power. 3. Prayer is Christlike. It was the custom of Jesus to pray. What the Master needed to do, his followers need the more. 4. Prayer is essential to growth. "Lord, what a change within us one short hour spent in thy presence doth avail to make!"

SUNDAY: AUGUST FIRST

MORNING SERVICE

Theme: Building Battlements.

SUGGESTED SCRIPTURE READING: Ezek. 33:1-19. After-petition: May God bless to our understanding and profit these great truths.

SELECTED HYMNS: "Christ our true and only light."—J. Heermann. "Lord, speak to me that I may speak."—F. R. Havergal. "Go labor on, spend and be spent."—H. Bonar. Stand up, stand up for Jesus."—G. Duffield. "Take my life, and let it be."—F. R. Havergal.

PRE-PROCESSIONAL PRAYER WITH CHOIR: O thou who hast said, "Whoso offereth praise glorifieth me," grant unto thy servants this day grace to sing with the spirit and understanding, to make melody in their hearts unto thee, and to be able to lead others into the same devotion. In the name of Christ we ask. Amen.

CALL TO WORSHIP: "O God, thou art my God; early will I seek thee: my soul thirsteth for thee, my flesh longeth for thee in a dry and thirsty land, where no water is; to see thy power and thy glory, so as I have seen thee in the sanctuary."

INVOCATION PRAYER: Almighty and all-merciful God, the Source of all life, the Father of our spirits, the Author of all good, grant us thy blessing as we wait together in thy house this day. Thou art Love. Thy nature is

Love. May love find its expression through us this day, O Christ, eternal Lover of the Father and of man. May love become loving-kindness and long-suffering, and self-sacrifice, and steadfastness. When the day closes may we be found well-pleasing in thy sight because we have manifested unto the world that which is thine own eternal nature, Love. Amen.—M. K. W. H.

Theme: Building Battlements.

TEXT: "When thou buildest a new house, then thou shalt make a battlement for thy roof, that thou bring not blood upon thine house, if any man fall from thence." Deut. 22:8.

INTRODUCTORY: The Hebrew code of laws, based upon God's great ten words at Sinai, was a code singularly gentle and humanitarian. It was different from the Egyptian, whose slaves the Hebrews had long been. It is said the ancient Egyptian language is not known to have contained a word corresponding to the familiar term "people." But that word blazes on almost every page of the Hebrew literature. In this Hebrew code of laws you see the value and the dignity of the individual man beginning to appear. The unknown toiling subject, the man at the bottom of society, gets to be worth thinking about and caring for.

Men may call the Bible antiquated, but the seeds of the wisest and most humane laws by which men have found the best ruling for themselves are planted in this Hebrew code. The beginning of democratic institutions of the best sort stirs first in these old Mosaic statutes. The fundamental idea of our own government, separated states managing their own concerns but presided over by a central national authority in charge of national concerns, is the very Hebrew idea of distinct tribes, yet all gathered into the organized Hebrew nation.

The Scripture we are studying is a specimen of this humanitarian caring for the individual man.

The tops of the houses in the East were flat. These roofs were useful parts of the houses for other purposes than merely that of shelter. They were for walking on, for sleeping on. Especially in the evening the pleasant coolness would call the people to the roofs. There would be danger of falling from them. But with the thoughtful care for the individual man which characterizes this whole Hebrew code, Moses directed that when the Hebrew built a house he should also build battlements or parapets about its roof, lest somebody fall from the roof.

I. The principles underlying this old legislation about building battlements around the roof are principles vital still. The principles are plainly these:

1. First, as far as you possibly can, you are bound to prevent harm and evil.

2. Second, if you neglect to prevent such harm and evil when you can you are responsible for the results of such neglect.

For its own sake, and for others' sakes, the house of the individual life needs battlements. Turn to the apostle's statement of the method of the noble life (Romans 14:16-21). But the only way you can live such a safe life for yourself, and a safe life for others also, is to use the suggestion of our text: by building battlements around it.

II. And notice these battlements are to be builded beforehand. You are not to wait till you and a lot of other people have tumbled and then build your battlements. Beforehand you are to build them. "When thou buildest a new house," etc.

III. Let us specify a little some of these battlements one ought to build about the individual life for his own sake lest he fall and for others' sakes lest he be the means of their fall.

1. The battlement of prayer. Daniel an example. Prayer kept him and helped him keep others. Build this battlement. Daily. Habitually. Remember that "as he did aforetime" concerning Daniel.

2. The battlement of the Bible. How vast and various a battlement

Holy Scripture is! Against temptation. Against impatience. Against despondency. Against cowardice. Against fear of death.

3. The battlement of a religiously observed Sunday.

4. The battlement of a brave confession of Christ.

Do any of these battlements need repairing in your case?

Have you yet begun to build such battlements?—W. H.

PRAYER OF ASPIRATION: Make taut our heart strings, Lord, that they may vibrate with compassion in the presence of a brother's distress. Help us to live in such close touch with thee that we may become channels of grace and power. Help us to redeem our times unto the good of others. After the example of Jesus we would live. Amen.—M. K. W. H.

Illustrative Material

OFFERTORY SENTENCE: "And this commandment have we from him, That he who loveth God love his brother also."

OFFERTORY PRAYER: We thank thee, our Father, that thy heart is so wonderfully kind. We thank thee that thou dost not break the bent reed, nor quench the spark in the smoking flax. The slightest aspiration is known of thee, the smallest, hidden deed of good. Let thy blessing rest upon the offering we bring thee this morning and upon each of the givers. In Jesus' name. Amen. —M. K. W. H.

Illustrative Material

SEED THOUGHTS, HOMILETIC AND EXPOSITORY. Putting Up Parapets: The houses referred to were covered with flat roofs. On these roofs conversations, amusements, business and worship were frequently carried on. I. In this requirement of parapets a great principle is suggested; namely, the sacredness of human life. "That thou bring not blood upon thine house." II. Another principle underlying the text is the inhumanity of selfishness. Implications: 1. Our homes ought to have every moral and spiritual safeguard. 2. These guards are most needed where there are pleasant

places—the heights from which too many fall. 3. When evil comes through neglect the builder's soul is stained with blood —J. F.

Modern Battlements: I. The sacredness of human life. II. The importance of family life. III. Some safeguards which should be placed about the home. 1. The Christian Sabbath. 2. Family prayer. 3. Reverence for God's Word. 4. Gospel temperance. 5. Good reading. 6. Making home pleasant, the happiest place on earth.—R. L. B.

Choice Illustrations on the Theme

RESPONSIBILITY FOR OTHERS. The man from an agency brought a car early one morning to an individual for the purpose of teaching him to drive an automobile. Together they drove to the country. Within an hour the new driver was starting, stopping, backing and turning with ease. When he remarked that the difficulties of handling a car had surely been exaggerated, his mentor merely suggested that they return to the main highway and try the traffic. Early morning city-bound traffic was heavy. The new driver began to perspire. Cars ahead, cars behind, cars passing at great speed made him forget the instructions that a few minutes before had seemed simple. At the first opportunity he took a side road, and stopped. Mopping his brow, he exclaimed, "If it were not for the other people. . . ." "Yes," smiled his teacher, "that's about all there is to driving a car: the other people." There is more to living the Christian life than "the other people," but they are essentially involved at every turn.—Lloyd Douglas.

FOR THE SAKE OF OTHERS. "For their sakes" might be called Jesus' motto. "For their sakes" was part of the "joy set before him" when "he endured the cross." "For their sakes" will carry men and women through hardships otherwise difficult, if not impossible to handle. This world is full of people who need girding for their own battles. They need the help that comes from associating with glowing souls. They need the aspect of good cheer. Mrs. Alice Freeman Palmer, who knew much hardship, had a way of radiating courage and cheer which gave others support. After her death a farmer's wife, who used to be cheered and comforted by meeting her at Boxford Station, wrote: "Even her pictures speak. I cut one from a Boston paper. It is framed on the wall over my table. I often look at it and promise 'I will be a better woman, Mrs. Palmer, because you have lived.'" Are you building battlements for the sake of others?

THOUGHT OF OTHERS. WHAT A GOAL! In this glorious land, with its opportunities for life, liberty and the pursuit of happiness, there is no more amazing story than that of Booker T. Washington. He states that "success is to be measured not so much by the position that one has reached in life as by the obstacles which he has overcome while trying to succeed." That lad rising from slavery to freedom, from illiteracy to education, from obscurity to fame, stirs our hearts to renewed effort to do our best. And success did not turn his head. It gave him his chance to make life happier for others. What a goal!—*Christian Herald.*

EVENING SERVICE

Theme: Ordeal and Outcome.

TEXT: "Then Shadrach, Meshach, and Abednego came forth out of the midst of the fire," etc. Dan. 3:26, 27.

INTRODUCTORY: Here is the story of true souls, immensely tried (walking in the midst of the fire), morally unconquerable ("you cannot conquer a true soul"), essentially uninjurable ("and they had no hurt"), divinely accompanied ("The form of the fourth is like the Son of God").

I. Ordeal is inevitable. Ordeal tests. Within the ordeal one may discover the presence of God.

II. The ordeal is to be gone through, not stayed in. The day that Singapore fell Winston Churchill said: "We go into the storm; we go through the storm." A man came back from the battle line and said, "I went through hell and I did not flinch."

III. These ancient heroes Shadrach, Meshach and Abednego were cast into a furnace seven times hotter than it was accustomed to heat it. They were supported in the ordeal by the presence of Another. They came forth unscathed.

IV. An ordeal endured, one comes forth with songs of joy and triumph upon one's lips. While one endures one finds oneself to be under the "power of a great expectation." One knows that the hour of deliverance follows, the day of victory lies ahead. Thanks be unto God who giveth us the victory through our Lord Jesus Christ!

V. An outcome of ordeal is the rearrangement of one's values. In hard experience first things fall into first place, secondary things find their secondary place, and ever after the wise man knows that great wisdom has been given him in and through his tribulation. Walking through the valley of the shadow of death: discovery, God is with me; I will fear no evil. Ordeal tribulation: discovery, the presence of Christ. Good cheer.—After M. K. W. H.

Suggestive Texts and Themes

The Chrism of Fire: "He that cometh after me is mightier than I, whose shoes I am not worthy to bear: he shall baptize you with the Holy Ghost, and with fire." Matt. 3:11.

The Silence of Consent: "And he saith unto them, Is it lawful to do good on the sabbath days, or to do evil? to save life, or to kill? But they held their peace." Mark 3:4.

The Presence That Makes Failure Impossible: "And all they that heard them laid them up in their hearts, saying, What manner of child shall this be! And the hand of the Lord was with him." Luke 1:66.

A Life That Was Never Dark: "As long as I am in the world, I am the light of the world." John 9:5.

Useless Quests of Unwise Love: "And while they looked stedfastly toward heaven as he went up, behold, two men stood by them in white apparel; which also said, Ye men of Galilee, why stand ye gazing up into heaven?" Acts 1:10, 11.

MIDWEEK FELLOWSHIP MEETING TOPIC

(Church Night or Suggested Sermon Subject)

Theme: Crossing at Eventide.

TEXT: "When even was come, he saith unto them, Let us go over unto the other side." Mark 4:35.

Evening—how it makes us pause; how much beauty, rest and peace there is in it! It was then that Jesus said: "Go and get the boat and let us cross over." In the morning they had gone out upon the waters. Now, the work of healing and the press of the multitudes were over.

I. It is a call at eventide to the other side of life; not a call to drift, for Jesus never taught men to do that. He said, "Set the rudder; heavy on the right oar for the other side."

II. There is another side where it is quiet, where there is prayer and detachment and spiritual fellowship. We hear the Master say: "Let us go over." Enough for today of this side of life.

III. Let us go with him into the night. Let us remember, too, that there is also another side to life, to which we shall someday cross when the boatman with the muffled oar will come. May we not drift then, but go gladly, because the Pilot shall be with us when we cross the bar as he was with those first disciples.—A. E. G.

CHRISTIAN ENDEAVOR SOCIETY TOPIC

Aug. 1. Prayers That Grow Their Answers. Ps. 90:12-17; Luke 11:11-13.

BULLETIN BOARD SLOGANS FOR THE MONTH

By EARL RINEY

It is possible to live a large life on little capital.

Sin may be clasped so close that we cannot see its face.

You have no right to consume happiness without producing it.

Courage is fear that has said its prayers.

What makes life dreary is want of motive.

One good type of education is self-knowledge.

God is, and nothing good is impossible.

Fear God and have no other fear.

A prejudiced man puts out his own eyes.

A tame tiger is still a tiger.

A Sabbath well spent brings a week of content.

Contentment makes a fat feast.

SUNDAY SCHOOL LESSON

Aug. 1. Christian Worship and Fellowship. Acts 2:46-47; Col. 3:12-17; Heb. 10:23-25.

MEMORY VERSE: "Let us consider how to stir up one another to love and good works, not neglecting to meet together." Heb. 10:24-25 (R.S.V.).

A Fellowship of Worship. 1. A fellowship of worship is a fellowship of worthship. Worship is a proclamation of each one's worth. Each one is a child of God.

2. A fellowship of worship is a fellowship of togetherness. "Where two or three are gathered together there am I in the midst of them."

What life have you if you have not life together?
There is no life that is not community,
And no community not lived in praise of God.—T. S. Eliot.

Togetherness releases power, overcomes coldness and induces warmth, deepens contrition.

3. A fellowship of worship is a fellowship of wonder. "Where nine or ten are gathered in holiness there is the majesty of God" (Jewish Proverb).

4. A fellowship of worship is a fellowship of motivation. You are motivated to "let your manner of life be worthy of the Gospel of Jesus Christ."

SUNDAY: AUGUST EIGHTH

MORNING SERVICE

Theme: The Strength That Comes Through Quietness.

SUGGESTED SCRIPTURE READING: Ps. 46:1-11; Isa. 26:1-4.

SELECTED HYMNS: "Calm me, my God, and keep me calm."—H. Bonar. "While Thee I seek, protecting Power."—H. M. Williams. "In heavenly love abiding."—A. L. Waring. "God is the Refuge of his saints."—I. Watts. "We bless thee for thy peace, O God."—Anon.

CALL TO WORSHIP: "All nations whom thou hast made shall come and worship before thee, O Lord; and they shall glorify thy name, for thou art great, and doest wondrous things: thou art God alone."

INVOCATION PRAYER: Almighty God, ever blessed, ever holy, whose mercy is from everlasting to everlasting, and whose strength is perfected in our weakness, help us now to draw near to thee, that with united mind and heart we may worship thee. We bring to thee the thirst we cannot quench at any other spring, and the hunger that can be satisfied only by thyself. Lift us out of our shadows into thy light, out of our fears into thy comfort, out of our perplexities into thy clear truth. Give us that faith in thee which will fill us with peace with the known that surrounds us, and with the unknown that is above and beyond us. We thank thee for this hour of worship. May we in this sacred place have spiritual fellowship with all those who in the sanctuaries of the world draw near to thee. Bless them and bless us. Make this place a mount of vision and an altar of consecration. We ask in Jesus' name. Amen.

Theme: The Strength That Comes Through Quietness.

TEXT: "Be still, and know that I am God." Ps. 46:10.

INTRODUCTORY: The root meaning of that word "Be still" is "to slacken," slacken your pace, slow up, don't be in such a hurry. In Havana one summer, while I was dashing down the street in typical American fashion, a shopkeeper grabbed me by the arm and said: "Wait a minute, you don't have to hurry in Cuba. Come on in and look around awhile."

Someone mentioned to me that when our forefathers in their travels missed a stage, they sat down complacently and waited a week! Now we are impatient if we miss one of the sections in a revolving door.

If all of our speed really produced results, if it made for more successful, happy living, then it would be justified. But alas, too often, our speed is just hurry and bustle, and the real values of life are left lingering by the roadside.

Archibald Rutledge, the nature writer, tells how his father "went slowly down the way of life; not because he was indolent, but because he did not want to miss the wonder by its wayside. 'Every time you hurry to get to a place,' he used to tell me, 'you run the chance of missing more than you gain. The wild things in nature rarely hurry unless they are in danger. How can life be rich for us if we dash through it? Speed will take you somewhere, but when you say you have arrived, that's about all you can say. Speed often takes us away from the very things that would do our souls the most good.' "

I. The Psalmist wrote: "Be still, and know." There are some things that inevitably result from quietness: poise, depth of character, stability of purpose. And there are some things that inevitably result from feverish hurry: anxiety, shallowness of character, instability. "Men ought always to pray and not to faint," the Scriptures admonish, inferring that when men pray they are strong and equipped to meet the varied experiences of life; but when men forget to pray and are driven by rush and hurry, they faint, they lack that steadying grace which holds one in the time of storm.

"We must remember," wrote Charles Kingsley, "that without solitude, without contemplation, without habitual collection and recollection of our own selves from time to time, no great purpose is carried out, and no great work can be done; and that it is the hustle and hurry of our modern life which causes shallow thought, unstable purpose, and wasted energy, in too many who would be better and wiser, stronger and happier, if they would devote more time to silence and meditation; if they would commune with their own heart in their chamber, and be still."

Where did God train Moses for his great work but in the silences of the wilderness? Jesus, before assuming his public ministry, spent forty days and forty nights in the desert alone with his thoughts and God. The Apostle Paul, that greatest of all Christian missionaries, following his sudden conversion, went off into the deserts of Arabia, there to think through his Christian position. John Bunyan gave to the world his immortal *Pilgrim's Progress* out of the solitude of his Bedford jail. Lincoln successfully carried through the overwhelming anguish and burden of the Civil War because he knew the strength of prayer in the stillness of his own room. It was said of the prophet Amos that his desert life had trained his eye so that "he knew a mirage when he saw one; . . . he had no illusions." How often God has had to draw men and women aside from the fog and confusion of life into quiet places before they could see life in its true proportions.

II. "Be still, and know that I am God." That I, the Creator, hold the world in the palm of my hand, that the world is sustained by the strength of my power. Know that God is still in control, that great spiritual laws rule and prevail which cannot be broken. Nations and men only break themselves against these laws. Let us take heart in the fact that God will accomplish his purpose and his plans in his own way and time.

If man has no time for God or for prayer or for spiritual goals then he is to be pitied. He is missing the very genius of life. He is like an eagle in a cage, like a lion pacing back and forth behind iron bars. The eagle was not created to spend its days in a cage. The lion was not created to be confined; he was created for the deep forests. And so man has been created, not for a life of feverish rush and hurry, but for communion and fellowship with his heavenly Father. "Be still, and know that I am God."—Rev. Haven N. Davis.

THEME PRAYER: O Master of the Living Word and the victorious silence, so teach us the secret of thy peace that we, being garrisoned by it in mind and spirit, shall be wise in all our silences, and, being at peace within, evoke peace without. In his name who held his peace. Amen.

OFFERTORY SENTENCE: "Vow, and pay unto the Lord your God: let all that be round about him bring presents unto him that ought to be feared."

OFFERTORY PRAYER: We recognize, our Father, that we are not our own, that we are bought with a price; we would therefore glorify thee in our bodies and in our spirits, which are thine. It is to this end we bring our offerings today and dedicate them to the furthering of thy kingdom in the world. Wilt thou graciously accept and use them. We ask in Christ's name. Amen.

Illustrative Material

SEED THOUGHTS, HOMILETIC AND EXPOSITORY. "Be still, and know." You cannot know deep and eternal truth unless you are still.—F. D. Maurice.

"Be still, and know that I am God" sound like strange words in the ears of most of us. "How can we be still," we ask, "while all things are in movement, while all things are unsettled? How can we be still while everyone is hastening to be rich, hastening to get beyond his neighbor? How can we be still when all the political world is full of slumbering fires, ready to break forth? How can we be still when the religious world is full of controversies and tumults?"— F. D. Maurice.

"Be still, and know." I. The command is assuring. God will not fail. II. Be still on account of our ignorance. We see but a fragment of God's design and work. III. The stillness enjoyed is not that of indolence. Be still, and believe. IV. Be still, and see God in all riding to victory.—H. R.

Choice Illustrations on the Theme

GETTING LOST IN THE WORLD. One of the last official public duties that Mr. Coolidge performed as President of the United States was to journey to Florida and there at Mountain Lake to dedicate a superlatively beautiful tower as the central landmark of a bird sanctuary. This magnificent structure was conceived and made possible by Edward W. Bok, who years before came to this country as a poor immigrant boy. The sanctuary, the tower, its carillon, were dedicated to beauty. Beauty and the satisfaction of the soul are the only dividends expected from this investment. Visitors are invited to come and share in its restful, quiet and peaceful atmosphere. And as you approach this beautiful tower, with its superb architecture, the music of the bells and the sylvan setting, these words from the pen of John Burroughs catch your attention: "I come here to find myself. It is so easy to get lost in the world."

WHY HURRY? A tourist from China pretty well analyzed our feverish situation. He was being shown the wonders of New York City and was taken to a subway. With his guide he boarded a local train, and when they reached Fourteenth Street, he was hurried off this local to take an express. "Why did we do that?" inquired the Chinese. "To save five minutes," was the reply. He looked puzzled for a moment, and then questioned: "And what shall we do with the five minutes?"

RESERVES IN ACTION. William James, writing some fifty years ago, tells of Dr. Clouston, a Scottish physician, and of his impressions after visiting this country. "You Americans," he said, "wear too much expression on your faces. You are living with all your reserves in action. The duller countenances of the British people betoken a better scheme of life— suggest stores of reserved nervous forces to fall back upon if the occasion should require it. This unexcitability I regard as the greatest safeguard of the British people. The other thing in you," he continues, "gives me a sense of insecurity. You really ought somehow to tone yourselves down. You take too intensely the trivial moments of life."

ONE THING IS NEEDFUL. Some years ago, Anton Lang, who for many years played the part of the Christus in the world-famous Oberammergau Passion Play, visited America. In New York he was interviewed by Bruce Barton. Answering the question, "What do you think of America?" Lang replied: "Your city overwhelms me a bit; you are so hurried; so worried. You want so many things that are unnecessary. In my little village we have a few things: a living and the love of our families and our work and our faith in God—just a few simple things, but they are enough." Bruce Barton commented on this answer: "You could almost imagine you heard another voice, that of the original Christ, 'Martha, Martha, thou art anxious and troubled about many things: but one thing is needful.' "—Rev. Haven N. Davis.

BE STILL

In every life
There's a pause that is better than onward rush,
Better than hewing or mightiest doing;
'Tis the standing still at sovereign will.
There's a hush that is better than ardent speech,
Better than sighing or wilderness crying;
'Tis the being still at sovereign will.
The pause and the hush sing a double song,
In unison low and for all time long,
O human soul, God's working plan

Goes on, nor heeds the aid of man!
Stand still, and see!
Be still, and know!
—Author Unknown

EVENING SERVICE

Theme: Mountain Lessons of the Divine Goodness (Vacation Time).

TEXT: "Thy righteousness is like the great mountains." Ps. 36:6.

INTRODUCTORY: "Righteousness" might equally be translated "goodness."

I. The mountains are firm, based and solid-hearted. God's goodness similarly is not fickle. It is solid and certain.

II. The mountains are unchangeable. There are foliage, and surface changes, but they endure.

III. The mountains are self-evident; do not have to be labeled. The goodness of God needs no proof. It shines in all things.

IV. Mountains cannot be measured with small standards. God's goodness is not to be comprehended in full by our finite calculations.

V. Mountains are awe-inspiring—incite to reverence. So there is sublimity in the active goodness of God.

VI. Mountains are difficult of ascent. So out of a worldly life it is difficult to rise to the level of the divine goodness.

VII. The mountains are regulative, namely, of streams, local climate, as barriers between countries, etc. So divine goodness comes down and regulates human morals and affairs.

VIII. The mountains enlarge and destroy petty boundaries—local strife. So God's goodness when we rise to it makes petty creeds and dogmas ridiculous.

IX. The mountains are full of sublimity and poetry. Equally a large view of God's goodness shows it as a sublime inspiration.

X. Mountains hide their secrets from the indolent and the absent. Those who dwell at their base know not the treasures and summits. So to many content with sin's valleys the goodness of God has little meaning.

XI. The mountains rise above the clamor of the world. God's goodness is silent, majestic, not moved by the demands of men.

XII. Attack on the mountains does not demolish them. Men may doubt, deny, revile the goodness of God, but it remains from age to age.

XIII. Mountains are the storehouses of precious gems and stones. Whoever will quarry in the mountains of Providence will find God's goodness full of precious things.

XIV. Mountains are often lighted with glory when all else is dark. When the shadows of evil cover the world, the mountains are firm and comforting.—S. H. V.

Suggestive Texts and Themes

The Grandest Eulogy Ever Given: "She hath done what she could." Mark 14:8.

Christ the Real Magnet: "And I, if I be lifted up from the earth, will draw all men unto me." John 12:32.

Ancient and Modern Spiritualism: "Then said the woman, Whom shall I bring up unto thee? And he said, Bring me up Samuel." I Sam. 28:11.

Obedience Essential in Christianity: "Ye shall walk after the Lord your God, and fear him, and keep his commandments, and obey his voice, and ye shall serve him, and cleave unto him." Deut. 13:4. "If ye love me keep my commandments." John 14:15.

Robbers of Men: "Thou shalt not steal." Ex. 20:15.

Robbers of God: "Will a man rob God? Yet ye have robbed me. But ye say, Wherein have we robbed thee? In tithes and offerings." Mal. 3:8.

MIDWEEK FELLOWSHIP MEETING TOPIC

(Church Night or Suggested Sermon Subject)

Theme: The Larger Vision.

TEXT: "Where there is no vision, the people perish." Prov. 29:18.

A young man poring over his book in

a New York City skyscraper, was told by the occulist, "You do not need glasses, but distance. Every noon hour go to the top of the building and spend a half hour looking up and down the Hudson and across the river to New Jersey. Give your eyes a chance at distance."

I. When there is no faraway vision, the eyesight will perish; so, when the soul is wholly occupied with the near, the little and the low, it is perishing for want of a wider outlook. Looking at self instead of the need of the wide world, looking down instead of up at the stars, looking at the earth instead of at the heavens, tend to make the soul blind.

II. Is not the best portion of some books their suggestiveness, giving clue to lofty ideas not in the writing, visions of inexpressible beauty beyond us? It is then that the mortal begins to put on immortality; things are seen beyond the horizon of time. We come to know that there are open doors in our Father's house above, inviting our entrance. Our sky is full of stars if we would but consider the heavens, give the eye of faith a chance; let it sweep through the universe of God and bring back visions immortal.

III. Nations, as well as individuals, perish without the wider, loftier vision of God's universe of all peoples and worlds. Looking down continually, we sag into anarchy, atheism and materialism. We use Bunyan's muckrake more than we do the telescope.—E. W. C.

CHRISTIAN ENDEAVOR SOCIETY TOPIC

Aug. 8. Gardens of the Bible. Gen. 2:7-17; Mark 14:32-42.

SUNDAY SCHOOL LESSON

Aug. 8. Choosing the Best. Matt. 6:25-33; Phil. 1:9-11; 4:8.

MEMORY VERSE: "It is my prayer that your love may abound more and more, with knowledge and all discernment, so that you may approve what is excellent." Phil. 1:9-10 (R.S.V.).

The dictionary definitions of the word *appreciate* are suggestive in relation to this matter of choosing the best. We must approve and appreciate what is excellent before we can choose. Here are the definitions: 1. "To set a just value on; to esteem to the full worth of." 2. "To be grateful for." The expression of thanks for a value actually enhances the value. 3. "To be sensitive to ·the aesthetic values of; as, to *appreciate* music. 4. "To be fully sensible of." 5. "To increase the value of," opposite, *depreciate*.

Apply this to that "first" value which Jesus pointed out—"the kingdom of God." Do we esteem the kingdom at its full worth? Are we grateful for the kingdom? Are we sensitive to its beauty? Are we fully sensible or aware of the kingdom? Do we so live as actually to increase the value of the kingdom? Do we really appreciate the kingdom? If so, we would choose it first.

SUNDAY: AUGUST FIFTEENTH

MORNING SERVICE

Theme: Conquerors Plus.

SUGGESTED SCRIPTURE READING: Rom. 8:24-39.

SELECTED HYMNS: "Stand up, my soul, and shake off thy fears."—I. Watts. "Am I a soldier of the cross."—I. Watts. "For all thy saints in warfare."—E. Nelson. "Oft in danger, oft in woe."—H. K. White. "Lift up, lift up your voices now."—J. M. Neale.

CALL TO WORSHIP: "Praise ye the Lord; for it is good to sing praises unto our God; for it is pleasant, and praise is comely. . . . Great is our Lord and mighty in power; his understanding is infinite."

INVOCATION PRAYER: Blessed be thy name, O God, for this holy day and sacred place. May this Sabbath be a day full of strength and comfort. May this be true for all who have assembled here to worship in thy courts and for all those also who are prevented from such privileges. Incline the hearts of thy people everywhere to commune with thee in the beauty of holiness. Out of the world's noise and confusion, and out of our own cares and worries we come. Make thy presence, we pray, very near and manifest unto us in this hour. Let the words of our mouths and the meditation of our hearts be acceptable unto thee, O Lord, our strength and our Redeemer. In our Redeemer's name we ask. Amen.

Theme: Conquerors Plus.

TEXT: "In all these things we are more than conquerors through him that loved us." Rom. 8:37.

INTRODUCTORY: The text sounds like the words of a professional boaster. Yet think of the little half-blind man who uttered them! Compare him to the ruthless warriors of his day. Would he be looked upon as a conqueror? Beaten, stoned, left for dead, persecuted, nevertheless daring to cry aloud, "We are more than conquerors!" How foolish his words must have sounded. Yet he was right. This was not an idle boast. He was giving expression to that which he had experienced.

There are varied ways in which we can face life with its trying experiences. One is meekly to accept defeat, to succumb, to allow the experiences of life to overwhelm us. Or to be defeated could mean remaining indifferent. Or we are defeated when we attempt to flee from life. And we are already defeated whenever we express a willingness to turn ourselves over to the enemy. Why be good? Why be faithful? So we

hoist the white flag. This is the way Judas reasoned. Whenever we become submissive to the forces arrayed against Christ, regardless of the reason, we have met defeat. A still further way to meet defeat is to be conquered. Whether we turn to the enemy, or allow him to rush in and capture us, the result is the same. Whenever we allow sin to assume mastery of our lives, slavery begins.

I. One way to face life is to be a conqueror and nothing more. Life is full of individuals who can never rise above the level of mere conquest. Some have advanced to unprecedented heights in the material realm and have reaped a financial harvest; yet the tragedy is that a great proportion are conquerors only, because they have gained no victories in the realm of the spirit. To be a conqueror is better than to fall short, but it is not enough.

II. Another way to face life is to be a conqueror, plus. That is what the apostle is saying in our text. A victory is not enough. We must do something with it after it is won.

1. First, we are more than conquerors when we refuse to lower our ideals in the face of opposition. The ideals of Jesus have never been surpassed. They never will be. We are more than conquerors when we assume ideals worthy of a Christian and maintain them at all costs.

2. We are more than conquerors when we deny self in the midst of selfishness. The fact that Jesus insisted upon this does not make it easy. Nothing is easy that calls for stern denial.

3. We are more than conquerors when we achieve victory in the presence of apparent defeat. Whatever else is lost we must courageously hold everything virtuous.

4. We are more than conquerors when we go the extra mile. The first mile makes us conquerors; the second adds the "plus." "Except your righteousness shall exceed," etc.

5. To love and forgive when hated and wronged makes us more than conquerors.

6. And we are more than conquerors

when we dare to place our most treasured possessions in the Master's arms and leave them there. This is extremely hard, but the road to conquest is never easy.

III. But how are we to become more than conquerors? It is one thing to suggest what should be done; it is another to determine how we can do it. Paul gives the answer in our text. "We are more than conquerors through Christ," he says. Conquest is impossible apart from Christ the Conqueror. This means that he first must conquer us. We must yield ourselves to him and by his strength, not ours, victory is gained. Every Christian can add the "plus," if he so desires, because he is empowered by the One who has power.

When we become more than a conqueror through Christ we gain a Companion in victory. We are not alone. The victorious Christ is with us, surrounding us with his love and becoming more intimate with the days.

I do not know what your burdens of the moment are, but you have them and feel their weight. Whatever their nature, is not this the time when our Companion in victory is indispensable? Will you not, with me, dedicate yourself anew to this conquering Christ, who makes us more than conquerors in every area of life's experiences?—Rev. George W. Wiseman.

THEME PRAYER: O God the strength of all that put their trust in thee, grant that we may be more than conquerors over all that makes war upon our souls, and being furnished rightly in love and goodness, may by our steadfastness hasten the triumph of all those things that make for peace both of body and of soul. Through Jesus Christ, our Lord. Amen.

OFFERTORY SENTENCE: "Trust in the Lord and do good, so shalt thou dwell in the land, and verily thou shalt be fed."

OFFERTORY PRAYER: Gracious God who giveth seed to the sower and bread to the eater, we thank thee for all the necessities of daily life. In gratitude we give of our substance that those who hunger for righteousness may be filled.

Accept our offering in the name of Jesus Christ our Lord. Amen.

Illustrative Material

SEED THOUGHTS, HOMILETIC AND EXPOSITORY. More than Conquerors: Conquerors although victorious are often all but defeated. The battle of Waterloo was won by a hair's breadth. The conquering army had nothing to spare. The believer in Christ has many foes and they are fierce to war against, but he has no doubt as to the result. God is with him and he cannot fail. He is more than conqueror.

More than Conquerors: I. Christians are conquerors. II. Christians are more than conquerors. 1. The means by which they overcome are such as enhance the glory of their conquests. 2. The manner in which they overcome makes them more than conquerors. III. Let them not be dismayed at any opposition. IV. But, Christian, take heed of pride or self-sufficiency.—B. B.

More than Conquerors: I. Victories that have been won by Christians. 1. Over "tribulation." 2. Over "distress." 3. Over "persecution." 4. Over "famine." 5. Over "nakedness." 6. Over "peril." 7. Over "the sword." II. The laurels of the fight. The words "more than conquerors" might be rendered "more exceeding conquerors." The Vulgate has a word which means "over overcomers," that is over and above overcoming.—C. H. S.

Choice Illustrations on the Theme

FAITHFULNESS PLUS. Sir Arthur Rostron was captain of the *Carpathia* which was first upon the scene after the sinking of the *Titanic* and rescued 706 persons. In his book, *Home from the Sea*, Captain Rostron tells how the Marconi operator on the *Carpathia* was supposed to go off duty at exactly midnight. But on this particular night he had stayed at his post until 12:35 A.M. With his headset still in place, he stooped to unlace his shoes, preparing to retire, when the S.O.S. came from the *Titanic*. Under forced draught the *Carpathia* rushed to the aid of the sinking ship, and the rescue of the 706 persons was completed. Had not an English radio operator remained at his job a half hour longer than he was supposed to be there, and a half hour for which he would receive no pay, 706 lives would have been lost.

CONQUEROR BY STRATEGY. Robert Louis Stevenson tells the story of a young man traveling in Spain and in a lonely part finding lodgment in an old castle. In the room he occupied there hung on the wall the picture of a beautiful but sensuous woman. Gradually the woman's face inflamed his imagination; it became an obsession he could not shake off, poisoning his heart and mind. In this castle in which he lived he had only met the señor and his wife, both of noble origin but poor. One day, passing up the staircase, he met face to face their daughter, of whose existence even he was ignorant. Young and beautiful, their eyes met and in that momentary glance love, fresh and pure, awoke in his heart. Filled with its strange glow and amazement he entered his room and looked up at the picture. Then he found the spell was gone. Instead of holding him he felt hatred and shame. The pure affection had done what no mental struggle could do.

Such is the power of a pure affection. Victory over sin is not gained by self-effort, but by opening the heart to the love of Christ. His love rushing in sweeps all foul affections out and raises the whole being into the heights of peace and victory. We become "more than conquerors through him that loved us."—*2,500 Best Modern Illustrations.*

CONSECRATION PLUS. From a Christian missionary we received this account of a Chinese Christian recently. He was a leader among young Christians in a village near Shanghai. He was severely wounded in a battle to defend his home. Several members of his family were killed, others shamefully treated; he lost his right leg and one eye. He was visited by a missionary to whom he expressed his desire to get well and to do the work God required of him. When reminded of his lost leg and eye, he said: "Thank God, I've still got my mouth left; I can speak for him."— Archer Wallace.

CHRISTIAN PLUS. A missionary in China writes of a girl in the mission school under her care. One night the girl came to her and said, "Teacher, I want you to pray that I may be a whole Christian." Struck by the expression, the teacher inquired what she meant. So the girl told her of certain things she had done that day that she felt to be wrong, and of things she had failed to do, which her teacher had commanded her. All this she instinctively felt was not in keeping with the spirit of the Gospel. So she came with tears in her eyes at the close of day, saying, "Oh, teacher, I want you to pray for me that I may be a whole Christian."—*Christian Age.*

NOT OVERCOMING, DEFEATED. A millionaire turned bootlegger was serving a long prison term when a friend of his visited him one day. The millionaire was sitting cross-legged, and with an enormous needle and a ball of twine was sewing burlap bags. "Hello," said the friend. "Sewing, eh?" "No," said the prisoner, with a grim smile. "Reaping."

EVENING SERVICE

Theme: Want of Sympathy.

TEXT: "We have piped unto you, and ye have not danced," etc. Matt. 11:17.

INTRODUCTORY: Christ got this picture from some children at play. The children of two thousand years ago were very like the children of today, even in their sports. Whatever the game they happened to play it was pretty sure to have in it some mimicry or quaint imitations or comic burlesque of what they had seen their elders do. Nothing more natural than for them to say, "Let us play wedding!" or "Let us play funeral!" That is what the children whom Jesus watched had been doing. His use of the illustration spoke of some sullen or contrary ones who would not respond for either game. The other and lively ones complained: "Whatever is the matter with you today? We have piped unto you, and ye have not danced; we have mourned unto you, and ye have not wept." They had offered to play "wedding" or "funeral," and they would play neither. They were sullen, morose, clear out of sympathy, and would not play the game.

What Jesus was telling these men who were listening to him was this, that they were like those refusing children in their own treatment of John the Baptist and of himself. He implied that it is no use trying to please everybody. John was a recluse and they said he had a devil. Jesus came eating and drinking and they said, "Behold a gluttonous man and a winebibber." The trouble with these men to whom Jesus was speaking was that they were entirely out of sympathy. They were like the contrary children complained against, to whom their companions said, "We have piped unto you, and ye have not danced; we have mourned unto you, and ye have not wept."

We will not at this time discuss the more difficult theme of the difference in treatment of John the Baptist and Christ, but more especially the lack of sympathy that too often exists between the most closely related and sincerely attached.

I. First, what are some of the causes of such want of sympathy? It is not owing to ignorance. "We have piped." We have appraised you of our joy or sorrow. It is not due to inability to understand the nature of our feelings. Nor is it to a willful intention to pain us. It is more likely to be due to carelessness of mind or absorption in other matters. Our recital does not affect our friends because their minds are engrossed with their own cares or pleasures.

II. Proofs of this lack of sympathy. "Ye have not danced." "Ye have not wept." The trouble is not personal estrangement. Our friends are personal spectators of us. Nor is there absence of kindly words. There may be loud professions without real manifestations of sympathy. True sympathy makes us weep with those who weep, and rejoice with those who rejoice.

III. The effects of this lack of sympathy. If we experience sorrow it is increased. No one bears our burden with us. If we experience joy it is diminished. For who cares to eat a feast alone? The effect should be to drive us to our heavenly Father, who ever sympathizes, and to our "sympathizing Saviour." To the burdened he says, "Come unto me," etc. To the happy his message is, "Make a joyful noise unto the Lord."

Suggestive Texts and Themes

The Christian Accent: "And after a while came unto him they that stood by, and said to Peter, Surely thou art one of them; for thy speech betrayeth thee." Matt. 26:73.

Sources of Weakness in the Body Politic: "And as the toes of the feet were part of iron, and part of clay, so the kingdom shall be partly strong, and partly broken." Dan. 2:42.

Life-Bestowers: "And Paul went down, and fell on him, and embracing him said, Trouble not yourselves; for his life is in him." Acts 20:10.

Personal Responsibility Before God: "Thou art weighed in the balances, and art found wanting." Dan. 5:27.

The Man Who Cuts the Bible: "And he cut it with the penknife." Jer. 36:23.

MIDWEEK FELLOWSHIP MEETING TOPIC

(Church Night or Suggested Sermon Subject)

Theme: The Profit of Godliness.

TEXT: "Godliness is profitable unto all things." I Tim. 4:8.

The subject of profit and loss in the kingdom of heaven is one which we would do well to study. It is the theme of several of the parables, and we meet it again and again on the pages of the new Testament.

I. A great many people cannot calculate profit and loss unless they are expressed in terms of dollars and cents. They make the mistake of substituting money values for spiritual values. That is the reason so many businessmen have divorced their religion from their business, have never really brought their business to Jesus.

II. On top of that, the businessman becomes distrustful when we preachers begin to talk about business. They say we haven't much business sense. Whether that is true or not, the Bible has sense about business and Jesus has sense about business. He took charge of Peter's fishing business one day for about fifteen minutes, and caught more fish at one haul than Peter had ever seen in that old net before.

III. Godliness is profitable; but there are some losses. What are they? Let Paul answer: "I have suffered the loss of all things that I may win Christ." We lose things, but we gain Christ.— E. V. C.

CHRISTIAN ENDEAVOR SOCIETY TOPIC

Aug. 15. Rivers and Seas of the Bible. Josh. 3:14-17; Matt. 3:13-17; 4:18-20; 8:23-27.

SUNDAY SCHOOL LESSON

Aug. 15. Self-discipline for Growth. Matt. 16:24-25; I Cor. 9:24-27; Heb. 12:1-4.

MEMORY VERSE: "If any man would come after me, let him deny himself, and take up his cross, and follow me." Matt. 16:24 (A.S.V.).

If any man *would* come after me. The earnest wish is, of course, a necessity. But if the volition remains only a wish nothing happens. Dreaming of a higher life does not achieve it. The volition must bring action. Intense action which is the redirection of life away from self and toward Christ is necessary. The passage from Paul suggests that a man must train for the higher life. Training will give a man control of his mind and his body, as well as of his soul and spirit. He will have the continual ennoblement of his intentions. A set of simple training rules will help him.

The passage from Hebrews, which calls us to "run with perseverance the race that is set before us, looking to Jesus," points us to the magnetism of a great life. The ideal is itself dynamic to draw us to right living. We keep our eyes on the goal and the goal quickens our pace.

SUNDAY: AUGUST TWENTY-SECOND

MORNING SERVICE

Theme: A Glimpse into Heaven.

SUGGESTED SCRIPTURE READING: Rev. 22:1-21.

SELECTED HYMNS: "Jerusalem the golden."—Bernard of Cluny. "For thee, O dear, dear country."—Bernard of Cluny. "Ten thousand times ten thousand."—H. Alford. "O Paradise, O Paradise."—F. W. Faber. "O Mother dear, Jerusalem."—F. B. P.

CALL TO WORSHIP: "We have thought of thy lovingkindness, O God, in the midst of thy temple. As is thy name, O God, so is thy praise unto the ends of the earth: Thy right hand is full of righteousness."

INVOCATION PRAYER: O God, Father of all goodness, we thank thee for the call to united worship. And for the promise of thy presence we thank thee. Let us know and feel that thou art here. Draw us with the cords of love and make us glad of heart as we commune with thee. We come to thee, O Father, for the benediction of thy grace. Help us to realize that thou art more willing to give than we are to ask. Out of thine infinite riches be pleased to bestow a blessing that shall sustain and strengthen us for the bearing of burdens and the discharge of duty during the coming days. And, O thou whose nearness is the answer to all our needs, help us in worshiping thee to lift our spirits above their weariness and littleness to thy eternal presence; and when our hour of worship is ended may the peace of it still possess us and its vision not grow dark. In Jesus' name we ask. Amen.

Theme: A Glimpse into Heaven.

TEXT: "Let not your heart be troubled," etc. John 14:1-3.

INTRODUCTORY: These are among the most loved words ever spoken. Jesus left the best for the last. We commonly speak of this last night as the final chapter of his life. To him it was only the beginning and he was informing his disciples of what was ahead. "In my Father's house," he says, "are many mansions: if it were not so, I would have told you. I go to prepare a place for you."

I. In the first place, Jesus describes heaven in terms not alone familiar but dear to the human heart. The very thought of its being the Father's House is enticing. When Jesus finished it seemed as though the Father's House was so near one could reach it by a few steps. We think of it in terms of distance. For Jesus it was an especially familiar place. He always lived in it. This is the reason for the confidence he engendered when he talked about it. Notice also the emphasis he placed upon the word "Father." There is nothing in that word to frighten us. It makes God real and his house inviting. "Father's House" means home, and home is the dearest place we know. There are treasures in a home that cannot be bought at any price. Love, faith, joy, sorrow, tears, suffering, lov-

ing ministry—these are but a few of the unpurchasables. Heaven is a home and the treasures no purchaser can buy are stored there.

II. In the second place, he indicates the preparation he is to make. "I go to prepare a place for you." Let us be thankful it is Jesus who does the preparing, for that will afford the greatest surprise our eyes can behold.

We have all had the experience of preparing for someone. There is another side we cannot overlook. It is seen from our angle. The greatest preparation in a home is, after all, the person we are about to see. And to prepare a place for one signifies we expect that person. When he arrives we are on hand with warm, friendly greetings. When Jesus prepares a place for us he expects us. But another thought is essential, that although the Master prepares a place for us, we must prepare ourselves for that place.

III. In the third place, he discloses that his departure is not final. "I will come again." We are amazed at his thoughtfulness. The coming of Jesus is not confined to life's varied experiences. He comes not merely unto us, but for us, in that experience we call death. Are we afraid of death? When the moment arrives we will hear his voice assuring us, "It is I, be not afraid." Death is not the cruel thing the world presents it to be. As we were received by loving arms and every possible attention when we came into this world, we may be sure our reception will be even more elaborate when we leave.

IV. Finally, he presents his reason for this extensive preparation. "That where I am, there ye may be also." We can be with him here and have his companionship now. But there is reserved for us the glad surprise of seeing him as he is, listening to his voice, and remaining in his presence always; and to be with him is to be with all our loved ones gone before.

Let us take heart and rejoice! We have a hope not devised by man, but by

God. We have a Saviour who is alive forevermore. Where he is there shall we be also.—Rev. George W. Wiseman.

THEME PRAYER: Almighty God who in a world of change has planted eternity in our hearts, grant unto us so to grow in grace and the knowledge of the mind of Jesus Christ that our goodness may be always reaching toward that perfection which, though we cannot reach it, we must be always seeking. We ask through Jesus Christ, our Lord. Amen.

OFFERTORY SENTENCE: "And God is able to make all grace abound toward you; that ye always having all sufficiency in all things, may abound to every good work."

OFFERTORY PRAYER: O Lord, renew our spirits and draw our hearts unto thyself, that our giving may not be to us a burden, but a delight; and give us such a love to thee as may sweeten all our obedience. We ask in the name of Christ. Amen.

Illustrative Material

SEED THOUGHTS, HOMILETIC AND EXPOSITORY. The Father's House: I. Christ discovers heaven to us. 1. Its nature. His home. The gathering place of God's children. 2. Its extent. "Many mansions." Plenty of room. "Mansions," beautiful dwelling places. 3. Its reality. "If it were not so, I would have told you." Finding us cherishing a hope of life over there, Christ says that were we cherishing a delusion he would have told us, undeceived us. II. Christ reveals it as a prepared place. "I go to prepare a place for you." It is a prepared place for prepared people. 1. He prepares it by making it accessible. 2. By gathering its people. 3. By supplying its blessings. III. The place, where is it? It is where he is. "That where I am there ye may be also." Not located; but to be where Christ is, that makes heaven for his followers. This was Paul's idea of heaven, to "depart and be with Christ."—W. H. B.

"Many Mansions": I. The magnitude of heaven. II. And vastness suggests variety. Suggests also the charm of variety. III. The hominess of heaven.

"Father's house." IV. Assurance. Its reality. "If it were not so, I would have told you." He is truth. Cannot deceive. If we were cherishing a mistaken hope he would have undeceived us. —A. R.

Choice Illustrations on the Theme

HEAVEN. "I go to prepare a place for you." Heaven is a prepared place for prepared people.

STRONGEST ASSURANCE. "If it were not so, I would have told you." Jesus found his disciples cherishing a hope of life beyond the grave, a heavenly home. He practically said, "I never would have allowed you to go on with such expectation were it to have no fulfillment. I would have undeceived you. 'If it were not so, I would have told you.' " Such words directly from him make strongest possible assurance.—H.

THE ROAD TO IT. A traveler in Switzerland tells of asking a little lad where Kandersteg was. The reply was significant: "I do not know where Kandersteg is, but there is the road to it."

BUILDING OUR OWN HEAVEN. There is a familiar legend of a wealthy woman who when she reached heaven was shown to a very plain cottage. She objected. "Well," she was told, "that is the house prepared for you." "Whose is that fine mansion across the way?" she asked. "It belongs to your gardener." "How is it that he has one so much better than mine?" "The houses here are prepared from the materials sent up. We do not choose them; you do that by your earthly deeds."

Upon the tomb of Atolus of Rheims it was written: "He exported his fortune before him into heaven by his charities. He has gone thither to enjoy it."

Best Modern Illustrations.

THINK OF THE PROSPECTS. A clergyman was once summoned to a deathbed in one of the slums of South London. Flight after flight of stairs he mounted, till he came to the topmost flat, and found his way into a miserable room with hardly any furniture, where a poor, half-starved old man lay dying in great pain. As he entered the room he could not help saying, "Oh, I am so sorry for you!" "Sorry for me?" the old man replied. "Why, think of my prospects!" —Rev. G. R. Balleine.

THE HEAVEN LIFE. When we wonder about the life which is to come, I think that perhaps the most helpful and suggestive statement about that life is that sentence of St. Paul, "As we have borne the image of the earthly, so we shall bear the image of the heavenly." Here in this life we have borne the image of the earthly, which was perfectly adapted to our earthly existence. In the life to come we shall bear the image of the heavenly, which will be perfectly adapted to our heavenly life, and whatever that life is to be like, we know that we shall be satisfied when we awake in His likeness.—Clarence E. Macartney, D.D.

EVENING SERVICE

Theme: Christian Suffering.

TEXT: "Doth Job fear God for nought?" Job 1:9.

INTRODUCTORY: There is a definite ministry in suffering. Job is the leading example in this regard. "Is Job serving God because he really loves him or just for the material blessings received from him?" came the question. The answer: "Because he loves me." And to prove it God allowed Job to be subjected to a period of trial seldom if ever equaled.

What was Job's reaction to this? "The Lord gave and the Lord hath taken away, blessed be the name of the Lord." When advised to curse God and die, he simply asked, "What? Shall we receive good at the hand of God, and shall we not receive affliction?" And again: "Though he slay me, yet will I trust in him." That is the type of faith that honors the Lord. Job's love was tried in a furnace of suffering and was found pure.

The Bible is full of other examples of those whose love for God was severely tested. Moses, Jeremiah, Daniel, Paul. So we might go down the roster of the heroes of faith and find those whose love for God was tried through affliction.

But there are other phases of the ministry of suffering.

I. Suffering purifies. What good would ore be if it were not subjected to the terrific heat which separates the dross from the pure metal? Our all-wise Father knows when there is dross in our lives which must be purged by fire. Again Job speaks: "I cannot see him; but he knoweth the way that I take; when he hath tried me I shall come forth as gold."

II. Suffering provides opportunity to manifest the indwelling Christ. As the rose petal must be crushed before it surrenders its most fragrant perfume, so the crushing trials we must endure are designed to bring out the characteristics of Christ in us—his long-suffering gentleness, his joyful self-control, and his calm resignation to the Father's will. Dare we complain and murmur when God is merely subjecting us to those things which provide an opportunity for the out-living of the in-living Christ?

III. Suffering glorifies God if received patiently. God was glorified when the three Hebrews entered the fiery furnace rather than deny him. And likewise he is accorded glory and honor every time a Christian accepts affliction and remains joyfully triumphant and peacefully resigned through it all.

Are you accepting your cross in such a way that God is glorified in the eyes of your friends?

IV. Suffering provides fellowship with Christ. Paul's great desire was that he might "know him and the fellowship of his sufferings." The more intense our suffering the more nearly we are able to feel, and in some small degree, the infinite suffering our Saviour experienced in giving his life for our redemption. And thus feeling it we appreciated it as never before.

V. We know it is for the best. We cannot understand at the present why we should be the one chosen to suffer, but we know by faith that it is for our benefit and God's glory. God doeth all things well, his way is perfect, and he makes all things work together for our good. He is our loving heavenly Father and never causes his child a needless tear. We see now only the wrong side of the tapestry of our life that is being woven; in that day when knowledge is perfected we shall see the right side and marvel at the design God hath wrought.

Until that day dawn, let us with patience bear our affliction with the quiet confidence that, no matter how dark the picture now, our times are in his hands and we are the objects of his love and shepherd-care.—W. E. G.

Suggestive Texts and Themes

A Fearless Pulpit: "We were bold in our God to speak unto you the gospel." I Thess. 2:2.

Social Outcasts: "Lover and friend hast thou put far from me." Ps. 88.18.

A Way to Avoid Death: "Verily, verily, I say unto you, If a man keep my saying, he shall never see death." John 8:51.

Christ's Manifold Dominion: "On his head were many crowns." Rev. 19:12.

The Curtailment of Life: "I will cause the sun to go down at noon." Amos 8:9.

The Question of Educated Youth: "The young man saith unto him, All these things have I kept from my youth up: what lack I yet?" Matt. 19:20.

MIDWEEK FELLOWSHIP MEETING TOPIC

(Church Night or Suggested Sermon Subject)

Theme: The Brotherhood of Jesus.

TEXT: "There is a friend that sticketh closer than a brother." Prov. 18:24.

One of two brothers, fighting in the same company in the French army, fell by a German bullet. The one who escaped asked permission of his officer to go and bring in his brother. "He is probably dead," said the officer, "and there is no use in risking your life to bring in his body." After further

pleading, the officer consented. Just as the soldier reached camp with his brother on his shoulders, the wounded man died. "There, you see," said the officer, "you risked your life for nothing." "No," replied Tom, "I did what he expected of me and I have my reward. When I crept up to him and took him in my arms, he said: "Tom, I knew you would come; I just knew you would come!'"

I. What a noble picture is this of faithful friendship, of heart kinship. All great friendship is sacrificial. Jonathan left his father's kingly palace for the sake of his beloved David. Damon gave up his liberty and life that his friend Pythias might go free. But supreme above all other friendships is that of Jesus leaving his throne, giving his life to rescue a race.

II. When he finds us dying in sin his touch brings new life to the soul. When he brings us in from the battlefield of death, we are alive forevermore with him. He is closer than a brother, nearer than any earthly kin; he is Creator, Restorer, Everlasting Friend. He ministers unto each one for the blessing of all; he is the brother of everybody in the family of God.

III. The Elder Brother has come and calleth for thee. He goes to rescue thee; he cries to the fallen one, "Come forth into newness of life, into fellowship of friends." O matchless friendship, O eternal companionship! —E. W. C.

CHRISTIAN ENDEAVOR SOCIETY TOPIC

Aug. 22. Wells of the Bible. Gen. 26:17-25; John 4:6-14.

SUNDAY SCHOOL LESSON

Aug. 22. Christian Giving. I Cor. 16:1-2; II Cor. 8:1-9.

MEMORY VERSE: "It is more blessed to give than to receive." Acts 20:35.

A small folder entitled "Yes" was distributed by a church at the time of its Every Member Canvass. It read as follows:

"Do you think giving has any connection with the spiritual side of religion?"

"Most certainly! In fact that is our interest in the matter. We do not want to know how much you or other members give. But we do want to know that God's will shall be done and that your soul shall grow through the way you use your money."

"How can I make sure that my giving will help me spiritually?"

1. "Pledge generously—not less than you feel in your heart God expects of you. If this is one tenth, exercise some faith and go ahead as a tither. Nine tenths for self with God will go farther than ten tenths without God.

2. "Give weekly—thus you may worship with your offering.

3. "Give personally—let every member of your family share in the joy of Christian Stewardship.

4. "Give prayerfully—pray daily for the causes to which your gifts go and for yourself that you may be a faithful trustee of the money God has entrusted to you.

5. "So live each day that your giving shall be but a symbol of the fact that you as well as your possessions belong to God."

SUNDAY: AUGUST TWENTY-NINTH

MORNING SERVICE

Theme: Vantage Points and Vision.

SUGGESTED SCRIPTURE READING: James 2:1-26.

SELECTED HYMNS: "Blest are the pure in heart."—J. Keble. "When I can read my title dear."—I. Watts. "Rise, my soul, and stretch thy wings."—R. Seagrave. "O Light, whose beams illumine all."—E. H. Plumptre. "Walk in the light, so shalt thou know."—B. Barton.

CALL TO WORSHIP: "Thus saith the high and lofty One that inhabiteth eternity, whose name is Holy: I dwell in the high and holy place, with him also that is of a contrite and humble spirit, to revive the spirit of the humble, and to revive the heart of the contrite."

INVOCATION PRAYER: O God, our heavenly Father, let the light of thy countenance rest upon us this day that we may truly worship and rejoice and be glad in thee. We lift up our eyes unto thee, O thou that dwellest in the heavens. Make us to know by the warming of our hearts and the quickening of our zeal that thou art here with a blessing. O thou ever-present Companion, we could not go on were it not for thy abiding presence with us. Help us to know that thou art ever by our side, close to us, helping us, making our hearts to burn within us. Reveal thyself to us so fully that our hearts and lives may be transformed by thy presence. Deliver us also from ignoble fears, arm us with faith and hope, send out thy light and thy truth, let them so lead us, that we may face the seen and unseen with tranquil courage; we ask all in the name of Christ. Amen.

Theme: Vantage Points and Vision.

TEXT: "Where there is no vision, the people perish." Prov. 29:18.

INTRODUCTORY: The story is told of how Sir Francis Drake and his men were once lost in the swamps of Panama. Eventually, after hours of wandering and growing alarm, one of them climbed to the top of a tree and looking out across the swamps and jungle he saw the waters of the Pacific calling them to launch out into a new and unexplored world.

Isn't that a parable of human life? The vast majority of people can be likened to Drake's men, caught in a jungle swamp. Life to them is a baffling and frightening mystery. They are lost, unhappy, imprisoned, hopeless. The real trouble with them is that they have never climbed to a vantage point and looked out beyond their immediate burdens and temptations and problems which hem them in to where glistening waters call them to new and glorious ventures in an unexplored world.

I believe that Christianity can make this a real experience for each of us; that it can give to men a vantage point and a vision, making them conscious of a new world and a new life beyond any which they have known.

I. In the first place, Christianity has always given men a glimpse beyond this world of time and space. Because we believe in God as Jesus Christ has revealed him, a God of love and power, we cannot believe that life ends in death. We see it stretching out beyond the grave, a fuller and more glorious life than we have ever known or dreamed. We cannot believe that the eternal purposes of God can be defeated. We have Jesus' own words to give us this assurance. "Because I live, ye shall live also."

II. But that is not all. The fact is that unless a man is a Christian he is depriving himself of half the world that could be his here and now. Christianity is not simply concerned with a life hereafter. Life on this earth can be an immeasurably richer and fuller thing than most people are aware. The very word "life" has a thrilling sound. Say it over to yourself a few times. "Life! Life!" It speaks of action, color, reality, joy. Yet for how few people life is really like that?

1. I suggest two such vantage points which Christianity can give us. First, there is the vantage point of worship. So, when the burden of the world presses heavily upon us, when we are baffled and lost, hemmed in by circumstance, let us climb to the vantage point of worship, where we breathe a rarer air, catch a glimpse of things eternal, and returning to the world again press on to those new realms in the inspiration of the vision we beheld in worship.

2. The other vantage point which Christianity gives us is that of service. That too takes us beyond ourselves, and widens the scope of our vision. You see, when we do something for someone else—give some word of encouragement, do some piece of service—we are setting in motion forces which go on and on, beyond all our planning and imagining.

Do you see what I mean by calling service a vantage point? It lifts us above any sense of futility in our lives, unspectacular though they may be. It reminds us that our love and loyalty and faith may have an influence far beyond our dreaming.

It is this sense of being sharers in the eternal purposes of God which gives life meaning and zest. Our life however humble, our service however inconspicuous, is being taken up and woven into the agelong and world-wide purposes of God.

This is the sort of vision which makes life worth living, delivering it from futility and hopelessness, sending us forth with zeal and faith to do God's will. —J. B. N.

THEME PRAYER: O Jesus Christ, Lord of all good life, do thou enrich and purify us in thought and desire. Deliver us from all false pride, intolerance, contempt and whatever in us hides thy light, who are the Light of the world. Amen.

OFFERTORY SENTENCE: "Thanks be unto God for his unspeakable gift!"

OFFERTORY PRAYER: Almighty God, grant us grace that we may fulfill our duty toward our neighbor, by loving others as ourselves, and doing unto all men as we would they should do unto us. Be pleased also to accept our offerings brought in a desire for the coming of thy kingdom. We ask through Christ. Amen.

Illustrative Material

SEED THOUGHTS, HOMILETIC AND EXPOSITORY. The Vitality of Vision: I. Where there is no vision of the present working of Christ in the world charity and life fade. II. Where there is no vision of the Divine Fatherhood devotion decays. III. Where there is no vision of Divine Providence practiced energy declines. IV. Where there is no vision of truth and fact knowledge decays. V. Where there is no vision of the possibilities of human nature sympathy decays. VI. Where there is no vision of duty holiness declines. VII. The vision of heaven saves hope from perishing. The inspiration of all progress is hope.—T. M.

The Vitality of Vision: I. The restraining power of vision. II. The sustaining power of vision. III. The ennobling power of vision. It purifies thought. It elevates the spirit. IV. The blessedness of obedience to the heavenly visions. If we would know the highest joy of visions we must obey them.—Z. M.

Choice Illustrations on the Theme

THANK GOD FOR THE STARS. "O God, we thank thee for the stars." Thus prayed a young boy on the closing night of one of our intermediate camps, as the group joined the prayer circle around the campfire. That boy had been impressed with the mystery of the stars, which illumine the night skies and guide men across the trackless seas and deserts. We, too, should thank God for the stars, the men who have lighted the pathway of mankind through the ages. "Where there is no vision the people perish."

LONG VIEWS OF LIFE. Dr. C. L. Goodell writes: "When Paul bade good-by to Demas, Demas went to the purple vineyards of Macedonia. Paul turned to the cold, damp prison and a little later to his martyrdom at the block." To those who take a short view, Demas may have seemed prudent. After twenty centuries we know that Demas took the wrong turn and went the wrong way. Religion enables us to take long views of life. We know that life must not be lived for any fleeting moment.— Archer Wallace.

THE VANTAGE POINT OF WORSHIP. No one who reads the Gospels can doubt that Jesus himself gained his own immeasurable strength and faith and poise from those long vigils in the desert and in the mountain, when he was alone with his Father, saw the vision glorious, and returned in the strength and inspiration of it to the world again. Like him, through such a vision, we too can be in the world and yet not of the world.

DREAM TRUE! A famous politician of a former generation, knowing that he had but a short time to live, was meditating upon his past. His career had been highly successful according to the standards of the world. Starting out in his boyhood with a determined ambition to secure money and power, he had achieved his aims. He had elected governors and helped to elect presidents; and he had enriched himself while doing so. All the tricks of politics had been used to attain his purposes, and he had justified the means by the end.

But his success, as he now looked back upon it, had brought no happiness. "In a few months I shall be dead," he said, "and the papers will say, 'Boss Matt Qualey is dead.' Had I lived my life differently, they would say, 'Statesman Matthew Stanley Qualey is dead.'" Then he gave a farewell message to the world which was summed up in the words "Dream True!"

We Americans have always been dreamers—but of what do we dream? Are we cherishing the false ideas of the politician and thinking mainly in terms of harnessing atomic energy and maintaining military might that will make us the most powerful and most hated nation in the world? Or do we dream like Christian statesmen of using our power and resources to satisfy the world's hunger for food and brotherhood?

And we preachers and religious leaders have always been dreamers. "Behold the dreamer cometh" might be said of almost everyone in religious work. Are we having the dreams of the ecclesiastical politician whose chief concern is for a larger salary, denominational prestige, and more publicity? Or have we become "fools for Christ's sake" who aspire only to shape our lives and our world according to the revelation of eternal truth in Jesus Christ? This is a time for greatness in state and church. Dream true!—Rev. Walter D. Cavert.

THE VANTAGE POINT OF SERVICE. In one of his books Leslie Weatherhead quotes an interesting example of this vantage point of service. A little more than two hundred years ago an old Puritan doctor wrote a book, and he died without knowing that it had been of use to anybody. As to who he was we are in doubt, but he called the book *The Bruised Reed*. Richard Baxter was converted by *The Bruised Reed*, and he wrote a book entitled *A Call to the Unconverted*. Philip Doddridge was converted by reading Baxter's book, and he wrote *The Rise and Progress of Religion in the Soul*. William Wilberforce read Doddridge's book, and he wrote *A Practical View of Christianity*. Thomas Chalmers read it and is said to have "set all Scotland on fire with God."

And who knows that that is the end of the story? Now you and I may not write great books, but the same principle holds good in every piece of Christian service we do, however quiet and humble.—Rev. John B. Nettleton.

EVENING SERVICE

Theme: Self-pity.

TEXT: "All these things are against me." Gen. 42:36.

INTRODUCTORY: Tell the story as here recorded. Really these things were not against but for him.

I. Now this malady of self-pity is quite a common one, and is certainly not confined to worried Jacobs and woebegone Jobs; but its frequency does not minimize its foolishness and harmfulness. Self-pity is a reflection on Providence, an infliction on neighbors and a deflection from the path of faith.

II. The root of self-pity. It is to be found in an exaggerated sense of self-regard. No one who has wholly given himself up to doing the will of God and serving his fellow men will find place or time for self-pity. This is a weed that grows in a neglected soil. Fill the garden of your life with the worship of God and the work of self-sacrificing service and you will soon choke out this poisonous plant.

Of course there is a self-regard which is not only commendable but essential. But this commendable attitude is concerned with one's holiness and helpfulness and not with one's happiness. It says not, "I must be happy," but, "I must be worthy."

III. Then we come to the harm of self-pity. It is a handicap and presupposes defeat. Such a person comes to think of himself as being unlucky and foredoomed to failure. He looks all around him and cries, "All these things are against me." Such a view of life leads of itself to the failure which it fears and brings about the fulfillment of its own prognostications. For an army to march to battle expecting defeat is the surest way to bring about defeat. Such a one is really setting circumstances against himself. "All things work together for evil" is the way in which he misreads Paul's great text. The quarrel with circumstances becomes also a quarrel with Providence till the wisdom, knowledge and love of God fade from view.

IV. The cure. Before this sickness of the mind can be successfully dealt with it must be rightly diagnosed. It will then be invariably found out that the patient is in the grip of a false philosophy of life. He is out to be happy, when he ought rather to aim at being holy and helpful. It is self-centeredness that has him in its deadly grip. This is the cancer destroying the tissue of his spiritual life. It means the death of all true joy, of all real peace and every high and holy hope.

Romans 8:28 may be claimed as the panacea for this sickness. That great verse reads as follows: "All things work together for good to them that love God." Then you will believe, whatever happens, that he is always good and true and just.

If you seek happiness she will shun you; but if instead you seek holiness and helpfulness you will find happiness slipping in unawares. The knowledge that you are pleasing God and serving your fellow men will bring with it peace and pleasure and growing power.— F. C. L.

Suggestive Texts and Themes

Pessimism and Some of Its Causes: "There be many that say, Who will show us any good?" Ps. 4:6. "Vanity of vanities: all is vanity." Eccles. 1:2.

Antagonism to Truth: "And the king of Israel said unto Jehoshaphat, There is yet one man, Micaiah the son of Imlah, by whom we may inquire of the Lord: but I hate him; for he doth not prophesy good concerning me, but evil." I Kings 22:8.

The Offensiveness of Ceremonialism: "Bring no more vain oblations; incense is an abomination unto me; the new moons and sabbaths, the calling of assemblies, I cannot away with; it is iniquity, even the solemn meeting."—Isa. 1:13.

The Success of Failure: "Yea verily, and I count all things to be loss for the excellency of the knowledge of Christ Jesus my Lord: for whom I suffered the loss of all things, and do count them but refuse, that I may gain Christ." Phil. 3:8 (A.S.V.).

The Failure of Success: "But they that are minded to be rich fall into a temptation and a snare and many foolish and hurtful lusts, such as drown men in destruction and perdition." I Tim. 6:9 (A.S.V.).

MIDWEEK FELLOWSHIP MEETING TOPIC

(Church Night or Suggested Sermon Subject)

Theme: Garden Revelations.

TEXT: "Therefore the Lord himself shall give you a sign." Isa. 7:14.

The Incarnation is no more a mystery than the unfolding blossoms in our gardens. The power of God is revealed in both.

I. Miracles cannot be limited to the sphere of religion. Nature, in her changing charms, is nothing else but the miraculous. The blossoming bud is an emblem of God's unfolding plan. No crimson rambler, no clinging morning-glory, no trailing nasturtium can be explained by a black clod of earth and a pint of water. The soil is athrob with the divine energy. The air is vibrant with whispers of the Infinite.

II. By the laws of association our thoughts leap from the roses everywhere to the "Rose of Sharon," how, by virtue of his great teachings and splendid idealism, desert places are made glad.

III. The Christ has traveled from the manger of Bethlehem to the firesides of nations. He has broken the fetters of the oppressed. He has put beauty in life and humanity in government. His presence is in the garden of our environments, and the world by the alchemy of his love is being transformed into an Eden of rest and peace, hope and joy.—R. B.

CHRISTIAN ENDEAVOR SOCIETY TOPIC

Aug. 29. Mountains of the Bible. Ex. 19:16-20; Matt. 5:1, 2, 26-30.

SUNDAY SCHOOL LESSON

Aug. 29. Growth through Christian Service. Gal. 6:1-2; James 1:22, 26-27; 2:14-17.

MEMORY VERSE: "Bear one another's burdens, and so fulfil the law of Christ." Gal. 6:2.

Growth, achieving maturity, is a most important matter not only for the individual but for the whole human race. Only mature persons will replace the hostility and suspicion in the world with growing appreciation and responsible love for other persons. Maturity is the aim of all growth. Christians should become mature in love.

Dr. Paul E. Johnson tells us that "the mature person is interdependent. . . . By outgrowing the indulgent dependence of childhood and the assertive independence of adolescence he comes into a larger appreciation of others as well as of himself. He honestly recognizes his need of others at the same time he realizes their need of him. He is ready to help others in a responsible comradeship that does not hesitate to bear each other's burdens or to go a second mile in useful service for the larger good."

SUNDAY: SEPTEMBER FIFTH

MORNING SERVICE

Theme: The Carpenter's Son (Labor Day).

SUGGESTED SCRIPTURE READING: John 15:1-27.

SELECTED HYMNS: "Ye servants of the Lord."—P. Doddridge. "Go labor on, spend and be spent."—H. Bonar. "God of the earnest heart."—S. Johnson. "Jesus, thou divine companion."— Henry van Dyke. "Rise up, O men of God."—W. P. Merrill.

CALL TO WORSHIP: "And many people shall go and say, Come ye, and let us go up to the moutnain of the Lord, to the house of the God of Jacob; and he will teach us of his ways, and we will walk in his paths: for out of Zion shall go forth the law, and the word of the Lord from Jerusalem."

INVOCATION PRAYER: Our Father, we thank thee for life and love and work to do, for life that is for serving, for love that sends us to our task, and for the large place thou hast given us in the world's work. Help us to realize how large a place it is. May we find our chiefest joy in useful labor wherein we join our hand and brain and heart to thy powers and thy laws and thy love. May the work of our hands be accomplished with such joy, such skill, such efficiency that it may have the qualities of thy great works. Thus may we be not mere creatures but creators with thee; not one of thy works, but one of thy workers. If we seem to succeed may we not be puffed up, but rather grateful to thee for conditions under which to work that make success possible. Thou art the living God. The cause is thy cause and thy voice hast called us to it. May we cast all our care upon thee who carest for us. Through Christ we offer these petitions. Amen.—Paul Moore Strayer, D.D.

Theme: The Carpenter's Son (Labor Day.)

TEXT: "Is not this the carpenter?" Mark 6:3.

INTRODUCTORY: "Is not this the carpenter?" As though no words of wisdom or works of power could come from a carpenter! If Jesus had been a rabbi in a scholar's robe it would have been another thing. Yes, and what another thing for us, and for all the world's workers! Celsus sneered at the carpenter, and said that word proved that Jesus was an imposter. How could God so demean himself? But the world has left Celsus behind, along with the critics of Nazareth, and blesses God for the gentleness and comfort, the sympathy and hope, which were given to us by the hands of the Carpenter.

It suits our best sense that the one who spoke of "putting the hand to the plow" and "taking the yoke upon us" should have made plows and yokes himself, and men do not think his words less heavenly for not smelling of books and lamps. Let us not make the mistake of those Nazarenes. That Jesus was a carpenter was to them poor credentials of divinity, but it has been divine credentials to the poor ever since. Let us not be deceived by social ratings and badges of the schools. Hundreds of doors are not to be unlocked by Phi Beta Kappa keys.

Carey was a cobbler, but he had a map of the world on his shop wall and outdid Alexander the Great in dreaming and doing. Many a weaver and tinker and stonecutter and hand worker has had open windows and a sky, and a mind with wings. What thoughts were in the mind of Jesus at his workbench! One of them was that the kingdoms of this world should become the kingdoms of God—at any cost!

Let us go into the Carpenter's shop and learn some lessons:

I. The dignity of toil. The Architect of the universe, by whom all things were created, when for love's sake he baceme a man, made plows and yokes. The loftiest soul did lowliest work. Hard hands belonged to the gentlest heart. The Son of God would not have an exceptional lot, but a common one. He must know how most men feel, and so he became a wage earner and a day laborer.

1. Now let all men know that work, the duty of Eden, the condition of health, the law of progress, the salt of manhood, the safeguard of virtue, bears forever the sign manual of God.

2. Now let all men feel the disgrace of idleness and hail the infinite dignity of the words that came from the heart of the Creator and the lips of the Carpenter: "My Father worketh hitherto, and I work."

II. Divine sympathy in toil. What this means to men, may mean to us, is beyond words. "What does the unseen Framer of the world know or care about my daily tasks?" Dare you look the Carpenter of Nazareth in the face and say that again? The words, "He that hath seen me hath seen the Father," brings to us immediately the assurance of the divine sympathy. Of course, the Omniscient knows every-

thing, but now we know that he knows with a new certainty and nearness. See the lackluster eye of the worker who knows not the love of God as Christ revealed it. Now see him after he has known Christ. He is resting at noon in his shop, reading the words, "Is not this the carpenter?"

Yes, yes, a Carpenter; same trade as mine.
It warms my heart as I read that line.
I can stand the hard work, I can stand the poor pay,
For I'll see that Carpenter at no distant day.

How like the Lord are the words of the *Logia*, lately found in Egypt: "Lift the stone and thou shall find me; cleave the wood and there am I!" Lift up your head, lift up your heart, toiler of the common day; your Saviour has drunk the cup you are drinking. He knows how it tastes. Let the thought of his loving sympathy stir your heart to new hope and love and loyalty.— M. D. B.

THEME PRAYER: O Thou who hast given us the great and precious trust of life, help us, we pray thee, so to live and love and labor that we may give of all our days and deeds a good accounting. May we so begin in wisdom, continue on in duty and end in love, that the whole course of our lives may in the end be blessed by thee. Through Jesus Christ, our Lord. Amen.

OFFERTORY SENTENCE: "Now that ye have consecrated yourselves unto the Lord, come near and bring sacrifices and thank offerings into the house of the Lord."

OFFERTORY PRAYER: O Lord, who didst call by name men to work upon the tabernacle in the wilderness, we thank thee for the dignity of labor and for the blessing thou dost bestow upon the producers. May this day remind us of the interdependence of all parts of the human family. Receive thine own, our Father, in this offering; yet thine own freighted with our love and winged by our prayers. We ask it in the name of Christ. Amen.

Illustrative Material

SEED THOUGHTS, HOMILETIC AND EXPOSITORY. Christ the Carpenter: I. How the fact that Jesus was a carpenter was a hindrance to the faith of his fellow countrymen. 1. The objection was natural. 2. It was wrong. 3. But in reality in his favor. II. How this fact should be a help to our faith. 1. It is a sign of Christ's humility. 2. It is a proof that he went through the experience of practical life. 3. It sheds a glory over the life of manual industry. 4. It should attract working men to Christ.—W. F. A.

The Dignity of Labor: I. It is a suitable occupation of time. 1. Profitable. 2. Healthful. 3. Saves from the bad effect of indolence. 4. It is a source of pure and useful enjoyment. II. It is an honorable means of maintenance. 1. Nothing degrading in it. 2. Deserves and commands fair remuneration. 3. Preserves a man's independence. III. It is a worthy service to others. 1. Products of industrial toil serviceable in the highest degree. 2. Such service is worthy of all honor. —R. G.

Choice Labor Day Illustrations

HIS ORIGINAL SIN. A clergyman tells of an Indian who was a candidate for the ministry, and was asked before the presbytery the important question, "What is original sin?" He answered that he didn't know what other people's might be, but he rather thought that his was laziness. There are no doubt at the present time many who are suffering from the same disease. Truly, he is to be pitied who has nothing to do. He is like a barnacle on a ship, or a floating derelict, useless to himself and dangerous to others.—Rev. E. W. Caswell.

THE CHRISTIAN VIEW OF VOCATION. It is said that in the obituary records of the old Moravians there are to be found many such phrases as: "He served the Lord as a farmer"; "He served the Lord as a merchant"; "He served the Lord as a carpenter." This is the truly Christian attitude toward the vocations of life. According to the New Testament, some are called to be "apostles, and some prophets, and some evangelists, and some pastors and teachers." But just as truly are men called to be businessmen and doctors and workers in other branches of human endeavor, some in places of leadership and prominence, others in humbler walks, but all to lives of Christian service. Such a view gives a greater meaning to the so-called secular occupations of the world. Whatever our task, it should be done "as unto the Lord." Serving the Lord, not making a living, is the chief business of life.—*Christian Observer.*

WORKING TO SHARE. One sultry summer night Dr. Merton Rice stopped at a cold-drink stand and asked the clerk for a large glass of orangeade. The clerk proceeded to prepare the drink, squeezing out the juice of a large orange, putting in some cracked ice, adding sugar, and stirring well. Dr. Rice, ready to put it to his lips, suddenly felt a tug at his coattail. Looking around he saw a small, bent, wizened old lady. She was looking pathetically into his face; and pointing at the glass in his hand, she said, "Please, sir, I'm thirsty too!" That little word "too" struck Dr. Rice's heart. He was thirsty on a hot night; she was thirsty too. He realized that before he could be happy in taking his drink, he must help her to enjoy some orangeade too.

Millions of needy hands are reaching across the immense distances of this globe today, tugging at our heartstrings. Voices are saying: "Please, sir, we want an education too!" "Please, sir, we want enough to eat too, enough to wear to keep us warm in the cold winter too!" "Please, sir, we should like to know about Jesus and the true God too!"

To all these voices we must answer, "I cannot be happy in enjoying my privileges and comforts until I have exhausted every possibility to bring similar privileges and comforts within reach of every other boy and girl, man and woman, in the world too." It is not enough to be sorry for others. We will work and strive that others may have those same good things in life which we demand for ourselves.

Quotable Labor Day Poetry

THE TOILERS

Day after day the great procession takes
  its way;
The army of the toilers, young and old
  and sad and gay;
The loom on which our smoothly
  running web of life is run
Functions by grace of these brown
  toilers in the sun.
> —Delphia Phillips.

THE GOSPEL OF LABOR

This is the Gospel of Labor—
  Ring it, ye bells of the kirk—
The Lord of love came down from above
  To live with the men who work.
This is the rose that he planted
  Here in the thorn-cursed soil—
Heaven is blessed with perfect rest;
  But the blessing of earth is toil.
> —Henry van Dyke.

EARNING TO GIVE

I thank thee, Lord, for strength of arm
  To win my bread,
And that beyond my need is meat
  For friend unfed.

I thank thee much for bread to live,
  I thank thee more for bread to give.
I thank thee, Lord, for snug-thatched
  roof
  In cold and storm,
And that beyond my need is room
  For friend forlorn.

Thy love to me I ill could spare,
  Yet dearer is Thy love I share.
> —E. M. Dornbush.

WORK!

Thank God for the might of it,
The ardor, the urge, the delight of it—
Work that springs from the heart's de-
  sire,
Setting the brain and the soul on fire—
Oh, what is so good as the heat of it.

And what is so glad as the beat of it,
And what is so kind as the stern com-
  mand,
Challenging brain and heart and hand?
  Work!
> —Angela Morgan.

NEVER GIVE UP

There's a time to part and a time to
  meet,
There's a time to sleep and a time to
  eat,
There's a time to work and a time to
  play,
There's a time to sing and a time to
  pray,
There's a time that's glad and a time
  that's blue,
There's a time to plan and a time to
  do,
There's a time to grin and to show your
  grit,
But there never was a time to quit.
> —Anon.

WORK

Work is the fresh air of the soul!
It clears the heavy brain,
Quickens the pulses of the mind,
Warms thought to action, and the blind
And sluggish will sunk into ease
Of ineffectual lethargies
It stirs to life again.
> —Susan Coolidge.

EVENING SERVICE

Theme: The Selfish and Unworthy Scramble (Labor Day).

TEXT: "I judge between cattle and cattle," etc. Ezek. 34:17-22.

INTRODUCTORY: These verses present to us a scene far too often enacted in human life. It is that of selfish and unworthy scramble—scramble for position, scramble for money, scramble for plivilege and enjoyment. It may be found in business, in professions, in art, in politics, in pleasure, and, it must be admitted, sometimes in the sphere of religion.

The prophet has here a message for God's flock. He has been speaking to the shepherds, but now he speaks to the flock, God's people. He says God will judge between the fat and the strong in the flock, between those who lacked and were weak, and those who being rich and wealthy made use of the opportunity which this gave them to trample down and bear hard on their poor neighbors. "And as for you, O my flock, thus saith the Lord God; Behold, I judge between cattle and cattle. . . . Seemeth it a small thing unto you to have eaten up the good pasture, but ye must tread down with your feet the residue of your pastures? . . . foul the residue with your feet?" It is, in fact, a graphic picture of selfish and most unworthy scramble.

I. Consider first that such scramble is utterly sinful. There is no suggestion that self-elevation is wrong. It may be right and good. To make the most of one's powers and opportunities, to rise by honest and patient industry, to walk the high level of honorable usefulness—this is admirable. But this is very different from an unworthy scramble, like pigs at a trough, for selfish advantage and preferment. The picture in the text is of struggling cattle in a pasture, each making a scramble for all he can get, in the meantime fouling, trampling into the dirt, that which they had muddied. It is a picture of a shameful "pushing the weakest to the wall."

II. The second consideration is that of the hardening result of such selfish action. The struggling cattle in the field are no worse for their heedlessness. They suffer no spiritual harm. They are not moral beings. They do not rise and fall in a moral sense. But people do. Scramble, selfish scramble, destroys all the finer and nobler elements of our nature. It is sinking to the level of the beasts themselves.

III. The third thing presented is thought of the happy contrast there is in Christian service. Thought of others, unselfish service of others, is the very opposite of the unworthy scramble we have been considering. The teaching of Christ, the example of Christ, is the very opposite. He came not to be ministered unto but to minister. He came not alone to serve men, but to give his life a ransom to the end of their eternal salvation.—W. C.

Suggestive Labor Day Texts and Themes

Does the Bible Represent Labor as a Curse? Gen. 1:28.

The Labor Principles: "To each one his work." Mark 13:34 (A.S.V.).

Sweat and bread: "In the sweat of thy face shalt thou eat bread." Gen. 3:19.

Love as Overtime Service: "We are unprofitable servants: we have done that which was our duty to do." Luke 17:10.

The Divine Toilers: "My Father worketh even until now, and I work." John 5:17 (A.S.V.).

Triumphant Trudging: "They shall walk, and not faint." Isa. 40:31.

Causes of Poverty: "The destruction of the poor is their poverty." Prov. 10:15.

The Dignity of Service: "I am among you as he that serveth." Luke 22:27.

MIDWEEK FELLOWSHIP MEETING TOPIC

(Church Night or Suggested Sermon Subject)

Theme: Seeking First.

TEXT: "Seek ye first the kingdom of God, and his righteousness." Matt. 6:33.

Jesus spoke a group of parables to call our attention to a phase of the kingdom of God which we often ignore; namely, its seekableness.

I. The shepherd sought his lost sheep. The woman sought her lost coin. In the words, "Seek ye first the kingdom of God," the primary emphasis is on "seek." He has been speaking about seeking worldy goods. He does not say they are not to be sought but he does say we must observe a priority in seeking spiritual good.

II. It was said of Plato that he "saw life clearly and as a whole." Supremely is this true of Jesus Christ. He never said the things the Gentiles seek are not worth seeking. But he made it plain that we are all in danger of making primary things secondary. The grave error of the world is in confusing things that are central and things that are subcentral.

III. What is the kingdom of God? It is not geographical, not economic, not mechanical, not formal. From several distinct sayings of Jesus we conclude that the kingdom of God is interior, invisible, vital and present. What is it, then? It is the reign of God's spirit in human life, the recognition of his kingship; conscious co-operation with him in the establishment of righteousness and peace and joy.

IV. These are the things we are to seek. Let us look again at that word "seek." There is in it a significance of care, of close scrutiny, of willingness to stoop in order to look into things that are obscure, a humility all characteristic of the mental attitude of the Christian. We are to seek good in unlikely places. We are to seek it when we would rather be doing something else. What are we seeking? What has priority in our lives?—C. C. A.

CHRISTIAN ENDEAVOR SOCIETY TOPIC

Sept. 5. "A Workman That Needeth Not to be Ashamed." John 5:17; Col. 3:17, 22-24.

BULLETIN BOARD SLOGANS FOR THE MONTH

By EARL RINEY

The social gospel is the gospel of Christ given practical application.

The man who minds his own business generally has a good one.

A miser is a rich pauper.

Be always on time; too late is a crime.

Contentment makes a fat feast.

Christ is a great Saviour for great sinners.

Debts and sins are more than we think them.

Charity lives at home, but walks abroad.

Better than a star on the breast is a conscience at rest.

Even a spark is fire.

Honest toil is no disgrace, but pride is always out of place.

Mercy's gate opens to those who knock.

SUNDAY SCHOOL LESSON

Sept. 5. Growth through Useful Work. Col. 3:23-24; I Thess. 4:10b-11; II Thess. 3:6-13.

MEMORY VERSE: "Whatever your task, work heartily, as serving the Lord and not men." Col. 3:23 (R.S.V.).

The word "vocation" is derived from the Latin voco, "I call." It means a calling. Someone or something calls and the person gives answer, he accepts a calling.

Christian ministers have a deep sense of calling. They believe that they are called by God to do a particular work. Their work becomes an answer to a word previously spoken to them by God himself.

Why should not every man doing useful work follow the same ideal as the Christian minister? Each worker would feel that God has a purpose for his life and he is fulfilling that purpose. There would come a new glory to work. In it the worker would grow into a new dignity.

How does a call from God come to any particular work? An interesting and profitable discussion can be based upon this question.

SUNDAY: SEPTEMBER TWELFTH

MORNING SERVICE

Theme: **Power to Create.**

SUGGESTIVE SCRIPTURE READING: II Cor. 5:1-21.

SELECTED HYMNS: "City of God, how broad and fair."—S. Johnson. "Glorious things of thee are spoken."—J. Newton. "Come to our poor nature's night."— G. Rawson. "O Christ, our King, Creator."—Gregory the Great. "Jesus, my strength, my Hope."—C. Wesley.

CALL TO WORSHIP: "Bless the Lord, O my soul: and all that is within me, bless his holy name. Bless the Lord, O my soul, and forget not all his benefits."

INVOCATION PRAYER: We come into the house of worship, O God, with desire to hear thee speak unto us. Grant unto us the ear of a learner, the heart of a child, to listen to thy voice. We desire to know thy will and way. Teach us the lessons that we ought to know. Deepen our knowledge of thee. Broaden our sympathy with our fellow men. Speak unto us of our salvation. And as we receive thy gospel, O Lord, help us also to accept the responsibilities which are upon us to witness unto others the good news of the Christ. By word and manner of life may we manifest him. Help us to reveal him to our children, to commend him to our friends, to proclaim him near and far, and to bring him into every area of human life. We ask in his name. Amen.—M. K. W. H.

Theme: **Power to Create.**

TEXT: "This beginning of miracles did Jesus in Cana of Galilee, and manifested forth his glory; and his disciples believed on him." John 2:11.

INTRODUCTORY: Today the wide earth over there is the urge to create. There is the desire to create new cities, a new social order, a new and better world and, on the part of races formerly subject to other powers, to create a new and independent national life. Yet there is a widespread sense of frustration.

In the miracle of Cana of Galilee, however, the answer is supplied. For John told that story not that there might be endless and futile arguments as to whether Jesus preferred wine to water, nor whether the wine in question was fermented or unfermented. He narrated the story because it was a "sign" that revealed the glory of Christ, and his glory was his Godhead, and the essence of Godhead is creative power. The transformation of water into wine was a great creative act "and manifested forth his glory."

I. A new religion. Far from being the only creative act of Christ's, however, this was but the beginning. The measureless creative power of Jesus was seen in his creation of a new religion. The water of Judaism was turned into the wine of Christianity. The waters of every quest after God which men have pursued throughout the passing ages were transformed into the wine of the Christian way. But Jesus came and opened up before their eyes the new and living way. He created a new religion. For there is none other name given among men whereby we may be saved. In this his glory was manifested.

II. A new society. Jesus revealed his creative power by creating a new society. He created the Church of the living God, the pillar and bulwark of Truth. It was, and is, a unique society with a unique mission. Its uniqueness consists in the fact that it is a divine creation and therefore an imperishable one. The gates of hell shall not prevail against it, asserted its Creator, and they never have, and they never will. However disfigured the Church may be by the unfaithfulness of men, it is a society that never loses the marks of its divine origin; the stamp of its Creator remains upon it. Because it is his, it still stands and will continue to stand, the eternal, imperishable city.

III. New men. Above all, the creative power of our Lord Jesus Christ is to be seen in his creation of new men. Christ creates new men; not different men or improved men, but new men, and no other power can do that. In all the centuries and in all the lands the creative power of Christ has been doing what no other person and no other power can ever hope to do, creating new men and women.

In the daily walk of our lives we are trying to create, to create character, to create homes and countless other things. In many ways and several directions the creative impulse rises within us, because we are of God's image. Well, this creative power that turns so many different waters into wine, that created a new bond between God and men, that created the new society and created new men in Christ, avails for you and for me.— G. W. H.

THEME PRAYER: Make and keep us thine, our Father, and strengthen us in the way of thy commandments. And may we be helpers of others in the way of life. We live by thy guidance and we trust in thy watchful care. Use our lives unto some great purpose. We commit them unto thee for Jesus' sake and in his name. Amen.

OFFERTORY SENTENCE: "Ye are not your own. For ye are bought with a price: therefore glorify God in your body, and in your spirit, which are God's."

OFFERTORY PRAYER: It is with grateful hearts, our Father, that we bring our offerings this day. New every morning and fresh every evening have been thy good gifts to us. Wilt thou graciously receive these as our token gifts of gratitude for thine unnumbered mercies and use them for the upbuilding of thy kingdom in the world. We ask in Christ's name. Amen.—H.

Illustrative Material

SEED THOUGHTS, HOMILETIC AND EXPOSITORY. Christ's Miraculous Act: I. The fact. II. The mode. III. The motive. IV. It was a creation-miracle.—J. L.

A Representative Miracle: I. Its essential character. A sign of soverign power wrought on inorganic nature. II. Its circumstantial character. Change of the simpler into the richer element. III. Its moral character. 1. The answer of love to faith. 2. Ministering to human joy. 3. It was a new creation. 4. The source of the sign was a marriage feast. —W.

The Miracle as a Sign: I. Of Christ's mission. Gladdening, joyous. II. Of the character of Christ. 1. Of his naturalness. 2. Of his mindfulness. 3. Of his grace and power.—G. T. P.

Some Lessons of the Miracle: I. That marriage is honorable. Jesus will not refuse his presence on such an occasion. II. On such occasions the presence and approbation of Christ should be sought. III. On such occasions and all others our conduct should be such that the presence of Jesus would be no interruption or disturbance. IV. That Jesus delighted to do good.—A. B.

Choice Illustrations on the Theme

CHRIST'S POWER TO TRANSFORM. An educated young Mohammedan came to me in Cairo and said: "I am a student in the law school, sir. What must a man do when he is conscious that he can write a better copy than his master?" I asked him what he meant, and he replied, "I am conscious that I have a better character than Mohammed." If this could truly be said of a disciple of Christ, the structure of Christianity would fall.—Samuel M. Zwemer.

CREATOR AND SAVIOUR. One of the most powerful and terrible of Rossetti's pictures is entitled "Found." It belongs to a realm which art has seldom the power effectively to touch and to raise into a pure atmosphere. A countryman and a country lass have loved each other, and to each other have plighted their troth. But she, lured into the city, has sunk under its temptation and has become lost to her past and to him whom once she loved. His love, however, still remains, and he ever searches for her face. One day as he is coming into market, he meets on Blackfriars Bridge a woman of gay attire, and seizing her by the wrist, to her shame and terror, he confronts her with the lover whom she has abandoned. He has sought and found. It was with such a look that Christ walked the streets of Jerusalem, peering into the faces of the passers-by, seeking the lost. It is with such a look that he walks the city's streets still, seeking his own, pursuing them until he finds them, and, having found them, entreating them to return. "I am come to seek and to save that which was lost."—J. Burns.

CHRISTIANITY A RELIGION OF PLUS. Christianity is a religion of Plus. In Jesus' Inaugural Address, commonly called the Sermon on the Mount, he lays down his principles for life. That was his platform, and it may be summed up thus: A Plus Program. He let it be known that more should be expected of Christians than of other people who make no profession. "What do ye more than others?"

Turn to the fifth chapter of Matthew and consider some of his plus suggestions. After comments on certain sins and customs, six times he says, "But I say unto you. . . ," and always it is a plus demand that he makes of his followers. Take revenge, for example. It is no longer to be "an eye for an eye," but "whoever shall smite thee on thy right cheek, turn to him the other also." Forgiveness is no longer "Love thy neighbor, and hate thine enemy," but "Love your enemies, bless them that curse you." Again, there is the "second mile." "What do ye more than others?"—Robert S. Tate.

WE ARE ALL CREATORS. We are all builders. Every day, according to the blueprints of the divine Architect, or in foolish disregard of God's will; with the best materials, or with the base and perishable that can never stand the tests of time, certainly not those of eternity; we are engaged on this momentous task. The foundation is Christ. All our hopes for now and hereafter are based on him.—Christian Herald.

THE CHURCH THE PALACE BEAUTIFUL. The finest name ever given outside the Bible to the church is the name Bunyan gave it—the "Palace Beautiful." Yet the churches with which he was acquainted were only the Baptist meeting houses in Bedfordshire. No better than barns they seemed to common eyes, but in his eyes each of them was a "Palace Beautiful," because, when seated on one of its benches, the eye of his imagination would look up through the dingy rafters and see the gorgeous roof and shining pinnacles of the Church Universal. Love to God, whose house it is, can make the humblest material structure a home of the Spirit.—Rev. F. Stalker.

EVENING SERVICE

Theme: Look to Yourselves.

TEXT: "Look to yourselves, that we lose not those things which we have wrought, but that we receive a full reward." II John 8.

INTRODUCTORY: "Look to yourselves." Looking after one's own interests is a thing most people believe in. But looking after Number One is hardly the teaching of this Scripture. However, it does suggest a caution, a care for self-preservation. There are dangers in inattention.

"Her pilot was asleep below" was once given as the simple and sufficient explanation of a ship's disaster. It was to the steamer *Montana*, which was grounded and wrecked upon a rock off the English coast. Of how many shipwrecked souls might the same thing be said, "The pilot was asleep below!" To men who are delaying in religion the caution might well be given, "Look to yourselves. You have a priceless treasure, your soul. 'What shall it profit a man if he shall gain the whole world and lose his own soul?'" "Look to yourselves" is a most proper and very important caution, but it is not quite the application of these words of the Apostle John. His is definitely giving a caution to those who are already Christians: "Look to yourselves, that we lose not those things which we have wrought, but that we receive a full reward." It has to do with the duty of self-inspection, with an inner look, with the watchful attitude.

I. Christians, look to yourselves concerning your beliefs, concerning your grasp of the truth, lest you let it slip, lest your faith grow weak. This is fundamental. Its importance is beyond expression. Look to yourselves that ye lose not those vivid and vigorous impressions of divine truth which marked the early part of your Christian career.

II. Or the application may be concerning our spiritual condition. "Look to yourselves" as to the reality of your religion. Look to yourselves as to the vitality of your religion. Look to yourselves that ye lose not the spirit of secret prayer and proper seasons for attending to it. And what as to the use of all the other means of grace? Have we grown lax, or formal, or cold? Have we lost taste and relish for the public ordinances of the gospel?

III. Or the application may be concerning our chosen associations. "Look to yourselves" as to whether your companionships are such as will lessen or interfere with the degree of Christian conduct? We all need to take heed to such a statement as this: "He that is a righteous man shall hold on his way, and he that hath clean hands shall wax stronger and stronger."

IV. Look to yourselves also that ye lose not the possession of a good conscience, the favor of God, and the power of bearing full witness for Christ on behalf of others.—H.

Suggestive Texts and Themes

Searchings and Resolves: ". . . By the watercourses of Reuben there were great resolves of heart. . . . at the watercourses of Reuben there were great searchings of heart." Judg. 5:15, 16.

Morning—and After: "In the morning sow thy seed, and in the evening withhold not thine hand." Eccles. 11:6.

The Cost of a Little Honey: "I did but taste a little honey with the end of the rod that was in mine hand, and lo, I must die." I Sam. 14:43.

Crucified or Consecrated: "They that are Christ's have crucified the flesh with the affections and lusts." Gal. 5:24. "Sanctify them through thy truth." John 17:17.

Sifted but Saved: "For, lo, I will command, and I will sift the house of Israel among all nations, like as corn is sifted in a sieve, yet shall not the least grain fall upon the earth." Amos 9:9.

MIDWEEK FELLOWSHIP MEETING TOPIC

(Church Night or Suggested Sermon Subject)

Theme: The Knock at the Door.

TEXT: "But Peter continued knocking." Acts 12:16.

I. Prayer had delivered Peter from prison. Iron doors opened at his call, but the door of the prayer meeting in the house of Mary, the mother of John, was closed. The praying company forgot to leave the latchstring out. They had more faith than expectation. How many formally pray to God and keep the door of the heart closed against him?

II. Rhoda, hearing the knock and the voice of Peter, goes to the door, but, in her joy, forgets to admit him. Relating the fact of Peter's being at the door to the company, they declare it must be his spirit. They thought Herod had already killed him. How often we believe everything but the fact of the direct answer!

III. When the church, under the baptism of Pentecost, goes forth to win the world for Christ all iron doors of unbelief and opposition in heathendom will open to her. We may be the Lord's ministering angels to liberate the nations locked in the prisons of darkness and doubt; miracles will be performed every day, if we will but believe.

IV. The angel could have opened the door of Mary for Peter, but God will not do for us what we can do for ourselves. The knocking continues, for Peter longs to tell them all about his wonderful deliverance. He is in a hurry to get doors open everywhere for his Lord's coming into men's hearts.

Christ is knocking more persistently than Peter, at the door of human hearts. Shall we let him in?—E. W. C.

CHRISTIAN ENDEAVOR SOCIETY TOPIC

Sept. 12. Forward with Christ through Christian Endeavor. Ex. 14:13-18; Phil. 4:13.

SUNDAY SCHOOL LESSON

Sept. 12. Christian Citizenship and Co-operation. Rom. 13:1-10; I Cor. 3:4-9.

MEMORY VERSE: Love does no wrong to a neighbor; therefore love is the fulfilling of the law. Rom. 13:10 (R.S.V.).

A Christian views every person as a child of God in one family. The significance of every person is thus marvelously increased and enhanced. It is natural to respond to significant persons. We appreciate them. We learn to love them. We seek to serve them.

When each person becomes infinitely valuable to us, as he is in the sight of God, not only do we do no wrong to our neighbor, but we feel responsible for our neighbor. We seek to exhibit love in all our personal relationships with him. We miss no opportunity to love our fellow men by doing them good. We seek new ways of making commitments of love.

Gandhi and Schweitzer are modern examples of persons who felt responsible love and made great personal commitments.

SUNDAY: SEPTEMBER NINETEENTH

MORNING SERVICE

Theme: Residual Religion.

SUGGESTED SCRIPTURE READING: Isa. 44:1-28.

SELECTED HYMNS: "The world is very evil."—Bernard of Cluny. , "The Lord is King! Lift up thy voice."—J. Conder. "Great God, how infinite art Thou."— I. Watts. "My God, how wonderful Thou art."—F. W. Faber. "God, my King, thy might confessing."—R. Mant.

CALL TO WORSHIP: "Let the people praise thee, O God; let all the people praise thee. . . . Then shall the earth yield her increase; and God, even our own God, shall bless us. God shall bless us; and all the ends of the earth shall fear him."

INVOCATION PRAYER: On this thy day, O Lord, be pleased to lift up the light of thy countenance upon us and give us

peace. Let this hour be full of thy presence and this sacred place as the gateway of heaven to our souls. Refresh us in mind and heart and spirit as we wait before thee. Enable us to worship thee in the beauty of holiness. Open thy Word before us. Help us to read, mark, learn and inwardly digest its truths. Manifest thy presence unto us all. And, our Father, who by thy Spirit dost put into our hearts such deep desires that we cannot be at rest until we rest in thee, so inspire us that our hunger for righteousness may control our thoughts and our needs, and therein may we find the true secret of our wellbeing. We ask in the name of Christ who blesses every seeking soul. Amen.

Theme: Residual Religion.

TEXT: "And the residue thereof he maketh a god." Isa. 44:17.

INTRODUCTORY: The prophet Isaiah here gives us a striking picture of an ignorant pagan who practiced residual religion. He gave his remnants, his leftovers to an idol, to a self-made god. The man cuts down a tree. With part of it he builds a fire to keep himself warm. With part of it he roasted meat, and ate until he was satisfied. In his satisfaction he rubbed his hands before the fire and said, "Aha, I am warm!" So with warmth and food he has satisfied two simple wants and instincts of nature. But there is yet another instinct which demands satisfaction. He is conscious that he is a weak creature in the midst of a strange and wonderful world. Mysterious powers that he cannot fathom seem to float about his life. Beyond simple food and warmth in some degree to meet a third human instinct, he takes the residue of his tree and fashions an idol, "maketh a god," and falls down and worships it.

I. Let us first notice this man's decision to make a god according to his own fancy. It was the kind of god that appealed to him. The same instinct carries many people of our own late day very far in the same direction. There are people not a few who create in their imagination their own god with attributes according to their own preferences.

II. In another respect there are people of today who resemble this pagan worshiper. This man of earlier times made a god out of a remnant, a remainder. Is not this still an accurate picture of the religion of many people? They arrange their homes as comfortably as they can, provide for all the necessities and most of the luxuries of life, and give to the true God the money, time and interest which they can easily spare. They go to church on Sunday if there is nothing else they particularly desire to do; they contribute to the church and its world-wide enterprise the little that remains after they have spent generously on themselves. God is not given priority; he is allowed only the remnants, the leftovers of their lives. Theirs is a residual religion.

Now, is it wholly untrue to describe some modern religion thus? To say that there are men and women of our day who live after this fashion? That when they have supplied their own wants, when their bodies have been amply fed, when the conditions of their lives have been so fell cared for that they are well provided with the warming comforts of life, then, out of the residue of their time, out of the residue of their money, out of the residue of their thought they will, perchance, consecrate something to God?

III. What is the natural conclusion? Plainly it is this: that we should learn to know the true God, our heavenly Father, and to love and worship and serve him. This is the central difference between idolatry in all its forms and true religion.—H.

THEME PRAYER: May we, our Father, have undivided hearts, worshiping no other gods before thee. Forgive us the altars we build to what we ought not to worship and the altars we leave unbuilt to the high and the holy. Save us from misdirected loyalties. May we maintain holy altars in our homes and offer to thee always the sacrifices of humble and contrite hearts. We ask in the name of Christ. Amen.

OFFERTORY SENTENCE: "All power is given unto me in heaven and in earth. Go ye therefore, and teach all nations, baptizing them in the name of the Father, and of the Son, and of the Holy Ghost: . . . and lo, I am with you always, even unto the end of the world." Amen.

OFFERTORY PRAYER: O Thou who openest thine hand and fillest thy creatures with good, forgive us our foolish wasteful ways with the stored wealth of this, thy world. So instruct us in the true wealth of life that seeking the welfare of all thy children, we may no longer be anxious for our daily needs having found the secret of the abounding life. Bless these offerings we bring today. We dedicate them to thy cause in the world. Amen.

Illustrative Material

SEED THOUGHTS, HOMILETIC AND EXPOSITORY. Idolatry: I. Its vanity. II. Neither the idol nor its god knows anything, while Jehovah knows all. III. Neither the idol nor its god can do aught, while Jehovah is almighty. IV. Neither the idol nor its god is aught, while Jehovah is the living God, God of the entire universe and the God of love. V. The worship of idols or their gods is degrading, while that of Jehovah exalts and saves the soul.—W. S. A.

The Idolater's Folly: With a dash of pungent satire Isaiah shows how silly a man can be. We have in this account the whole process of god-manufacture. The man is an utter fool only to be held up to the derision of all sensible men.—J. T. D.

"He burneth part thereof in the fire," which is to far better purpose than the other part made into an idol.—J. T.

Choice Illustrations on the Theme

WORSHIP TRUE AND FALSE. There is much residual religion connected with both Christian and pagan lands. There are examples of worship both true and false. The director of religious education in one of our great city churches noticed that a young boy frequently came into the sanctuary to engage in a brief period of prayer and meditation. "I like to come here," the boy explained, "because it makes me feel bigger than I am."

That is what worship should accomplish in our lives. Often the outside world belittles us, and gives us an inferiority complex. At other times it flatters us, and tempts us to conceit. But in the presence of Almighty God, we are made to feel our greatness in the truest sense—the rightful dignity of those who are citizens of an eternal world.

An example of the contrary is indicated by a missionary from Japan. He tells us that in one of the great temples of that country the devotion of the worshiper consists in running around the sacred building one hundred times dropping a piece of wood into a box at each round. When the wearisome exertion is ended the worshiper goes home tired but very happy at the thought of having done his god such a worthy service. We think this unspeakably silly. Yet is there much difference between running around a temple a certain number of times and the walking to church, sitting quietly through the service, and walking back, unless we go with a definite purpose of worship, unless we listen reverently and obediently to the voice of God speaking through his Word and Minister, unless we truly approach God when we bow in prayer? Are we not just as foolish and unreasonable as the Japanese runner? "Let the words of my mouth and the meditation of my heart be acceptable in thy sight, O Jehovah, my rock and my redeemer."

DESTROYING IDOLS. Missionaries in India are confronted by much the same conditions which Paul must have been meeting when he wrote to his new converts, "Little children, keep yourselves from idols." As a help in this work a native hymn has been used throughout the district. Translated, the title of it is "King Jesus Has Come," and these words are repeated in the refrain. One stanza is:

King Jesus has come, King Jesus has come,
To tear down the idols King Jesus has come.

This song has been immensely helpful in arousing the people's enthusiasm to tear down their idols with their own hands. Of course, this willingness comes after preaching has convinced them of the wrong of Christians keeping such things. One day in Sherkot, where two hundred Christians lived, five idols were torn down at one time. One of these was a very old and large one. It had been the great trial of the workers, and a hindrance to the work for many years. There is but one God and his glory he will not give to another.

IDOLS DETHRONED. Mrs. Howard Taylor of China tells how Pastor Hsi taught his fellow villagers that there is no other God but God. Suspicious of him when he became a Christian, their respect for him grew as they noted his upright life, and when they required an official to collect the taxes, take care of the temples, and so on, they decided that he, a scholar and no longer an opium smoker, was the man. Before accepting, he made two stipulations: that he should have nothing to do with the temple sacrifices, but should pray only to the true God; and that no one in the village should, during his term, worship the gods in the temple or bring gifts to them. The temple must be closed for a year. Finally the citizens agreed, and Hsi prayed to the true God that the village might prosper. At the close of the year it was found that the affairs of the village had never been more prosperous, and Hsi was re-elected. For three whole years the temple was closed. When congratulated on the service he had rendered, he smilingly replied that perhaps the village had been saved some needless expense, adding: "By this time the idols must be quite starved to death. Spare yourselves now any effort to revive them."—*Sunday School Times.*

WORSHIPING A TREE. The Rev. L. Lloyd, a missionary in China, saw a curious object of worship in a small temple near Peking, a log of wood such as is sawed into planks for building. He learned that this timber was being hauled to Peking by a number of mules, and when it reached this spot a hitch occurred and the log refused to move another inch. Some of the Chinese "wise men" were called in, and they declared the log possessed by a spirit and that it would be best to build a temple over it and make it an object of worship. This was done, and wayfarers continue to offer incense at this strange shrine and two or three priests live off the offerings.—*2,500 Best Modern Illustrations.*

BANISHMENT OF IDOLS. Christianity allows no idols. As Dagon fell before the ark of the covenant, so have all the gods of the Pantheon fallen before the power of the cross. So shall they continue to fall till the kingdoms of this world are reclaimed to Christ.—*New Cyclopedia of Illustrations.*

EVENING SERVICE

Theme: The Church Realizing Itself.

TEXT: "And he is the head of the body," etc. Col. 1:18.

INTRODUCTORY: This is no time for despair about the church. The Jeremiahs who talk of the church as a finished institution are quite unaware of its true nature. The real church is stronger than ever before. Just as the problems confronting the nations are more complex than ever, so are the problems confronting the church. But instead of despair, there is hope, and instead of fear, there is faith that Jesus Christ has the solution for every human problem.

I. The church of the first century was an enterprising, experimenting church. In the first flush of joy following Pentecost, the Christian community entered upon an experiment in communal living. This was the spontaneous outcome of their belief in the imminent return of the Lord. The outbreak of persecution served only to strengthen the bonds which bound them to one another. As time went on, they realized two things: the apparent postponement of the Lord's second coming, and the necessity of engaging in productive work. The passing of the years also meant that there were fewer and fewer people who had seen and heard the Lord in the days of his flesh. Consequently, it was necessary to write down what was still remembered of his words and work. Thus the Gospels were written.

II. Even in the first century the church was by no means all that it ought to have been. In the first chapter of Romans, St. Paul gives a rapid sketch of the wickedness prevailing in the pagan world of his day, but he refuses to allow the Christians to pose as judges since they did the very same things themselves.

The church has never been and is not now what it ought to be. The marvel is that in the face of incredible obstacles, within and without, it has not only persisted but made headway, morally as well as numerically.

III. It is inconceivable what the world would be like if there were no church. "Christ loved the church and gave himself for it." He is the Head of the church, its beginning, the first-born from the dead, its inspiration, its glory, the fountainhead from whom all living waters flow.

It is my conviction that the church is gradually realizing itself. Its greatest foe is not opposition, but apathy.

The last chapter of the church's history is still to be written. It will be a chapter of triumph upon triumph. The Saviour who started the church will bring it to a glorious conclusion.—L. R. F.

Suggestive Texts and Themes

Nations That Are Minus Quantities: "All nations before him are as nothing; and they are counted to him less than nothing, and vanity." Isa. 40:17.

A Pilgrim Saviour: "O the hope of Israel, the saviour thereof in time of trouble, why shouldest thou be as a stranger in the land, and as a wayfaring man that turneth aside to tarry for a night?" Jer. 14:8.

A Thought to Silence Complaint: "Wherefore doth a living man complain, a man for the punishment of his sins?" Lam. 3:39.

A Puritanism Desirable Today: "I proclaimed a fast there, at the river of Ahava, that we might afflict ourselves before our God, to seek of him a right way." Ezra 8:21.

The Meeting of Two Kings: "I think myself happy, king Agrippa, that I am to make my defence before thee this day touching all the things whereof I am accused by the Jews." Acts 26:2 (A.S.V.).

MIDWEEK FELLOWSHIP MEETING TOPIC

(Church Night or Suggested Sermon Subject)

Theme: The Highest Bondage.

TEXT: "Ye are my friends, if ye do the things which I command you." John 15:14 (A.S.V.).

We are ever slaves and some master ever rules our lives. Lust, greed of gold, or base political or selfish ambitions stretch forth their evil scepters, and we become their toiling slaves.

I. Our life, all life, consists in going out to meet the duties, the laws and the obligations which living thrusts upon us.

II. You may be the servant of the angels of love and helpfulness, the minister of the kingdom of God, the steward of human brotherhood, the cup-bearers of a purer civilization. But you must serve something or somebody. There is no alternative. Some ideal of life must draw us through toil, sacrifice and pain to be the blessing or the curse of mankind.

III. To substitute a higher for a lower obligation is the only way of human progress. The only free souls are those who have escaped from their ignoble interests and passions, to live under the scepter of unselfish thought.

IV. Through Christ, life has been given its true meaning. Through him, the strength of soul has come to us to dare the championship of great causes. Through him, we have visioned a goal for civilization. Through him, there brightens the immortal hope which lights our pathway.—W. S. S.

CHRISTIAN ENDEAVOR SOCIETY TOPIC

Sept. 19. Making Our Christian Endeavor Click. I Cor. 14:40; I Tim. 3:12-16; II Tim. 2:15.

SUNDAY SCHOOL LESSON

Sept. 19. Growing in Christian Love. Matt. 5:43-48; I John 4:11-19.

MEMORY VERSE: "Above all these put on love, which binds everything together in perfect harmony." Col. 3:14 (R.S.V.).

The climax of Christian growth is in the area of love. Jesus set a high standard for growth when he said, "Be ye therefore perfect [mature], even as your Father which is in heaven." God is love. Our maturity, our growth-climax, is in becoming a loving person. In becoming loving men we become true sons of our Father.

We must learn to love. The best place to learn to love is in a family. The Christian home is a natural setting for learning love. It is established by two lovers who pledge their faith to each other and take vows to hold their faith forever sacred. In the Christian home daily tasks become services of love one to another. There is opportunity to practice forgiveness. The Christian home reaches out in service to the community. It develops love for God. The Christian church trains in love. Its activities give opportunity for practice in love. "Love is not learned until it is practiced. To love God is a social act which moves one to love the children of God and devote one's life with them in social experiences of sharing and serving."

SUNDAY: SEPTEMBER TWENTY-SIXTH

MORNING SERVICE

Theme: Heart Religion.

SUGGESTED SCRIPTURE READING: II Chron. 25:1, 2. (Note a new translation of "but not with a perfect heart"—"but his heart was not in it.") II Chron. 29:1, 2; 31:20, 21.

SELECTED HYMNS: "I love thy kingdom, Lord."—Timothy Dwight. "Take my life, and let it be."—Frances R. Havergal. "Lord, speak to me, that I may speak."—F. R. Havergal. "My Jesus, I love thee."—Anon.

CALL TO WORSHIP: "This is God's church and he is here. This is Christ's body and he is in the midst. At any moment the Sword of his Spirit may descend upon us to pierce the armor of our pride and self-righteousness and leave us naked and defenceless. At this hour his voice may sound in our hearts and electrify us into action, sending us forth to challenge the world and do battle with the principalities and powers that seek to rule it."—A. I. B.

Or, "The Lord seeth not as man seeth; for man looketh on the outward appearance, but the Lord looketh on the heart."

INVOCATION PRAYER: By the presence and the power of thy Spirit, O God, may this unadorned service be filled with everlasting significance and high destiny for all who worship here. In Jesus' name. Amen.

Theme: Heart Religion.

TEXTS: "Amaziah did that which was right in the sight of the Lord, but not with a perfect heart" ("but his heart was not in it"). II Chron. 25:2.

"Hezekiah . . . wrought that which . . . right . . . and he did it with all his heart." II Chron. 31:20, 21.

INTRODUCTORY: Two kings of Judah. Both became kings at twenty-five years of age. Both reigned twenty-nine years. Both died at fifty-four. But they are in vivid contrast.

I. Amaziah. "He did that which was right in the sight of the Lord, but his heart was not in it." How did that come about? There is something wrong here. What could be wrong? We can only surmise.

1. Perhaps he was seduced by the sensate. Sensate—not sensuous, not sensual, these words carry the idea of the lustful; by sensate we mean reaching only the senses, the eyes, ears, nose, mouth, hands.

A man of sensate religion becomes satisfied with that which he sees, hears, exhibits in gestures—it is secular, this worldly religion.

Amaziah did right. That means that he followed all religious observances. He made the proper sacrifices at the temple. He kept the designated feast days. He observed the new moons and the sabbaths. He brought his tithes to the priests. He bowed his head and kneeled at the right moments . . . but his heart was not in it. It was surface experience, only gestures, motions.

This was religion of the eyes, vision, but no idealization or meditation. Ears, hearing, but no interpretation, no deep significance. Nostrils, the incense rising at the altar, but no deep prayer to God.

Hands making signs, but the soul bearing no burdens. He went through the motions, but his heart just wasn't there.

2. Or it may be Amaziah was put to sleep by the familiar. Religion can put a man to sleep. A Russian criticism of the church—religion became an opiate. It was going through the same old sleep-producing ritual. It didn't stab people awake. It never reached their minds, hearts, wills.

This morning we sang the Gloria, the Doxology, and repeated the Lord's Prayer. These are climactic in a service. The people rise up in worship. But we might well ask the question, Does familiarity with them reduce them to the automatic? Are our souls numb when we cry out "Glory be to the Father"? What about the Doxology? The Lord's Prayer? Were these forms without substance? Lip service but not heart service? It is easy to succumb to the familiar.

3. Perhaps Amaziah became a victim of hypocrisy. Doing right but his heart not in it, he was making a show of something he did not really have. He was only playing a part.

Hypocrisy is off-balance, imbalance. An automobile wheel that is not in balance subjects the tires to a cross or oblique friction which wears them out very quickly. Hypocrisy creates soul friction. Unconsciously it wears a man's soul pretty thin.

4. Amaziah may have had a vacuum heart. We know what that means—something foreign rushes in. Jesus put it in a parable. He said that when an unclean spirit is gone out of a man, and a man's life is empty, even though it be swept and garnished, then the devils come back, seven of them, and enter into the man and dwell there. The last state of the man is worse than the first.

It seems that this is exactly what happened to Amaziah. "Now it came to pass, after that Amaziah was come from the slaughter of the Edomites, that he brought the gods of the children of Seir, and set them up to be his gods, and bowed down himself before them, and burned incense unto them." II Chron. 25:14. Where God was not, the false gods took possession. If God is not in the heart the seven deadly demons make their dwelling place there.

II. Hezekiah. The secret of his life we find in the 38th Chapter of Isaiah in his own prayer, "Remember now, O Lord, I beseech thee, how I have walked before thee in truth and with a perfect heart." "His heart was in it."

1. Hezekiah's occupied heart. All his life he permitted God to enter his heart, and the heart of the man was safe and sure. His was no vacuum heart. The devils might come up to the windows of his life, but looking in they would not enter, for God was ruling there. (Catch the contrasts with Amaziah).

2. Hezekiah's life rang consistent and true. He was not perfect. No man is. The ideal is always beyond our grasp. But he who reaches for the better life and cannot attain it is not a hypocrite. The quest is sincere.

It became the lifework of Hezekiah to

bring his life, his nation's life, the worship of the temple into integration, harmony, consistency with the will of god. (II Chron. 29 to 32; Isaiah 36 to 39.)

3. Hezekiah, in contrast with Amaziah, put his heart into his religious devotion and it never became commonplace and sleep-producing. (See the Call to Worship as related to this point.)

4. Hezekiah's religion in contrast with Amaziah's was cordial rather than sensate. Cordial—from the heart. It was real, unfeigned, warm, ardent, zealous, vigorous religion. Its tendency was to revive, invigorate and cheer.

With only one life to live shall I put my heart into the things of God, or shall I fritter life away in hypocrisies? —M. K. W. H.

THEME PRAYER: Out of a dim and ancient past, O God, we hear thy great commandments: "Thou shalt love the Lord thy God with all thy heart, and with all thy soul, and with all thy strength, and with all thy mind; thou shalt love thy neighbour as thyself." We hear them again from the lips of Jesus whose words bear the mighty impact of his character.

We thank thee that thou hast made us so that heart and soul and strength and mind can be exercised in love. We are made to love and to be loved—this we learn from our Saviour.

Then deal with our hearts, O God, that they may be emptied of all that is not love, all pride and wickedness, all selfishness and greed, all envy and malice, all hatred and ill will, that our hearts may be full of love, full of lovingkindness and tender mercies.

Deal with our souls, the birthplace of our intentions, that we may seek only after love.

Inspire our minds that they may meditate only upon the good, the just and the loving. Rid them of all error and untruth and false imaginings. And ever move our hands and feet to serve thee in loving deeds and our neighbors in a ministry of service.

Hear, O Lord, our intercessions. Every moment we believe that thou art doing for everyone all that thou canst do in consistency with love and wisdom. If our indifference toward others or our inaction for them delays or frustrates thy will, if in thy Providence thou dost need our co-operation and effort, then, O God, make us quick to give unto thee. Dost thou need our minds, our thoughts? Dost thou need our sympathies? Dost thou need our serving hands and feet to bring thy good will to pass? Then may we be filled with joy to offer thee all that we can be or do in order that thy will may be done. In Jesus' name. Amen.

OFFERTORY SENTENCE: "And whatsoever ye do, do it heartily, as to the Lord, and not unto men."

OFFERTORY PRAYER: Help us, O Lord, to put our heart into our offering, to go beyond the token-gift and give from our inmost selves, gifts of true gratitude, deep consecration and sincere love. Amen.

Illustrative Material

OTHER TEXTS ON THEME: "I have given thee a wise and an understanding heart." I Kings 3:12. "The Lord searcheth all hearts and understandeth all the imaginations of the thoughts." I Chron. 28:9. "Create in me a clean heart, O God; and renew a right spirit within me." Ps. 51:10. "Keep thy heart with all diligence; for out of it are the issues of life." Prov. 4:23. "A sound heart is the life of the flesh." Prov. 14:30. "Every way of a man is right in his own eyes: but the Lord pondereth the hearts." Prov. 21:2. "I the Lord search the heart." Jer. 17:10. "Blessed are the pure in heart: for they shall see God." Matt. 5:8. "With the heart man believeth unto righteousness." Rom. 10:10. "God . . . hath shined in our hearts." II Cor. 4:6.

Formalism—A Painted Fire. A curse of the people of God in every century has been the exaltation of forms rituals, worldly wisdom above the spiritual.

I. Formalists are often evangelical, but not evangelistic.

II. Formalism in worship, though correct in pattern and though it performs ceremonies, appointed by God himself, calls forth the sternest rebukes from the Almighty.

III. The opposite of formalism is not formlessness, but spirituality—O. G. W.

Choice Illustrations on the Theme

BENDED KNEES. Bended knees, whilst you are clothed with pride; heavenly petitions, whilst you are hoarding up treasures upon earth; holy devotions whilst you live in the follies of this world; prayers of meekness and charity, whilst your heart is the seat of spite and resentment; hours of prayer, whilst you give up days and years to idle diversions, impertinent visits, and foolish pleasures; are as absurd, unacceptable services to God, as forms of thanksgiving from a person that lives in repining and discontent.—William Law.

THE SELECTIVE POWER OF PERSONALITY. [Amaziah and Hezekiah contrasted.] One of the noblest odes in literature is the ode of Coleridge written at sunrise at Chamonnix. The poet is gazing upwards at the Alps, and he hears a mighty song of praise to God. The torrent praises him. There is no discord in that forest of pine and the snowy summit praises him. There is no discord in that mighty chorus—"earth with her thousand voices praises God." But now there comes reeling on to that same scene some poor drunkard with his sodden brain. And the same torrents are sounding in his ears, and the same peaks are white against the heaven. But for him, ruined by his vice, and fashioned by his past, neither in cataract nor snow nor forest is there heard one syllable of heaven.—G. H. M.

TWO KINDS OF RELIGION. What I want is not to possess religion, but to have a religion that possesses me.—Charles Kingsley.

SENSATE EXPERIENCE. [Having eyes we see not.] It is more difficult to teach ignorance to think than to teach an intelligent blind man to see the grandeur of Niagara. I have walked with people whose eyes are full of light, but who see nothing in wood, sea, or sky, nothing in city streets, nothing in books. What a witless masquerade is this seeing! It were better far to sail for ever in the night of blindness, with sense and feeling and mind, than to be this content with the mere act of seeing. They have the sunset, the morning skies, the purple of distant hills, yet their souls voyage through this enchanted world with a barren stare.—Helen Keller, *The World I Live In.*

THE EMPTY LIFE. Have you ever observed how a vacant house goes to wrack and ruin much more quickly than does a house that is occupied?

An empty house is an invitation to marauders, trespassers and tramps. Its windows soon become targets for miscreant and rowdy youths, a nesting place for pigeons, bats and sparrows, and a menace to the health and well-being of the community.

Our lives are like that. They also soon go to pieces unless they are occupied with noble purposes, worthy ideals, annd positive goodness. . . . An empty life is a constant invitation to everything that is bad. And "the last state of any such person will be worse than the first."—R. C. H.

EVENING SERVICE

Theme: Teach All (Religious Education Week).

TEXT: "Go ye therefore, and teach all." Matt. 28:19.

INTRODUCTORY: This is the great command which our Lord laid upon his disciples in his farewell message. No one who evades it has a right to consider himself a Christian.

I. Teach all the Christian gospel. Do not dilute it, nor water it down. Emphasize both its personal and social aspects; but do not become a fanatic on a single issue, always stressing one aspect of the truth and overlooking other aspects equally vital. Be sure that you teach the gospel as a revelation of the inherent nature of the universe in which we live. Christianity is not an ideal. It is the truth.

II. Teach all the gospel to all the people in your community. Teach the adults who are in control of the world today, and the youth who are the hope of tomorrow. Do not overlook those who live in the alley or on the avenue. Teach the illiterate, and also the college graduate, for the man with the best secular education may be the most ignorant of what it means to be a Christian. All are in need of a deeper knowledge of Christ and of a more complete commitment to his will.

III. Go out into the highways and hedges and by your earnestness compel the people to come in. Let them know the urgency of your desire to share with them your Christian faith. If some people will not come to the church, we must have enthusiasm enough to try to reach them where they are. Do your best to develop a program that will take Christian teaching into the home, the school, the factory, and the places where people naturally are to be found.

IV. Teach all nations. Never forget that the field is the world. No one should be allowed to remain a spiritual isolationist in an atomic age. Do not permit people to become parochial in their outlook, but keep alive a vision of the ecumenical church binding all mankind into a Christian brotherhood. Our basic, inescapable responsibility is to communicate our faith to every person in every land.—Walter D. Calvert, D.D.

Suggestive Religious Education Week Texts

"Thou shalt teach them diligently unto thy children." Deut. 6:7.

"Learn of me." Matt. 11:29.

"What manner of child shall this be?" Luke 1:66.

"Canst thou speak Greek?" Acts 21:37.

"These things command and teach." I Tim. 4:11.

"Teaching them to observe all things whatsoever I have commanded you." Matt. 28:20.

"We know that thou art a teacher come from God." John 3:2.

"The Lord give thee understanding in all things." II Tim. 2:7.

"Out of heaven he made thee to hear his voice, that he might instruct thee." Deut. 4:36.

"Stand thou still a while, that I may shew thee the word of God." I Sam. 9:27.

"One of the priests . . . taught them how they should fear the Lord." II Kings 17:28.

"Wisdom . . . crieth in the chief place of concourse." Prov. 1:20, 21.

"Let us therefore follow after the things . . . wherewith one may edify another." Rom. 14:19.

"Whatsoever things were written aforetime were written for our learning." Rom. 15:4.

MIDWEEK FELLOWSHIP MEETING TOPIC

(Church Night or Suggested Sermon Subject)

Theme: Christ and Education (Religious Education Week).

TEXT: "Remember Jesus Christ." II Tim. 2:8 (A.S.V.).

"I want to say to you," wrote Dostoevski to his brother, "that I am a child of this age, a child of unbelief and skepticism. And yet . . . I believe that there is nothing lovelier, deeper, more sympathetic, more rational, more human and more perfect than the Saviour." This is something for all of us to think about.

I. There is nothing "lovelier" than Christ. That takes in art and aesthetics.

II. There is nothing "deeper" than Christ. That includes philosophy and science.

III. There is nothing "more sympathetic" than Christ. That takes account of economics, sociology and political science.

IV. There is nothing more "rational" than Christ. That includes logic, psychology and metaphysics.

V. There is nothing more "human" than Christ. That embraces anthropology, ethnology, history, engineering, ancient and modern languages.

VI. There is nothing more "perfect" than Christ. That takes in all education and all life in and out of college. —Hugh Thomson Kerr, D.D.

CHRISTIAN ENDEAVOR SOCIETY TOPIC

Sept. 26. Am I a player or Spectator? Luke 20:9-16.

SUNDAY SCHOOL LESSON

Sept. 26. Living Witnesses. Matt. 5:13-16; Acts 8:4-6; II Cor. 5:14-20.

MEMORY VERSE: "Let your light so shine before men, that they may see your good works and give glory to your Father who is in heaven." Matt. 5:16 (R.S.V.).

The lights with which Jesus was familiar were burning wicks in oil or perhaps some kind of candle. The lights he saw were lights of open flame. It was important that such lights burned clearly, steadily, brightly and revealingly.

As lights shining before men we ought to shed a clear light because we are Christ-kindled, because we know the effect of a smoky flame, because we know the effect of a clear flame, because we want to glorify God.

SUNDAY: OCTOBER THIRD

MORNING SERVICE

Theme: Triumphant Faith.

SUGGESTED SCRIPTURE READING: Heb. 11:1-40.

SELECTED HYMNS: "Lord, I believe; Thy power I own."—J. R. Wreford. "O for a faith that will not shrink."— W. H. Bathurst. "Rock of Ages, cleft for me."—A. M. Toplady. "Jesus, thou art the sinner's Friend."—R. Burnham. "I heard the voice of Jesus say."—H. Bonar.

CALL TO WORSHIP: "Blessed be the name of the Lord from this time forth and forevermore. From the rising of the sun unto the going down of the same the Lord's name is to be praised."

INVOCATION PRAYER: Our Father, who intrudeth not the sacred precincts of our lives, who knocketh at the doors of our hearts that we may open them, today we give thee entrance not as a stranger, but as Father; unto the Christ as our Saviour and Friend; and unto thy Spirit as our Guide and Comforter. We close no inner door, we bid thee welcome, and may thy presence fill our

lives with purity and peace and power. Amen.—M. K. W. H.

Theme: Triumphant Faith.

TEXT: "By faith Abraham, when he was called to go out into a place which he should after receive," etc. Heb. 11:8.

INTRODUCTORY: There is always a certain fascination about the man who cuts out a new path. What fascinates this writer in the story of Abraham is not the simple fact that he left his home in Ur and moved to the land of Canaan. It was a step that seemed to lack the guarantee of any tangible result. The only evidence to which Abraham could refer was the fact that God had spoken.

I. The importance of faith. To Abraham belongs the credit of taking a first step in a lifelong adherence to an invisible spiritual Supreme. For this reason the writer of this epistle singles him out as one of the great pioneers in the life of faith, a noble example of unquestioning trust in God. The example of Abraham was used in this letter to spur on men who are showing signs of dropping out of the race which they had set themselves to run. When they became Christians they had probably expected a speedy transformation of the world order, but many things had befallen them contrary to their expectation and they were beginning to lose faith in the goal for which they had set out.

II. The venture of faith. The life of faith always involves a venture, a stepping out into the unknown way with a profound conviction that the purpose of God will never fail. That was the kind of conviction Abraham possessed when he heard the voice of God telling him to leave his country and kinsfolk. "And he went out not knowing whither he went." We are all familiar with what may be called ventures of faith in many aspects of our life. Acting on this principle men have embarked upon enterprises which to many have seemed madness and they have done so because they have confidence in their judgment. The venture is grounded in a faith that the enterprise is worth while and that the present sacrifice will be compensated by subsequent success.

And for the Christian there is the sure word of Christ which declares that there is no man who has left home and kindred and friends but shall receive a hundredfold and inherit life eternal. Oftentimes the prospect may seem a poor one, but I believe that the man who is willing to make the venture will find that in him who made the promise resides also the fulfilment. The venture of faith will be justified by the result.

III. The vision of faith. The venture of faith, which is undertaken in response to God's challenge, is ever sustained and nourished by the vision of its final result. It is one of the great characteristics of faith that it actualizes or makes real to the believer the thing that is hoped for; it is "the substance of things hoped for, the evidence of things not seen." I try sometimes to visualise the situation when

Abraham decided to break with the old life to embark on a journey with prospects as barren as the desert through which he so often would pass. But Abraham, looking through the telescope of faith, could see beyond the barren wastes of the desert the realization of the promise. "He looked for a city which hath foundations, whose builder and maker is God."

I think it was Victor Hugo who once said, "The ideal is the real. I live with my eye fixed upon the vision." So it was with Abraham. Present circumstances were often grim and seemed to contradict all his hopes, but he looked in faith to God and caught the sustaining vision, and that was all the evidence he needed of the things not seen. There are doubtless many things which discourage us in our life today, and daunt us as we think of the manifold problems of our time. But if we are willing to make the venture of faith, and truly believe that God is calling us on to a more concentrated effort for his kingdom, we shall not be denied the vision that such a kingdom really exists. We shall know that there are things which cannot be shaken, that there is a city whose foundations are in the holy mountains whose builder and maker is God. The same truth is found in a quaint Indian story which tells how an old traveler was once asked by a certain peasant, "Whither goest thou?" The old man replied, "To a city far away." When asked further where it was, whether in India, or in Asia, or one of the Western lands, he said, "Further, further, my friend, much further, for the city I seek is Truth, and it is hidden in the heart of God."

Far off I see the goal,
 O Saviour, guide me.
I feel my strength is small,
 Be Thou beside me.
With vision ever clear,
With love that conquers fear,
And grace to persevere,
O Lord, provide me.
—S. H. H. P.

THEME PRAYER: Almighty and everlasting God, who not only givest every good and perfect gift, but dost also increase those thou hast given; we most humbly beseech thee to increase in us the gift of faith, that we may truly believe in thee, and in thy promises; and that neither by our negligence or infirmity of the flesh, nor by grievousness of temptation, nor by the subtle crafts and assaults of the enemy, we be driven from faith in our Saviour and Lord Jesus Christ. Amen.

OFFERTORY SENTENCE: "But this I say, He which soweth sparingly shall reap also sparingly; and he which soweth bountifully shall reap also bountifully."

OFFERTORY PRAYER: O Thou Who hast committed to us the great and solemn trust of life, we thank thee for the goods thou hast put into our keeping. Forgive us our derelictions, give us wisdom and strength for what thou dost expect of us, and, being true to thee, may we be true to all who trust us. Accept and bless these offerings we bring thee now and use them for the advancement of thy kingdom in the world. We ask in Jesus' name. Amen.

Illustrative Material

SEED THOUGHTS, HOMILETIC AND EXPOSITORY. The Obedience of Faith: I. The kind of faith that produces obedience. 1. Faith in God. 2. In the rightness of all he says. 3. In his care for and over us. II. The kind of obedience that faith produces. 1. Prompt. 2. Exact. 3. Practical. 4. Far-seeing. 5. Unreckoned and implicit. "He went out not knowing whither he went." III. The sort of life that will come of this faith and obedience. 1. The life of honor. 2. Of communion with God.—S.

Abraham's Faith: I. The hard task to which Abraham was called. 1. Involved painful separation. 2. The risk of being misunderstood. 3. Uncertainty for the future. II. The simple faith by which this hard task was fulfilled. 1. Based on a divine call. 2. Sustained by abundant promises. 3. Expressed by absolute surrender. III. The wonder-

ful blessing to which this simple faith led. Think of what came of this act of obedience!—C. N.

Choice Illustrations on the Theme

THE ADVENTURES OF FAITH. In his famous description of the boat race Vergil says of the winning crew: "They can because they believe they can."

FAITH TO SEE ONE THROUGH. Following the attempt to climb Mt. Everest in 1922, the participants drew up a list of three qualifications essential to such an undertaking. The first, to be sure, was physical fitness. But the other two, interestingly enough, were concerned with attitudes of mind. A would-be climber of Mt. Everest had to have "singleness of purpose" and "unswerving faith in the possibility of its achievement." He had to be able to say, "This one thing I do, and I am confident that it can be accomplished."

How often have these two qualities of life—concentration and faith—been the means of seeing men through! Handicaps of every kind fade before them.

DOUBT AND FAITH

Doubt sees the obstacles;
    Faith sees the way!
Doubt sees the darkest night;
    Faith sees the day!
Doubt dreads to take a step;
    Faith soars on high,
Doubt questions, "Who believes?"
    Faith answers, "I!"
       —*Jewish Missionary Magazine*

FAITH CONQUERS INDECISION. One night in the Pacific five men from a torpedoed ship rode in an open boat. There was scarcely food for four. So the fifth decided to slip overboard in the night. He did what a Salvation Army lass years before had done from an overcrowded lifeboat after the *Titanic* sank, in order that a man and his wife might be rescued together. Faith conquers indecision. When Luther was ordered before the Diet of Worms without assurance of safety, and his friends warned him that John Huss had not been saved from the stake under similar circumstances, he replied: "I am called in the name of God to go, and I would go though I were certain to meet as many devils in Worms as there are tiles on the houses." When the secret police offered Martin Niemoeller freedom if only he would refrain from preaching, and when a prison mate told him how to bribe the guards and get lenient prison treatment, he refused again and again, and once he said: "I will not have a better fate than any other man in this camp." Having decided he kept true to his course. Faith conquered indecision and every temptation to escape from the painful consequences of high decision.—Elkmore M. McKee.

FAITH FOR THE FUTURE. In those dark days when the Constitutional Convention was in session, more than once the meeting was at the point of breaking up amid bitter quarrels. But as the last members were finally signing that immortal document, Benjamin Franklin looked toward the President's chair, at the back of which was painted a flaming sun, and observed to those near him: "I have often and often, in the course of this session, and the vicissitudes of my hopes and fears as to its issue, looked at that sun behind the President, without being able to tell whether it was rising or setting; but now, at length, I have the happiness to know that it is a rising, and not a setting sun."

Armed with a confidence of faith born out of the deep and abiding experience of the past, and sure that God is just and merciful, we may face the future with hope assured that tomorrow we shall see a rising and not a setting sun. After all, it *may* be a better world tomorrow—and it will be if God's will is done on earth.—Rev. Donald H. Tippet.

EVENING SERVICE

Theme: The Spider-web Trust.

TEXT: "Whose hope shall be cut off, and whose trust shall be a spider's web." Job 8:14.

INTRODUCTORY: In physics, in morals, in religion reality has no respect for those who have no regard for truth and fact. In religion reality might seem to reign, for it is backed by revelation. But it is not true, for not a few men think they can sip the sensual sweet and decline the sensual bitter. These are the hypocrites. Their hope shall be cut off. Their trust is as a spider's web. While very beautiful in structure it is equally fragile in texture. It suits the builder's purposes, yet being self-spun, self-built, it is destined to be swept away.

I. Beautiful as to its structure; admirable is the fairy architecture of the spider's web. Beautiful too is the religion of the hypocrite's trust. His religion satisfies the eye. Strung with beads of dew, it is a bright cloud which for the moment passes for the sun itself.

II. But when tried, though so beautiful in structure, the hypocrite's religion is found to be very fragile in its texture. This is no disparagement of the spider's web. For such a tiny weaver it is remarkably strong and wonderful. But hypocrisy is a frail reliance.

III. The spider's web is adequate to its purpose. The spider ensnares his prey. The hypocrite does make a gain of godliness, sometimes an apparently successful ladder of religion.

IV. The hypocrite's trust, being false, with all that rests upon it, shall be utterly swept away. The pious dissembler will exhaust his last resource, wear out his last disguise.

V. But a true hope is an anchor to the soul. 1. It connects its possessor with an unseen world. It takes hold "within the veil." 2. It possesses enduring strength. Suggests the strength of a true hope. "Sure and steadfast." 3. It gives the soul calmness and security.—W. C. J.

Suggestive Texts and Themes

Personality and Providence: "As the Lord hath distributed to each man, as

God hath called each, so let him walk."
I Cor. 7:17 (A.S.V.).

Man as God's Interpreter: "If ye then, being evil, know how to give good gifts unto your children, how much more shall your Father which is in heaven give good things to them that ask him?" Matt. 7:11.

How to Find One's Lifework: "And he thought within himself, saying, What shall I do? . . . And he said, This will I do." Luke 12:17, 18.

The Upper Room: "And when they were come in, they went up into an upper room, where abode both Peter, and James, and John, and Andrew." Acts 1:13.

Tragedy of a Soul: "And he went his way." Luke 22:4.

MIDWEEK FELLOWSHIP MEETING TOPIC

(Church Night or Suggested Sermon Subject)

Theme: True Education (Religious Education Week).

TEXT: "And Moses was learned in all the wisdom of the Egyptians, and was mighty in words and in deeds." Acts 7:22.

Moses was one of the most learned men of his time. His education embraced the whole range of Greek, Chaldee, Assyrian and Egyptian literature. There is much in his experience to commend the subject of education to all classes. In his training we see: I. God's testimony in favor of education. 1. By God's providence Moses was placed where he could enjoy all the advantages of a good secular education. God's will in favor of education is also seen. 2. In the establishment of the schools of the prophets. 3. In the teaching of the Bible. See especially the book of Proverbs. 4. In the capacity and cravings of the human mind. The education of the mind, then, is a sacred duty. II. The great value of education. 1. Think on the cost of Moses' education, the sufferings of the Israelites, and

the dangers of a heathen court. 2. Think of the increased power his education gave him. By education mental diamonds are polished and nuggets of gold are converted into current coin. III. Secular education is not itself sufficient. We have a twofold nature, mental and moral. Educate both. Moses received a religious training, first from his mother, and afterward from God in the desert. IV. Eminence in secular education may be combined with eminence in religious education. Moses was distinguished for both. Also Paul, Milton, Ruskin, etc. Intelligent piety is the best of piety. 1. The Christian church should seek the education of the masses. 2. All educated minds should be consecrated to Christ.

CHRISTIAN ENDEAVOR SOCIETY TOPIC

Oct. 3. Facing Uncertainty. Matt. 24:3-13.

BULLETIN BOARD SLOGANS FOR THE MONTH

By EARL RINEY

The best Thanksgiving is Thanksliving.

The religion of joy gives joy in religion.

A man's life is worth while so long as his enthusiasm lasts.

The great object in life is to do our best and be kind.

The gospel is the balance wheel of character.

Tomorrow will be a better day if you begin this morning to improve it.

Affliction is the school of faith.

Brokenhearted penitents and wholehearted seekers please God well.

He has bad food who feeds on others' faults.

Faith in God is never out of season.

He talks much who has least to say.

Prayer and pains bring best of gains.

Search the Scriptures and let them search you.

SUNDAY SCHOOL LESSON

Oct. 3. Man's Struggle to Understand Life. Job. 1:1; 19:7-10; 23:3-10.

MEMORY VERSE: "Ye shall seek me, and find me, when ye shall search for me with all your heart." Jer. 29:13.

Job is typical of modern man— troubled, perplexed, helpless. 1. His perplexity. In his perplexity he may question God's goodness, even rebel against God's government of the universe. 2. His need. His supreme need is to be assured of God's loving concern for his creatures and to turn to God in faith. 3. In the face of such perplexity and such need the truth of the memory verse can be emphasized—that those who seek God sincerely will surely find him.

SUNDAY: OCTOBER TENTH

MORNING SERVICE

Theme: The Duty of Observing the Lord's Supper (Holy Communion).

SUGGESTED SCRIPTURE READING: Matt. 26:17-30.

SELECTED HYMNS: "Here, O my Lord, I see thee face to face."—H. Bonar. "Jesus, thou joy of loving hearts."— Bernard of Clairvaux. "Bread of the world, in mercy broken."—Reginald Heber. "Saviour, who thy flock art feeding."—W. G. Muhlenberg. "A parting hymn we sing around thy table, Lord."—Aaron R. Wolfe.

CALL TO WORSHIP: "I will come into thy house in the multitude of thy mercy: and in thy fear will I worship toward thy holy temple."

INVOCATION PRAYER: We come unto thee, O God, in our endeavor to make this service of worship a simple and sincere expression of our love and loyalty to thee. It is a token, also, of our hearts' desire for a measure of thy grace sufficient unto this day's deepest need. Accept, our Father, our hymns and prayers and meditations as an offering of love, and use them, we pray, as a means of manifesting thy loving-kindness toward us. In this service lift us above the usual spiritual levels of our lives to the place where we have clearer perceptions and broader visions. Grant us an awareness of and a fuller communion with thee; a deeper fellowship with our fellow men and a larger knowledge of our own lives and possibilities in relation to thy purposes. In Jesus' name. Amen.—M. K. W. H.

Theme: The Duty of Observing the Lord's Supper (Holy Communion).

TEXT: "I must by all means keep this feast that cometh in Jerusalem." Acts 18:21.

INTRODUCTORY: It is a duty. It is also a great privilege. So Paul thought of it. But just now we will think of the observance of the Lord's Supper especially as a duty, though it is at the same time a wonderful aid and privilege.

When our Lord was baptized he satisfied John by saying, "Suffer it to be so now, for thus it becometh us to fulfil all righteousness." That is, it becomes us to observe every righteous ordinance of God. The same spirit that animated the Master directed the conduct of his disciples. Everywhere they were distinguished by a reverence for the ordinances of religion. And if there be an instance in which this spirit was most strikingly exemplified we see it now in the case of Paul. Surrounded as he was by the people of Ephesus, who entreated him to remain among them for a longer period, he still felt the moving influence of the obligation to observe the feast of Pentecost in Jerusalem. I trust that everyone among us here responds to this same feeling of the apostle. A Christian will surely say, "I must by all means keep this feast, that of the Lord's Supper." There are many and supremely important reasons.

I. First, because it is the wish and commandment of Christ. Were it a mere conventional ordinance, merely one of those outward circumstances which are not essential to the existence of Christianity, it might be left to our own discretion whether we should observe it or not. But it comes to us on the authority of the Saviour himself, who said, "This do in remembrance of me." There is not any precept more explicitly laid down, and we cannot refuse to observe it without setting aside the authority of Him to whom we are indebted for all that we now are or hope hereafter to enjoy.

II. It is a duty, further, that we may be the better warned of the evil of sin. There is in this ordinance a manifestation of the evil of sin that is not to be found elsewhere; for we commemorate that great sacrifice which the Father required in order to render the exercise of mercy to the penitent consistent with the exercise of his justice in the moral administration of the world. When, therefore, the believer sits down at the table of the Lord and has his eyes turned to the cross of Christ, his heart is smitten with a sense of the evil nature and destroying tendency of sin, and he feels that the world is crucified unto him and he to the world. He realizes afresh the reality and evil of sin, and resolves anew against it.

III. It is a duty to observe the feast because it is a most important means of grace. There is no feeling to which the heart is more ready to respond than our need of strength greater than our own for the varied duties and trials and sorrows of our nature. And God has promised that his grace shall be sufficient for us, that his strength shall be made perfect in our weakness. But we must wait upon him for this strength and grace in the way of his appointment. We are not, therefore, to expect the blessing unless we employ the means. And the Lord's Supper is one of the appointed means by which the Spirit of God meets the believer to renew, to sanctify, to encourage and to direct him.

IV. It is a duty to observe the feast also because it is one of the most direct means of uniting the family of God in the bonds of peace and love. At this table the rich and the poor meet together. There we learn to love mankind when we see that love which embraced the world as "one world." There we learn to forgive our enemy when we see Christ bleeding for his foes.

V. It is our duty to observe this feast because we know not that we shall have another opportunity. We are all frail creatures, and we know not what a day shall bring forth. Let us by all means keep this feast of obedience and love and grace and wondrous privilege.—J. J.

THEME PRAYER: Our Heavenly Father, how wonderful thy power and wisdom and holiness and love in thy work of redemption through thy Son! No wisdom or power in heaven or earth could have delivered us but thine. O set our affections on things above. May we go out from this Communion Service to serve thee in deeper love and in newness of life. We ask all in our Redeemer's name. Amen.

OFFERTORY SENTENCE: "To do good and to communicate forget not; for with such sacrifices God is well pleased."

OFFERTORY PRAYER: We would bring to thee, our Father, these our token gifts of gratitude for all thy mercies. Thou dost open thine hand and satisfy the wants of every living thing. Out of thy fulness have we all received. Wilt thou graciously accept these expressions of our thanks and use them for the good of others. We ask in Christ's name. Amen.

Illustrative Material

SEED THOUGHTS, HOMILETIC AND EXPOSITORY. Broken Things: "Take, eat: this is my body which is broken for you." I Cor. 11:24. How often we have heard these beautiful words in the Communion of the Lord's Supper, where we have offered the sacrifices of a broken heart and contrite spirit. I. Is there not a blessing in broken things? Too often we would keep them whole for our selfish enjoyment; but unbroken alabaster boxes are valueless, as many uncrushed flowers are odorless. II. Broken earthly hopes make room for heavenly riches. Breaking the marble makes the statuary beautiful; breaking the grain gives bread to the hungry; breaking the rocks opens the way to gold and precious stones; breaking the earth gives oil and coal for commerce and comfort. So breaking the body of Jesus on Calvary gives the Bread of Life to famishing millions. III. To become like our Saviour we break the alabaster boxes of loving sacrifice for others.—E. W. C.

Choice Lord's Supper Illustrations

RENEWING OF EXPERIENCE. No one has lived the inner life without seasons of early passions when the romance of Jesus has captured the soul, without experiencing seasons of later declension when the greenery of spring grew gray in the city dust. It is in such hours of coldness and weariness we ought to reinforce our souls with the sacrament of the bread and wine. As one makes a journey to some country kirkyard where the dust of his departed is lying, and cleanses away the moss that has filled up the letters of his mother's name, so do we in the holy communion again assure ourselves of a love so amazing that it passes knowledge, but so utterly divine that it must be true.—John Watson, D.D.

EXPERIENCE AT THE LORD'S TABLE. What if the Master had left us without instituting this Supper? How many precious lessons and experiences we would have lost. The scene is a most beautiful one when, reclining at the table with those who had been his nearest followers, he tells them the meaning of his love and sacrifice. This experience may be ours when we meet at his table.—John Timothy Stone, D.D.

VALUE OF COMMUNION. Observance of the sacrament of the Lord's Supper has blessed values and results. It is said that the Mohammedans used to bring so much incense into the Mosque of Omar at Jerusalem that anyone going from it carried everywhere the sweet odor, and men could tell where he had been. So men will know where we have been, if we spend much time with God. Let us not neglect the coming to the Lord's Table. It will prove a blessing to us and will help us to prove a blessing to others.

COMMUNING AS COVENANTERS. "This is my blood of the new covenant." We should go away from the feast as covenanters. We have taken the new covenant in his blood, and the holy sacrament will be fresh upon our lips; and there must be something about us akin to the Scottish Covenanters when they emerged from Greyfriars Churchyard, having entered into holy bond and covenant with the Lord. There must be something in our very demeanor telling the world that we have been at a great tryst, and our lives must be bravely, grandly quiet, confident in the glorious Ally with whom the covenant has been made. There must be nothing dubious in our stride.—John H. Jowett, D.D.

NOTE OF TRIUMPH. We must not forget that even in this sad night of the establishment of the sacrament of the Lord's Supper there was a note of triumph. The feast ended with a hymn. What they sang probably was the concluding portion of the Hallel, the special group of Psalms assigned to the Passover. It would contain such verses as Psalm 116:13, "I will take the cup of salvation, and call upon the name of the Lord"; and Psalm 118:29, "O give thanks unto the Lord; for he is good: for his mercy endureth for ever." The remembrance of what Christ has done for us should always fill our hearts with love and our lips with song. "The joy of the Lord is your strength."

Suggestive Lord's Supper Texts and Themes

A Message First: "I will not eat, until I have told mine errand." Gen. 24:33.

A Dying Wish Respected: "This do in remembrance of me." Luke 22:19.

At the Last Supper: "Now when the even was come," etc. Matt. 26:20-22.

The King's Guests: "When the king came in to see the guests." Matt. 22:11.

Meditation Kindling Love: "My meditation of him shall be sweet." Ps. 104:34.

The Lord's Desire: "With desire I have desired to eat this Passover with you before I suffer." Luke 22:15.

Preparation for the Feast: "There make ready." Luke 22:12.

Love for the Unseen Saviour: "Whom having not seen, ye love." I Pet. 1:8.

EVENING SERVICE

Theme: The Good Fight of Faith.

TEXT: "Fight the good fight of faith." I Tim. 6:12.

INTRODUCTORY: This figure of speech is often used in the Scriptures, in our hymns, and in Christian conversation. Why? There are many reasons.

I. Notice, first, that war is a terribly earnest business. Of all things under the sun this work of fighting, if it is to be done at all, is one that must be done with all our heart and mind. It is no mere political parade affair of plumes and epaulets and drums and flags and trumpets. Only certain ruin will come to those who go into it in that spirit, with light and careless heart. But it is definitely to such a work as that that Paul likens the Christian life, and it is in the same earnest spirit that he would have us deal with it.

Of course, the whole thing differs from the warfares of the world. They work sorrows and desolation and death. They do call forth heroic qualities, such as courage and devotion. But the Christian warfare works no evil. This conflict of ours, while it demands equal courage and devotion, is gentle also, and merciful, ready to suffer loss, but not to inflict it. Witness the early martyrs, as Paul and Timothy knew them. Wild beasts at Ephesus. Stonings at Jerusalem. The prison and the stake and the cross of those days.

II. What men fight for. They fight for existence, bread. They fight for wealth. They fight for position. If Christians, men fight to "lay hold on eternal life."

III. Why is this fight called a "good fight"? True Christianity is a good fight, though "good" is a curious word to apply to our warfare. All worldly warfare is more or less evil. We can think of many reasons why the Christian warfare is called a good fight. We fight under the best of Commanders, the Lord Jesus Christ. Our contest is carried on with the best of Help, the blessed Holy Spirit. The Christian's fight is good, too, because it is fought for the best of purposes, for the best issues and results. Furthermore, it is a good fight because it does good to the soul of him that fights it. The Christian fight is the good fight of faith in which he lays hold on eternal life.

IV. In closing, let us consider the method, or how to fight the good fight of faith. There must be the reconnaissance, the outlook, the decision, the enlistment. There must be preparation, the armor, the equipment, the drill. There must be the conflict, which will include both defense and attack. "Am I a soldier of the Cross?"—H.

MIDWEEK FELLOWSHIP MEETING TOPIC

(Church Night or Suggested Sermon Subject)

Theme: Getting Clear.

TEXT: "And they immediately left the ship and their father, and followed him." Matt. 4:22.

Mrs. Howard Taylor, addressing Student Volunteers at Toronto, said she had been willing to go anywhere in the world for Christ—except China. But in China the door opened, and she was much depressed. As the ship was clearing the Bay of Naples and the shores of Europe were fading, a sailor in the prow sang out to the captain: "All is clear now, sir." And the captain shouted: "Full steam ahead!" Instantly it seemed as though the anchor that held the missionary had been taken aboard, and she said: "O Christ, all is clear now for thee. Full power ahead!"

I. It was so with these four fishermen. They did what multitudes of modern disciples never seem able to do—they got clear for Christ. Young, brave and enthusiastic, they immediately left all and followed him.

II. There is a great parable of life here. Ship and nets may stand for material prospects and possessions. They are analogous to worldly appeals —not wrong in themselves, but wrong if they crowd out the superior claims of Jesus. The Christian life is an enlistment for the whole man and for life.

III. The call of Christ is a call to detach ourselves from many things that we may attach ourselves to one thing. Fishing, henceforth, was to be incidental; following Jesus was always first. May God help us to get rid of the dragging anchors of the world.

IV. Happy is the Christian who gets clear at the very start. It is a miserable existence to attempt halfway measures with God. We cannot dictate the terms of our surrender to Jesus. The victorious life is simply the life in which we cease to dictate and direct, and hand over the command to Jesus. —H. P. H.

CHRISTIAN ENDEAVOR SOCIETY TOPIC

Oct. 10. Faith to Conquer Uncertainty. Rom. 8:31-39; I Cor. 15:55-58.

SUNDAY SCHOOL LESSON

Oct. 10. God's Answer to Man's Perplexity. Job 38:1-7; 42:1-6, 10a.

MEMORY VERSE: "Be still, and know that I am God." Ps. 46:10.

God reveals himself to Job, and Job is overwhelmed by God's power and Glory. He sees God to be infinitely more wonderful than he had imagined. God does not answer Job's questions, but Job is satisfied with what he has seen. He knows that God is one whom he can approach as a Friend, one to whom he may speak, one who can answer prayer. Those who are troubled and perplexed today can find in Job's final understanding of God renewed confidence in the adequacy of God's government of his universe.

SUNDAY: OCTOBER SEVENTEENTH

MORNING SERVICE

Theme: Measuring Altars.

SUGGESTED SCRIPTURE READING: Matt. 23:1-28.

SELECTED HYMNS: "I would be true." —H. A. Walter. "Father in heaven, who lovest all."—R. Kipling. "True-

hearted, whole-hearted, faithful and loyal."—F. R. Havergal. "Draw thou my soul, O Christ."—L. Larcom. "O God of earth and altar."—G. K. Chesterton. "When the weary, seeking rest." —H. Bonar.

CALL TO WORSHIP: "My voice shalt thou hear in the morning, O Lord; in the morning will I direct my prayer unto thee, and will look up."

INVOCATION PRAYER: In deep reverence, O God, we bow before thee in worship. In the presence of thy holiness we feel unworthy and without any right to stand before thee; but in the presence of thy love we come with hearts that are full of joy. Accept our worship, O thou holy and loving Father. Be thou in our midst, and grant unto us awareness of thy presence. Create in us clean hearts and renew a right spirit within us. By contact with thee may we be strengthened in our inward man and may our hearts be made more loving. Unite us as a church ever aspiring toward the good life and ever seeking more fruitful ways of service. Bless this day all who undergo pain and suffering. Rejoice with those who rejoice. Lead us all into pathways of service and peace. In Jesus' name. Amen.— M. K. W. H.

Theme: Measuring Altars.

TEXT: 'And these are the measures of the altar after the cubits." Ezek. 43:13.

INTRODUCTORY: Looked upon geometrically there are the measurements, vv. 13-17. Thus broad, thus high, etc. Thus it is a mechanical structure. But that says nothing of it as a spiritual symbol. In that respect the altar is immeasurable.

But we should remember that in dealing with the altar we are not merely dealing with a geometrical figure. The altar has its finite side, but it has its infinite aspect also. It looks toward things beyond ken, things of plus quality, things of the unknown, of the divine.

Let us think of our tendency to measure things by cubits.

I. Some would measure a home by cubits, by the size or appointments of a house. There may be a relation between the two, but in many cases there is no relation. One cannot measure wedded love by the carat-size of the engagement diamond or weight in gold of the wedding ring. It is the spirit within that makes a house into a home, that makes it warm in winter and glorious in summer. A home is not measured by cubits. A visit to your mother is not measured by the number of miles traveled.

II. One cannot measure churches by cubits. Who can measure what even the humblest church is doing for a town or a village? It may have no beauty of architecture, no impressive furnishings. It may make very little if any noise and excitement. But seen in its spiritual significance it may be the salvation of the place. Our sanctuaries, not the banks and chambers of commerce, good as they are, give glory to our towns and security to our cities.

III. One cannot measure personal religion by cubits. Its forms and ceremonies may be most exact. But form may exist while denying the power thereof. So much fidelity in attendance, so much in gifts, the fulfillment of forms may be but cubit measurements. In some old European cathedrals there was a board with punched holes and pegs. Piety was measured by making so many rounds of the building, the tally being kept by advancing the pegs. Cubit measures! So many rounds so much religion! Impossible! It is rankest self-deception. You cannot measure poetry by the size of the volume. You cannot measure a painting by the size of the canvas. You cannot measure the meaning of the flag by a measuring of the bunting.

IV. One cannot measure missions or preaching of the gospel by cubits. Someone calculated the income of one of our great denominational mission boards and then the number of conversions reported. He found that each conversion cost some thousands of dollars. What a man that would have been for measuring altars. How very ingenious was the application of the footrule! But what about the measure of a soul?

V. How about a measurement by cubits of the Cross of Christ? The Roman footrule was laid upon it. So wide, so high, so much in weight—was that the Cross? No! Never! The true Cross is immeasurable. It is something infinitely beyond specification.

THEME PRAYER: *Forgive us, Lord,* the altars we build to what we ought not to worship and the altars we leave unbuilt to the high and the holy. Save us from misdirected loyalties. May we maintain holy altars in our homes and offer to thee always the sacrifices of humble and contrite hearts. In His name who hast revealed thee to us. Amen.

OFFERTORY SENTENCE: "Thanks be unto God for his unspeakable gift!"

OFFERTORY PRAYER: O thou blessed God, who hast enriched us with thy grace, help us not only to rejoice in our spiritual wealth but to share it with others. Thou hast broken for us the living Bread; help us to give the hungry to eat. Enlarge our hearts. Save us from selfishness. Use us to thy glory. Accept and bless these offerings of thy people and use them for the furtherance of thy cause in the world. We ask in the name of Christ. Amen.

Illustrative Material

SEED THOUGHTS, HOMILETIC AND EXPOSITORY. Measuring by Cubits: God is a great measurer. God has a line, a reed, a pole. God makes his cities foursquare, and he will not see the law of the square violated.—J. P.

"These are the measures of the altar after the cubits." Yes, after the cubits. That is to say, if you look upon the thing geometrically here it is, so long, so broad, so high. After that manner the altar is measurable. When you have given cubits you have given nothing. But in dealing with an altar we are not dealing with geometrical figures. We are dealing with the immeasurable.

Measuring by Cubits. A man may build a cathedral and yet never pray. —J. P.

Choice Illustrations on the Theme

THE DANGER OF FORMALISM. You cannot magnify the little external things of religion without thereby minimizing the great and vital things.—Author Unknown.

WHAT DO YOU DO WHEN YOU GO TO CHURCH? In one of our great cities there is a section called Chinatown, where many Chinese people live and carry on their business. A group of Christian visitors was being shown through this section by a Chinese friend. They visited a shrine in a small room where now and then a Chinese paused quietly to worship. Someone happened to remark that the room was small and would not accommodate very many people, to which the friendly guide replied: "We have worship without a congregation. You have a congregation without worship." The answer caused a great deal of discussion and heart-searching among those who were there. Do you think the Chinese guide was right? What do you do when you go to church? What, after all, is worship? Does it depend upon the presence of a crowd? Are we slaves of the crowd? Are we in danger of mistaking the sensation that comes in the presence of a mass of people for that other deeper sensation which comes when the "still small voice" speaks to us? Do you worship God when you are alone as easily as when you are with others? Real worship is one of the most revealing and testing experiences which we can share.—Ernest Bourner Allen.

MEASURING ALTARS. Let us beware of thinking of religion as a matter of going through with forms. The old monks of York Minster used to think that duty could be done and merit massed by walking around the arches of the solemn cathedral in sedate procession. According to their accurate measurement, twelve rounds made one mile of marching virtue. There yet may be seen holes in a board at the great portal supplied with pegs with which they checked off their religion. But those old monks are not the only people who have made the mistake of supposing that going through so many forms meant just that much religion. You may go through forms and have religion; but let us guard carefully against the mistake of thinking that religion itself consists in going through the forms.—H.

LIFELESSNESS AND FORMS. The artist may mold matter into forms of surprising beauty, and make us feel their elevating and purifying influences; but what is the marble Moses of a Michelangelo, or the cold statue of his living Christ, compared to the embodiment of Jesus in the sculpture of a holy life? What are all the forms of moral beauty in the Pharisee of religion compared with the true and holy life of the heart of the devoted Christian?—*New Cyclopedia of Illustrations.*

GEOMETRICAL ALTARS. In an old church at Valsbol the men have for centuries had a queer habit. They went to the altar to receive the sacrament and on returning they each made a bow, standing always on the same spot, in the direction of the women. Why they did it no one knew; but lately, in cleaning one of the walls a picture of the Virgin Mary was discovered. It was covered up by whitewash four centuries ago, and the worshipers had continued to bow toward it long after everyone had forgotten that it was there. It will be well for all Christians everywhere if this story cannot be applied to them; if they are not bowing in apparent reverence before some religious experience of their youth or other ages whose significance they have forgotten.—*2,500 Best Modern Illustrations.*

EVENING SERVICE

Theme: The Flight into the Wilderness.

TEXT: "He arose, and went for his life." I Kings 19:3.

INTRODUCTORY: This is a sad sequel to the triumph on Mt. Carmel. Elijah had forgotten Jezebel. We are in danger of forgetting our chief adversary. Elijah, too, had taken his eyes off God. He acted in a panic. "He arose, and went for his life."

I. Elijah's weakness. He was a man of like passions with us. He suffered from a terrible reaction. Overwrought nerves, a tired brain and physical exhaustion had much to do with the prophet's fall. Those who go up go down. Reaction set in. He suffered from a terrible disappointment, for Jezebel was still seeking his life. His wish, "O Lord, take away my life," was folly. He fled from death yet prayed for death! Then, too, his reason for the wish was untrue.

II. Consider God's tenderness to him. 1. He allowed him to sleep. This was better than medicine, or inward rebuke, or spiritual instruction. 2. He fed him with food convenient and nourishing. 3. He made him aware of angelic care. "An angel touched him." 4. He allowed him to tell his grief. This is often a ready relief. 5. God revealed himself and his ways—wind, earthquake, fire, still small voice. 6. He told him good news: "Yet I have seven thousand in Israel." His sense of loneliness was thus removed. 7. He gave him more to do. Anoint others.

III. Learn some useful lessons. 1. First, it is seldom right to pray to die. We have no right to destroy our own lives or to ask the Lord to do so. 2. When we do wish to die, the reason must not be impatience, petulance, pride or insolence. 3. We have no idea of what may yet be in store for us in this life. 4. In any case let us trust in the Lord and do good, and we need not be afraid. Take courage. "Thou shalt not die but live."—C. H. S.

Suggestive Texts and Themes

The Great Companion: "Now the God of peace be with you all. Amen." Rom. 15:33.

Trusteeship of the Ministry: "Let a man so account of us, as of the ministers of Christ, and stewards of the mysteries of God." I Cor. 4:1.

Utterance, the Supreme Spiritual Gift: "Follow after charity, and desire spiritual gifts, but rather that ye may prophesy." I Cor. 14:1.

What Follows the Heart's Unveiling: "But we all, with open face beholding as in a glass the glory of the Lord, are changed into the same image from glory to glory, even as by the Spirit of the Lord." II Cor. 3:18.

Life Values: "Let not the wise man glory in his wisdom, neither let the mighty man glory in his might, let not the rich man glory in his riches: But let him that glorieth glory in this, that he understandeth and knoweth me." Jer. 9:23, 24.

MIDWEEK FELLOWSHIP MEETING TOPIC

(Church Night or Suggested Sermon Subject)

Theme: God's Remedy.

TEXT: "Thus saith the Lord, I have healed these waters; there shall not be from thence any more death or barren land." II Kings 2:21.

Unlike the miserable village which now occupies the site, Jericho of old was a pleasant place in which to live. Situated in the Jordan valley about five miles from the end of the Dead Sea, it was surrounded by a territory unusually fertile and productive. The city itself was well located and protected. But there was one great drawback. The water was bad. The men of the city were in desperation. They had exhausted every available means to sweeten the water. Still it was not good for man or beast, and still it caused the trees to cast their fruit prematurely. In their predicament they came to Elisha and he went forth to the springs of the waters and healed them.

I. Ours is a pleasant situation. We would trade our country for none on earth. Most of us are well satisfied with our community, our town, our state and our nation. But, even as in Jericho, there are things in our individual, and community, and state and national lives which are not as they should be. There are bitter streams which cause premature casting of fruit.

II. We may try our best, we may exhaust every possibility of human endeavor, and we shall be at our wits' end to sweeten the streams of life, unless we turn to God, for he alone can purify and make altogether pleasant.

III. God's remedy applied at the spring of the waters will heal all bitterness.—J. A. M.

CHRISTIAN ENDEAVOR SOCIETY TOPIC

Oct. 17. The Christian Shares His Faith. Acts 3:1-11.

SUNDAY SCHOOL LESSON

Oct. 17. **Wisdom for Daily Living.** Prov. 3:1-6; 4:10-15, 18-19.

MEMORY VERSES: Trust in the Lord with all thy heart, and lean not upon thine own understanding: in all thy ways acknowledge him, and he will direct thy paths. Prov. 3:5-6 (A.S.V.).

There are three kinds of wisdom proclaimed and taught in the book of Proverbs. I. Prudential Wisdom. This is the wisdom of common sense. So-called practical wisdom. This includes sagacity in dealing with affairs, the knowledge of men and things that comes from experience. This is worldly wisdom in the best sense of the term. It is imperfect when taken by itself.

II. There is basically Moral Wisdom. This is wisdom looked upon as identical with the law of God. "This inner, deeper wisdom judges human nature and human conduct by the religious ideal set forth in the law of God. It probes down to the causes which produce such tragic failure in the lives of men. It sees that life is built on law: so that to break law is not merely folly that incurs punishment but is to sin against our own nature and wrong our own self."

III. There is Incarnate Wisdom. "Wisdom is a glorious Personality, the first born of creation, not only presiding over the fortunes of men and disposing of human destiny, but aiding God in creation, the divine Wisdom set up from everlasting, from the beginning or ever the earth was."

SUNDAY: OCTOBER TWENTY-FOURTH

MORNING SERVICE

Theme: Failure's Loss.

SUGGESTED SCRIPTURE READING: Heb. 11:1-16. After-petition: May God's blessing attend this reading of his Word. SELECTED HYMNS: "Lord, I believe; thy power I own."—J. R. Wreford. "O for a faith that will not shrink."—W. H. Bathurst. "Walk in the light: so shalt thou know."—B. Barton. "O gift of gifts! O grace of faith!"—F. W. Faber.

PREPROCESSIONAL CHOIR PRAYER: Through our offering of praise this morning bless us each and the congregation gathered. Give us the spirit of devout worship. May our hearts be in tune with thee while our lips utter thy praise. We ask in Christ's name. Amen.

CALL TO WORSHIP: "The hour cometh, and now is when the true worshipers shall worship the Father in spirit and in truth; for the Father seeketh such to worship him."

INVOCATION PRAYER: Almighty God, who hast caused the light of eternal life to shine upon the world, we beseech thee that our hearts may be so kindled with heavenly desires, and thy love so shed abroad in us by thy Holy Spirit, that we may continually seek the things which are above; and, abiding in purity of heart and mind, may at length attain unto thine everlasting kingdom, there to dwell in the glorious light of thy presence, world without end. Amen.

Theme: Failure's Loss.

TEXT: "Neither did Asher drive out the inhabitants of Accho." Judg. 1:31.

INTRODUCTORY: At first thought there does not seem to be much in this text except the Asherites' failure to do what was expected of them. But there is much more. The Children of Israel were commanded to drive out the inhabitants of the Promised Land and have nothing to do with them, their gods or their customs. Almost all the tribes of Israel failed to take full possession of the land which God had given. They allowed the inhabitants to remain —some of them as servants, or slaves, some of them as tributary peoples, and some of them as independent peoples. Also, sad to relate, the Israelites often imitated them and fell into their evil ways morally and spiritually.

Much of the history of Israel is made up of falling away, then suffering the punishment, then repenting, coming back to God, and his delivering them out of their distresses. Our text gives an instance where the failure of one tribe was worse than of others. "Neither did Asher drive out the inhabitants of Accho."

I. Consider, first, what they missed.

1. They missed possessing a wonderful seaport. It was a seaport so important that it has been fought for for centuries. It was the key to Galilee. Assyrians fought for it. Arabs fought for it. Egyptians fought for it. Later Turks fought for it, England at one time helping them. Napoleon fought for it, failed and had to leave Palestine in consequence. The Asherites missed a seaport that they really might have had.

2. They therefore missed a wonderful opportunity of easy communication with all the then known world. They could have become a great seafaring nation, but they drove not out the heathen inhabitants of Accho.

3. They missed opportunity for the wealth their ships might have brought from many parts of the world. Instead they remained perhaps one of the poorest of the tribes of Israel.

4. They also lost the opportunity for fame that this strategic position might have given them.

II. Not only did the Asherites fail in grasping wonderful opportunities and advantages; but their failure brought great evils. Their failure left an enemy within which is the worst kind of an enemy. You can guard against an outside enemy; but who can guard against an inside, ever-present enemy? Accho was a continual thorn in the Israelites' sides, a continual danger, a continual worry, and worst of all a continual tempter. The gods of Accho were ever a snare unto Asher, for Asher bowing before the gods of the inhabitants provoked the Lord to anger. I think Asher's history and the history of the world would have been far different had Asher grasped the opportunity and driven out the inhabitants of Accho.

But, friends, as I study Asher's failure and mourn because of it, the thought comes to me that many of us make similar failure. God has given us opportunity to possess boundless blessings. But we fail of possession because we fail to drive out some evil from our life, some pet sin, some enemy that would dwell in our heart-land where God only should dwell. God has promised great blessings if we drive the enemy from our hearts; but because of lack of purpose, or of faith, or of love for an unsurrendered sin, we fail to drive out the intruder and we miss the supremest good.

III. Now, yet more important, note what we miss when we compromise as Asher did. We miss communion with God. We miss communion with God's people. By not driving out sin and self we lose fame—the only fame worth while, that of being known as the children of God. Enoch was famous because he "walked with God." Abraham was famous because he was a "friend of God." Moses was famous because God "spake unto Moses face to face as a man speaketh unto his friend." David was famous for "he was a man after God's own heart." These men "drove out the inhabitants of Accho." And we can be famous, in a good sense, if we drive every sin from our hearts.

By failing to drive out sin we fail in the great privilege of being a blessing to the world. Unsaved ourselves, we cannot save others, or work to that end. Uncleansed ourselves, we cannot lead others to the cleansing Fountain. Unvictorious ourselves, we cannot tell others how to be victorious.

Do we wish to be spiritually useful? This can be only when sin is out and God is in.—Henry G. C. Hallock, PH.D., missionary in China.

THEME PRAYER: We bow before thee, O God, with our hearts full of sorrow, our souls stabbed with pain. How often we have been untrue to the dream, disobedient unto the vision. Forgive us and lift again that which is high before our eyes. We will wait. We will listen. We will obey. Amen.—M. K. W. H.

OFFERTORY SENTENCE: "God so loved the world, that he gave his only begotten Son, that whosoever believeth in him should not perish, but have everlasting life."

OFFERTORY PRAYER: For life we thank thee, O God, and for all that life does for us and in us when we submit to thy will. We would not conform unto the world, we would be transformed that we may prove what is the good and acceptable will of God. Bless us and the offerings we bring this day. In the name of Christ. Amen.—M. K. W. H.

Illustrative Material

SEED THOUGHTS, HOMILETIC AND EXPOSITORY. Forsaking the Lord's Work: The tribes did not fail because they had begun imprudently, but because they did not continue believingly. I. Men forsaking a work which had been begun after long preparation. II. Men forsaking a work which had already been prosecuted with great energy and at great cost. III. Men forsaking a work about which they had cherished ardent hopes. IV. Men forsaking a work in which they had already won splendid triumphs. V. Men forsaking a work to which God had commanded them, in which he had marvelously helped them and in which he no less waited to help them still. They did not "remember the years of the right hand of the Most High." "They forgot his works."

—F. G. M.

Choice Illustrations on the Theme

NOT AT HOME. One day Fortune knocked at a fellow's door. But the fellow wasn't at home. He was over at his neighbor's across the street telling a hard-luck story.

BUT ONE TRIP. Standing by the railroad I watched the postmaster as he hung out the bag to be caught by the mail express soon to pass. A few minutes after and the train came thundering round the curve. The mail agent looked out of his car, and then, thrusting out an iron arm attached to the side of it, snatched the bag, and the train sped on its way. So God is hanging out opportunities along the pathway of our lives. If we are alert and watchful, we may appropriate them for the glory of God and the advancing of his kingdom. If we are careless and indifferent, we pass them by, and they are lost to us forever, as we make but one trip on this line.—*Sunday School Chronicle.*

GRAINS FALL THROUGH. Many do with opportunities as children do at the seashore; they fill their little hands with sand, and then let the grains fall through,, one by one, till all are gone. —Rev. T. Jones.

OPPOSITE THE PORT. The Rev. Frank Fox tells of a foggy day spent on the ocean on one of the great liners. Cautiously, throughout the entire day they crept along to the mournful sounding of the foghorn, until 6:00 P.M. At that hour the fog lifted for just three minutes and the captain found that they were opposite the port. But some of the men were not at their posts, and before they reported for duty the fog had again fallen and a whole night of peril followed just outside the harbor.

LOST OPPORTUNITIES. A minister, passing a big department store, followed a sudden impulse to go in and talk to the proprietor on the subject of his salvation. Finding him, he said, "Mr. T., I've talked beds and carpets and bookcases with you, but I've never talked my business with you. Would you give me a few minutes to do so?" Being led to the private office, the minister took out his New Testament and "preached unto him Jesus." After some conversation the storekeeper said to the minister, "I'm seventy years of age. I was born in this city, and more than five hundred church officers have known me as you have, but in all these years you are the only man who ever spoke to me about my soul."—*New Century Leader.*

EVENING SERVICE

Theme: Effectual Help.

TEXT: "Grace to help in time of need." Heb. 4:16.

INTRODUCTORY: There are two kinds of causes—instrumental and immediate causes (or proximate causes, as they are sometimes called) and ultimate causes, generally spoken of as effective causes. When a baseball bat strikes a ball, the bat is the proximate or instrumental cause, but the arm of the player, or rather his will, is the effective cause. The words "effective" and "effectual" are synoynmous.

I. There is the story of a lame beggar at the temple gate. Seeing two men approach he asked alms, exposing a distorted foot. One of the men said: "We have no money, but we have power to heal you. In the name of Jesus Christ of Nazareth, rise up and walk." Looking down the beggar saw he had been cured, and rose up and walked. If the apostles had given him the alms he asked that would have been immediate help. But when they gave him a good ankle, power to help himself, they gave him effectual help.

II. Jesus Christ came to the world to give help to the needy race. There is little difference between the words "saviour" and "helper." "Mighty to save" means "mighty to help." But Jesus Christ has a method in saving—in helping. He is an effectual helper. In this he is like God—he is ever the Godlike Christ.

III. Here is a man in trouble. He is in debt or in need. Creditors are pressing. He prays for help. If God will only send him money now, he will be grateful. Perhaps God does send him money. That has happened many a time. But it does not always happen. Suppose it does not happen. Suppose, instead, God permits him to suffer, and in a sudden access of wisdom the man sees there are other methods of meeting the demands, or with desperate courage he goes to work to earn the money he needs. Or, he fails—compromises with his creditors. There is many an honest bankrupt. Then slowly he goes to work to rebuild his fortune. As time passes, he sees his failure was a blessing; he has learned a valuable lesson.

IV. He is a better man because once he failed. Is it not possible to see the effectual help of God in that sudden access of wisdom or in that wonderful exercise of courage, or in the fine spirit in which the man rebuilt upon the ruins of an old business the structure of a better? Instrumental help would have solved a temporary problem, but effectual help solves a problem that is lifelong, and that may be eternity-long. —C. C. A.

Suggestive Texts and Themes

An Error in Accounting: "Ye have said, It is vain to serve the God." Mal. 3:14.

Through Grief to Grace: "For the Lord will not cast off for ever: but though he cause grief, yet will he have compassion according to the multitude of his mercies." Lam. 3:31, 32.

The Living and Giving Christ: "I am the living bread which came down from heaven: if any man eat of this bread, he shall live for ever: and the bread that I will give is my flesh, which I will give for the life of the world." John 6:51.

The Wasted Years: "I will restore to you the years that the locust hath eaten . . . my great army which I sent among you." Joel 2:25.

The Gift of the Unattainable: "I will give him the morning star." Rev. 2:28.

MIDWEEK FELLOWSHIP MEETING TOPIC

(Church Night or Suggested Sermon Subject)

Theme: Holy Ground.

TEXT: "The place whereon thou standest is holy ground." Ex. 3:5.

I. When God wants leaders, he finds them in the places of their faithful toil. Moses led his flock on the hills of Midian, as a preparation for leading the people of the Lord. Saul was to find a kingdom, when he was looking for his flock.

II. Yet work alone will not suffice. Above the labor there must be a certain mood. If that condition be not present, the workers become mere drudges. Moses knew how to tend the flock, but he knew more. God found his leader in the desert, a man who listened to the divine voice and had a genius for "holy ground." In such a man the divine fire always glows without being consumed.

III. There is always an advantage in solitude. In Michelangelo's palace in Florence, your guide leads you across the salon to what appears a blank wall. He touches a covered button and a panel swings out. A small cell in the wall is revealed. It is lighted by a slim window, and is furnished with a wooden stool, and a shelf set aslant against the wall. There Michelangelo was alone with God, and his high ideals—on "holy ground." It was there he worked out how to swing the Pantheon in the air, and to give us the dome of St. Peter's. There he learned to limn the statue of David, and to spread such glories on the Sistine ceiling as make its common plaster more precious than gold. Great are the gains of solitude. What the artist had in Florence the Lawgiver had in Horeb.—W. S. S.

CHRISTIAN ENDEAVOR SOCIETY TOPIC

Oct. 24. A Channel of Thy Peace (World Order Sunday). Luke 8:23-26; Matt. 15:24-27.

SUNDAY SCHOOL LESSON

Oct. 24. Making Home Life Successful. Prov. 4:1-4; 6:20-23; 19:13-14; 31:10-12.

MEMORY VERSE: "My son, keep the commandment of thy father, and forsake not the law of thy mother." Prov. 6:20 (A.S.V.).

Christian love is learned. "The home is a natural setting for love. Established by two lovers who pledge their faith in each other and take vows to hold love forever sacred, whose daily tasks are services of love one to another —here if anywhere love can be learned."

"Learning is present from birth; and any human capacity, whether to love or to hate, is learned by seeking goals with other persons. . . . Children learn to love by receiving and participating in a family or group where Christian attitudes of kindness, tender care, faithful service, forgiving and reconciling, acceptance, unfailing interest, honest appreciation, and sustaining responsibility predominate."—Quotations from *Christian Love* by Paul E. Johnson.

SUNDAY: OCTOBER THIRTY-FIRST

MORNING SERVICE

Theme: A Child of the Reformation (Reformation Sunday).

SUGGESTED SCRIPTURE READING: Rom. 8:1-17, 31-39.

SELECTED HYMNS: "A mighty fortress is our God."—Martin Luther. "Arm those, thy soldiers, mighty Lord."— C. Wordsworth. "Rejoice, ye pure in heart."—E. H. Plumptre. "Just as I am, without one plea."—C. Elliott. "Onward, Christian soldiers."—S. Baring-Gould.

CALL TO WORSHIP: "He that cometh to God must believe that he is, and that he is a rewarder of them that diligently seek him."

CALL TO WORSHIP (non-Biblical): "Faith means trust. Trust is the act, in which a man may rely upon the faithfulness of Another, that His promise holds and that what He demands He demands of necessity. 'I believe' means 'I trust.' I believe not in myself; I believe in God."

INVOCATION PRAYER: In Thee, O God, we put our trust. Unto thee as Sovereign Will we come that we may render fuller obedience. Unto thee as Holy Love we come that we may satisfy the needs of our hearts. And unto thee as Sacrificial Servant we come that our sins may be forgiven and that we may have peace. And when we go forth from this house may it be as witnesses and ambassadors of Christ the great revealer of thyself to us. Teach us this day the greater and deeper lessons of life. From little faith lead us to great faith. In pain or suffering, in disappointment or loss, release the hero in our souls. By larger trust may we find serenity of spirit. Help us to acknowledge thee in all our ways. Direct thou our paths. In Jesus' name. Amen.— M. K. W. H.

Theme: A Child of the Reformation (Reformation Sunday).

TEXT: "The house of Jacob shall possess their possessions." Obad. 1:17.

On the 31st day of October, 1517, Martin Luther nailed upon the door of the Castle Church at Wittenberg in Germany a document which contained ninety-five Theses concerning indulgences. He did this in defiance of the Pope in Rome. Thomas Carlyle in a stirring and dramatic chapter states that the whole world and its history was waiting for this man and this act. Elsewhere he declares that "the moment in which Martin Luther defied the wrath of the Diet of Worms was the greatest moment in the modern history of men." Luther's courageous act is being celebrated on this Reformation Sunday throughout the Protestant world.

What we are and what we think and do and believe is to a great extent a heritage. It is something that has been handed down to us. We have most likely a Protestant heritage. If it is a good heritage we should appreciate it. If is is a valuable heritage we should hold it in trust. If it is a worthy heritage we should pass it on to our children and our children's children. If it is a heritage which holds human destiny we should weigh it and, if not found wanting, give it to our fellow man. If it is a divine heritage then it should be treasured as the greatest possession of our souls. Let us possess our possession.

I. A a child of the Reformation I have a heritage of truth to possess, and I am free to possess it.

We are not now thinking of any dogma that has been laid down by the Reformation or any Reformer or any Reformation Church saying, "This is the truth, you must believe it." Before truth becomes dogmatic it must be submitted to the highest criticism it is possible to give it and each of us has the right to engage in the criticism. As a child of the Reformation I have a heritage of truth which I am free to arrive at, possess and cherish without the stultification of my own mind and without the denial of my own conscience. If there is truth to be found I have the right to discover it wherever it is to be found.

As a child of the Reformation I am not kept in ignorance. It was through the influence largely of Martin Luther that the Bible was placed in the hands of the common people of Europe and by that into my hands and yours, and through the influence of the Bible societies into the hands of people speaking more than a thousand different languages. You may not accept the Bible as truth or as containing truth but there it is—at least you have no excuse for being ignorant of what it says. Nor as a child of the Reformation are you denied the right to read the Hindu sacred books, nor the Koran, nor the Analects of Confucius. Let truth be discovered, let it be weighed by the reason to find out whether it is genuine. Truth that one is forbidden to test is thrown into doubt.

As a child of the Reformation I am not kept in ignorance by the Bull of any pope or by any Canon Law or by any index of prohibited books. My mind is not pushed into a medieval mold; it can reach out with wonder and experiment and explore to discover and appreciate and use any truth that appears.

As a child of the Reformation I am not steeped in superstition. Almost every influence of the Protestant church has been to deliver its members from the stultifying effects of superstitious practice.

In the Church of the Lateran in Rome people creep up the Lateran staircase on their knees with the expectation of receiving indulgence or acquiring merit. These steps are said to be those of Pilate's staircase miraculously transported from Jerusalem to Rome. It was from this staircase that Martin Luther arose when the words came to his mind, "The just shall live by faith." He arose out of the superstition of medievalism into the free inquiry of a new day.

III. As a child of the Reformation I have a heritage of grace to accept and I am free to accept it. By grace I mean the mercy, the loving-kindness, the steadfast love of God offered unto me freely to meet my soul's need.

Let us glory in the fact that the grace of God is immediate—it is always right here in time and place. Let me sin, as I do, and forgiveness can be accepted immediately if I have a contrite heart. No hocus-pocus, no magic, no human intermediary is necessary to secure this blessing.

We glory in the fact that the grace of God for the forgiveness of sin rests in Christ himself. No one holds a receptacle of merit which can be turned on or off like a water faucet.

We glory in the fact that any person can pray for us and that prayer can be used by God as a channel of grace to meet our soul's need. In this matter of grace we rejoice in the priesthood of all believers as taught by the Apostle Peter.

Grace is free. That grace which shall bring one into the presence of God with exceeding great joy is not to be bought and paid for, nor does one's rapid progress into the presence of God depend upon any payments.

We rejoice that grace is abundant. It is not limited. Or as stated in the scripture, "My grace is sufficient for thee." It is strange that both Martin Luther and John Wesley had difficulties with that text. It seems almost absurd now. The trouble was that they put a period at the wrong place. They thought of the text as "My grace is sufficient," period. Martin Luther believed implicitly and preached confidently that Christ died for all mankind, long before he could persuade himself that Christ died for Martin Luther. John Wesley crossed the Atlantic that he might proclaim the forgiveness of sins to the Indians of America; but it was not until he was verging on middle life that he adequately realized the possibility of the forgiveness of his own.

III. As a child of the Reformation I have a heritage of love to experience and I am free to love in return.

Martin Luther's great text was, "The just shall live by faith." That's right —faith in the love of God. That is the life of trust.

I once visited a home where an aged woman was facing death. I discovered her to be troubled and I think that I brought her some comfort and peace. How did I do that? I quoted the 23rd Psalm. I used the words of Jesus, "Come unto me. . . . Ye believe in God, believe also in me. . . . Peace I leave with you, my peace I give unto you. . . . Lo, I am with you always. . . . Then I said, "God is faithful. God is love! God loves you!" There was a heritage of love which she could experience.

"God so loved. . . . Greater love has no man. . . . The love of God is perfect . . . and perfect love casteth out fear."

Such love I can return, not in the same measure, not in the same degree, but in kind—"We love because he first loved us." In this spirit we worship not in fear. We worship not because worship is imposed upon us. We worship in spontaneous reaction to the love of God who first loved us.

And so I give; truly it would be much cheaper to buy masses and charms, I could get them much cheaper than I pay Sabbath after Sabbath into my church treasury. But I do not give to buy, nor under any compulsion; my giving is a free, open expression of my faith and love.

This heritage of which we have spoken, a heritage of truth, of grace and of love, is opened to us by our own free acts. We have a heritage of freedom. Freedom is the key word. Freedom is the thrilling word. This freedom is a heritage which carries obligation to transmit it, extend it, and oppose the forces that threaten it.

Prayer. Almighty God, whose power is free, whose power is superior to all other powers, whose power is love activated and revealed in Jesus Christ, we rejoice that we can affirm, "We believe in God the Father Almighty!" We rejoice in the words of Scripture which we have read—"Who shall separate us from the love of Christ? shall tribulation, or distress, or persecution, or famine, or nakedness, or peril, or sword? . . . Nay, in all these things we are more than conquerors through him that loved us."

Help us, O God, to transmute our faith into trust. Thus in our days of restlessness may we find peace, in our days of ignorance find wisdom, after sinful thought and deed find for-

He was a good man, and full

giveness, in our sorrow find comfort, in every experience of life find meaning, and in death find life.

Help us to transmute our faith and trust into good works. May the everyday and necessary things be done, not from a drab and dull sense of duty, but with appreciation and meaning as we relate them to the welfare of others and the service of God. May we undertake the great works which prove that we we have a great and living faith. By faith and works, O Lord, may we build thy kingdom, transmit a rich heritage to our children, establish the nation in justice and righteousness and secure the peace of the world. In Jesus' name. Amen.

Illustrative Material

Obadiah 1:17, the text of the preceding sermon, might be used with Ephesians 1:3-14 as listing the "spiritual blessings," v. 3, which the Christian may possess: holiness, sonship, our redemption, the mystery of his will, ourselves become a heritage, v. 11.

The house of Jacob shall possess its own possessions, not the possessions of Edom and of the heathen. "When the children of Israel shall have returned from exile God will, at the same time, restore to them their ancient country, so as for them to possess whatever had been promised to their father Abraham."—Calvin.

Choice Illustrations on the Theme

THE ONE FREEDOM. I know but one freedom and that is the freedom of the mind. As for any other freedom, it is but a mockery and a delusion, for however free you may think yourself, you have to use the door when you go out of the room, nor are you free to make yourself young at will or to profit by the sun at night.—Antoine de Saint-Exupéry.

LUTHER'S THESIS. "That if the Pope has the power for a paltry sum of money to redeem souls from purgatory, he ought on account of most holy charity and the utmost need of souls, to empty purgatory."

"MY GRACE IS SUFFICIENT FOR THEE." "Why, I said to myself, I should think it is!" and I burst out laughing. I never understood what the holy laughter of Abraham was like until then. It seemed to make unbelief absurd. It was as though some little fish being very thirsty was troubled about drinking the river dry; and Father Thames said, "Drink away, little fish, my stream is sufficient for thee." Or as if a little mouse in the granaries of Egypt, after seven years of plenty, feared lest it die of famine, and Joseph said, "Cheer up, little mouse; my granaries are sufficient for thee!" Again I imagined a man away up yonder on the mountains saying to himself: "I fear I shall exhaust all the oxygen in the atmosphere." But the earth cries, "Breathe away, O man, and fill thy lungs; my atmosphere is sufficient for thee."—Charles Spurgeon.

DEVOTION AND SUPERSTITION. "It is not easy to draw the line between devotion and superstition, but there are places at home and abroad where devotions are practiced and promoted as a means to gather money. . . . Catholics are ashamed and non-catholics are horrified. It is a crime to gather money—even to build a church—at such a cost to real religion. . . . The use of relics is of course approved by the Church. In that use we profess unqualified faith, but we do loath, despise and condemn the contemptible practice of applying the relic with one hand and collecting money with the other."—Monsignor ———.

EVENING SERVICE

Theme: The Portrait of a Christian.

TEXT: "He was a good man, and full of the Holy Ghost and of faith." Acts 11:24.

INTRODUCTORY: Our text gives us the materials for a portrait: "He was a good man, and full of the Holy Ghost and of faith." A good man! What a fine testimonial that is! Barnabas was a good man, and his goodness expressed itself in all his actions.

I. The first thing reported of him is an act of great generosity. Barnabas had that kind of goodness. He could not see another in want while he had something to give him. So he sold his farm and laid the money at the feet of the apostles for distribution. He did not even seek the glory of distributing it himself.

II. But that was not the only kind of goodness he had. He was one of those lovely people who are always eager to see the best in everybody and with insight enough to discern between the genuine and the insincere. So when the young church was afraid of Saul "Barnabas took him, and brought him to the apostles, and declared unto them how he had seen the Lord in the way." When he saw that he was genuine he stood by him without asking whether it would be popular or not.

III. When the church in Jerusalem wanted to get a sound report of the work that was beginning in Antioch, it was Barnabas they sent. With that clear vision that belongs to those who are free from jealousy and self-seeking, Barnabas immediately saw that the work at Antioch was the real thing. But he knew he had not the gifts that were needed for the difficult work in Antioch, and he also knew someone who had. "So Barnabas went off to Tarsus to look for Saul, and on finding him he brought him to Antioch." The work of God was always first with Barnabas; he considered it and never considered himself at all.

IV. Barnabas was a good man. He was capable and sane; he had personality; there was nothing sour or shady in his life; there was no skeleton in his closet; he was always patient, always kind; never jealous, never snobbish, never rude. Barnabas was never glad when others went wrong. He was always gladdened by goodness. He was always eager to believe the best about everybody, always hopeful about everybody, always patient with everybody. He was a good man; and no man is good who is not in sympathy with his fellow men, who has not a largehearted tolerance for their weaknesses and failures and a passionate interest in their welfare.

V. Barnabas was a good man plus. He was a good man and full of the Holy Ghost and faith. What was that extra? He was not just a good man; he was a man of God; and when he came to your door you felt God had come there too.

Barnabas was like that. He was a good man, in the widest sense of that great word. But he was more than that. He was a man in whom God lived. That was why the apostles called him the Son of Encouragement. You just could not go near him without being helped, renewed, restored. If you were in the depths of discouragement and failure, and you met Barnabas, you left him with your head high and your eyes shining, believing that life was worth while and that you would make something lovely out of it yet. He radiated encouragement and life and hope and power and love, because God was in him.—J. M.

Suggestive Texts and Themes

Mysterious Failure in Character: "A righteous man falleth seven times, and riseth up again." Prov. 24:16 (A.S.V.).

The Abdication of Self: "I have been crucified with Christ; and it is no longer I that live, but Christ liveth in me: and that life which I now live in the flesh I live in faith, the faith which is in the Son of God, who loved me, and gave himself up for me." Gal. 2:20.

The Uncrowned Queen of Moral Courage: "But the queen Vashti refused to come at the king's commandment by the chamberlains." Esther 1:12.

Threefold Deliverance: "For thou hast delivered my soul from death, mine eyes from tears, and my feet from falling." Ps. 116:8.

The Impossible Purchase: "But Peter said unto him, thy money perish with thee, because thou has thought that the gift of God may be purchased with money." Acts 8:20.

MIDWEEK FELLOWSHIP MEETING TOPIC

(Church Night or Suggested Sermon Subject)

Theme: **Living in the Divine Presence.** Text: "That those things which cannot be shaken may remain." Heb. 12:27.

Eighteen centuries have passed since these words were written. What changes have taken place in these years! Christianity has passed through ages of mysticism, dogmatism, reform and evangelism. There is a "spiral movement" in history. We come back where we started, but we are higher than when we started. Each succeeding form carries with it that which is best in the form below.

I. Many modern Christians believe in the possibility of a living, present, personal friendship with God through Christ. A recent writer, meditating upon the pathetic inquiry of the Master, "Could ye not watch with me an hour?" writes:

Yea, Lord, and I will watch with Thee
Throughout the night,
Till dawns the morning light,
Whilst Thou are praying for the world and me.

My night approaches—my Gethsemane;
Deep falls the shade,
But I am not afraid,
For lo, Thou watchest through the dark with me.

II. A conviction of Christ's reality and of his presence with us is characteristic of the faith of the present age. It is an age of uncertainty about many things, an age of change, an age of shifting emphasis—but what of that? The things which cannot be shaken remain.

III. We have Christ. We are sure of him, and all things else essential are sure because of him. We are sure of God and immortality and redemption. "How shall he not freely with him give us all things?"—C. C. A.

CHRISTIAN ENDEAVOR SOCIETY TOPIC

Oct. 31. Luther, the Reformer. Matt. 3:7-12.

SUNDAY SCHOOL LESSON

Oct. 31. **The Dignity of Work.** Proverbs 6:6-11; 18:9; 24:30-34.

Memory Verse: "Seest thou a man diligent in his business? he shall stand before kings; he shall not stand before mean men." Prov. 22:29.

Dr. John H. Jowett pointed out that "our Lord throws a halo over common toil." We recall that the angels' visit at the time of the birth was to the shepherds in the fields. "The very birth-hour of Christianity irradiated the humble doings of humble people. . . . Common work was encircled with an immortal crown."

It is good to remember that Jesus learned the trade of carpenter and followed this as his vocation during the years of his young manhood.

In the upper room "he took a towel, and girded himself, . . . and began to wash the disciples' feet." He did not disparage humble services. He has given us an example. When a man begins to despise the "towel" he is losing his kingly dignity.

SUNDAY: NOVEMBER SEVENTH

MORNING SERVICE

Theme: God's Ideal for Nations (Armistice Day).

SUGGESTED SCRIPTURE READING: Ps. 46:1-11.

SELECTED HYMNS: "Let there be light, Lord God of Hosts."—W. M. Vories. "O Zion haste, thy mission high fulfilling."—M. A. Thomson. "We've a story to tell to the nations."—C. Sterne. "In Christ there is no East nor West."—J. Oxenham. "Jesus shall reign where'er the sun."—I. Watts. "O God of love, O King of peace."—H. W. Baker.

CALL TO WORSHIP: "Glory to God in the highest, and on earth peace, good will toward men." "Blessed are the peacemakers, for they shall be called sons of God."

INVOCATION PRAYER: Almighty God, who holdeth the world in the hollow of thy hand, who setteth the bounds of the nations, who causeth the earth to clothe itself with loveliness and fruitfulness, Creator of us all, our hearts are restless until they rest in thee. May thy greatness be unto our smallness as the great ocean unto the little boats that ply upon it; lift us up and set us free for usefulness and venture. In thee we live and move and have our being.

Yet teach us, our Father, that in coming unto thee we come unto One with mind and heart and will, whose thought and love and purpose is toward us, thy children. In such knowledge we come unto thee today to receive thy wisdom, to experience thy love, to follow thy guidance. We come, too, as suppliants for grace. Grant unto us forgiveness of our sins and comfort in our sorrows. In our weakness may we become strong

and in the midst of tribulation may we have peace.

We turn our minds, O Lord, unto our country and pray for its welfare. May our President do justly, love mercy, and walk humbly with thee. Bless with wisdom and vision all who hold office in our land. May every citizen find opportunity in his daily task to build a better state and establish here thy kingdom.

As we approach the anniversary of the armistice of the World War we bow in repentance before thee; our hearts are burdened with our shame; because we planted the grapes of wrath which brought forth another war. Forgive all humanity; forgive us all together; forgive each one. Deliver us, O God. In days of old thou wast a God of deliverance; deliver us in our day, O Lord. We ask in Jesus' name. Amen. —M.

Theme: God's Ideal for Nations (Armistice Day).

TEXT: "Nebuchadnezzar the king, unto all people, nations, and languages, that dwell in all the earth; Peace be multiplied unto you," etc. Dan. 4:1-3.

INTRODUCTORY: War boasts many monuments. On the Acropolis at Athens there is a temple of Victory commemorating Marathon and other battles won by Greek soldiers. In Rome the Forum has no nobler ruins of the empire than its triumphant arches erected in celebration of successful battles. Higher than the pylons of Karnak whose margnificent temple was designated "the throne of the world" are the granite obelisks in memory of Pharaoh and his brown-skinned warriors who ruled Egypt several millenniums ago. And if this history is too ancient, you will find similar monuments depicting martial glory in the main isle of the Cathedral of Notre Dame in Paris, on the pavements and on every wall of Westminster Abbey, and in both the castle and the cathedral of Edinburgh. Walk around our own national capitol, read the inscriptions on the gallery, of greatness in the capitol building itself, and we can see that our own country is not lax in lauding national heroes and commemorating victorious battles.

I. But peace has few memorials. There is one notable monument high apart from civilization and seen by few travelers, "Christ of the Andes." A most beautiful, immortalized sermon on peace in stone, depicting the Man of peace.

II. In a moral universe, ruled over by a great God, no question is settled finally until it is settled right. For the nations to be at peace among themselves means that wrongs, national and international, must be earnestly, intelligently and fully righted. A civilization that could permit such colossal calamities as World Wars I and II has little to boast of.

III. If we are to cast civilization into a new mold we must come to a new will to peace. Disarmament must come, but disarmament is not enough. You will never bring peace by the negative process of destroying military equipment. You can no more bring in a lasting peace by scrapping battleships and fortifications than you can make a weedless garden by destroying the hoe and the harrow. War is a matter of the soul. Disarmament is largely a state of mind. I fear that we have been too much concerned about the machinery for peace and not the desire for it. We are overmuch concerned about the technique for a warless world rather than the triumph of an age of peace. Do not misunderstand me. There is place for the machinery of peace, but it does not come first. What is the use of making a machine if there is nothing to produce? If war is a matter of the soul, then the soul must be built to the will to peace.

IV. No prayer has been prayed more often since the day of the prophet Isaiah than the prayer for peace. No hope has been so strong in the soul of man as the hope that one day earth may realize the glory song sung by angels in the Syrian night sky over the plains of Bethlehem: "Peace on earth." Yet so little has come of it. For every one year of peace the would has had thirteen years of war.

Why is that prayer so slow of fulfillment and why is that hope so late in coming? It is because we have not willed peace. The church will truly honor the nation's soldier dead, and its soldiers living, by dedicating itself to the great enterprise of ending war. Our ex-soldiers themselves will respond to this note. They do not glorify war. They loathe and hate it. And they will honor the church that rejects war as a way of settling international differences. Here are two stanzas written by E. D. Schonberger entitled "The Great Armistice":

The joy that leaped into thy waiting
    sight
From that wee bit of swaddling prophecy
When thou didst lift it on thy eager
    hands,
Is but a gleam to that transcendent light
That bursts my heart and loosens all the
    bands
Which bind me to the earth. I, too,
    have seen,
O ancient Simeon, and sing with thee:
    "Nunc Dimittis!"

Long ages have I carried on my breast:
Not only these last years of misery,
But all the years since Jesus heard thy
    song—
Dark bloody years, by bloody kings
    oppressed.
They seem to crush me with their load
    of wrong,
Today, they say, all strife is at an end!
I, too, have prayed, and now I sing with
    thee:
    "Nunc Dimittis!"

THEME PRAYER: In faith we set our eyes upon thee, O God. We see thee in the face of Christ. We know thee through the ministry of thy Holy Spirit. As we behold Jesus crowned with glory and honor we pray for the subjection of all things unto him. We await the day when the whole earth shall be covered with the knowledge of the Lord as the waters cover the sea. Inspire us to do our duties in the world and leave our destinies with thee. May we find a sense of victory in lifting up our hearts unto thee, and there, too, our forgiveness, our joy and our peace. Amen.—M.

OFFERTORY SENTENCE: "Vow and pay unto the Lord your God."

OFFERTORY PRAYER: Forgive us, our Father, that in our vain restlessness we have sought so much other than peace and pity us in that we have so sadly failed as we have sought it. Grant us wisdom, faith and courage to seek it anew and in thine own good time win it for ourselves and all men. These things we pray as we bring our offerings to help bring in thy kingdom in all the earth. We ask in the name of Christ. Amen.

Illustrative Material

SEED THOUGHTS, HOMILETIC AND EXPOSITORY. "How great are his signs! and how mighty are his wonders!" Dan. 4:3. Man touching the inexpressible. I. All true religious exaltation is overpowering. II. No religion is complete that does not simply defy the believer to tell what it is in all its scope, in all its indications, in all its exalting enthusiasms. III. We are the better for those great billows of enthusiasm which roll through the soul. It does us good to be brought into the sanctuary of the unutterable.

"His kingdom is an everlasting kingdom." Dan. 4:3. I. God's kingdom is perfectly distinct from all the kingdoms of this world. Compare Nebuchadnezzar's. II. It is a kingdom that has always been advancing, according to the absolute sovereignty of God's own will. III. It is a grace kingdom. It has privileges for all its subjects. IV. It is a kingdom of unchangeable character.

Choice Illustrations on the Theme

ARE WE GOD'S SONS? The other day a great dirigible floated over our city. It was so beautiful in the sunlight that we forgot it was built to drop bombs, and not bouquets. Suppose Jesus had been in command of it and released its burden of death upon the men and women and little children below? Would the heavens have opened and a voice declared, "This is my beloved Son in whom I am well pleased"? And is there reason to suppose the Father would be better pleased if the bombs were dropped by any of his other sons? And would it make any difference to him whether they fell on New York or Boston or Berlin or Tokyo or Peking? —Harold Marshall.

WHY

The men of the earth said, "We must arm,
For so we would reveal
The nobler part of the human heart,
The love of the nation's weal."
But they who had sung their lullaby,
The mothers of men, they answered,
"Why?"

AN ARMISTICE DAY PRAYER. O God of peace, unite in a dream of brotherhood all those who worship thee. Begin with ourselves. Take from our hearts enmity and strife, and give us the humility which is fitting to thy sons. Help us so to control our economic life that the pressure for profits shall not triumph over the ideals of Christian service. Supplant the intolerance of nationalism with a program of brotherly affection. Give us courage to support our convictions. Consecrate our lives to the coming of thy kingdom. And may grace, mercy and peace be multiplied to all men and nations. We ask in the name of Christ, the Prince of Peace. Amen.

WHAT MAKES A NATION GREAT?

Not serried ranks with flags unfurled,
Not armoured ships that gird the world,
Not hoarded wealth, nor busy mills,
Not cattle on a thousand hills,

Not sages wise, nor schools, nor laws,
Not boasted deeds in freedom's cause—
All these may be, and yet the State
In the eye of God be far from great.

That land is great which knows the
    Lord,
Where songs are guided by His Word,
Where justice rules 'twixt man and man,
Where love controls in act and plan,
Where, breathing in this native air,
Each soul finds joy in praise and
    prayer—
Thus may our country, good and great,
Be God's delight—man's best estate.
                —Alexander Blackburn.

EVENING SERVICE

Theme: The Story of an Unknown Prophet (Armistice Day).

TEXT: "A prophet of the Lord was there, whose name was Oded." II Chron. 28:9.

INTRODUCTORY: Man's inhumanity to man is not new in the world. Read the story, II Chron. 28:1-15. Oded, an almost unknown prophet, lived in the time of the wicked king Ahaz, who brought misfortune and misery on himself and his kingdom of Judah. In a cruel war Syria and Ephraim triumphed over Judah, the Israelites carrying away captive of their brethren "200,000 women, sons, and daughters," along with much spoil. When they reached Samaria with their captives they were suddenly confronted by the prophet Oded, who went forth and addressed not the chiefs alone with whispers of policy, but the whole host in general, great and small. He calls upon them to forego their pleasure of revenge and financial gains and to abstain from reducing to slavery their brethren whom the fortunes of war had put into their power.

I. His argument was striking. He solemnly points out that Judah's defeat is the penalty of her sin. Also that in the slaughter of such immense numbers as they had already put to death they had committed crimes enough, and that

to enslave their brethren would be to provoke the anger of God still more. He called upon them, therefore, to liberate those they had intended to enslave.

II. His single voice prevailed. Alone in making the suggestion Oded is not long left alone. "Certain heads of the children of Ephraim" stood up stoutly against the more violent that opposed Oded's word. They said "Ye shall not bring in the captives hither" with the courage of their nobler mood. Remarkable result. With that openness to generous and noble appeals that sometimes marks a multitude, the whole host suddenly caught the glow of nobler feeling, and at once the resolve to set the captives free was decided upon and put into operation. The treasure of the spoil was used to relieve the captives' needs.

III. An incident of this kind is much too rare. It was too seldom seen, if at all, in the two great World Wars we have passed through. Its occurrence indicates to us how much of noble service might be rendered if all did their part toward making the world a little brighter and better than it is. The several after-the-war "Restoration Funds" were actions in the right direction.

IV. There is a further suggestion here as to the duty and responsibility of leaders. A prophet worthy of his calling, and the chief men of Israel having the courage of their convictions, together swayed the whole people with a generous impulse. No greater mercy could come from our heavenly Father than leaders whose worth adorns their eminence. Generous leaders, even in times of peace, may win results no less noble. Let leaders in Church or State, or in society in general, study this excellent and lonely prophet Oded until they learn, like him, to forego all flattery and all care for popular acceptance and find the stately courage which can urge the worthy cause upon their fellow men.—After R. G.

Suggestive Armistice Day Texts and Themes

War Forbidden. "Thus saith the Lord, Ye shall not go up, nor fight against your brethren." II Chron. 11:4.

A place in the Sun: "I saw an angel [servant of God] standing in the sun." Rev. 19:17.

The Man for the Gap: "I sought for a man among them, that should build up the wall, and stand in the gap before me for the land, that I should not destroy it." Ezek. 22:30 (A.S.V.).

The Ministry of Comfort: "Comfort ye, comfort ye my people, saith your God." Isa. 40:1.

The way of the Brokenhearted: "And they went and told Jesus." Matt. 14:12 (A.S.V.).

The Call to the Colors and the Call to the Cross: "And I, if I be lifted up from the earth, will draw all men unto me." John 12:32.

The Gospel of Good Cheer: "Be of good cheer; it is I; be not afraid." Matt. 14:27.

"There shall be no night." Rev. 21:25.

"Judge not, that ye be not judged." Matt. 7:1.

"God . . . hath made of one blood all nations of men for to dwell on all the face of the earth." Acts 17:26.

"Wherefore putting away lying, speak every man truth with his neighbour: for we are members one of another." Eph. 4:25.

MIDWEEK FELLOWSHIP MEETING TOPIC

(Church Night or Suggested Sermon Subject)

Theme: Concerning the Will of God.

I. We should pray for the knowledge of the will of God: "We . . . do not cease to pray for you, and to desire that ye might be filled with the knowledge of his will in all wisdom and spiritual understanding." Col. 1:9.

II. We should understand the will of God: "Wherefore be ye not unwise, but understanding what the will of the Lord is." Eph. 5:17.

III. We should obey the will of God

with the whole heart: "Not with eyeservice, as men-pleasers; but as the servants of Christ, doing the will of God from the heart." Eph. 6:6.

IV. We should obey the will of God at any cost: "And he went a little farther, and fell on his face, and prayed, saying, O my Father, if it be possible, let this cup pass from me: nevertheless not as I will, but as thou wilt." Matt. 26:39.

BULLETIN BOARD SLOGANS FOR THE MONTH

By EARL RINEY

Charity begins right where you are.

Sweetness of disposition hides a multitude of sins.

"Forget not all his benefits."

The best Thanksgiving is Thanksliving.

Jesus had a message for society as well as for the soul.

Christianity is religion at its deepest and most universal.

Plant life's furrows with the seeds of thanksgiving.

He who loves God most loves his creatures most.

"The things which are seen are temporal." Look beyond today!

Argument thrives where facts are scarce.

Make up your mind to do the thing you dream of doing.

He who deserves nothing should be content with anything.

He who grumbles picks his own pocket.

It takes many a load of earth to bury the truth.

To sweeten your morsel share it.

CHRISTIAN ENDEAVOR SOCIETY TOPIC

Nov. 7. Tyndale, the Translator. Luke 1:1-4; Rev. 1:9-11.

SUNDAY SCHOOL LESSON

Nov. 7. The Splendor of Self-control.

Prov. 14:29; 15:1-3; 16:32; 20:1; 23:29-35.

MEMORY VERSE: He that is slow to anger is better than the mighty; and he that ruleth his spirit than he that taketh a city. Prov. 16:32.

For an example of *magnificent control* study David in his fight with the giant Goliath. A little girl made comment concerning David. "He used only one stone."

There are three types of man that need magnificent control. I. The man of bad temper. Bringing temper under control gives a man meekness. One scholarly authority assures us that the Greek word used in the Gospels and translated "meekness" describes "a colt which was broken in and harnessed. It was once a wild horse careening over the waste, and now it is disciplined for service. Its strength is not reduced; but its real value has been developed."

II. The man of inordinate desire. Joseph's control when he was in the house of Potiphar is magnificent. The lesson has much to say about control over the self when tempted to drink intoxicants.

III. The man with fear in his heart. Consider Nehemiah when he said, "Should such a man as I flee?"

No man should despair of himself. "The finding of the man in you is one of the glorious capacities of the Gospel of Christ."

SUNDAY: NOVEMBER FOURTEENTH

MORNING SERVICE

Theme: The Joy of the Lord (Financial Canvass).

SUGGESTED SCRIPTURE READING: Mal. 1:6-14; II Cor. 9:1-9.

SELECTED HYMNS: "Saviour, thy dying love."—S. D. Phelps. "We give thee but thine own."—W. W. How. "O Lord of heaven and earth and sea."—C. Wordsworth. "O God of mercy, God of might."—G. Thring. "Soldiers of the cross, arise."—W. W. How.

CALL TO WORSHIP: "Seeing then that we have a great high priest, that is passed into the heavens, Jesus the Son of God: . . . Let us therefore come boldly unto the throne of grace, that we may obtain mercy, and find grace to help in time of need."

INVOCATION PRAYER: O God and Master of us all, teach us to render day by day an account of our stewardship to thee. All we have of time and talents and possessions are thine; and we are thine, bought with a price. We come with contrite hearts to acknowledge that we have often wasted time that should have been spent with and for thee; we have used thoughtlessly and for our own purposes talents that should have been used in thy service; and our possessions have been so little at thy disposal. Consecrate us and all that we have more truly to thyself. Give us opportunities for serving thee and our fellow men, and grant to us courage to use these opportunities aright. Teach us the joy of time spent in thy presence and service. We long to be good stewards of thy manifold gifts rendering an account to thee as our Master. At the close of life's day may we hear thee say: "Well done, good and faithful servant, enter into the joy of thy Lord." In the name of our Redeemer Christ we pray. Amen.

Theme: The Joy of the Lord (Financial Canvass).

TEXT: "Enter thou into the joy of thy Lord." Matt. 25:21.

INTRODUCTORY: This is the joy that Jesus would give us. Always available and available to all. If, however, hoarding life and money for self we let instincts of self-preservation and possessiveness destroy our liberality, we will miss the joy of our Lord.

I. But at what cost! Some people never know the joy of their Lord because begrudging what God and the church ask of them their thoughts of him become twisted: "Lord, I know that thou art a hard man. . . ." Refusing the fellowship of giving your life becomes a complex of fear: "I was afraid. . . ." Refusing your talents to God's work, your life shrivels through disuse: "I went and hid my talent. . . ." E.g., a worshiper singing, "Were the whole realm of nature mine, that were a present far too small," while fingering pocket coins to find smallest for collection plate! A small gift from a small heart makes "the whole realm of nature," especially human nature, shrivel and shrink.

II. On the other hand, you can "enter into the joy of your Lord" by serving him with loyalty. The loyalty of the good stewards: "Well done, good and faithful servant!" The meaning of stewardship. Loyal stewardship results in joy for Christian disciples.

Joy comes through committal to a cause—Christ's cause. Francis of Assisi's joy from that. See Chesterton's *Francis of Assisi*; Kossak's *Blessed Are the Meek*. Joy of good soldier signing enlistment papers to defend his country against his enemies, signing your enlistment papers (pledge card) today.

III. You can "enter into the joy of your Lord" by serving him with imagination. Five and two-talent men had joy because they let their imagination make them ten and five-talent men for their Lord. "Lord, thou deliverest unto me five talents; behold, I have gained. . . ."

Jesus left no specific instructions as to how men were to use their talents for him. Yet, throughout the centuries, the Christians' joy of accomplishment came from application of Christian imagination to needs of Christ and his kingdom. Imagination always multiplies the Christian investment.

So today use your imagination to see your Christ-invested money as a swift-winged bomber, not dropping explosives, but the "dynamis," the power of God for saving men, into every hamlet and city of the world. Through foreign and national missions, etc. Today use your imagination to see what your church could do with more money (not the tithe the Bible says is God's portion, but the 15 per cent the government says is your portion for God); to see larger service your church could render youth, men and women in this hour of crisis. Use your imagination to be like the woman who, in a meeting when people were asked to give as though they were placing their money in the pierced hands of Christ, came up and said, "I was going to give fifty cents, but now I am going to give ten dollars!" Do this, and you will "enter into the joy of your Lord."

IV. Finally, you can "enter into the joy of your Lord" by serving him with enthusiasm. The stewards eagerly came to their returning Lord with evidences of what they had done for him. Much of Jesus' power came from the enthusiasm men found in doing his work in reaching and redeeming broken, bitter men. No greater happiness can you find than enthusiastic generosity in the work of Christ in your church through the coming year. Prof. Henry Link, in both his books, says: "One of the greatest sources of happiness for modern men and women is to give themselves with enthusiasm to the church and church work." This is the universal experience of all who try it.

Such enthusiasm is contagious. When you have it: every victory of your church, your achievement; every gain, something you have done; every new piece of equipment, something you helped get; its warmth and welcome, something you have wrought; every new member, someone you helped win. This enthusiasm an open sesame to "joy of your Lord."

On the first Palm Sunday the disciples, with loyalty, imagination and enthusiasm, acclaimed Jesus as King and Lord over all by waving their palms. Today let us acclaim him in loyalty, imagination and enthusiasm, not with palms, but with pens, pencils and pledges; not waving them, but weaving them into a great congregational signature and signification that Christ is King and Lord of our community and of the world. It all lies in your hands. A Chinese philosopher was once approached by some mischievous boys. "What do we have in our hands?" they asked. "A bird," he replied. "Is it alive or dead?" they shouted. And he, being a wise philosopher and knowing that they would either kill or allow it to live in accordance with his answer, said, "It is up to you; it is in your hands!"—C. M. M.

THEME PRAYER: Touch our eyes with insight, O Lord, that we may see shining through our possessions, our security and our freedom the toil and sacrifice of those to whom we owe them. Forbid that we shall take anything thus hallowed ungratefully, or abuse by our selfishness that others have made sacred by their high devotion. Through Jesus Christ. Amen.

OFFERTORY SENTENCE: "Remember the words of the Lord Jesus, how he said, It is more blessed to give than to receive."

OFFERTORY PRAYER: We are glad to believe, our Father, that is is indeed more blessed to give than to receive—that it not alone enlarges the heart and builds up character; but that it is a source of great happiness and transforms us more like unto thyself, the giving God. Wilt thou graciously receive the offerings we bring this day and use them to the forwarding of thy cause and kingdom in the world. We ask in the name of Christ. Amen.—H.

Illustrative Material

SEED THOUGHTS, HOMILETIC AND EXPOSITORY. Imperfect Sacrifice: Men act toward God as they would not to an earthly ruler. I. How men stand before his presence and profane his name. "Let them offer that to their governor!" (Mal. 1:8). II. How they mistreat his authority and disregard his commands.

III. How many pretend to make sacrifices for his cause and give only "the halt and the blind," only that which is worthless and cost them nothing. IV. How many render only heartless homage and selfish service. Our conduct toward God may be tested by the way in which it would be received by an earthly ruler.—W. O. L.

Anything Good Enough for God! I. "If ye offer the blind for sacrifice, is it not evil?" They had plenty of cattle without blemish. II. "If ye offer the lame and sick, is it not evil?" III. "Offer it now to thy governor!" IV. Imperfections. 1. Spiritless worship. 2. Blind sacrifice. 3. Lame offerings. 4. Sick gifts.—W. R. F.

Choice Illustrations on the Theme

MATERIAL POSSESSIONS. Material possessions, as such, are not condemned in the Bible. Emphatic, however, are the warnings concerning our attitude toward them. Covetousness and anxiety, and even idolatry, may possess our souls, whether our possessions be great or little. Our spiritual safety lies only in the dedication both of ourselves and all that we have to God. The soul thus dedicated cannot be smothered under an abundance of material things, nor can it be led astray by their glamor, because it is seeking first the kingdom of God and his righteousness.—*Christian Observer*.

SCRAP IS NOT ENOUGH. Have we sought to mobilize our total resources when we teach our children to give pennies in Sunday School and provide them with fifty-cent movie tickets? How deep is our concern for the kingdom when we spend dollars for dinners and drop dimes on the offering plate? How genuine is our Christian profession when we save seventeen dollars for ourselves against each dollar we invest in the world-saving Gospel of Christ? When the cause of Christ requires the "first fruits," can we expect his blessing if we give only the remnants? The kingdom of heaven cannot be built on scrap. "Bring ye the whole tithe into the storehouse, that there may be food in my house, and prove me now herewith, saith Jehovah of hosts."—Alva V. King.

HER ALABASTER BOX. Hudson Taylor tells us that after a great missionary meeting at Cardiff he received a letter from a widow, who said: "I could not put into your hand yesterday any money or jewels, for my husband is dead and we have hard shifts to live. But I have one jewel—my daughter. She has long wanted to go. I could not let her go from my care, but last night I gave my alabaster box of very precious ointment to Christ; and if you will see to her going out now, I will be glad to send her."—Southern Presbyterian Journal.

GIVING WEIGHS THE GIVER. Evangelist Sam Jones went out one Sunday afternoon from Atlanta to preach in a country church. Just before beginning his sermon he looked all around at the unceiled walls, at the broken window panes, up through broken places in the roof, and then looking into the faces of his audience said, "Well, I know what kind of a crowd I am to preach to this afternoon."—One who heard him.

GIVING IS PAYING. Is there hope for a man when it is reported that he prayeth? How much more when it is said, "Behold, he payeth also."—Daniel Dorchester, D.D.

GIVING BLESSES THE GIVER. "Every flower that you plant along some other man's track sheds its fragrance on you." One cannot give fully, freely of himself and his substance to others without reaping the reward. Nor can one be miserly of himself and his possessions without suffering for it. You remember Scrooge and how dismal his outlook upon life was until the Christmas spirit entered his heart and it was warmed and mellowed. The old man who cared for nothing but money and for nobody but himself was utterly transformed. Just as far as we are like the old Scrooge in our indifference to humanity, just so far shall we reap bitterness and gall; just as far as we are like the new Scrooge shall the blessings we bestow come back

to us a thousandfold. "No man liveth to himself."—5,000 Best Modern Illustrations.

EVENING SERVICE

Theme: Commitment, Loyalty and Sacrifice (Financial Canvass).

TEXT: "Upon the first day of the week let every one of you lay by him in store, as God hath prospered him." I Cor. 16:2.

INTRODUCTORY: A Buddhist prince once said to a missionary, "If you Christians would only live your Christianity it would sweep the world. There's nothing else like it on the face of the earth." The recent World War was a sad but eloquent testimony to the fact that professing Christians had not lived according to the principles set forth by the Prince of Peace. The wave of totalitarianism which has swept over some nations in the past two decades and threatened to engulf the whole world, found its greatest source of power in the practical use of terms which are strangely familiar to Christian people —commitment, loyalty, sacrifice.

I. The Nazi regime set up a detailed plan to indoctrinate the youth as well as adults in a program which at frequent intervals provided pompous ceremonies at which every may, woman and child was committed to the cause of the war lords.

II. Having been committed to the totalitarian way of life, a loyalty was required which made home and loved ones of secondary importance. The Gestapo invaded the sanctities of the home in the interest of the government to which every last soul was to be loyal regardless of what that loyalty might cost.

III. Thoroughly committed to the program and sworn to loyalty, the totalitarian people must be ready for any sacrifice. The giving of time, talent, property and life itself was not too much for the advancement of a government which taught its people to hate all other races.

IV. As long as the people could be held to such a program—even by force —the war machine swept on with remarkable success. But when high-ranking generals, as well as citizens in the more quiet walks of life, began to feel the sacrifice too great, and when disloyalty crept into their lives and there was an unwillingness to be completely and wholeheartedly committed to the national cause, the advance of their armies halted and the retreats began.

V. It is so in the kingdom of God on earth. The armies of the Captain of our salvation are halted and begin their retreats when its soldiers are not completely committed to the cause of Christ —when their genuine loyalty to Christ is undermined by loyalties to other causes, and when they refrain from renewing their commitment at regular and frequent intervals.

One missionary who eagerly returned to the Philippines when war with Japan seemed imminent, and who afterward died in a prison camp near her field of labor, before returning asked a group of well-to-do Christian women if they would make some sacrifice for the cause of Christ in the Philippines. The women were interested in her story and responded by contributing an average sum of money equal to the price of a show, some discarded spectacles, some last year's Christmas greeting cards which the native children enjoyed, and some unfinished fancy work which the women did not want.

Compare such so-called sacrifice with the price which nations paid to wage war instead of a campaign of love! No wonder Christianity is not "sweeping the world." Too many Christian soldiers make practically no sacrifice but give the unwanted, discarded tag ends of time, effort and money. Too many Christian soldiers do not have a loyalty which makes all other causes of little consequence by comparison. Too many Christian soldiers do not renew their commitment regularly as Paul suggested, by laying aside on the first day

of the week an offering for the support of Christ's kingdom.

A great spiritual advance will take place and Christianity will "sweep the world," as the Buddhist prince said, when Christians are thoroughly committed to Christ's cause, loyal to the Prince of Peace, and willing to make some real sacrifice in the spirit of love for him who first loved us.—Clair B. Gahagen, D.D.

Suggestive Financial Canvass Texts and Themes

Giving a Condition of Getting: "Charge them that are rich in this world," etc. I Tim. 6:17-19.

The Pleasure of Giving: "I have shewed you all things, how that so labouring ye ought," etc. Acts 20:35.

Stewardship: "It is required in stewards, that a man be found faithful." I Cor. 4:2.

The Law of Benevolence: "Thou shalt not delay to offer the first of thy ripe fruits." Ex. 22:29.

Giving as an act of Worship: "Thy prayers and thine alms are come up for a memorial before God." Acts 10:4.

Self-denial an Element of Worship: "Bring an offering, and come into his courts." Ps. 96:8.

Dealing Honestly with God: Mal. 3:8-10. A man admitted that he owed everything to God. "But God isn't pressing me as my other creditors are," he said. Thus to take advantage of God's long-suffering is robbery.

A Christian's Possessions: Luke 12:13-21. Refugees could take with them only what they could carry. What, after all, are the things that supremely matter?

The Rich Young Ruler: Luke 18:18-24. A mother complains that her son does not love her. He is a good provider, but without love, nothing else matters.

The Use and Abuse of Wealth: James 2:15, 16; 5:1-6. None was more concerned than Jesus that all should be fed and clothed—and none more insistent that to live for food and clothing was fatal to one's true life.

MIDWEEK FELLOWSHIP MEETING TOPIC

(Church Night or Suggested Sermon Subject)

Theme: Consecrated Property (Financial Canvass).

TEXT: "Honour the Lord with thy substance, and with the first fruits of all thine increase," etc. Prov. 3:9, 10.

Our religion is a mockery unless it affects the way in which we spend our money, as well as all other concerns of life.

I. We can honor God with our property.

II. God has a claim on our property. 1. Originally came from him. 2. He created the materials and powers of nature, gave us our faculties; we sow the seed but God gives the increase. 3. Our property is only lent to us for a season.

III. Our whole property should be consecrated to God. It was all given us by him. We are accountable for the use of all of it. We have control of the property. We are stewards, not beggars.

IV. The best of our property should be more directly offered to the service of God. God expects the best. Should have the first fruits.

V. It is well to dispose of our property on some well-considered method. 1. Can thus give most readily and justly. 2. Consider needs. 3. Consider ability. 4. Consider proportion. 5. Consider that lack of method will result in lack or laxity of giving.

VI. The consecration of property to God brings a blessing to the owner. If not always rewarded with temporal riches it is repaid in better treasures. 1. The pleasures of sympathy and benevolence. 2. The smile of God.—P. C.

CHRISTIAN ENDEAVOR SOCIETY TOPIC

Nov. 14. Livingstone, the Missionary. Acts 13:1-5.

BULLETIN BOARD SLOGANS FOR THE MONTH

By EARL RINEY

True religion affords government its surest support.

The nation that fears God need fear no other power.

Christ did not come to make life easy, but to make men strong.

The church is the bulwark of civilization.

The Bible is common sense inspired.

Human improvement is from within outward.

Sin may be clasped so close that we cannot see its face.

You are not strong when you are wrong.

If God is your partner make your plans large.

Nothing is simpler than faith and nothing more sublime.

Christ in the heart is heaven on earth.

Truth will keep your heart steady in the storm.

SUNDAY SCHOOL LESSON

Nov. 14. A Study in Values. Prov. 11:27-28; 13:7; 15:13-17; 20:11-12; 22:1-4.

MEMORY VERSE: "A good name is rather to be chosen than great riches, and loving favour rather than silver and gold." Prov. 22:1.

This study in values is a study in contrasts—right over against wrong, uprightness over against wickedness, spiritual values over against material values.

Wallace McPherson Alston points out that the clear-cut difference between right and wrong has become blurred in the thinking of many of our day and generation. For many honest and well-meaning people matters of right and wrong have become confused and complicated.

Many factors are responsible. Here are some of them: revolt against authority, the prevalent insistence upon self-expression, the complex social situation, loss of faith in a personal God.

"How can we settle what is right and what is wrong? . . . The test of experience will help us in specific issues to settle for ourselves what is right." Other tests which can be applied are "the test of publicity." Would you be willing to have the whole world know what you are doing? "The test of general application"—What if people everywhere should do as I am doing, as I propose to do? What would be the result? "The test of foresight"—Where is this sort of conduct leading? "The test of influence." "The test of Christlikeness."

SUNDAY: NOVEMBER TWENTY-FIRST

MORNING SERVICE

Theme: Our National Blessings (Thanksgiving).

SUGGESTED SCRIPTURE READING: Ps. 65:1-13.

SELECTED HYMNS: "We plow the fields and scatter."—Matthias Claudius. "Come ye thankful people, come."—Henry Alford. "Now thank we all our God."—M. Rinkhart. "Now sing we a song for the harvest."—J. W. Chadwick. "Praise to God and thanks we bring."—W. C. Gannett.

CALL TO WORSHIP: "Praise waiteth for thee, O God, in Zion; unto thee shall the vow be performed. O thou that hearest prayer, unto thee shall all flesh come."

INVOCATION PRAYER: Father, with thankful and humble hearts we appear before thee. We would thank thee for all the benefits that we have received from thy goodness. It is to thy blessing we owe what success we have found. Every opportunity for doing good; every impulse in the right way; each victory we have gained over ourselves; every thought of thy presence, O Father; every silent but loving glance on the example of our pattern, thy Son our Lord, all are alike thy gifts to us. Give us strength and wisdom to walk faithfully and joyfully in the way of willing obedience to thy laws and cheerful trust in thy love. The best thanksgiving we can offer to thee is to live according to thy holy will; grant us every day to offer it more perfectly, and to grow in the knowledge of thy will and the love thereof, forevermore. Amen.—Michael Sailer.

Theme: Our National Blessings (Thanksgiving).

TEXT: "Oh let the nations be glad and sing for joy!" Ps. 67:4.

INTRODUCTORY: It is not easy to be grateful. Gratitude is, first of all, a feeling, and feelings do not come and go at will. We may know we ought to feel grateful, but knowing this does not bring the desired feeling.

I. It is not easy to be grateful for national blessings. Blessings which are general and which come alike to millions of human beings do not readily touch the heart. The sunshine, for instance, falls on everybody and how seldom it awakens a song of thanksgiving in the heart. A child will feel grateful for an apple, but how difficult it is for a man or woman to feel grateful for a bumper crop of apples which grow in somebody else's orchard. The story of the harvesting of millions of bushels of grain ought to move the heart, but it does not. We can read pages of statistics without the slightest emotion. Fruitful fields and flourishing industries and booming commerce and high wages are all fuel for the fire of thanksgiving, but not many persons are capable of feeling gratitude for such colossal and nation-wide blessings.

It is not easy to feel gratitude in a time of abounding prosperity. When the cup runs over is not the most propitious moment for the uttering of praise; it is when the cup is almost empty, and one does not know when or how it can be filled again, that the heart appreciates the few remaining drops and begins to glow with gratitude that the cup is not entirely empty. It is not the rich but the poor who know best the meaning of gratitude.

II. It is not easy to feel gratitude for material blessings. Such blessings seem to come of themselves and along lines which can be easily recognized and explained. When we receive an automobile, or a radio set, or a moving-picture machine, it comes, as a rule, as the result of our own industry or good luck.

III. It is not easy to express thanks, even to a human being. The words of thanksgiving seem to stick in our throat. The people who do the most for us seldom receive from us any word of appreciation. We take all their kindness for granted. This is true of many husbands and wives, many sons and daughters. It is likewise true of many neighbors and friends.

IV. It is more difficult to thank God than to thank man. God seems so far away and so indifferent to human praise. Who are we that we should weary him with our offerings of thanks? With this excuse in our hearts we say nothing. Moreover, we do not know how to phrase properly our expression of thanksgiving. It is because of our sense of incompetency in the realm of appreciation and praise that we excuse ourselves for remaining dumb before the Lord.

For all these reasons there is no day in the year more difficult to observe properly than our national Thanksgiving Day. There is probably no other holiday which is more shabbily celebrated. The day is generally observed as a day of recreation and social enjoyment, but not as a day of thanksgiving. A day is given to us for the express purpose of cultivating one of the most beautiful of all the graces, but most of us allow the opportunity to pass unappreciated and unused.

V. The result is that we are, on the whole, an ungrateful people! Even Christians are, as a rule, deficient in the grace of gratitude. We do not live enough in the Psalter, nor do we understand how to use the vocabulary which the Hebrew poets coined.

One of the reasons why we are so impoverished in our thanksgiving faculties is because of the haste in which we live. We rush through the days, and this pell-mell form of existence gives us scant chance for meditation. It is only when we lay our minds upon a mercy and allow it to lie there for a while, that the mind passes into a grateful mood. The Psalmist says that one day while he was musing, the fire began to burn. Gratitude is a kind of fire which can be kindled only by vivid memories. Whenever we forget His benefits, we lose the power of singing praise to Him.

We are in sore need, therefore, of a national Thanksgiving Day every year. It does not come as Christmas comes or as Easter or as Whitsunday; it does not come as the Fourth of July comes or as Washington's Birthday, or as the birthday of Lincoln; it comes by proclamation of the President of our country. At one season of the year the President is permitted, by a custom which runs back to the beginning, to speak to us as if he were our spiritual leader. Once a year he dares to speak to us about God; he even goes so far as to ask us to pray to God. He does not order or command it, but he recommends it. He tells us he wishes we would do it. He does not speak to us as churches, but as individuals, as a people, as a nation, and although a layman, he does not hesitate to ask all of the officials of the churches as well as all the laymen, and also all human beings outside the churches, to speak to God about his great goodness to them.

VI. If we are wise, we act on our President's suggestion. We keep the day sacred to the idea of Thanksgiving. If we have permitted the memory of our sorrows and hardships and misfortunes to overshadow the memory of our mercies and blessings, we will crowd the dark things aside long enough to take a steady look at the things which are bright. We will take a vacation for at least a day from all grumblings and growlings and fault-findings. We will seek diligently for the things that are lovely and of good report.

And we will also keep the day as a national day. It is, of course, a home day also, a day on which to think of the blessings which have come to our own family, such as life and health and strength and success and happiness, and we do well when we meditate on our own individual gladness and victories. But Thanksgiving Day is not a day solely for the individual or family or community, but for the entire nation. On that day we ought to think of the whole American people; their character, their spirit, their ideals and their achievements. We ought to think of our government, what it has done well and what it has done amiss within the last twelve months. We should cultivate not a parochial mind but a national mind. We should train ourselves to think not narrowly but broadly, not sectionally but continentally. Someday soon we shall need a more fully developed international mind, and the only way to secure that sort of a mind is to build up a sound and active national mind. A nation has a soul and a mission and a destiny.

God is a God of nations as well as of individuals; he has his plans for nations as well as for families.

We Americans are prone to criticize our government and to assume that nearly everything it does is foolish or wrong. Let us, on our national Thanksgiving Day, search in the record of our national life for evidences of the superintending guidance of God, and return thanks for whatsoever our public servants have been able to accomplish toward making this a better world.— C. E. J.

THEME PRAYER: O God, we praise thee for the dream of the golden city of peace and righteousness which has ever haunted the prophets of humanity, and we rejoice with joy unspeakable that at last the people have achieved the freedom and knowledge and power which may avail to turn into reality the vision that so long has beckoned in vain. May we who now live see the oncoming of the great day of God, when all men shall stand side by side in equal worth and real freedom, all toiling and all reaping, masters of nature but brothers of men, exultant in the tide of the common life, and jubilant in the adoration of thee, the source of their blessings and the Father of all. Amen.

OFFERTORY SENTENCE: "I will be exalted among the heathen; I will be exalted in the earth."

OFFERTORY PRAYER: Our Father, we ask thee to multiply and magnify this our offering even as Jesus multiplied and magnified the five loaves and two fishes, that it may become mighty to do much good. In Jesus' name. Amen.

Illustrative Material

SEED THOUGHTS, HOMILETIC AND EXPOSITORY. Religion in Full Exercise: "O give thanks unto the Lord; for he is good; for his mercy endureth for ever." I Chron. 16:34. Godly thankfulness is the music of the soul under the Master's touch, with full power on, and all the stops out. I. How rendered? 1. With personal reverence—worshipful. 2. With the incense of offerings. 3. In holy array—the apparel most becoming to saints. 4. With solemnity—stillness and receptiveness of spirit. II. Why the song of Thanksgiving? Gratitude is rent we owe our God. The larger the acreage, the greater the rent due him. 1. God is good. In his faithfulness and dealings. 2. He is merciful. Evidenced by his abounding blessings, by his provisions, and by penalties deferred. III. Benefits. By our thankfulness we add glory or luster to God, but benefits abound to us. Buds, blossoms, fragrance to those about us.—Rev. C. A. Terhune.

Choice Thanksgiving Ilustrations

MONUMENTS TO GOD'S PROVIDENCE. Chester, England, has a celebrated structure, known as "God's Providence House," which was errected in 1652. The relief ornamentation in the spaces between the wood framing presents a feeling of richness, which is in marked contrast with the modern brick houses that adjoin this admired building. The front, as it now appears, is a modern restoration of the original, but the visitor is assured that everything modern about it is in exact conformity with the old work. The house evidently belonged to a family of considerable importance, for a coat of arms ornaments the beam under the upper window. Under the gable, on the main beam, is the inscription: God's Providence Is Mine Inheritance.

From this inscription the house derives its name. According to the popular belief, the inscription was added after the plague which ravaged the city during the seventeenth century. Tradition says that this was the only building in Watergate Street which the plague passed over; and in gratitude for that remarkable deliverance, the owner had the inscription carved on the main beam. There is nothing impossible or even improbable in the tradition.

For how many deliverances is it our privilege to build monuments to God's providence, to express in some tangible way our thanks!

GOD OUR CONDUCTOR. The other day when I got into a bus I noticed a little girl, all alone but radiantly happy, humming a little tune to herself. She was a picture of joy. I leaned forward and said, "Why, my little girl, aren't you afraid of riding all alone in this bus?" Her eyes went wide at my folly, her lips bubbled with laughter. "Oh," she said, "they can't hurt me on this bus; my father's the conductor." We are thundering through the universe at inconceivable speed, swept through joy and grief, sickness and health, death and life, while all the time our heavenly Father is the conductor—only we don't trust and sing in that way. If we trusted God more there would be more songs of praise upon our lips.—*Golden Hours.*

GIVING THANKS BY ENJOYING WHAT WE HAVE. Some years ago a leading magazine sent telegrams to celebrities all over the world asking them what they really wanted for Christmas. They were asked, "What, if you could have anything you wanted, would you really want most?" There were many kinds of answers. One of the most significant was from a lady who said, "If Santa Claus deals in other than material things for Christmas, may I be given an ever greater ability to appreciate all that I now have."

Has it ever struck you how many people are miserable because of what they do not have instead of happy because of what they do have? The one thing most of us lack is what this lady asked for: ability to appreciate what we already possess. The more we measure the blessings we have the less we feel the lack of what we do not have. There is no finer way to show gratitude than to enjoy the blessings which are already ours.—Author Unknown.

THANK GOD FOR GOD. In one of his short stories, "The Lost Word," Henry van Dyke tells of a young man who supposed this would be a happier world if one did not believe in God. So one day he bargained with a wise old man to eliminate the word "God" from his life on condition that he would receive wealth, pleasure and success. He found all three, but also found that his happiness was incomplete because there was no one to thank. Furthermore, adversity came, and he had no one to go to for strength and help. At the last he and his wife again wholeheartedly spoke the words, "O God, our Father," and in so doing found life complete and their joy full.

We do not stop often enough to consider how dependent we are upon God. God is the background, the source, the sustenance of the universe and of our physical, mental, moral and spiritual lives. He explains us and the mysteries of our lives and of the universe. He is our Father, our Comrade, our Redeemer. Without him we are orphans in the world. Daily, as Joyce Kilmer did, we ought to say, "Oh, thank God for God."—Unidentified.

A THANKSGIVING STRATEGY. Instead of counting sheep when unable to sleep, why not count your blessings? The numbers will run so high, you will fall asleep from sheer exhaustion.—*King's Business.*

Quotable Thanksgiving Poetry

THANKSGIVING

Praise the Lord for grain abundant,
   On the hills and o'er the plains;
Praise the Lord for sheep and cattle,
   Fruit and fowl, and merchant-gains.
Praise the Lord for health of body,
   For our colleges and schools;
Praise the Lord for home and country,
   When no despot-power rules.
Praise the Lord that here the people,
   As one family, abide,
Jew and Gentile, white and black,
   Living daily side by side.
Praise the Lord for peace that's ours,
   Born of justice, sane and wise;
Praise the Lord for this our Nation,
   Precious in Jehovah's eyes.
—Rev. Walter H. Brooks. Written in his 88th year.

THANKSGIVING

I humbly kneel and give Thee thanks, O Lord,
   For strength to till my little rocky field;
For all the blessings that Thy love has poured
   Upon me in the harvest's mystic yield;
For calm and storm; for sun and snow and rain;
   For dawning's clarion; for weary dusk;
For hope that ever leans to solace pain;
   For dewy gardens sweet with myrrh and musk;
But most of all for faith that steels my soul

Against each mocking doubt, that lifts and leers
Across the dark, and makes me see my goal
Beyond the anguish of these fleeting years,
A shining glory in whose splendor gleams
Fulfillment, Lord, of all my cherished dreams.
   —Edgar Daniel Kramer.

EVENING SERVICE

Theme: Reasons for Thanksgiving (Thanksgiving).

SUGGESTED SCRIPTURE READING: Deut. 16:10-15.

INVOCATION PRAYER: God of our Fathers, known of old: We thank thee for thy providence over us for three centuries as a people. We thank thee for our heritage of freedom, so dearly won; for those who were pioneers in the beginnings of this Republic; for the daring and genius of statesmen and seers; for the loyalty and devotion of humble men and women; for all who dreamed the American Dream and who fashioned the dream into visible shape and form.

Help us to keep faith with our heroic dead. Save us from the waste of their sacrifice, from carelessness and indifference, from softness and smug complacency. Fashion us into a united people, devoted to the ideals of freedom and justice. Give to us the lighted mind and well-considered courage of those who march breast forward.

We pray for quickened and enlarged sympathies. We would share the sufferings and sorrows of the world. Help us to reach our hands of help to thy disinherited children everywhere.

We pray for our President, the Congress, and all who guide the affairs of this nation that they may govern well.

We pray for the outpouring of thy Spirit in all the world that the Spirit of Christ may yet rule in the hearts of men everywhere; so shall we be led into that co-operative Commonwealth of God in which all the families of the earth shall be blessed. In Jesus' name we ask. Amen.—Merle N. Smith, D.D.

TEXT: "O give thanks unto the Lord, for he is good: for his mercy endureth for ever. Let the redeemed of the Lord say so." Ps. 107:1, 2.

INTRODUCTORY: Gratitude is a grace that struggles for expression. It does not shut itself up in the heart. It does not allow itself to be merely felt. It wants to speak. It wants to say something. The writer of this 107th Psalm shows us that he thinks well of this tendency to give expression to grateful feeling; yes, that he regards it as duty. He says, Let those who are among the redeemed of the Lord, those who have experienced God's mercies, those who have tasted of his goodness— let them "say so." Let them give voice to, recount the number of favors and their grateful feelings in regard to them. "O give thanks unto the Lord, for he is good: for his mercy endureth for ever. Let the redeemed of the Lord say so."

Giving thanks to the Lord for his mercies is always a comely thing for us to do; but especially at this period of our national Thanksgiving ought we to stir ourselves to this delightful duty.

Let us suggest some among the many reasons we have for thanksgiving:

1. Thank God for consciousness. On that hinges all joy, all experience, all personality. A human being is better than a stone.

2. Thank God for home. Only those that have no home know the preciousness of home and home life. Think of the thousands of boarders and their lonely evenings!

3. Thank God for love. Riches are for the few; love is for all. The poor can enjoy its blessings fully as much as the rich.

4. Thank God for open doors. There is something in life for everyone to do. We go forward in faith, and opportunities open up before us: employment, friendships, service.

5. Thank God for books. All the past ages spread before us a mental feast; the best minds in the world serve us. No soul need be starved intellectually with books available.

6. Thank God for your critics. They usually speak a good deal of truth, and are worth listening to.

7. Thank God for Christian fellowship. It makes one family of all Christians, unites them in service, emphasizes their unity rather than their differences, binds them together in love.

8. Thank God for education. We may not have too much of it, but just to be able to read intelligently opens up the treasures of the ages to us and sharpens the mind to reason clearly.

9. Thank God for courtesy shown by you and shown to you. Courtesy makes life pleasant. It is sunshine, summer weather, and makes for good humor and good will all around.

10. Thank God for the ability to enjoy things. Some minds are diseased and cannot do aught but worry. Thank God that like the bee you can extract sweetness from many flowers along your way.

11. Thank God for music. You cannot sing or play? What matter? There are others that can, and you can enjoy their gift. Songs in the heart make life's burdens light.

12. Thank God for science. Without it we should be in the dark ages. Science is a great light. It has given us health through sanitation, built our bridges, our ships, our steamengines, our automobiles, our airplanes, and it has given us, among countless other things, the radio.

13. Thank God for missionaries. Without them the world would be in worse darkness than it is in today. We know now that our own people cannot rise while the nations of the earth remain in ignorance. All mankind must rise together, or fail to rise. Missionaries are real uplifters.

14. Thank God for the safety of our shores and the riches of our land; for the right to think as we please, speak as we feel, and vote as we believe best; for the chance to build better for our children than our fathers knew; for

our country's peaceful attitude toward all nations, and for her self-contained power to maintain that attitude with dignity and calm.

We have only started to present reasons for our giving thanks, for the whole region of religion and its supreme benefits and blessings remain to be recounted.

Suggestive Thanksgiving Texts

"The Lord thy God bringeth thee into a good land." Deut. 8:7.

"Let the people praise thee, O God; let all the people praise thee." Ps. 67:3.

"It is a good thing to give thanks unto the Lord, and to sing praises unto thy name, O most High." Ps. 92:1.

"Let us come before his presence with thanksgiving." Ps. 95:2.

"Giving thanks always for all things." Eph. 5:20.

"Remember all the way which the Lord thy God led thee." Deut. 8:2.

"Praise is comely for the upright." Ps. 33:1.

"Oh that men would praise the Lord for his goodness, and for his wonderful works to the children of men!" Ps. 107:8.

"It is good to sing praises unto our God; for it is pleasant; and praise is comely." Ps. 147:1.

"Where are the nine?" Luke 17:17.

"Do ye thus requite the Lord?" Deut. 32:6.

"His praise shall continually be in my mouth." Ps. 34:1.

"He thanked God and took courage." Acts 28:15.

"Blessed are they that dwell in thy house: they will be still praising thee." Ps. 84:4.

"Enter into his gates with thanksgiving." Ps. 100:4.

MIDWEEK FELLOWSHIP MEETING TOPIC

(Church Night or Suggested Sermon Subject)

Theme: The Baseness of Murmuring (Thanksgiving).

TEXT: "I have heard the murmurings." Num. 14:27.

Have any of us a tendency to murmur? This Thanksgiving season is a good time to look into the matter.

1. Because murmuring is not a mere fault or a simple sin. It is a serious thing. 1. It involves presumption. 2. It involves ingratitude. 3. It involves rebellion.

II. Our murmuring is without a just cause. For our blessings are multitudinous. Murmuring ignores blessings, is most ungracious, and is both without reason and against reason.

III. Furthermore, murmuring is against the best Being. 1. Think who and what he is, the supremely wise and good God—our heavenly Father. 2. Think of what he has done for those Israelites, and what he has done for us. Redeemed, guarded, sustained—crowned our days with loving-kindness and tender mercies. 3. Think of what he had promised Israel, and has promised us. How base to murmur against our Great Benefactor! 4. Many are habitual grumblers. How great their sin!

IV. Murmuring is known of God. "I have heard the murmurings." 1. Israel's murmurers were excluded from the Promised Land. 2. The murmurers of today exclude themselves from the Canaan of joy and peace and contentment. 3. Murmuring is a self-punishing sin.—W. J.

CHRISTIAN ENDEAVOR SOCIETY TOPIC

Nov. 21. "Now Thank We All Our God" (Thanksgiving Sunday). II Cor. 9:15.

SUNDAY SCHOOL LESSON

Nov. 21. God's Provision for His Creatures. Ps. 104:1-5, 10-14, 24, 23.

MEMORY VERSE: "The earth is the Lord's, and the fulness thereof; the world, and they that dwell therein." Ps. 24:1.

Make a Thanksgiving inventory. Count your blessings. Do it in terms of the 36th Psalm, vv. 5-10. The

Psalmist is no little two by four individual who things that you can measure things with a tape-line. Note the blessings which can be tabulated under:

I. Loving-kindness. God's love doing kindly deeds. Loving-kindness is a heart word. It has grace in it. Measure it by the heavens.

II. Faithfulness. It means a "grip on things." It is an arm word, a hand word. Count the blessings that we have because of the faithfulness, the stability of God. Measure God's faithfulness by the skies.

III. Righteousness. It means "straight," the opposite of "crooked." It is a great character word. It is God's character. Tabulate the blessings which are ours because of God's righteousness. Use the mountains as a measuring line to measure God's righteousness, says the Psalm.

IV. Judgments. This is a clear thinking, keenly discriminating, mind word. It says that God sees things perfectly; he sees them whole. He can cut like a two-edged sword between right and wrong. He balances to a hair's weight. He shows knowledge and justice. There are blessings which are the judgments of God. Measure them as one would measure the depth of the ocean.

V. "Thou preservest man and beast." This does not mean for man just enough to eat and drink—it means life abundant. It means fullness, deliverance, salvation. Here is our journal of mercies. God's loving-kindness, faithfulness, righteousness, judgments, salvation.

SUNDAY: NOVEMBER TWENTY-EIGHTH

MORNING SERVICE

Theme: Say So.

SUGGESTED SCRIPTURE READING: Mark 5:1-20; Acts 1:1-8.

SELECTED HYMNS: "I've found a Friend, O such a Friend."—J. G. Small. "People of the living God."—J. Montgomery. "I'm not ashamed to own my Lord."—I. Watts. "I love to tell the story."—K. Hankey.

CALL TO WORSHIP: "O come, let us worship and bow down: let us kneel before the Lord our Maker. For he is our God; and we are the people of his pasture, and the sheep of his hand."

INVOCATION PRAYER (or Pastoral Prayer): We thank thee, O God, that thou hast endowed us, thy creatures, with the capacity for worship. The privilege of prayer is a gift of thy goodness and in its exercise we render unto thee our gratitude.

We come unto thee with no virtue of our own, with all our imperfections upon our heads, with few deeds of worth in our hands, and with a very shallow and fickle love in our hearts. But we do come with sincerity to seek thy ministry and blessing.

We pray for the forgiveness of our sins. Forgive the open deed, so presumptuous, which we knew was evil before we did it, that which brought no peace for ourselves and only sorrow for others. We beseech thee, too, to cleanse our inner natures from which arise the tempers and attitudes and moods which are ill-pleasing to thee. Grant unto us the mind of Christ. We covet his wisdom, his judgment, his sense of what is vital. We pray, too, for his heart that we may more perfectly love thee, and love our fellow man as our brother. Direct our wills that we may be steadfast in good works, ever seeking thy kingdom, ever abounding in love.

Help us, our Father, to live as Christians should within all the areas of life. May our homes be full of love and therefore full of peace. Into business may we carry the Christian virtues of truth and honesty. In our professions may we show the higher skill because we are Christians. In school may we become more studious because we prepare for service in Christ's name. In play may we be joyous because we find it recreative of the strong body and the healthy mind and radiant spirit.

Our hearts are full of praise for the manifold blessings which we enjoy, for thy presence with our sick, thy comfort unto our bereaved, and thy good pleasure toward us all. In Jesus' name. Amen.—M. K. W. H.

Theme: Say So.

TEXT: "That which we have seen and heard declare we unto you." I John 1:3.

INTRODUCTORY: This short epistle is an apostolic testimony. In this third verse John declares that he is giving testimony concerning things which he had "seen and heard." This implies also what he had thought and felt and knew. He is giving experience. He would agree with the Psalmist who said, "Let the redeemed of the Lord say so."

Each friend of Christ living close to him learns from him and of him that which no one has learned before, and which it is his duty and privilege to tell out to others. God puts into the heart of every one of his people something he would have that one utter.

I. Let us think first of the influence of testimony. Testimony has influence. Consider an example of this from the secular field.

Before the Australian gold fields were opened a party of experts were sent to explore the district. They made their survey and sent in their report that gold would be found. But somehow nobody was greatly interested. Some time after some lads came from the Bush to Melbourne with some lumps of yellow ore in their pockets. "Why," said those to whom they showed it, "that's gold; where did you get it from?"

"Oh," said they, "there's plenty of it up our way." Next morning everyone who could was off to the diggings. As witnesses to Christ our lives must show that we have the "nugget." Yes, testimony has influence.

II. Now let us think of the charm of testimony. A report of a report, the mere repetition of a report, is a cold thing and of small value; but a report of what we have witnessed and experienced ourselves comes warmly upon men's hearts. So a mere formal description of faith and its blessings fall flat on the ear; but when a sincere believer tells of his own experience of the Lord's faithfulness, it has a great charm about it. We like to hear the narrative of a journey from the man himself. In a court of law no hearsay evidence is ever accepted. "Tell us," says the judge, "not what your neighbor said, but what you saw yourself." So personal evidence of the power of God's grace, or of what one has experienced, has a wonderfully convincing force upon the mind and heart and resolution of others. When the Psalmist said, "I sought the Lord, and he heard me, and delivered me from all my fears," he gave a far more powerful testimony than any amount of formal argument concerning prayer.

III. We may well think also of the great need of testimony. One reason is because of the lack of it, the want of an intelligent, warmhearted and true expression of testimony to what the Lord has done for us. Said the Psalmist, "Come and hear, all ye that fear God, and I will declare what he hath done for my soul" (Ps. 66:16). That is good for Christians. Or, as we quoted in the beginning, "Let the redeemed of the Lord say so" (Ps. 107:2). That is good for everybody. Redemption and all that is implied in it is surely a gift that demands acknowledgment. If you were struggling in the grip of some mysterious or deadly disease and after many disappointments at last you found a doctor who understood your case, conquered the disease and set you in perfect health again, what would you do? You would announce that doctor's name abroad, telling all you could of his skill, and mentioning yourself as an example of his healing power. You would do that as a debt of gratitude; but you would do it also for the sake of those who needed similar help. One duty of testimony grows out of the need of others.

IV. It is scarcely necessary to go on to mention the power of testimony. All that has been said implies it. There is surely great power in personal testimony. There is also great happiness in its expression, both from a sense of duty done and of help rendered. It also, most important, gives due glory to God and to Christ our Saviour.—H.

THEME PRAYER: Our Father God, may thy kingdom be powerfully preached by thy believing children. Let the minds of men be open to thy gospel, their attention arrested and their minds subdued. Teach us faithfulness in the work of witnessing to others. Forgive us our so many vain and contentious words and help us to live that our deeds may defend our faith and what we are witness to thy grace. In Jesus' name. Amen.

OFFERTORY SENTENCE: "If there be first a willing mind, it is accepted according that a man has, and not according to that he has not."

OFFERTORY PRAYER: Touch our eyes with insight, O Lord, that we may see shining through our possessions, our security and our freedom the toil and sacrifice of those to whom we owe them. Forbid that we shall take anything thus hallowed ungratefully, or abuse by our selfishness what others have made sacred by their high devotion. Wilt thou graciously accept our morning offerings and bless us as we bring them; we ask in Jesus' name. Amen.

Illustrative Material

SEED THOUGHTS, HOMILETIC AND EXPOSITORY. The Duty to Declare: I. The need of testimony. II. The influence of testimony. III. The inner blessedness of giving testimony and witness-bearing. Say so. Tell of that which

we have seen and heard and experienced. It is a great, almost supreme way of doing good.—H.

Witness-bearing: God gives to every human soul a message to deliver. Each friend of Christ, living close to him, learns something from him which no one has learned before, which he is to forthtell to the world.—J. R. M.

Witnessing: If you can do nothing else for God, you can carry a shining face. Charles Kingsley once said, "If you wish your neighbors to see what God is like, let them see what he can make you like."—N. W. C. A.

Choice Illustrations on the Theme

THE VALUE OF TESTIMONY. One night that rugged and wonderful worker among men whose lives had been broken by sin, Sam Hadley, was speaking to a large gathering of poor wrecks who had come into the doors of his mission hall. A trained physician sat among the men as an observer of a condition which drew him merely out of curiosity. The vigorous appeal of the preacher for immediate decision for a new life finally so impressed the physician that he could not restrain the protest of his scientific objection to it all, and he arose and speaking feelingly said: "Mr. Hadley, you have been appealing here with a glowing passion to these drunkards for a new and made-over life. I speak as a physician to say that you would not talk to these men thus if you had ever seen what the inside of a drunkard's stomach looks like." As quick as a flash from the experience which was the basis of all the great mission worker's preaching, he replied, "Sir, I had a drunkard's stomach, and Jesus Christ saved me from it, and saves me from it now." How eloquently does genuine experience always meet life! It is the most convincing preachment we have. Oh, for a witnessing church! Your experience—don't leave it out—M. S. Rice.

WITNESSING TESTIMONY. Frederick the Great was once ridiculing Christianity in the presence of his generals. Most of them were convulsed with laughter at his coarse jests. One of them, however, Joachim von Zietan, remained silent, and after a time could bear it no longer. "Your majesty knows well," said he, "that in war I have never feared any danger, and everywhere I have boldly risked my life for you and my country. But there is One above us who is greater than you and I—greater than all men. The Holy One I can never allow to be mocked or insulted; for on him repose my faith, my comfort, and my hope in life and death. I salute your Majesty." The great emperor looked at the man in astonishment and admiration, and then and there apologized for what he had said. Jochim von Zietan had spoken the right word at the right time and it has made his name illustrious.—H. B. Hunting.

THE VALUE OF TESTIMONY. Bishop Thoburn was a man so widely traveled, so humanly approachable, so crisp and keen of speech, and so penetrative of other people's individuality that his long life made a lasting impression in India, America, and among those who went down to the sea in ships in his company. Bishop F. J. McConnell says: "He was once crossing the Indian Ocean on a boat on which were two English-women who avowed themselves atheists and who argued atheism for days in his presence. As the journey came near to its end one of the women said: 'Bishop Thoburn, we do not wish to be impertinent, but we wonder that you could listen respectfully to our arguments for two weeks without being convinced.' The bishop replied: 'Madam, I have greatly enjoyed your conversation. I have never heard the case for atheism more brilliantly put. I am sorry the journey is so nearly over. But I have enjoyed the conversation merely as an intellectual exercise. There was no more likelihood of convincing me of the non-existence of God than of the non-existence of myself. For I have known God for forty years.'"—*The Christian Advocate*.

AN OUTLET ALSO BY WITNESSING. The electrician had stopped at the street cor-ner to renew carbons in the arc lamp. A small boy was watching him. As the day was bright and sunny the boy was astonished to see that the man wore rubber boots. "Why do you wear those boots?" he asked. "Do you think it's going to rain?" The workman laughed good-naturedly. "No, sonny, I wear them so as to be safe from electric shocks when I handle these lamps. Electricity can't go through rubber very well, and one of the funny things about electricity is that it can't get into a person unless it can get out again." Is that not true about other things in life? Take love. It can't get into a human heart unless it can get out again. It must either find an outlet in service or die. Yet many persons forget that truth.—*The Otterbein Teacher*.

YOUR TONGUE, YOUR HANDS

Christ has no hands but our hands
To do His work today;
He has no feet but our feet
To lead men in His way;
He has no tongues but our tongues,
To tell men how He died;
He has no help but our help,
To bring them to His side.
—Annie J. Flint.

EVENING SERVICE

Theme: Narrow Windows.

TEXT: "And there were narrow windows . . . and palm trees." Ezek. 40:16.

INTRODUCTION: This picturesque phrase in the book of Ezekiel about narrow windows and palm trees summarizes in a few words a "right philosophy." Many people are looking out on life through narrow windows. They feel the restriction of their circumstances. Their ambitions have not been realized; their dreams have not been fulfilled. Opportunity has passed them by. They have never had a chance to do great things, or to develop their latent talents. The great tide of life has left them high and dry. Others have gone out to triumph and achievement; they are left with "the daily round and common task." Life has become monotonous —even meaningless, and (either openly or secretly) they have said, "Oh, to get out of this rut, this village, this town, this job, this prison—to get away from the pettiness and narrowness of it all." If we are looking at life today through the narrow windows of circumstances, what do we see? Or, to use a modern expression, what is our reaction? That depends upon ourselves—upon our philosophy of life. We see what we look for. The mud is there—plenty of it. But thank God, so are the stars, and palm trees, and open flowers. We can see them from the narrowest windows—if we look in the right direction. It depends upon the "view" we are taking of life. Each one of us makes our own world, and the world we make depends very largely upon how we see the things around us.

I. Some of the finest work for the kingdom of God is being done by men and women who are looking out on life through the narrow windows of restricted circumstances. Because they are people with a right philosophy—people with vision and faith—they are seeing from their narrow windows stars, palm trees, and open flowers. I think, for instance, of the folk who are working in countless country churches up and down the land—steadily plodding on amidst the big difficulties of small churches. Not for them the inspiration of great sermons and large congregations, the well-trained choir, the beautiful organ. Instead, often an indifferent sermon, a handful of people—probably a harmonium which has long since lost its harmony; generally one good lady, at least, in the congregation who takes it upon herself to lead the singing—all out of tune! But in nearly every small village Bethel one finds some person who, for years, has borne all this, kept the church alive, and the witness for the kingdom going.

Why have they done it? What has been their inspiration to do this uninspiring work? Is it not because they have been able to see through the narrow windows a vision of the kingdom?

The vision is sometimes blurred—can one be surprised? It is their faith in God and in the ultimate triumph of his kingdom that inspires them to go on.

II. Then again, many people are looking out at life through the narrow windows of physical infirmity—blindness, deafness, crippling diseases, chronic ill-health, and so on. Some have allowed these things completely to defeat and overwhelm them. Others have overcome the physical disablement, and have achieved greatness, even happiness, in spite of it. Moses had an impediment of speech—but he did not let that prevent him from leading his people out of captivity. St. Paul was a cripple—but it did not prevent him from travelling far and wide preaching the gospel of Jesus Christ. John Keats and Robert Louis Stevenson suffered from consumption. Milton was blind, and Beethoven deaf. President Roosevelt had infantile paralysis. Catherine Booth, the mother of the Salvation Army, was always ailing. George Matheson was stricken with blindness. When he took farewell of his Edinburgh congregation in 1899, he described himself as "Barred by every gate of fortune, yet refusing to give in; overtaken by night, yet confident of the morning." "Overtaken by night . . ." Isn't that the spirit of his hymn?

O joy that seekest me through pain,
I dare not ask to fly from thee.
I trace the rainbow through the rain,
And trust the promise is not vain
That morn shall tearless be.

Happiness depends upon a right philosophy of life. And a right philosophy of life depends upon our faith in God. If we are sure of God, then none of the blows of life will overwhelm and defeat us. Unless we are sure of him, sooner or later life will conquer us and perhaps utterly crush us. By being sure of God I don't mean that we shall always understand his ways. There are many things we never shall understand in this world. But we can all understand Jesus when he points out time and again, in parable after parable, that God is our Father. I believe that the whole secret of happiness and peaceful assurance is to believe in God —not as a dim and distant Ruler of the Universe—not as a First Cause—but as a Father, a Father who cares, and loves and gives.—John Dunford.

Suggested Texts and Themes

The Highest Peak in the Range: "But in the last days it shall come to pass, that the mountain of the house of the Lord shall be established in the top of the mountains, and it shall be exalted above the hills; and people shall flow unto it." Mic. 4:1.

Forces That Ruin Cities: "Woe to the bloody city; it is all full of lies and robbery; the prey departeth not; the noise of a whip, and the noise of the rattling of the wheels, and of the prancing horses, and of the jumping chariots." Nah. 3:1.

The Ready Christian: "For I am ready not to be bound only, but also to die at Jerusalem for the name of the Lord Jesus." Acts 21:13.

The Fame of Faith: "First, I thank my God through Jesus Christ for you all, that your faith is spoken of throughout the whole world." Rom. 1:8.

Radiations of Moral Influence: "And ye, in any wise keep yourselves from the accursed thing, lest ye make yourselves accursed, when ye take of the accursed thing, and make the camp of Israel a curse, and trouble it." Jos. 6:18.

MIDWEEK FELLOWSHIP MEETING TOPIC

(Church Night or Suggested Sermon Subject)

Theme: The Deepest Need of Civilization.

TEXT: "Tell me, I pray thee, where the seer's house is." I Sam. 9:18.

We know where the man of fame lives. One can find his address in almost any telephone book. We know where the wealthy man dwells. It is easy to find out where honor or love or knowledge lives.

I. But where is the wise man's house? This is a serious question of our times. Is it at Washington, London, Moscow? From time immemorial the human race has asked, "Where can wisdom be found?"

II. Nothing is more desperately needed than just what the Bible calls wisdom, moral insight, ability to discriminate between values, understanding of what things are worth living for and ability to put them into practice. For centuries the Christian church was the custodian of the world's values. Now this crucial function of our civilization has for the most part been taken over by others who have largely failed. There is growing dissatisfaction with their leadership.

III. We need the rare, creative and practical wisdom described in the book of Proverbs. This wisdom became personal according to the Christian idea. As the love of God was shown forth in Christ so also was the wisdom of God.

IV. Wisdom can become any man's possession. It is the gift of God to men who will ask for it and consistently seek it. The deepest need of our civilization is for the common man to be wise. And wisdom is within his reach. Where does the wise man live? Does he live at your address?—M. K. W. H.

CHRISTIAN ENDEAVOR SOCIETY TOPIC

Nov. 28. The Money I Have to Spend. Mal. 3:10; I Chron. 29:11-13; Matt. 25:14-30.

SUNDAY SCHOOL LESSON

Nov. 28. **Our Ever-present Help.** Ps. 46, Ps. 142.

MEMORY VERSE: "God is our refuge and strength, a very present help in trouble." Ps. 46:1.

The 46th Psalm has three stanzas. In the first God is the lord of creation.

Changing earth, shaking mountains, roaring and troubled waters should not cause man to fear. The Creator is our refuge and strength, our very present help.

In the second stanza God is lord of history. Though nations rage and kingdoms move, God's voice has authority and his presence is with his people.

In the third stanza God is the lord of eternal peace. It is useless to resist the power of the almighty ruler. He who commands the hosts of heaven is with us.

This Psalm inspired Martin Luther to compose his greatest hymn, "A Mighty Fortress Is Our God."

SUNDAY: DECEMBER FIFTH

MORNING SERVICE

Theme: Illusions and Expectations (Advent).

SUGGESTED SCRIPTURE READING: Luke 1:68-79; Heb. 10:19-25.

SELECTED HYMNS: "Come, thou long-expected Jesus."—C. Wesley. "Hark, the sound, the Saviour comes."—P. Doddridge. "Draw nigh, draw night, Emanuel."—Latin. "Lift up your heads, ye gates of brass."—J. Montgomery. "O come, O come, Emmanuel."—Latin. "Watchman, tell us of the night."—J. Bowring.

CALL TO WORSHIP: "Behold, I will send my messenger, and he shall prepare the way before me: and the Lord, whom ye seek, shall suddenly come to his temple, even the messenger of the covenant, whom ye delight in: behold, he shall come, saith the Lord of hosts."

INVOCATION PRAYER: We bow in awe before thee, O God, whom space and time cannot bound nor limit. We marvel at thine unchangeableness, the same yesterday, today, tomorrow. And so with thy love. We cannot think of thee the God of righteousness being less righteous tomorrow, nor as a God of love less loving tomorrow. In thine eternal righteousness and thine everlasting love we live and move and have our being.

We hail the advent of our Lord and Saviour whose coming in Bethlehem we

remember. Does he not come unto his people now? Does he not always come to his people? Ever come into our community. Ever come, Lord Jesus, into our hearts. Ever come into our homes. Give us eyes to see thee, hearts to love thee, hands and feet to serve thee. In thine own name we ask.— M. K. W. H.

Theme: Illusions and Expectations (Advent).

TEXT: "Let your moderation be known unto all men. The Lord is at hand." Phil. 4:5.

INTRODUCTORY: The special note of the Advent season is expectation. We cultivate the habit of looking forward that we may come to Christmas time with the happy spirit of expectancy in our hearts. For this spirit of expectancy is like a golden thread, linking together the children of God of all ages. Ask the early Christians what they are doing, and they will reply: "The Lord is at hand! We are waiting for him!" And that same unconquerable spirit of expectation still lives in human hearts. Still men wait and dream of a good to come—a new coming of Christ.

I should like, this morning, to trace that golden thread of expectation, and to see what message it has for us today.

I. You will see at once that this spirit of expectation was the master-instinct of the prophets. They moved through the world of their day with something of the far-off look of men who have trained themselves in the rapture of the forward view. And gradually their vision came to center in one thing—the promise of the coming of Christ. Always there arose some prophet to stir the slumbering embers and kindle the expiring flame. The mighty expectation of many centuries ended in "a child wrapped in swaddling clothes and lying in a manger."

II. And as with the prophets of the Old Testament, so with the apostles of the New. For their eyes, too, were fixed on the future—on what they called the "coming of Christ"—with them, too, "The Lord was at hand." And here, also, we notice the same mingling—the same necessary and inevitable mingling —of error and illusion. Whatever else may be said of the early church, this is undoubtedly true, that its back was toward the world and its face toward the coming of the Lord.

What are we to say to it all? Are we to regard his coming as a vain illusion? Are we to cease to expect his coming? No; for both illusion and expectation have a genuine value in the Christian life. Indeed, every Christian life should be a life of expectation; a life lived in the belief that as we grow older, God will, through the teaching of experience, make himself more and more known to us; an earnest and eager desire for fresh revelations of his will, his power and his love.

III. Here is the true faith of Christ's coming; a faith that expects great things of God, and attempts great things for God; a faith that discovers in Christ, amid the confusion of these times, the foregleams of a great and better tomorrow; a faith that dares to pray for the coming of his kingdom, not in words only, but also, and much more, in works, watching for it the while as those who wait for the morning.

And the thought is not one for us only as individuals. This is a faith for the whole church, and for the world at large.

What we require is the quiet temper, which, refusing to sink into apathy, or despair because of the evils of our times, is ever looking for and expecting some new and more glorious coming of Christ.

I say these words with special meaning this morning. For once more the time draws near the birth of Christ. Once more we prepare to celebrate the Christmas festival. We would do well to do so, but we must not merely look backward, we must look forward. For "the Lord is at hand," yes, indeed, he is always coming; and we must pray and hope and expect that the bells of Christmas may not only recall the manger of Bethlehem but may also, more and more as the years roll by, "ring in the Christ that is to be."— W. R. M.

THEME PRAYER: Let this coming Christmas, our Father, mark truly a bringing of grace for each house, for each person, young and old, for poor and rich, for high and low, but primarily for the lowly and the abandoned, the tired and the despondent, the bowed down and the worried! Let us deeply experience the holy Christ festival of this year; let it be to us a blessing now and for all time! Amen.

OFFERTORY SENTENCE: "There shall come a star out of Jacob, and a sceptre shall rise out of Israel."

OFFERTORY PRAYER: Our Father, grant that those necessary works wherein we are engaged, whether in the affairs of thy church or of this world, may not prevail to hinder us; but that at the appearing and advent of thy Son we may hasten with joy to meet him. Bless the offerings we bring to the end that his kingdom may be hastened. In his name we ask. Amen.

Illustrative Material

SEED THOUGHTS, HOMILETIC AND EXPOSITORY: The Lord Is at Hand: This is not primarily an Advent text. I. The Lord is at hand providentially. II. Spiritually. III. Personally. He is at hand in the operations of nature. In the events of history. In redemptive power.

In Expectation: I. Therefore be joyful.

II. Be gentle. III. Be trustful. IV. Be prayerful. V. Be peaceful.—C. J. P. E. Advent: I. The fullness of time. 1. The time appointed by the Father. 2. Time has a fullness. II. The filling of time. "God sent his Son." III. The fullness of benefit to us. Redemption. Liberation. IV. The fullness of duty by us. 1. Christmas should be a time of fullness of joy on our part. 2. A fullness of gratitude. 3. A fullness of benevolence.—B. A.

Choice Advent Illustrations

EXPECTATION

They all were looking for a king
 To stay their foes and lift them high;
Thou cam'st, a little baby thing,
 That made a woman cry.
                —George MacDonald.

LIVING IN EXPECTATION. An old Negro woman was once questioned as to the whereabouts of her dead husband. She replied, "I hope he is whar I 'spec' he ain't!" Too much of our Christian hope is like that. We hope for peace on earth but we do not really expect it. We hope for better relations between races and classes of people, but we do not really see how it can come about. We wish that we ourselves could be finer—purer in thought, more courageous in upholding our Christian ideals —but it seems too much honestly to believe possible.

Thousands in Jesus' own country were hoping for a Messiah when Jesus was born into the world. But they didn't recognize their Saviour when he came to them. Only a few, like the saintly Anne in the temple, "were living in expectation." But it is because of these few that the world moves ahead. Jesus Christ works wonders in this world through lives that face themselves and the world with hope.—Ganse Little.

WHY THE INCARNATION? Two friends were one day walking in the fields talking as they walked of the inscrutable mystery of God's doings. One of them was a man of some intellectual force, whose heart, however, had never been opened to the divine light. He said petulantly, "How can a man of finite mind know God? How can he discover what God is doing? How can he understand God's will? And pointing contemptuously to an anthill where thousands of insects were busy at their toil, he asked, "How can those ants understand what is in my mind?" Like a flash the answer came. "There is only one way—by becoming an ant and declaring it to them!" And in that answer lies everything that we need for the enlightment of our minds and the establishment of our hearts. For God became man in the person of his Son, that we might have a calm, unshaken confidence in him.—J. Stuart Holden.

THE RISING ADVENT STAR. A band of fugitives was crossing an eastern desert. The night was dark; but they determined to push on. Soon they lost their way, and had to spend the night in anxiety and fear. It seemed as if the night would never pass. But almost all at once the sun arose, bringing daylight and showing the way of safety. Not one of them ever forgot that sunrising. So too the people of this world in their wanderings. They were lost— lost in the darkness of sin. But the Day-spring from on high visited them, has risen upon us, making plain the way of eternal safety. Christ is the Dawn. Christ is our Day-spring, and the purpose of his coming was to give us the light that would lead to eternal life.—5,000 Best Modern Illustrations.

ADVENT PREPARATION

Have you any old grudge you'd like
 to pay,
Any wrong laid up from a bygone day?
Gather them all now, and lay them
 away
  When Christmas comes.

Hard thoughts are heavy to carry, my
 friend,
And life is short from beginning to end;
Be kind to yourself, leave nothing to
 mend
  When Christmas comes.
                —William Lytle.

THE WHY OF THE ADVENT. The most wonderful event in all the world's history was the Son of God becoming man. This happened when he was born as a Babe in Bethlehem. He came into the world that he might get nearer to the people, and tell them of God's love. A story is told of a Moravian missionary who went to the West Indies to preach to the slaves. But they were toiling all the day in the fields, and he could not get near to them. So he had himself sold as a slave and went among the other slaves, toiling with them in the fields, that he might tell the story of God's love. This illustrates in a way what Christ did.—J. R. Miller, D.D.

EVENING SERVICE

Theme: Ambassadors of Christ.

TEXT: "We are ambassadors therefore on behalf of Christ." II Cor. 5:20 (A.S.V.).

INTRODUCTORY: Being ambassadors of Christ implies our conscious acceptance of active membership in the Christian fellowship.

I. Ambassadors of Joy. Luke 2:10; Galatians 4:4-7; Matthew 6:28-31; Col. 1:12-14. Our message, which is the echo and the continuation of the message of Christ, is nothing less than the announcement of a new world order, the kingdom of God. We are ordained to proclaim the Law of Love, of Brotherhood among men, of Sacrifice, and of Purity—the Law which alone has the power to transform humanity. Our message is characterized by the joy which it reflects; the joy of men who have become conscious of their divine Sonship.

II. Ambassadors of Life. Psalm 16:11; John 20:31, 17:3; Revelation 22:2. Our world is being torn by one revolution after another, and teems with those who—and with justification—are demanding the right to live. If we are true ambassadors, we are sent also to those who are rebellious and who have lost heart. It is our mission to give meaning to this earthly life, to give direction to the outbursts of the human conscience, and in the place of hatred to sow the seeds of fraternal life.

III. Ambassadors of Liberty. Psalm 119:45; John 8:36; Galatians 5:1; Romans 8:21. In permitting the reality of the consciousness of his divine origin to escape him, man has lost the true conception of liberty, the full appreciation of his personal worth, and his understanding of the true meaning of the obedience which he owes to his Father. Man attains the fullness of his personality only when he has acquired complete human liberty through his perfect union with God. Jesus, in his absolute obedience to God, and his complete union with him, dominates from the cross by virtue of the freedom that comes only through obedience.

IV. Ambassadors of Light. Isaiah 42:16; Psalm 43:3; John 14:6; Matthew 5:14-16. Impurity robs the eye of its luster. The purification of the heart and of the conscience, realized through union with Christ, gives a new radiance to every human countenance. For man to understand the truths and the principles of which he has need in order to live abundantly, he has but to grasp the meaning of the simple message of salvation contained in Christ's Gospel. The true ambassador of Christ leaves a train of light in his wake.

V. Ambassadors of Deliverance. Psalm 32:7; Psalm 107:6; Matthew 10:7-8; II Corinthians 3:16-17. The lame walked and proclaimed their recovery, the blind sang a hymn of thankfulness for the restoration of their sight. We are indeed surrounded by spiritual impotents; by men and women who groan in moral and physical distress. We are true ambassadors only if in the midst of such a multitude miracles are being wrought.

Since the beginning of divine Revelation, God's ambassadors have been chosen and called by him. Those on whom the spirit of God reposes become his ambassadors. What is demanded of ambassadors is a complete consecration to their mission, perfect obedience to the divine inspiration. The true ambassadors of Christ are capable of surpassing every human effort, through their understanding of human needs, and of entering vitally into every human distress, because their source of inspiration is the divine Power of God.

Suggestive Advent Texts and Themes

Redemption Drawing Nigh: "Lift up your heads; for your redemption draweth nigh." Luke 21:28.

Advent Preparation: "I am the voice of one crying in the wilderness, Make straight the way of the Lord." John 1:23.

Advent Messenger: "Behold, I send my messenger before thy face, which shall prepare thy way before thee." Matt. 11:10.

Advent Prophesied: "Behold, a virgin shall conceive, and bear a son, and shall call his name Immanuel." Isa. 7:14.

Incarnation Prophesied: "They shall call his name Emmanuel, which being interpreted is, God with us." Matt. 1:23.

MIDWEEK FELLOWSHIP MEETING TOPIC

(Church Night or Suggested Sermon Subject)

Theme: Without Me—Nothing.

TEXT: "Without me ye can do nothing." John 15:5.

Christian character and Christian service are not the results of accidental circumstances. They are always the fruits of Christian faith. "Without me," said Jesus to the disciples, "ye can do nothing." He did not mean, of course, that without him one could not walk, or breathe, or work, or engage in one's daily activities. He was thinking rather of the things that have an abiding value; the things that make for nobility of soul and fruitfulness in service—those things, in a word, that we think of as the crowning glory of life. Without him, such high achievements cannot be attained. To have faith in him—that is the way by which are built into life those things that enable us to fulfill the divine purpose.

No man lives a true and useful life apart from Christ. We need his eye to guide us, his hand to uphold us, his arm to lean upon.

I. We have here a vision of failure. Without Christ—nothing.

II. We have here an aspiration of hope. That word "do" has music in it. It suggests great possibilities.

III. We have here a voice of wisdom. Without Christ nothing, but with him all things are possible. Join with him. Abide in the Vine. Fruit-bearing results.

CHRISTIAN ENDEAVOR SOCIETY TOPIC

Dec. 5. The Time I Have to Spend. I Pet. 4:11; I Cor. 10:31.

BULLETIN BOARD SLOGANS FOR THE MONTH

By EARL RINEY

The stars still point the way for the wise men.

Working toward a future goal sets your life in a higher key.

The elevator to heaven is not running; take the stairs.

To find your own comfort carry it to another.

A man's wealth is the good he does in the world.

Christ was the supreme endeavor of God to make himself known.

Get out of the daily grind; go to church on Sunday.

No man can avoid his own company so he had better make it as good as possible.

To live in triumph is better than to live in luxury.

There are no deductions from the wages of sin.

Christ's presence in the heart spells Christmas to the individual.

Self-righteousness is making a bridge of our own shadow.

SUNDAY SCHOOL LESSON

Dec. 5. A Prayer for Forgiveness. Ps. 130:86.

MEMORY VERSE: "Thou, Lord, art good, and ready to forgive, and abundant in lovingkindness unto all them that call upon thee." Psalm 86:5. (A.S.V.).

"Out of the depths"; thus begins the 130 Psalm. "Under every deep a lower deep opens" said Emerson. In what depths was the Psalmist. Notice the plural—he was in more than one. He is in the depth of sin for he is in need of forgiveness. This may also be a depth of shame, loneliness, despair. His physical being may also be in its own depth of ill, as well as his soul.

Though cast down he is not utterly defeated. He has expectation. He knows where forgiveness is to be found. He will hope in the word of God. He will wait for the mercy of God to lift him out of the depths. He waits, tense and impatient, more than watchmen—wait for the morning, but he waits in hope.

The Psalm ends on a high level. He calls upon his people, the community of Israel to share in his expectation. There is mercy for the people of the promise, as there is forgiveness for himself, a single penitent.

SUNDAY: DECEMBER TWELFTH

MORNING SERVICE

Theme: God's Revelation in Christ (Advent).

SUGGESTED SCRIPTURE READING: Heb. 1:1-14.

SELECTED HYMNS: "O Christ, our King, Creator."—Gregory the Great. " 'Tis for conquering kings to gain."—Anon. "O Jesus, King, most wonderful."—Bernard of Clairvaux. "O for a thousand tongues to sing."—C. Wesley. "To our Redeemer's glorious name." —A. Steele.

CALL TO WORSHIP: "Behold, I will send my messenger, and he shall prepare the way before me: and the Lord, whom ye seek, shall suddenly come to his temple, even the messenger of the covenant, whom ye delight in."

INVOCATION PRAYER (Advent): Almighty and ever-blessed God, who in the fullness of time didst send forth thy Son to be the Saviour of the world, as at this time through thy long-suffering patience with us we are permitted once again to observe the season of Advent, we pray that we may give good heed to the warning voices which call us to repentance and preparation of heart, so that we may come to the brightness of his rising who for our salvation was incarnate on this earth. May we all bring forth fruits meet for repentance. O thou who art ever coming to us in the events that befall us, forbid that with untrimmed lamp and ungirt loin we should but hear thy voice from behind the shutting door. Grant unto us that, spending the time of our sojourning here in godliness and holy fear, we may be like men that look for their Lord. We ask in the name of the Christ we look for. Amen.

Theme: God's Revelation in Christ (Advent).

TEXT: "God, who at sundry times and in divers manners spake in time past unto the fathers by the prophets, hath in these last days spoken unto us by his Son." Heb. 1:1, 2.

INTRODUCTORY: Revelation, in the Old Testament, means to unveil, or to lay bare. In the New Testament it has the added implication, to disclose what was before unknown.

Man's attempts to discover God end in failure. The door must be opened from the other side. What we know of God is not due to reason or logic or any human means.

I. God only reveals himself when we are ready. This is the experience of the race. The first revelations were elementary. The author of the Epistle to the Hebrews caught the significance of progressive revelation when he wrote, "God, who at sundry times and in divers manners spake in time past unto the fathers by the prophets, hath . . . spoken unto us by his Son." It is the testimony of the Bible that revelation is made strictly in the degree to which people are able to receive it. Gradually, and in differing ways, God has unveiled himself through the long centuries before Christ. When the world was ready to apprehend him, he revealed himself as Immanuel.

II. It is always "when the fulness of the time" has been taken into account that God makes his appearance. We must be ready to receive him. All the great souls of the church have seen God in "the fulness of the time" (Gal. 4:4). When we are ready, he is revealed "by his Spirit, who searcheth all things."

III. God reveals himself supremely in Christ. Jesus is the answer to our endless questions. What is God like? The Saviour's reply discloses what was before unknown—God is like a father. What are his intentions toward us? Jesus says, God desires that each person "might have life, and . . . have it more abundantly." Apart from Jesus, mankind can do no more than guess the answers to fundamental questions. The revelation of God in Jesus is unique. Even his enemies are constrained to admit that "never man spake like this Man!"

IV. The true revelation of what one thinks of another is found in what he is willing to endure for the other's sake. Here is the divine record in Christ: "God so loved the world that he gave his only begotten Son"; "God spared not his own Son, but delivered him up for us all"; "I am the Good Shepherd, and know my sheep . . . I lay down my life for the sheep."

William Spurgeon was once approached by an old man who said, "Dr. Spurgeon, I am glad to meet you. I am the father of Henry Drummond." "Oh," replied the preacher, "then I already know you, for I know your son so well." Those who know the Lord Jesus Christ well, already know God. "He that hath seen me," he said to Philip on that solemn day when he spoke of himself as the Way, the Truth, and the Life, "hath seen the Father." "It is written, 'Eye hath not seen nor ear heard, neither have entered into the heart of man, the things God hath prepared for them that love him.' But God hath revealed them unto us by his Spirit, for the Spirit searcheth all things, yea the deep things of God."—Rev. Douglas M. Carhart.

THEME PRAYER: Almighty God, our heavenly Father, who in thy providence hast made all ages a preparation for the kingdom of thy Son; we beseech thee to make ready our hearts for the brightness of thy glory and the fulness of thy blessing in Jesus Christ our Lord. Amen.

OFFERTORY SENTENCE: "Take heed, and beware of covetousness: for a man's life consisteth not in the abundance of the things which he possesseth." "Seek ye first the kingdom of God, and his righteousness; and all these things shall be added unto thee."

OFFERTORY PRAYER: Grant unto us, O Lord, divine wisdom that we may live life well, in the consecration of our talents, in the dedication of our time, and in the stewardship of our wealth. Save us from the folly of spending life as men put wages into a bag full of holes; rather may we lay up treasure in heaven where moth cannot corrupt, where thieves cannot break through and steal. Amen.—M. K. W. H.

Illustrative Material

SEED THOUGHTS, HOMILETIC AND EXPOSITORY. God Revealed in Christ: I. God's revelation of himself supernaturally communicated. II. Gradually and variously revealed. III. In Christ his final and full revelation.—D. R. J.

God's Revelation to Man: I. To man. II. Through man. III. In a variety of ways. IV. Has made Christ the final revelation of himself. V. The superiority of this man.

Advent Anticipations: From the remotest ages prophetic utterances announcing better times and a coming deliverance had pervaded the ancient world. Such mutilated and ancient prophecies are found among the most widely differing nations.

The Advent: Near events have remote causes. The majestic river that sweeps by freighted with commerce cannot be explained without going back to distant hills and hidden springs.

Choice Advent Illustrations

ADVENT NOTES. In a world of darkness and sin Isaiah rang the bells of prophecy, which was fulfilled when the sound of those bells reverberated among the Judean hills on that solemn midnight when Jesus was born in Bethlehem. The first note of Isaiah's prophetic chime was, "His name shall be called Wonderful." And he was most wonderful in his birth, life, death and resurrection. The second note was that he should be called "Counselor." Surely he answers the world's need for guidance. The third note was, "The mighty God, the everlasting Father." The power and presence of God were exemplified for man in the birth of the Christ. The fourth note was, "The Prince of Peace." At the Christmas season we still hear the echo of those bells of prophecy, for we have God's promise that of "the increase of his government and peace there shall be no end."—Rev. Myron E. Hayes.

THE DIAMOND OF DAYS. The year keeps its best holiday until the last. Other days may be bright with June skies, or rich with autumn colors; or they may be charged with personal meaning as they mark birthdays or other anniversaries, or they may be big with national significance as they commemorate historic events; but greater than all these is the day we are soon to celebrate. Its skies may be somber and its leaves all dead, but it marks the greatest event of all time and hides in its heart the greatest joy. Its meaning is more than personal or national, and its joy overflows all lines and in some degree floods the globe. It is celebrated on more continents and islands and by more millions of people than any other, and rises into the grandeur of a cosmopolitan day. The great world knows deep down in its heart that this day, beneath all its merrymaking, means more for it than any other on the calendar. Christmas is the diamond of days, and it is fitting that the year should bring it forth as its finest gem to sparkle on the robe of its departing glory.—J. H. Snowden, D.D.

EXPECTATION. Since the creation of the world there has occurred no greater event than the birth of Jesus. It was the beginning of the creation of man anew. To it all the ages looked forward. Patriarchs had "seen his day" in hours of spiritual exaltation; poets had dreamed of his coming; and prophets had been granted visions of the promised Messiah. The expectation of the Jewish race had been awakened until many a mother looked into the eyes of her babe and wondered if in him might not be the Deliverer of the people. Surrounding nations absorbed the spirit of expectancy, and not alone in Judea, but in Rome and Arabia, the advent of a statelier king than had ever wielded scepter upon the earth was cherished in the hearts of men.—Charles C. Albertson, D.D.

THE ADVENT PROMISE. Among the curiosities of the Bank of England may be seen some ashes, the remains of some banknotes that were burned in the great fire of Chicago. After the fire they were found and carefully put between boards and brought to the bank. Various tests were applied, the numbers and value were ascertained, and the Bank of England paid the money to the owners. If a human promise can be worth so much, how much more is the promise of God.

The Advent promise too was one of infinite value.

BEYOND THE TELLING. An Alaskan girl was found by her teacher admiring a beautiful sunset. When it was suggested that she try to put the scene on canvas, she replied: "Oh, I can't draw glory." So the most expressive words are utterly inadequate when one would describe to another his own personal vision of the Christ. Let us get a new vision of him at this Advent season.

Suggestive Advent Texts and Themes

The Messiah of Prophecy: Isa. 52:13-54:12.

The Messiah of Vision: Luke 2:29, 32.

The Messiah of Faith: Matt. 16:12-17.

The Messiah of Accomplishment: Rom. 8:34-35.

The Eternal Christ: Rev. 1:17-18.

The Greatest Quest: "Where is he?" Matt. 2:2.

The Rising Star: "There shall come a Star out of Jacob," etc. Num. 24:17.

The Day Star in the Heart: II Pet. 1:10.

EVENING SERVICE

Theme: The Word of God.

God is the Father of all men. All men are his children.

His divine fatherhood must be in some and perhaps many respects like human fatherhood. He would desire to speak to his children. He would desire to express his love. He would reveal his love and fatherhood in guidance, in wisdom, in providence.

God has many means at his disposal to do this. Among these means is the use of language. He gave his children power of communicating one with another through words. He might use the same means of speaking to his children.

This leads to a child's perplexity. A small boy of this church asked for a conference with me. He came with a hard problem to solve. He said, "God speaks to his children, doesn't he?" "Yes." "How does God know all the languages so that he can speak to all of his children." "Oh!" I said, "God speaks to us in our minds and hearts." Then, said the boy, "I can understand that."

I. So the translations began—God speaking to his children in their minds and hearts—and these men transcribing in their own language and for their own people the Word of God. Thus across many centuries inspired men wrote out in the Hebrew language the thirty-nine books which constitute the Old Testament. The Word of God is translated thus into Hebrew.

And then in due course of time after the coming of Christ when men had not only heard but seen the Word of God —they put it down in language, the language which was read across a wide area in the world—the New Testament was written down in Greek.

And so it came to pass that the Word of God, in the language of the heart and mind, was translated into Hebrew and Greek. There are sixty-six books in this translation, thirty-nine of the Old Testament in Hebrew; twenty-seven of the New Testament in Greek.

This Word of God should belong to all men—those who spoke neither Hebrew nor Greek. It must reach the minds and hearts of all men—and so continues the fascinating story of the manuscripts.

Our interest today is in the English Bible, but what of the stories of translation into more than one thousand other languages, the Latin, Coptic, Arabic, French, German, Japanese, Chinese, Tagalog, Bulu, Navajo—on and on. I'm thrilled that I have a little share in this—in Tokyo, Japan, Takeo Matsumoto is now translating the Bible into colloquial Japanese for the American Bible Society. For five years I taught him the English language. As he bends over his Hebrew O.T. and his Greek N.T. he also scrutinizes the English versions for exact meanings. My first preaching was on the streets of Japanese towns with Matsumoto Sau as my interpreter. I speak only of this to bring the matter a little closer.

Consider that in the early days after the translation was made the multiplication of manuscripts was by hand, for the art of printing was not. Many old parchments can be seen at the Huntington Library. I wished to study one some years ago. I was given permission but a guard was by my side all the time, so priceless are these parchments. Not only must translation be made from language to language, but the same language changes from century to century.

It was a man named John Wycliffe who was born in 1320 "who saw that the true emancipation of the souls of his fellow men lay in the opportunity to read the Bible in his own tongue and in his own home." He gave his attention to putting the Bible into the language of the everyday man and woman—not withholding it from them by keeping it in Latin, and to be expressed by a careless, indolent and haughty priesthood.

This translation crystallized the various dialects of England into the English language for the future use of the English-speaking and writing world. But language changes—from 1383 to 1611 is a long time. When James I came to the throne of England in 1603, it was in the midst of a galaxy of scholars and writers which made the period unique in English history. It was the age of Shakespeare, Spenser, Bacon and many others. The English language had been given a purity, style and beauty that has never been sur-

passed. It is a fascinating story how King James organized a group of scholars who translated the Bible anew and gave us the version which we shall always read and treasure and love. The influence of the King James version of the Bible upon the English-speaking peoples of the world is inestimable.

Now 433 years have passed since 1611. Many discoveries have been made which throw new light on the Bible text. (The words of many 1611 passages are out of use or sound archaic—thou and thee, thy and thine, have dropped out of our common speech. Meanings of English words have changed: "Conversation" in King James means "conduct" now. "Communicate" in King James mean "share" at the present time.

Errors in translation have been found. "We loved him because he first loved us" may be true; but it is not the exact meaning; "We love because he first loved us." All Christian love depends on God's love for men.

And now it comes to pass that ninety-one men working together, men of our time, some of whom we know, have again translated the Bible into our own present-day language. That which God would say to his children comes to them in words that they can easily understand.

This is a great event, perhaps far greater than we think.

II. Translation is not enough. The multiplication of Bibles in languages and in the English language is important, but in our hands the Bible must be interpreted. Coming from the mind and heart of God into a language that reaches the eye and ear it must also reach the mind and the heart. This process let us call interpretation.

This right of interpretation belongs to you and me. The translation of the Bible by Protestantism carries with it the distribution of the Bible into the hands of all men, that they themselves may read, ponder, interpret and live by it.

You must know that this is one of the foundation principles of the Reformation and the Protestant church. In the words of Martin Luther: "It is a wickedly devised fable that it is for the pope alone to interpret the Scriptures or to confirm the interpretation of them." And as Luther further said, "There is not a single letter in the Bible to confirm the Roman assumption."

Wycliffe put the Bible into the hands of the people that each man might read and interpret in his own right. Thirty years after his death, the Council of Constance condemned Wycliffe for this and ordered that his bones be dug up and burnt. This was done and the ashes cast into the River Avon. His enemies, who thought they had now finished him, did not foresee history's verdict:

The Avon to the Severn runs
And Severn to the sea;
And Wycliffe's dust shall spread abroad
Wide as the waters be.

Other names are associated with the attempt to give the Bible to the people.

The Council of Constance which spread the ashes of Wycliffe burned the Bohemian John Hus at the stake, his wickedness being that he prepared a new translation of the Scriptures into his mother tongue.

William Tyndale was another who, in the face of fierce opposition on the part of the church authorities, determined to give the Bible to the common people in their native tongue, the English language. Four hundred and eighteen years ago he was tied to the stake and strangled and burned.

When you take up your Bible to read it, when we openly read it from the desk on a Sunday morning, let us remember that this privilege was bought at a great price. This Bible is a part, the major part, of our American and Christian heritage. Its authority as the Word of God is supreme. It becomes authoritative by edict of no church or pope; rather does it call upon all to recognize its own authority.

You and I have the liberty to interpret this Bible as we will. Under this liberty and privilege many things have happened. For example, by this we established in America the great universities such as Yale, Harvard, Princeton and many others. We have the great denominational churches which may look like divisions in the Body of Christ, but by them destructive truths found in this Word of God have been given emphasis and the nation and the world have felt their influence.

Our right of interpretation places men in the Protestant pupils of the nation who vicariously read, study and meditate that they may rightly interpret God's holy Word—that the people may carry its truth into their homes and vocations and daily lives.

The teenage boy has the right to prop his body in bed at night and read his chapter—and come to his own conclusions. Let him be aware that while doing so God's spirit works in his mind and heart. The aged man has the right to sit in his armchair and seek to discover a good end to life and a good entrance into the heavenly kingdom, not dependent upon any announcement or pronouncement of pope or priest.

We have the book—we ourselves are interpreters, a holy priesthood, with authority derived from the Book, the Christ who is our companion and the Holy Spirit working in our hearts.

III. But now we come to another matter—translation is not enough; interpretation is not enough.

These may give us ideas, God-given ideas, not to be despised, but ideas are poor ghosts. They need to be clothed with flesh and blood. This we call incarnation.

Translation, Interpretation, Incarnation are God's methods. The Word of God is made flesh. The thing God wants to say he says in flesh and blood, even in the life of Jesus.

Only thus does the Word of God have maximum impact and influence. The word spoken, explained is not enough; we must see the word lived. As John wrote in his epistle: "We have seen with our eyes, we have looked upon the word, we have touched the word with our hands." Then the word is powerful, dymanic. Love that is a word of language is one thing; love that is a word of living life is far more.

Here then is a new translation; it is for your new interpretation; it is for our incarnation. A book that is paper and print and binding is one thing; we must see it lived in daily walk and action.

This book carries the word "law"— that law becomes vital only as it is lived out in obedience. This book carries the word "love"—it must be lived out in the lives of men and women.

The Christ is the center of the book —the historic Christ of long ago, the present spiritual Christ of now—but the world will see and hear and know and understand and heed and surrender only as it seems it will transform our lives unto the stature of the manhood of Jesus Christ.

"See what love the Father has given us, that we should be called children of God, and so we are. . . . Beloved, we are God's children now; it does not yet appear what we shall be, but we know that when he appears we shall be like him, for we shall see him as he is."

Then will the Word of God become incarnation.

Translation, Interpretation, Incarnation, these three, and the greatest of these is Incarnation.

MIDWEEK FELLOWSHIP MEETING TOPIC

(Church Night or Suggested Sermon Subject)

Theme: The Fullness of Time (Advent).

TEXT: "When the fulness of the time was come, God sent forth his Son." Gal. 4:4.

What were the elements of the fullness of time?

I. Expectation had been wakened by the Old Testament Scriptures. The prophecies looked to Christ as their goal.

II. The dispersion had carried the Jews into all the nations around Palestine, and thus was there a people prepared to understand the Gospel. They had the Scriptures, the synagogue worship, and a lofty idea of God.

III. The Greek language had spread in all lands as a common speech, and its literature and philosophy were a preparation for the Gospel message.

IV. Roman conquest had broken down the wall between East and West and established universal peace. Roman roads made highways for missionaries as well as for armies and merchants.

V. The religious needs of the world were at the greatest. Faith in the national gods was shattered, and human wisdom had failed to save the family in civilized lands or to hold together the social order.

Then God sent forth his Son.

CHRISTIAN ENDEAVOR SOCIETY TOPIC

Dec. 12. Our "Uncommon" Book (Bible Sunday). Heb. 4:12; II Pet. 1:21.

SUNDAY SCHOOL LESSON

Dec. 12. **Yearning for the Living God.** Ps. 42:1-8; 84-4, 5; 102:25-27.

MEMORY VERSE: "This God is our God for ever and ever." Ps. 48:14.

Read and study Psalms 42 and 43 together. They are probably by the same author, and it may be that Psalm 84 is by the same sensitive individual. Psalm 42 is one man's yearning for the living God. These facts can be discovered concerning him.

He lived far away from the temple.

He had once taken part in a temple ceremonial, v. 4.

He was a musician, a harpist (Ps. 43:4).

He lived near the sources of the Jordan, in the mountainous region of Mt. Hermon, v. 6.

He was acquainted with the wild life of the region, "as the hart panteth . . ." v. 1. "The back drop of wild nature reflects in the poet's mind the tempests of his soul," v. 7. Acquainted with the Psalmist, his own feelings break over one, and one shares his desire for a realization of the eternal and unchanging God.

SUNDAY: DECEMBER NINETEENTH

MORNING SERVICE

Theme: The Gospel of the Incarnation (Christmas).

SUGGESTED SCRIPTURE READING: Luke 2:1-20.

SELECTED HYMNS: "Good Christian men, rejoice."—Holst. "Angels o'er the fields."—Old French Carol. "I hear along our street."—Old English Carol of the Hearth, MacKinnon. "O come, all ye faithful."—Latin. "Joy to the world, the Lord is come."—Isaac Watts. "O little town of Bethlehem."—Phillips Brooks. "The first Noel."—Traditional. "It came upon the midnight clear."—E. H. Sears.

PREPROCESSIONAL PRAYER WITH THE CHOIR: On this glad Christmas morning may we bring offerings of rich praise to our Lord. May we ourselves experience the Christmas spirit that all who hear us may rejoice. In Christ's name we ask. Amen.—H.

CALL TO WORSHIP: "Unto us a child is born, unto us a son is given: and the government shall be upon his shoulder: and his name shall be called Wonderful, Counsellor, The Mighty God, The everlasting Father, The Prince of Peace. Of the increase of his government and peace there shall be no end."

INVOCATION PRAYER: Our heavenly Father, we come into thy presence with hearts that are grateful for the gift of thy Son. We are filled with thanksgiving that he came not with pomp and in glory, but as the Babe of Bethlehem, taking our human nature upon him, meeting our temptations, bearing our burdens, sharing our common life. We bless thy name for this revelation of thy love, which suffereth all things, even unto the cross. Wilt thou forgive the coldness of our hearts, the uncertainty of our minds, our feebleness of purpose, our narrowness of vision.

By the manger of Bethlehem make us as little children in thy house; stay the fever in our hearts; center all our purposes in thy will. We thank thee for the sweet human significance of the festival which we are celebrating. We thank thee for home and childhood, and for all our dear human fellowships and friendships. Forgive our enemies, if we have any, and help us to forgive them. Take from us all narrow and bitter thoughts and feelings; our vanity and pride, and all dislike, doubt and jealously of others, that this day we may enter the kingdom as little children. Soften and fill our hearts with love and gratitude, with tenderness and peace. Consecrate our joy; help us to serve thee with mirth, and whether we eat or drink, or whatsoever we do, may we do all to thy glory. We ask in Christ's name. Amen.

Theme: The Gospel of the Incarnation (Christmas).

TEXT: "The Word was made flesh, and dwelt among us, (and we beheld his glory, the glory as of the only begotten of the Father,) full of grace and truth." John 1:14.

INTRODUCTORY: There are many elements that go to make up Christmas. There are the very ancient customs that come to us from the pagan midwinter festivals, with their bonfires and feasting, their ritual use of mistletoe, and so on. It is a fascinating study to trace out the origins of the many quaint customs of Christmas time. But for us Christians the very center of it all is the wonder of Advent, the coming of the Saviour, God becoming flesh and dwelling among us. It is that supreme miracle of history that gives the Christmas season its glow, its wonder.

Far be it from me to try to "explain" Jesus, to reduce him, as it were, to a formula, to make the profundities of his nature clear. That simply cannot be done. All the same we do very well to try to understand in some measure what we mean by the Incarnation, so that we may worship with our minds as well as with our hearts, and that we may help others to come to him.

I. We start where the disciples started, with the man Jesus, the carpenter and prophet of Nazareth in Galilee. "Behold the man." Yes, Jesus was a real man. That was how the disciples knew him—to start with—as a man. But what a man!

As the disciples beheld, and lived with Jesus, they began to see beyond his common humanity. Some see simply an ordinary peasant, some see just a formidable opponent, who by hook or by crook must be destroyed. Others, those nearest to him in fellowship and love, see something beyond, flashes as it were of the glory of God. They, and we following in their footsteps and developing their thought, find in Jesus Christ the door to a new region of truth and experience—the nature of God and his dealings with mankind.

II. How can we sum up what we have seen through Christ? All the devotion of the Christian ages cannot express it all. But perhaps two phrases can express a great deal of that discovery. The first of these is Christ, the Image of God.

Men must have some image of the God they adore. If men are not allowed to make images of God with their hands, they will make them with their imaginations. So the Hebrews sometimes thought of God as a great warrior-judge seated on a glorious throne above the clouds. As the disciples lived with Jesus he became for them the image of God. They looked and looked and beyond the human form and personality they saw the divine nature. In his love and purity they saw the Holy Love of Almighty God. In him the glory of God was revealed. "No man hath seen God at any time: the only begotten Son, which is in the Father, he hath declared him." Philip saith unto Jesus, "Lord, show us the Father." Jesus answers, "He that hath seen me hath seen the Father." They come to realize that in him God was active, present. At last Paul gave perfect utterance to their intuition when he wrote, "God was in Christ, reconciling the world unto himself." That is why the church has always seen Jesus as the fulfillment of the ancient prophecy of the coming of Immanuel, God-with-us.

The first disciples saw this in the mighty acts of Jesus, in what we call his miracles, when he assumed divine authority and exercised Godlike power. He said, and they acknowledged, that in him the kingdom of God had come.

IV. At last they were able even to see God in Jesus dying on Calvary. That had seemed the most glaring revelation of Jesus' human frailty and defeat—when his enemies bound and broke him, when the glory departed utterly and they saw just a suffering man dying in agony and ignominy. Yet, as they thought about that dreadful tragedy it dawned upon them that God was there, too. God had come, and he was there even on Calvary, in action still.

That is all part of the joy of this season, for we see the simple, pathetic happenings of Bethlehem as part of the universal drama of salvation. What the disciples saw in and through Jesus we can see, and our vision is reinforced by the thought and experience of the Christian centuries.

O come, let us adore him, Christ the Lord!—H. T.

THEME PRAYER: O Father, who hast declared thy love to men by the birth of the Holy Child at Bethlehem; help us to welcome him with gladness and to make room for him in our common days; so that we may live at peace with one another and in good will with all thy family. And O thou, who are love and light, we thank thee above all for the gift of the Christmas Christ. Help us to keep our hearts open to receive thy joy that we may ever be channels of "good tidings" in his name. Amen.

OFFERTORY SENTENCE: "And when they had opened their treasures, they presented unto him gifts; gold, and frankincense, and myrrh."

OFFERTORY PRAYER: Gracious Giver of all good, as we celebrate again the birth of Christ we would renew the joy of giving in a deeper appreciation of his Incarnation, whereby thou hast revealed thy love for all people. Direct our giving through this glad season, that it may carry the good news of peace on earth and good will to all men, through Christ our Lord. Amen.

Illustrative Material

SEED THOUGHTS, HOMILETIC AND EXPOSITORY. The Incarnation: I. God becomes man. 1. The fact itself. The Word—personal, eternal, divine, the active energy of the divine nature, Author of creation, Source of life and light, the Medium of all revelation. II. Two seemingly discordant ideas "Word" and "flesh." III. How he became thus. It involved willing transformation by the energy of the Person himself. "Became," not assumed. The living heart of Christianity is supernatural. IV. The various purposes of the Incarnation. 1. To reveal God. 2. To show what man ought to be. 3. That he might die. 4. That he might have full sympathy with us. 5. That manhood might be glorified. He stooped down to lift us, to save us. What he is he will make us.—A. M.

The Incarnation: I. Plainly asserted. 1. The Person assuming, "The Word."

2. The nature assumed, "flesh." 3. The assumption itself. Not *fuit*, but *factus et* —the true human nature united with his divine Person. II. This assertion strongly confirmed. He dwelt among us and we saw his glory. He "tabernacled" with us. We were eye-witnesses of it, I John 1:1-3.—J. F.

The Incarnation: I. Its relation to man. Shows the dignity of the human body. 2. And the dignity and worth of the human soul. 3. And links man to God. II. Its relation to God. 1. Reveals the Fatherhood of God. 2. Reveals the redeeming character of God. Gave his Best to save us.—C. J. J.

Choice Christmas Illustrations

INCARNATION IS IDENTIFICATION. It is said that when Mrs. Booth, who even more than her husband was the life of the Salvation Army, was a little girl, running along the road with hoop and stick, she saw a prisoner dragged away by a constable to the lockup. A mob was hooting at the unfortunate culprit, and his utter loneliness appealed at once to her heart; it seemed to her that he had not a friend in the world. Quick as thought she sprang to his side and marched down the street with him, determined that he should know that there was one soul that felt for him whether he suffered for his own fault or that of another.

Even so Jesus, who was the brightness of the Father's glory, condescended to come down to this world, not only to manifest the Father's love for us, but also to identify himself with us in our suffering. He was touched with the feeling of our infirmities, and could not bear to see us suffer alone; and so he has come to give help to the helpless, comfort to the sorrowing, and peace to the penitent. "The Word was made flesh and dwelt among us." He identified himself with us in our need.

THE WORD MADE FLESH. A group of college girls in a Sunday School class in a southern city decided to send Christmas presents to the children in an orphan asylum. Each took the name of a youngster and wrote asking what gift was most desired. One child who felt lonely and misunderstood replied, "What I want most is a sister." The young woman was at first startled by the answer, but after an inner struggle was equal to the occasion, and wrote back, "I will see that you get the present you ask for. I will be your sister. I am coming to see you soon and will see you often. From today, I am, your loving Sister."

Thousands of boys and girls, many from homes of financial comfort, have a similar feeling of loneliness amid the disturbed conditions of modern life. They need sympathy and understanding friendship, but all too often are failing to find it.

A major sin of the average so-called Christian is his failure to identify himself with human need. He is not much moved with compassion by the sight of the multitude of youth and children who are like sheep and lambs without a shepherd.

When God wanted to save mankind, he went to them in person. This is the central meaning of the Incarnation. It is the heart of the Christmas message. "The Word was made flesh and dwelt among us." Christmas comes again to remind people of the necessity for the sacrificial giving of themselves.—Rev. Walter D. Cavert.

GOD'S CHRISTMAS OFFER. It is stated that on a wager a man once stood on London Bridge for a whole day trying to give away golden sovereigns. Only two persons accepted them. Equally foolish is the world in refusing the greatest of all gifts—God's Christmas Gift.

NO WELCOME GIVEN. There were shepherds in Judea who did not hear the angels sing their song of royal welcome, and there were many of earth's wise men who were not guided to Bethlehem by the star. So today there are those whose ears and eyes and hearts are closed to God's blessed communications and who go on in life with no saving faith in him as their Saviour.

INCARNATION. A father who was on a trip to the Far East had a child at home over whose bed hung the father's portrait. Every morning the child looked lovingly at it, and one day said to his mother, "Mother, I wish father would come out from the frame!" Jesus is the portrait of our Omnipotent Father and Friend as revealed in the Word of God. He is God incarnate. "The word was made flesh and dwelt among us." "He that hath seen me hath seen the Father." It is his place to "come out from the frame" and incarnate himself in our lives. By that fellowship we are "transformed into the same image from glory to glory."—H.

OLD NEWS, NEW NEWS, GOOD NEWS. It is told of Alfred, Lord Tennyson, that one day, as he was out walking, he happened on a poor old woman, whom he greeted with the common question: "What's the news today?" Her reply was that the only news worth telling was that Jesus Christ came into the world to save sinners. "Ah," returned the great poet, "that is old news and new news and good news."—East and West.

Quotable Christmas Poetry

CAROL JOYFULLY

The whole world is a Christmas tree,
And stars its many candles be.
O sing a carol joyfully,
The world's great feast in keeping;
For once on a December night,
An angel held a candle bright,
And led three Wise Men by its light,
To where a Child was sleeping.
> —Unidentified.

I WOULD CELEBRATE

O I would celebrate my Lord
With every gift my means afford,
And I would wreathe His name around
With every joy I ever found,
And I would light a candled tree
For everyone on earth to see,
And I would send a Star to greet
My brother soul on every street,
And I would sing my love among

The carolers in every tongue,
And I would wish at last to be
On Christmas Day as poor as He.
—Jean Kenyon Mackenzie.

YOUR CHRISTMAS

A bright and blessed Christmas Day,
  With echoes of the angels' song,
And peace that cannot pass away,
  And holy gladness, calm and strong,
And sweet heart carols, flowing free,
  These form my Christmas wish for
  thee.
—Unidentified.

ALL ON A CHRISTMAS DAY

Out of the heart of God there came
  To a dark, despairing world
The gift of a Life of light and hope
  And the banner of love unfurled.
Into the heart of man there came,
  As he went his weary way,
A song of cheer and a gift of love,
  All on a Christmas Day.
It is for those who know the joy
  Of the Gift of God's great heart,
To share with the world that knows it
  not
The bliss it doth impart;
To spread good-will and kindliness
  Along life's toilsome way,
And make the heart of man rejoice,
  All on a Christmas Day.
—Robert Brewster Beattie.

EVENING SERVICE

Theme: If Jesus Had Not Been Born.

TEXT: "For there is born to you this day in the city of David a Saviour, who is Christ the Lord."—Luke 2:11 (A.S.V.).

I. If Christ had not been born we would have little revelation of God, and what we did have would be meaningless. As Christ is the key to the Old Testament it would have no interpretation. The world of nature would be a puzzle. It seems to reveal a God of power and wisdom and goodness, but without Christ we would know little of his Person. We would not know that he loves sinners and is willing to give his life for their redemption; that he loves all the people in all the world. There would be no understanding of Psalm 23 and Isaiah 53. Men would still be crying, "Show us the Father," for no one had said, "He that hath seen me hath seen the Father."

II. If Christ had not been born we would face the guilt of personal sin without hope of mercy and no assurance of forgiveness. The decree would still stand: "The soul that sinneth it shall die." In our conscience we would feel the sting of our guilt. The deepest yearnings of the soul would find no satisfaction. There would be no peace in the assurance of divine forgiveness and reconciliation with God. The word "Saviour" would be unknown. There would be no gospel of redemption. Mankind would be lost, without a mediator, without a substitute, without an atonement, without a Saviour.

III. If Christ had not been born there would be little light on life's problems. We would not know the meaning of life or how we ought to live. We would not have the perfect Example of manhood, its criterion of moral character, its supreme figure of moral excellence. The matchless teachings of the Great Teacher would be missing, and the best of men would be wandering without an acceptable revelation of authority and without a dynamic for worthy living. The world would have been without its greatest figures, its outstanding personalities, its greatest music, poetry, art, literature and songs. Life would have been a burden, an affliction, without a motive to serve or survive.

IV. If Christ had not been born there would be no relief from suffering, sorrow or death. Without him there would be no explanation of suffering. We would not know that God suffers, sympathizes, cares. There would be no real joy, no ground of peace, no consolation. Facing death, there would be no hope in our hearts and no comfort when the dear ones are taken away. The life beyond would be the blackness of despair, anguish and uncertainty.

V. If Christ had not been born we

would face a Godless, lifeless, hopeless world. We would not know God, could not know that he cared, that sin would be forgiven; there would be no light for our way and no light thrown on the future; there would be no one to redeem, no one to lead, no one to empower. Women would remain under a cloud, children under a curse, the poor despised and the weak helpless. Life would be a struggle, seeking only the survival of the fittest.

VI. But Jesus was born. The darkness of the picture gives way to a glorious light. We do not live in a Godless, hopeless world. The Christmas story is the supreme fact of the universe. God loved the world. God revealed himself in his Son. Jesus came to save his people from their sins. Life's pathway is lighted by the life and teachings of Jesus. The light of the world keeps on shining and darkness cannot put it out. Life's meaning is clear. Life's power is available. Life's victory is sure.—R. L. L.

Alternate Theme: The Sign of the Babe (Christmas).

TEXT: "And this shall be a sign unto you; Ye shall find the babe," etc. Luke 2:12.

INTRODUCTORY: "This shall be a sign unto you; Ye shall find a babe." A babe! A babe, almost unnoticed, crowded out, while the world continued its busy way without a pause to notice, or adore. Yet what a significant sign it is.

I. Remember, too, that it is a sign. It is not just an isolated event in history, this coming of God to earth in Christ Jesus. If you saw the film *Green Pastures* you will remember how God was depicted as paying an occasional visit to his world, looking around, and returning to heaven. This is not the meaning of the Incarnation. Emmanuel means God with us here, now, always, everywhere. The Babe is the sign of the Eternal Presence.

II. It was in the wisdom of God that he revealed himself to the world as a Babe. And why? Surely to teach men that what he desired of men was not simply worship and obedience, but love and service. Christ came as a helpless baby, needing care and love and nurture of human beings. He needed the shelter of a human home, the tender care of a mother, the upright example of a father, the fellowship of brothers and sisters, the wisdom of teachers to guide his growing powers, the influence of friends. A little child is at the mercy of those into whose care it is committed, and whose lives come into contact with it. And God, in his wisdom, chose to clothe himself with that helplessness, that utter dependency on human love and service.

The characters of the Christmas story fall into two groups—those who ministered in some way or other to the needs of the Christ Child, and those who neglected him. On the one hand there are Joseph and Mary, giving him love, nurture and protection; the magi bringing their costly gifts; the shepherds coming in simple adoration. Each in his own way recognized that the Gift of God brought with it a personal responsibility for giving and serving. On the other hand there is the innkeeper, concerned only with filling his inn with the most profitable guests, the census crowds busy about their own affairs, Herod intent upon himself and his own reputation.

III. The Christ Child is not only the sign of God's gifts to us, it is also the sign of God's demands upon us. Christmas still divides men into those two groups—those who see the sign, and those who are blind to it; and those who respond to it, and those who ignore it.

We all need God, but the Babe in the manger is the sign of God's need of us —our worship, our love, our service. All that we sing in our hymns about the power, the greatness, the goodness of God is gloriously true, but the Christmas story reminds us that men have their response to make to God, their gifts to offer him, their service to give him. He came as a little Babe that men might realize his need of them. A Babe, that is God's sign to us. A sign of the new life, the utter revolution that Christ makes; a sign of the divine working and presence in human life; a sign of God's need of our love and service. "O come, let us adore him, Christ the Lord."—J. B. N.

Suggestive Christmas Texts

"Behold, a virgin shall conceive, and bear a son, and shall call his name Immanuel." Isa. 7:14.

"Unto us a child is born . . . and his name shall be called Wonderful." Isa. 9:6.

"She brought forth her firstborn son, and wrapped him in swaddling clothes, and laid him in a manger." Luke 2:7.

"Unto you is born this day in the city of David a Saviour, which is Christ the Lord." Luke 2:11.

"Let us now go even unto Bethlehem, and see this thing which is come to pass." Luke 2:15.

"God . . . hath in these last days spoken unto us by his Son." Heb. 1:1, 2.

The Rising Star: "There shall come a Star out of Jacob, and a Sceptre shall rise out of Israel," etc. Num. 24:17.

The Bethlehem of the Heart: "Until Christ be formed in you." Gal. 4:19.

Endowing the Christ: "And when they had opened their treasures, they presented unto him gifts; gold," etc. Matt. 2:11.

MIDWEEK FELLOWSHIP MEETING TOPIC

(Church Night or Suggested Sermon Subject)

Theme: Bethlehem Speaks to Our World (Christmas).

TEXT: "Now when Jesus was born in Bethlehem of Judaea." Matt. 2:1.

Bethlehem speaks of promise and triumph. I know how disappointing and even terrible this world can be, but let it be remembered that this is also the world which celebrates Christmas. I feel genuinely sorry for those who, in threatening times, lack the faith which gives this season its glorious significance.

I. This day commemorates the birth of the King of kings. With right we observe it in exultation. Only let us be sure, as we face a difficult world, that the banner we carry is the banner of the Lord. A man asked me recently, "Are not your claims for the power of Christ too high?" No, even in imagination I cannot reach a point that transcends him.

II. Our trouble is that we hold him in too low esteem. Bear in mind that "it pleased the Father that in him should all the fullness dwell." The meaning of Christmas is that God is active in the affairs of the world.

III. Christ has made a profound change for the better in the history of civilization. What seems a temporary check must never be viewed as a defeat. Those who proceed on the assumption that Christianity is through are preparing for a fearful collapse. The Supreme Power in this universe does not make much noise, nor are his activities without their mystery.

IV. Our calendar dates events from the birth of Jesus. The Christian philosophy of life is part of our daily thought. The Spirit of Christ has entered our human situation. His life belongs to the history of our world. He has demonstrated his power to forgive sin and set death at naught. The most stupendous forces of the world have been arrayed against him without accomplishing his defeat. The world is under the sway of his redeeming Spirit, and he is the Master of the human soul. —Teunis E. Gouwens, D.D.

CHRISTIAN ENDEAVOR SOCIETY TOPIC

Dec. 10. Great Joy to All Men (Christmas Sunday). Luke 2:1-14.

SUNDAY SCHOOL LESSON

**Dec. 19. Glory to God in the Highest.
Ps. 148; Matt. 1:18-25.**

MEMORY VERSE: "O come, let us worship and bow down: let us kneel before the Lord our maker." Ps. 95:6.

The use of Psalm 148 may give a fresh and joyous approach to the narratives in Luke and Matthew which belong especially to the Christmas season. The Matthew passage links New Testament fulfillment with Old Testament anticipation.

Psalm 148 is a splendid vehicle for praise to God for his glorious gifts, above all for the gift of his Son. Many of its features—"angels," "Stars of light," "beasts and all cattle," "kings of the earth," "old men and children"—accord beautifully with the Nativity story.

SUNDAY: DECEMBER TWENTY-SIXTH

MORNING SERVICE

Theme: Time the Great Weaver (End of Year).

SUGGESTED SCRIPTURE READING: Eccles. 3:1-15; I Cor. 7:29-31.

SELECTED HYMNS: "Days and Moments quickly flying."—E. Caswell. "Ring out, wild bells."—A. Tennyson. "Our God, our help in ages past."—I. Watts. "While with ceaseless course the sun."—J. Newton. "O God, the Rock of Ages."—E. H. Bickersteth.

CALL TO WORSHIP: "And Samuel took a stone and set it between Mizpah and Shen, saying, Hitherto hath the Lord helped us."

INVOCATION PRAYER: O thou who hast given us the great and precious trust of life, help us, we pray thee, so to live and love and labor that we may give of all our days and deeds a good accounting. May we so begin in wisdom, continue on in duty and end in love, that the whole course of our lives may in the end be blessed by thee. We humbly bow before thee in thanksgiving for the privilege of living in these tremendous times. Forgive us for the lamentable failures whereby we have contributed to the tragedy of our day. Quicken us by thy Holy Spirit that we may do our duty and claim our opportunity in fellowship and service with thy children everywhere, near and far and of all classes, all nations, all races. Use us, we beseech thee, according to thy Holy Will, for the propagation of thy Gospel, wherein there is redemption for our souls, peace for the world, and salvation for all mankind. Hasten the day, we earnestly pray, O King of kings and Lord of lords, when righteousness shall govern the nations, when suffering and sin shall be done away, and when the earth shall be full of the knowledge of God as the waters cover the sea.

Now unto Him that is able to do exceeding abundantly above all that we ask or think, according to the power that worketh in us, unto Him be glory in the Church by Christ Jesus throughout all ages, world without end. Amen.

Theme: Time the Great Weaver (End of Year).

TEXT: "My days are swifter than a weaver's shuttle." Job 7:6.

INTRODUCTORY: Few things are more fascinating than the loom and the weaver's shuttle and all the things that go with them. Hundreds of strands of thread are carefully prepared and set into the loom. This is called the warp. The other thread is wound upon bobbins or quills and placed in shuttles which are inserted on each side in such a manner that when the machine is operated these shuttles fly back and forth between the threads of the warp and the cloth is woven a thread at a time.

Job, who wrote these words of our text, was greatly fascinated by this whole process of weaving, though in simpler form in his day, of course. But it was exactly this picture which he had in mind when he exclaimed, "My days are swifter than a weaver's shuttle." The figure of weaving has been a favorite illustration of poets and writers of all ages, as when they speak of the "loom of time," "the warp and woof of life," the "weaving of one's destiny." Let us see what this illustration suggests to us as we think today about those things of greatest importance to us all, such as Christian decision, Christian growth, and power and guidance for daily living.

I. The swiftness of the shuttle. How swiftly the days pass! "My days are swifter than a weaver's shuttle." Watch the shuttles fly back and forth, in some cases at the rate of 210 times a minute! See the whirling machinery! Listen to the din, the noise, the clatter! That is a picture of life. How swiftly the days pass for all of us. That is why time is such a precious thing. That is why we ought to feel the impelling duty to be investing it for goodness and for God right now.

II. Importance of little things. Job's figure of the loom also suggests the fact that many little things go into the making of life. How many threads there are in a bolt of cloth on the loom! One can hardly count the many threads of the warp, not to mention the thousands upon thousands of threads in the filling. How very small and weak any one of them seems to be by itself. Even so life for each of us is made up of countless little threads of habit, of activity, and of inspiration. How many steps you take in a single day! How many millions in the past year. How many millions upon millions of words, acts and thoughts! Just as the cloth is made up of almost countless tiny threads, you cannot say that a single thread is unimportant.

III. Mending broken threads. In this business of weaving there are broken threads which must be caught up and mended. Every now and then in the weaving room we see a machine stop, and the weaver comes, picks up a broken thread, mends it, and the machine is started on its way again. In fact, the principal business of the weaver while the cloth is being made is to keep the machine going and to look for faulty or broken threads. Watchfulness and diligence are necessary. And watchfulness and diligence are necessary, too, for Christian living and upright character.

IV. Weaving to a pattern. Once more, the loom reminds us that a weaver follows a pattern. And God intends that our lives and characters be woven to a pattern. He is a poor disciple of the Master who is content to live aimlessly, who chooses no lofty goals which he wants to reach, who forgets that he has a divine Pattern after which to shape his life. When Jesus said, "Follow me," he meant what he said—"Emulate me," "Take me as your pattern." "If any man would come after me, let him deny himself, and take up his cross, and follow me." In Jesus God has given us the right pattern for our lives.

V. Power and output. A final suggestion from the loom concerning life is the relation of the driving power to the amount of work and quality of work turned out. If you went to the weaving rooms of many of the old Eastern countries, you would find quite a different arrangement and the process slow. But enter one of our modern mills and there you see one girl attending four or five looms, all going at high speed, and turning out hundreds of times as much cloth as that one girl can turn out who has to propel her own machine. What is the difference? These modern looms are driven with electricity. Their motors are in contact with the great dynamo and the powerhouse.

Are you trying to live in your own strength alone, trying to run the loom of life by man power only? If you are, you are certain to be finding it a sorry business—weary, discouraging and hopeless.

There is a better way; and that way is to keep in touch with the Supreme Dynamo, the source of divine Power. Such lives are the hope of the church and of the world!—Rev. A. D. Cloud.

THEME PRAYER: O God of the seasons, thou giver of days and years, we witness thy providence in the coming of ever-marvelous times in the hurrying calendar of our lives. We remember the years of thy right hand, O God, as thou didst lead us along our way. We meditate upon thy goodness. And as we remember so we put our trust in thee. Each day wilt thou guide us. Set our hearts forward. Grant us high purpose and high hope. With cheerfulness we follow the road. Amen.

OFFERTORY SENTENCE: "Blessed be the Lord God, who daily loadeth us with benefits, even the God of our salvation."

OFFERTORY PRAYER: Through the whole of this passing year, our Father, thy bounties have been new every morning and fresh every evening. Here and now we would raise our Ebenezer and say, Hitherto hath the Lord helped us. With grateful hearts we bring these our morning offerings and pray for thy blessing upon the gifts and the givers. In Christ's name we ask. Amen.

Illustrative Material

SEED THOUGHTS, HOMILETIC AND EXPOSITORY. The Web of Life: The words of the text fitly describe the quickness with which the days of our life glide away. Job compares human life to the shuttle's motions. I. The swiftness of our days. II. Each day has added another thread to the web of life. What is life but a collection of days? Each day adds something to the color and complexion of the whole life, and for good or evil. The importance of every day. III. We weave now what we wear in eternity. How is the day of our life being spent?
—E. B.

Time and Change: We are thankful, dear Lord, that in the midst of change thou changest not!

What the Sun Dial says: "Traveller, it is later than you think!"
The use of time is fate.—Chapman.

Choice End-of-Year Illustrations

THE HOURGLASS WARNING. There was an ancient custom of putting an hourglass into the coffin of the dead, to signify that their time had run out. A useless notification to them. Better to put the hourglass into the hands of the living and show them the grains gliding steadily out.—New Cyclopedia of Illustrations.

FLIGHT OF TIME. Our common view of time is of its passing with slow and measured tread; but the truer conception is to think of it as a "flight." The artist Crane, in a picture entitled "The Chariots of the Fleeting Hours," represents the hours being drawn by four wild horses and driven by remorseless youths, who earnestly urge their horses on, lashing them to a greater speed. Meanwhile sinks the sun, and the night hurries to meet the rushing chariots. To those in earnest, this is the view to take. "I must work while it is today, for the night cometh." Only by this sense of urgency can we do anything worth doing in the short span of our earthly life. This also carries a lesson for the closing days of the closing year.—2,500 Best Modern Illustrations.

OPPORTUNITY CANNOT BE RECALLED. The Rev. Dr. Frederick W. Robertson presented a startling picture of lost opportunity when he said: "Have you ever seen those marble statues in some public square or garden which art has so finished into a perennial fountain that through the lips or through the hands the clear water flows in a perpetual stream? And the marble stands there passive, cold, making no effort to detain the gliding water? It is so that time flows through the hands of men, swift, never pausing till it has run itself out; and there is the man petrified into a marble sleep, not feeling what it is that is passing away forever."—5,000 Best Modern Illustrations.

FINDING TIME. Charles Buxton says, "You will never 'find' time for anything. If you want time you must make it."

THE IMPORTANCE OF NOW. The Dean of Christ Church, Oxford, England, in a sermon to the junior members of the University, gave them this suggestive motto: "Plan your life as if you had long to live; live it as if you expected to die soon." We should well heed those words. In planning there should be breadth and depth of purpose; in carrying out the plans there should be intensity of execution. Above all, we should remember that now is the golden time. No regrets can atone for past time wasted. No future time is promised in which to make up for neglect of present opportunities.—*5,000 Best Modern Illustrations.*

EVENING SERVICE

Theme: The Christian's Taking Account of Time (Watch Night).

TEXT: "A wise man's heart discerneth both time and judgment." Eccles. 8:5.

INTRODUCTORY: Of all seasons of the year this present one inclines us most to thought. If when the old year is dying or when the new one is being born men will not think, it is very doubtful if they will ever think at all. This section of Scripture is in praise of the wisdom of the wise man.

I. Who is the wise man? What are some of his characteristics? He is the good man. He is an amiable man, who has the respect of his neighbors. He shows prudence and judgment. He is a useful man, rendering service to his community and the world. He is skilled to know and promote what ought to be done. His conversation is wholesome and his actions are such as win commendation. "A wise man's heart discerneth both time and judgment."

II. The wise man's heart discerneth time. This is the last night of the year. Any man who is not utterly unwise must realize that this is a time for re-view. Too much looking back is not good, but he is very thoughtless who does not ever review the past for its lessons.

III. And the wise Christian, the man of spiritual discernment, will not fail to note the development of God's purposes in the world.

IV. He will also mark and recognize the shortness of time. The Christian, "knowing the time," learns to cherish more and more the pilgrim spirit.

V. The wise man's heart also discerneth the swiftness of time. Life is "like a tale that is told." It is compared to "a weaver's shuttle," flying rapidly across the web.

VI. Also the wise Christian discerns that time is a precious talent for which he must give an account.

We live in a world of change. Learn from the year that is past. How important is the year to come!—H.

END OF PRAYER YEAR: Our Father, thy promises to us, thy children, have been thoroughly tested. We review our lives and rediscover thee. At every turn of the way thou hast been with us. Dangers we have known and trials and sorrows and fears; but thou hast not forsaken us. Through all our experiences thou hast spoken peace to our hearts. On we go into the unfolding moments of a new day, confident that thy providence runs before us just as it has outrun us hitherto. Amen.— John Marvin Rast.

Choice End-of-Year Illustrations

YEAR'S END

What is soiled, make Thou pure;
What is wounded, work its cure;
What is parched, fructify;
What is rigid, gently bend;
What is frozen, warmly tend;
Strengthen what goes erringly.
—"Veni, Sancte Spiritus"
(13th Century).

THE GATE. And I said to the man who stood at the gate of the year: "Give me a light, that I may tread safely into the unknown!"

And he replied: "Go out into the darkness and put your hand into the Hand of God. That shall be to you better than light and safer than a known way."—M. L. Haskins.

YEAR'S END SYNAGOGUE SERVICES. The Jews have a tradition which gives great sacredness to the synagogue services of the last day of their year. It is held that if the ritual of that solemn day is faithfully observed from the early assembling till the day wears to its close, God will hear the prayers of his penitent people and will wipe out the score against them for the whole year past. The day is observed by large gatherings, and it is an impressive sight to see the great numbers of men and boys standing together with the white tallith (scarf) over their shoulders and earnestly following the service with their prayer books in their hands. One of them, who had been educated to be a rabbi but afterward became a Christian minister, described to us these solemn services which in his youth he attended every year. He told how the earnestness of prayer deepened as the day drew toward its close, and in the last hour, and the last moments of the hour, the prayer rose into an agonized cry for pardon and deliverance. But our friend confessed that often he had come away from that solemn service with a painful doubt whether his prayer had been heard and he really forgiven.—Franklin Noble, D.D.

Suggestive Texts for the Year's End

"Days should speak, and multitude of years should teach wisdom." Job 32:7.

"Then cometh the end." I Cor. 15:24.

"They went every one straight forward." Ezek. 10:22.

"Let us go on unto perfection." Heb. 6:1.

"Behold, the former things are come to pass, and new things do I declare." Isa. 42:9.

"The Lord shall be thy confidence, and shall keep thy foot from being taken." Prov. 3:26.

"My times are in thy hand." Ps. 31:15.

"Ye have not passed this way heretofore." Josh. 3:4.

"As thy days, so shall thy strength be." Deut. 33:25.

"Ye shall henceforth return no more that way." Deut. 17:16.

"Thine ears shall hear a word behind thee, saying, This is the way, walk ye in it." Isa. 30:21.

"The books were opened." Rev. 20:12.

"Thou art worthy to take the book, and to open the seals thereof." Rev. 5:9.

"He hath sent me . . . to proclaim the acceptable year of the Lord." Isa. 61:1, 2.

MIDWEEK FELLOWSHIP MEETING TOPIC

(Church Night or Suggested Sermon Subject)

Theme: A New Spirit for a New Time (End of Year).

TEXT: "He hath put a new song in my mouth, even praise unto our God." Ps. 40:3.

I. A better disposition we ought to carry into the new year's greetings.

II. We owe a grateful spirit for our happy experiences. We can enumerate enough to waken our thankfulness.

III. We can begin to pay this debt. Some debts are discouraging, but gratitude to God is uplifting.

IV. A grateful gladness will help our work. Some laughter is "like the crackling of thorns under a pot," but gladness in God's love makes the heart eager for active service.

V. We have watched and prayed against temptation: but we should watch for the answers to our prayers, and they will fill our mouths with singing.

CHRISTIAN ENDEAVOR SOCIETY TOPIC

Dec. 26. Right Turn Ahead! (The New Year.) Phil. 3:13, 14.

SUNDAY SCHOOL LESSON

Dec. 26. The Whole Duty of Man.
Eccles. 1:2-3, 13; 2:1, 18; 3:16; 4:1; 5:10-13; 12:1, 13-14.

MEMORY VERSE: "This is the end of the matter; all hath been heard: Fear God, and keep his commandments; for this is the whole duty of man." Eccles. 12:13 (A.S.V.).

The passages given above direct attention to the ancient philosopher's trial-and-error experiments in living. They include work, seeking after knowledge, pleasure, wealth. He sought to discover what would produce the most lasting satisfaction.

The reasoned conclusion of his experiments is found in 12:13-14. This is the "Q.E.D." at the end of the problem —"Fear God, and keep his commandments."

The word "fear" needs to be given its true meaning as used by the writer. In the minds of many persons the emphasis is on being afraid of. This may be corrected by an explanation of the meaning of filial fear.

This lesson can be used to suggest a helpful approach to the new year.

SECTION VIII. The Junior Pulpit. A Church-School Year of Suggestive Sermons for Children and Youths

JANUARY 3. Topic: Now (New Year).

TEXT: "Put them in mind. . . . to be ready to every good work." Tit. 3:1.

It was a great day when you learned to tell time. I remember how happy I was when I did not have to ask the time but could read the clock myself. And when we learn to tell the time, it is surprising how many chances there are to read it. There is your own watch, the clock in the living room, the clocks in the bedrooms, clocks on the street, in towers, in store windows, outside of banks and inside, time announced over the radio. Why, there are clocks everywhere! People must think that time is very important. And it is. It is one of the most important things about our life. And yet for all the clocks everywhere, so that about all we have to do is to turn our head to see one, there are not many people who know the time.

We talk often as if there were three kinds of time. We speak of yesterday, and today, and tomorrow. We mean the past—that is gone; the future is coming; but the only time we really have is the present. And the thing for you to learn about telling time is not only that the present is the only time there is but also that it is your time.

You will agree with me, I am sure, that you hear entirely too much about the future. Everybody is telling you about what you may become, and that you must get ready for it. So you have to learn this and learn that. You have to spend a lot of time at school. You have to practice your music. And in Sunday School you are told to get ready to be useful men and women. It is all about getting ready. It is all about the time to come. How tired you grow of it all, this hearing about getting ready for other days, when all the time you know that today is your day!

And I believe that you are right. You young folks are not just men and women growing up. You are boys and girls. You are not just getting ready to live; you are living now! You are not just going to be somebody someday; you are somebody now!

You are not getting ready to live; you are living. Do not think you must get ready to be a Christian man or woman. Be a Christian boy or girl. Just getting ready is never to be ready. What you are is what counts, not what you are getting ready to be. Paul wrote to Titus and said: "Put them in mind . . . to be ready to every good work." Every watch and every clock tells the same story. Can you really tell the time?

335

Well, the only thing the clock says is "Now."—P. H. Pleune, D.D.

JANUARY 10. Topic: Jesus Blessing Little Children: His Arms.

Let us think together for a few moments this morning about that story of Jesus' calling little children to his arms and blessing them (Mark 10:16). Our word is for the very youngest of our families who are here. But why not for the moment include all of us, even those older being "made a child again just for today"? We grown people are all too adult. The kingdom of heaven is for those who are childlike—not childish—but like young children in teachableness, in simplicity and in confiding trust. It will do us good and only good to go back to the spirit of our childhood for the time being.

I have heard of a little boy who once said, "When I am well I like to be carried by my father, but when I am sick I like my mother to carry me." When asked the reason, he said, "When I am well my father carries me on his back, and it is lots of fun; but when I am sick my mother carries me in her arms, and it makes me well." That little boy did not know that when he was expressing this very natural thought he was helping to preach the gospel. Jesus was like a good mother. "He took them up in his arms, put his hands upon them, and blessed them."

Now let us think for a few moments about the arms of Jesus.

I. First of all think of the arms of Jesus as stretched-out arms. In one of the Psalms God is pictured as with "stretched-out arms." Jesus' outstretched arms show that children are welcome to him, that he is very ready to receive them. He invites them. He asks them to come. He longs to take them in his embrace. That is what arms outstretched mean.

II. Then, too, the arms of Jesus are loving arms. They are like the dearest mother's arms. Mothers love us toward all that is good. I have heard of a young boy who was taken from a drunken home to a children's refuge. He said one day to the matron, "I wish my father were here, for I think I would love him good." This is what Jesus does for all the children who come to his arms. He loves them good. When they are in his arms bad tempers, wrong thoughts, pride and selfishness and all that is unlovely is loved out, and they are helped to be pure and true and good.

III. Then I think I ought to say also that Jesus' arms are strong arms. I have heard of a shipwreck at sea. A little child, a great favorite with all on board, was with the weeping mother in the cabin. A strong sailor rushed to the place, took up the little fellow, wrapped his oilskin coat about him, folded him to his bosom, and jumped into the raging waters. He saved the boy's life. That was love. And that was strength. Jesus has strong arms to save even the youngest of us from all threatening danger.

There are at least three things we can say about Jesus and the children. He is attractive to children. He takes a deep interest in children; and he wants them to be safe and happy.

IV. Now there is one thing more I think ought to be said. It is that Jesus takes up in his arms *willing* children. He wants the children he takes to his bosom to trust him, and to be ready to have him love and help and save them.

I think when I read that sweet story
    of old,
When Jesus was here among men,
How He called little children as lambs
    to His fold,
I should like to have been with them
    then.

I wish that His hands had been placed
    on my head,
That His arms had been thrown around
    me,
And that I might have seen His kind
    look when He said,
"Let the little ones come unto me."

Yet still to His footstool in prayer I
may go,
And ask for a share in His love;
And if I now earnestly seek Him below,
I shall see Him and hear Him above.

—H.

JANUARY 17. Topic: Paths Cross-Lots.

It is a very old topic I have for you
this morning, young friends, but it is
a very important one. It is all the more
important because it is so old. I call
the topic cross-lots paths, but the real
subject is habits. You all know how
cross-lots paths are formed. Maybe
you have at some time helped to make
them. Somebody begins by going in
just one way around certain bushes and
between certain trees. At first it doesn't
seen to make any difference, but before long the grass gets worn off in
certain places, and other people finding the way a little smoother there begin to follow in the worn places. And
then, before anyone realizes it, the path
is made, a hard brown strip through
the green.

Now, young people, did you know it,
that is just what happens in our brains.
Every time we repeat an action or a
thought, we wear little paths in our
brains, making it easier for the thought
to go that way the next time, until
finally it seems to go of its own accord,
and we do things "before we think,"
as we say.

That is what we call habit. Habit
is something you have until it has you.
How can we manage about habit? I
have read a story about an old stage
driver who used to boast that in over
twenty-five years on the road he had
never hurt a passenger, nor a horse. In
explanation, he used to affirm that
he always held on to the reins, and
that any horse could run away if he
were only permitted to get the start.
"But," said he, "I never let them get
the start! That's the whole secret."

Yes, holding the reins is a safe thing
to do. Any horse can run away once

he gets the start. And the most trival
thing may start the runaway.

A boy or a girl may feel that he or
she can control a habit. But it is a good
deal safer not to risk a habit getting
a possible start. Certain habits have
run away with a good many and have
produced very much personal wreckage
hitherto—that is, in the past. It is
better to hold the reins rather tight
and, like the old stage driver, "never
let the horses get out of hand."

Then you know, too, that habits
have a way of becoming fixed, so that
the time arrives when you cannot
change them.

While shaking hands with an old
man a friend noticed that some of the
old man's fingers were quite bent inward, and he had not the power of
straightening them. Alluding to this
fact, the man said, "In these crooked
fingers there is a good text for a talk
to young boys and girls. For fifty
years I used to drive a stage, and these
bent fingers show the effects of holding
the reins for so many years."

This story is our text. Is it not a
suggestive one? Does it not teach us
how oft-repeated acts become a habit,
and, once acquired, remain generally
through life?

The old man's crooked fingers are but
an emblem of the crooked tempers,
cross words and queer actions that
some boys and girls have shown until
they had the habit and the habit had
them.

Right now, so near the beginning of
the New Year, is a good time to break
off old bad habits and form good new
ones. It is not easy work but it ought
to be done, and now is the time to do
it.—H.

JANUARY 24. Topic: Asking, Find-ing Out, and Getting In.

Text: "Ask, and it shall be given
you; seek, and ye shall find; knock, and
it shall be opened unto you." Luke
11:9.

This is one of the places in the Gospels where Jesus teaches about prayer,
and encourages us to keep on praying.

Ask, seek, find, is the order. Not long ago I read an Eastern story which I think makes plain this thought. It is said that once upon a time a great king in the East was thinking about his coming birthday. He resolved to invite his people to his palace and make them his guests for the day. When the day came many visited the palace intent upon having a happy holiday.

From one village came three boys who were great chums. Entering the gates and walking about in the royal gardens and grounds, by and by they turned to the grand entrance of the palace itself. They were amazed to see the majestic hall, its crystal dome, and the jewels and other treasures displayed for their admiration.

By and by they came to a place where a notice read, "To the Refreshment Rooms." One of the boys said, "Ah, that is what I want." The other two said, "No, not yet. Let us see more of the palace first." But the first boy went in and was soon enjoying every luxury his taste could desire. The king's servants waited on him until he had all he could eat. "Can't we bring you something more?" they asked. "I'm afraid not," he answered, still looking at the tables. "Would it be allowable to take some home?" he asked. "Oh, certainly; it's all for you, and it's all free." So now he tightened the girdle of his loose robe, and stuffed the fronts like great pockets, as full as they could hold, until at last he could take no more inside or outside.

In the meantime his two friends had gone one, but soon came to another notice, "To the King's Libraries." This greatly excited the second boy, and he exclaimed, "My, that is just what I was hoping for. There are so many questions and problems I want to solve. Here's the very chance for me." He became so engaged in the books that he forgot all about his lunch and the flight of time, until a great gong boomed about the palace and warned all it was time to go. He looked so disappointed that one of the servants asked: "What is the matter? Can I do anything for you?" Said the boy, "Why, I have just begun this book. It seems just what I need." The servant said, "Just take it with you. The books are for you, and are entirely free." Though greatly surprised, he tucked the book under his arm and went out to find his friends. They were to meet in front of the grand entrance when the gong boomed. There he found the others. The first boy patted his sides, pulled out some of his dainties and said, "Look what I've got!" The second showed his book trophy. Then they both turned to the third boy and asked, "What did you get?" He only seemed dazed, though his eyes had a shining, faraway look. At last he was able to tell them. "After you both left me I went on till I came to a door that stood ajar. I knocked and looked in and a lovely voice said, "Come in, my friend, come in." So I entered and found myself in the presence of the king. He spoke with me in such a friendly way and listened to me so graciously that I seemed to be in an esctasy, and hardly knew whether I was on earth or in heaven until the great bell tolled and I knew I must go." But his face was still shining, and his eyes were lighted with a great radiance, for he had seen the king in his beauty and had enjoyed fellowship with him. —H.

JANUARY 31. Topic: A Bag of Gems.

Text: "A bag of gems laid on a heap of stones." Prov. 26:8 (MOFFATT).

That was a queer place for gems, was it not? Who would look for gems in a heap of stones by the roadside? And yet there they were all safely tied up in a bag. Perhaps somebody laid them down and forgot about them, or perhaps they were hidden in a hurry, and then their owner died and the secret of their hiding place died with him. We do not know, but there they were, and when I came upon them in the book of Proverbs they gave me two messages for you young folks this morning.

I. First, they told me not to forget to look for the gems amid the stones. What does that mean? Of course it doesn't mean that you are to pull down every heap of stones you meet on a country roadside, or that you are to expect to find a bag of jewels among them. No, it means that you are to look for beauty among things that seem plain and ugly; that you are to look for brightness among things that seem dull or disagreeable; that you are to look for goodness amid things that seem unattractive or even worthless.

You are to look for beauty among the things that seem ugly and plain. Once a gentleman was walking along the seashore. He was accompanied by an old, old man who had lived there all his days. And as they walked along the visitor complained of the blackness and bleakness of the beach at that part. But the old man only smiled. "Have you ever stooped down, sir?" he asked. And when the stranger stooped, he saw that what had before seemed a black mess was crowded with thousands upon thousands of exquisite little shells.

Have you found the shells amidst the pebbles, young friends? Have you looked for the gems amidst the stones? Have you used the eyes God gave you to discover all the marvels with which he has crowded this wonderful world? You are missing some of the best things in life if you have not. And then you are to look for brightness among the things that seem dull or disagreeable. You are to look for goodness amidst things that seem unattractive or even worthless. Boys, girls, there is never a heap of stones without its gems. Look for the gems. There is never anyone so bad but he has some good in him. Look for the gems. And if you look for the gem perhaps you will be the means of helping it to shine in the glorious light of day.

II. I have only a minute left for the other message of the jewels, but I must not leave it out. For the second thing they told me was this: not to throw away my gems on a heap of stones. And what does that mean? "Well, it just means that you and I are not to throw away things that are valuable on things that are worthless. We are not to waste our energies on trifles; we are not to waste our minds in reading bad books; we are not to waste our friendship on bad companions.

And, young people, there is one priceless jewel you each possess. It is your life here on earth. What are you going to do with it? Are you going to cut it and polish it and make it gloriously worth while? Or are you going to throw it away on a heap of stones?—Author Unknown.

FEBRUARY 7. Topic: The Bronze Lions in Shanghai.

I have a brother who for many years has been a missionary in China, and a daughter who was there for nineteen years. My brother has a number of Sunday Schools under his care, and makes friends with great numbers of Chinese children. Often they run to him on the streets, take hold of his fingers, sometimes one to each finger, and call him "Jesus man"! He loves them very much and says that the Chinese boys and girls are just as lively, affectionate and lovable as our American boys and girls, and that when they once begin to come to Sunday School they attend regularly, just delight to come and to sing the hymns they learn, like "Jesus loves me, this I know, For the Bible tells me so," and others the missionaries teach them.

I want to give you boys and girls this morning an account my brother recently sent me. He says:

"At the front of the Hong Kong and Shanghai Bank's new building here in Shanghai there are two large crouching bronze lions. As one goes by he notices that the legs and paws of the lions are quite shiny, as though people in passing had rubbed up against them. But they are far enough back from the sidewalk to render this explanation unlikely.

"But wait a bit. Soon you will see Chinese come, stop and look at one of the lions, and then rub the great bronze beast's shiny parts with their hands and then turn and rub themselves!

"The people believe that if they eat the flesh of lions, tigers, leopards and other strong animals it will make themselves also strong. It is for this reason also that medicines made of tiger bones, sinews, claws and other parts are highly prized for cures and are always expensive.

"It is much the same idea that leads them to rub the bronze lions in Shanghai. Lions are strong. Rubbing, they think, must make the person who rubs them receive imparted strength from the thing rubbed. That is their thought.

"I once saw a little boy in Russia rub the face of the silver image of Jesus and then rub his own face. I wondered if he wished and believed that in doing so he would perhaps become a little more like Christ! I hope that may have been his thought.

"One thing I do know is that if we come in close contact with Christ in the fellowship of prayer, in the reading of his word, in thought and affection, we shall not alone truly receive strength from him, but we shall also grow more like him."

That is my brother's story, all the way from China; I have brought it to you this morning. I am sure you will appreciate the story, and that it makes you wish to come into close touch with Christ and to become increasingly like him.—H.

FEBRUARY 14. Topic: Would You Like to Know a Secret?

Now, young friends, would you like to know a secret? It is a real secret, similar to what some people learn when they are initiated into a secret society or fraternal organization. I want to initiate you this morning into a society whose members know the secret.

But first let me tell you a story. It is a legendary story that comes from far-away Japan. It is about a man whose name was Hofus.

Hofus was a poor stonecutter in Japan. His food was coarse and his clothing plain, but he was happy and content until one day he took a load of stone to the house of a rich man. When he saw the fine things the rich man had he cried out, "Oh, that Hofus were rich!"

As Hofus said this a fairy cried, "Have your wish!" and immediately Hofus was rich. He ceased work and lived in luxury and contentment until one day he saw a prince with a snow-white carriage, snow-white horses, a golden umbrella, and many, many servants. Then cried Hofus, "Oh, that Hofus were a prince!" No sooner had Hofus uttered his wish than he became a prince. He was happy and content as a prince until one day, while riding in his beautiful carriage under his golden umbrella, he sweltered and burned in the rays of the sun.

"The sun is greater than I," cried Hofus. "Oh, that Hofus were the sun!" Immediately Hofus became the sun, and he was happy and content until a great cloud came and entirely hid the sun. Then cried Hofus, "The cloud is greater than I. Oh, that Hofus were the cloud!" Immediately Hofus became a cloud. He was happy and content as a cloud until the cloud fell as rain and swept everything before it except a great rock which stood unmoved by the great rush of water.

Then cried Hofus, "The rock is greater than I. Oh, that Hofus were a rock!" Immediately Hofus became a rock and he was happy and content as a rock until one day a stonecutter came to the rock and began to split it. Then cried Hofus, "The stonecutter is greater than I. Oh, that Hofus were a stonecutter!" Immediately Hofus became a stonecutter, as he had been before, at the beginning; and this time Hofus was really happy and content, for he had learned that there are disadvantages in every lot in life, and that the best place for each of us is exactly where God has put us. And here comes the text for this sermon, "I have learned, in whatsoever state I am, therewith to be content" (Phil. 4:11). It was the Apostle Paul who said this. He did not have any easy time, but said he had been initiated into a secret, as some men we know have been initiated into a secret society, or some fraternal organization. Would you like to know the secret? How would you like to join the Society of Contented Boys and Girls today?—H.

FEBRUARY 21. Topic: The Light in the Window.

The other night I was coming home when an eastern storm was at its worst. There seemed not a star in the sky; the night was so dark. I was wishing that I might get home as quickly as possible to sit by the fire with an interesting book. No one loves to be out in such a storm, which was the worst of the winter. I made my way along as best I could; but as I came down the little hill to the parsonage my eye caught sight of a little light, which seemed to be all alone in the midst of one of our hills.

Though I had seen the light in the window of this cottage many a time, I came to see it truly only in the storm. As I looked at it this is what it seemed to mean to me. The light in that hillside cottage was giving brightness and beauty to a place called home. And so I began to think of that greater light of God put in the window for us in the person of his son Jesus Christ, our Lord. A light which had been shining ever since the world began became most bright when we saw it in the manger of Bethlehem and afterward on the cross of Calvary. That was a light to lead all the children of men home to God. And though many people live as if that Light had never been, still it is ever shining and will shine on to lead and bring people home to God.

Dear young friends, I want you to know and ever remember, wherever you go or whatever you do, that God's Light of Love is ever shining and will shine for you, shining to lead you home. "For God so loved the world, that he gave his only begotten Son, that whosoever believeth in him should

not perish, but have everlasting life." The light in God's window of love is for you.—Rev. James E. Brimelow.

FEBRUARY 28. Topic: About a Minister's Young Daughter.

There is one thing I know about boys and girls, especially about those that are quite young. It is that when they want anything they want it very much. I know of a boy who once said, "I want what I want when I want it." Of course that was quite rude. But I know another true story about a little girl, the daughter of a minister. There came upon her a little illness, which caused her to be put to bed quite early one night. In a little while she called her mother. "Mamma," said she, "I want to see my dear Papa!" "No, dear," said her mother; "Papa is working in his study and is not to be disturbed just now."

Presently came the pleading voice again: "I want to see my Papa!" No," was the answer, "I cannot disturb him."

Then the four-year-old parishioner rose to a question of privilege. "Mamma," she said, "I am a sick woman, and I want to see my minister!"

It certainly is true that children do sometimes say very striking and interesting things. I heard of a little girl who said: "How am I supposed to button my dress behind when I am all in front?"

I have read of a Philadelphia woman who recently went calling accompanied by her five-year-old boy. He was a rather good-looking little fellow, of the Fauntleroy type, and more than one of the women she visited said complimentary things about him, all of which he took in with due modesty. Before the afternoon ended, however, he revealed his ideas of maternal pride. One of the women said jokingly, but with serious face: "My little man, I think I will just keep you here with me. I have no little boy of my own. Don't you think your mother would sell you to me?"

"No ma'am," he replied promptly.

"You don't?" she asked in affected surprise. "Why, don't you think I have enough money to buy you?"

"It isn't that," he answered, politely, "but there are just five of us, you see, and she would not care to break the set!"

Now, I wonder what teachings I can draw from these incidents? Well, I think I have said enough!—H.

MARCH 7. Topic: The Power of Example (Chinese Folk Tale).

My brother, who has been for many years a missionary in China, recently sent me a story which I am going to give to you young folks this morning. This is the way the story goes:

"Once upon a time there was a king in the country Zee called Way-koong. He liked to wear purple-colored robes. Naturally, all the people and officials in the land began to wear purple, following his example. Because of this, purple clothes and materials became five times as expensive as those of other colors, at which the king was much displeased.

"One day he said to Koo-zoong, one of his ministers, 'I like to wear purple. But now purple clothes have become too expensive for the people. Everyone in the land wants to wear purple clothes. How can I stop it?'

"The minister said, 'Your majesty, why do you not try discarding purple garments yourself? If you do so, and say to your ministers of state that you are tired of purple and do not like the odor of it, and request those who wear purple to stand a little farther from you, it will probably have the effect you desire.'

"The king did as was suggested. After even the first day no one in the palace wore purple! Next day no one in the capital was wearing purple! On the third day no one in his kingdom was wearing purple!

"Moral: If a man wishes to advise others to be good he must first be good himself. Many are good at giving advice to others but do not practice what they preach. How can they expect others to do what they advise with the lips only?"

Even for boys and girls, I suppose example is better than precept. I am sure you believed that even before you heard this interesting Chinese story.—H.

MARCH 14. Topic: The Wind and the Sun.

This month of March is quite generally known as "the windy month." It is this being the windy month, yet the sun beginning to struggle against the winds, which makes the very old story I bring this morning seem quite appropriate. The story is one of the oldest in the world. You doubtless know it perfectly well. Yet is may be so old that it is new, and I am going to risk telling it to you. It is one of Aesop's fables. It belongs to a period more than twenty-five hundred years ago, for Aesop was an old Greek writer of a time over five hundred years before Christ.

Of course you know that in his stories the birds and animals and forces of nature are represented as talking to one another and acting a good deal like some people, some humans, etc.

This story tells of a contest between the wind and the sun. A dispute arose between the north wind and the sun as to which was the stronger of the two. Then they saw a traveler on his way, and agreed to try which could the sooner get his cloak off from him.

The north wind began, and sent a furious blast, which at the onset nearly tore the cloak from its fastenings. But the traveler, seizing the garment with a firm grip, held it around his body so tightly that the north wind spent his remaining force in vain.

The sun, driving away the clouds that had gathered, then poured his most sultry beams on the traveler's head. Growing faint with the heat, the man flung off his cloak and ran for protection to the nearest shade.

The moral of the fable is this: "Kindness effects more than severity." And that is true. There is an old saying: "Vinegar never catches flies." Kindess wins. That is a good lesson for us to learn while we are young. "Kindness effects more than severity." Young folks, don't forget the fable of the wind and the sun.—H.

MARCH 21. Topic: Know Your Church: The True Ruby (1).

Today I want to talk to you young folks about glass of a particular color. In our church and in many other churches there are one or more stained-glass windows. In each such window there is glass of many colors. But I am to speak at this time of only one color, the true ruby. One of our members recently gave me a pamphlet which has given me information which I am going to pass on to you. But at this time I speak only of that especially beautiful color known as true ruby.

This booklet says that the most difficult colored glass to make is that deep red which we call ruby. The true ruby glass is made of the whitest sand. You know that glass is made of sand, don't you? Well, it is, and the brilliancy of the glass goes right back to the sand pit. Someone said once that you can't make a silk purse out of a pig's ear. Well, you can't make true ruby glass out of poor sand.

Now, there is something to think about. If we have good stuff, as we say, from our fathers and mothers, good bodies and keen minds and sympathetic hearts, then we surely ought to be thankful—that means we have the clear base of sincerity and truth. That's the beginning of the true ruby. White sand for brilliant glass!

Now listen to this. You can get ruby-red glass by putting copper into the pot metal when you mix the glass. But it is not the true ruby. It produces a sort of orangey yellow or a violet pink. What do you suppose makes the true ruby the most beautiful color known to art? Gold. Solid gold is put into the glass to get the true sunset flame ruby.

Now there is a question for us. What am I putting into my life—cheap copper or expensive gold? When we are tested by life, will we have some poor off-color stuff or true ruby made of pure gold? And one more thing. Here's a secret

of glass color. It is a lot easier to get the color by putting in borax; but the color fades in ten or fifteen years. When you want true ruby—no borax!

When someone tries to get us to take an easy cheap road to character or position in life, then we must say, "No, no borax!" True ruby! That's the glory of the window. That will be the charm of your life, young friends. True ruby.

True ruby! White sand! Pure gold! No borax!—M. K. W. H.

MARCH 28. Topic: Know Your Church: Colored Glass: The Furnace (2).

Last Sunday we talked about the deep red glass in church windows called true ruby. We found that true ruby is the very finest of the glassmaker's art. Let us recall three things I told you about it. First, true ruby glass is made of the purest white sand. Second, the color is given to it by gold placed placed in the melting pot. Third, no borax must be used in making the true ruby. We also mentioned that there is such a thing as true ruby characters, and that young people can have such characters.

Now this morning I want to tell you a little more about this "no borax" idea. It is this way. When you put sand and gold in the melting pot and then add this substance called borax, then you do not need to heat the mixture as hot as you otherwise would to get the color in the glass. "Well," you might say, "that is a good thing, isn't it? Makes it easier. Might as well take the easy way."

Yes, but the color doesn't last as long. It fades out after ten years or so. If you don't use borax you have to make the glass terribly hot. It must go into the hottest furnace. But then it comes out true ruby. And the true ruby never fades.

Now may I tell you about some boys that I know? One boy went swimming in the river one spring where he had swum the previous summer. He thought the water was deep at that

THE MINISTERS MANUAL FOR 1954

place, but instead it was shallow. And when he dived in he broke a bone in his neck and was taken to the hospital. I used to visit him there. One day when I came he was all excited. "Mr. H., Mr. H., I can move my finger!" And he showed me that he could move one finger just the fraction of an inch. You see he was paralyzed and he had to learn all over again how to use his limbs. He was like glass in the furnace and the furnace was hot. He was having a hard time of it. But I am told that he came through true ruby, and sometimes when I take up a magazine I read the writings of this boy and I believe he is true ruby.

A few years ago a boy lived two houses from us. One summer day infantile paralysis struck him. He went right into a furnace of suffering and while there he didn't waste his time. With one hand in water he would work with the other. And he never whimpered. He never asked for things to be made easier. He didn't want borax! He would stand the heat. He is now a man with true ruby character.

I suppose that you all know young friends, who, if they have to stand the furnace fire, will come out true ruby personalities.

And that is just exactly what Jesus did. He went to the cross. And he came out true ruby!—M. K. W. H.

APRIL 4. Topic: Know Your Church: The Meaning of Its Name.

Someone has well said that "words are things." Another says that "syllables govern the world." Still another that "words are but pictures of our thoughts." It was the Chinese Confucius who said, "For one word a man is often deemed to be wise, and for one word he is often deemed to be foolish. We ought to be careful indeed what we say."

I wonder whether you boys and girls know that every word we use has a beginning and a history. And with most words it is not difficult to find out the story of them.

Anybody has the right to make up

words, and if he can get everybody else to use them, finally the word will get into the dictionary.

Let me give you examples of some common words with interesting histories. Here is the word "book." Why is a book called "book"? It is this way: Back in Europe an old name for a beech tree was buc, b-u-c. A beech tree has nice smooth bark and before there was good paper the bark of the beech tree was used to write on. And so the word for beech tree became the word for book.

Let me tell you another word that is interesting. You all know the word "boulder" for a large stone. How did it get that name? Well, many centuries ago perhaps people watched the great stones roll down the moutnain streams when there was a storm and flood. And they heard the great stones make a crashing sound and they called them buller, buller-steens, that is, bullerstones. They came down the stream going "buller, buller, buller," like thunder. And now we call big stones boulders, because they went "buller, buller, buller." And so a boy came home and said, "Mother, I heard a stone go 'buller, buller'!" That boy gave us the word "boulder."

But why should this church be called [insert denominational name]. It is the name of a Christian denomination as we say.

One day a little girl went to the post office to buy some stamps. And the clerk said, "What denomination?" He meant, do you want one cent, or two cent, or three cent stamps? But she said, "Presbyterian." He knew where she went to Sunday School.

[Conclude this little talk by explaining the name of your denomination.]—M. K. W. H.

APRIL 11. Topic: Know Your Church: Two Interesting Windows.

I know a church which has two very interesting stained-glass windows. The first represents a fine-looking old man. I can imagine that when that good man got to talking, as men sometimes do, about his mother, he would say, "She made me a little coat every year when I was a boy."

I'll tell you another thing that happened when he was a boy. He was going to be a minister in the temple of God and in those days the ministers and the boys in training lived right in the temple. They kept the little temple lamps burning all night before the altar, and I can imagine this boy sleeping in one part of the Church and Eli, the old minister, sleeping on the other side.

One night when the light was making long shadows through the temple and everything was quiet, dead quiet and still, this boy heard a voice call his name "Samuel!" And he ran to to the priest and said, "Here am I." But Eli said, "I didn't call you."

He lay down again, but soon he heard a voice, "Samuel!" So Samuel ran over to Eli again. "Here I am. You called me." But Eli said, "I called thee not, my son; lie down again."

But the third time the voice came, "Samuel!" And Samuel ran to Eli again. Then Eli knew that the voice of God was coming to the boy's heart. And he said, "Go, lie down, and it shall be, if he call thee that thou shalt say, 'Speak, Lord, for thy servant heareth.'"

Well, the voice called again and Samuel heard and answered. And God told Samuel something he was going to do and by that and what followed Samuel became a great leader and prophet.

Now almost every time you hear a story like that you know that the boy had a good mother. And just beside her boy, in another window of that church, is a picture of Hannah. Now in these stained-glass windows Samuel and Hannah are dressed in strange dress to us, but you must remember that they lived a long time ago and in another land.

Hannah was a good mother, I'm sure of it. She gave her boy a good name. Samuel means "Asked of God." She had asked God for a boy, so she called him "Asked of God." It's a fine thing to have a good name and to live up to it. She gave her boy a good name.

Then "she took him to the house of God." Maybe he didn't care about that at first, but soon he was glad for that is the place to hear the word and voice of God. "She made him a little coat every year." That's in the Bible for that's just like a mother.

And when Samuel was an old man I can hear him say, "My mother made me a little coat every year when I was a boy."—M. K. W. H.

APRIL 18. Topic: The Meaning of Easter (Easter).

It does not seem well for you young folks to think much about death. Because you are young it is better for you to think about life. And that is what Easter means, life, not death.

There is a little poem about death and Easter which I think you are old enough to appreciate. It is called "The Inn by the Road," and was written by C. E. Warner. I am going to repeat it to you:

Ne'er was the sky so deep a hue
But that the sun came breaking through;
There never was a night so dark
But wakened to the singing lark;
Nor was there ever a lane so long
It had no turn for the weary throng;
Nor heart so sad that sometime after
There came no sound of lilting laughter;
And Death's not the end—'neath the
    cold black sod—
'Tis the Inn by the Road on our way
    to God.

The other day I read an article written by a minister, and I want to quote to you the substance of a part of it. It is really about Easter, though the title is "Night and Morning." The writer says:

"There was a man I knew who had a daughter. There came a time when she was to be married. Ever since she was a little girl her father's custom had always been to tuck her into bed at night. Whatever time of the night he came in he would always go in softly and tuck her in and kiss her. And sometimes she would partly awaken and say, "Hello, daddy," and he would say, "Good-night, sweetheart." And so it came to the last night that she was to be under his roof. As before, he went in that last night she was to be under his roof and under the shadow of his love, and he tucked her in. She put her arms around his neck and drew him close, and he put his arms around her and said, "My daughter"; and she just said, "Daddy."

I wonder if God, in the last night that we are to be in our home on earth, will not come down and tuck us in. When our eyelids droop and our voices falter, and we can hear no sound, I think Someone will be there. It will be God. He will tuck us in; he will say, "Sleep sweetly"; then he will stay right there and will not go away, and after a time will awaken us with a kiss and say, "It is morning."

Remember, boys and girls, Easter does not mean death; it means life. This is no memorial day. Nobody thinks of Jesus as being dead. Nowhere have Christian folk met merely to pay their respects to his memory and to hear and say a few kind words about him. The word that goes around the world today is "He lives!" From near and far, from every habitation of man where the Bible is known, from tropic forest and frozen north, from mountain heights and sea-washed islands, from populous city and country hamlet is raised in glorious chorus the cry, "He is risen indeed! Alleluia!"—H.

APRIL 25. Topic: Know Your Church: A Study of Backgrounds.

We know a church which has a dark red curtain hanging back of the Communion table, and on the table in front of the curtain stands a cross. Why is the curtain there? It is to make a good background for seeing the cross. Suppose we were to take the dark red curtain down and put in its place a gray curtain. Why that would not do at all. You all realize that. If one should stand the cross in front of a gray curtain then the people in the other end of the church would scarcely be able to see the cross

at all. The cross would not stand out as it does against the dark red.

You see, young friends, that a lot depends on the background. Let me give you another example. You go out some night when the moon is not shining and see how much brighter the stars are on the dark nights. Maybe you don't know that the stars are shining in the sky just now. Yes, but we cannot see them in daytime because there is no dark background. That is the reason the poets speak about the "curtain of the night."

Backgrounds are very interesting. Someday take a red rose and hold it out by itself. It will be lovely. But then get the greenest leaves you can find and hold the red rose in the midst of the green leaves and see how much lovelier it is.

My friend has a woolly white dog and when he is rolling in the green grass you might say in passing, "Look at the nice white dog." But if a snow came and covered everything with fresh clean snow and the dog came out into the snow, I know that you might say, "Look at the dirty white dog." You see, a lot depends upon the background.

Now I want to call your attention to one of the greatest verses in the Bible. It is this: "In God we live and move and have our being." It means that you and I have a background. Here we are, but back of us always ready to give us life and strength and more life is God.

Many people have the happy faculty of seeing God back of things. They look up at the stars and they see God in the background. They see a field of flowers and then they think of God. They look at their own lives and know that God is back of them. They look up at the cross and see God. These are good things for even quite young boys and girls to think about. They will mean more as you grow older. Backgrounds in life are very important.—M. K. W. H.

MAY 2. Topic: From a Chinese Window.

When the Union Railroad Station in Los Angeles, California, was built a few years ago, several blocks of Chinese homes and stores had to be demolished to make room for it. A new section called China City is an outgrowth of this development.

There the tourist may wander at will through little streets bearing such delightful names as Dragon Road and Lotus Pool Road. Everywhere attractive restaurants are serving Chinese food steaming hot from its immersion in shallow copper bowls of sizzling peanut oil. Small stores crowd one another in the display of treasures from old China, together with products of modern native craftsmanship.

In the window of one of those shops recently appeared two written letters fastened against the glass. With them was an exquisite bracelet, a ten-dollar bill, and an elaborately bound book. The letters read thus:

"On the 7th of August I took this bracelet from your store. On returning a little later, I heard you questioning a young couple as to its disappearance. I would not like to have anyone else accused of a wrong I did. If I knew the value of the bracelet I would return the price, but as I have no idea as to its worth, I am returning it."

This letter was unsigned. The other was written by the owner of the shop, and addressed to the writer of the first letter, evidently a conscience-stricken thief, in this manner:

"The bracelet you took was not mine; all material things belong to God. We brought nothing into the world when we came, and can take nothing out when we go. Therefore, all material is His. But, my friend, I am happy that you have made this decision to be honest with yourself. I wish you would come into the store and make yourself known to me. I would like to take you by the hand and congratulate you. I also want to offer you a gift of friendship. Here is a ten-dollar bill, and also a ten-dollar book of wise sayings of one of my country's noble philosophers. They are yours —with my good will."

The man who stole the bracelet had an accusing conscience. The conscience which God has given us is the soul's sentinel. If we always give heed to the voice of conscience we shall be kept in the right way. The other day a man speaking of certain things which other people sometimes practice, said, "I cannot do such things. If I do there is someone inside of me who talks to me nights." How many have been withheld from sin, from folly, from rashness and bitterness by that voice within! Be quick, young friends, to obey the voice of conscience.

MAY 9. Topic: Teddy's Automobile.

This morning I am going to tell you a story. It is not called religious, but I am sure you will get from it its own religious meaning.

Teddy sat on the front steps of his home and watched the dark-skinned men digging a ditch out in the street. They wore such funny clothes. Some of the coats and trousers didn't match, and some of the men had gay-colored handkerchiefs tied loosely around their necks. But somehow, Teddy did not feel like laughing at them, even though they did seem queer, and talked in strange language.

Teddy wondered if these men had any little boys at home. He thought he would like to find out, but didn't know how.

Just then he noticed one of the men waving a dipper and calling to another for water, as near as he could understand. "No more, no more," the other man said.

When Teddy heard that, he felt so sorry for the man who was thirsty that he jumped up and ran as fast as he could around the house and into the kitchen to ask mother for a pail of cool water for the men out in front.

Of course, mother gladly filled the pail, and Teddy took it eagerly and hurried out to the street. "Won't you have a drink?" he called, as he held the water up for them to see. How their dark eyes shone! And how quickly they came to get some water! One patted Teddy on the head. "Have you a little boy?" Teddy asked. "Yeh—six-year-old. No brudder—sister—no play udder chiles." Teddy saw that his eyes grew sad as he thought about his lonesome little boy at home.

Teddy gave all the men a drink and then he went slowly back to the kitchen, thinking deeply all the way. And after he had given mother the pail, he went to the big drawer that held his toys. He wondered what he would like best if he were a little boy in a strange land.

Finally he chose his automobile, one that went all by itself when it was wound. He took it to his mother, and explained to her about the little Italian boy who was lonesome. He asked if he might send it to him by his daddy for his very own. Mother was pleased, and readily gave her consent.

Teddy's face beamed as he handed the shiny toy to the man who had patted him on the head. "For your little boy," he said. "Yeh, for my leedle boy? No, no, you mama not like." But mother was looking through the window and she nodded her head.

How happy the Italian man was! He took the little shining toy and wrapped it carefully in the big handkerchief he took from his neck. "You good boy. My leedle boy love."

Teddy was up early next morning. He wondered if the Italian man would tell him what his little boy said.

Sure enough, the man's face was covered with smiles when he saw Teddy come out on the front steps. He dropped his pick, and coming up close, said, "My leedle boy! He so glad! He play much. He laugh and laugh. He go to sleep laughing!"

And Teddy was so happy because he had made the little Italian stranger happy.—F. Upson.

MAY 16. Topic: Cultivation of Acquaintance with Our Animal Friends.

Not a few boys and girls have tamed very interesting animal pets. It is quite a hobby with some of you, and delightful fun. Some of these pets are quite unusual creatures, though others are more common. I have known of pets of canary birds, rabbits, mice, lambs, chickens, ducks, goats, pigs, monkeys, parrots, squirrels, guinea pigs, woodchucks, raccoons, and others. One of my brothers as a boy had a pet raccoon that became almost too insistent and mischievous. Another had a canary that would come to him at any time and sit on his head or shoulders and sing when he asked it. Once when our family were on a visit to India we were at a hotel in the city of Jaipur. A man came along with a cageful of tiny birds. My wife, who was sitting on the hotel porch, was taken by surprise when the whole cageful of birds was suddenly in her lap. Again in a little bit they were all back in their cage. The man allured them where he wished by the tossing of exceedingly small birdseed. The same man had also a larger bird which he commanded to fly into a tree and bring him a leaf. This it did, putting the tree leaf into the man's hand.

Once in China we met a young man one morning in Tsing Tau who had a covered bird cage. He placed the cage on a wall, lifted the curtain, and a somewhat large bird of the mockingbird variety began at once to sing with astonishing energy, variety of notes and enthusiasm.

We mention these cases only to instance how these animal creatures can be tamed and taught to perform. At the present time one of our daughters has an interesting squirrel friend. In the city park nearby there are many squirrels. This one is not a pet, but it will come to her bedroom window and scratch upon it in the morning to wake her up to give it peanuts. If she does not answer soon enough it will often bump its head on the pane to make a more insistent demand.

A notable historic instance is one related of some swans that belonged to a bishop in England. The swans were in the moat of the palace of the Bishop of Wells. The old gatehouse with its gray, ivy-grown walls still stands, and it is said swans in their successors still sail up and down the dark waters of the moat, which centuries ago was a defense of the castle.

The peculiar thing about these swans

is that they ring a dinner bell whenever they are hungry, and expect to have it answered at once. A long string hangs out of the gatehouse window and, as the story is told, when the swans are hungry the leader swims up to the bell rope, pulls at it, and then waits quietly for the lodgekeeper's wife to bring out her basket of food.

It is said that eighty years ago the daughter of the bishop who lived there then taught the swans this trick with great patience and care. The swans that have come since then have apparently in turn learned the secret of the bell rope, so that a swan that is able to perceive the connection between the pulling of the string and the appearing of the bread basket has always been among them.

These stories of the cultivation of acquaintance with our animal friends may bring us several suggestions. One is that of the duty and privilege of kindness to animals. The last story, about the swans, may suggest the privilege of the prayer, "Give us this day our daily bread." We are taught, "Ask and ye shall receive." Let the swans teach us this lesson—the lesson of prayer.—H.

MAY 23. Topic: **About Saving Money.**

Every boy and every girl at some time tries to save money. Saving is certainly a fine habit to form very early in life. There are many people who are poor today who would not be in need if they had started to save when they were young.

But in order to save one must have a real reason for doing so. Just to save for the sake of having money is to be a miser. Money was meant to be saved and used for good purposes. So when we try to save let us remember some of the good things for which we may put aside our money.

I. First, let us save to help ourselves. In what way? One big way comes into my mind just now. No one of us wants to be ignorant. Each of us would like to have a good education. You may help yourself to a college education by begin-

ning to save while you are young. I know of boys who have peddled papers, mowed lawns, cleaned out cellars, and have done all sorts of work and saved some of the money they earned while they were in grammar school and high school, and when they entered college they had enough money to help quite a lot.

II. That is reason number one. And here is reason number two: save to help others. There are many people who saved money all through the years while they were earning who when the chance came to help someone were able to do so. Some of them have sent missionaries across the sea. Others have built churches. Still others have helped poor and needy people.

Each summer as I go through Philadelphia, I pass a beautiful church and a lot of fine college buildings. I once asked how these buildings came to be, and someone told me that they were built with fifty-seven pennies! Think of it; fifty-seven copper pennies built a college in which there are hundreds of students, a church worth a quarter of a million dollars, and a great hospital caring for thousands of little children! Do you want the story? Well, here it is.

Years ago there was a little girl who went to a Sunday School in Philadelphia and found the classes so full that there seemed to be no room for her. She was very much disappointed and so began to save her pennies so that her church might be bigger and other poor little children might have a chance to go to Sunday School. No one knew she was doing this until one day when she was taken ill, and she told her pastor of the money she was saving to build the church. When God took her out of her sufferings, they found under her pillow a little red pocketbook in which there were fifty-seven pennies and a scrap of paper on which she had written the reason why she had saved her pennies. The pastor who visited her was a good man and knew how valuable those fifty-seven pennies were. Soon the story of those pennies got into the papers and the people read about them with tears in their eyes. And then people began to give and before long the great Baptist Temple, Temple College, and the Samaritan Hospital were built in Philadelphia. So six-year-old little Hattie May Wiatt saved her money and it was used to lead other people to do what they had failed to do.—A. H. Limouze, D.D.

MAY 30. Topic: Looking Down and Seeing Up.

One of the loveliest places in the world is Yosemite Valley in California. Every visitor to the Golden State tries to see Yosemite. Surely some of you have been there.

In Yosemite the mountains stand straight up for thousands of feet. The streams come tumbling over the mountains and come straight down in magnificent waterfalls. The valley floor is a wonderful meadow carpeted with grasses and flowers. The trees grow straight and tall as though they were trying to reach higher than the mountains. A small river cuts through the meadow in a hurry; it seems to get down to the plain and water the ranches and gardens of the people.

There is one place in Yosemite where the visitor has a most interesting and fascinating experience. He looks down to see up. It is a little mountain lake, almost round in circumference, and in this lake is mirrored not only the stones and grasses and flowers on its shore, but also the trees and standing about them the mountains. This lake is called Mirror Lake. The reflection in the lake equals in beauty the real valley and mountains above it. If a photograph is taken it is difficult to tell which side is up; the two images, one above the lake, the other in the lake, are exactly alike.

Looking down and seeing up—there is a chapel in Rome in Italy called the Sistine Chapel. There are rich and famous paintings on the ceiling of the chapel, but it is difficult to see them by stretching the neck and tilting the head. The best way is to carry a mirror into the chapel, look down into the mirror and see up to the paintings.

The astronomers do this as they sit at their telescopes. Their heads are not craned upward. They are turned downward to see the planets and the stars which are mirrored in the telescope.

There are some people who can look down with their eyes and see up with their minds. A poet once looked down at a little flower and then he wrote these lines:

Flower in the crannied wall,
I pluck you out of the crannies,
I hold you here, root and all, in my hand,
Little flower—but *if* I could understand
What you are, root and all, and all in all,
I should know what God and man is.

Alfred, Lord Tennyson was looking at a little flower with his eyes; he was seeing God with his mind.

Do you remember the wise men who visited Jesus when he was a babe at Bethlehem? They looked down at the babe and with their minds they saw God. I think that maybe this is the reason they were called *wise* men—they could look down and see up.

There is a text in the Bible, II Corinthians 3:18 (A.S.V.), which tells of "beholding as in a mirror the glory of the Lord," looking down and seeing up.

JUNE 6. Topic: Margins.

This is the school commencement season. Young people from children up are thinking about success in life. Our topic this morning is Margins, which has to do with getting on in the world. I know a woman who is a schoolteacher and a good one. She has been teaching now for more than twenty years. She has had a good salary and no dependents, but she has spent as she went along all that she got. She has now no margin. She says that she expects to spend her last days in some public institution.

I know another woman, past middle life, who is a secretary in a Christian benevolent institution. She has had an excellent salary, but never saves any money. In fact when she gets this month's salary she always has debts from last month that demand it all. She buys an automobile on time, and it is about worn out by the time she has it paid for and must purchase another. She never has any margin.

Another, a secretary in the same institution, has resolutely put aside month by month 10 per cent of her salary, and now has a safe margin for the remainder of her days. The Rev. Frank D. McAlister is authority for a rather tragic story on this theme of margins. Its meaning will be plain as I go along. It is about a mining prospector by the name of Cranna. At the age of seventeen this man had left his home in Scotland to seek a fortune in the island continent "way down under." With a companion he plunged into the heart of wild and hitherto untraversed country to look for gold. The two young men found several valuable claims, but were always forced to sell out for a song in order to get enough to eat.

Finally Cranna stumbled on the great gold field at Mount Morgan, in the State of Queensland. The man's claim looked like a veritable bonanza. His chronic poverty, however, compelled him to sell for whatever he could get, and the highest bid was fifty-four pounds, or about one hundred and seventy dollars. Since then Mount Morgan claim has yielded a hundred million dollars' worth of gold, and is still producing. In other words, had Cranna controlled money enough to feed and clothe himself for a single year he might have become one of the world's richest men.

A margin of money, even though it be slight, makes available opportunities that otherwise must be missed. And surely there are goods of life besides money that ask for a measure of surplus, if they are to be effective helps to well-being. For example, a little more time than is absolutely necessary to do the errand or catch the train is probably advisable for most people. Some unforeseen interruption may occur. Auto tires occasionally encounter bent nails, or fire alarms may slow up traveling schedules. In any event, there would seem to be no particular point in barely

meeting life's engagements by split seconds, and gasping for breath.

How desirable is some excess of physical vigor over and above the requirements of the day! If one burns up all reserves each twenty-four hours, there is nothing left for one to draw upon in times of special demand. Young people often feel that they can beat the rules at this point, but later they learn better. Perhaps the most thriftless people of all are those whose spiritual supplies stand chronically at low-water mark. A merely traditional religion may serve in life's uneventful routine. But what of hours when earth seems to tremble beneath the feet, and stars grow dim in the night sky? In such experiences of loss or bereavement a robust and full-bodied faith is all that saves one. No conventional form of words will do. Margins? Yes, indeed, in all ranges of life and activity. They make the difference between poverty and abundance.

JUNE 13. Topic: The Beauty and Significance of Our Flag (Flag Day).

[Note: The second Sunday of June is almost universally observed as Children's Day. A Children's Day talk will be found in the Sermon Section on this date.]

Tomorrow, the fourteenth of June, is known as Flag Day. It is given that name because it was on that day in the year 1777 that the Continental Congress chose the flag which now waves over all our broad land. Besides, the Fourth of July, Independence Day, occurs so soon, that I thought you would like to think about our beloved flag today. Both these days remind us of the beauty and significance of our national flag.

Flags have been the symbols of national life and honor, of patriotism and love of country, for more than three thousand years. The Chinese had flags as early as the twelfth century before Christ. Ensigns, standards and banners were in constant use among the Assyrians, Egyptians, Hebrews, and other Oriental peoples from the earliest times. Much is said in Roman history of the

Roman standards. Among these the most famous was that of Constantine, which consisted of a long gilded spear, on the top of which was a crossbar, from which hung a purple cloth beautifully decorated with a monogram of Christ and the Greek letters Alpha and Omega. It commemorated the emperor's conversion to Christianity.

We think our "red, white and blue" is the most beautiful flag in the world. When the Chinese first saw it they called it the "flower flag."

The thought of it was not born in the heart of any of our great statesmen, but in the heart of a loving, loyal, gifted woman, and the mere designing of the "stars and stripes" is enough to give the name of Betsy Ross, of Philadelphia, a place of permanent fame in our nation's history.

As we have said, our flag is a symbol. It signifies that we are a free people, and a united people, "the United States of America." It represents sacrifice. At a great cost we obtained this our "land of the free." The flag is also a security. It guarantees the safety of every citizen. And it is a sanctification. It hallows and consecrates the national sentiment. It consecrates us to our nation's ideals and purifies our patriotism.

There are two special flags I want to mention this morning. One is a gift that was made to Wellesley College. The gift was made by General Pershing, which was his own service flag in the first World War. It consists of a red ground with four white stars. He gave also his war helmet and the personal battle pennon of the German ex-Kaiser. The flag will go down in history as among Wellesley's most prized possessions.

There is another flag I want to mention. It is in the library of the Presbyterian Board of Foreign Missions at 156 Fifth Avenue, New York. It too will go down in history as the emblem of the United States of America which saved the lives of missionaries and native Christians alike in the awful days in Urumia, Persia, before the United States entered the first World War.

Our flag has gained many triumphs since those days of the first World War, but we must leave mention of these until some later time.

> Above the flags of all nations,
>   Our beautiful banner floats high;
> Its stars like the stars of heaven,
>   And its blue as blue as the sky.
>
> Long may it wave in its beauty,
>   The symbol of Freedom and Right;
> Not a star be lost from its azure,
>   Not a blot stain its spotless white.
>   —H.

SEPTEMBER 5. Topic: God's Trademark (Object Sermon).

[Object: A Brick.]

In the ruins of ancient Babylon have been found many bricks bearing the stamp of Nebuchadnezzar the king. The brick which I hold in my hand also has something stamped upon it. Here we find the name or the initials of the company that manufactures it. These letters were stamped on this brick when it was soft, when it was being made. Then it was easy. It is made of clay. The soft clay was pressed into a mold, then baked in an oven.

You and I, too, are made of clay. We may not look like bricks, but our bodies are made of clay. The Bible says that man was made from the dust of the earth. To be sure, your body is flesh; but your flesh comes from the food that you eat and that grows in the ground, or comes from it. When a person dies his body crumbles back into the clay from which it was made.

Now, the manufacturer of this brick stamped his trade-mark on it when it was made from clay. And God put his trade-mark upon us when he made us out of clay. In the Bible we read, "God created man in his own image." That means that he stamped himself on us. We know who made this Brick, for the manufacturer's name is on it. We know who made us, for God's stamp is on us. God has made us souls like himself. We have bodies, but we are souls—souls that can love, be kind, be just, be honest and do good.

When I was a boy on my father's farm we used to use a red brick like this to scour and clean the rust from a plow that had become rusty. A plow does not turn a furrow well if the mold-wing is rusty. We would rub it with a brick until it was clean and bright. When the brick was used long in this way the name of the maker would become worn away and the trade-mark gone.

Young friends, it is possible to wear off God's trade-mark, his image on our souls. Rubbing with sin and wrong will wear down God's stamp upon us. We wear away God's trade-mark from us when we do things that are wrong and which he cannot approve.

There is one other thing that can be said about this brick. It is hard to think of something that just one brick can do. But it is easy to think of what many bricks can do. Many bricks can be built into a wall, a pavement, a house, or a tall building. But one brick cannot do very much alone.

In that way, too, we are like bricks. Many people working together can do great things that one person cannot do. One person cannot make a good strong church, but many people can. Many people working together can make this a good world in which God is loved and the right is done. One brick alone cannot make a wall; we need many bricks. One Christian alone cannot make the world right; we need many Christians. But, at the same time, let us do each his or her part.—Rev. J. J. Sessler (Adapted).

SEPTEMBER 12. Topic: Christian Worship.

TEXT: "O come, let us worship and bow down: let us kneel before the Lord our Maker." Ps. 95:6.

What do we mean by worship? It means having some thought and idea of God; a yearning after God; praise and prayer before God; seeking a likeness to God.

Nearly everybody worships, but do people all worship aright? Heathen people worship. Usually they think of a god to be feared, or to be satisfied, or to be bought off. Some pagans beat drums to attract the attention of their god. They chant songs, offer sacrifices, cut their bodies, or dance to win the favor of their gods.

The Mohammedan is anxious when he worships that his own body is clean. He will not wear shoes or gold or silver, and when the hour of prayer comes he bows down, wherever he is, and says, "There is one God, and Allah is his prophet."

We Christians worship in many ways. We come into the church and worship by confessing God and loving him, by believing in Christ and praising him. Deaf people understand this. Some who can never hear a word spoken are glad to go to God's house. They have secret thoughts of God and his love. They honor him in his house of prayer.

I sometimes preach in the church of the deaf. It is a tender and precious service. I have found there three men who are like Helen Keller, deaf, dumb and blind. The service is interpreted to them on their hands, and by their manner and countenance they show that they know what it means to worship God. Worship is of the heart and life. We confess our love in our worship.

Jane, a little girl, had just finished her prayer. She had thanked God for many friends and many things, and last of all she thanked God for her father and her mother. Then saying good-night, she turned to her mother and said: "I do love you, mother, but of course I love God best, for if it hadn't been for God, I wouldn't have you, would I?" I think she had a right idea of God, and if you know God it is not difficult rightly to worship him.

You cannot worship God without prayer. You cannot worship God without faith. A child can believe in God, know him, and love him, and speak to him in prayer, and that is worshiping God.—Rev. C. W. Watch.

SEPTEMBER 19. Topic: The Cock and the Fox.

Of course you know that in all the ancient stories the fox is made out a very sly old fellow and up to all sorts of tricks, but he generally loses out. One of the interesting old stories is about the cock and the fox. This is one of Aesop's fables, where the birds and animals are represented as talking to one another and acting a good deal like some people act. You know, too, that the story is very ancient, for it has come down through more than twenty-five centuries. It is so old that it may be new to you. Anyway I am going to risk telling it.

The story states that a cock perched among the branches of a lofty tree crowed aloud. The shrillness of his voice echoed through the wood, and the well-known note brought to the spot a fox, who was prowling in quest of prey. The fox, seeing that the cock was at so great a height, set his wits to work to find some way of bringing him down.

He saluted the cock in his mildest voice and said, "Have you not heard, cousin, of the proclamation of universal peace and harmony among all kinds of beasts and birds? We are no longer to prey upon and devour one another, but love and friendship are to be the order of the day. So do come down, and we will talk over this great news at our leisure."

The cock, who knew that the fox was only at his old tricks, pretended to be watching something in the distance. The fox asked him what it was he was looking at so earnestly. "Why," said the cock, "I think I see a pack of hounds yonder." "Oh, then," said the fox, "your humble servant must be gone." "Nay, cousin," said the cock, "pray do not go; I am just coming down. You surely are not afraid of dogs in these peaceable times when love and friendship are to be the order of the day." "No," said the fox; "but it is ten to one whether these dogs have heard of the proclamation yet."

The moral of this fable is: "Cunning often outwits itself." The fox's sly talk about a peace proclamation did not give him much confidence when dogs came in sight. To be tricky, young friends, is not alone foolish and wrong, but generally results in self-defeat. "Cunning often outwits itself." Don't forget it.

Remember the story of the cock and the fox.—H.

SEPTEMBER 26.   Topic: Like a Tree.

TEXT: "And he shall be like a tree planted by the rivers of water." Ps. 1:3.

Who shall be like a tree? The good man, anyone who loves God, and loves to do right. How many kinds of trees are there? How many kinds of people are there? One person is a dead tree in God's great field of earth. He is a hindrance to those who teach the truth and of those who do good. His influence and example do much evil.

But our text does not talk about the dead trees; it tells of the live ones. In the 104th Psalm it is said: "The trees of the Lord are full of sap." They are not dead trees, they are all alive.

The trees can teach us many lessons:

I.   Grow straight and beautiful. Live a life of good report. Have a good reputation. Do not let any sin make you grow crooked and full of knots and gnarls.

II.   Be sound to the heart. Some beautiful trees are rottenhearted, hollowhearted. They are dying trees. They are hypocrites. The lumberman cuts one down, it cannot be used. Be honest, be true, be sincere, be what you want people to think you are.

III.   Be strong. Do not let any little wind of temptation blow you over. Overcome evil with good. Sometimes the winds blow over even live trees in the forest, but God is better to his children than to trees. "Ye shall not be tempted above that ye are able."

IV.   Keep growing. Last winter was cold, last summer was hot, but every live tree grew a little; it added one more ring to the trunk, a few more twigs to the branches. Do not let trouble keep you from growing in faith; do not let hard work keep you from growing in love; keep growing every year.

V.   Give help to others. All live trees are of some use—shade, timber, nuts or fruit. Every Christian can be of some use in the world. Find your work and do it well.

VI. God cares for all. For every tree there is a place to grow, plenty of air, light and rain. There is also for you all that you need. God cares for all his children. He never has forgotten one; he will never fail you nor forsake.

VII. Be contented. No tree ever worries, frets or grumbles. Does it grow in a winderness? It may yet be made a part of a city palace.

The trees look in at your window, they smile down upon you along the streets. Learn the lessons that they teach, and may you be like a tree planted by the rivers of water.—Rev. E. P. Michel.

OCTOBER 3. Topic: How Littles Make Bigs.

I want to tell you young friends three stories this morning. They are all short. And they are all true. The first is about a boy in Rochester, New York. He heard his pastor talking about the need of a new church and Sunday School building. The minister said that if each member of the church and Bible school would bring a few bricks the new church could be built.

Next morning the pastor heard a knock at his door. When he opened he found a bit of a boy outside with three bricks in his little wagon. The boy said: "I have brought a load of bricks to build the church." The pastor thanked him and then went down town to call upon some of his officers. He said, "We are going to build the church right away; the first load of bricks has come."

When the people of the church heard that boy's gift they set about giving and working in dead earnest. Before long the great Brick Church of Rochester was erected, and there it stands today.

Now for my second true story. There was a little girl in a certain Sunday School. The pastor and people were exceedingly anxious for a building, so that they would not need longer to rent. In the midst of the talk a little girl became so much interested that she brought all her savings—thirty-seven cents— toward the new house of worship. By the Lord's blessing that thirty-seven cents grew to be sixty thousand taels, for this was in Shanghai, China. With that money a comfortable church with Bible-school building was purchased. Thirty-seven cents was not a large amount; but it was the seed that produced that result.

Now, my third story. There was a little boy who lived in the land we call Palestine—the Holy Land. It was when Jesus was here among men. This boy had a small basket of food, in which there were two small fishes, and he went out with the others to hear Christ preach. There was a great crowd of people listening to the Preacher, and they were so interested that they forgot all about how time was flying until it drew toward night. That little boy offered his basket of lunch to the Preacher and the Preacher blessed it and fed five thousand people. That was a very little boy, and he had a very little basket; but it did a very great deal of good—had great results.

Now, why do I tell you these stories?— about three bricks and a boy, thirty-seven cents and a girl, two small fishes and a small boy? Because I want you to know that though you may not think you can do much, yet Jesus blesses littles into bigs. If you give what little you have of time or talent to Jesus, he will make your little offering turn out to great good. It is not how big your offering is that matters. It is the power, the blessing of Jesus back of it, that makes it count for the glory of God and the good of men. "She hath done what she could" (Mark 14:8). That is our text. Do what you can, boys and girls, and Christ will bless it and bless you in doing it. He can and will bless your littles into bigs.—H. G. C. H.

OCTOBER 10. Topic: A Forest Deer and its Curious Behavior (Mercy Sunday).

In some parts of our country a day is set apart for the observance of what is called Mercy Sunday. The purpose of the observance is to promote the practice of kindness to animals. It is the thought and meaning of this observance which leads me to tell the story I have for you boys and girls this morning. It is about a very interesting and beautiful naturally wild animal and its actions. I am to tell you about a deer we saw in the woods.

One warm day last summer our family decided to drive to a distant woods in the country for a picnic. We went about twenty miles to a rather dense forest in a region very sparsely settled. After the noon lunch our two daughters were exploring a little stream with a view of finding the spring at its source. In the wildest part they came upon it, bubbling up cool and clear, when, to their utter astonishment, they came upon a deer. It was a fawn or doe, very sleek and beautiful, possibly a little less than two years of age. The deer looked at them, and they looked at it. Then the animal allowed them to approach it slowly.

Soon it seemed to enjoy their company and followed them to where the family was camped. It became very friendly, allowing us all to rub its nose, pat its back and scratch its ears, with much apparent enjoyment of the attention. Twice it ran away, jumped a fence or two with graceful ease, but soon came back to the group.

Now here is the most interesting thing. When we started the auto to leave, it did not nervously jump or offer to run away. What do you think it did? It put its two forefeet into the auto and wanted to get in!

There was not any farmhouse near. There was no sign of any ownership. The whole occurrence seemed to us all most mysterious.

Now, let me go on. A few months later we learned the history of the deer. In the gunning season of nearly two years previous, when it was a little fawn, the baby animal in some way suffered a broken leg. The children of a farmer's family in the region found the little thing, took it home, bound up its broken limb, and nursed it well. While it was very young it was often taken along in the family auto for a ride. They treated it as a real pet and the little doe liked it.

So you see why, though it was now two years old and weighing nearly two hundred pounds, it so surprised us all

by wanting to get into our car for a ride. You see also how capable a wild and naturally timid animal is of being petted and tamed, and of showing a beautiful gratitude for such kindly treatment.

I am sure you have no need to be reminded of what was said in the beginning concerning Mercy Sunday and kindness to animals. You may be a little surprised to know that the Bible has somewhat to say on this theme of kind treatment to animals. In the book of Proverbs (12:10), there is a verse which says, "A righteous man regardeth the life of his beast." We will count that as our text for this little talk.—H.

OCTOBER 17. Topic: About Fairies.

TEXT: "Keep in mind whatever is true, whatever is worthy, whatever is just, whatever is pure, whatever is attractive, whatever is high-toned, all excellence, all merit." Phil. 4:8 (Moffatt).

"Alice and Mary don't believe in fairies, Mother. Alice says they are only alive in stories, and Mary says it just goes to show how silly you are if you believe in 'em."

Jane was perched on the kitchen stool with a bowl in her lap, from which she scraped frosting. Although her mother had left a generous layer of sweetness Jane could not quite enjoy it, for her mind was distressed with thinking over her two playmates' unbelief in fairies.

"It isn't silly to believe in fairies," said her mother comfortingly.

"But," said Jane, "I have never seen one."

"Well, I have," said her mother. "When you brought home that little white puppy and bound up his sore paw I saw a fairy named Kindness. And when you smiled instead of pouting because I called you to tend the baby, even when you were so eager to keep on with your play, I saw two fairies. One was Willingness, and one was Unselfishness."

"You are a darling, Mother, but you know you just saw the fairies in your mind. You didn't see any really truly fairies with golden dresses and silver wings, now, did you?"

Jane's mother opened the cupboard

JUNIOR PULPIT

357

door and carefully set away the new cake so that the frosting would be hard by suppertime, then she answered her little girl. "Did you ever notice the lovely light come into people's eyes when they do good deeds? It is as beautiful as any golden dress, and a contented smile will carry its owner into the hearts of others as easily as silver wings could carry a storybook fairy straight to the heart of a flower."

"Oh, I understand now," cried Jane, clapping her hands. "Our deeds are real fairies. Good deeds are good fairies, but when we are naughty it is like choosing wicked, black gnomes for our company."—E. A. Wilcox.

OCTOBER 24. Topic: Use Your Own Yardstick.

Safely stored in a government vault in Washington, D. C., is a steel yardstick which is the standard for all lineal measurement in the United States.

Where shall we look, however, for a yardstick that is the standard for measuring individual character or success or failure?

Only within ourselves can such a standard be found. Every one of us possesses an infinitely precise and accurate yardstick with which to measure our own achievements, but we too seldom use it. We are lazy and do not take the trouble to get it out from the deep vaults of our spirit where it is stored. It lies there all our lives, its brilliance buried under rubbish and obscured by dust.

Instead of using this accurate, dependable standard of measurement that is our own, we take the faulty yardstick which is in common use about us. Perhaps, according to its decree, we are failures, so we are cast down, discouraged, even despairing.

This yardstick we have unthinkingly used is probably incorrect. At best, it measures only material things and often guages them inaccurately. It takes no cognizance of spiritual accomplishments nor of mental ones, unless they can be turned into making money. Yet spiritual and mental successes are our only truly important and permanent achievements.

It carries no markings for determining growth of character. It cannot be used to ascertain strength of soul or goodness of purpose.

Let us no longer measure our individual success or failure by the warped, inaccurate yardstick which the world offers us. Instead, let us search within ourselves for the authentic standard of measurement to be found in our own hearts, waiting to give us the true answer to the question, "Have we succeeded, or have we failed?"—O. Davenport.

OCTOBER 31. Topic: The Lord's Prayer.

Once very early in his ministry Jesus was praying and his disciples heard him. There was something about his prayer that made them wish to pray as he did. So they said to him (and I am sure it was not hard at all to say this to him, he was so kind and easy to talk to), "Lord, teach us to pray." And I am sure he was as ready to do what they asked as they had found it easy to ask him. So he said to them, "After this manner therefore pray ye," etc. (Matt. 6:9).

Now I wonder how many of you can repeat what he said? How many can? Let me see your hands. Yes. Now let us all repeat it together.

Now, because he taught it, what do we call it? Yes, "The Lord's Prayer." Sometimes it is called by the first two words, "Our Father." And there is a great branch of the Church of Christ which calls it not "Our Father" but "Pater Noster," which is the Latin for "Our Father," because the Roman Catholic Church uses Latin in its services, instead of English or French or German or Spanish or Italian, etc.

Every good Catholic says the Lord's Prayer many times a day—so many "Pater Nosters" counted with beads. And I wish all you young friends, if you do not already do so, to say the Lord's Prayer every morning and evening of your lives. You may offer the prayer without counting beads; but every time you say it remember that Jesus himself taught it to his disciples.

There is no time to explain much about this prayer this morning, but there are a few things I especially hope you young people will remember about it.

I. It is a prayer against swearing. "Our Father who art in heaven, hallowed be thy name." That means that his name is holy and we are to keep it holy and help others to keep it holy.

II. It is a prayer for making disciples, or a missionary prayer. "Thy kingdom come." The followers of Christ are to get other disciples.

III. It is a prayer for food. "Give us this day our daily bread."

IV. It is a prayer for forgiveness and forgivingness. "Forgive us our debts as we forgive our debtors."

V. It is a prayer against temptation. "Lead us not into temptation, but deliver us from evil." How much we need to offer that petition, that we may be kept from temptation, or strengthened to overcome when we are tempted!

Then there are the closing words, sometimes called the Doxology. They are an ascription of praise: "For thine is the kingdom and the power and the glory, for ever."

Then we say "Amen," which means, "So be it." "So may it be." "We want it."—Rev. William Tatlock (Adapted).

NOVEMBER 7. Topic: Possess Your Possessions.

I want to talk to you boys and girls about possessing your possessions. A story will tell you what I mean by that.

One day in Chicago a man was busy in his shop polishing pieces of colored stone to be used in cheap necklaces and bracelets. The bright pebbles one finds at the seashore or in mountain brooks are often very lovely when polished. People often came to his shop to have pebbles polished so that they might use them as pocket pieces or put them in rings.

This morning a stranger entered his shop. He was a laborer. He drew from

his pocket a rough red stone and handed it to the shopkeeper.

"I want you to cut and polish this," he said.

Gustaf Gillman, the shopkeeper, could scarcely believe what he saw.

'Where did you get this?" he gasped.

'My father picked it up in Hungary more than fifty years ago. He thought it was a pretty pebble. When I landed in America in 1903 I found it in my valise. I guess my mother had put it in. "It has been lying around our house ever since. The children played with it. My last baby cut his teeth on it. Once a rat dragged it into a hole, but I found it again by accident. It was lost several times but always turned up again. I came to look at it as my luck stone.

"One night I dreamed it was a diamond and worth a lot of money. But it's no diamond—it's red."

"No," said the shopkeeper, "it's a pigeon's-blood ruby."

"What might it be worth?" asked the owner, John Mihok.

"I'd say anywhere from $100,000 to $250,000," answered Gillman. Mihok almost fainted. He leaned against the door.

The stone was cut into a flawless ruby. It is believed to be the largest ruby in this country, and possibly the largest ruby in the world.

John Mihok had been a laborer all his life. Michael Mihok, his father, was a laborer before him. For fifty years they worked almost day and night to keep the wolf from the door. And all the while they had in their careless possession a gem which an emperor might have coveted.

They did not possess their possession.

Boys and girls, think this true story over. Think about the things which you have—material things and spiritual things, God's Word, liberty, the privilege of learning, the love of Christ in your heart, and many other priceless possessions. Are you really possessing your possessions?

NOVEMBER 14. Topic: The Stolen Hen (Chinese Story).

As I have told you before, I have a brother who has lived and worked in China as a missionary for many years. He has sent me many stories as recounted to him by the Chinese themselves. They are not in print, not found in books, but are just the folktales that circulate among the people. One of these I am going to tell you young folks this morning. It illustrates the Chinese idea of strategy in detecting evil.

The story states that once upon a time a woman had one of her fowls escape from her and fly into a neighbor's yard. She went over and asked the man for her hen. But the neighbor said, "I did not see your hen." The woman knew better. After a bitter quarrel she took the neighbor to the magistrate saying, "He has hidden my fowl and will not return it to me." The man denied again, saying, "I did not see her hen. I don't know where it is." The magistrate said, "All right; you may both go home. I will investigate the matter."

As the two were going out at the door the official said in a loud voice to someone standing by: "What a fool that thief is! He not only steals the woman's hen, but puts the chicken feathers in his hair to let others see that he has stolen it!" The neighbor, overhearing the remark, put his hand quickly to his hair!

The official, noting the action, called him back and said, "If you did not steal the hen, why did you put your hand to your hair?" The neighbor was speechless and stood condemned.

"Be sure your sin will find you out."
"Conscience makes cowards of us all."
—H.

NOVEMBER 21. Topic: On Being Thankful (Thanksgiving).

Next Thursday is Thankgiving Day. I am quite sure all you young folks know that, and are already smacking your lips with the thought of the good things you are to have to eat—turkey and dressing and cranberry sauce and mince pie. This morning let me remind you that next to a pure heart is the blessing of a thankful heart.

There is a story told of a good minister in Scotland. He was of rather a conservative type, somewhat quiet and particular. He had in his congregation a poor old woman who when anything particularly helpful was said would shout and say, "Praise the Lord! Amen!" This practice greatly disturbed the minister, and one New Year's day he went to see her. "Betty," he said, "I'll make a bargain with you. You call out 'Praise the Lord!' just when I get to the best part of my sermon, and it upsets my thoughts. Now if you will stop doing this all this year, I'll give you a pair of wool blankets." Betty was poor, and the offer of the blankets looked good; so she did her very best to earn them. Sunday after Sunday she kept quiet.

But one day a minister of another type came to preach, a man bubbling over with joy. As he preached on the forgiveness of sin and all the blessings that follow, the vision of the blankets began to fade, and the joys of salvation became brighter and brighter. At last Betty could stand it no longer, and, jumping up, she cried, "Blankets or no blankets, praise the Lord. Amen."

I suppose we do not need to shout in church, but I want to say that gratitude is a grace that struggles for expression. It does not shut itself up in the heart. It does not allow itself to be merely felt. It wants to speak. It wants to say something. The writer of the 107th Psalm exclaims, "Let the redeemed of the Lord say so." Why return thanks unto God for mercies if they have not come from him? If Thanksgiving Day means anything it means that we say to God, "Our blessings are from thee and unto thee do we now return thanks."

But not only should we give thanks to God because he is the Giver of our blessings, but we have much additional reason to do so when we consider the abundance of them.

We are all too much prone to forget

God's benefits. We have excellent memories for all our trials and sorrows and losses, but fail to recall our blessings. It seems that the very abundance of God's favors and their ever-unbroken flow tend to make us all the more forgetful of the Giver of them all. But it is our duty to remember, to be thankful. So doing we will soon find ourselves ready to adopt the words of the Psalmist and say, "How many are thy gracious thoughts to me, O Lord! How great is the sum of them! When I count them they are more in number than the sand."—H.

NOVEMBER 28. Topic: The Satyr and the Traveler.

The story I have for you this morning is entitled "The Satyr and the Traveler." It is one of Aesop's fables. Aesop was an old Greek writer of a time more than twenty-five hundred years ago. There must have been some value in a piece of writing that has come down generation after generation for that length of time. Don't you think so? The fact is that not alone boys and girls and young people, but older people still read and enjoy Aesop's fables.

Another fact you know is that in Aesop's fables the birds and animals are represented as talking to one another and acting a good deal as some people act.

This fable is called "The Satyr and the Traveler." As you know, in the olden times a satyr was supposed to be a sort of woodland deity, or sprite. He is depicted as a sly, cunning creature, with goatlike ears, pug nose and short tail and branching horns. A satyr is not looked upon as being good, or moral, or as delighting in good things. Rather otherwise.

In this fable a satyr is respresented as ranging in the forest in the winter. He came across a traveler half-starved and shivering with cold. The satyr took pity on him and invited him to go to his cave. On the way the man kept blowing his fingers. "Why do you do that?" asked the satyr, who had seen little of the world. "To warm my hands; they are nearly frozen," replied the man.

Arrived at the cave, the satyr poured out a mess of smoking pottage and laid it before the traveler, who at once commenced blowing it most vigorously. "What, blowing again!" exclaimed the satyr. "Is it not hot enough?"

"Yes, in faith," answered the man, "it is hot enough in all conscience, and that is just the reason why I blow it."

"Be off with you!" said the satyr, in alarm. "I will have nothing to do with a man who can blow hot and cold from the same mouth!"

The moral of this fable is in this wise statement: "The man who talks for both sides is not to be trusted."

That is a common saying even today when we hear people spoken of as "blowing both hot and cold." "The man who talks for both sides is not to be trusted." You can't be for the right and wrong both at the same time. Young friends, be definitely, distinctly on the side of right. Don't be milk and water people. Don't try to be on both sides of the fence at the same time. And when you are Christians be out-and-out Christians. You cannot serve two masters. You cannot serve God and Mammon.—H.

DECEMBER 5. Topic: Two Christmas Trees (Advent).

It is three weeks yet until Christmas. But this is called the Advent Season when people begin to think about Christmas and get ready in mind and heart and the presents they are going to give at Christmas. Of course we have Christmas trees at Christmas, and so I am going to tell you a story this morning about two kinds of trees, Christmas Trees and Apple Trees. The story is from a minister whose name is H. L. Williams. Listen carefully and see if you get the lesson the story teaches.

The first frosts of autumn had touched the earth. Leaves had turned to red and brown and dropped to the ground. Golden corn had ripened in the shock. The barns and cellars were bursting with the good things of the earth. On the hillside, one at the edge of the orchard, and the other at the edge of the woods, stood two trees.

One was an apple tree. It shivered in the wind without its clothes, the leaves. The other was the evergreen cedar as beautiful as in the days of summer.

At this time of the year trees as well as children look forward to a great day, the coming birthday of Jesus. It had happened that just about this time two boys had passed through the orchard. They had seen the cedar at the edge of the woods. "What a marvelous Christmas tree that will make," one had said. "We will remember and it shall be our Christmas tree," said the second.

So the evergreen tree was jubilant. "Do you know what a Christmas tree is, Apple Tree?" asked the evergreen. Then without waiting for an answer the evergreen went on. "I will tell you. They take a Christmas tree and they put it in the largest room of the house. Then upon it they hang colored ornaments and stars and tinsel. Bright little electric lights are hung from the branches. They twinkle through the windows. Then they hang presents on the tree. And sometimes at Christmas everyone in the whole neighborhood comes and stands around the tree, and the people all say, 'Isn't it beautiful?' "

The apple tree shivered and bowed her head. Then she thought of the months past when her boughs had borne beautiful flowers. She thought of the apple-picking time when she yielded bushels of finest apples. That made it possible for her to raise her head. The spruce was still gaily swinging in the breeze and humming a popular song.

"You will be beautiful, Cedar Tree, I am sure," the apple tree said. "But there is a difference in the kinds of beauty. My flowers and my fruits came from within me. You are to be made beautiful by having things hung onto you."

Now, there are people just like these trees. There are some who are happy and beautiful because of what they themselves are. And there are some who are made happy only by the things which are "hung onto them."

DECEMBER 12. A Korean Girl's Christmas Story (Advent).

Next Sunday in our church we will celebrate as Christmas, but the real Christmas Day comes nearly a week later. The date is Saturday, December 25. But we celebrate it here in our church the Sunday before. This time for several weeks ahead of Christmas is known as Advent; so I think a story about Christmas this morning will be appropriate. Before the second World War our family visited in Korea, and the story I have is from that country and is as told by a native Korean minister's daughter.

She says, "Whenever I think of Christmas I am filled with reverence for the one carol which I know I shall never forget. Even now I can hear the sharp but musical sound of a violin which came from out of the darkness of the poor section of Seoul. I have heard many Christmas carols, and I have sung many, for my father is a pastor, but no other hymn can touch me in the way that 'Silent Night' does. It is my favorite among all the Christmas songs, and whenever I feel unhappy at any time I hum it.

"My sister, who died three years ago, went with me through the business section of Seoul one Christmas Eve. It was a snowy night. We hunted in shops for gifts, and after we had finished our shopping we walked along the streets just for fun. It was a perfect night; the night of the birthday of Jesus, Christmas Eve.

"On passing a dark alley my sister and I heard a faint but clear sound. We stopped and listened. The melody was as velvet. Slowly we began to walk around its source. Suddenly a thatched hut obstructed our path. A mud wall, a town paper window, and a twig door greeted us. The music grew fainter and ceased. A dim voice filtered through the window of oiled paper.

" 'Brother, tomorrow is Christmas, isn't it? People are all gay and giving, but we must have a lonely time, fatherless and motherless. No presents to give or receive. I wish I were dead!'

" 'Oksoon, you promised me you would not say that again. Here, let's put the record on again, and enjoy Christmas Eve a bit before we have to sell father's victrola.'

"Then we heard the disc beginning to whirr again. The music of 'Silent Night' once more filled that muddy, stench-filled alley, and lighted up my sorrowful heart. I could not stand there without wanting to help in some way.

" 'Sister, I will give this sweater to that girl. It will be far better than to send it to my friend who is sure to have a happy Christmas with many gifts,' I said. 'Yes, you can give the sweater to the girl, and I will give a necktie to her brother,' my sister replied.

"We wrapped the garment and tie together, using the newspaper we had intended to take home to father. I opened the outer twig gate and slipped the package under the eves and in front of the inner door, where the wind could not drift the snow. Then we walked quietly and quickly through the slush and back to the street. The last note of the violin had ceased.

"From that day to this, whenever I celebrate Christmas, I am always reminded of that poor brother and sister, their dark home, my sainted sister, and the gifts we two fortunate girls were able to leave at that hovel door. The music of that holy hymn touches the cords of memory. It is always with me—'Silent Night, Holy Night, all is calm, all is bright'—ah, I can never forget it."

DECEMBER 19. Topic: The Legend of St. Christopher (Christmas).

This year Christmas does not come until next Saturday, but we are holding our Christmas services today. I think it appropriate that I should tell you young friends the legend of St. Christopher. It is a very ancient and familiar story and I am quite sure that all you boys and girls have heard it. But it is well to bring such a story often to mind. So I am going to tell it to you again this morning. This is the way the story is told.

Once upon a time there lived a great giant named Offerus all alone by the banks of a mighty river. He was so strong that he was able to pull up the forest trees by the roots, and he was so tall that he could easily step from one hill to another. He could have crushed a man with his little finger, but he never hurt so much as a tiny sparrow, for he was a good giant.

It was a very swift river near which Offerus had built his hut. It was wide and deep, and it rushed and tumbled along, ready to break the boats and drown the poor travelers who wished to cross. But Offerus was stronger than the river. He took a huge pine tree for a staff, and whenever it was a dark, stormy night, and he heard cries of distress from the river, he would plunge into the water and carry the travelers safely to the other side. And he was always ready, and never weary.

One night there was a more terrible storm than usual. The forest trees moaned and sighed, and the river roared as it beat against the shore. Offerus sat in his hut, and he heard a tiny voice crying through the storm: "Offerus, Offerus, come and carry me over!"

It did not seem as if any one could be out in such a wild storm, but the giant heard the small voice again calling: "Offerus, come and carry me across!"

So Offerus took his pine-tree staff and reached for his lantern which hung upon the wall, and he opened the door to go out into the night. It was very dark and the rain beat into his face so that he could scarcely see. But he looked up and down, holding his lantern high above his head, and he came to a little Child, all drenched with the rain, waiting for him on the bank of the river.

"Offerus, you must carry me over this night," he called.

So Offerus lifted the little Child in his strong arms, and took his staff, and waded into the stream, thinking what a light burden he carried.

But the waves rose higher and higher, the waters came up to his shoulder, and the wind blew fiercely. The strangest thing of all was this: at every step the little Child upon his shoulder grew heavier, until it seemed to Offerus that he would never be able to cross the river—he must turn and go back.

But he was brave, as all giants are, and he struggled on, tottering as he went and aiding his steps with his stout staff; and at last he reached the other side. As he set down his burden, safely and gently, he said: "Child, who art thou? The whole world upon my shoulders could not have been heavier."

And the Child looked up and said softly, as he laid his little hand in Offerus' great one: "In helping every poor traveler thou hast been helping me. Blessed shalt thou be, St. Christopher! This night thou hast carried over the Christ Child."

Then the Christ Child slipped away into the night and St. Christopher stood and looked after him, leaning upon his staff and thinking of the wonderful thing which had happened to him.

And the staff suddenly took root in the ground—although it was the bleak winter season—and it flourished and sent forth branches and leaves, and it towered over the other trees in the forest to show to every traveler who should pass that way the place where St. Christopher had carried over the little Christ Child.

Now, boys and girls, I have thought of a Christmas text for all of you. Get it by heart. Remember it. Act upon it. This is it: "Inasmuch as ye have done it unto one of the least of these my brethren, ye have done it unto me" (Matt. 25:40).—H.

DECEMBER 26. Topic: The Russian Legend of Babouscka (Christmas).

Yesterday was the real Christmas date. Last Sunday we celebrated Christmas in our church. I told you young folks then the legend of St. Christopher.

Because this is so near to Christmas, and we still have the Christmas spirit, it seems appropriate to tell you another Christmas legend. This, too, is probably very familiar to you all, or to most of you; but it is well to tell such stories over and over again and keep them familiarly in our minds. This one is from Russia, or told as the Russians express it. It is called The Legend of Babouscka.

It was the night the dear Christ Child came to Bethlehem. In a country far away from him, an old, old woman named Babouscka sat in her snug little house by her warm fire. The wind was drifing the snow outside and howling down the chimney, but it only made Babouscka's fire burn more brightly.

"How glad I am that I may stay indoors!" said Babouscka, holding her hands out to the bright blaze.

But suddenly she heard a loud rap at her door. She opened it and her candle shone on three old men standing outside in the snow. Their beards were as white as the snow, and so long that they reached the ground. Their eyes shone kindly in the light of Babouscka's candle, and their arms were full of precious things—boxes of jewels, and sweet-smelling oils, and ointments.

"We have traveled far, Babouscka," they said, "and we stop to tell you of the Baby Prince born this night in Bethlehem. He comes to rule the world and teach all men to be loving and true. We carry him gifts. Come with us, Babouscka!"

But Babouscka looked at the driving snow, and then inside at her cozy room and the crackling fire. "It is too late for me to go with you, good sirs," she said, "the weather is too cold." She went inside again and shut the door, and the old men journeyed on to Bethlehem without her. But as Babouscka sat by her fire, rocking, she began to think about the little Christ Child, for she loved all babies.

"Tomorrow I will go to find him," she said; "tomorrow, when it is light, and I will carry him some toys."

So when it was morning Babouscka put on her long cloak, and took her staff, and filled a basket with the pretty things a baby would like—gold balls, and wooden toys, and strings of silver cobwebs—and she set out to find the Christ Child.

But oh! Babouscka had forgotten to ask the three old men the road to Bethlehem, and they had traveled so far through the night that she could not overtake them. Up and down the roads she hurried, through woods and fields and towns, saying to whomsoever she met: "I go to find the Christ Child. Where does he lie? I bring some pretty toys for his sake."

But no one could tell her the way to go, and they all said: "Farther on, Babouscka, farther on." So she traveled on, and on, and on for years and years— but she never found the little Christ Child.

They say the old Babouscka is traveling still, looking for him. When it comes Christmas Eve, and the children are lying fast asleep, Babouscka comes softly through the snowy fields and towns, wrapped in her long cloak and carrying her basket on her arm. With her staff she raps gently at the doors and goes inside and holds her candle close to the little children's faces. "Is he here?" she asks. "Is the little Christ Child here?" And then she turns sorrowfully away again, crying: "Farther on, farther on." But before she leaves she takes a toy from her basket, lays it beside the pillow for a Christmas gift. "For his sake," she says softly and then hurries on through the years and forever in search of the little Christ Child.

That is the Russian legend of Babouscka, young friends. Very beautiful, is it not? But I hope none of you boys and girls, or older people either, will miss finding the Christ Child because of delay. This is my text for this little after-Christmas sermon: "Behold, now is the accepted time; behold, today is the day of salvation" (II Cor. 6:2). —H.